ORGANIZATIONAL BEHAVIOR

Improving Performance and Commitment in the Workplace

JASON A. COLQUITT
University of Florida

JEFFERY A. LEPINE
University of Florida

MICHAEL J. WESSON
Texas A&M University

McGraw-Hill Irwin

Boston   Burr Ridge, IL   Dubuque, IA   New York
San Francisco   St. Louis   Bangkok   Bogotá   Caracas   Kuala Lumpur
Lisbon   London   Madrid   Mexico City   Milan   Montreal   New Delhi
Santiago   Seoul   Singapore   Sydney   Taipei   Toronto

ORGANIZATIONAL BEHAVIOR: IMPROVING PERFORMANCE
AND COMMITMENT IN THE WORKPLACE

2 3 4 5 6 7 8 9 0 CTP/CTP 0 9 8

ISBN   978-0-07-353008-6
MHID   0-07-353008-5

Editorial director: *Brent Gordon*
Publisher: *Paul Ducham*
Executive editor: *John Weimeister*
Senior developmental editor: *Christine Scheid*
Marketing manager: *Krista Bettino*
Project manager: *Bruce Gin*
Production supervisor: *Gina Hangos*
Senior designer: *Artemio Ortiz Jr.*
Senior photo research coordinator: *Jeremy Cheshareck*
Photo researcher: *Jennifer Blankenship*
Senior media project manager: *Matthew Perry*
Cover design: *Dave Seidler*
Cover image: © *Photofest Inc.*
Typeface: *10/12 Times New Roman*
Compositor: *Laserwords Private Limited*
Printer: *CTPS*

Library of Congress Cataloging-in-Publication Data

Colquitt, Jason.
    Organizational behavior: improving performance and commitment in
the workplace / Jason A. Colquitt, Jeffery A. Lepine, Michael J. Wesson.
        p. cm.
    Includes index.
    ISBN-13: 978-0-07-353008-6 (alk. paper)
    ISBN-10: 0-07-353008-5 (alk. paper)
    1. Organizational behavior. 2. Personnel management. 3. Strategic planning. 4. Consumer
satisfaction. 5. Job satisfaction. I. Lepine, Jeffery A. II. Wesson, Michael J. III. Title.
HD58.7.C6255 2009
658.3--dc22
                                2007038807

Dedication

To Catherine, Cameron, Riley, and Connor, and also to Mom, Dad, Alan, and Shawn. The most wonderful family I could imagine, two times over.

-J.A.C.

To my parents who made me, and to Marcie, Izzy, and Eli, who made my life complete.

-J.A.L.

To Liesl and Dylan: Their support in all I do is incomparable. They are my life and I love them both. To my parents: They provide a foundation that never wavers.

-M.J.W.

ABOUT THE AUTHORS

JASON A. COLQUITT

Is a Professor in the Management Department at the University of Florida's Warrington College of Business. He received his Ph.D. from Michigan State University's Eli Broad Graduate School of Management and earned his B.S. in Psychology from Indiana University. He teaches organizational behavior and human resource management at the undergraduate, masters, and executive levels and also teaches research methods at the doctoral level. He was recognized as one of the Warrington College's Teachers of the Year due to his high marks in the classroom.

Jason's research interests include organizational justice, trust, team effectiveness, and personality influences on task and learning performance. He has published more than 20 articles on these and other topics in *Academy of Management Journal, Academy of Management Review, Journal of Applied Psychology, Organizational Behavior and Human Decision Processes,* and *Personnel Psychology.* He is currently serving as an Associate Editor for *Academy of Management Journal* and has served (or is serving) on a number of editorial boards, including *Academy of Management Journal, Journal of Applied Psychology, Organizational Behavior and Human Decision Processes, Personnel Psychology, Journal of Management,* and *International Journal of Conflict Management.* He is a recipient of the Society for Industrial and Organizational Psychology's Distinguished Early Career Contributions Award and the Cummings Scholar Award for early to mid-career achievement, sponsored by the Organizational Behavior division of the Academy of Management. He was also elected to be a Representative-at-Large for the Organizational Behavior division.

Jason enjoys spending time with his wife, Catherine, and three sons, Cameron, Riley, and Connor. His hobbies include playing basketball, playing the trumpet, watching movies, and rooting on (in no particular order) the Pacers, Colts, Cubs, Hoosiers, Spartans, and Gators.

JEFFERY A. LEPINE

Is the Darden Restaurants Diversity Management Professor at the Warrington College of Business, University of Florida. He received his Ph.D. in Organizational Behavior from the Eli Broad Graduate School of Management at Michigan State University. He also earned an M.S. in Management from Florida State University and a B.S. in Finance from the University of Connecticut. He teaches organizational behavior, human resource management, and management of groups and teams at undergraduate and graduate levels.

Jeff's research interests include team functioning and effectiveness, individual and team adaptation, citizenship behavior, voice, and occupational stress. He has published more than 20 articles on these and other topics in *Academy of Management Journal, Academy of Management Review, Journal of Applied Psychology, Organi-*

zational Behavior and Human Decision Processes, and *Personnel Psychology.* He is currently serving or has served on the editorial boards of *Academy of Management Journal, Journal of Applied Psychology, Organizational Behavior and Human Decision Processes, Personnel Psychology, Journal of Management, Journal of Organizational Behavior,* and *Journal of Occupational and Organizational Psychology.* He is a recipient of the Society for Industrial and Organizational Psychology's Distinguished Early Career Contributions Award and the Cummings Scholar Award for early to mid-career achievement, sponsored by the Organizational Behavior division of the Academy of Management. He was also elected to the Executive Committee of the Human Resource Division of the Academy of Management. Prior to earning his Ph.D., Jeff was an officer in the U.S. Air Force.

Jeff spends most of his free time having fun with his family. He also enjoys playing guitar, avoiding sharks, devising ways to keep mole crickets off his lawn, and watching NCAA championship games.

MICHAEL J. WESSON

Is an associate professor in the Management Department at Texas A&M University's Mays Business School. He received his Ph.D. from Michigan State University's Eli Broad Graduate School of Management. He also holds an M.S. in human resource management from Texas A&M University and a B.B.A. from Baylor University. He has taught organizational behavior and human resource management based classes at all levels but currently spends most of his time teaching Mays MBAs, EMBAs, and executive development at Texas A&M. He was awarded Texas A&M's Montague Center for Teaching Excellence Award.

Michael's research interests include organizational justice, goal-setting, organizational entry (employee recruitment, selection, and socialization), person–organization fit, and compensation and benefits. His articles have been published in journals such as *Journal of Applied Psychology, Personnel Psychology, Academy of Management Review,* and *Organizational Behavior and Human Decision Processes.* He currently serves on the editorial boards of the *Journal of Applied Psychology* and the *Journal of Organizational Behavior* and is an ad hoc reviewer for many others. He is active in the Academy of Management and the Society for Industrial and Organizational Psychology. Prior to returning to school, Michael worked as a human resources manager for a *Fortune* 500 firm. He has served as a consultant to the automotive supplier, healthcare, oil and gas, and technology industries in areas dealing with recruiting, selection, onboarding, compensation, and turnover.

Michael spends most of his time trying to keep up with his wife Liesl and son Dylan. He is a self-admitted food and wine snob, home theater aficionado, and college sports addict (Gig 'em Aggies!).

PREFACE

Why did we decide to write this textbook? Well, for starters, organizational behavior (OB) remains a fascinating topic that everyone can relate to (because everyone either has worked or is going to work in the future). What makes people effective at their job? What makes them want to stay with their employer? What makes work enjoyable? Those are all fundamental questions that organizational behavior research can help answer. However, our desire to write this book also grew out of our own experiences (and frustrations) teaching OB courses using other textbooks. We found that students would end the semester with a common set of questions that we felt we could answer if given the chance to write our own book. With that in mind, *Organizational Behavior: Improving Performance and Commitment in the Workplace,* was written with the following questions in mind.

DOES ANY OF THIS STUFF REALLY MATTER?

Organizational behavior might be the most relevant class any student ever takes, but that doesn't always shine through in OB texts. The introductory section of our book contains two chapters not included in other books: *Job Performance* and *Organizational Commitment.* Being good at one's job and wanting to stay with one's employer are obviously critical concerns for employees and managers alike. After describing these topics in detail, every remaining chapter in the book links that chapter's content to performance and commitment. Students can then better appreciate the practical relevance of organizational behavior concepts.

IF THAT THEORY DOESN'T WORK, THEN WHY IS IT IN THE BOOK?

In putting together this book, we were guided by the question, "What would OB texts look like if all of them were first written in 2007?" We found that many of the organizational behavior texts on the market include outdated (and indeed, scientifically disproven!) models or theories, presenting them sometimes as fact or possibly for the sake of completeness or historical context. Our students were always frustrated by the fact that they had to read about, learn, and potentially be tested on material that we would tell them in class we knew to be wrong. Although we believe that historical context can be important at times, we believe that focusing on what we really know at this point is paramount in today's fast-paced classes. Thus, this textbook includes new and emerging topics that others leave out and excludes flawed and outdated topics that some other books leave in.

HOW DOES ALL THIS STUFF FIT TOGETHER?

Organizational behavior is a diverse and multidisciplinary field, and it's not always easy to see how all its topics fit together. Our book deals with this issue in two ways. First, all of the chapters in our book are organized around an integrative model that

FIGURE 1-1	Integrative Model of Organizational Behavior

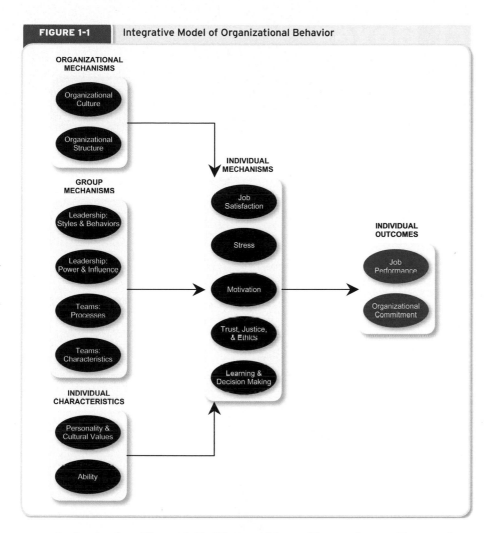

opens each chapter (see Figure 1-1). That model provides students with a roadmap of the course, showing them where they've been and where they're going. Second, our chapters are tightly focused around specific topics and aren't "grab-baggish" in nature. Our hope is that students (and instructors) won't ever come across a topic and think, "Why is this topic being discussed in this chapter?"

DOES THIS STUFF HAVE TO BE SO DRY?

Research on motivation to learn shows that students learn more when they have an intrinsic interest in the topic, but many OB texts do little to stimulate that interest. Put simply, we wanted to create a book that students enjoy reading. To do that, we used a more informal, conversational style when writing the book. We also tried to use company examples that students will be familiar with and find compelling. We included insert boxes, self-assessments, and exercises that students should find engaging (and sometimes even entertaining!).

These questions come up in OB classes of all types, including undergraduate, masters, and executive courses. We therefore believe that *Organizational Behavior: Improving Performance and Commitment in the Workplace* will be appealing to OB students of all varieties, regardless of the class level, university type, or course format.

Special Features: OB Insert Boxes

OB on Screen

This feature uses movie quotes and scenes from recent and classic films to illustrate OB concepts. From *Office Space* to *300*, *Talledega Nights* to *The Queen*, Hollywood continues to offer rich, vivid, examples of OB in action.

OB at the Bookstore

This feature links the content in each chapter to a mainstream, popular business book. Books like *Blink*, *Fish*, and *Now, Discover Your Strengths* represent the gateway to OB for many current and future employees. This feature helps students put those books in a larger context.

OB Assessments

This feature helps students see where they stand on key OB concepts in each chapter. Students gain insights into their personality, their emotional intelligence, their style of leadership, and their ability to cope with stress, which can help them understand their reactions to the working world.

OB for Students

Whether undergraduates, masters, or executives, everyone enrolled in an OB class has one thing in common: They're students. This feature applies OB theories and concepts to student life. It examines questions like, "What makes students satisfied with their university?", "What personality traits improve performance in student groups?", and "Should student grades be kept secret from recruiters?"

OB Internationally

Changes in technology, communications, and economic forces have made business more global and international than ever. This feature spotlights the impact of globalization on the organizational behavior concepts described in this book. It describes cross-cultural differences in OB theories, how to apply them in international corporations, and how to use OB to manage cultural diversity in the workplace.

OB ON SCREEN

MONSTERS, INC.

I'm in the zone today, Sullivan. I'm gonna do some serious scaring, putting up some big numbers.

With these words, Randall (the evil-looking purple monster) challenged Sulley (the big, blue, furry lug) to match his task performance in *Monsters, Inc.* (Pixar, 2001, released by Disney).[8] You see, the source of electricity in the monster world is the screams provoked by highly specialized monster "scarers" who enter the bedroom doors of unsuspecting human children at night.

Sulley and Randall would both score well in terms of task performance. They are the two best scarers at Monsters, Inc., and compete with each other throughout the film for the all-time "scare" record. The similarity between Sulley and Randall ends there however.

Sulley has a positive attitude about his job and is more than willing to go above and beyond to help his coworkers and the organization. For example, in one scene, Sulley offers [...] his coworker Mike (the green, pear-shaped guy) so [...] his demanding, serpent-haired girlfriend. In another [...] very pathetic new scarers. Late in the film, he even [...] that fundamentally improves the operations and prof- [...] ley would score high on citizenship behavior.

OB AT THE BOOKSTORE

Jack: Straight from the Gut
by Jack Welch with John Byrne (New York: Warner Business Books, 2001).

I'm over the top on lots of issues, but none comes as close to the passion I have for making people GE's core competency.

With this statement, Jack Welch, *Fortune*'s Manager of the 20th Century[33] and possibly the most influential CEO of the second half of the twentieth century,[34] reveals the key to his managerial philosophy. In reflecting on his career at General Electric, beginning with his first job in the GE plastics division in 1960 to his rise to CEO in 1981 and then to the appointment of his successor in 2000, Welch reports that GE was all about finding and building great people.

One of the most notable strategies Welch used to build great people involved managing job performance. Although there was a formal performance evaluation cycle at GE, informal performance reviews could occur anywhere and anytime. The purpose of the formal and informal evaluations was to create differentiation among the employees. Although Welch considered sev- [...] eral term [...] tiv [...] (A p [...] ers), [...] Es o [...]

DIFFERE [...]
"Vitalit [...]

OB ASSESSMENTS

HELPING

How helpful are you? This assessment is designed to measure helping, an interpersonal form of citizenship behavior. Think of the people you work with most frequently, either at school or at work. The questions below refer to these people as your "work group." Answer each question using the scale below, then sum up your answers.

1 STRONGLY DISAGREE	2 MODERATELY DISAGREE	3 SLIGHTLY DISAGREE	4 NEITHER DISAGREE NOR AGREE	5 SLIGHTLY AGREE	6 MODERATELY AGREE	7 STRONGLY AGREE

1. I volunteer to do things for my work group. _____
2. I help orient new members of my work group. _____
3. I attend functions that help my work group. _____
4. I assist others in my group with their work for the benefit of the group. _____
5. I get involved to benefit my work group. _____
6. I help others in this group learn about the work. _____
7. I help others in this group with their work responsibilities. _____

OB FOR STUDENTS

What does performance mean to you as a student? For many of you, performance is likely to boil down to exam grades, course grades, and, ultimately, grade point average. Although grades are certainly an important indicator of your effectiveness as a student, they are actually the results of your performance. So instead, think for a moment about the important types of performance behaviors that contribute to your effectiveness as a student. It is likely that most of you think about activities such as attending class, paying attention to lectures, completing assigned readings and other assignments, and studying for exams. Note that these activities could all be considered task performance. Each activity is focused on transforming information from readings, lectures, and experiences into knowledge, which is assessed using quizzes, exams, and other assignments. But did you ever consider how citizenship behavior and counterproductive behavior might contribute to your effectiveness as a student?

First, in classes that require teamwork, these two dimensions of performance are crucial. Your team will likely perform at a much higher level if you and your teammates are helpful to one another, actively participate in team meetings, and suggest improvements to the team's routine. Similarly, your team will likely perform at a lower level if you and your teammates gossip about one another, refuse to share information, or blame one another for errors.

OB INTERNATIONALLY

As we have already explained, citizenship behavior tends to be viewed as relatively voluntary because it is not often explicitly outlined in job descriptions or directly rewarded. However, people in organizations vary in their beliefs regarding the degree to which citizenship behavior is truly voluntary, and these differences have important implications.[36]

As an example, consider a situation in which an employee chooses not to engage in certain citizenship behaviors because of his or her belief that the behaviors are voluntary. However, this employee works for a supervisor who believes that the behaviors are part of the job. If the supervisor were to give this employee a poor performance evaluation for failing to engage in citizenship behaviors, the employee would believe that the evaluation was unfair and likely protest. As another example, consider a situation in which an employee engages in citizenship behaviors because of his or her belief that the behaviors are part of the job. However, this employee works for a supervisor who believes that citizenship behaviors are unnecessary. Assuming that the supervisor would not consider the citizenship behaviors on a performance evaluation, the employee would likely react negatively because he or she has not been recognized for putting effort into activities that help other member of the organization.

So what types of factors cause differences in beliefs regarding whether or not citizenship behavior is discretionary? One factor that would appear to be important is national culture. It is widely believed that the culture in countries like the United States, Canada, and the Netherlands encourages behaviors that support competition and individual achievement, [...]

Special Features: End-of-Chapter Sections

Takeaways

Students are always asking, "What are the most important 'takeaways' from this chapter?" This section gives a point-by-point review of the Learning Goals found at the beginning of each chapter.

Key Terms

Summarizes the most critical terms covered in the chapter, with definitions of all terms available in the Glossary.

Discussion Questions

Not only for review purposes, our Discussion Questions ask students to apply concepts in the chapter to their own lives and experiences.

Cases

To help bring students full circle, a case appears at the end of every chapter that provides a follow-up to the company highlighted in the Opening Vignette.

Exercises

In addition to the self-assessments within the chapter, we have included exercises at the end of each chapter. Some of them we have created ourselves over the years, but we also feature some "classics" that are tried and true and that nearly everyone we know uses in class.

TAKEAWAYS

2.1 Job performance is the set of employee behaviors that contribute to organizational goal accomplishment. Job performance has three dimensions: task performance, citizenship behavior, and counterproductive behavior.

2.2 Task performance includes employee behaviors that are directly involved in the transformation of organizational resources into the goods or services that the organization produces. Organizations can determine task performance behaviors by using j...

2.3 Citizen... reward... of the... helpin...

2.4 Count... nizatio... sabota... ment, i...

2.5 A num... ing the...

2.6 The M...

KEY TERMS

• Job performance	p. 00	• Property deviance	p. 00
• Task performance	p. 00	• Sabotage	p. 00
• Routine task performance	p. 00	• Theft	p. 00
• Adaptive task performance	p. 00	• Production deviance	p. 00
• Job analysis	p. 00	• Wasting resources	p. 00
• Occupational information		• Substance abuse	p. 00
network	p. 00	• Political deviance	p. 00
• Citizenship behavior	p. 00	• Gossiping	p. 00
• Interpersonal citizenship		• Incivility	p. 00
behavior		• Personal aggression	p. 00
• Helping	p. 00	• Harassment	p. 00
• Courtesy	p. 00	• Abuse	p. 00

DISCUSSION QUESTIONS

2.1 Describe the job that you currently hold or hope to hold after graduation. Now look up that job in O*NET database. Does the profile of the job fit your expectations? Are any task behaviors missing from O*NET's profile?

2.2 Describe a job in which citizenship behaviors would be especially critical to an organization's functioning and one in which citizenship behaviors would be less critical. What is it about a job that makes citizenship more important?

2.3 Figure 2-3 classifies productive deviance and political deviance as more minor in nature than property deviance and personal aggression. When might those types of counterproductive behavior prove especially costly?

2.4 Consider how you would react to 360 degree feedback. If you were the one receiving the feedback, whose views would you value most: your managers's or your peers'? If you were asked to assess a peer, would you want your opinion to affect

CASE   ST. JUDE CHILDREN'S HOSPITAL

Given the complexity and cost of fixing them, most organizations knowingly choose to ignore dysfunctions within their performance management system. St. Jude Children's Research Hospital is unlike most organizations. By 2001, it realized that its current performance management system was no longer effective and a new system was needed to improve the organization.

Working with Watson Wyatt, a consulting firm, St. Jude Children's Research Hospital created a new system that addressed all the concerns of the old system. First, the rating system that skewed the performance of employees was replaced by a continuum. Managers now can give employees honest feedback without categorizing them within the confines of a ranking system. Second, customization of job performance replaced one-size-fits-all evaluations. Now a lab scientist will not be evaluated with the same criteria...

EXERCISE   PERFORMANCE OF A SERVER

The purpose of this exercise is to explore what job performance means for a server in a restaurant. This exercise uses groups of six participants, so your instructor will either assign you to a group of six or ask you to create your own group of six. The exercise has the following steps:

1. Conduct a job analysis for a restaurant server. Begin by drawing a circle like the one below. Use that circle to summarize the major job dimensions of a restaurant server. For example, one job dimension might be "Taking Meal Orders." Divide the circle up with four additional job dimensions. Now get more specific by listing two behaviors per job dimension. For example, two behaviors within the "Taking Meal Orders" dimension might be "Describing the Menu" and "Making Recommendations." At the end of Step 1, you should have a list of eight specific behaviors that summarize the tasks involved in being a restaurant server. Write your group's behaviors down on a transparency, laptop, or chalkboard, leaving some space for some additional behaviors down the line.

Taking Orders

2. Take a look at the resulting list. Did you come up with any behaviors that would be described as "citizenship behaviors"? If you didn't include any in your list, does that mean that citizenship behavior isn't important in a restaurant setting? If your group includes someone who has worked as a server, ask him or her to describe the importance of citizenship behavior. Come up with two especially important citizenship behaviors and add those to your list.

Special Features: Supplements

Instructor's Resource CD-ROM
(ISBN: 0073296546, 13-digit
ISBN: 9780073296548)

Allowing instructors to create a customized multimedia presentation, this all-in-one resource incorporates the Instructor's Manual, Computerized Testbank, PowerPoint Slides, and downloaded figures from the text.

Instructor's Manual

Prepared by Carol Moore of California State–East Bay, this manual was developed to help with organizing your classroom presentation. It contains an extensive "chapter roadmap" with an outline of the chapter, Teaching Tips (e.g., hints on how to handle difficult topics), suggestions on the usage of assessments/exercises in the text, suggestions on self-assessments/group exercises found in the Group and Video Resource Manual (see below), and suggestions on where to use Management in the Movies videos (see below). The manual also contains *Business-Week* articles that could be used as cases or "lecturettes," and notes and answers to the end-of-chapter exercises. The video notes that accompany the end-of-chapter videos can be found as a separate folder on the Instructor's Resource CD or on our Web site at **www.mhhe.com/colquitt.**

Testbank and EZ Test Online

Testbank: Our Testbank contains a variety of true/false, multiple choice, and short and long essay questions, as well as "scenario-based" questions, which are application based and use a situation described in a narrative, with 3–5 multiple-choice test questions based on the situation described in the narrative. We've aligned our Testbank questions with Bloom's Taxonomy and AACSB guidelines, tagging each question according to its knowledge and skills areas. Categories include Global, Ethics and Social Responsibility, Legal and other External Environment, Communication, Diversity, Group Dynamics, Individual Dynamics, Production, and IT. Designations aligning questions with Learning Objectives and features exist as well.

EZ Test Online: McGraw-Hill's EZ Test Online is a flexible and easy-to-use electronic testing program. The program allows instructors to create tests from book-specific items, accommodates a wide range of question types, and enables instructors to add their own questions. Multiple versions of the test can be created, and any test can be exported for use with course management systems such as WebCT, BlackBoard, or any other course management system. EZ Test Online is accessible to busy instructors virtually anywhere via the Web, and the program eliminates the need to install test software. Utilizing EZ Test Online also allows instructors to create and deliver multiple-choice or true/false quiz questions using iQuiz for iPod. For more information about EZ Test Online, please see the Web site at **www.eztestonline.com.**

PowerPoint Presentation Slides

Based on instructor feedback, the PowerPoint Presentation slides (prepared by Liesl Wesson, Texas A&M University) will consist of 2 types of presentations: **Outline** and **Detailed** formats that give instructors the flexibility to tailor their presentations to their class needs. The Outline format follows a "don't give them everything" philosophy, which requires students to attend class and take notes to have all the information available to them. The Outline format therefore leaves a significant amount of room on the slides for students to take notes but still maintains the use of tables and figures straight from the book. The Detailed set builds on the outline format to include full definitions and descriptions for the topics covered. This format is designed for instructors who prefer that the students be listening to them instead of taking basic, definition-oriented notes during class. Each format has advantages and disadvantages, but the provision of multiple sets of slides should make it easier for instructors to access ready-made presentations designed to fit their teaching style.

Organizational Behavior Video DVD
(ISBN: 0073337285, 13-digit ISBN: 9780073337289)

For instructors who want to incorporate more "real-world" examples into the classroom, *Organizational Behavior: Improving Performance and Commitment in the Workplace* offers this compilation video DVD, which features news clips on organizational behavior–related topics from NBC, PBS, and *BusinessWeek* TV. Videos are organized by topic and include such companies as Disney Imagineering, 1154 Lil, Johnson & Johnson, and Xerox, as well as topics such as Outsourcing, Work/Life Balance, Layoffs and their psychological effects, Discrimination, and Employees with Passion. Instructor Notes can be found in the Instructor Center of the Web site at **www.mhhe.com/colquitt.** Quizzes on each video can also be found in the Student Center of the Web site.

Online Learning Center at www.mhhe.com/colquitt

If you're looking for a one-stop shopping area for all things OB, look no further than our Web site. Separated into both Instructor and Student areas, each section holds a variety of material for instructors to develop and use in their course and for students to use to review. Instructors will find supplements, additional course materials including video notes, and links to the Group and Video Resource Manual and Manager's HotSeat Online. Students will find basic material like chapter quizzes and the basic PowerPoint outline slides free to use. For a nominal fee, they can access premium content, including interactive Self-Assessments and Test Your Knowledge quizzes, iPod downloadable content of narrated PowerPoint slides along with chapter quizzes, quizzes to review the end-of-chapter videos, a link to the Guide to Online Research, and more.

Management in the Movies
(ISBN: 0073317713, 13-digit ISBN: 9780073317717)

Looking for another way to engage your students in the classroom? The *Management in the Movies* DVD is available exclusively to adopters of McGraw-Hill textbooks and contains a collection of "Big Screen" Hollywood films that students will recognize. Each movie has been clipped to highlight a specific scene (each is less than two and a half minutes) and linked to specific topics.

Some of the topics include:

- Groups—*13 Going On 30.*
- Ethics—*John Q.*
- Diversity—*Inside Man.*
- Attitudes, Values, Culture—*Hoosiers.*
- Control and Change—*Gung Ho.*
- And more!

Along with the DVD, McGraw-Hill provides instructor notes with suggestions for using the clip, clip summaries, and discussion questions to accompany each segment! Material for both you and your students can be found on the OLC.

Manager's HotSeat Online www.mhhe.com/mhs

In today's workplace, managers are confronted daily with issues involving ethics, diversity, working in teams, and the virtual workplace. The Manager's HotSeat offers interactive software that allows students to watch as 15 real managers apply their years of experience to confront these issues. Students assume the role of the manager as they watch the video and answer multiple choice questions that pop up, forcing them to make decisions on the spot. They learn from the manager's mistakes and successes, then write a report critiquing the manager's approach by defending their reasoning. Reports can be e-mailed or printed out for credit. These video segments are a powerful tool for your course that truly immerses students in the learning experience. Ask your McGraw-Hill sales representative how you can obtain access.

Group and Video Resource Manual: An Instructor's Guide to an Active Classroom (in print ISBN: 0073044342, or online at www.mhhe.com/mobmanual)

This manual, created for instructors, contains everything needed to integrate activities successfully into the classroom. It includes a menu of items to use as teaching tools in class. All of our interactive Self-Assessment exercises, Test Your Knowledge quizzes, Group Exercises, and Manager's HotSeat videos are located in this one manual, along with teaching notes and PowerPoint slides to use in class. Group exercises include everything you might need to use the exercise in class—handouts, figures, and so forth.

This manual is organized into 25 topics including ethics, decision making, change, and leadership for easy inclusion in your lecture. A matrix appears at the front of the manual that references

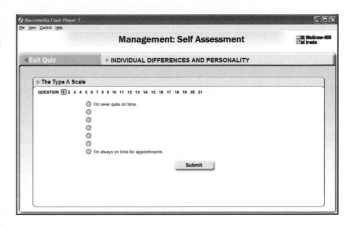

each resource by topic. Students can access all of the exercises and self-assessments on their textbook's Web site. The Manager's HotSeat exercises are located online at www.mhhe.com/MHS

"Enhanced" Cartridge for WebCT and Blackboard

Do you already use WebCT or Blackboard? Are you hoping to put more of your course materials online? Are you looking for an easy way to assign more materials to your students and manage a gradebook? If so, *Organizational Behavior: Improving Performance and Commitment in the Workplace* offers the answer, because it comes equipped with McGraw-Hill's new Enhanced Cartridge.

The Enhanced Cartridge is designed to help you get your course up and running with much less time and effort. The content, enhanced with more assignments and more study materials than a standard cartridge, is prepopulated into appropriate chapters and content categories. Now there's no need to cut and paste our content into your course—it's already there! But you can still choose to hide content we provide and add your own, just as you have in WebCT and Blackboard. The *Organizational Behavior: Improving Performance and Commitment in the Workplace* enhanced cartridge content includes:

- iPod/MP3 content.
- Chapter pre- and posttests.
- Gradebook functionality.
- Discussion boards.
- Additional assignments.
- Personalized graphics/banners/icons for your school.
- And much more!

You can choose to package a password card with your text, or students can buy access via e-commerce through the book's Web site for $10. Ask your McGraw-Hill sales representative about how to get the enhanced cartridge to accompany *Organizational Behavior: Improving Performance and Commitment in the Workplace* for your course.

Acknowledgments

An enormous number of persons played a role in helping us put the first edition of this textbook together. Truth be told, we had no idea that we would have to rely on and put our success in the hands of so many different people! Each of them had unique and useful contributions to make toward the publication of this book, and they deserve and thus receive our sincere gratitude.

A special thanks goes out to Carol Moore (California State University–East Bay) for her outstanding work on our Instructor's Manual and for helping us develop some of the end-of-chapter exercises; Amit Shah (Frostburg State University) for helping with the end-of-chapter cases; Kathleen Barnes (East Stroudsburg University) for her authorship of the Testbank file; and Liesl Wesson (Texas A&M University) for her development of the PowerPoint presentations.

We are overly indebted to John Weimeister, our sponsoring editor, for his encouragement to write the textbook and his steadfast belief in our doing things in a more "unorthodox" way at times. John has been taking good care of us all the way back to our graduate school days. Thanks also go out to Christine "Chipper" Scheid, our Senior Development Editor, who did her best to keep us on track in terms of actually getting things done and provided valuable feedback throughout the process. We also owe much gratitude to our Marketing Managers, Meg Beamer and Krista Bettino, whom we always felt were behind us 100 percent. We also would like to thank Bruce Gin, Gina Hangos, Artemio Ortiz, Jeremy Cheshareck, Elisa Adams, Matthew Perry, and Susan Lombardi at Irwin/McGraw Hill, as they are the masterminds of much of how the book actually looks as it sits in students' hands; their work and effort were spectacular.

We have also had the great fortune of having had over 50 faculty members from colleges and universities around the country provide feedback on various aspects of the First Edition of this textbook. Whether by providing feedback on chapters or attending focus groups, their input made this book substantially better:

Grace Auyang, *University of Cincinnati*

Joy Beatty, *University of Michigan-Dearborn*

Bryan Bonner, *University of Utah*

James H. Browne, *Colorado State University-Pueblo*

Deborah Butler, *Georgia State University*

Jerry Carbo, *Fairmont State University*

Macgorine Cassell, *Fairmont State University*

Fred Dorn, *University of Mississippi*

Ken Dunegan, *Cleveland State University*

Kathy Edwards, *University of Texas-Austin*

Berrin Erdogan, *Portland State University*

Linda Evans, *University of Dayton*

David Fearon, *Central Connecticut State University*

Mark Fichman, *Carnegie Mellon University*

Laura Fuller, *Wilmington College*

Megan Gerhardt, *Miami University of Ohio*

Treena Gillespie, *Cal State University-Fullerton*

Ron Humphrey, *Virginia Commonwealth University*

Christine Jackson, *Purdue University*

Paul H. Jacques, *Western Carolina University*

Sheryl Joshua, *University of North Carolina, Greensboro*

Dong Jung, *San Diego State University*

Christian Kiewitz, *University of Dayton*

Robin Lightner, *University of Cincinnati*

Donna Mickens, *Southern Illinois University-Edwardsville*

Nathan Moates, *Valdosta State University*

Karthik Namasivayam, *Pennsylvania State University*

Rhonda Palladi, *Georgia State University*

Elizabeth Ravlin, *University of South Carolina*

Clint Relyea, *Arkansas State University*

Barbara Ritter, *Coastal Carolina University*

Joe Santora, *Essex County College*

James Schmidtke, *Cal State University-Fresno*

Don Schreiber, *Baylor University*

Holly Schroth, *University of California, Berkeley*

Bret Simmons, *University of Nevada-Reno*

Randi Sims, *Nova Southeastern University*

Ronald Sims, *College of William and Mary*

Karen J. Smith, *Columbia Southern University*

Dan Spencer, *University of Kansas-Lawrence*

Lynda St. Clair, *Bryant University*

David Tansik, *University of Arizona*

Ed Tomlinson, *John Carroll University*

Joy Turnheim Smith, *IUPUI-Fort Wayne*

William Turnley, *Kansas State University*

Sean Valentine, *University of Wyoming*

Jim Whitney, *Champlain College*

Joana Young, *Baylor University*

We would also like to thank our students at the undergraduate, masters, and executive levels who were taught with early versions of these chapters for their constructive feedback toward making them more effective in the classroom. Thanks also to our Ph.D. students for allowing us to take time out from research projects to focus on this book.

Finally, we thank our families, who gave up substantial amounts of time with us and put up with the stress that necessarily comes at times during an endeavor such as this.

Jason Colquitt

Jeff LePine

Michael Wesson

BRIEF CONTENTS

PART 1 INTRODUCTION TO ORGANIZATIONAL BEHAVIOR 3

CHAPTER 1 4
What is Organizational Behavior?

CHAPTER 2 34
Job Performance

CHAPTER 3 64
Organizational Commitment

PART 2 INDIVIDUAL MECHANISMS 101

CHAPTER 4 102
Job Satisfaction

CHAPTER 5 140
Stress

CHAPTER 6 176
Motivation

CHAPTER 7 216
Trust, Justice, and Ethics

CHAPTER 8 254
Learning and Decision Making

PART 3 INDIVIDUAL CHARACTERISTICS 289

CHAPTER 9 290
Personality and Cultural Values

CHAPTER 10 334
Ability

PART 4 GROUP MECHANISMS 369

CHAPTER 11 370
Teams: Characteristics

CHAPTER 12 406
Teams: Processes

CHAPTER 13 438
Leadership: Power and Influence

CHAPTER 14 470
Leadership: Styles and Behaviors

PART 5 ORGANIZATIONAL MECHANISMS 513

CHAPTER 15 514
Organizational Structure

CHAPTER 16 544
Organizational Culture

GLOSSARY 577

PHOTO CREDITS 595

INDEX 597

NAME 597

COMPANY 608

SUBJECT 610

TABLE OF CONTENTS

PART 1 INTRODUCTION TO ORGANIZATIONAL BEHAVIOR 3

CHAPTER 1 4
What Is Organizational Behavior?

What Is Organizational Behavior? 6

Organizational Behavior Defined 7

An Integrative Model of Organizational Behavior 7

Does Organizational Behavior Matter? 12

Building a Conceptual Argument 12

Research Evidence 15

So What's So Hard? 18

How Do We "Know" What We Know about Organizational Behavior? 21

SUMMARY: MOVING FORWARD IN THIS BOOK 25

TAKEAWAYS 27

KEY TERMS 28

DISCUSSION QUESTIONS 28

CASE 29

EXERCISE 29

CHAPTER 2 34
Job Performance

Job Performance 36

What Does It Mean to Be a "Good Performer"? 38

Task Performance 38

Citizenship Behavior 43

Counterproductive Behavior 46

Summary: What Does It Mean to Be a "Good Performer"? 50

Trends Affecting Performance 51

Knowledge Work 52

Service Work 53

Application: Performance Management 53

Management by Objectives 55

Behaviorally Anchored Rating Scales 55

360 Degree Feedback 56

TAKEAWAYS 57

KEY TERMS 57

DISCUSSION QUESTIONS 58

CASE 58

EXERCISE 59

CHAPTER 3 64
Organizational Commitment

Organizational Commitment 66

What Does It Mean to Be a "Committed" Employee? 67

Types of Commitment 68

Withdrawal Behavior 76

Summary: What Does It Mean to Be a "Committed" Employee? 83

Trends That Affect Commitment 83

Diversity of the Workforce 83

The Changing Employer-Employee Relationship 85

Application: Commitment Initiatives 88

TAKEAWAYS 90

KEY TERMS 90

DISCUSSION QUESTIONS 91

CASE 91

EXERCISE 92

PART 2 INDIVIDUAL MECHANISMS 101

CHAPTER 4 102
Job Satisfaction

Job Satisfaction 104

Why Are Some Employees More Satisfied Than Others? 105

    Value Fulfillment: Value-Percept Theory 107

    Satisfaction with the Work Itself: The Job Characteristics Model 111

    Mood and Emotions 118

    Summary: Why Are Some Employees More Satisfied Than Others? 125

How Important Is Job Satisfaction? 125

    Life Satisfaction 128

Application: Tracking Satisfaction 131

TAKEAWAYS 132

KEY TERMS 133

DISCUSSION QUESTIONS 134

CASE 134

EXERCISE 135

CHAPTER 5 140
Stress

Stress 142

Why Are Some Employees More "Stressed" Than Others? 144

    Types of Stressors 145

    How Do People Cope with Stressors? 151

    The Experience of Strain 154

    Accounting for Individuals in the Stress Process 156

    Summary: Why Are Some Employees More "Stressed" Than Others? 159

How Important Is Stress? 160

Application: Stress Management 161

    Assessment 163

    Reducing Stressors 163

    Providing Resources 163

    Reducing Strains 165

TAKEAWAYS 166

KEY TERMS 167

DISCUSSION QUESTIONS 167

CASE 168

EXERCISE 168

CHAPTER 6 176
Motivation

Motivation 178

Why Are Some Employees More Motivated Than Others? 180

    Expectancy Theory 180

    Goal Setting Theory 186

    Equity Theory 191

    Psychological Empowerment 197

    Summary: Why Are Some Employees More Motivated Than Others? 200

How Important Is Motivation? 202

Application: Compensation Systems 204

TAKEAWAYS 206

KEY TERMS 206

DISCUSSION QUESTIONS 207

CASE 207

EXERCISE 208

CHAPTER 7 216
Trust, Justice, and Ethics

Trust, Justice, and Ethics 219

Why Are Some Authorities More Trusted Than Others? 220

    Trust 220

    Justice 224

    Ethics 233

    Summary: Why Are Some Authorities More Trusted Than Others? 238

How Important Is Trust? 240

Application: Social Responsibility 241

TAKEAWAYS 243

KEY TERMS 244

DISCUSSION QUESTIONS 244

CASE 245

EXERCISE 245

CHAPTER 8 254
Learning and Decision Making

Learning and Decision Making 256

Why Do Some Employees Learn to Make Decisions Better Than Others? 257

    Types of Knowledge 257

    Methods of Learning 258

    Methods of Decision Making 265

    Decision-Making Problems 268

    Summary: Why Do Some Employees Learn to Make Decisions Better Than Others? 275

How Important Is Learning? 276

Application: Training 278

TAKEAWAYS 279

KEY TERMS 280

DISCUSSION QUESTIONS 281

CASE 281

EXERCISE 282

PART 3 INDIVIDUAL CHARACTERISTICS 289

CHAPTER 9 290
Personality and Cultural Values

Personality and Cultural Values 292

How Can We Describe What Employees Are Like? 293

    The Big Five Taxonomy 293

    Other Taxonomies of Personality 306

    Cultural Values 307

    Summary: How Can We Describe What Employees Are Like? 311

How Important Are Personality and Cultural Values? 313

Application: Personality Tests 314

TAKEAWAYS 320

KEY TERMS 321

DISCUSSION QUESTIONS 322

CASE 322

EXERCISE 323

CHAPTER 10 334
Ability

Ability 336

What Does It Mean for an Employee to Be "Able"? 339

    Cognitive Ability 339

    Emotional Ability 344

    Physical Abilities 348

    Summary: What Does It Mean for an Employee to Be "Able"? 354

How Important Is Ability? 354

Application: The Wonderlic 357

TAKEAWAYS 360

KEY TERMS 360

DISCUSSION QUESTIONS 361

CASE 361

EXERCISE 362

PART 4 GROUP MECHANISMS 369

CHAPTER 11 370
Teams: Characteristics

Team Characteristics 372

What Characteristics Can Be Used to Describe Teams? 373

    Team Types 373

    Variations within Team Types 377

    Team Interdependence 379

    Team Composition 384

    Summary: What Characteristics Can Be Used to Describe Teams? 390

How Important Are Team Characteristics? 393

Application: Team Compensation 393

TAKEAWAYS 395

KEY TERMS 396

DISCUSSION QUESTIONS 396

CASE 397

EXERCISE 397

CHAPTER 12 406
Teams: Processes

Team Processes 408

Why Are Some Teams More Than the Sum of
Their Parts? 409

Taskwork Processes 412

Teamwork Processes 416

Team States 418

*Summary: Why Are Some Teams More Than
the Sum of Their Parts? 421*

How Important Are Team Processes? 422

Application: Training Teams 424

Transportable Teamwork Competencies 424

Cross-Training 425

Team Process Training 426

Team Building 426

TAKEAWAYS 427

KEY TERMS 428

DISCUSSION QUESTIONS 428

CASE 429

EXERCISE 429

CHAPTER 13 438
Leadership: Power and Influence

Leadership: Power and Influence 441

Why Are Some Leaders More
Powerful Than Others? 441

Acquiring Power 442

Using Influence 447

Power and Influence in Action 450

*Summary: Why Are Some
Leaders More Powerful Than Others? 457*

How Important Is Power and Influence? 459

Application: Negotiations 460

TAKEAWAYS 461

KEY TERMS 462

DISCUSSION QUESTIONS 463

CASE 463

EXERCISE 464

CHAPTER 14 470
Leadership: Styles and Behaviors

Leadership: Styles and Behaviors 474

Why Are Some Leaders More
Effective Than Others? 476

Leader Decision-Making Styles 477

Day-to-Day Leadership Behaviors 481

Transformational Leadership Behaviors 487

*Summary: Why Are Some Leaders More
Effective Than Others? 492*

How Important Is Leadership? 495

Application: Leadership Training 497

TAKEAWAYS 499

KEY TERMS 499

DISCUSSION QUESTIONS 500

CASE 500

EXERCISE 501

**PART 5 ORGANIZATIONAL
MECHANISMS** 513

CHAPTER 15 514
Organizational Structure

Organizational Structure 516

Why Do Some Organizations Have
Different Structures Than Others? 517

Elements of Organizational Structure 518

Organizational Design 525

Common Organizational Forms 527

*Summary: Why Do Some
Organizations Have Different Structures
Than Others? 534*

How Important Is Structure? 534

Application: Restructuring 536

TAKEAWAYS 537

KEY TERMS 538

DISCUSSION QUESTIONS 538

CASE 539

EXERCISE 540

CHAPTER 16 544
Organizational Culture

Organizational Culture 546

Why Do Some Organizations Have
Different Cultures Than Others? 547

   Culture Components 548

   General Culture Types 552

   Specific Culture Types 553

   Culture Strength 554

   Maintaining an Organizational Culture 557

   Changing an Organizational Culture 560

   *Summary: Why Do Some
   Organizations Have Different Cultures Than
   Others? 561*

How Important Is Organizational Culture? 564

Application: Managing Socialization 564

TAKEAWAYS 569

KEY TERMS 569

DISCUSSION QUESTIONS 570

CASE 570

EXERCISE 571

GLOSSARY 577

PHOTO CREDITS 595

INDEX 597

   NAME   597

   COMPANY   608

   SUBJECT   610

PART 1

INTRODUCTION TO ORGANIZATIONAL BEHAVIOR

CHAPTER 1:
What Is Organizational Behavior?

CHAPTER 2:
Job Performance

CHAPTER 3:
Organizational Commitment

What Is Organizational Behavior?

 LEARNING GOALS

After reading this chapter, you should be able to answer the following questions:

1.1 What is the definition of "organizational behavior"?

1.2 What are the two primary outcomes in studies of organizational behavior? What factors affect those two primary outcomes?

1.3 Do firms that are good at organizational behavior tend to be more profitable? Why might that be, and is there any research evidence to support this tendency?

1.4 What is a theory, and what is its role in the scientific method?

1.5 What does a "correlation" represent, and what are "big," "moderate," and "small" correlations? What is a meta-analysis?

Starbucks's phenomenal success is due in large part to its mastery of organizational behavior, enabling it to hire enthusiastic and motivated employees who perform their jobs consistently well.

STARBUCKS

Wherever you are as you read this book, chances are good that a Starbucks isn't too far away. By the start of 2006, there were about 10,000 Starbucks locations worldwide, including a mall, campus, airport, or highway exit near you.[1] Although some people may worry about the fate of their local, independent coffee shops or the high price of Starbucks coffee, consider the answers to these questions: When was the last time your Starbucks was messy? When was the last time you were treated rudely by the person across the counter? When was the last time your order of choice tasted wrong (or even just a bit different)?

One reason for Starbucks's success is that such occurrences are quite rare, especially compared with other service, retail, or dining venues. Who receives much of the credit for the consistency in Starbucks's service? The rank-and-file employees who run the stores and interact directly with the customer. Somehow Starbucks has been able to find employees who are conscientious and intelligent, who seem motivated and satisfied with their jobs, who remain committed to their stores for a longer-than-normal period of time, and who perform their job duties reliably and enthusiastically. Put simply, Starbucks seems to be doing a good job managing organizational behavior.

Some support for that claim comes from *Fortune* magazine's list of the "100 Best Companies to Work For" in 2007, on which Starbucks placed 16.[2] Generous benefits and health care coverage—even for part-time workers and for spouses and partners—seem to have instilled a sense of commitment, as Starbucks's voluntary turnover rate is 120 percent lower than the average quick service restaurant business.[3] Guiding principles like "provide a great work environment" and "treat each other with respect and dignity" seem to have fostered a sense of satisfaction with the culture of the organization.[4] Indeed, a recent survey showed that 82 percent of employees were either "satisfied" or "very satisfied" with the company.[5] In addition, the social activism of the company—Starbucks contributed $15 million to local nonprofits in 2004—seems to have built a sense of trust and ethics among the rank-and-file employees. Taken together, such policies and practices are increasing the likelihood that your next Starbucks visit will be a pleasant one.

WHAT IS ORGANIZATIONAL BEHAVIOR?

Before we define exactly what the field of organizational behavior represents, take a moment to ponder the following: Who was the single *worst* coworker you've ever had? Picture fellow students with whom you've worked on class projects; colleagues from part-time or summer jobs; or peers, subordinates, or supervisors working in your current organization. What did this coworker do that earned him or her "worst coworker" status? Was it some of the behaviors shown in the right column of Table 1-1 (or perhaps all of them)? Now take a moment to consider the single *best* coworker you've ever had. Again, what did this coworker do to earn "best coworker" status—some or most of the behaviors shown in the left column of Table 1-1?

If you ever found yourself working alongside the two people profiled in the table, two questions probably would be foremost on your mind: "*Why* does the worst coworker act that way?" and "*Why* does the best coworker act that way?" Once you understand why the two coworkers act so differently, you might be able to figure out ways to interact with the worst coworker more effectively (thereby making your working life a bit more pleasant). If you happen to be a manager, you can formulate plans for how to improve attitudes and behaviors in the unit. Such plans may include how to screen applicants, train and socialize new organizational members, manage evaluations and rewards for performance, and deal

TABLE 1-1	The Best of Coworkers, the Worst of Coworkers	
THE BEST	**THE WORST**	
Have you ever had a coworker who usually acted this way?	Have you ever had a coworker who usually acted this way?	
√ Got the job done, without having to be managed or reminded	√ Did not got the job done, even with a great deal of hand-holding	
√ Adapted when something needed to be changed or done differently	√ Was resistant to any and every form of change, even when changes were beneficial	
√ Always was a "good sport," even when bad things happened at work	√ Whined and complained, no matter what was happening	
√ Attended optional meetings or functions to support colleagues	√ Optional meetings? Was too lazy to make it to some required meetings and functions!	
√ Helped new coworkers or people who seemed to need a hand	√ Made fun of new coworkers or people who seemed to need a hand	
√ Followed key rules, even when the reasons for them were not apparent	√ Broke virtually any rule that somehow made their work more difficult	
√ Felt an attachment and obligation to the employer for the long haul	√ Seemed to always be looking for something else, even if it wasn't better	
√ Was first to arrive, last to leave	√ Was first to leave for lunch, last to return	

Million Dollar Question:
Why do these two employees act so differently?

with conflicts that arise between employees. Without understanding why employees act the way they do, it is very difficult to find a way to change their attitudes and behaviors at work.

ORGANIZATIONAL BEHAVIOR DEFINED

Organizational behavior (OB) is a field of study devoted to understanding, explaining, and ultimately improving the attitudes and behaviors of individuals and groups in organizations. Scholars in management departments of universities and scientists in business organizations conduct research on OB. The findings from those research studies are then applied by managers or consultants to see whether they help meet "real-world" challenges. In addition, OB can be contrasted with two other courses commonly offered in management departments: human resource management and strategic management. **Human resource management** takes the theories and principles studied in OB and explores the "nuts-and-bolts" applications of those principles in organizations. An OB study might explore the relationship between learning and job performance, whereas a human resource management study might examine the best ways to structure training programs to promote employee learning. **Strategic management** focuses on the product choices and industry characteristics that affect an organization's profitability. For example, a strategic management study might examine the relationship between firm diversification (when a firm expands into a new product segment) and firm profitability.

1.1

What is the definition of "organizational behavior"?

The theories and concepts found in OB are actually drawn from a wide variety of disciplines. For example, research on job performance and individual characteristics draws primarily from studies in industrial and organizational psychology. Research on satisfaction, emotions, and team processes draws heavily from social psychology. Sociology research is vital to research on team characteristics and organizational structure, and anthropology research helps inform the study of organizational culture. Finally, models from economics are used to understand motivation, learning, and decision making. This diversity brings a unique quality to the study of OB, as most students will be able to find a particular topic that is intrinsically interesting and thought provoking to them.

AN INTEGRATIVE MODEL OF ORGANIZATIONAL BEHAVIOR

Because of the diversity in its topics and disciplinary roots, it is common for students in an organizational behavior class to wonder "How does all this stuff fit together?" How does what gets covered in Chapter 3 relate to what gets covered in Chapter 13? To clarify such issues, this textbook is structured around an integrative model of OB, shown in Figure 1-1, that is designed to provide a roadmap for the field of organizational behavior. The model shows how the topics in the next 15 chapters—represented by the 15 ovals in the model—all fit together. We should stress that there are other potential ways of combining the 15 topics, and Figure 1-1 likely oversimplifies the connections among the topics. Still, we believe the model provides a helpful guide as you move through this course. Figure 1-1 includes five different kinds of topics.

INDIVIDUAL OUTCOMES. The right-most portion of the model contains the two primary outcomes of interest to organizational behavior researchers (and employees and managers in organizations): *job performance* and *organizational commitment.* Most employees have two primary goals for their working lives: to perform their jobs well and to remain a member of an organization that they respect. Likewise, most managers have two primary goals for their employees: to maximize their job performance and to ensure that they stay with the firm for a significant length of time. As described in Chapter 2, there

1.2

What are the two primary outcomes in studies of organizational behavior? What factors affect those two primary outcomes?

FIGURE 1-1   Integrative Model of Organizational Behavior

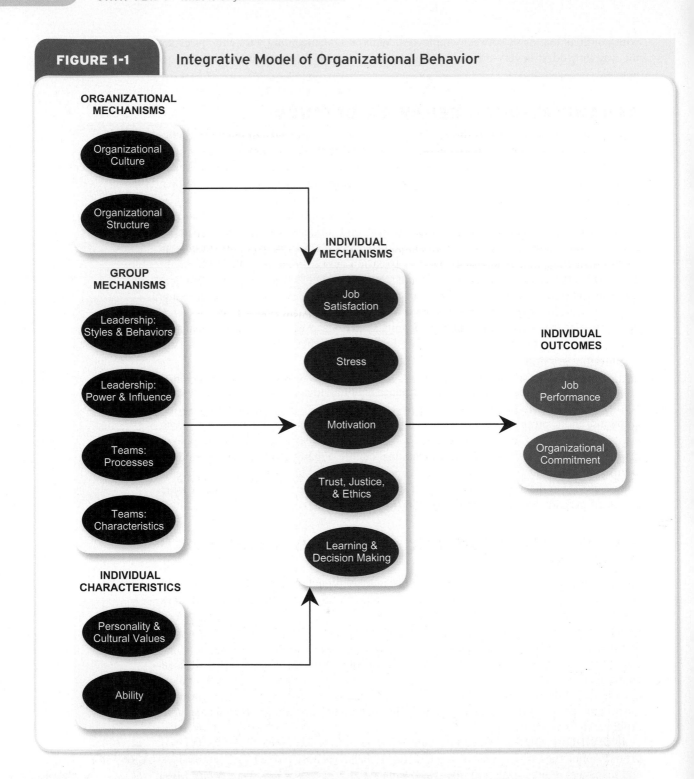

are several specific behaviors that, when taken together, constitute good job performance. Similarly, as described in Chapter 3, there are a number of beliefs, attitudes, and emotions that cause an employee to remain committed to an employer.[6]

This book starts by covering job performance and organizational commitment so that you can better understand the two primary organizational behavior goals. Our hope is that by using performance and commitment as starting points, we can highlight the practical importance of OB topics. After all, what could be more important than having employees who perform well and want to stay with the company? This structure also enables us to conclude the other chapters in the book with sections that describe the relationships between each chapter's topic and performance and commitment. For example, the chapter on motivation concludes by describing the relationships between motivation and performance and motivation and commitment. In this way, you'll learn which of the topics in the model are most useful for understanding your own job performance and your own desires to stay with (or leave) your company.

INDIVIDUAL MECHANISMS. Our integrative model also illustrates a number of individual mechanisms that directly affect job performance and organizational commitment. These include *job satisfaction,* which captures what employees feel when thinking about their jobs and doing their day-to-day work (Chapter 4). Another individual mechanism is *stress,* which reflects employees' psychological responses to job demands that tax or exceed their capacities (Chapter 5). The model also includes *motivation,* which captures the energetic forces that drive employees' work effort (Chapter 6). *Trust, justice, and ethics* reflect the degree to which employees feel that their company does business with fairness, honesty, and integrity (Chapter 7). The final individual mechanism shown in the model is *learning and decision making,* which deals with how employees gain job knowledge and how they use that knowledge to make accurate judgments on the job (Chapter 8).

Many organizations view these mechanisms as critical to job performance and organizational commitment. For example, The Container Store—a Texas-based retailer that specializes in storage and organization products—stresses the need to create an "air of excitement" within its stores, so that employees feel a sense of satisfaction and fun day in and day out.[7] Facilities within the company are designed to manage workplace stress, with bright colors, large displays of artwork, good lighting and windows, and a focus on safety that has minimized workplace accidents.[8] Motivation is fostered both formally and informally, with wages that are 50–100 percent higher than the industry average, supplemented by a "celebration mailbox" voicemail system that compliments employees for especially good performance.[9] Perceptions of trust, justice, and ethics are created by sharing financial

The Container Store provides employees with higher-than-average wages and gives significant support to charitable causes. These strategies foster a sense of motivation and trust and helped the company place fourth on *Fortune's* "100 Best Companies to Work For" list.

information openly with all employees and donating significant sums of money to charities and causes that are important in each store's community.[10] The Container Store also stresses learning and decision making. One of its guiding principles—"Intuition does not come to an unprepared mind"—captures the importance of learning everything needed to help a customer.[11] Indeed, the organization offers 235 hours of training in a full-time employee's first year (the industry average is only 7 hours).[12] The end result is an organization noted for its effective customer service with a turnover rate only one-fourth the industry average.[13]

INDIVIDUAL CHARACTERISTICS. Of course, if satisfaction, stress, motivation, and so forth are key drivers of job performance and organizational commitment, it becomes important to understand what factors improve these individual mechanisms. Two such factors reflect the characteristics of individual employees. *Personality and cultural values* reflect the various traits and tendencies that describe how people act, with commonly studied traits including extraversion, conscientiousness, and collectivism. As described in Chapter 9, personality and cultural values affect the way people behave at work, the kinds of tasks they are interested in, and how they react to events that happen on the job. The model also examines *ability,* which describes the cognitive abilities (verbal, quantitative, etc.), emotional skills (other awareness, emotion regulation, etc.), and physical abilities (strength, endurance, etc.) that employees bring to a job. As described in Chapter 10, ability influences the kinds of tasks an employee is good at and those with which an employee may struggle.

The Container Store also points to individual characteristics as part of its recipe for success. The founders of the company espouse a "one equals three" principle, which suggests that one great worker is as valuable as three good ones.[14] The interviewing and screening process used by the organization is much more intensive than the industry norm, so The Container Store can identify the outgoing, creative, talented, and curious people who will excel in its organization. As a result, one employee who had been with the company for 10 years noted, "You can't help but feel special and proud, knowing you're surrounded by the best, most talented individuals in the business."[15]

GROUP MECHANISMS. The integrative model in Figure 1-1 also acknowledges that employees do not work alone. Instead, they typically work in one or more work teams led by some formal (or sometimes informal) leader. Like the individual characteristics, these group mechanisms shape satisfaction, stress, motivation, trust, and learning. Chapter 11 describes the *team characteristics* that summarize the qualities that teams possess, such as their norms, their roles, and the way members depend on one another. Chapter 12 then describes the *team processes* that summarize how teams behave, including topics like cooperation, conflict, and communication. The next two chapters focus on the leaders of those teams. We first describe how individuals become leaders in the first place and consider *leader power and influence* to summarize the process by which individuals attain authority over others (Chapter 13). We then describe how leaders behave in their leadership roles; *leader styles and behaviors* capture the specific actions that leaders take to influence others at work (Chapter 14).

Issues of teamwork and leadership are also critical at The Container Store. The company stresses that all employees work for a common cause and that no one can succeed without helping other employees succeed. One of the founders, Garrett Boone, challenges employees to ask, "Whom can I help today, communicate with, and share with to make their work better?"[16] Effective leadership has helped instill this focus on teamwork, because the founders spend much of their time actually working in stores and getting to know employees' first names, hobbies, and family details.

ORGANIZATIONAL MECHANISMS. Finally, our integrative model acknowledges that the teams described in the prior section are grouped into larger organizations that themselves affect satisfaction, stress, motivation, and so forth. For example, every company has an *organizational structure* that dictates how the units within the firm link to (and communicate with) other units (Chapter 15). Sometimes structures are centralized around a decision-making authority, whereas other times, structures are decentralized, affording each unit some autonomy. Every company also has an *organizational culture* that captures "the way things are" in the organization—shared knowledge about the rules, norms, and values that shape employee attitudes and behaviors (Chapter 16).

The Container Store also has managed issues of structure and culture to achieve its record of success. As the company has expanded, it has divided its stores according to the regional markets they serve and created general area directors that can focus specifically on the needs of specific markets.[17] However, the company has taken great care to ensure that the expansion does not alter its organizational culture. The founders make celebrations and award presentations key components of the fun, quirky, and folksy culture of the company; attend as many store anniversary parties as they can; and transmit costumed skits to those ceremonies they can't make.[18] With these kinds of practices, it's not surprising that The Container Store placed fourth on *Fortune*'s "100 Best Companies to Work For" list in 2007.[19]

SUMMARY. Each of the chapters in this textbook will open with a depiction of this integrative model, with the subject of each chapter highlighted. We hope that this opening will serve as a guide for where you are in this book, as well as where you've been and where you're going. Some of you will be able to apply those topic areas to your current working life, whether you're working full-time or part-time and whether you occupy a managerial or nonmanagerial role. Of course, some of you are full-time students or between jobs at the moment. Regardless of your work status, one thing all of you have in common is that you're students. As it turns out, many of the same concepts that predict success in an organization also predict success in a classroom. We will explore some of those commonalities in our **OB for Students** feature, which appears in each chapter and illustrates how OB concepts can be applied to improve academic success.

OB FOR STUDENTS

This feature is designed to demonstrate the generalizability of many OB principles by applying them to another area of life: life as a student. Each chapter will explore how a particular topic occurs in the classroom. This inaugural edition highlights some of the things you can expect in the chapters to come:

Job Satisfaction (Chapter 4). How do students judge how satisfied they are with their university life? How do they weigh things like where they live, how much they like their classmates, and how much they enjoy what they're studying?

Stress (Chapter 5). The working world doesn't corner the market on stress; juggling several classes along with life's other responsibilities can be quite stressful in its own right. We'll explore how various kinds of stressful demands affect student learning and class performance.

Team Characteristics (Chapter 11). Several classes use team projects. We'll explore two factors that are important drivers of the effectiveness of student teams, in the hope that you can use this discussion to improve your own team's functioning.

Organizational Structure (Chapter 15). What kinds of organizational structures do most students find attractive when they are on the job market? Do some students have different structural preferences than others?

Organizational Culture (Chapter 16). How do new students learn about the culture of a university? Are there benefits of socializing new students in the same way that organizations socialize new employees? What would such socialization efforts look like?

DOES ORGANIZATIONAL BEHAVIOR MATTER?

Having described exactly what OB is, it is time to discuss another fundamental question: Does it really matter? Is there any value in taking a class on this subject, other than fulfilling some requirement of your program? (You might guess that we are biased in our answers to these questions, given that we wrote an entire book on this subject!) Few would disagree that organizations need to know principles of accounting and finance to be successful; it would be impossible to conduct business without such knowledge. Similarly, few would disagree that organizations need to know principles of marketing, as consumers need to know about the firm's products and what makes those products unique or noteworthy.

However, people sometimes wonder whether a firm's ability to manage OB has any bearing on its bottom-line profitability. After all, if a firm has a good-enough product, won't people buy it regardless of how happy, motivated, or committed its workforce is? Perhaps for a time, but effective OB can help keep a product good over the long term. This same argument can be made in reverse: If a firm has a bad-enough product, isn't it true that people won't buy it, regardless of how happy, motivated, or committed its workforce is? Again, perhaps for a time, but the effective management of OB can help make a product get better, incrementally, over the long term.

Consider this pop quiz about the automotive industry: Name the four best-selling foreign nameplates in the United States from 2002 to 2005. You earn a B if you knew that Toyota was #1 (1.67 million) and Honda was #2 (1.2 million). You earn an A if you knew that Nissan was #3 (855,002). But who is #4? Mazda? Volkswagen? Mercedes? Nope—the answer is Hyundai (418,615).[20] Hyundai's offerings were once criticized as being "cheap," with Jay Leno famously comparing a Hyundai to a bobsled ("It has no room, you have to push it to get going, and it only goes downhill!").[21] More recent models—including those built in a new manufacturing plant in Montgomery, Alabama—are regarded as good looking and well made, and the Sonata was labeled the most reliable car in America by *Consumer Reports* in 2004.[22] This shift represents Hyundai's increased emphasis on quality; work teams devoted to quality have been expanded eightfold, and almost all employees have enrolled in special training programs devoted to quality issues.[23] Hyundai represents a case in which OB principles are being applied to multiple cultures. Our **OB Internationally** feature spotlights such international and cross-cultural applications of OB topics in each chapter.

After it enrolled its employees in quality training programs and dramatically increased its reliance on work teams, Hyundai produced *Consumer Reports'* "most reliable car of the year" for 2004—the Sonata.

BUILDING A CONCEPTUAL ARGUMENT

Of course, we shouldn't just accept it on faith that OB matters, nor should we merely look for specific companies that appear to support the premise. What we need instead is a logical conceptual argument that captures exactly why OB might affect the bottom-line profitability

OB INTERNATIONALLY

Changes in technology, communications, and economic forces have made business more global and international than ever. To use Thomas Friedman's line, "the world is flat." The playing field has been leveled between the United States and the rest of the world.[24] This feature spotlights the impact of globalization on the organizational behavior concepts described in this book. More specifically, this feature will cover a variety of topics:

Cross-Cultural Differences. Research in cross-cultural organizational behavior has illustrated that national cultures affect many of the relationships in our integrative model. Put differently, there is little that we know about OB that is "universal" or "culture free."[25]

International Corporations. An increasing number of organizations are international in scope, with both foreign and domestic operations. Applying organizational behavior concepts in these firms represents a special challenge—should policies and practices be consistent across locations or tailored to meet the needs of the culture?

Expatriation. Working as an expatriate—an employee who lives outside his or her native country—can be particularly challenging. What factors influence expatriates' job performance and organizational commitment levels?

Managing Diversity. More and more work groups are composed of members of different cultural backgrounds. What are the special challenges involved in leading and working in such groups?

of an organization. One such argument is based on the **resource-based view** of organizations. This perspective describes what exactly makes resources valuable—that is, what makes them capable of creating long-term profits for the firm.[26] A firm's resources include financial (revenue, equity, etc.) and physical (buildings, machines, technology) resources, but they also include resources related to organizational behavior, such as the knowledge, decision making, ability, and wisdom of the workforce, as well as the image, culture, and goodwill of the organization.

The resource-based view suggests that the value of resources depends on several factors, shown in Figure 1-2. For example, a resource is more valuable when it is *rare*. Diamonds, oil, Babe Ruth baseball cards, and Action Comics #1 (the debut of Superman) are all expensive precisely because they are rare. Good people are also rare—witness the adage "good people are hard to find." Ask yourself what percentage of the people you have worked with have been talented, motivated, satisfied, and good team players. In many organizations, cities, or job markets, such employees are the exception rather than the rule. If good people really are rare, then the effective management of OB should prove to be a valuable resource.

The resource-based view also suggests that a resource is more valuable when it is **inimitable,** meaning that it cannot be imitated. A new form of technology can help a firm gain an advantage for a short time, but what happens when a competing firm adopts the same technology? Many of a firm's resources can be imitated, though it is sometimes expensive. Manufacturing practices can be copied, building layouts can be mimicked, equipment and tools can be approximated. Good people, in contrast, are much more difficult to imitate. As shown in Figure 1-2, there are three reasons why people are inimitable.

HISTORY. People create a **history**—a collective pool of experience, wisdom, and knowledge that benefits the organization. History cannot be bought. Consider an example

FIGURE 1-2   What Makes a Resource Valuable?

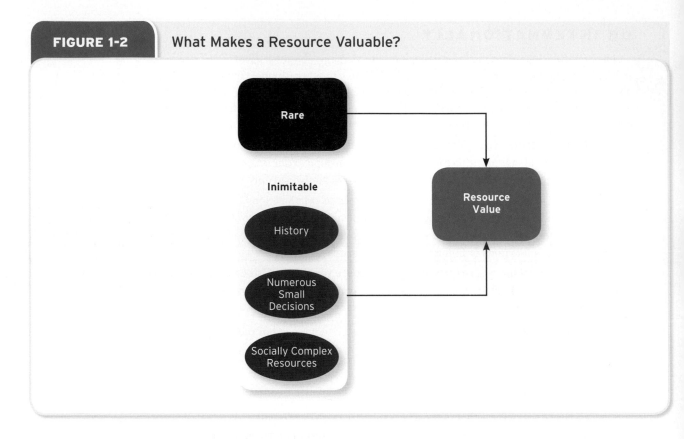

from the discount airline industry. Southwest and JetBlue are the market leaders in this industry, profiting from more frequent point-to-point daily schedules routed into less expensive airports. Delta launched its own discount brand—Song—to compete in this market, though the brand was ultimately abandoned and folded back into Delta's regular operations.[27] One challenge facing Song was that it was competing, for the first time, in a market in which Southwest had existed for decades. Their respective positions on the "industry learning curve" were quite different.

NUMEROUS SMALL DECISIONS. The concept of **numerous small decisions** captures the idea that people make many small decisions day in and day out, week in and week out. "So what?" you might say, "Why worry about small decisions?" Ask yourself how much time elapsed between the arrival of *Diet Coke with Lime* on grocery store shelves and the arrival of *Diet Pepsi Lime*. Answer? About two months.[28] Big decisions can be copied; they are visible to competitors and observable by industry experts and analysts. In the case of Song, the company was able to copy one of JetBlue's signatures— a television for every seat—so that Song passengers were able to watch pay-per-view movies or play video games.[29] However, it would be more difficult to copy one of Southwest's signatures—the playful, whimsical style displayed by flight attendants and service personnel.[30] Officials from Song may not have the opportunity to observe a Southwest flight attendant turning the seatbelt instructions into a comedy routine on a given day or finding a way to make an anxious toddler laugh on a particular flight. Those decisions are invisible to competitors but not to the travelers who make mental notes about their next trip.

SOCIALLY COMPLEX RESOURCES. People also create **socially complex resources,** like culture, teamwork, trust, and reputation. These resources are termed "socially complex" because it is not always clear how they came to develop, though it is clear which organizations do (and do not) possess them. An upper manager at Song could have exited a Southwest flight convinced that the company would benefit from adopting the competitor's playful and fun culture. But how exactly would that be done? A new culture cannot just be implemented like a change in software systems. It springs from the social dynamics within a given firm at a given point in time.

RESEARCH EVIDENCE

Thus, we can build a conceptual argument for why OB might affect an organization's profitability: Good people are both rare and inimitable and therefore create a resource that is valuable for creating competitive advantage. Conceptual arguments are helpful, of course, but it would be even better if there were hard data to back them up. Fortunately, it turns out that there is a great deal of research evidence supporting the importance of OB for company performance. Several research studies have been conducted on the topic, each employing a somewhat different approach.

One study began by surveying executives from 968 publicly held firms with 100 or more employees.[31] The survey assessed so-called "high performance work practices"— OB policies that are widely agreed to be beneficial to firm performance. The survey included 13 questions asking about a combination of hiring, information sharing, training, performance management, and incentive practices, and each question asked what proportion of the company's workforce was involved in the practice. Table 1-2 provides the questions used to assess the high performance work practices (and also shows which chapter of the textbook describes each particular practice in more detail). The study also gathered the following information for each firm: average annual rate of turnover, productivity level (defined as sales per employee), market value of the firm, and corporate profitability. The results revealed that a one-unit increase in the proportion of the workforce involved in the practices was associated with an approximately 7 percent decrease in turnover, $27,000 more in sales per employee, $18,000 more in market value, and $3,800 more in profits. Put simply, better OB practices were associated with better firm performance.

Although there is no doubting the importance of turnover, productivity, market value, and profitability, another study examined an outcome that is even more fundamental: firm survival.[32] The study focused on 136 nonfinancial companies who made initial public offerings (IPOs) in 1988. Firms that undergo an IPO typically have shorter histories and need an infusion of cash to grow or introduce some new technology. Rather than conducting a survey, the authors of this study examined the prospectus filed by each firm (the Securities and Exchange Commission requires that prospectuses contain honest information, and firms can be liable for any inaccuracies that might mislead investors). The authors coded each prospectus for information that might suggest OB issues were valued. Examples of valuing OB issues included describing employees as a source of competitive advantage in strategy and mission statements, emphasizing training and continuing education, having a human resources management officer, and emphasizing full-time rather than temporary or contract employees. By 1993, 81 of the 136 firms included in the study had survived (60 percent). The key question is whether the value placed on OB predicted which did (and did not) survive. The results revealed that firms who valued OB had a 19 percent higher survival rate than firms who did not value OB.

A third study focused on *Fortune*'s "100 Best Companies to Work For" list, which has appeared annually since 1998.[33] Table 1-3 provides the 2007 version of the list. If the 100 firms on the list really do have good OB practices, and if good OB practices really do influence firm profitability, then it follows that the 100 firms should be more profitable.

1.3

Do firms that are good at organizational behavior tend to be more profitable? Why might that be, and is there any research evidence to support this tendency?

TABLE 1-2	Survey Questions Designed to Assess High Performance Work Practices
SURVEY QUESTION ABOUT OB PRACTICE	**CHAPTER IN WHICH PRACTICE IS DISCUSSED**
1. What is the proportion of the workforce who are included in a formal information sharing program (e.g., a newsletter)?	Chapter 7 (Trust, Justice, & Ethics)
2. What is the proportion of the workforce whose jobs have been subjected to a formal job analysis?	Chapter 2 (Job Performance)
3. What proportion of nonentry-level jobs have been filled from within in recent years?	Chapter 6 (Motivation)
4. What is the proportion of the workforce who are administered attitude surveys on a regular basis?	Chapter 4 (Job Satisfaction)
5. What is the proportion of the workforce who participate in Quality of Work Life (QWL) programs, Quality Circles (QC), and/or labor-management participation teams?	Chapter 11 (Teams: Characteristics)
6. What is the proportion of the workforce who have access to company incentive plans, profit-sharing plans, and/or gain-sharing plans?	Chapter 6 (Motivation)
7. What is the average number of hours of training received by a typical employee over the last 12 months?	Chapter 8 (Learning & Decision Making)
8. What is the proportion of the workforce who have access to a formal grievance procedure and/or complaint resolution system?	Chapter 7 (Trust, Justice, & Ethics)
9. What proportion of the workforce are administered an employment test prior to hiring?	Chapters 9, 10 (Personality & Cultural Values, Ability)
10. What is the proportion of the workforce whose performance appraisals are used to determine compensation?	Chapter 6 (Motivation)
11. What proportion of the workforce receive formal performance appraisals?	Chapter 6 (Motivation)
12. Which of the following promotion decision rules do you use most often? (a) merit or performance rating alone; (b) seniority only if merit is equal; (c) seniority among employees who meet a minimum merit requirement; (d) seniority.	Chapter 6 (Motivation)
13. For the five positions that your firm hires most frequently, how many qualified applicants do you have per position (on average)?	Chapter 10 (Ability)

Source: M.A. Huselid, "The Impact of Human Resource Management Practices on Turnover, Productivity, and Corporate Financial Performance," *Academy of Management Journal* 38 (1995), pp. 635–72. Copyright © 1995 Academy of Management. Reproduced via permission from Copyright Clearance Center.

TABLE 1-3	The "100 Best Companies to Work For" in 2007	
1. Google	35. Children's Healthcare Atl.	69. Nike
2. Genentech	36. Goldman Sachs	70. Paychex
3. Wegman's Food Markets	37. Northwest Comm. Hosp.	71. AstraZeneca
4. The Container Store	38. Robert W. Baird	72. Medtronic
5. Whole Foods Market	39. J. M. Smucker	73. Aflac
6. Network Appliance	40. Amgen	74. American Express
7. S.C. Johnson & Son	41. JM Family Enterprises	75. Quad/Graphics
8. Boston Consulting	42. PCL Construction	76. Deloitte & Touche USA
9. Methodist Hospital	43. Genzyme	77. Principal Financial Grp.
10. W.L. Gore	44. Yahoo	78. Timberland
11. Cisco Systems	45. Bain & Co.	79. TDIndustries
12. David Weekley Homes	46. First Horizon National	80. Lehigh Valley Hospital
13. Nugget Market	47. American Fidelity Assur.	81. Baptist Health S. Florida
14. Qualcomm	48. SAS Institute	82. CDW
15. American Century Invest.	49. Nixon Peabody	83. EOG Resources
16. Starbucks	50. Microsoft	84. Capital One Financial
17. Quicken Loans	51. Stew Leonard's	85. Standard Pacific
18. Station Casinos	52. OhioHealth	86. National Instruments
19. Alston & Bird	53. Four Seasons Hotels	87. Texas Instruments
20. QuikTrip	54. Baptist Health Care	88. CarMax
21. Griffin Hospital	55. Dow Corning	89. Marriott International
22. Valero Energy	56. Granite Construction	90. Men's Wearhouse
23. Vision Service Plan	57. Publix Supermarkets	91. Memorial Health
24. Nordstrom	58. PricewaterhouseCoopers	92. Bright Horizons
25. Ernst & Young	59. Pella	93. Milliken
26. Arnold & Porter	60. MITRE	94. Bingham McCutchen
27. Recreational Equip. (REI)	61. SRA International	95. Vanguard
28. Kimley-Horn & Assoc.	62. Mayo Clinic	96. IKEA North America
29. Edward Jones	63. Booz Allen Hamilton	97. KPMG
30. Russell Investment Grp	64. Perkins Coie	98. Synovus
31. Adobe Systems	65. Alcon Laboratories	99. A.G. Edwards
32. Plante & Moran	66. Jones Lang LaSalle	100. Stanley
33. Intuit	67. HomeBanc Mortgage	
34. Umpqua Bank	68. Procter & Gamble	

To explore this premise, the study went back to the original 1998 list and found a "matching firm" for the companies that were included.[34] The matching firm consisted of the most similar company with respect to industry and size in that particular year, with the added requirement that the company had not appeared on the "100 Best" list. This process essentially created two groups of companies that differ only in terms of their inclusion in the "100 Best." The study then compared the profitability of those two groups of companies. The results revealed that the "100 Best" firms were more profitable than their peers. Indeed, the study's authors noted that an investment portfolio based on the 1998 "100 Best" list would have earned an 82 percent cumulative investment return from 1998–2000 compared with only 37 percent for the broader market.

SO WHAT'S SO HARD?

Clearly this research evidence seems to support the conceptual argument that good people constitute a valuable resource for companies. Good OB does seem to matter in terms of company profitability. You may wonder then, "What's so hard?" Why doesn't every company prioritize the effective management of OB, devoting as much attention to it as they do accounting, finance, marketing, technology, physical assets, and so on? Some companies do not do a good job managing their people. Why is that?

Work by Jeffrey Pfeffer provides one potential answer. Pfeffer has written extensively about the OB practices that tend to be used by successful organizations. Some of these practices are highlighted in our **OB at the Bookstore** feature, which appears in each chapter to showcase a well-known book that discusses OB concepts. Pfeffer also has described why more organizations do not use seemingly "commonsense" practices. One reason is that there is no "magic bullet" OB practice—one thing that, in and of itself, can increase profitability. Instead, the effective management of OB requires a belief that several different practices are important, along with a long-term commitment to improving those practices. This premise can be summarized with what might be called the **Rule of One-Eighth:**

> One must bear in mind that one-half of organizations won't believe the connection between how they manage their people and the profits they earn. One-half of those who do see the connection will do what many organizations have done—try to make a single change to solve their problems, not realizing that the effective management of people requires a more comprehensive and systematic approach. Of the firms that make comprehensive changes, probably only about one-half will persist with their practices long enough to actually derive economic benefits. Since one-half times one-half times one-half equals one-eighth, at best 12 percent of organizations will actually do what is required to build profits by putting people first.[35]

The integrative model of OB used to structure this book was designed with this Rule of One-Eighth in mind. Figure 1-1 suggests that high job performance depends not just on employee motivation but also on fostering high levels of satisfaction, effectively managing stress, creating a trusting climate, and committing to employee learning. Failing to do any one of those things could hinder the effectiveness of the other concepts in the model. Of course, that systemic nature reveals another reality of organizational behavior: It is often difficult to "fix" companies that struggle with OB issues. Such companies often struggle in a number of different areas and on a number of different levels. One such (fictitious) company is spotlighted in our **OB on Screen** feature, which appears in each chapter and uses well-known movies to demonstrate OB concepts.

OB AT THE BOOKSTORE

This feature is designed to spotlight some OB books that are available at your local bookstore. You will have heard of some of these books but be less familiar with others. We included this feature because these books are much more widely read than academic and practitioner OB journals (and most OB textbooks!). Each chapter highlights a book whose content is (for the most part) supported by scholarly research on OB. This inaugural edition spotlights *The Human Equation: Building Profits by Putting People First* by Jeffrey Pfeffer (Boston, MA: Harvard Business School Press, 1998).

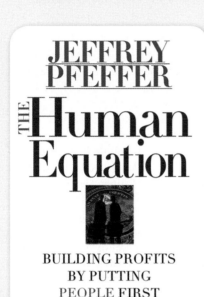

Something very strange is occurring in organizational management.

With these words, Pfeffer identifies a growing paradox in which managers extol the importance of their employees while engaging in mass layoffs and increasing their use of temporary workers. To counteract such trends, Pfeffer describes his Seven Principles of Successful Organizations (listed here, along with the chapter in this book that discusses such concepts in detail).

1. **Employment Security.** Employees must feel confident in their job security to remain committed and motivated (see Chapter 2 on Organizational Commitment).
2. **Selective Hiring.** Employers must work hard to measure individual characteristics that cannot be supplied by training, such as personality (see Chapter 9 on Personality and Cultural Values).
3. **Self-Managed Teams.** Work should be structured around teams so that employees can pool their work-related knowledge (see Chapter 11 on Team Characteristics).
4. **High and Contingent Compensation.** Employers should pay more than their competitors and base that pay on individual, group, or organizational performance (see Chapter 6 on Motivation).
5. **Extensive Training.** Organizations must invest in their staff to impart general skills that are valuable in a variety of jobs (see Chapter 10 on Ability).
6. **Reduction of Status Differences** The culture should use symbols, language, physical space, dress, and compensation structures to remove some of the status differences that discourage teamwork (see Chapter 16 on Organizational Culture).
7. **Sharing Information** Employers must share business numbers and results with all employees to reduce secrecy and increase knowledge of company operations (see Chapter 7 on Trust, Justice, & Ethics).

Pfeffer's focus on reducing differences in compensation may undermine individual achievement in some circumstances, and his condemnation of temporary workers may be too universal. However, each of the practices listed is firmly rooted in OB research and sound practice. He also underscores how none of the seven is sufficient in and of itself, as truly successful organizations use the practices in tandem.

OB ON SCREEN

OFFICE SPACE

This feature is designed to allow you to imagine OB in action on the silver screen. Once you've read about an OB topic, you'll find that you see it play out all around you, especially in movies. This inaugural edition spotlights (what else?) *Office Space* (Dir: Mike Judge. 20th Century Fox, 1999).

> *Since I started working, every single day has been worse than the day before, so that every day you see me is the worst day of my life.*

With these words, Peter Gibbons summarizes what it is like to work at Initech, the computer programming firm where he updates bank software. Peter doesn't exhibit particularly good job performance (he works very slowly and breaks company rules), nor is he very committed to the organization (he comes in late, leaves early, and misses a lot of work).

Of course, the key question from an OB perspective is, "Why does Peter act that way?" At Initech, the better question might be, "Why doesn't everybody?" From the perspective of our integrative model of OB, the problem starts at the top and flows down. The culture of the organization is rigid and emotionless, with management seeming to delight in pointing out mistakes (like Peter's failure to use a cover sheet on his reports). The structure of the organization somehow assigns eight different bosses to Peter (providing eight opportunities to relive the cover sheet conversation). From a leadership perspective, the evil Bill Lumbergh seems to relish the power that comes with his title but does little to improve the functioning of his unit. The result is a workforce that feels little to no motivation, because performance has no impact on the money they earn. All this is worsened by the arrival of "the two Bobs," consultants whose job it is to choose which employees to fire and which to retain. The imminent layoffs combine with all the other problems to create a sense of distrust in the office.

Clearly it would take a lot of time and effort to turn Initech around. The effort would require several changes to several different practices to address several different components of our OB model. And those changes would need to be in place for a long period of time before the company could turn the corner. An uphill climb, to be sure, but Initech has one thing going for it: The Bobs are on the job!

HOW DO WE "KNOW" WHAT WE KNOW ABOUT ORGANIZATIONAL BEHAVIOR?

Now that we have described what OB is and why it is an important topic of study, we now turn to how we "know" what we know about the topic. In other words, where does the knowledge in this textbook come from? To answer this question, we must first explore how people "know" about anything. Philosophers have argued that there are several different ways of knowing things:[36]

- **Method of Experience:** People hold firmly to some belief because it is consistent with their own experience and observations.
- **Method of Intuition:** People hold firmly to some belief because it "just stands to reason"—it seems obvious or self-evident.
- **Method of Authority:** People hold firmly to some belief because some respected official, agency, or source has said it is so.
- **Method of Science:** People accept some belief because scientific studies have tended to replicate that result using a series of samples, settings, and methods.

Consider the following prediction: Providing social recognition, in the form of public shows of praise and appreciation for good behaviors, will increase the performance and commitment of work units. Perhaps you feel that you "know" this claim to be true because you yourself have always responded well to praise and recognition. Or perhaps you feel that you "know" it to be true because it seems like common sense—who wouldn't work harder after a few public pats on the back? Maybe you feel that you "know" it to be true because a respected boss from your past always extolled the virtue of public praise and recognition.

However, the methods of experience, intuition, and authority also might have led you to the opposite belief—that providing social recognition has no impact on the performance and commitment of work units. It may be that public praise has always made you uncomfortable or embarrassed, to the point that you tried to hide especially effective behaviors to avoid being singled out by your boss. Or it may seem logical that social recognition will be viewed as "cheap talk," with employees longing for financial incentives rather than verbal compliments. Or perhaps the best boss you ever worked for never offered a single piece of social recognition in her life, yet her employees always worked their hardest on her behalf.

From a scientist's point of view, it doesn't really matter what a person's experience, intuition, or authority suggests; the prediction must be tested with data. In other words, scientists don't simply assume that their beliefs are accurate; they acknowledge that their beliefs must be tested scientifically. Scientific studies are based on the scientific method, originated by Sir Francis Bacon in the 1600s and adapted in Figure 1-3.[37] The scientific method begins with **theory,** defined as a collection of assertions—both verbal and symbolic—that specify how and why variables are related, as well as the conditions in which they should (and should not) be related.[38] More simply, a theory tells a story and supplies the familiar who, what, where, when, and why elements found in any newspaper or magazine article.[39] Theories are often summarized with theory diagrams, the "boxes and arrows" that graphically depict relationships between variables. Our integrative model of OB in Figure 1-1 represents one such diagram, and there will be many more to come in the remaining chapters of this textbook.

A scientist could build a theory explaining why social recognition might influence the performance and commitment of work units. From what sources would that theory

1.4

What is a theory, and what is its role in the scientific method?

FIGURE 1-3 | **The Scientific Method**

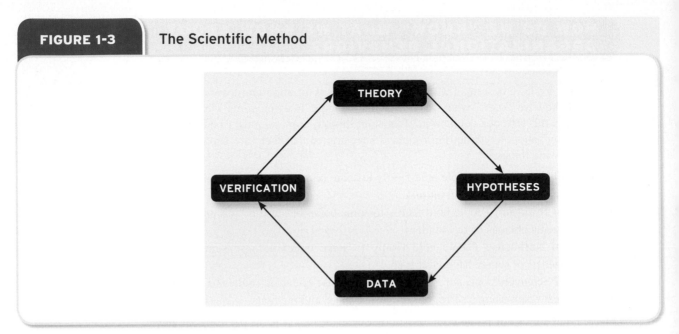

Source: Adapted from F. Bacon, M. Silverthorne, and L. Jardine, *The New Organization* (Cambridge: Cambridge University Press, 2000).

be built? Theories may be built from interviews with employees in a work setting, which provide insights into their views about the strengths and weaknesses of social recognition. They also may be built from observations of people at work, in which case scientists take notes, keep diaries, and pore over company documents to find all the elements of a theory story.[40] Alternatively, theories may be built from research reviews, which examine findings of previous studies to look for general patterns or themes.[41]

Although many theories are interesting, logical, or thought provoking, many also wind up being completely wrong. After all, scientific theories once predicted that the earth was flat and the sun revolved around it. Closer to home, OB theories once argued that money was not an effective motivator and that the best way to structure jobs was to make them as simple and mundane as possible.[42] Theories must therefore be tested to verify that their predictions are accurate. As shown in Figure 1-3, the scientific method requires that theories be used to inspire **hypotheses.** Hypotheses are written predictions that specify relationships between variables. For example, a theory of social recognition could be used to inspire this hypothesis: "Social recognition behaviors on the part of managers will be positively related to the job performance and organizational commitment of their units." This hypothesis states, in black and white, the expected relationship between social recognition and unit performance.

Assume a family member owned a chain of 21 fast-food restaurants and allowed you to test this hypothesis using the restaurants. Specifically, you decided to train the managers in a subset of the restaurants about how to use social recognition as a tool to reinforce behaviors. Meanwhile, you left another subset of restaurants unchanged to represent a control group. You then tracked the total number of social recognition behaviors exhibited by managers over the next nine months by observing the managers at specific time intervals. You measured job performance by tracking drive-through times for the next nine months and used those times to reflect the minutes it takes for a customer to approach the restaurant, order food, pay, and leave. You also measured the commitment of the work unit by tracking employee retention rates over the next nine months.

So how can you tell whether your hypothesis was supported? You could analyze the data by examining the **correlation** between social recognition behaviors and drive-through times, as well as the correlation between social recognition behaviors and employee turnover. A correlation, abbreviated r, describes the statistical relationship between two variables. Correlations can be positive or negative and range from 0 (no statistical relationship) to ±1 (a perfect statistical relationship). Picture a spreadsheet with two columns of numbers. One column contains the total numbers of social recognition behaviors for all 21 restaurants, and the other contains the average drive-through times for those same 21 restaurants. The best way to get a feel for the correlation is to look at a scatterplot—a graph made from those two columns of numbers. Figure 1-4 presents three scatterplots, each depicting differently sized correlations. The strength of the correlation can be inferred from the "compactness" of its scatterplot. Panel (a) shows a perfect 1.0 correlation; knowing the score for social recognition allows you to predict the score for drive-through times perfectly. Panel (b) shows a correlation of .50, so the trend in the data is less obvious than in Panel a but still easy to see with the naked eye. Finally, Panel (c) shows a correlation of .00 no statistical relationship. Understanding the correlation is important because OB questions are not "yes or no" in nature. That is, the question is not "*Does* social recognition lead to higher job performance?" but rather "*How often* does social recognition lead to

1.5

What does a "correlation" represent, and what are "big," "moderate," and "small" correlations? What is a meta-analysis?

FIGURE 1-4 | **Three Different Correlation Sizes**

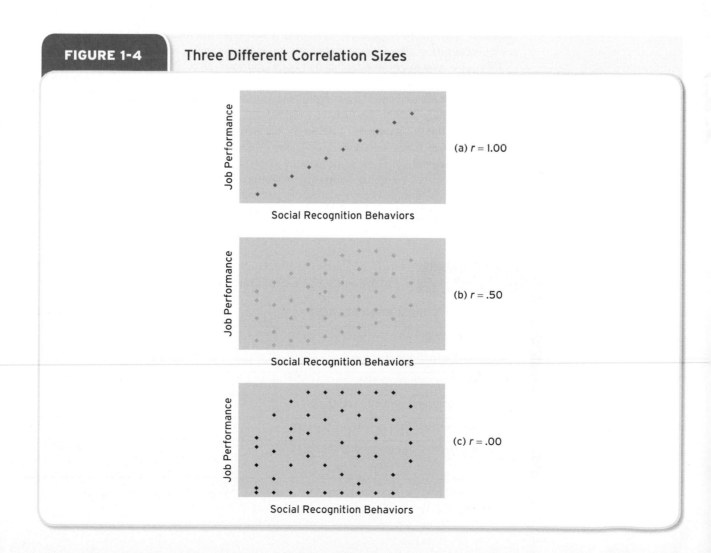

(a) $r = 1.00$

(b) $r = .50$

(c) $r = .00$

A study of Burger King restaurants revealed a correlation between social recognition—praise and appreciation by managers—and employees' performance and commitment. Such studies contribute to the growing body of organizational behavior knowledge.

higher job performance?" The correlation provides a number that expresses an answer to the "how often" question.

So what is the correlation between social recognition and job performance (and between social recognition and organizational commitment)? It turns out that a study very similar to the one described was actually conducted, using a sample of 21 Burger King restaurants with 525 total employees.[43] The correlation between social recognition and job performance was .28. The restaurants that received training in social recognition averaged 44 seconds of drive-through time nine months later versus 62 seconds for the control group locations. The correlation between social recognition and retention rates was .20. The restaurants that received training in social recognition had a 16 percent better retention rate than the control group locations nine months later. The study also instituted a financial "pay-for-performance" system in a subset of the locations and found that the social recognition effects were just as strong as the financial effects.

Of course, you might wonder whether correlations of .28 or .20 are impressive or unimpressive. To understand those numbers, let's consider some context for them. Table 1-4 provides some notable correlations from other areas of science. If the correlation between height and weight is only .44, then a correlation of .28 between social recognition and job performance doesn't sound too bad! In fact, a correlation of .50 is considered "strong" in organizational behavior research, given the sheer number of things that can affect how employees feel and act.[44] A .30 correlation is considered "moderate," and many studies discussed in this book will have results in this range. Finally, a .10 correlation is considered "weak" in organizational behavior research. It should be noted, however, that even "weak" correlations can be important if they predict costly behaviors such as theft or ethical

TABLE 1-4	Some Notable Correlations		
CORRELATION BETWEEN. . .		*r*	**SAMPLE SIZE**
Height and weight		.44	16,948
Viagra and sexual functioning		.38	779
Ibuprofen and pain reduction		.14	8,488
Antihistamines and reduced sneezing		.11	1,023
Smoking and lung cancer within 25 years		.08	3,956
Coronary bypass surgery and 5-year survival		.08	2,649

Source: R. Hogan, "In Defense of Personality Measurement: New Wine for Old Whiners," *Human Performance* 18 (2005), pp. 331–41.

violations. The .08 correlation between smoking and lung cancer within 25 years is a good example of how important small correlations can be.

Does this one study settle the debate about the value of social recognition for job performance and organizational commitment? Not really, for a variety of reasons. First, it included only 21 restaurants with 525 employees. Maybe the results would have turned out differently if the study had included more locations. Second, maybe there is something unique about fast-food employees or restaurant employees in general that makes them particularly responsive to public praise and recognition. Third, it may be that social recognition affects drive-through times but not other forms of job performance, like customer service ratings or the accuracy of completed food orders.

The important point is that little can be learned from a single study. The best way to test a theory is to conduct many studies, each of which is as different as possible from the ones that preceded it.[45] So if you really wanted to study the effects of social recognition, you would conduct several studies using different kinds of samples and different measures. After completing all of those studies, you could look back on the results and create some sort of average correlation across all of the studies. This process is what a technique called **meta-analysis** does. It takes all of the correlations found in studies of a particular relationship and calculates a weighted average (such that correlations based on studies with large samples are weighted more than correlations based on studies with small samples). It turns out that a meta-analysis has been conducted on the effects of social recognition and job performance and indicates an average correlation of .21 across studies conducted in 96 different organizations in the service industry.[46] That meta-analysis offers more compelling support for the potential benefits of social recognition than the methods of experience, intuition, or authority could have provided.

SUMMARY: MOVING FORWARD IN THIS BOOK

The chapters that follow will begin working through the integrative model of OB in Figure 1-1, beginning with the individual outcomes and continuing with the individual, group, and organizational mechanisms that lead to those outcomes. Each chapter begins by spotlighting a company that historically has done a good job of managing a given topic or is currently struggling with a topic. Theories relevant to that topic will be highlighted and discussed. The concepts in those theories will be demonstrated in the **OB on Screen** features to show how OB phenomena have "come to life" in film. You'll also get to see how those concepts can be applied to student life in the **OB for Students** feature. In addition, the **OB Internationally** features describe how those concepts operate differently in different cultures and nations.

Each chapter ends with three sections. The first section provides a summarizing theory diagram that explains why some employees exhibit higher levels of a given concept than others. For example, the summarizing theory diagram for Chapter 4 will explain why some employees are more satisfied with their jobs than others. As we noted in the opening of this chapter, knowledge about *why* is critical to any employee who is trying to make sense of his or her working life or any manager who is trying to make his or her unit more effective. How often have you spent time trying to explain your own attitudes and behaviors to yourself? If you consider yourself to be a reflective person, you've probably thought about such questions quite a bit. Our **OB Assessments** feature will help you find out how reflective you really are. This feature also appears in each chapter of the textbook and allows you to gain valuable knowledge about your own personality, abilities, job attitudes, and leadership styles.

OB ASSESSMENTS

This feature is designed to illustrate how OB concepts actually get measured in practice. In many cases, these OB assessments will provide you with potentially valuable insights into your own attitudes, skills, and personality. The OB assessments that you will see in each chapter consist of multiple survey questions. Two concepts are critical when evaluating how good the OB assessments are: *reliability* and *validity*. Reliability is defined as the degree to which the survey questions are free from random error. If survey questions are reliable, then similar questions will yield similar answers. Validity is defined as the degree to which the survey questions seem to assess what they are meant to assess. If survey questions are valid, then experts on the subject will agree that the questions seem appropriate.

PRIVATE SELF-CONSCIOUSNESS

How reflective or introspective are you? This assessment is designed to measure private self-consciousness—the tendency to direct attention inward to better understand your attitudes and behaviors. Answer each question using the response scale provided. Then subtract your answers to the bold-faced questions from 4, with the difference being your new answers for those questions. For example, if your original answer for question 5 was "3," your new answer is 1 (4 – 3). Then sum your answers for the six questions.

0	1	2	3	4
EXTREMELY UNCHARACTERISTIC OF ME	SOMEWHAT UNCHARACTERISTIC OF ME	NEUTRAL	SOMEWHAT CHARACTERISTIC OF ME	EXTREMELY CHARACTERISTIC OF ME

1. I'm always trying to figure myself out. _____

2. Generally, I'm not very aware of myself. _____

3. I reflect about myself a lot. _____

4. I'm often the subject of my own daydreams. _____

5. I never scrutinize myself. _____

6. I'm generally attentive to my inner feelings. _____

7. I'm constantly examining my motives. _____

8. I sometimes have the feeling that I'm off somewhere watching myself. _____

9. I'm alert to changes in my mood. _____

10. I'm aware of the way my mind works when I work through a problem. _____

SCORING

If your scores sum up to 26 or above, you do a lot of self-reflection and are highly self-aware. You may find that many of the theories discussed in this textbook will help you better understand your attitudes and feelings about working life.

Source: A. Fenigstein, M.F. Scheier, and A.H. Buss, "Public and Private Self-Consciousness: Assessment and Theory," *Journal of Consulting and Clinical Psychology* 43 (1975), pp. 522–27. Copyright © 1975 by the American Psychological Association. Adapted with permission. No further reproduction or distribution is permitted without written permission from the American Psychological Association.

The next concluding section will describe the results of meta-analyses that summarize the relationships between that chapter's topic and both job performance and organizational commitment. Over time, you'll gain a feel for which of the topics in Figure 1-1 have strong, moderate, or weak relationships with these outcomes. This knowledge will help you recognize how everything in OB fits together and what the most valuable tools are for improving performance and commitment in the workplace. As you will discover, some of the topics in OB have a greater impact on how well employees perform their jobs, whereas others have a greater impact on how long employees remain with their organizations. Finally, the third concluding section will describe how the content of that chapter can be applied, at a specific level, in an actual organization. For example, the motivation chapter concludes with a section describing how compensation practices can be used to maximize employee effort. If you're currently working, we hope that these concluding sections help you see how the concepts you're reading about actually could be used to improve your own organizations. Even if you're not working, these application sections will give you a glimpse into how you will experience OB concepts once you begin your working life.

In closing, we hope you come to believe that OB is an interesting subject, because almost everyone can relate to the concepts discussed within it. Almost everyone has experienced a bad boss, instructor, or other authority figure. Almost everyone has grappled with issues of trust or had to find a way to cope with stress. You will read about how noteworthy companies have dealt with these issues, but you can also ask yourself how you would react in the same situation. We suspect you might find yourself more intrinsically interested in some topics than others and hope that the **OB at the Bookstore** feature inspires you to read other books on those subjects. In summary, happy reading—we hope you enjoy the book!

TAKEAWAYS

1.1 Organizational behavior is a field of study devoted to understanding and explaining the attitudes and behaviors of individuals and groups in organizations. More simply, it focuses on *why* individuals and groups in organizations act the way they do.

1.2 The two primary outcomes in organizational behavior are job performance and organizational commitment. A number of factors affect performance and commitment, including individual mechanisms (job satisfaction; stress; motivation; trust, justice, and ethics; learning and decision making), individual characteristics (personality and cultural values, ability), group mechanisms (team characteristics, team processes, leader power and influence, leader styles and behaviors), and organizational mechanisms (organizational structure, organizational culture).

1.3 The effective management of organizational behavior can help a company become more profitable, because good people are a valuable resource. Not only are good people rare, but they are also hard to imitate. They create a history that cannot be bought or copied, they make numerous small decisions that cannot be observed by competitors, and they create socially complex resources such as culture, teamwork, trust, and reputation. Many scientific studies support the relationship between effective organizational behavior and company performance. Good OB policies have been linked to employee productivity, firm profitability, and even firm survival.

1.4   A theory is a collection of assertions, both verbal and symbolic, that specifies how and why variables are related, as well as the conditions in which they should (and should not) be related. Theories about organizational behavior are built from a combination of interviews, observation, research reviews, and reflection. Theories form the beginning point for the scientific method and inspire hypotheses that can be tested with data.

1.5   A correlation is a statistic that expresses the strength of a relationship between two variables (ranging from 0 to ± 1). In OB research, a .50 correlation is considered "strong," a .30 correlation is considered "moderate," and a .10 correlation is considered "weak." A meta-analysis summarizes the results of several research studies. It takes the correlations from those research studies and calculates a weighted average to give more weight to studies with larger samples.

KEY TERMS

- Organizational behavior   *p. 7*
- Human resource management   *p. 7*
- Strategic management   *p. 7*
- Resource-based view   *p. 13*
- Inimitable   *p. 13*
- History   *p. 13*
- Numerous small decisions   *p. 14*
- Socially complex resources   *p. 14*
- Rule of one-eighth   *p. 18*
- Method of experience   *p. 21*
- Method of intuition   *p. 21*
- Method of authority   *p. 21*
- Method of science   *p. 21*
- Theory   *p. 21*
- Hypotheses   *p. 22*
- Correlation   *p. 23*
- Meta-analysis   *p. 25*

DISCUSSION QUESTIONS

1.1   Can you think of other service businesses that, like Starbucks, seem to do an effective job with customer service? If you managed a franchise for one of those businesses, which organizational behavior topics would be most important to maintaining that high service level?

1.2   Think again about the worst coworker you've ever had—the one who did some of the things listed in Table 1-1. Think about what that coworker's boss did (or didn't do) to try to improve his or her behavior. What did the boss do well or poorly? What would you have done differently, and which organizational behavior topics would have been most relevant?

1.3   Which of the individual mechanisms in Figure 1-1 (job satisfaction; stress; motivation; trust, justice, and ethics; learning and decision making) seems to drive your performance and commitment the most? Do you think you're unique in that regard, or do you think most people would answer that way?

1.4   Create a list of the most successful companies that you can think of. What do these companies have that others don't? Are the things that those companies possess rare and inimitable (see Figure 1-2)? What makes those things difficult to copy?

1.5   Think of something that you "know" to be true based on the method of experience, the method of intuition, or the method of authority. Could you test your knowledge using the method of science? How would you do it?

CASE   STARBUCKS

What lures 40 million customers to visit Starbucks each week? Customers will pay a higher price for a cup of coffee, compared with that in other local establishments, because Starbucks delivers consistent product and service quality to give customers a "Starbucks Experience" that is inimitable in the industry. The ability to set a new benchmark in product quality and customer service has been the cornerstone of its business.

Starbucks's excellent global reputation developed from management's belief in human capital and in treating employees as the company's greatest asset. Jim Donald, CEO and President of Starbucks, believes that human resources should attend every strategic discussion concerning the company. By aligning human resources management and strategic management, the corporation created a corporate culture that focused on delivering world-class customer service to customers. Employees at Starbucks are expected to cooperate and work together to meet the demands of their customers. Starbucks attracts and retains the best and the brightest in the industry due to the high level of satisfaction that employees receive while on the job. To increase employees' passion to deliver high levels of customer service, Starbucks offers a multitude of training options to employees so they may become coffee masters. Starbucks has created a competitive advantage by creating a workforce that is very knowledgeable and passionate about what it does.

1.1 Do you believe that Starbucks's corporate culture has given the organization a competitive advantage in the industry? Explain.

1.2 What makes Starbucks more desirable to work for than other coffee shops? Would you prefer to work at Starbucks? Why or why not?

Sources: J.A. Michelli, "Starbucks Experience," *Leadership Excellence,* November 2006; W. Sheri, "Profitability Is in the People," *Black Enterprise,* January 2006; "Starbucks Corporation," Datamonitor, May 2006; and "Views from the Top," *HR Magazine* 51, no. 11 (November 2006), pp. 80–83.

EXERCISE   IS OB COMMON SENSE?

The purpose of this exercise is to take some of the topics covered in this textbook and examine whether improving them is "just common sense." This exercise uses groups of six participants, so your instructor will either assign you to a group of six or ask you to create your own group of six. The exercise has the following steps:

1. Consider the theory diagram shown below. It explains why two "independent variables" (the quality of a movie's script and the fame of its stars) affect a "dependent variable" (how much the movie makes at the box office).

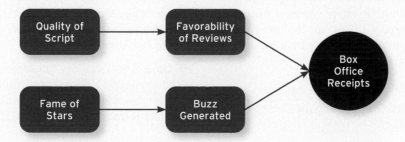

2. Now build your own theory diagram about organizational behavior. In groups of 4–6 students, choose one of the following four topics to use as your dependent variable:

- *Job Satisfaction:* The pleasurable emotions felt when performing job tasks.
- *Strain:* -The headaches, fatigue, or burnout resulting from workplace stress.
- *Motivation:* The intensity and persistence of job-related effort.
- *Trust in Supervisor:* The willingness to allow a supervisor to have significant influence over key job issues.

Using a transparency, laptop, or chalkboard, build a theory diagram that summarizes the factors that affect your chosen dependent variable. To be as comprehensive as possible, try to include at least four independent variables. Keep your books closed! You should build your diagrams using only your own experience and intuition.

3. Each group should present its theory diagram to the class. Do the predicted relationships make sense? Should anything be dropped? Should anything be added?

4. Now compare the theory diagram you created with the diagrams in the textbook (Figure 4-7 for Job Satisfaction, Figure 5-5 for Strain, Figure 6-7 for Motivation, and Figure 7-8 for Trust in Supervisor). How does your diagram compare to the textbook's diagrams (search the bold-faced key terms for any jargon that you don't understand)? Did you leave out some important independent variables or suggest some variables that have not been supported by the academic research summarized in the chapters? If so, it shows that OB is more than just common sense.

ENDNOTES

1.1 Gold, E. "Commentary: With Roughly 9000 Stores, Starbucks Serves It Up by Design." *St. Louis Daily Record,* May 13, 2005. Retrieved September 17, 2005, from the LexisNexis database.

1.2 Levering, R., and M. Moskowitz. "In Good Company." *Fortune,* January 22, 2007, pp. 94–114.

1.3 Weber, G. "Preserving the Counter Culture. *Workforce Management,* February 1, 2005, p. 28. Retrieved September 17, 2005, from the Lexis-Nexis database.

1.4 Gold, "Commentary."

1.5 Weber, "Preserving the Counter Culture."

1.6 Meyer, J. P., and N.J. Allen. *Commitment in the Workplace.* Thousand Oaks, CA: Sage, 1997.

1.7 Nelson, B. "The Buzz at The Container Store." *Corporate Meetings and Incentives,* June 1, 2003, p. 6. Retrieved September 18, 2005, from the LexisNexis database.

1.8 Forger, G. "Good Today, Better Tomorrow." *Modern Materials Handling,* October 1, 2004, p. 22. Retrieved September 18, 2005, from the LexisNexis database.

1.9 Gale, S.F. "Everyday Praise, Swanky Dinners, and Hiking Trips with the Honchos: Here's How The Container Store Recognizes Employees' Hard

Work, Which Has Fueled the Chain's Growth." *Workforce Management,* August 1, 2003, p. 80. Retrieved September 18, 2005, from the Lexis-Nexis database.

1.10   Mazzetti, M. "Managing, Texas-Style." *Texas Monthly,* December 2000, p. 64. Retrieved September 18, 2005, from the LexisNexis database.; "The Container Store Fights AIDS." *Retail Merchandiser,* December 12, 2003. Retrieved September 18, 2005, from the LexisNexis database.

1.11   Nelson, "The Buzz."

1.12   Mazzetti, "Managing, Texas-Style."

1.13   Gale, "Everyday Praise."

1.14   Ibid.

1.15   "Take this Job and Love It! Much Can Be Learned from the Best Employers in the U.S." *Successful Meetings,* July 2003, Vol. 52, p. 33. Retrieved September 18, 2005, from the LexisNexis database.

1.16   *Incentives,* April 1, 2003. Retrieved September 18, 2005, from the LexisNexis database.

1.17   "Container Store Realigns Staff as It Plans Growth Push." *HFN,* August 4, 2003, p. 38. Retrieved September 18, 2005, from the LexisNexis database.

1.18   Gale, "Everyday Praise."

1.19   Levering and Moskowitz, "In Good Company."

1.20   Hart, R. "Born in the USA: Think You Know What Hyundai Is About? Think Again." *Autoweek,* May 23, 2005, p. 20. Retrieved August 19, 2005, from the LexisNexis database.

1.21   Ihlwan, M., and C. Dawson. "Building a 'Camry Fighter': Can Hyundai Transform Itself into One of the World's Top Auto Makers?" *BusinessWeek,* September 6, 2004, p. 62.

Retrieved August 19, 2005, from the LexisNexis database.

1.22   "A Better Drive: Hyundai Motor." *The Economist,* May 21, 2005. Retrieved August 19, 2005, from the LexisNexis database.

1.23   Ihlwan, M.; L. Armstrong; and M. Eldam. "Kissing Clunkers Goodbye." *BusinessWeek,* May 17, 2004, p. 45. Retrieved August 19, 2005, from the LexisNexis database.

1.24   Friedman, T.L. *The World Is Flat: A Brief History of the Twenty-First Century.* New York: Farrar, Straus, & Giroux, 2005.

1.25   Aguinis, H., and C.A. Henle. "The Search for Universals in Cross-Cultural Organizational Behavior." In *Organizational Behavior: The State of the Science,* ed. J. Greenberg. Mahwah, NJ: Lawrence Erlbaum Associates, 2003, pp. 373–411.

1.26   Barney, J.B. "Looking Inside for Competitive Advantage. In *Strategic Human Resource Management,* ed. R. S. Schuler and S. E. Jackson. Malden, MA: Blackwell, 1999, pp. 128–41.

1.27   Mokoto, R. "Designing an Identity to Make a Brand Fly." *New York Times,* November 6, 2003, p. 10. Retrieved August 20, 2005, from the Lexis-Nexis database.

1.28   "Lime Coke Dashes to Launch." *The Grocer,* March 5, 2005, p. 76. Retrieved August 20, 2005, from the LexisNexis database.

1.29   Mokoto, "Designing."

1.30   Serwer, A. "Southwest Airlines: The Hottest Thing in the Sky." *Fortune,* March 8, 2004. Retrieved August 20, 2005, from http://www.mutualofamerica.com/articles/Fortune/March04/fortune.asp.

1.31 Huselid, M.A. "The Impact of Human Resource Management Practice on Turnover, Productivity, and Corporate Financial Performance." *Academy of Management Journal* 38 (1995), pp. 635–72.

1.32 Welbourne, T.M., and A.O. Andrews. "Predicting the Performance of Initial Public Offerings: Should Human Resource Management Be in the Equation?" *Academy of Management Journal* 39 (1996), pp. 891–919.

1.33 Levering and Moskowitz, "In Good Company."

1.34 Fulmer, I.S.; B. Gerhart; and K.S. Scott. "Are the 100 Best Better? An Empirical Investigation of the Relationship Between Being a "Great Place to Work" and Firm Performance." *Personnel Psychology* 56 (2003), pp. 965–93.

1.35 Pfeffer, J., and J.F. Veiga. "Putting People First for Organizational Success." *Academy of Management Executive* 13 (1999), pp. 37–48.

1.36 Kerlinger, F.N., and H.B. Lee. *Foundations of Behavioral Research.* Fort Worth, TX: Harcourt, 2000.

1.37 Bacon, F.; M. Silverthorne; and L. Jardine. *The New Organon.* Cambridge: Cambridge University Press, 2000.

1.38 Campbell, J P. "The Role of Theory in Industrial and Organizational Psychology." In *Handbook of Industrial and Organizational Psychology,* Vol. 1, eds. M.D. Dunnette and L. M. Hough. Palo Alto, CA: Consulting Psychologists Press, 1990, pp. 39–74.

1.39 Whetten, D.A. "What Constitutes a Theoretical Contribution?" *Academy of Management Review* 14 (1989), pp. 490–95.

1.40 Locke, K. "The Grounded Theory Approach to Qualitative Research." In *Measuring and Analyzing Behavior in Organizations,* eds. F. Drasgow and N. Schmitt. San Francisco, CA: Jossey-Bass, 2002, pp. 17–43.

1.41 Locke, E.A., and G.P. Latham. "What Should We Do About Motivation Theory? Six Recommendations for the Twenty-First Century." *Academy of Management Review* 29 (2004), 388–403.

1.42 Herzberg, F.; B. Mausner; and B.B. Snyderman. *The Motivation to Work.* New York: John Wiley & Sons, 1959; Taylor, F.W. *The Principles of Scientific Management.* New York: Harper & Row, 1911.

1.43 Peterson, S.J., and F. Luthans. "The Impact of Financial and Nonfinancial Incentives on Business-Unit Outcomes over Time." *Journal of Applied Psychology* 91 (2006), pp. 156–65.

1.44 Shadish, W.R.; T.D. Cook; and D.T. Campbell. *Experimental and Quasi-Experimental Designs for Generalized Causal Inference.* Boston, MA: Houghton-Mifflin, 2002.

1.45 Ibid.

1.46 Stajkovic, A.D., and F. Luthans. "A Meta-Analysis of the Effects of Organizational Behavior Modification on Task Performance, 1975–1995." *Academy of Management Journal* 40 (1997), pp. 1122–49.

Job Performance

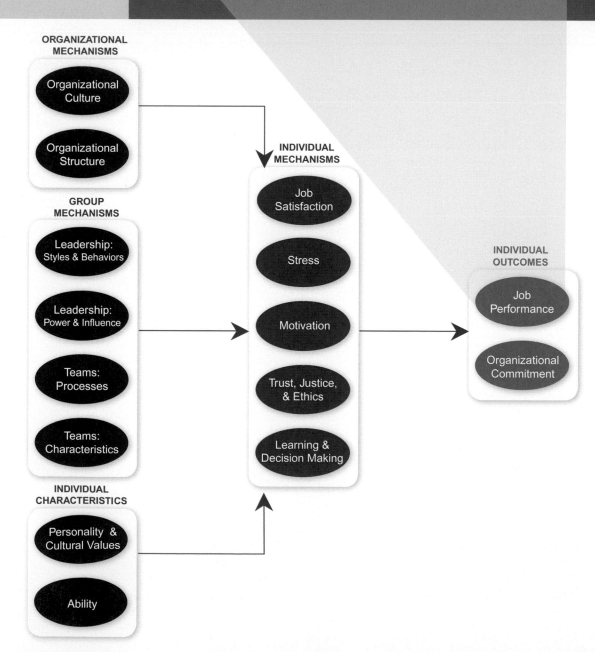

ORGANIZATIONAL MECHANISMS
- Organizational Culture
- Organizational Structure

GROUP MECHANISMS
- Leadership: Styles & Behaviors
- Leadership: Power & Influence
- Teams: Processes
- Teams: Characteristics

INDIVIDUAL CHARACTERISTICS
- Personality & Cultural Values
- Ability

INDIVIDUAL MECHANISMS
- Job Satisfaction
- Stress
- Motivation
- Trust, Justice, & Ethics
- Learning & Decision Making

INDIVIDUAL OUTCOMES
- Job Performance
- Organizational Commitment

After growth made St. Jude Children's Research Hospital the third largest health care charity in the United States, the organization developed employee performance problems that it eventually traced to an inadequate rating and appraisal system. Hundreds of employees gave input to help a consulting firm solve the problems.

LEARNING GOALS

After reading this chapter, you should be able to answer the following questions:

2.1 What is the definition of job performance? What are the three dimensions of job performance?

2.2 What is task performance? How do organizations identify the behaviors that underlie task performance?

2.3 What is citizenship behavior, and what are some specific examples of it?

2.4 What is counterproductive behavior, and what are some specific examples of it?

2.5 What workplace trends affect job performance in today's organizations?

2.6 How can organizations use job performance information to manage employee performance?

ST. JUDE CHILDREN'S RESEARCH HOSPITAL

The next time you order a pizza from Domino's, check the pizza box for a St. Jude Children's Research Hospital logo. If you're enjoying that pizza during a NASCAR race, look for Michael Waltrip's #99 car, which Domino's and St. Jude jointly sponsor. These collaborations spotlight the mission of the Tennessee-based hospital, which works to save children by finding cures for catastrophic illnesses through research and treatment. St. Jude currently has more than 4,000 active patients, and each day, approximately 200 children visit St. Jude for clinical visits or admission as a patient to one of the hospital's 60 rooms. The managers and employees at St. Jude have worked hard to build

America's third largest health care charity, where "no one pays for treatment beyond what is covered by insurance, and those without insurance are never asked to pay."[1]

The very existence of St. Jude depends on the public's perception that their contributions to the hospital will be used effectively. According to Chief Operations Officer John Nash, approximately 30 donations are needed for each $1,000 the hospital spends.[2] The leaders of St. Jude believe that the effective use of donations and the reputation of St. Jude depend very much on the performance of each and every employee. However, after experiencing tremendous growth in the 1990s, St. Jude began to suffer several performance problems, many of which were traced to employees' performance evaluations.[3] Managers only used the top two rating categories when evaluating their subordinates' performance, virtually ignoring the bottom three categories. As a result, all employees appeared to be exceeding performance standards, and the rating system could not identify areas in need of improvement or separate high from low performers. Picture a class in which every student gets an A or A−, regardless of how much they actually learn. It may seem appealing for a while, but students need to know what they've mastered and what they're still struggling with, and those students who work harder need to be rewarded with better grades.

Another problem with the job performance evaluations at St. Jude was that the rating system did not distinguish between different types of jobs in terms of the task and interpersonal activities that were necessary for success. Although academics, scientists, doctors, medical students, nurses, fund raisers, accountants, and human resources and public relations personnel employed by St. Jude carried out many different types of tasks in many different contexts, the evaluation system was not flexible enough to tailor feedback to each employee. Picture a calculus class that is forced to use the same kinds of exams as an English class. It's hard to use essays and creative writing to evaluate the amount of calculus learned, just as it's hard to use equations and statistics to evaluate the amount of English learned.[4]

In response to these problems, St. Jude began working with a consulting firm to develop an improved performance management system.[5] The overall goal of the new system was to motivate managers and employees to think about job performance in a way that would promote the life-saving mission of St. Jude. In developing the revamped system, hundreds of employees across different job levels and functional areas gave input. The system's components now include documentation of performance goals for each employee within specific jobs and a roadmap for how to accomplish those goals. The evaluation system also encourages communication throughout the year between supervisors and subordinates. Whether a performance shortfall issue has to do with core task responsibilities or more general behaviors like cooperativeness and teamwork, employees now have the information and support they need to improve. Although instituting the new system was not easy, the effort was worthwhile. Improved employee performance translates into better usage of donated funds—all of which are necessary to save the lives of the small children who roam the hallways of St. Jude.

JOB PERFORMANCE

We begin our journey through the integrative model of organizational behavior with job performance. Why begin with performance? Because understanding one's own performance is a critical concern for any employee, and understanding the performance of one's unit is a critical concern for any manager. Consider for a moment the job performance of your university's football coach. If you were the university's athletic director, you might gauge the coach's performance by paying attention to various behaviors. How much time does the coach spend on the road during recruiting season? How effective are the coach's practices? Are his offensive and defensive systems well designed, and is his play calling during games appropriate? You might also gauge some other behaviors that fall outside the strict domain of football. Does the coach run a clean program? Do his players graduate on time? Does he represent the university well during interviews with the media?

Of course, as your university's athletic director, you might be tempted to ask a simpler question: Does he win? After all, fans and boosters may not care how good the coach is at the previously listed behaviors if the team fails to make it to a prestigious bowl game. Moreover, the coach's performance in terms of wins and losses has important implications for the university because it affects ticket sales, bowl revenues, licensing fees, and booster donations. Still, is every unsuccessful season the coach's fault? What if the coach develops a well-conceived game plan but the players repeatedly make mistakes at key times in the game? What if the team experiences a rash of injuries or inherits a schedule that turns out to be much tougher than originally thought? What if one or two games are decided at the last moment and influenced by fluke plays or bad calls by the officials?

This example illustrates one dilemma when examining job performance. Is performance a set of behaviors that a person does (or does not) perform, or is job performance the end result of those behaviors? You might be tempted to believe that it is more appropriate to define performance in terms of results rather than behaviors, because results seem more "objective" and are more connected to the central concern of managers—"the bottom line." For example, the job performance of salespeople is often measured by the amount of sales revenue generated by each person over some time span (e.g., a month, a quarter, a year). For the most part, this logic makes perfect sense: Salespeople are hired by organizations to generate sales, and therefore, those who meet or exceed sales goals are worth more to the organization and should be considered higher performers.

However, as sensible as this logic seems, using results to indicate job performance creates a problem because results are often influenced by factors that are beyond the employee's control—product quality, competition, equipment, technology, budget constraints, coworkers, and supervision, just to name a few. Even if these uncontrollable factors are less relevant in a given situation, there is another problem with a results-based view of job performance, in that results don't indicate how to reverse a "bad year." That is, performance feedback based on results does not generally provide people with enough information to learn what they need to change in their behavior to improve. Given that OB as a field of study aims to understand, predict, and improve behavior, we will refer to job performance as behavior. The outcomes associated with those behaviors will therefore be termed "job performance results."

So what types of employee behaviors constitute job performance? To understand this question, consider that **job performance** is formally defined as the value of the set of employee behaviors that contribute, either positively or negatively, to organizational goal accomplishment.[6] This definition of job performance includes behaviors that are within the control of employees, but it places a boundary on which behaviors are (and are not) relevant to job performance. For example, going to get a can of *Diet Coke with Lime* from the soda machine during a break is not usually relevant (in either a positive or negative sense) to organizational goal accomplishment. That behavior is therefore not relevant to job performance. However, taking that can of *Diet Coke with Lime* and pouring it all over one of the company's customers is relevant (in a negative sense) to organizational goal accomplishment. That behavior is therefore relevant to job performance.

2.1

What is the definition of job performance? What are the three dimensions of job performance?

WHAT DOES IT MEAN TO BE A "GOOD PERFORMER"?

Our definition of job performance raises a number of important questions. Specifically, you might be wondering which employee behaviors fall under the umbrella heading of "job performance." In other words, from an employee's perspective, what exactly does it mean to be a "good performer"? We could probably spend an entire chapter just listing various behaviors that are relevant to job performance. However, those behaviors generally fit into three broad categories.[8] Two categories are task performance and citizenship behavior, both of which contribute positively to the organization. The third category is counterproductive behavior, which contributes negatively to the organization. In our **OB on Screen** feature, you'll find an example of employees who demonstrate various levels of all three aspects of job performance. The sections that follow describe these broad categories of job performance in greater detail.

TASK PERFORMANCE

2.2

What is task performance? How do organizations identify the behaviors that underlie task performance?

Task performance includes employee behaviors that are directly involved in the transformation of organizational resources into the goods or services that the organization produces. If you read a description of a job in an employment ad online, that description will focus on task performance behaviors—the tasks, duties, and responsibilities that are a core part of the job. Put differently, task performance is the set of explicit obligations that an employee must fulfill to receive compensation and continued employment. For a flight attendant, task performance includes announcing and demonstrating safety and emergency procedures and distributing food and beverages to passengers. For a firefighter, task performance includes searching burning buildings to locate fire victims and operating equipment to put out fires. For an accountant, task performance involves preparing, examining, and analyzing accounting records for accuracy and completeness. Finally, for an advertising executive, task performance includes developing advertising campaigns and preparing and delivering presentations to clients.[9]

Although the specific activities that constitute task performance differ widely from one job to another, task performance also can be understood in terms of more general categories. One way of categorizing task performance is to consider the extent to which the context of the job is routine or changing. **Routine task performance** involves well-known responses to demands that occur in a normal, routine, or otherwise predictable way. In these cases, employees tend to act in more or less habitual or programmed ways that vary little from one instance to another. As an example of a routine task activity, you may recall watching an expressionless flight attendant robotically demonstrate how to insert the seatbelt tongue into the seatbelt buckle before your flight takes off. Seatbelts haven't really changed since . . . oh . . . 1920, so the instructions to passengers tend to be conveyed the same way, over and over again.

In contrast, **adaptive task performance,** or more commonly "adaptability," involves employee responses to task demands that are novel, unusual, or, at the very least, unpredictable.[10] For example, on August 2, 2005, Air France Flight 358, carrying 297 passengers and 12 crew members from Paris, France, to Toronto, Canada, skidded off the runway on landing and into a ravine. Amid smoke and flames, the flight attendants quickly responded to the emergency and assisted three-quarters of the 297 passengers safely off the plane within 52 seconds, before the emergency response team arrived. One minute later, the remaining passengers and 12 crew members were out safely.[11] From this example, you can see that flight attendants' task performance shifted from activities such as providing safety demonstrations and handing out beverages to performing emergency procedures to save passengers' lives.

OB ON SCREEN

MONSTERS, INC.

I'm in the zone today, Sullivan. I'm gonna do some serious scaring, putting up some big numbers.

With these words, Randall (the evil-looking purple monster) challenged Sulley (the big, blue, furry lug) to match his task performance in *Monsters, Inc.* (Pixar, 2001, released by Disney).[8] You see, the source of electricity in the monster world is the screams provoked by highly specialized monster "scarers" who enter the bedroom doors of unsuspecting human children at night.

Sulley and Randall would both score well in terms of task performance. They are the two best scarers at Monsters, Inc., and compete with each other throughout the film for the all-time "scare" record. The similarity between Sulley and Randall ends there however.

Sulley has a positive attitude about his job and is more than willing to go above and beyond to help his coworkers and the organization. For example, in one scene, Sulley offers to stay late to do some paperwork for his coworker Mike (the green, pear-shaped guy) so that Mike can keep his date with Celia, his demanding, serpent-haired girlfriend. In another scene, Sulley offers to help train some very pathetic new scarers. Late in the film, he even comes up with a valuable suggestion that fundamentally improves the operations and profitability of Monsters, Inc. Clearly, Sulley would score high on citizenship behavior.

In terms of counterproductive behavior, much of the film centers on Sulley's covert attempts to return a 2-year-old girl, whom Sulley names Boo, back to her bedroom after she finds her way into the monster world. Direct contact with human children is strictly forbidden at Monsters, Inc., because the monsters believe that even the slightest touch from a child can be lethal. Although you would probably agree that Sulley's behavior is ethical because he is acting in the best interest of Boo's safety, from Monsters, Inc.'s, perspective, the behavior is counterproductive; the company wants Sulley to turn the girl over to the government's Child Detection Agency. However, Randall puts any of Sulley's indiscretions to shame. In conjunction with his evil boss, Randall assaults and kidnaps others to test an illegal (and potentially deadly) new method for extracting energy from children. Fortunately, Sulley (and Mike) are around to try to save the day. Do they return Boo safely to her bedroom? You'll have to watch to find out.

Although flight attendants receive training so they can handle emergency situations such as this one, executing these behaviors effectively in the context of an actual emergency differs fundamentally from anything experienced previously. Because of the increasing pace of change in the workplace due to globalization, technological advances, and the greater prevalence of knowledge-intensive work, adaptability is becoming increasingly important as a type of performance in and of itself.[12] As a consequence, organizations are beginning to implement practices that promote the types of behaviors associated with adaptability. As you should be able to discern from the list in Table 2-1,[13] the behaviors

TABLE 2-1	Behaviors Involved in Adaptability
BEHAVIOR TITLE	**EXAMPLE OF ACTIVITIES**
Handling emergencies or crisis situations	Quickly analyzing options for dealing with danger or crises and their implications; making split-second decisions based on clear and focused thinking
Handling work stress	Remaining composed and cool when faced with difficult circumstances or a highly demanding workload or schedule; acting as a calming and settling influence to whom others can look for guidance
Solving problems creatively	Turning problems upside-down and inside-out to find fresh new approaches; integrating seemingly unrelated information and developing creative solutions
Dealing with uncertain and unpredictable work situations	Readily and easily changing gears in response to unpredictable or unexpected events and circumstances; effectively adjusting plans, goals, actions, or priorities to deal with changing situations
Learning work tasks, technologies, and work situations	Quickly and proficiently learning new methods or how to perform previously unlearned tasks; anticipating change in the work demands and searching for and participating in assignments or training to prepare for these changes
Demonstrating interpersonal adaptability	Being flexible and open-minded when dealing with others; listening to and considering others' viewpoints and opinions and altering own opinion when it is appropriate to do so
Demonstrating cultural adaptability	Willingly adjusting behavior or appearance as necessary to comply with or show respect for others' values and customs; understanding the implications of one's actions and adjusting approach to maintain positive relationships with other groups, organizations, or cultures

Source: E.D. Pulakos, S. Arad, M.A. Donovan, and K.E. Plamondon, "Adaptability in the Workplace: Development of a Taxonomy of Adaptive Performance," *Journal of Applied Psychology* 85 (2000), pp. 612–24. Copyright © 2000 by the American Psychological Association. Adapted with permission. No further reproduction or distribution is permitted without permission from the American Psychological Association.

involved in adaptability are diverse and may be involved in a variety of jobs in today's economy.

Now that we've given you a general understanding of task performance behaviors, you might be wondering how organizations identify the sets of behaviors that represent "task performance" for different jobs. Many organizations identify task performance behaviors by conducting a **job analysis.** Although there are many different ways to conduct a job analysis, most boil down to the following three steps. First, a list of all the activities involved in a job is generated. This list generally results from data from several sources, including observations, surveys, and interviews of employees. Second, each activity on this list is rated by "subject matter experts" according to things like the importance and frequency of the activity. Subject matter experts generally have experience performing the job or managing people who perform the job and therefore are in a position to judge the degree to which specific activities contribute to the organization. Third, the activities that are rated highly in terms of their importance and frequency are retained and used to define task performance.

Those retained behaviors often find their way into the measures that managers use to evaluate the task performance of employees. Men's Wearhouse provides a good example of an organization that uses task performance information in this way.[14] The company first gathers information about the employee's on-the-job behavior. Table 2-2 lists some of the factors included in the performance evaluation for wardrobe consultants at Men's Wearhouse. After the behavior information is gathered, senior managers provide feedback and coaching to the employee about which types of behaviors he or she needs to change to improve. The feedback is framed as constructive criticism meant to improve an employee's behavior. Put yourself in the place of a Men's Wearhouse wardrobe

TABLE 2-2 Performance Review Form for a Wardrobe Consultant at Men's Wearhouse

IMPORTANT TASK BEHAVIORS

Greets, interviews, and tapes all customers properly.

Participates in team selling.

Is familiar with merchandise carried at local competitors.

Ensures proper alteration revenue collection.

Treats customers in a warm and caring manner.

Utilizes tailoring staff for fittings whenever possible.

Involves management in all customer problems.

Waits on all customers, without prejudging based on attire, age, or gender.

Contributes to store maintenance and stock work.

Arrives at work at the appointed time and is ready to begin immediately.

Dresses and grooms to the standards set by TMW.

Source: C.A. O'Reilly III and J. Pfeffer, *Hidden Value: How Great Companies Achieve Extraordinary Results with Ordinary People* (Boston: Harvard Business School Press, 2000). Reprinted by permission of Harvard Business School Press. Copyright © 2000 by the Harvard Business School Publishing Corporation; all rights reserved.

consultant for a moment. Wouldn't you rather have your performance evaluated on the basis of the behaviors in Table 2-2 rather than some overall index of sales? After all, those behaviors are completely within your control, and the feedback you receive from your boss will be more informative than the simple directive to "sell more suits next year than you did this year."

When organizations find it impractical to use job analysis to identify the set of behaviors needed to define task performance, they can turn to a database the government has created to help with that important activity. The **Occupational Information Network** (or O*NET) is an online database that includes, among other things, the characteristics of most jobs in terms of tasks, behaviors, and the required knowledge, skills, and abilities (http://online. onetcenter.org).[15] Figure 2-1 shows the O*NET output for a flight attendant's position, including many of the tasks discussed previously in this chapter. Of course, O*NET represents only a first step in figuring out the important tasks for a given job. Many organizations ask their employees to perform tasks that their competitors do not so their workforce performs in a unique and valuable way. O*NET cannot capture those sorts of unique task requirements—the "numerous small decisions" that separate the most effective organizations from their competitors.

For example, the authors of a book entitled *Nuts* identify "fun" as one of the dominant values of Southwest Airlines.[16] Southwest believes that people are willing to work more productively and creatively in an environment that includes humor and laughter. Consistent with this belief, flight attendant task performance at Southwest includes not only generic flight attendant activities, such as those identified by O*NET, but also activities that reflect a sense of humor and playfulness. As an example, effective flight attendants tell jokes over

FIGURE 2-1 O*NET Results for Flight Attendants

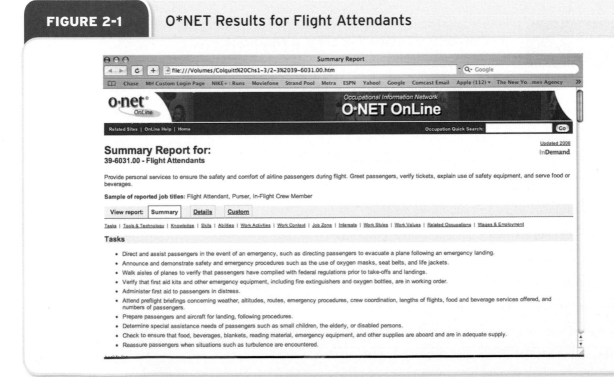

O*NET, or Occupational Information Network, is an online government database that lists the characteristics of most jobs and the knowledge required for each. This sample is for the job of flight attendant.

the intercom such as, "We'll be dimming the lights in the cabin . . . pushing the light-bulb button will turn your reading light on. However, pushing the flight attendant button will not turn your flight attendant on."[17] Thus, though O*NET may be a good place to start, the task information from the database should be supplemented with information regarding behaviors that support the organization's values and strategy.

Before concluding our section on task performance, it is important to note that task performance behaviors are not simply performed versus not performed. Although poor performers often fail to complete required behaviors, it is just as true that the best performers often exceed all expectations for those behaviors. The most valuable employees in any organization are those who "go the extra mile" by engaging in levels of task performance that previously were unheard of. As an example, the task performance behaviors required of a major league pitcher are to take the mound every fifth day and face the opposing team for as many innings as he remains effective. During Game 1 of the 2004 American League Championship Series (ALCS) against the New York Yankees, Boston Red Sox pitcher Curt Schilling was unable to push off the mound with his right foot and, as a result, had to leave the game after three innings. After the game, Schilling met with Dr. William Morgan and the Red Sox medical staff to discuss courses of actions that might allow him to pitch again in the postseason. Dr. Morgan suggested a procedure that involved suturing tendons in Schilling's ankle together, something that had been tried only once before on a cadaver.[18]

Despite the risk that the injury could worsen and possibly end his career, Schilling decided to go ahead with the procedure so that he could pitch effectively and achieve a Sox win. Schilling went on to pitch seven innings of one-run ball that led Boston to a 4–2 victory in Game 6 against the Yankees, and the Red Sox ended up winning the ALCS. Schilling also wanted to pitch in Game 2 of the World Series against the St. Louis Cardinals, but to do so, the Red Sox medical staff needed to resolve the numbness in Schilling's ankle. The staff found that one of the sutures that provided support for the ankle needed to be removed because it was pressing against a nerve. Again, despite personal risk, Schilling displayed great dedication and decided to go ahead with the procedure. Shilling went on to pitch six innings of no-hit ball in a blood-soaked sock. Schilling's "above and beyond" levels of task performance played a large part in the Red Sox's victory in Game 6 and, ultimately, their first World Series championship in 86 years.

These sorts of "extra mile" stories can be found in traditional organizational contexts as well. For example, the task performance behaviors for hotel employees consist of caring for guests and making sure they have everything they need to enjoy their stay. However, the employees at the Hilton New Orleans Riverside Hotel "went the extra mile" as the city was ravaged by Hurricane Katrina. The 450 employees in the hotel cared for approximately 4,500 guests during the storm, guarding their safety while the hurricane blew through the city and afterward when the levees failed. One employee carried elderly guests down 16 flights of stairs because of the oppressive heat on the higher floors. Hotel executives even arranged for charter buses to make the trip from Texas to evacuate guests.[19] If you asked the hotel employees, they might be tempted to understate their actions by saying, "We were just doing our jobs." And that's true—but they were doing their jobs at an exceptionally high level that will not soon be forgotten by those hotel guests.

CITIZENSHIP BEHAVIOR

Sometimes employees go the extra mile by actually engaging in behaviors that are not within their job description—and thus that do not fall under the broad heading of task performance. This situation brings us to the second category of job performance, called citizenship behavior. **Citizenship behavior** is defined as voluntary employee activities that may or may not be rewarded but that contribute to the organization by improving the

2.3

What is citizenship behavior, and what are some specific examples of it?

overall quality of the setting in which work takes place.[20] Have you ever had a coworker or fellow student who was always willing to help someone who was struggling? Who always attended optional meetings or social functions to support his or her colleagues? Who always maintained a good attitude, even in trying times? We tend to call those people "good citizens" or "good soldiers."[21] High levels of citizenship behavior earn them such titles. Although there are many different types of behaviors that might seem to fit the definition of citizenship behavior, research suggests two main categories that differ according to who benefits from the activity: coworkers or the organization (see Figure 2-2).[22]

The first category of citizenship behavior is the one with which you're most likely to be familiar: **interpersonal citizenship behavior.** Such behaviors benefit coworkers and colleagues and involve assisting, supporting, and developing other organizational members in a way that goes beyond normal job expectations.[23] For example, **helping** involves assisting coworkers who have heavy workloads, aiding them with personal matters, and showing new employees the ropes when they first arrive on the job. Do you consider yourself a helpful person? Check the **OB Assessments** feature to see how helpful you really are. **Courtesy** refers to keeping coworkers informed about matters that are relevant to them. Some employees have a tendency to keep relevant facts and events secret. Good citizens do the opposite; they keep others in the loop because they never know what information might be useful to someone else. **Sportsmanship** involves maintaining a good attitude with coworkers, even when they've done something annoying or when the unit is going through tough times. Whining and complaining are contagious; good citizens avoid being the squeaky wheel who frequently makes mountains out of molehills.

Although interpersonal citizenship behavior is important in many different job contexts, it may be even more important in contexts in which employees work in small groups or teams. A team with members who tend to be helpful, respectful, and courteous is also likely to have a positive team atmosphere in which members trust one another. This type of situation is essential to foster the willingness of team members to work toward a common

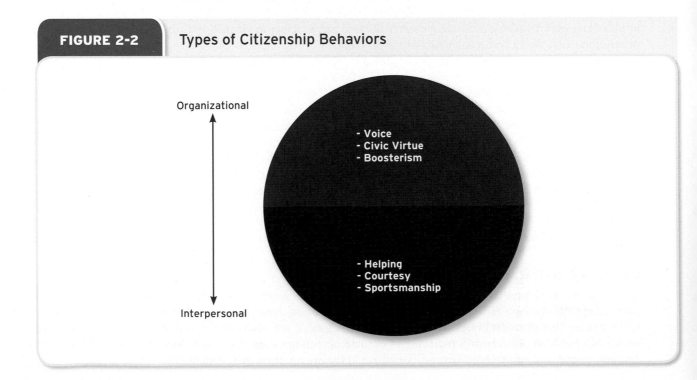

FIGURE 2-2   Types of Citizenship Behaviors

Organizational

- Voice
- Civic Virtue
- Boosterism

- Helping
- Courtesy
- Sportsmanship

Interpersonal

OB ASSESSMENTS

HELPING

How helpful are you? This assessment is designed to measure helping, an interpersonal form of citizenship behavior. Think of the people you work with most frequently, either at school or at work. The questions below refer to these people as your "work group." Answer each question using the scale below, then sum up your answers.

1	2	3	4	5	6	7
STRONGLY DISAGREE	MODERATELY DISAGREE	SLIGHTLY DISAGREE	NEITHER DISAGREE NOR AGREE	SLIGHTLY AGREE	MODERATELY AGREE	STRONGLY AGREE

1. I volunteer to do things for my work group. _____

2. I help orient new members of my work group. _____

3. I attend functions that help my work group. _____

4. I assist others in my group with their work for the benefit of the group. _____

5. I get involved to benefit my work group. _____

6. I help others in this group learn about the work. _____

7. I help others in this group with their work responsibilities. _____

SCORING

If your scores sum up to 40 or higher, you perform a high level of helping behavior, which means you frequently engage in citizenship behaviors directed at your colleagues. This is good, as long as it doesn't distract you from fulfilling your own job duties and responsibilities. If your scores sum up to less than 40, you perform a low level of helping behaviors. You might consider paying more attention to whether your colleagues need assistance while working on their task duties and pitching in when appropriate.

Source: L.V. Van Dyne and J.A. LePine, "Helping and Voice Extra-Role Behaviors: Evidence of Construct and Predictive Validity," *Academy of Management Journal* 41 (1998), pp. 108–19. Copyright © 1998 Academy of Management. Reproduced via permission from Copyright Clearance Center.

team goal rather than goals that may be more self-serving.[24] In fact, if you think about the behaviors that commonly fall under the "teamwork" heading, you'll probably agree that most are examples of interpersonal citizenship behavior.[25]

The second category of citizenship behavior is **organizational citizenship behavior**. These behaviors benefit the larger organization by supporting and defending the company, working to improve its operations, and being especially loyal to it.[26] For example, **voice** involves speaking up and offering constructive suggestions for change. Good citizens react to bad rules or policies by constructively trying to change them as opposed to passively complaining about them (we return to the subject of voice in Chapter 3 on Organizational Commitment).[27] **Civic virtue** refers to participating in the company's operations at a deeper-than-normal level by attending voluntary meetings and functions, reading and keeping up with organizational announcements, and keeping abreast of business news that affects the company. **Boosterism** means representing the organization in a positive way when out in public, away from the office, and away from work. Think of friends you've had who worked for a restaurant. Did they always say good things about the restaurant when talking to you and keep any "kitchen horror stories" to themselves? If so, they were being good citizens by engaging in high levels of boosterism.

Two important points should be emphasized about citizenship behaviors. First, as you've probably realized, citizenship behaviors are relevant in virtually any job, regardless of the particular nature of its tasks,[28] and there are clear benefits of these behaviors in terms of the effectiveness of work units and organizations.[29] As examples, research conducted in a paper mill found that the quantity and quality of crew output was higher in crews that included more good citizens.[30] Research of 30 restaurants also showed that higher levels of citizenship behavior promoted higher revenue, better operating efficiency, higher customer satisfaction, higher performance quality, less food waste, and fewer customer complaints.[31] Thus, it seems clear that citizenship behaviors have a significant influence on the bottom line.

Second, citizenship behaviors become even more vital during organizational crises, when beneficial suggestions, deep employee involvement, and a positive "public face" are critical. For example, Southwest Airlines relied on high levels of organizational citizenship behaviors after 9/11. Top corporate leaders worked without pay through the end of 2001, while rank-and-file employees voluntarily gave up days or weeks of paid vacation so that the employee profit-sharing plan could remain fully funded. The end result of this good citizenship was that Southwest suffered no layoffs after 9/11 and was the only major airline to make a profit that year.[32]

From an employee's perspective, it may be tempting to discount the importance of citizenship behaviors—to just focus on your own job tasks and leave aside any "extra" stuff. After all, citizenship behaviors appear to be voluntary and optional, whereas task duties are not. However, discounting citizenship behaviors is a bad idea, because supervisors do not always view such actions as optional. In fact, research on computer salespeople, insurance agents, petrochemical salespeople, pharmaceutical sales managers, office furniture makers, sewing machine operators, U.S. Air Force mechanics, and first-tour U.S. Army soldiers has shown that citizenship behaviors relate strongly to supervisor evaluations of job performance, even when differences in task performance are also considered.[33] As we discuss in our **OB Internationally** feature, the tendency of supervisors to consider citizenship behaviors in evaluating overall job performance appears to hold even across countries with vastly different cultures.[34] Of course, this issue has a lot of relevance to you, given that in most organizations, supervisors' evaluations of job performance play significant roles in determining pay and promotions. Indeed, employee citizenship behavior has been found to influence the salary and promotion recommendations people receive, over and above their task performance.[35] Put simply, it pays to be a good citizen.

COUNTERPRODUCTIVE BEHAVIOR

2.4

What is counterproductive behavior, and what are some specific examples of it?

Now we move from the "good soldiers" to the "bad apples." Whereas task performance and citizenship behavior refer to employee activities that help the organization achieve its goals and objectives, other activities in which employees engage do just the opposite. The third broad category of job performance is **counterproductive behavior,** defined as employee behaviors that intentionally hinder organizational goal accomplishment. The word "intentionally" is a key aspect of this definition; these are things that employees

OB INTERNATIONALLY

As we have already explained, citizenship behavior tends to be viewed as relatively voluntary because it is not often explicitly outlined in job descriptions or directly rewarded. However, people in organizations vary in their beliefs regarding the degree to which citizenship behavior is truly voluntary, and these differences have important implications.[36]

As an example, consider a situation in which an employee chooses not to engage in certain citizenship behaviors because of his or her belief that the behaviors are voluntary. However, this employee works for a supervisor who believes that the behaviors are part of the job. If the supervisor were to give this employee a poor performance evaluation for failing to engage in citizenship behaviors, the employee would believe that the evaluation was unfair and likely protest. As another example, consider a situation in which an employee engages in citizenship behaviors because of his or her belief that the behaviors are part of the job. However, this employee works for a supervisor who believes that citizenship behaviors are unnecessary. Assuming that the supervisor would not consider the citizenship behaviors on a performance evaluation, the employee would likely react negatively because he or she has not been recognized for putting effort into activities that help other member of the organization.

So what types of factors cause differences in beliefs regarding whether or not citizenship behavior is discretionary? One factor that would appear to be important is national culture. It is widely believed that the culture in countries like the United States, Canada, and the Netherlands encourages behaviors that support competition and individual achievement, whereas the culture in countries like China, Colombia, and Portugal encourages behaviors that promote cooperation and group interests over self-interests.[37] On the basis of these cultural differences, it is only natural to expect that people from the former set of countries would consider citizenship performance relatively unimportant compared with people from the latter set of countries. In reality, however, the findings from one recent study comparing Canadian and Chinese managers found that this cultural stereotype was simply not true.[38] Managers in both countries not only took citizenship behavior into account when evaluating overall job performance, but the weight they gave to citizenship behavior in their overall evaluation of employees was the same. One explanation for this result is that the realities of running effective business organizations in a global economy have a significantly stronger impact on managerial practices than do cultural norms.

So what is the lesson here? Although employees may view citizenship behavior as voluntary because it is not spelled out in job descriptions or explicitly rewarded, managers take these behaviors into account, and this evaluation appears to be true across countries with vastly different cultural traditions.

mean to do, not things they accidentally do. Although there are many different kinds of counterproductive behaviors, research suggests that—like task performance and citizenship behavior—they can be grouped into more specific categories (see Figure 2-3).[39]

Property deviance refers to behaviors that harm the organization's assets and possessions. For example, **sabotage** represents the purposeful destruction of physical equipment, organizational processes, or company products. Do you know what a laser disc is? Probably not—and the reason you don't is because of sabotage. A company called Disco-Vision (a subsidiary of MCA) manufactured laser discs in the late 1970s, with popular movie titles like *Smokey and the Bandit* and *Jaws* retailing for $15.95. Although this level

| FIGURE 2-3 | Types of Counterproductive Behaviors |

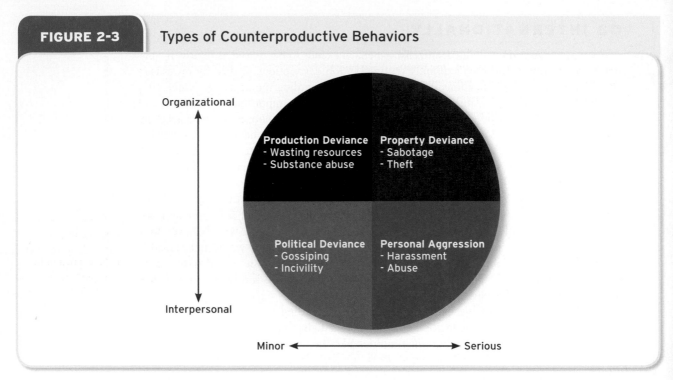

Source: Adapted from S.L. Robinson and R.J. Bennett, "A Typology of Deviant Workplace Behaviors: A Multi-dimensional Scaling Study," *Academy of Management Journal* 38 (1995), pp. 555–72.

matches the price of DVDs today, it was far less than the $50–$100 needed to buy video-cassettes (which were of inferior quality) at the time. Unfortunately, laser discs had to be manufactured in "clean rooms," because specs of dust or debris could cause the image on the TV to freeze, repeat, skip, or drop out. When MCA merged with IBM in 1979, the morale of the employees fell, and counterproductive behaviors began to occur. Specifically, employees sabotaged the devices that measured the cleanliness of the rooms and began eating in the rooms—even "popping" their potato chip bags to send food particles into the air. This sabotage eventually created a 90 percent disc failure rate that completely alienated customers. As a result, despite its much lower production costs and higher quality picture, the laser disc disappeared, and the organizations that supported the technology suffered incredible losses.[40]

Even if you've never heard of the laser disc, you've certainly eaten in a restaurant. The cost of counterproductive behaviors in the restaurant industry is estimated to be 2–3 percent of revenues per year, but what may be more disconcerting is the nature of those counterproductive behaviors.[41] Thirty-one percent of employees who responded to a survey knowingly served improperly prepared food, 13 percent intentionally sabotaged the work of other employees, and 12 percent admitted to intentionally contaminating food they prepared or served to a customer (yuck!). At a minimum, such sabotage of the restaurant's product can lead to a bad meal and a customer's promise to never return to that establishment. At a maximum, such behaviors can lead to food poisoning, health code violations, and a damaging lawsuit.

Theft represents another form of property deviance and can be just as expensive as sabotage (if not more). Research has shown that up to three-quarters of all employees have engaged in counterproductive behaviors such as theft, and the cost of these behaviors is staggering.[42] For example, one study estimated that 47 percent of store inventory shrinkage was due to employee theft and that this type of theft costs organizations approximately $14.6 billion per year.[43] Maybe you've had friends who worked at a restaurant or bar and been lucky enough to get discounted (or even free) food and drinks whenever you wanted. Clearly that circumstance is productive for you, but it's quite counterproductive from the perspective of the organization.

Counterproductive behavior by employees can be destructive to the organization's goals. In some settings, such as a restaurant, it can even be a problem for customers.

Production deviance is also directed against the organization but focuses specifically on reducing the efficiency of work output. **Wasting resources** is the most common form of production deviance, when employees use too many materials or too much time to do too little work. Manufacturing employees who use too much wood or metal are wasting resources, as are restaurant employees who use too many ingredients when preparing the food. Workers who work too slowly or take too many breaks are also wasting resources because "time is money" (we return to this particular subject in Chapter 3 on Organizational Commitment). **Substance abuse** represents another form of production deviance. If employees abuse drugs or alcohol while on the job or shortly before coming to work, then the efficiency of their production will be compromised because their work will be done more slowly and less accurately.

In contrast to property and production deviance, **political deviance** refers to behaviors that intentionally disadvantage other individuals rather than the larger organization. **Gossiping**—casual conversations about other people in which the facts are not confirmed as true—is one form of political deviance. Everyone has experienced gossip at some point in time and knows the emotions people feel when they discover that other people have been talking about them. Such behaviors undermine the morale of both friendship groups and work groups. **Incivility** represents communication that is rude, impolite, discourteous, and lacking in good manners.[44] The erosion of manners seems like a societywide phenomenon, and the workplace is no exception. Recall the classic scene from *Jerry Maguire,* in which Tom Cruise's character, after getting fired from his job, scoops the company fish out of the tank and takes them with him because "these fish have manners" (unlike everyone else in that particular company).

Taken one by one, these political forms of counterproductive behavior may not seem particularly serious to most organizations. However, in the aggregate, acts of political deviance can create an organizational climate characterized by distrust and unhealthy competitiveness. Beyond the productivity losses that result from a lack of cooperation among employees, organizations with this type of climate likely cannot retain good employees. Moreover, there is some evidence that gossip and incivility can "spiral"—meaning that they gradually get worse and worse until some tipping point—after which more serious forms of interpersonal actions can occur.[45]

Those more serious interpersonal actions may involve **personal aggression,** defined as hostile verbal and physical actions directed toward other employees. **Harassment** falls under this heading and occurs when employees are subjected to unwanted physical contact or verbal remarks from a colleague. **Abuse** also falls under this heading; it occurs when an employee is assaulted or endangered in such a way that physical and psychological injuries may occur. You might be surprised to know that even the most extreme forms of personal aggression are actually quite prevalent in organizations. For example, one employee is killed by a current or former employee on average each week in the United States.[46] Acts of personal aggression can also be quite costly to organizations. For example, Mitsubishi Motor Manufacturing of America settled a class action sexual harassment lawsuit in 1998 for $34 million after women at a plant in Normal, Illinois, complained of widespread and routine groping, fondling, lewd jokes, lewd behavior, and pornographic graffiti.[47]

Three points should be noted about counterproductive behavior. First, there is evidence that people who engage in one form of counterproductive behavior also engage in others.[48] In other words, such behaviors tend to represent a pattern of behavior rather than isolated incidents. In this sense, there really are "bad apples." Second, like citizenship behavior, counterproductive behavior is relevant to any job. It doesn't matter what the job entails; there are going to be things to steal, resources to waste, and people to be uncivil toward. Third, it is often surprising which employees engage in counterproductive behavior. You might be tempted to guess that poor task performers will be the ones who do these sorts of things, but there is only a weak negative correlation between task performance and counterproductive behavior.[49] Sometimes the best task performers are the ones who can best get away with counterproductive actions, because they are less likely to be suspected or blamed.

SUMMARY: WHAT DOES IT MEAN TO BE A "GOOD PERFORMER"?

So what does it mean to be a "good performer"? As shown in Figure 2-4, being a good performer means a lot of different things. It means someone is good at the particular job tasks that fall within his or her job description, whether those tasks are routine or require more adaptability. But it also means that the employee engages in citizenship behaviors directed at both coworkers and the larger organization. And it means that he or she refrains from engaging in the counterproductive behaviors that can so badly damage the climate of an organization. The goal for any manager is therefore to have employees who fulfill all three pieces of this good performer description.

As you move forward in this book, you'll notice that almost every chapter includes a description of how that chapter's topic relates to job performance. For example, Chapter 4 on Job Satisfaction will describe how employees' feelings about their jobs affect their job performance. You'll find that some chapter topics seem more strongly correlated with task performance, whereas other topics are more strongly correlated with citizenship behavior or counterproductive behavior. Such differences will help you understand exactly how and why a given topic, be it satisfaction, stress, motivation, or something else, influences job performance. By the end of the book, you'll have developed a good sense of the most powerful drivers of job performance. That knowledge will come in handy in your working life and, as described in our **OB for Students** feature, in your academic life as well.

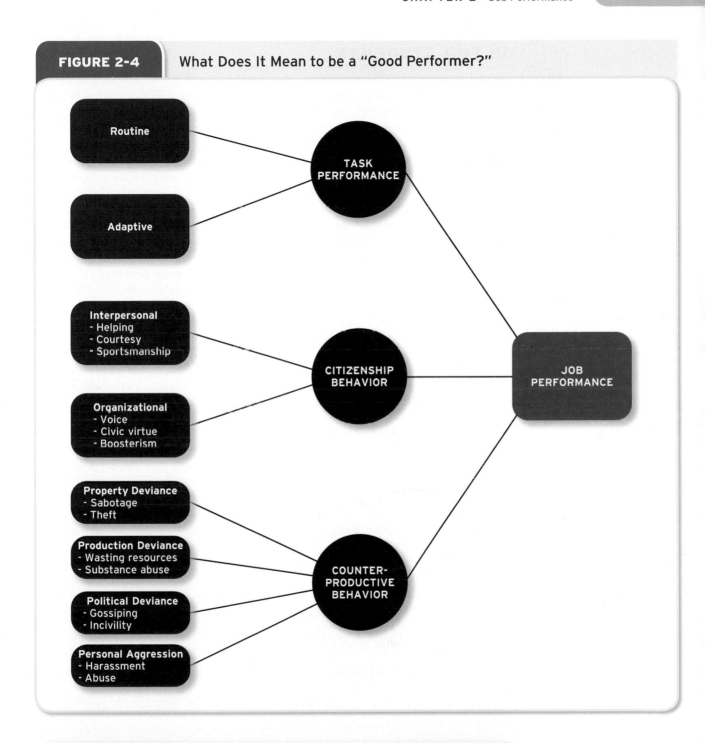

FIGURE 2-4 What Does It Mean to be a "Good Performer?"

- Routine
- Adaptive

→ TASK PERFORMANCE

- Interpersonal
  - Helping
  - Courtesy
  - Sportsmanship
- Organizational
  - Voice
  - Civic virtue
  - Boosterism

→ CITIZENSHIP BEHAVIOR

- Property Deviance
  - Sabotage
  - Theft
- Production Deviance
  - Wasting resources
  - Substance abuse
- Political Deviance
  - Gossiping
  - Incivility
- Personal Aggression
  - Harassment
  - Abuse

→ COUNTER-PRODUCTIVE BEHAVIOR

→ JOB PERFORMANCE

TRENDS AFFECTING PERFORMANCE

 2.5
What workplace trends affect job performance in today's organizations?

Now that we've described exactly what job performance is, it's time to describe some of the trends that affect job performance in the contemporary workplace. Put simply, the kinds of jobs employees do are changing, as is the way workers get organized within

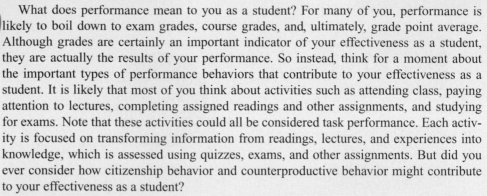

OB FOR STUDENTS

What does performance mean to you as a student? For many of you, performance is likely to boil down to exam grades, course grades, and, ultimately, grade point average. Although grades are certainly an important indicator of your effectiveness as a student, they are actually the results of your performance. So instead, think for a moment about the important types of performance behaviors that contribute to your effectiveness as a student. It is likely that most of you think about activities such as attending class, paying attention to lectures, completing assigned readings and other assignments, and studying for exams. Note that these activities could all be considered task performance. Each activity is focused on transforming information from readings, lectures, and experiences into knowledge, which is assessed using quizzes, exams, and other assignments. But did you ever consider how citizenship behavior and counterproductive behavior might contribute to your effectiveness as a student?

First, in classes that require teamwork, these two dimensions of performance are crucial. Your team will likely perform at a much higher level if you and your teammates are helpful to one another, actively participate in team meetings, and suggest improvements to the team's routine. Similarly, your team will likely perform at a lower level if you and your teammates gossip about one another, refuse to share information, or blame one another for errors.

Second, many courses devote points to participation. It may be that displays of citizenship and counterproductive behaviors can influence professors' assessments of participation points. Although we are not advocating using these behaviors as "impression management" tactics, you can probably understand why a professor might give more participation points to a student who had high attendance, participated above the norm, attended voluntary office hours, and did extra work to improve his or her class standing. Similarly, you can probably understand why a professor might give fewer participation points to a student who routinely showed up late for class, chatted with neighbors and read newspapers during lectures, and was confrontational or argumentative.

Third, it could be argued that the ultimate indicator of your effectiveness as a student is your ability to apply what you've learned to the "real world." So even in academic settings in which citizenship behavior and counterproductive behavior do not influence your grades, it may be crucial that you engage in these aspects of performance to develop the habit of doing so in situations in which they are not absolutely required. As we have noted elsewhere, citizenship behavior and counterproductive behavior will likely be considered by your employer when evaluating your overall performance. In essence, your career may depend on whether you routinely engage in the right behaviors on the job, even when the boss isn't around to watch.

companies. These trends put pressure on some elements of job performance while altering the form and function of others.

KNOWLEDGE WORK

Historically speaking, research on organizational behavior has focused on the physical aspects of job performance. This focus was understandable, given that the U.S. economy was industrial in nature and the productivity of the employees who labored in plants and factories was of great concern. However, by the early 1990s, the majority of new jobs required employees to apply theoretical and analytical knowledge acquired through formal education and continuous learning.[50] Today, statistics from the U.S. Department of Labor confirm the rise of **knowledge work,** in that jobs involving cognitive activity are becoming more prevalent than jobs involving physical activity.[51]

In addition to being more cognitive, knowledge work tends to be more fluid and dynamic in nature. Facts, data, and information are always changing. Moreover, as time goes by, people gain more and more access to

The rapid rise in the number of service jobs, such as retail sales and customer service, means that managers need more than ever to maintain a positive work environment with high citizenship behavior and low levels of counterproductive behavior.

those facts and data, using anything from Google to Yahoo to cell phones to PDAs. In addition, the tools used to do knowledge work change quickly, with software, databases, and computer systems updated more frequently than ever. As those tools become more powerful, the expectations for completing knowledge work become more ambitious. After all, shouldn't a presentation be finished more quickly when every book used in it is available online rather than at some library?

SERVICE WORK

Of course, not all jobs being created in today's economy are knowledge work jobs. In fact, one of the fastest growing sectors in the economy is service jobs. **Service work** involves the creation of a service rather than a good or product and involves direct verbal or physical interactions with customers. Projections suggest that almost 20 percent of the new jobs created between now and 2012 will be service jobs, trailing only professional services in terms of growth.[52] Retail salespersons, customer service representatives, and food service workers represent the bulk of that service job growth. By comparison, maintenance, repair, construction, and production jobs are only projected to account for 4–7 percent of new jobs over the next several years.

The increase in service jobs has a number of implications for job performance. For example, the costs of bad task performance are more immediate and more obvious. When a customer service representative does his or her job duties poorly, the customer is right there to notice. That failure cannot be hidden behind the scenes or corrected by other employees chipping in before it's too late. In addition, service work contexts place a greater premium on high levels of citizenship behavior and low levels of counterproductive behavior. If service employees refuse to help one another or maintain good sportsmanship, or if they gossip and insult one another, those negative emotions get transmitted to the customer during the service encounter. Maintaining a positive work environment therefore becomes even more vital.

APPLICATION: PERFORMANCE MANAGEMENT

Now that we've described what job performance is, along with some of the workplace trends that affect it, it's time to discuss how organizations use job performance information. As you saw in our chapter opening St. Jude example, an organization's performance management system can have a significant impact on employee behaviors and, in the end, an organization's ability to achieve its mission. Indeed, as our **OB at the Bookstore**

OB AT THE BOOKSTORE

JACK: STRAIGHT FROM THE GUT
by Jack Welch with John Byrne (New York: Warner Business Books, 2001).

I'm over the top on lots of issues, but none comes close to the passion I have for making people GE's core competency.

With this statement, Jack Welch, *Fortune*'s Manager of the 20th Century[53] and possibly the most influential CEO of the second half of the twentieth century,[54] reveals the key to his managerial philosophy. In reflecting on his career at General Electric, beginning with his first job in the GE plastics division in 1960 to his rise to CEO in 1981 and then to

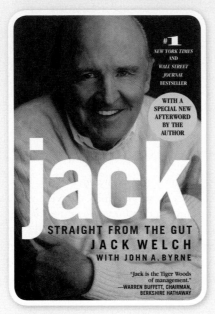

the appointment of his successor in 2000, Welch reports that GE was all about finding and building great people.

One of the most notable strategies Welch used to build great people involved managing job performance. Although there was a formal performance evaluation cycle at GE, informal performance reviews could occur anywhere and anytime. The purpose of the formal and informal evaluations was to create differentiation among the employees. Although Welch considered several systems that could differentiate people in terms of their performance, the most effective relied on the "vitality curve." The vitality curve forces managers to rank all of their people into one of three categories: the top 20 percent (A players), the vital middle 70 percent (B players), or the bottom 10 percent (C players).

The A players are thought to possess "the four Es of GE leadership": very high *energy* levels,

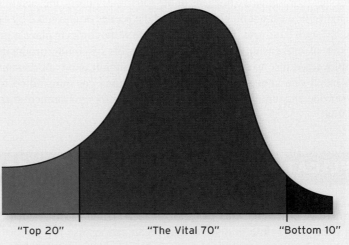

DIFFERENTIATION
"Vitality Curve"

"Top 20"   "The Vital 70"   "Bottom 10"

Source: JACK by Jack Welch and John Byrne. Copyright © 2001 by John F. Welch Jr. Foundation. Reprinted by permission of Grand Central Publishing/ Hachette Book Group USA.

the ability to *energize* others around common goals, the *edge* to make tough yes-and-no decisions, and finally the ability to consistently *execute* and deliver on their promises." (p. 158). The B players are developed. According to Welch, B players are the backbone of the company but lack the passion of A's. The C players are those who cannot get the job done and are let go. The system is taken so seriously that managers who cannot differentiate their people find themselves in the C category.

Today, approximately 20 percent of *Fortune* 500 companies use some variant of Welch's forced ranking system, which is popularly known as "rank and yank" or the "dead man's curve."[55] However, there are some important controversies to consider. For example, some believe the system is inherently unfair because it forces managers to give bad evaluations to employees who may be good performers, just to reach a preestablished percentage. As another example, employees may become hypercompetitive with one another to avoid finding themselves in a lower category. This type of competitiveness is the opposite of what may be needed in today's team-based organizations. Although Welch is still revered as the ultimate charismatic CEO, these and other problems have resulted in something of a backlash against "Jack's Rules."[56]

feature illustrates, job performance information plays a central role in management practices that have important consequences for employees and organizations alike. In this section, we describe how job performance information may be used to manage employee performance. Although organizations manage employee performance in a wide variety of ways, we'll spotlight three of the most representative: management by objectives, behaviorally anchored rating scales, and 360 degree feedback.

MANAGEMENT BY OBJECTIVES

Management by objectives (MBO) is a management philosophy that bases an employee's evaluations on whether the employee achieves specific performance goals.[57] How does MBO work? Typically, an employee meets with his or her manager to develop a set of mutually agreed-upon objectives that are measurable and specific. In addition, the employee and the manager agree on the time period for achieving those objectives and the methods used to do so. An example of a performance objective for a line manager in a factory might be something like, "Reducing production waste by 35 percent within three months by developing and implementing new production procedures." Employee performance then can be gauged by referring to the degree to which the employee achieves results that are consistent with the objectives. If the line manager cuts production waste by 37 percent within three months, the manager's performance would be deemed effective, whereas if the manager only cuts production waste by 2 percent, his or her performance would be deemed ineffective. However, MBO is best suited for managing the performance of employees who work in contexts in which objective measures of performance can be quantified.

2.6

How can organizations use job performance information to manage employee performance?

BEHAVIORALLY ANCHORED RATING SCALES

You might have noticed that MBO emphasizes the results of job performance as much as it does the performance behaviors themselves. In contrast, **behaviorally anchored rating scales** (BARS) assess performance by directly assessing job performance behaviors. The BARS approach uses "critical incidents"—short descriptions of effective and ineffective behaviors—to create a measurement instrument that managers can use to evaluate employee performance. Consider the job of a computer programmer as an example and assume that a manager wants to measure the adaptive task performance of employees. A BARS approach might use critical incidents to create the following response anchors, ranging from excellent adaptive performance (5) to poor adaptive performance (1):

- 5 = Open-minded; learns new methods easily.
- 4 = Willing to make changes without much need for persuasion or supervision.
- 3 = Able to make changes with average amount of instruction.
- 2 = Requires persuasion and supervision to make changes.
- 1 = Unwilling to accept changes; does not adjust readily.

Typically, supervisors rate several performance dimensions using BARS and score an employee's overall job performance by taking the average value across all the dimensions. In addition, because the critical incidents convey the precise kinds of behaviors that are effective and ineffective, feedback from BARS can help an employee develop and improve over time. That is, employees can develop an appreciation of the types of behaviors that would make them effective. Such information provides a nice complement to MBO, which is less capable of providing specific feedback about why an objective might have been missed.

360 DEGREE FEEDBACK

The **360 degree feedback** approach involves collecting performance information not just from the supervisor but from anyone else who might have firsthand knowledge about the employee's performance behaviors. These other sources of performance information typically include the employee's subordinates, peers, and customers. With the exception of the supervisor's ratings, the ratings are combined so that the raters can remain anonymous to the employee. Most 360 degree feedback systems also ask the employee to provide ratings of his or her own performance. The hope is that this 360 degree perspective will provide a more balanced and comprehensive examination of performance. By explicitly comparing self-provided ratings with the ratings obtained from others, employees can develop a better sense of how their performance may be deficient in the eyes of others and exactly where they need to focus their energies to improve.

Although the information from a 360 degree feedback system can be used to evaluate employees for administrative purposes such as raises or promotions, there are problems with that sort of application. First, because ratings vary across sources, there is the question of which source is most "correct." Even if multiple sources are taken into account in generating an overall performance score, it is often unclear how the information from the various sources should be weighted. Second, raters may give biased evaluations if they believe that the information will be used for compensation, as opposed to just skill development. Peers in particular may be unwilling to provide negative information if they believe it will harm the person being rated. As a result, 360 degree feedback is best suited to improving or developing employee talent, especially if the feedback is accompanied by coaching about how to improve the areas identified as points of concern.

TAKEAWAYS

2.1 Job performance is the set of employee behaviors that contribute to organizational goal accomplishment. Job performance has three dimensions: task performance, citizenship behavior, and counterproductive behavior.

2.2 Task performance includes employee behaviors that are directly involved in the transformation of organizational resources into the goods or services that the organization produces. Organizations gather information about relevant task behaviors using job analysis.

2.3 Citizenship behaviors are voluntary employee activities that may or may not be rewarded but that contribute to the organization by improving the overall quality of the setting in which work takes place. Examples of citizenship behavior include helping, courtesy, sportsmanship, voice, civic virtue, and boosterism.

2.4 Counterproductive behaviors are employee behaviors that intentionally hinder organizational goal accomplishment. Examples of counterproductive behavior include sabotage, theft, wasting resources, substance abuse, gossiping, incivility, harassment, and abuse.

2.5 A number of trends have affected job performance in today's organizations, including the rise of knowledge work and the increase in service jobs.

2.6 The MBO, BARS, and 360 degree feedback practices are three ways that organizations can use job performance information to manage employee performance.

KEY TERMS

- Job performance   *p. 37*
- Task performance   *p. 38*
- Routine task performance   *p. 38*
- Adaptive task performance   *p. 38*
- Job analysis   *p. 41*
- Occupational Information Network *p. 42*
- Citizenship behavior   *p. 43*
- Interpersonal citizenship behavior *p. 44*
- Helping   *p. 44*
- Courtesy   *p. 44*
- Sportsmanship   *p. 44*
- Organizational citizenship behavior *p. 45*
- Voice   *p. 45*
- Civic virtue   *p. 45*
- Boosterism   *p. 46*
- Counterproductive behavior   *p. 46*
- Property deviance   *p. 47*
- Sabotage   *p. 47*
- Theft   *p. 49*
- Production deviance   *p. 49*
- Wasting resources   *p. 49*
- Substance abuse   *p. 49*
- Political deviance   *p. 49*
- Gossiping   *p. 49*
- Incivility   *p. 49*
- Personal aggression   *p. 49*
- Harassment   *p. 49*
- Abuse   *p. 50*
- Knowledge work   *p. 53*
- Service work   *p. 53*
- Management by objectives   *p. 55*
- Behaviorally anchored rating scales *p. 55*
- 360-degree feedback   *p. 56*

DISCUSSION QUESTIONS

2.1   Describe the job that you currently hold or hope to hold after graduation. Now look up that job in O*NET database. Does the profile of the job fit your expectations? Are any task behaviors missing from O*NET's profile?

2.2   Describe a job in which citizenship behaviors would be especially critical to an organization's functioning and one in which citizenship behaviors would be less critical. What is it about a job that makes citizenship more important?

2.3   Figure 2-3 classifies productive deviance and political deviance as more minor in nature than property deviance and personal aggression. When might those types of counterproductive behavior prove especially costly?

2.4   Consider how you would react to 360 degree feedback. If you were the one receiving the feedback, whose views would you value most: your manager's or your peers'? If you were asked to assess a peer, would you want your opinion to affect that peer's raises or promotions?

CASE   ST. JUDE CHILDREN'S HOSPITAL

Given the complexity and cost of fixing them, most organizations knowingly choose to ignore dysfunctions within their performance management system. St. Jude Children's Research Hospital is unlike most organizations. By 2001, it realized that its current performance management system was no longer effective and a new system was needed to improve the organization.

Working with Watson Wyatt, a consulting firm, St. Jude Children's Research Hospital created a new system that addressed all the concerns of the old system. First, the rating system that skewed the performance of employees was replaced by a continuum. Managers now can give employees honest feedback without categorizing them within the confines of a ranking system. Second, customization of job performance replaced one-size-fits-all evaluations. Now, a lab scientist will not be evaluated with the same criteria as a cafeteria worker. Third, employee training establishes what the performance management system means for them. The performance management system is a tool used by management to help employees improve in areas in which they are weak.

The new system must be working. St. Jude Children's Research Hospital was named one of the best places to work in academia by *The Scientist Magazine* in 2006. Important factors contributing to this accolade were personal fulfillment, peer relations, institutional management, and tenure procedures. St. Jude is in great company, joining institutions such as the National Institute of Health, Stanford University, and Vanderbilt University on this prestigious list.

2.1   Can a job performance system be one-size-fits-all? Explain.

2.2   Did the benefits outweigh the costs of creating a new performance management system for St. Jude Children's Research Hospital?

Sources: "Best Places to Work in Academia 2006," *The Scientist Magazine,* October 2006; "How St. Jude's Gave Its Performance Mgmt. Process New Vigor," *Pay for Performance Report,* 2003; "St. Jude Children's Research Hospital 2006 Annual Report," 2006, www.stjude.org.

EXERCISE   PERFORMANCE OF A SERVER

The purpose of this exercise is to explore what job performance means for a server in a restaurant. This exercise uses groups of six participants, so your instructor will either assign you to a group of six or ask you to create your own group of six. The exercise has the following steps:

1. Conduct a job analysis for a restaurant server. Begin by drawing a circle like the one below. Use that circle to summarize the major job dimensions of a restaurant server. For example, one job dimension might be "Taking Meal Orders." Divide the circle up with four additional job dimensions. Now get more specific by listing two behaviors per job dimension. For example, two behaviors within the "Taking Meal Orders" dimension might be "Describing the Menu" and "Making Recommendations." At the end of Step 1, you should have a list of eight specific behaviors that summarize the tasks involved in being a restaurant server. Write your group's behaviors down on a transparency, laptop, or chalkboard, leaving some space for some additional behaviors down the line.

Taking Orders

2. Take a look at the resulting list. Did you come up with any behaviors that would be described as "citizenship behaviors"? If you didn't include any in your list, does that mean that citizenship behavior isn't important in a restaurant setting? If your group includes someone who has worked as a server, ask him or her to describe the importance of citizenship behavior. Come up with two especially important citizenship behaviors and add those to your list.

3. Take another look at your list. Did you come up with any behaviors that would be described as "counterproductive behaviors"? If you didn't include any in your list, does that mean that counterproductive behavior isn't an important concern in a restaurant setting? If your group includes someone who has worked as a server, ask him or her to describe the potential costs of counterproductive behavior. Come up with two especially costly counterproductive behaviors and add those to your list.

4. Class discussion (whether in groups or as a class) should center on how a restaurant owner or manager might use the resulting list to evaluate the performance of restaurant servers. How could this list be used to assess server performance? Would such an approach be valuable? Why or why not?

ENDNOTES

2.1   St. Jude Children's Hospital, "About St. Jude," n.d., http://www.stjude.org/aboutus, (August 26, 2005).

2.2   Atalla, A.M., "When Mission Is Life: Managing Performance at St. Jude Children's Research Hospital," *Strategy@Work,* August 2003, http://www.watsonwyatt.com/strategyatwork/article.asp?articleid=11558, (August 19, 2005).

2.3   Ibid.

2.4   "How St. Jude's Gave its Performance Management Process Renewed Vigor," *IOMA's Pay for Performance Report,* October 2003, pp. 7–11.

2.5   Atalla, "When Mission Is Life."

2.6   Campbell, J.P. "Modeling the Performance Prediction Problem in Industrial and Organizational Psychology." In *Handbook of Industrial and Organizational Psychology,* Vol. 1, 2nd ed., eds. M.D. Dunnette and L.M. Hough. Palo Alto, CA: Consulting Psychologists Press, 1990, pp. 687–732; Motowidlo, S.J.; W.C. Borman; and M.J. Schmit. "A Theory of Individual Differences in Task and Contextual Performance." *Human Performance* 10 (1997), pp. 71–83.

2.7   Borman, W.C., and S.J. Motowidlo. "Expanding the Criterion Domain to Include Elements of Contextual Performance." In *Personnel Selection in Organizations,* eds. N. Schmitt and W.C. Borman. San Francisco: Jossey-Bass, 1993, pp. 71–98.

2.8   Anderson, D.K. (Producer); P. Docter; L. Unkrich; and D. Silverman (Directors). *Monsters, Inc.* Emeryville, CA: Disney Pixar Studios, 2001.

2.9   Occupational Information Network (O*Net) Online. http://online.onetcenter.org/, (August 17, 2005).

2.10 LePine, J.A.; J.A. Colquitt; and A. Erez. "Adaptability to Changing Task Contexts: Effects of General Cognitive Ability, Conscientiousness, and Openness to Experience." *Personnel Psychology* 53 (2000), pp. 563–93.

2.11 CBC News, "Plane Fire at Pearson Airport. Flight 358," *Indepth Website,* August 8, 2005, http://www.cbc.ca/news/background/plane_fire/, (August 17, 2005).

2.12 Ilgen, D.R., and E.D. Pulakos. "Employee Performance in Today's Organizations." In *The Changing Nature of Work Performance: Implications for Staffing, Motivation, and Development,* eds. D.R. Ilgen and E.D. Pulakos. San Francisco: Jossey-Bass, 1999, pp. 1–20.

2.13 Pulakos, E.D.; S. Arad; M.A. Donovan; and K.E. Plamondon. "Adaptability in the Workplace: Development of a Taxonomy of Adaptive Performance." *Journal of Applied Psychology* 85 (2000), pp. 612–24.

2.14 O'Reilly, III, C.A., and J. Pfeffer. *Hidden Value: How Great Companies Achieve Extraordinary Results with Ordinary People.* Boston: Harvard Business School Press, 2000.

2.15 Occupational Information Network (O*Net) Online.

2.16 Freidberg, K., and J. Freidberg. *Nuts! Southwest Airlines' Crazy Recipe for Business and Personal Success.* Austin, TX: Bard Press, 1996.

2.17 Kaplan, M.D.G., "What Are You, a Comedian?" *USA Weekend.com,* July 13, 2003,

http://www.usaweekend.com/03_
issues/030713/030713southwest.html,
(September 15, 2005).

2.18 Curry, J. "A Doctor Is Keeping
Schilling in Stitches," *The New York
Times,* October 24, 2004, http://
query.nytimes.com/gst/abstract.html
?res=F50E16FD3D590C778EDDA
90994DC404482&n=Top%252fNe
ws%252fSports%252fBaseball%
252fMajor%2520League%252fBo
ston%2520Red%2520Sox, (August
18, 2005); MacMullan, J. "Schilling
Talked a Good Game—and Was
a Man of His Word," *The Boston
Globe,* October 31, 2004, http://
www.boston.com/sports/baseball/
redsox/articles/2004/10/31/pitch_
man?mode=PF, (August 18, 2005).

2.19 Weber, J., and C. Palmeri, " 'Vertical
Evacuation' at the Hilton," *Business-
Week,* September 19, 2005, http://
proquest.com, (March 14, 2007).

2.20 Borman and Motowidlo, "Expanding
the Criterion Domain."

2.21 Organ, D. W. *Organizational Citizenship Behavior: The Good Soldier
Syndrome.* Lexington, MA: Lexington Books, 1988.

2.22 Coleman, V. I., and W.C. Borman.
"Investigating the Underlying Structure of the Citizenship Performance
Domain." *Human Resource Management Review* 10 (2000), pp. 25–44.

2.23 Coleman and Borman, "Investigating
the Underlying Structure."

2.24 MacMillan, P. *The Performance Factor: Unlocking the Secrets of Teamwork.* Nashville, TN: Broadman &
Holman Publishers, 2001.

2.25 LePine, J.A.; R.F. Piccolo; C.L. Jackson; J.E. Mathieu; and J.R. Saul. "A
Meta-Analysis of Teamwork Process:
Towards a Better Understanding of
the Dimensional Structure and Relationships with Team Effectiveness

Criteria." Working Paper, University
of Florida, 2007.

2.26 Coleman and Borman, "Investigating the Underlying Structure."

2.27 Van Dyne, L., and J.A. LePine.
"Helping and Voice Extra-Role
Behavior: Evidence of Construct
and Predictive Validity." *Academy of
Management Journal* 41 (1998),
pp. 108–19.

2.28 Motowidlo, S.J. "Some Basic Issues
Related to Contextual Performance
and Organizational Citizenship
Behavior in Human Resource Management." *Human Resource Management Review* 10 (2000), pp. 115–26.

2.29 Podsakoff, P.M.; S.B. MacKenzie;
J.B. Paine; and D.G. Bachrach.
"Organizational Citizenship Behav-
iors: A Critical Review of the Theo-
retical and Empirical Literature and
Suggestions for Future Research."
Journal of Management 26 (2000),
pp. 513–63.

2.30 Podsakoff, P.M.; M. Ahearne; and
S.B. MacKenzie. "Organizational
Citizenship Behavior and the Quan-
tity and Quality of Work Group
Performance." *Journal of Applied
Psychology* 82 (1997), pp. 262–70.

2.31 Walz, S.M., and B.P. Neihoff. "Orga-
nizational Citizenship Behaviors
and Their Effect on Organizational
Effectiveness in Limited-Menu
Restaurants." In *Academy of Man-
agement Best Papers Proceedings,*
eds. J.B. Keys and L.N. Dosier.
Statesboro, GA: College of Business
Administration at Georgia Southern
University (1996), pp. 307–11.

2.32 McGee-Cooper, A., and G. Looper.
"Lessons on Layoffs: Managing
in Good Times to Prepare for Bad
Times." n.d., http://www.amca.com/
articles/article-layoffs.html, (August
17, 2005).

2.33 Allen, T.D., and M.C. Rush. "The Effects of Organizational Citizenship Behavior on Performance Judgments: A Field Study and a Laboratory Experiment." *Journal of Applied Psychology* 83 (1998), pp. 247–60; Avila, R.A.; E.F. Fern; and O.K. Mann. "Unraveling Criteria for Assessing the Performance of Sales People: A Causal Analysis." *Journal of Personal Selling and Sales Management* 8 (1988), pp. 45–54; Lowery, C.M., and T.J. Krilowicz. "Relationships Among Nontask Behaviors, Rated Performance, and Objective Performance Measures." *Psychological Reports* 74 (1994), pp. 571–78; MacKenzie, S.B.; P.M. Podsakoff; and R. Fetter. "Organizational Citizenship Behavior and Objective Productivity as Determinants of Managerial Evaluations of Salespersons' Performance." *Organizational Behavior and Human Decision Processes* 50 (1991), pp. 123–50; MacKenzie, S.B.; P.M. Podsakoff; and R. Fetter. "The Impact of Organizational Citizenship Behavior on Evaluation of Sales Performance." *Journal of Marketing* 57 (1993), pp. 70–80; MacKenzie, S.B.; P.M. Podsakoff; and J.B. Paine. "Effects of Organizational Citizenship Behaviors and Productivity on Evaluation of Performance at Different Hierarchical Levels in Sales Organizations." *Journal of the Academy of Marketing Science* 27 (1999), pp. 396–410; Motowidlo, S.J., and J.R. Van Scotter. "Evidence That Task Performance Should Be Distinguished from Contextual Performance." *Journal of Applied Psychology* 79 (1994), pp. 475–80; Podsakoff, P.M., and S.B. MacKenzie. "Organizational Citizenship Behaviors and Sales Unit Effectiveness." *Journal of Marketing Research* 3 (February 1994),
pp. 351–63; Van Scotter, J.R., and S.J. Motowidlo. "Interpersonal Facilitation and Job Dedication as Separate Facets of Contextual Performance." *Journal of Applied Psychology* 81 (1996), pp. 525–31.

2.34 Rotundo, M., and P.R. Sackett. "The Relative Importance of Task, Citizenship, and Counterproductive Performance to Global Ratings of Job Performance: A Policy Capturing Approach." *Journal of Applied Psychology* 87 (2002), pp. 66–80.

2.35 Allen and Rush, "The Effects of Organizational Citizenship Behavior on Performance Judgments"; Kiker, D.S., and S.J. Motowidlo. "Main and Interaction Effects of Task and Contextual Performance on Supervisory Reward Decisions." *Journal of Applied Psychology* 84 (1999), pp. 602–609; Park, O.S., and H.P Sims Jr. "Beyond Cognition in Leadership: Prosocial Behavior and Affect in Managerial Judgment." Working paper, Seoul National University and Pennsylvania State University, 1989.

2.36 Morrison, E.W. "Role Definitions and Organizational Citizenship Behavior: The Importance of the Employee's Perspective." *Academy of Management Journal* 37 (1994), pp. 1543–67.

2.37 Hofstede, G. *Cultures and Organizations: Software of the Mind.* New York: McGraw-Hill, 1991.

2.38 Rotundo, M., and J.L. Xie. "Understanding the Domain of Counterproductive Work Behavior in China." Working Paper, University of Toronto, 2007.

2.39 Robinson, S.L., and R.J. Bennett. "A Typology of Deviant Workplace Behaviors: A Multidimensional Scaling Study." *Academy of Management Journal* 38 (1995), pp. 555–72.

2.40 Cellitti, D.R., "MCA DiscoVision: The Record That Plays Pictures," June 25, 2002, http://www.oz.net/blam/DiscoVision/RecordPlaysPictures.htm, (August 16, 2005).

2.41 Hollweg, Lewis. *Inside the Four Walls of the Restaurant: The Reality and Risk of Counter-Productive Behaviors,* 2003, http://www.batrushollweg.com/files/Website.Inside_the_Four_Walls_of_the_Restaurant1.Reprint_9.pdf, (August 17, 2005).

2.42 Harper, D. "Spotlight Abuse—Save Profits." *Industrial Distribution* 79 (1990), pp. 47–51.

2.43 Hollinger, R.C., and L. Langton. *2004 National Retail Security Survey.* Gainesville, FL: University of Florida, Security Research Project, Department of Criminology, Law and Society, 2005.

2.44 Andersson, L.M., and C.M. Pearson. "Tit for Tat? The Spiraling Effect of Incivility in the Workplace." *Academy of Management Review* 24 (1999), pp. 452–71.

2.45 Ibid.

2.46 Armour, S., "Managers Not Prepared for Workplace Violence," *USA Today,* July 19, 2004, http://www.usatoday.com/money/workplace/2004-07-15-workplace-violence2_x.htm, (September 11, 2005).

2.47 PBS, "Isolated Incidents?" *Online Newshour,* April 26, 1996, http://www.pbs.org/newshour/bb/business/april96/mitsubishi_4-26.html, (September 11, 2005).

2.48 Sackett, P.R. "The Structure of Counterproductive Work Behaviors: Dimensionality and Performance with Facets of Job Performance." *International Journal of Selection and Assessment* 10 (2002), pp. 5–11.

2.49 Sackett, P.R., and C.J. DeVore. "Counterproductive Behaviors at Work." In *Handbook of Industrial, Work, and Organizational Psychology,* Vol. 1, eds. N. Anderson, D.S. Ones, H.K. Sinangil, and C. Viswesvaran. Thousand Oaks, CA: Sage, 2001, pp. 145–51.

2.50 Drucker, P. F. "The Age of Social Transformation." *The Atlantic Monthly* 274, no. 5 (1994), pp. 53–80.

2.51 U.S. Department of Labor, Bureau of Labor Statistics, "Tomorrow's Jobs," n.d., http://stats.bls.gov/oco/oco2003.htm, (August 27, 2005).

2.52 Hecker, D. "Occupational Employment Projections to 2012." *Monthly Labor Review* 127 (2004), pp. 80–105, http://proquest.com, (August 27, 2005).

2.53 "*Fortune* Selects Henry Ford Businessman of the Century," November 1, 1999, http://www.timewarner.com/corp/print/0,20858,667526,00.html, (August 27, 2005).

2.54 Auletta, K., "Jack Welch: The Lion Roars," *BusinessWeek,* September 24, 2001, http://proquest.com, (March 14, 2007).

2.55 Johnson, G. "Forced Ranking: The Good, the Bad, and the Alternative." *Training Magazine* 41 (May 2004), pp. 24–34.

2.56 Morris, B., "The New Rules," *Fortune,* July 24, 2006, http://proquest.com, (December 2, 2006).

2.57 Drucker, P.F. *The Practice of Management.* New York: Harper and Brothers, 1954.

CHAPTER

3

Organizational Commitment

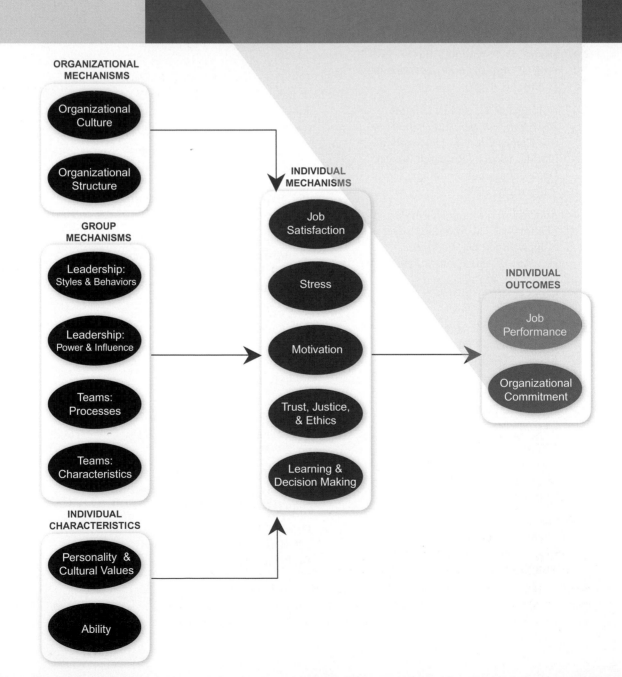

ORGANIZATIONAL MECHANISMS

- Organizational Culture
- Organizational Structure

GROUP MECHANISMS

- Leadership: Styles & Behaviors
- Leadership: Power & Influence
- Teams: Processes
- Teams: Characteristics

INDIVIDUAL CHARACTERISTICS

- Personality & Cultural Values
- Ability

INDIVIDUAL MECHANISMS

- Job Satisfaction
- Stress
- Motivation
- Trust, Justice, & Ethics
- Learning & Decision Making

INDIVIDUAL OUTCOMES

- Job Performance
- Organizational Commitment

Microsoft has had great success with its many computer products but has recently had trouble holding on to some of its software developers.

 LEARNING GOALS

After reading this chapter, you should be able to answer the following questions:

3.1 What is organizational commitment? What is withdrawal behavior? How are the two connected?

3.2 What are the three types of organizational commitment, and how do they differ?

3.3 What are the four primary responses to negative events at work?

3.4 What are some examples of psychological withdrawal? Of physical withdrawal? How do the different forms of withdrawal relate to each other?

3.5 What workplace trends are affecting organizational commitment in today's organizations?

3.6 How can organizations foster a sense of commitment among employees?

MICROSOFT

When was the last time you used a Microsoft product? Chances are, it was within the past few hours, whether you were surfing the Web using Internet Explorer, answering e-mail using Outlook Express, writing a paper or memo using Word, using a computer running Windows, or playing a videogame on an Xbox. How did Microsoft become successful enough to attain this presence in our day-to-day lives? If you were to ask the chairman of the company, Bill Gates, or the CEO of the company, Steve Ballmer, they'd likely explain that Microsoft hires the best computer science students from the best universities, year in and year out. After all, if a company wants to have the best products in a given market, it helps to have the best people. Microsoft has been able to hire the best people in part by being known as a great place to work. For example, Microsoft placed 50 on *Fortune*'s list of the "100 Best Companies to Work For" in 2007.[1]

However, for the first time in its history, Microsoft is having trouble holding on to its best and brightest.[2] Microsoft's annual rate of voluntary turnover, which captures the percentage of the workforce that decides to quit in a given year, is just 9 percent—still below the industry average.[3] But many of Microsoft's most respected software developers, engineers, managers, and marketers have recently left to go work for competing firms in the high-tech industry.[4] For example, Kai-Fu Lee, one of Microsoft's foremost experts on speech recognition, left for Google, as did Mark Lucovsky, Joe Beda, and Gary Burd, three of the company's most distinguished engineers.[5] The employees who have quit their jobs at Microsoft voice a wide range of complaints about the company, including a swelling bureaucracy, sagging morale among the rank-and-file employees, a lack of innovative spark, cuts in compensation and benefits, and an unfair performance evaluation system.[6] Many of these complaints are echoed on Web sites and blogs run by current Microsoft employees, which reinforce a culture of criticism within the company.

The challenge for Microsoft is to find a way to reverse these trends so that it can retain the most talented employees. After all, what could be more damaging than losing one of your best and brightest to a major competitor? Not only do you no longer have access to that employee's knowledge and experience, but now your competitor can draw on his or her wisdom to find a way to beat you. Microsoft is already taking steps to combat some of the complaints raised by former employees, including a reorganization of its business units designed to make the company more nimble and innovative.[7] Of course, there isn't likely to be a "magic bullet" that will single-handedly prevent further exit of more and more talented and valuable employees.

ORGANIZATIONAL COMMITMENT

Organizational commitment sits side by side with job performance in our integrative model of organizational behavior, reflecting one of the starting points for our journey through the concepts covered in this course. Why begin with a discussion of organizational commitment? Because as illustrated in the Microsoft example, it is simply not enough to have talented employees who perform their jobs well. You also need to be able to hang on to those employees for long periods of time so that the organization can benefit from their efforts. Put yourself in the shoes of a business owner. Let's say you spent a great deal of time recruiting a graduate from the local university, selling her on your business, and making sure that she was as qualified as you initially believed her to be. Now assume that, once hired, you took a personal interest in that employee, showing her the ropes and acting as mentor and instructor. Then, just as the company was set to improve as a result of that employee's presence, she leaves to go to work for a competitor. As an employer, can you think of many things more distressing than that scenario?

Unfortunately, that scenario, like the events at Microsoft, is not far-fetched. One recent survey by the Society for Human Resource Management showed that 75 percent of employees were looking for a new job.[8] Of those job seekers, 43 percent were looking for more money, and 35 percent were reacting to a sense of dissatisfaction with their current employer. Managers should be worried about these sorts of numbers, because the cost of turnover can be very high. Estimates suggest that it costs about .5 times the annual salary + benefits to replace an hourly worker, 1.5 times the annual salary + benefits to replace a salaried employee, and as much as 5 times the annual salary + benefits to replace an executive.[9] Why so expensive? Those estimates include various costs, including the administrative costs involved in the separation, recruitment expenses, screening costs, and training and orientation expenses for the new hire.[10] They also include "hidden costs" due to decreased morale, lost organizational knowledge, and lost productivity.

Organizational commitment is defined as the desire on the part of an employee to remain a member of the organization.[11] Organizational commitment influences whether an employee stays a member of the organization (is retained) or leaves to pursue another job (turns over). It is important to acknowledge that turnover can be both voluntary and involuntary. Voluntary turnover occurs when employees themselves decide to quit; involuntary turnover occurs when employees are fired by the organization for some reason. Our attention in this chapter is focused primarily on reducing voluntary turnover—keeping the employees that the organization wants to keep.

3.1

What is organizational commitment? What is withdrawal behavior? How are the two connected?

Employees who are not committed to their organizations engage in **withdrawal behavior,** defined as a set of actions that employees perform to avoid the work situation behaviors that may eventually culminate in quitting the organization.[12] The relationship between commitment and withdrawal is illustrated in Figure 3-1. Some employees may exhibit much more commitment than withdrawal, finding themselves on the green end of the continuum. Leaving aside personal or family issues, these employees are not "retention risks" for the moment. Other employees exhibit much more withdrawal than commitment, finding themselves on the red end of the continuum. These employees are retention risks—teetering on the edge of quitting their jobs. The sections that follow review both commitment and withdrawal in more detail.

FIGURE 3-1   Organizational Commitment and Employee Withdrawal

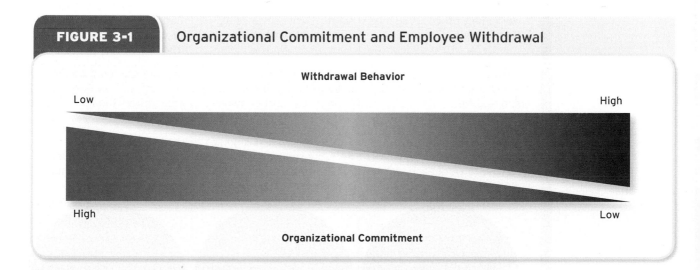

WHAT DOES IT MEAN TO BE A "COMMITTED" EMPLOYEE?

One key to understanding organizational commitment is to understand where it comes from. In other words, what creates a desire to remain a member of an organization? To explore this question, consider the following scenario: You've been working full-time for your employer for around five years. The company gave you your start in the business, and you've enjoyed your time there. Your salary is competitive enough that you were able to purchase a home in a good school system, which is important because you have one young child and another on the way. Now assume that a competing firm contacted you while you were attending a conference and offered you a similar position in its company. What kinds of things might you think about? If you created a list to organize your thoughts, what kinds of issues would appear on that list?

TYPES OF COMMITMENT

3.2

What are the three types of organizational commitment, and how do they differ?

One potential list is shown in Table 3-1. The left-hand column reflects some emotional reasons for staying with the current organization, including feelings about friendships, the atmosphere or culture of the company, and a sense of enjoyment when completing job duties. These sorts of emotional reasons create **affective commitment,** defined as a desire to remain a member of an organization due to an emotional attachment to, and involvement with, that organization.[13] Put simply, you stay because you *want* to. The middle column reflects some cost-based reasons for staying, including issues of salary, benefits, and

TABLE 3-1	The Three Types of Organizational Commitment	
What Makes Someone Want to Stay with their Current Organization?		
EMOTION-BASED REASONS	**COST-BASED REASONS**	**OBLIGATION-BASED REASONS**
Some of my best friends work in my office . . . I'd miss them if I left.	I'm due for a promotion soon . . . will I advance as quickly at the new company?	My boss has invested so much time in me, mentoring me, training me, showing me "the ropes."
I really like the atmosphere at my current job . . . it's fun and relaxed.	My salary and benefits get us a nice house in our town . . . the cost of living is higher in this new area.	My organization gave me my start . . . they hired me when others thought I wasn't qualified.
My current job duties are very rewarding . . . I enjoy coming to work each morning.	The school system is good here, my spouse has a good job . . . we've really "put down roots" where we are.	My employer has helped me out of a jam on a number of occasions . . . how could I leave now?
Affective Commitment	Continuance Commitment	Normative Commitment
Staying because you **want** to.	Staying because you **need** to.	Staying because you **ought** to.

promotions, as well as concerns about uprooting a family. These sorts of reasons create **continuance commitment,** defined as a desire to remain a member of an organization because of an awareness of the costs associated with leaving it.[14] In other words, you stay because you *need* to. The right-hand column reflects some obligation-based reasons for staying with the current organization, including a sense that a debt is owed to a boss, a colleague, or the larger company. These sorts of reasons create **normative commitment,** defined as a desire to remain a member of an organization due to a feeling of obligation.[15] In this case, you stay because you *ought* to.

As shown in Figure 3-2, the three types of organizational commitment combine to create an overall sense of psychological attachment to the company. Of course, different people may weight the three types differently. One person may be very rational and cautious by nature, focusing primarily on continuance commitment when evaluating his or her overall desire to stay. Another person may be more emotional and intuitive by nature, going more on "feel" than a calculated assessment of costs and benefits. The importance of the three commitment types also may vary over the course of a career. For example, you might prioritize affective reasons early in your work life before shifting your attention to continuance reasons as you start a family or become more established in a community. Regardless of how the three types are prioritized, however, they offer an important insight into *why*

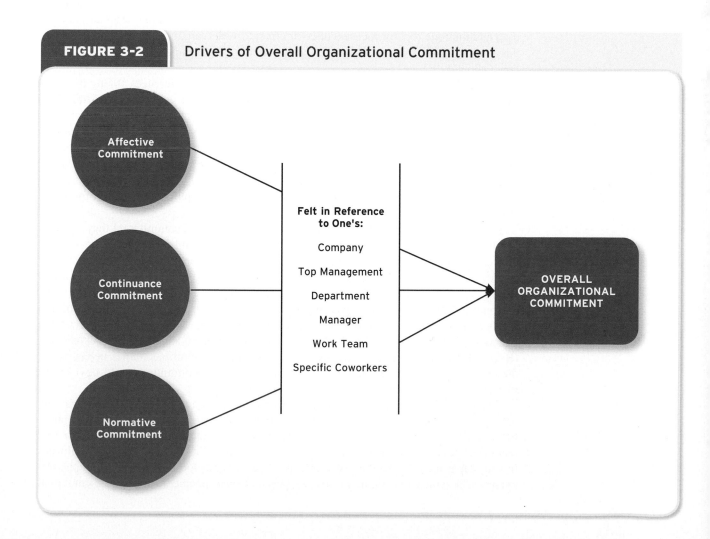

FIGURE 3-2   Drivers of Overall Organizational Commitment

Affective Commitment

Continuance Commitment

Normative Commitment

Felt in Reference to One's:

Company

Top Management

Department

Manager

Work Team

Specific Coworkers

OVERALL ORGANIZATIONAL COMMITMENT

Committed employees often have strong positive feelings about one particular aspect of their job, such as their colleagues, their manager, or the particular work they do.

someone might be committed and what an organization can do to make employees feel more committed.

Figure 3-2 also shows that organizational commitment depends on more than just "the organization." That is, people aren't always committed to companies; they're also committed to the top management that leads the firm at a given time, the department in which they work, the manager who directly supervises them, or the specific team or coworkers with whom they work most closely.[16] We use the term **focus of commitment** to refer to the various people, places, and things that can inspire a desire to remain a member of an organization. For example, you might choose to stay with your current employer because you are emotionally attached to your work team, worry about the costs associated with losing your company's salary and benefits package, and feel a sense of obligation to your current manager. If so, your desire to remain cuts across multiple types of commitment (affective, continuance, and normative) and multiple foci (or focuses) of commitment (work team, company, manager). Now that you're familiar with the drivers of commitment in a general sense, let's go into more depth about each type.

AFFECTIVE COMMITMENT. One way to understand the differences among the three types of commitment is to ask yourself what you would feel if you left the organization. Consider the reasons listed in the left-hand column of Table 3-1. What would you feel if, even after taking all those reasons into account, you decided to leave your organization to join another one? Answer: You'd feel a sense of *sadness*. Employees who feel a sense of affective commitment identify with the organization, accept that organization's goals and values, and are more willing to exert extra effort on behalf of the organization.[17] Is affective commitment something that you feel for your current employer or have felt for a past employer? Check the **OB Assessments** feature to find out.

It's safe to say that if managers could choose which type of commitment they'd like to instill in their employees, they would choose affective commitment. Moreover, when a manager looks at an employee and says "She's committed" or "He's loyal," that manager usually is referring to a behavioral expression of affective commitment.[18] For example, employees who are affectively committed to their employer tend to engage in more interpersonal and organizational citizenship behaviors, such as helping, sportsmanship, and boosterism. One meta-analysis of 22 studies with more than 6,000 participants revealed a moderately strong correlation between affective commitment and citizenship behavior.[19] (Recall that a meta-analysis averages together results from multiple studies investigating the same relationship.) Such results suggest that emotionally committed employees express that commitment by "going the extra mile" whenever they can.

Because affective commitment reflects an emotional bond to the organization, it's only natural that the emotional bonds among coworkers influence it.[20] We can therefore gain a better understanding of affective commitment if we take a closer look at the bonds that tie employees together. Assume you were given a sheet with the names of all the employees in your department or members of your class. Then assume you were asked to rate the frequency with which you communicated with each of those people, as well as the emotional

OB ASSESSMENTS

AFFECTIVE COMMITMENT

How emotionally attached are you to your employer? This assessment is designed to measure affective commitment—the feeling that you *want* to stay with your current organization. Think of your current job or the last job that you held (even if it was a part-time or summer job). Answer each question using the response scale provided. Then subtract your answers to the bold-faced questions from 6, with the difference being your new answers for those questions. For example, if your original answer for Question 3 was "4," your new answer is "2" (6–4). Then sum your answers for the six questions.

1 STRONGLY DISAGREE	2 DISAGREE	3 NEUTRAL	4 AGREE	5 STRONGLY AGREE

1. I would be very happy to spend the rest of my career in this organization. _____

2. I really feel as if this organization's problems are my own. _____

3. **I do not feel like "part of the family" at my organization.** _____

4. **I do not feel "emotionally attached" to this organization.** _____

5. This organization has a great deal of personal meaning for me. _____

6. **I do not feel a strong sense of belonging to my organization.** _____

SCORING

If your scores sum up to 20 or above, you feel a strong sense of affective commitment to your current or past employer, which means that you feel an emotional attachment to the company, or the people within it, that lessens the likelihood that you would leave voluntarily. If your scores sum up to less than 20, you have a weaker sense of affective commitment to your current or past employer. This result is especially likely if you responded to the questions in reference to a part-time or summer job, for which there is rarely enough time to develop a deep emotional bond.

Source: J.P. Meyer and N.J. Allen, 1997, *Commitment in the Workplace,* Sage Publications. Copyright © 1997 Sage Publications Inc. Reproduced via permission from Copyright Clearance Center.

depth of those communications. Those ratings could be used to create a "social network diagram" that summarizes the bonds among employees. Figure 3-3 provides a sample of such a diagram. The lines connecting the 10 members of the work unit represent the communication bonds that connect each of them, with thicker lines representing more frequent communication with more emotional depth. The diagram illustrates that some employees are "nodes," with several direct connections to other employees, whereas others remain at the fringes of the network.

FIGURE 3-3   A Social Network Diagram

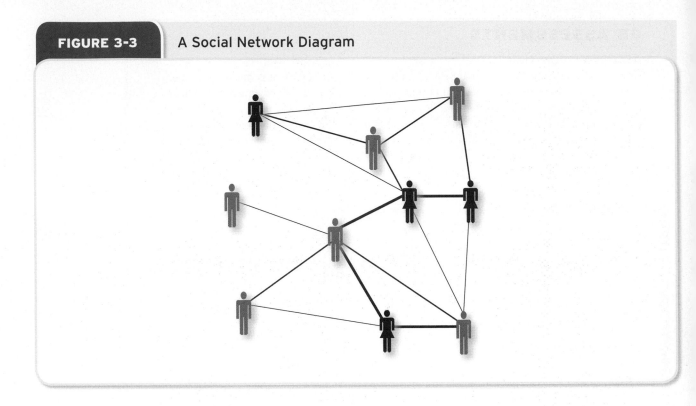

The **erosion model** suggests that employees with fewer bonds will be most likely to quit the organization.[21] If you look at Figure 3-3, who's most at risk for turning over? That's right—the employee who only has one bond with someone else (and a relatively weak bond at that). From an affective commitment perspective, that employee is likely to feel less emotional attachment to work colleagues, which makes it easier to decide to leave the organization. Social network diagrams can also help us understand another explanation for turnover. The **social influence model** suggests that employees who have direct linkages with "leavers" will themselves become more likely to leave.[22] In this way, reductions in affective commitment become contagious, spreading like a disease across the work unit. Think about the damage that would be caused if the central figure in the network (the one who has linkages to five other people) became unhappy with the organization.

Cisco Systems seems to understand the importance of affective commitment. The San Jose–based leader in networking hardware and software enjoys one of the lowest voluntary turnover rates among organizations surveyed by *Fortune* in 2004 (3 percent).[23] Cisco employees point to the fun workplace culture as a key factor, with company cafes offering movie-themed menus at Academy Awards time or "nerd lunches" during which experts discuss important tech topics. Harley-Davidson also appears to understand the importance of fostering an emotional attachment to the organization. The voluntary turnover rate at the Milwaukee-based motorcycle manufacturer is less than 2 percent, and employee surveys reveal that workers strongly identify with the culture of motorcycle riding. In fact, Harley-Davidson pays some employees to work at biker rallies.[24] These sorts of activities reinforce the emotional bonds between the company and its employees, fostering affective commitment.

CONTINUANCE COMMITMENT. Now consider the reasons for staying listed in the middle column of Table 3-1. What would you feel if, even after taking all those reasons

WELCOME RIDERS!

Not only are Harley riders loyal to their bikes, but employees are also dedicated to the company and identify with the culture of motorcycle riding. Some even get to work at biker rallies like this one.

into account, you decided to leave your organization to join another one? Answer: You'd feel a sense of *anxiety*. Continuance commitment exists when there is a profit associated with staying and a cost associated with leaving,[25] with high continuance commitment making it very difficult to change organizations because of the steep penalties associated with the switch.[26] One factor that increases continuance commitment is the total amount of investment (in terms of time, effort, energy, etc.) an employee has made in mastering his or her work role or fulfilling his or her organizational duties.[27] Picture a scenario in which you've worked extremely hard for a number of years to finally master the "ins and outs" of working at a particular organization, and now you're beginning to enjoy the fruits of that labor in terms of financial rewards and better work assignments. That effort might be wasted if you moved to another organization (and had to start over on the learning curve).

Another factor that increases continuance commitment is a lack of employment alternatives.[28] If an employee has nowhere else to go, the need to stay will be higher. Employment alternatives themselves depend on several factors, including economic conditions, the unemployment rate, and the marketability of a person's skills and abilities.[29] Of course, no one likes to feel "stuck" in a situation, so it may not be surprising that the behavioral benefits associated with affective commitment do not really occur with continuance commitment. There is no statistical relationship between continuance commitment and citizenship behavior, for example, or any other aspects of job performance.[30] Continuance commitment therefore tends to create more of a passive (as opposed to active) form of loyalty.[31]

It is important to note that some of the reasons in the middle column of Table 3-1 center on personal or family issues. Continuance commitment focuses on personal and family issues more than the other two commitment types, because employees often need to stay for both work and nonwork reasons. One concept that demonstrates the work and nonwork forces that can bind us to our current employer is **embeddedness,** which summarizes a person's links to the organization and the community, his or her sense of fit with that

TABLE 3-2	Embeddedness and Continuance Commitment	
"Embedded" People Feel:		
FACET	**FOR THE ORGANIZATION:**	**FOR THE COMMUNITY:**
Links	• I've worked here for such a long time. • I'm serving on so many teams and committees.	• Several close friends and family live nearby. • My family's roots are in this community.
Fit	• My job utilizes my skills and talents well. • I like the authority and responsibility I have at this company.	• The weather where I live is suitable for me. • I think of the community where I live as home.
Sacrifice	• The retirement benefits provided by the organization are excellent. • I would sacrifice a lot if I left this job.	• People respect me a lot in my community. • Leaving this community would be very hard.

Source: Adapted from T.R. Mitchell, B.C. Holtom, T.W. Lee, C.J. Sablynski, and M. Erez, "Why People Stay: Using Job Embeddedness to Predict Voluntary Turnover," *Academy of Management Journal* 44 (2001), pp. 1102–21.

organization and community, and what he or she would have to sacrifice for a job change.[32] As demonstrated in Table 3-2, embeddedness strengthens continuance commitment by providing more reasons why a person needs to stay in his or her current position (and more sources of anxiety if he or she were to leave).

Think about your current situation. If you're a college student who is working part-time, you likely don't feel very embedded. Your links to your job are probably only short term, and you may feel that the job is more routine than you'd like from a fit perspective. You probably also wouldn't feel you were sacrificing much if you left the job. From a community perspective, you may be going to school in a different city or state than where you grew up, again resulting in few links, low perceived fit, or a lack of felt sacrifice. However, if you're a full-time employee who is relatively established in your job and community, you may feel quite embedded in your current situation. To see how a Memphis law firm took advantage of the concepts of embeddedness and continuance commitment to retain its employees, see our **OB on Screen** feature.

Alcon Labs seems to understand the value of continuance commitment. The Fort Worth–based leader in eye care products enjoys a voluntary turnover rate of less than 2 percent.[33] One likely reason for that low rate is the benefits package Alcon offers its employees. For example, Alcon offers a 401(k) retirement plan in which it matches 240 percent of what employees contribute, up to a total of 5 percent of total compensation. So, for example, if an employee invests $500 toward retirement in a given month, Alcon contributes $1,200. That policy more than doubles the most generous rates of other companies, allowing employees to build a comfortable "nest egg" for retirement more quickly. Clearly employees would feel a bit anxious about giving up that benefit if a competitor came calling.

NORMATIVE COMMITMENT. Now consider the reasons for staying listed in the right-hand column of Table 3-1. What would you feel if, even after taking all those reasons

OB ON SCREEN

THE FIRM

The firm encourages children . . . because children bring stability.

By repeating a comment made to her during a recruitment event, Mitch McDeere's wife suggests that there's something spooky about the Memphis law firm that is about to hire her husband in *The Firm* (Dir: Sydney Pollack. Paramount Pictures, 1993), based on the book by John Grisham. Mitch (Tom Cruise) is somewhat confused by the strange comment but still decides to accept the job and make the move to Memphis.

Why does the firm care so much about how stable its employees are? Because the firm's only client is the Mafia, so it needs to know that its employees will remain committed once they learn that secret. The firm therefore wants Mitch to become embedded—to have kids and develop links in the community—so that he feels he needs to stay.

The firm creates a sense of continuance commitment in a number of ways. First, it pays 10 percent more than any other law firm, meaning that an employee would sacrifice a lot of money in any job change. Second, it provides a low-interest loan to make it easier for employees to buy a house, thereby enhancing their links to the community. In addition to encouraging children, the firm hires only married couples, providing more opportunity for family-related embeddedness to develop. Most important, though, is the understanding that anyone who decides to leave the firm will likely suffer a tragic "accident." Clearly such a threat creates the sense that one needs to stay, with commitment rooted in a strong feeling of fear and anxiety.

Unfortunately for the firm, continuance commitment is the only type of commitment it can foster. As a result, Mitch never develops the kind of affective or normative commitment that might result in behaviors that benefit the firm. To the contrary, Mitch spends all his time and energy in the quest to escape from his "trap" by finding a way to expose the firm to the FBI. Lesson #1 for employers: It's important to build all three types of commitment, not just continuance. Lesson #1 for students: Stay away from the mob!

into account, you decided to leave your organization to join another one? Answer: You'd feel a sense of *guilt.* Normative commitment exists when there is a sense that staying is the "right" or "moral" thing to do.[34] The sense that people *should* stay with their current employers may result from personal work philosophies or more general codes of right and wrong developed over the course of their lives. They may also be dictated by early experiences within the company, if employees are socialized to believe that long-term loyalty is the norm rather than the exception.[35]

In addition to personal work philosophies or organizational socialization, there seem to be two ways to build a sense of obligation-based commitment among employees. One way is to create a feeling that the employee is in the organization's debt—that he or she owes something to the organization. For example, an organization may spend a great deal of money training and developing an employee. In recognition of that investment, the employee may feel obligated to "repay" the organization with several more years of loyal service.[36] Picture a scenario in which your employer paid your tuition, allowing you to further your education, while also providing you with training and developmental job assignments that increased your skills. Wouldn't you feel a little guilty if you took the first job opportunity that came your way?

Another possible way to build an obligation-based sense of commitment is by becoming a particularly charitable organization. Did you ever wonder why organizations spend time and money on charitable things—for example, building playgrounds in the local community? Don't those kinds of projects take away from research and development, product improvements, or profits for shareholders? Well, charitable efforts have several potential advantages. First, they can provide good public relations for the organization, potentially generating goodwill for its products and services and helping attract new recruits.[37] Second, they can help existing employees feel better about the organization, creating a deeper sense of normative commitment.

The potential commitment benefits of charitable actions may be particularly appealing to younger employees. Some evidence indicates that members of Generation Y (those born between 1977 and 1994) are somewhat more charitably minded than other generations. As one example, membership in Netimpact.org, a network of socially conscious MBA graduates, rose to 10,000 in 2004.[38] Many organizations increasingly believe that social responsibility must become a more central feature of their organizational identity to retain such employees, even if their charitable actions do not have a tangible impact on sales of products or services.

Qualcomm recognizes the value of normative commitment. The San Diego–based firm, specializing in wireless technologies, has a voluntary turnover rate of just over 3 percent. After six Qualcomm employees lost their homes in a forest fire, other Qualcomm employees collected donations and contributed $60,000 to the Red Cross disaster relief fund.[39] Qualcomm matched that contribution and gives 1–2 percent of its pretax profits to charitable causes each year.[40] Charitable actions are also an important element of Microsoft's culture. Not only does Bill Gates himself donate a large percentage of his wealth to philanthropic efforts,[41] but his organization matches any charitable contribution made by its employees.[42] These sorts of activities create a sense that employees ought to remain in their current positions.

WITHDRAWAL BEHAVIOR

A recent survey revealed that only 25 percent of the largest 500 companies are confident that their current talent pool is sufficient.[43] Organizational commitment is therefore a vital concern, because the loss of even one talented employee can only worsen that situation. However, there are times when organizational commitment becomes even more critical, namely, in the face of some negative work event. To paraphrase the old saying, "When the going gets tough, the organization doesn't want you to get going." In tough times, organizations need their employees to demonstrate loyalty, not "get going" right out the door.[44] Of course, it's those same tough times that put an employee's loyalty and allegiance to the test.

Consider the following scenario: You've been working at your company for three years and served on a key product development team for the past several months. Unfortunately, the team has been struggling of late. In an effort to enhance the team's performance, the organization has added a new member to the group. This member has a solid history of product development but is, by all accounts, a horrible person with whom to work. You can easily see the employee's talent but find yourself hating every moment spent in the employee's presence. This situation is particularly distressing because the team won't finish its work for another nine months, at the earliest. What would you do in this situation?

Research on reactions to negative work events suggests that you might respond in one of four general ways.[45] First, you might attempt to remove yourself from the situation, either by being absent from work more frequently or by voluntarily leaving the organization. This removal is termed **exit,** defined as an active, destructive response by which an individual either ends or restricts organizational membership.[46] Second, you might attempt to change the circumstances by meeting with the new team member to attempt to work out the situation. This action is termed **voice,** defined as an active, constructive response in which individuals attempt to improve the situation.[47] Third, you might just "grin and bear it," maintaining your effort level despite your unhappiness. This response is termed **loyalty,** defined as a passive, constructive response that maintains public support for the situation while the individual privately hopes for improvement.[48] Fourth, you might just go through the motions, allowing your performance to deteriorate slowly as you mentally "check out." This reaction is termed **neglect,** defined as a passive, destructive response in which interest and effort in the job declines.[49] Sometimes neglect can be even more costly than exit because it is not as readily noticed. Employees may neglect their duties for months (or even years) before their bosses catch on to their poor behaviors.

3.3

What are the four primary responses to negative events at work?

Taken together, the exit–voice–loyalty–neglect framework captures most of the possible responses to a negative work event,[50] like the addition of a new colleague who makes work more difficult. Where does organizational commitment fit in? Organizational commitment should decrease the likelihood that an individual will respond to a negative work event with exit or neglect (the two destructive responses). At the same time, organizational commitment should increase the likelihood that the negative work event will prompt voice or loyalty (the two constructive responses). Research suggests that factors that promote affective and normative commitment indeed increase the likelihood of voice and loyalty while decreasing the likelihood of exit and neglect.[51]

If we consider employees' task performance levels, together with their organizational commitment levels, we can gain an even clearer picture of how people might respond to negative work events. Consider Table 3-3, which depicts combinations of high and low levels of organizational commitment and task performance. **Stars** possess high commitment and high performance and are held up as role models for other employees. Stars likely respond to negative events with voice because they have the desire to improve the status quo and the credibility needed to inspire change.[52] It's pretty easy to spot the stars in a given unit, and you can probably think about your current or past job experiences and identify the employees who would fit that description. **Citizens** possess high commitment and low task performance but perform many of the voluntary "extra-role"

TABLE 3-3	Four Types of Employees			
			Task Performance	
			HIGH	LOW
Organizational Commitment	HIGH		Stars	Citizens
	LOW		Lone wolves	Apathetics

Source: Adapted from R.W. Griffeth, S. Gaertner, and J.K. Sager, "Taxonomic Model of Withdrawal Behaviors: The Adaptive Response Model," *Human Resource Management Review* 9 (1999), pp. 577–90.

activities that are needed to make the organization function smoothly.[53] Citizens are likely to respond to negative events with loyalty because they may not have the credibility needed to inspire change but possess the desire to remain a member of the organization. You can spot citizens by looking for the people who do the little things—showing around new employees, picking up birthday cakes, ordering new supplies when needed, and so forth.

Lone wolves possess low levels of organizational commitment but high levels of task performance and are motivated to achieve work goals for themselves, not necessarily for their company.[54] They are likely to respond to negative events with exit. Although their performance would give them the credibility needed to inspire change, their lack of attachment prevents them from using that credibility constructively. Instead, they rely on their performance levels to make them marketable to their next employer. To spot lone wolves, look for the talented employees who never seem to want to get involved in the conflicts or squabbles within a unit. Finally, **apathetics** possess low levels of both organizational commitment and task performance and merely exert the minimum level of effort needed to keep their jobs. Apathetics should respond to negative events with neglect, because they lack the performance needed to be marketable and the commitment needed to engage in acts of citizenship.

It's clear from this discussion that exit and neglect represent the flipside of organizational commitment: withdrawal behavior. How common is withdrawal behavior within organizations? Quite common, it turns out. One study clocked employees' on-the-job behaviors over a two-year period and found that only about 51 percent of their time was actually spent working! The other 49 percent was lost to late starts, early departures, long coffee breaks, personal matters, and other forms of withdrawal.[55] As a manager, wouldn't you like to feel like there was more than a coin-flip's chance that your employees were actually working during the course of a given day?

As shown in Figure 3-4, withdrawal comes in two forms: psychological (or neglect) and physical (or exit). **Psychological withdrawal** consists of actions that provide a mental escape from the work environment.[56] When an employee is engaging in psychological withdrawal, "the lights are on, but nobody's home." Some business articles refer to psychological withdrawal as "warm-chair attrition," meaning that employees have essentially been lost even though their chairs remain occupied.[57] How big of a problem is psychological withdrawal? A recent Gallup poll revealed that more than 70 percent of employees feel "disengaged" from their work (suggesting that the 51 percent work time result discussed previously may be optimistic!).[58]

3.4

What are some examples of psychological withdrawal? Of physical withdrawal? How do the different forms of withdrawal relate to each other?

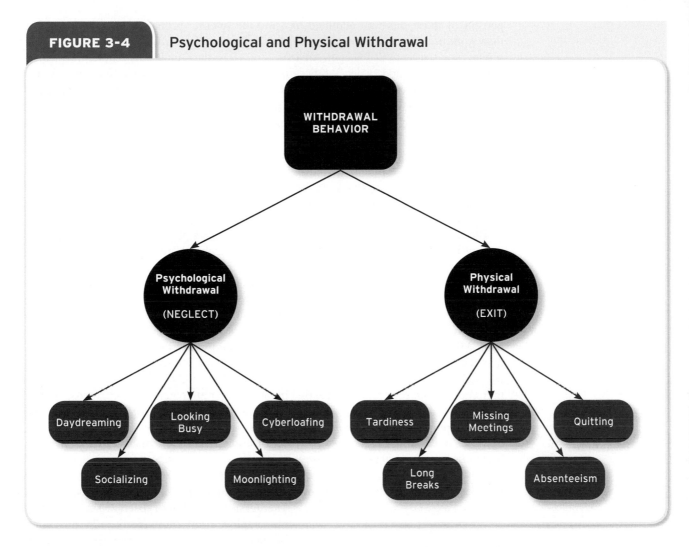

FIGURE 3-4   Psychological and Physical Withdrawal

Psychological withdrawal comes in a number of shapes and sizes. The least serious is **daydreaming,** when an employee appears to be working but is actually distracted by random thoughts or concerns. **Socializing** refers to the verbal chatting about nonwork topics that goes on in cubicles and offices or at the mailbox or vending machines. **Looking busy** indicates an intentional desire on the part of the employee to look like he or she is working, even when not performing work tasks.[59] Sometimes employees decide to reorganize their desks or go for a stroll around the building, even though they have nowhere to go. (Those who are very good at managing impressions do such things very briskly and with a focused look on their faces!) When employees engage in **moonlighting,** they use work time and resources to complete something other than their job duties, such as assignments for another job.[60]

Perhaps the most widespread form of psychological withdrawal among white collar employees is **cyberloafing**—using Internet, e-mail, and instant messaging access for their personal enjoyment rather than work duties.[61] One recent survey of more than 3,000 employees from 750 different organizations revealed that employees spend around 40 percent of their workday responding to personal e-mails or surfing the Web.[62] Ninety-seven percent of those surveyed admitted to using the Internet primarily for personal rather than work use. To see for yourself, go for a stroll around any office and count how many screens you see set to ESPN.com, Amazon.com, eBay, the iTunes music store, travel sites, stock-watch sites, and (when the boss is clearly not looking) job hunting sites. At the end of 2003, one estimate suggested that cyberloafing had cost the U.S. economy $250 billion in lost productivity.[63] Some employees view cyberloafing as a way of "balancing the scales" when it comes to personal versus work time. For example, one participant in a cyberloafing study noted, "It is alright for me to use the Internet for personal reasons at work. After all, I do work overtime without receiving extra pay from my employer."[64] Although such views are quite reasonable, other employees view cyberloafing as a means of retaliating against negative work events. One participant in the same study noted, "My boss is not the appreciative kind; I take what I can whenever I can. Surfing the net is my way of hitting back."

Physical withdrawal consists of actions that provide a physical escape, whether short term or long term, from the work environment. Physical withdrawal also comes in a number of shapes and sizes. **Tardiness** reflects the tendency to arrive at work late (or leave work early).[65] Of course, tardiness can sometimes be unavoidable, as when employees have car trouble or must fight through bad weather, but it often represents a calculated desire to spend less time at work.[66] **Long breaks** involve longer-than-normal lunches, soda breaks, coffee breaks, and so forth that provide a physical escape from work. Ben Hamper's classic book *Rivethead: Tales of the Assembly Line*[67] is filled with examples of General Motors manufacturing employees taking excessively long breaks. For example, employees would routinely take turns covering for one another on the assembly line for half a shift so that they could spend several hours sleeping in their cars or at home, running errands, or even drinking beer at local bars. Sometimes such breaks stretch into **missing meetings,** which means employees neglect important work functions while away from the office. As a manager, you'd like to be sure that employees that leave for lunch are actually going to come back, but sometimes, that's not a safe bet!

Absenteeism occurs when employees miss an entire day of work.[68] Of course, people stay home from work for a variety of reasons, including illness and family emergencies. There is also a rhythm to absenteeism. For example, employees are more likely to be absent on Mondays or Fridays.[69] Moreover, streaks of good attendance create a sort of pressure to be absent, as personal responsibilities build until a day at home becomes irresistible.[70] That type of absence can sometimes be functional, because people return to work with their "batteries recharged."[71] Group and departmental norms also affect absenteeism by signaling whether an employee can get away with missing a day here or there without being noticed.[72] These issues aside, a consistent pattern of absenteeism, month in and month out, is a symptom of the kind of low commitment that concerns most managers. Should absenteeism (in the form of missed classes) concern instructors as well? See our **OB for Students** feature to find out.

Finally, the most serious form of physical withdrawal is **quitting**—voluntarily leaving the organization. As with the other forms of

"Hewes, it's come to my attention that you've been using our internet access to troll for babes."

OB FOR STUDENTS

What does withdrawal mean for you as a student? The most obvious form of withdrawal for students is missed classes—the academic version of absenteeism. Why do students choose to stay home from class on a given day? One study identified the top six reasons for missing class, ranked as follows:[73]

1. Needing to complete work for another class.
2. The class is boring.
3. Severe illness (e.g., flu).
4. Minor illness (e.g., cold, sore throat).
5. Tired from social activities.
6. Oversleeping.

These reasons illustrate that there are a number of factors that cause people to be absent. Some are avoidable, some are unavoidable; some are related to the class, some are unrelated. Of the factors listed, the "class is boring" reason most clearly captures absenteeism as a response to a negative class-related event. Students don't like the class, so they engage in exit behaviors. There's also a rhythm and seasonality to absenteeism, as students are most likely to miss Friday classes or classes near the end of the semester (when project deadlines become most pressing).

Here's the million-dollar question for any student: Does absenteeism harm course grades? The clear answer is "yes." One study examined the correlation between class attendance and course grades across 17 different class sections and identified correlations ranging from .29 to .73.[74] Another study found that students who attend all classes average a .45 point higher GPA in the course than students who only attend half the classes.[75] This result appears even when taking into account a student's prior cumulative GPA and his or her motivation levels.

These sorts of results explain why some instructors build an attendance requirement into their classes, causing students to sign in each day to reduce absences. The benefits of this policy were tested in two sections of a psychology course.[76] One section required students to sign in to record attendance; the other section didn't. Absenteeism was one-third lower in the section that required sign-ins, and the students in that section performed significantly better on seven of the eight quizzes in the class.

The bottom line is clear for you as a student—come to class, and you'll get a better grade. Of course, showing up may be only half the battle, particularly if students are tempted to engage in neglect during lectures (e.g., reading the newspaper, surfing the Web, falling asleep). If you find yourself tempted to engage in those forms of psychological withdrawal, consider this result: Students who participate during class increase their course GPAs by an average of .23 points.[77] So there's a reason to pay attention!

withdrawal, employees can choose to "turn over" for a variety of reasons. The most frequent reasons include leaving for more money or a better career opportunity; dissatisfaction with supervision, working conditions, or working schedule; family factors; and health.[78] Note that many of those reasons reflect avoidable turnover, meaning that the organization could have done something to keep the employee, perhaps by offering more money, more frequent promotions, or a better work situation. Family factors and health, in contrast, usually reflect unavoidable turnover that doesn't necessarily signal a lack of commitment on the part of employees.

Regardless of their reasons, some employees choose to quit after engaging in a very thorough, careful, and reasoned analysis. Typically some sort of "shock," whether it be a critical job change or a negative work experience, jars employees enough that it triggers the thought of quitting in them.[79] Once the idea of quitting has occurred to them, employees begin searching for other places to work, compare those alternatives to their current job, and—if the comparisons seem favorable—quit.[80] This process may take days, weeks, or even months as employees grapple with the decision. In other cases, though, a shock may result in an impulsive, knee-jerk decision to quit, with little or no thought given to alternative jobs (or how those jobs compare to the current one).[81] Of course, sometimes a shock never occurs. Instead, an employee decides to quit as a result of a slow but steady decrease in happiness until a "straw breaks the camel's back" and voluntary turnover results.

Figure 3-4 shows 10 different behaviors that employees can perform to psychologically or physically escape from a negative work environment. A key question remains though: "How do all those behaviors relate to one another?" Consider the following testimonials from uncommitted (and admittedly fictional) employees:

- "I can't stand my job, so I do what I can to get by. Sometimes I'm absent, sometimes I socialize, sometimes I come in late. There's no real rhyme or reason to it; I just do whatever seems practical at the time."

- "I can't handle being around my boss. I hate to miss work, so I do what's needed to avoid being absent. I figure if I socialize a bit and spend some time surfing the Web, I don't need to ever be absent. But if I couldn't do those things, I'd definitely have to stay home . . . a lot."

- "I just don't have any respect for my employer anymore. In the beginning, I'd daydream a bit during work or socialize with my colleagues. As time went on, I began coming in late or taking a long lunch. Lately I've been staying home altogether, and I'm starting to think I should just quit my job and go somewhere else."

Each of these statements sounds like something that an uncommitted employee might say. However, each statement makes a different prediction about the relationship between the withdrawal behaviors in Figure 3-4. The first statement summarizes the **independent forms model** of withdrawal, which argues that the various withdrawal behaviors are uncorrelated with one another, occur for different reasons, and fulfill different needs on the part of employees.[82] From this perspective, knowing that an employee cyberloafs tells you nothing about whether that employee is likely to be absent. The second statement summarizes the **compensatory forms model** of withdrawal, which argues that the various withdrawal behaviors negatively correlate with one another—that doing one means you're less likely to do another.[83] The idea is that any form of withdrawal can compensate for, or neutralize, a sense of dissatisfaction, which makes the other forms unnecessary. From this perspective, knowing that an employee cyberloafs tells you that the same employee probably isn't going to be absent. The third statement summarizes the **progression model** of withdrawal, which argues that the various withdrawal behaviors are positively correlated: The tendency to daydream or socialize leads to the tendency to come in late or take long breaks, which leads to the tendency to be absent or quit.[84] From this perspective, knowing that an employee cyberloafs tells you that the same employee is probably going to be absent in the near future.

Which of the three models seems most logical to you? Although all three make some sense, the progression model has received the most scientific support.[85] Studies tend to show that the withdrawal behaviors in Figure 3-4 are positively correlated with one another.[86] Moreover, if you view the behaviors as a causal sequence moving from left (daydreaming) to right (quitting), the behaviors that are closest to each other in the sequence tend to be more highly correlated.[87] For example, quitting is more closely related to absenteeism than to tardiness, because absenteeism is right next to it in the withdrawal progression.[88] These results illustrate that withdrawal behaviors may begin with very minor actions but eventually can escalate to more serious actions that may harm the organization.

SUMMARY: WHAT DOES IT MEAN TO BE A "COMMITTED" EMPLOYEE?

So what does it mean to be a "committed" employee? As shown in Figure 3-5, it means a lot of different things. It means that the employee has a strong desire to remain a member of the organization, maybe because he or she wants to stay, needs to stay, or feels he or she ought to stay. Regardless of the reasons for their attachment though, retaining employees means stopping the progression of withdrawal that begins with psychological forms and escalates to behavioral forms. Note that the negative sign (−) in Figure 3-5 illustrates that high levels of overall organizational commitment reduce the frequency of psychological and physical withdrawal. Note also that psychological withdrawal goes on to affect physical withdrawal, which represents the progressive nature of such behaviors.

As you move forward in this book, you'll notice that every chapter includes a description of how that chapter's topic relates to organizational commitment. For example, Chapter 4 on Job Satisfaction describes how an employee's satisfaction level influences his or her organizational commitment. You'll find that some chapter topics are more strongly correlated with affective commitment, whereas other topics correlate more strongly with continuance or normative commitment. Such differences will help you see exactly how and why a given topic, whether it be satisfaction, stress, motivation, or something else, affects organizational commitment. By the end of the book, you will have developed a good sense of the most powerful drivers of commitment.

TRENDS THAT AFFECT COMMITMENT

Now that we've described exactly what organizational commitment represents, it's time to describe some of the trends that affect it in the contemporary workplace. Put simply, the composition of the workforce is changing, as is the traditional relationship between employees and employers. These trends put pressure on some types of commitment and alter the kinds of withdrawal seen in the workplace.

DIVERSITY OF THE WORKFORCE

One of the most visible trends affecting the workplace is the increased diversity of the United States' labor force. Demographically speaking, about 70 percent of the U.S. workforce was white in 2004.[89] That percentage is expected to drop to about 65 percent by 2012. Meanwhile, the percentage of minorities in the workforce is expected to rise as follows: African Americans (11 to 12 percent), Hispanics (13 to 15 percent), and Asians (4 to 6 percent). Thus, by 2012, minority groups will make up one-third of the workforce. Meanwhile, women have virtually matched men in terms of workforce percentages, with

 3.5

What workplace trends are affecting organizational commitment in today's organizations?

FIGURE 3-5   What Does It Mean to Be a "Committed" Employee?

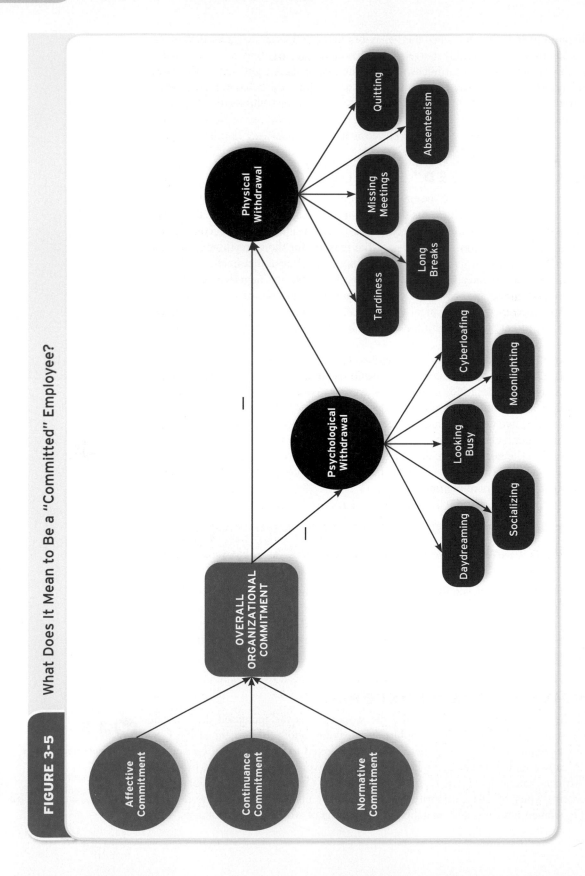

53 percent of jobs filled by men and 47 percent by women. These statistics show that the "white, male-dominated" workforce is becoming a thing of the past.

The workforce is becoming diverse in other ways as well. The percentage of members of the workforce who are 60 or older was 7 percent in 2004 and is predicted to grow to 10 percent in 2012.[90] As the 78 million Baby Boomers near retirement, they are expected to remain in the workforce significantly longer than previous generations.[91] Research suggests that remaining a member of the workforce is actually beneficial to older people's health, keeping them more mentally and physically fit. Moreover, medical advances are helping older employees stay vital longer, just as the physical labor component of most jobs keeps shrinking. The Baby Boomers are also one of the most educated generations, and research suggests that their continued participation in the workforce could add $3 trillion dollars a year to the country's economic output. That, combined with the uncertainty surrounding Social Security and stock market–based retirement plans, makes staying in the workforce a logical call. For more information on how this age diversity affects organizational commitment, see our **OB at the Bookstore** feature.

As the economy continues to become more global, U.S. businesses face another important form of diversity: More and more employees are foreign-born. Although stereotypes view immigrants as staffing blue collar or service jobs, many of the most educated employees come from abroad. Consider that half of the PhDs working in the United States are foreign-born, as are 45 percent of the physicists, computer scientists, and mathematicians.[92] At the same time, more and more American employees are working as expatriates who staff offices in foreign countries for long periods of time. Serving as an expatriate can be a very stressful assignment for employees as they adjust to a new country, a new style of working, and increased distance from family and friends. See our **OB Internationally** feature for more discussion of organizational commitment in multinational corporations.

These forms of diversity make it more challenging to retain valued employees. Consider the social network diagram in Figure 3-3. As work groups become more diverse with respect to race, gender, age, and national origin, there is a danger that minorities or older employees will find themselves on the fringe of such networks, which potentially reduces their affective commitment. At the same time, foreign-born employees are likely to feel less embedded in their current jobs and perceive fewer links to their community and less fit with their geographic area. This feeling may reduce their sense of continuance commitment. Recent trends suggest that the most educated and skilled immigrants are leaving the U.S. workforce at a rate of about 1,000 a day, particularly when their home country's economy begins to boom.[98]

THE CHANGING EMPLOYEE–EMPLOYER RELATIONSHIP

A few generations ago, many employees assumed that they would work for a single organization for their entire career. The assumption was that they would exchange a lifetime of loyalty and good work for a lifetime of job security. That perception changed in the 1980s and 1990s as downsizing became a more common part of working life. In 1992, downsizing statistics peaked as 3.4 million jobs were lost, and annual job losses have remained that high ever since.[99] Downsizing represents a form of involuntary turnover, when employees are forced to leave the organization regardless of their previous levels of commitment. The increase in downsizing has gone hand-in-hand with increases in temporary workers and outsourcing, fundamentally altering the way employees view their relationships with their employers.

OB AT THE BOOKSTORE

WORKFORCE CRISIS: HOW TO BEAT THE COMING SHORTAGE OF SKILLS AND TALENT

by Ken Dychtwald, Tamara J. Erickson, and Robert Morison (Boston, MA: Harvard Business School Press, 2006).

> *Our goal in this book is to enable organizations and their leaders to make the most of their talent supply today and to ensure their talent supply tomorrow . . . . We empha- size employment practices that will boost workforce commitment and performance immediately, at the same time that they position the organization to be an "employer of choice" in the tighter labor markets of the not-so-distant future.*

With these words, the authors summarize the central focus of their book: how to maintain organizational commitment in the face of increasing age diversity. The authors review two key trends: (a) the potential retirement of the Baby Boom generation and (b) the "birth dearth"—the declining birthrate in the United States and other industrialized nations. The authors suggest several specific strategies for dealing with these two trends, including strategies focusing on older and younger workers.

For older workers. Organizations need to retain older workers, not encourage them to retire. Their organizational knowledge and con- nections will be needed to cope with a skill shortage in the labor market.

For younger workers. Organizations need to recruit talented younger workers, just like always. However, retaining those workers will become more challenging if the younger employees see less potential for advancement as a result of the "Boomer bottleneck."

How exactly should organizations go about building commitment among these two distinct groups? For older workers, the authors suggest that organizations need to strive to bust "ageist" views about the productivity of that workforce segment. Organizations also should institute practices that allow for career "deceleration" or "downshifting" without formal retirement. For younger workers, organizations need to survey new employees about their potentially unique needs and desires. The authors suggest that younger employees are particularly attracted to the "three S's": *say* (having a voice in organizational affairs), *stake* (a sense of ownership in the busi- ness), and *stimulus* (a work environment that is interesting and engaging). The organiza- tions that can successfully foster commitment among the old and young alike could enjoy a significant advantage over their competitors.

OB INTERNATIONALLY

Fostering organizational commitment can be more complex in multinational corporations, for two primary reasons. First, multinational corporations provide two distinct foci of commitment. Employees can be committed to the local subsidiary in which they work, or they can be committed to the global organization. Research on commitment in multinational corporations suggests that employees draw a distinction between those two foci when judging their commitment.[93] Specifically, employees distinguish between the prestige of their local subsidiary and the reputation of the larger organization. They also distinguish between the support provided by their local supervisor and the support provided by the global organization's top management. Such results reveal that it is possible to be committed to the local office but not the overall organization or vice versa.

Second, multinational corporations require many employees to serve as expatriates for significant periods of time. Research suggests that the organizational commitment of expatriates depends, in part, on how well they adjust to their foreign assignments.[94] Research further suggests that expatriates' adjustment comes in three distinct forms:[95]

- *Work adjustment.* The degree of comfort with specific job responsibilities and performance expectations.
- *Cultural adjustment.* The degree of comfort with the general living conditions, climate, cost of living, transportation, and housing offered by the host culture.
- *Interaction adjustment. The degree of comfort when socializing and interacting with members of the host culture.*

A study of American multinational corporations in the transportation, service, manufacturing, chemical, and pharmaceutical industries showed that all three forms of adjustment relate significantly to affective commitment.[96] If expatriates cannot feel comfortable in their assignment, it's difficult for them to develop an emotional bond to their organization. Instead, they are likely to withdraw from the assignment, both psychologically and physically.

What factors contribute to an expatriate's adjustment levels? It turns out that work adjustment depends on many of the same things that drive domestic employees' job satisfaction and motivation.[97] Cultural and interactional adjustment, in contrast, are very dependent on spousal and family comfort. If an expatriate's spouse or children are unhappy in their new environment, it becomes very difficult for the expatriate to remain committed. Fortunately, research suggests that cultural and interactional adjustment can increase with time, as experiences in the host nation gradually increase expatriates' sense of comfort and, ultimately, their commitment to the work assignment.

Companies usually downsize to cut costs, particularly during a recession or economic downturn. Does downsizing work? Does it make the company more profitable? One study suggests that the answer is "not usually." This study examined 3,628 companies between 1980 and 1994, of which 59 percent downsized 5 percent or more of their workforce at least once and 33 percent fired 15 percent or more of their workforce at least once.[100] The most important result was that downsizing actually harmed company profitability and stock price. In fact, it typically took firms two years to return to the performance levels that prompted the downsizing in the first place. The exception to this rule was companies that downsized in the context of some larger change in assets (e.g., the sale of a line of business, a merger, an acquisition). However, such firms were relatively rare; only one-eighth of the downsizers were involved in some sort of asset change at the time the layoffs occurred.

Why doesn't downsizing tend to work? One reason revolves around the organizational commitment levels of the so-called "survivors." The employees who remain in the organization after a downsizing are often stricken with "survivor syndrome," characterized by anger, depression, fear, distrust, and guilt.[101] One study found that downsizing survivors actually experienced more work-related stress than did the downsizing victims who went on to find new employment.[102] Survivor syndrome tends to reduce organizational commitment levels at the worst possible time, as downsizing survivors are often asked to work extra hard to compensate for their lost colleagues.

The change in employee–employer relationships brought about by a generation of downsizing makes it more challenging to retain valued employees. The most obvious challenge is finding a way to maintain affective commitment. The negative emotions aroused by survivor syndrome likely reduce emotional attachment to the organization. Moreover, if the downsizing has caused the loss of key figures in an employee's social network, then his or her desire to stay will be harmed. However, a second challenge is to find some way to maintain normative commitment. The sense that people *should* stay with their employer may have been eroded by downsizing, with personal work philosophies now focusing on maximizing marketability for the next opportunity that comes along. Even if an employee felt obligated to remain at a firm in the past, seeing colleagues get dismissed in a downsizing effort could change that belief rather quickly.

APPLICATION: COMMITMENT INITIATIVES

3.6

How can organizations foster a sense of commitment among employees?

Now that you've gained a good understanding of organizational commitment, as well as some of the workforce trends that affect it, we close with a discussion of strategies and initiatives that can be used to maximize commitment. As the opening example of Microsoft illustrated, almost every company struggles to foster commitment at some time or another. What can they do to prevent withdrawal? From an affective commitment perspective, employer strategies could center on increasing the bonds that link employees together. Ben & Jerry's holds monthly "joy events" during which all production stops for a few hours, to be replaced by Cajun-themed parties, table tennis contests, and employee appreciation celebrations.[103] Monsanto, the St. Louis–based provider of agricultural products, groups staffers into "people teams" charged with designing employee-bonding activities like "snowshoe softball."[104] Such tight bonding among employees may explain why Monsanto's voluntary turnover rate is only 3 percent. Companies like PepsiCo and Procter & Gamble pay particular attention to mentoring and team-building programs for female and minority employees to create a sense of solidarity among employees who might otherwise remain on the fringe of social networks.[105]

From a continuance commitment perspective, the priority should be to create a salary and benefits package that creates a financial need to stay. One study compared the impact of a variety of human resource management practices on voluntary turnover and found that two of the most significant predictors were average pay level and quality of the benefits package.[106] Of course, one factor that goes hand-in-hand with salaries and

Ben & Jerry's, founded by Ben Cohen and Jerry Greenfield, goes to lengths to encourage employees to hang out together and have fun during their work-week. Such bonding activities lower turnover and encourage valued employees to remain.

benefits is advancements and promotions, because salaries cannot remain competitive if employees get stuck in neutral when climbing the career ladder.[107] Perhaps that's why companies that are well-known for their commitment to promotion-from-within policies, like A.G. Edwards and the Principal Financial Group, also enjoy especially low voluntary turnover rates.[108] Paying attention to career paths is especially important for star employees and foreign-born employees, both of whom have many options for employment elsewhere.[109]

From a normative commitment perspective, the employer can provide various training and development opportunities for employees, which means investing in them to create the sense that they owe further service to the organization. As the nature of the employee–employer relationship has changed, opportunities for development have overtaken secure employment on the list of employee priorities.[110] IBM is one company with a reputation for prioritizing development. Its "workforce management initiative" keeps a database of 33,000 resumes to develop a snapshot of employee skills. IBM uses that snapshot to plan its future training and development activities, with $400 million of the company's $750 million training budget devoted to giving employees the skills they may need in the future. If employees find developmental activities beneficial and rewarding, they may be tempted to repay those efforts with further years of service.

A final practical suggestion centers on what to do if withdrawal begins to occur. Managers are usually tempted to look the other way when employees engage in minor forms of withdrawal. After all, sometimes such behaviors simply represent a break in an otherwise busy day. However, the progression model of withdrawal shows that even minor forms of psychological withdrawal often escalate, eventually to the point of absenteeism and turnover. The implication is therefore to stop the progression in its early stages by trying to root out the source of the reduced commitment. Many of the most effective companies take great strides to investigate the causes of low commitment, whether at the psychological withdrawal stage or during exit interviews. As one senior oil executive acknowledged, the loss of a talented employee warrants the same sort of investigation as a technical malfunction that causes significant downtime on an oil rig.[111]

TAKEAWAYS

3.1   Organizational commitment is the desire on the part of an employee to remain a member of the organization. Withdrawal behavior is a set of actions that employees perform to avoid the work situation. Commitment and withdrawal are negatively related to each other—the more committed an employee is, the less likely he or she is to engage in withdrawal.

3.2   There are three types of organizational commitment. Affective commitment occurs when an employee *wants* to stay and is influenced by the emotional bonds between employees. Continuance commitment occurs when an employee *needs* to stay and is influenced by salary and benefits and the degree to which he or she is embedded in the community. Normative commitment occurs when an employee feels that he or she *ought* to stay and is influenced by an organization investing in its employees or engaging in charitable efforts.

3.3   Employees can respond to negative work events in four ways: exit, voice, loyalty, and neglect. Exit is a form of physical withdrawal in which the employee either ends or restricts organizational membership. Voice is an active and constructive response by which employees attempt to improve the situation. Loyalty is passive and constructive; employees remain supportive while hoping the situation improves on its own. Neglect is a form of psychological withdrawal in which interest and effort in the job decrease.

3.4   Examples of psychological withdrawal include daydreaming, socializing, looking busy, moonlighting, and cyberloafing. Examples of physical withdrawal include tardiness, long breaks, missing meetings, absenteeism, and quitting. Consistent with the progression model, withdrawal behaviors tend to start with minor psychological forms before escalating to more major physical varieties.

3.5   The increased diversity of the workforce can reduce commitment if employees feel lower levels of affective commitment or less embedded in their current jobs. The employee–employer relationship, which has changed due to decades of downsizing, can reduce affective and normative commitment, making it more of a challenge to retain talented employees.

KEY TERMS

- Organizational commitment   *p. 67*
- Withdrawal behavior   *p. 67*
- Affective commitment   *p. 68*
- Continuance commitment   *p. 69*
- Normative commitment   *p. 69*
- Focus of commitment   *p. 70*
- Erosion model   *p. 72*
- Social influence model   *p. 72*
- Embeddedness   *p. 73*
- Exit   *p. 77*
- Voice   *p. 77*
- Loyalty   *p. 77*
- Neglect   *p. 77*
- Stars   *p. 77*
- Citizens   *p. 77*
- Lone wolves   *p. 78*
- Apathetics   *p. 78*
- Psychological withdrawal   *p. 78*
- Daydreaming   *p. 79*
- Socializing   *p. 79*
- Looking busy   *p. 79*
- Moonlighting   *p. 79*
- Cyberloafing   *p. 79*
- Physical withdrawal   *p. 80*
- Tardiness   *p. 80*
- Long breaks   *p. 80*

- Missing meetings   *p. 80*
- Absenteeism   *p. 80*
- Quitting   *p. 80*

- Independent forms model   *p. 82*
- Compensatory forms model *p. 82*
- Progression model   *p. 82*

DISCUSSION QUESTIONS

3.1 Which type of organizational commitment (affective, continuance, or normative) do you think is most important to the majority of employees? Which do you think is most important to you?

3.2 Describe other ways that organizations can improve affective, continuance, and normative commitment, other than the strategies suggested in this chapter. How expensive are those strategies?

3.3 Consider times when you've reacted to a negative event with exit, voice, loyalty, or neglect. What was it about the situation that caused you to respond the way you did? Do you usually respond to negative events in the same way, or does your response vary across the four options?

3.4 Can organizations use a combination of monitoring and punishment procedures to reduce psychological and physical withdrawal? How might such programs work from a practical perspective? Do you think they would be effective?

3.5 Can you think of reasons the increased diversity of the workforce might actually increase organizational commitment? Why? Which of the three types of commitment might explain that sort of result?

3.6 Studies suggest that decades of downsizing have lowered organizational commitment levels. Can you think of a way that an organization can conduct layoffs without harming the commitment of the survivors? How?

CASE MICROSOFT

Microsoft has one of the lowest employee turnover rates in the IT industry; however, there is room for improvement. Top talent is currently leaving Microsoft to pursue Internet start-ups or jumping ship to Google. The loss of these key employees represents a serious threat to the success of the company in the future. Recognizing this problem, Microsoft is actively identifying its top talent and developing ways to make jobs more attractive.

Employee engagement appears to be the buzz in corporate America. Studies show that employees who are engaged are more productive, profitable, and customer focused and less likely to leave the organization. According to Dr. Beverly Kaye, an expert on career issues in the workplace, what employees want is a relationship with their managers, so managers have to act more like coaches, not bosses. Some of the factors that always rank at the top with regard to what gets employees engaged and what they value in a job include career opportunities and development, great people to work with, and a great boss.

Microsoft is meeting the challenge of improving worker morale head on to retain its employees. MyMicrosoft is a program introduced by the company to provide some of the attractive amenities that other IT companies offer employees. This program will include a wide range of incentives focused on improving the working conditions and culture of the company, such as a set of lifestyle perks and a management development program.

Microsoft's new program is an initial step to improve the morale of employees, but only time will tell if this program is attractive enough to retain employees.

3.1 What are the factors causing the brain drain at Microsoft? Explain.

3.2 Is Microsoft's organizational structure having an impact on its organizational commitment levels? Explain.

Sources: S. Harvey, "Getting the Stars Aligned at Microsoft," *Strategic HR Review,* March 2002; M. Goldsmith, "Engaging Employees," *BusinessWeek,* July 3, 2007; "Microsoft Struggles to Improve Worker Morale," *eweek,* June 5, 2006; M. Moeller and V. Murphy, "Outta Here at Microsoft," *BusinessWeek,* November 29, 1999; J. Persaud, "Keep the Faithful," *People Management,* June 12, 2003.

EXERCISE   REACTING TO NEGATIVE EVENTS

The purpose of this exercise is to explore how individuals react to three all-too-common scenarios that represent negative workplace events. This exercise uses groups of six participants, so your instructor will either assign you to a group of six or ask you to create your own group of six. The exercise has the following steps:

1. Individually read the following three scenarios: the annoying boss, the boring job, and pay and seniority. For each scenario, write down two specific behaviors in which you would likely engage in response to that scenario. Write down what you would actually

Annoying Boss	You've been working at your current company for about a year. Over time, your boss has become more and more annoying to you. It's not that your boss is a bad person, or even necessarily a bad boss. It's more a personality conflict—the way your boss talks, the way your boss manages every little thing, even the facial expressions your boss uses. The more time passes, the more you just can't stand to be around your boss.	Two likely behaviors:
Boring Job	You've been working at your current company for about a year. You've come to realize that your job is pretty boring. It's the first real job you've ever had, and at first it was nice to have some money and something to do every day. But the "new job" excitement has worn off, and things are actually quite monotonous. Same thing every day. It's to the point that you check your watch every hour, and Wednesdays feel like they should be Fridays.	Two likely behaviors:
Pay and Seniority	You've been working at your current company for about a year. The consensus is that you're doing a great job—you've gotten excellent performance evaluations and have emerged as a leader on many projects. As you've achieved this high status, however, you've come to feel that you are underpaid. Your company's pay procedures emphasize seniority much more than job performance. As a result, you look at other members of your project teams and see poor performers making much more than you, just because they've been with the company longer.	Two likely behaviors:

do, as opposed to what you wish you would do. For example, you may wish that you would march into your boss's office and demand a change, but if you would actually do nothing, write down "nothing."

2. In groups, compare and contrast your likely responses to the three scenarios. Come to a consensus on the two most likely responses for the group as a whole. Elect one group member to write the two likely responses to each of the three scenarios on the board.

3. Class discussion (whether in groups or as a class) should center on where the likely responses fit into the Exit–Voice–Loyalty–Neglect framework. What personal and situational factors would lead someone to one category of responses over another? Are there any responses that do not fit into the Exit–Voice–Loyalty–Neglect framework?

ENDNOTES

3.1 Levering, R., and M. Moskowitz. "In Good Company." *Fortune,* January 22, 2007, pp. 94–114.

3.2 Greene, J. "Troubling Exits at Microsoft." *BusinessWeek,* September 26, 2005, pp. 99–108.

3.3 Ibid.

3.4 Elgin, B. "Revenge of the Nerds— Again." *BusinessWeek,* August 8, 2005, pp. 28–31.

3.5 Greene, "Troubling Exits."

3.6 Greene, "Troubling Exits;" Greene, J. "Less Could Be More at Microsoft." *BusinessWeek,* October 3, 2005, p. 40.

3.7 Greene, "Less Could Be More."

3.8 "By the Numbers." *Fortune,* December 27, 2005, p. 32.

3.9 "Estimating Turnover Costs." http://www.keepemployees.com/turnover-cost.htm (October 20, 2005).

3.10 Ahlrichs, N.S. *Manager of Choice.* Mountain View, CA: Davies-Black Publishing, 2003.

3.11 Mowday, R.T.; R.M. Steers; and L.W. Porter. "The Measurement of Organizational Commitment."

Journal of Vocational Behavior 14, (1979), pp. 224–47.

3.12 Hulin, C.L. "Adaptation, Persistence, and Commitment in Organizations." In *Handbook of Industrial and Organizational Psychology,* Vol. 2, ed. M.D. Dunnette and L.M. Hough. Palo Alto, CA: Consulting Psychologists Press, Inc., 1991, pp. 445–506.

3.13 Meyer, J.P., and N.J. Allen. "A Three-Component Conceptualization of Organizational Commitment." *Human Resource Management Review* 1 (1991), pp. 61–89.

3.14 Ibid.

3.15 Ibid.

3.16 Meyer, J.P., and N.J. Allen. *Commitment in the Workplace.* Thousand Oaks, CA: Sage, 1997.

3.17 Mowday, Steers, and Porter, "The Measurement of Organizational Commitment."

3.18 Ibid.

3.19 Meyer, J.P.; D.J. Stanley; L. Herscovitch, and L. Topolnytsky. "Affective, Continuance, and Normative Commitment to the Organization: A

Meta-Analysis of Antecedents, Correlates, and Consequences." *Journal of Vocational Behavior* 61 (2002), pp. 20–52.

3.20 Mathieu, J.E., and D.M. Zajac. "A Review and Meta-Analysis of the Antecedents, Correlates, and Consequences of Organizational Commitment." *Psychological Bulletin* 108 (1990), pp. 171–94.

3.21 Johns, G. "The Psychology of Lateness, Absenteeism, and Turnover." In *Handbook of Industrial, Work, and Organizational Psychology,* eds. N. Anderson, D.S. Ones, H.K. Sinangil, and C. Viswesvaran. Thousand Oaks, CA: Sage, 2001, pp. 232–52.

3.22 Ibid.

3.23 Levering, R., and Moskowitz, M. "The 100 Best Companies to Work For." *Fortune,* January 24, 2005, pp. 64–94.

3.24 Kanter, R.M. "Commitment and Social Organization: A Study of Commitment Mechanisms in Utopian Communities." *American Sociological Review* 33 (1968), pp. 499–517.

3.25 Stebbins, R.A. "On Misunderstanding the Concept of Commitment: A Theoretical Clarification." *Social Forces* 48 (1970), pp. 526–29.

3.26 Becker, H.S. "Notes on the Concept of Commitment." *American Journal of Sociology* 66 (1960), pp. 32–42.

3.27 Rusbult, C.E., and D. Farrell. "A Longitudinal Test of the Investment Model: The Impact of Job Satisfaction, Job Commitment, and Turnover of Variations in Rewards, Costs, Alternatives, and Investments." *Journal of Applied Psychology* 68 (1983), pp. 429–38.

3.28 Meyer and Allen, *Commitment in the Workplace.*

3.29 Meyer, Stanley, Herscovitch, and Topolnytsky, "Affective, Continuance, and Normative Commitment."

3.30 Mowday, Steers, and Porter, "The Measurement of Organizational Commitment."

3.31 Mitchell, T.R.; B.C. Holtom; T.W. Lee; C.J. Sablynski; and M. Erez. "Why People Stay: Using Job Embeddedness to Predict Voluntary Turnover." *Academy of Management Journal* 44 (2001), pp. 1102–21.

3.32 Levering and Moskowitz, (2005). "The 100 Best Companies to Work For."

3.33 Wiener, Y. "Commitment in Organizations: A Normative View." *Academy of Management Review* 7 (1982), pp. 418–28.

3.34 Meyer, J.P.; N.J. Allen; and C.A. Smith. "Commitment to Organizations and Occupations: Extension and Test of a Three-Component Conceptualization." *Journal of Applied Psychology* 78 (1993), pp. 538–51.

3.35 Meyer and Allen, "A Three-Component Conceptualization."

3.36 Grow, B. "The Debate over Doing Good." *BusinessWeek,* August 15, 2005, pp. 76–78.

3.37 Ibid.

3.38 Levering and Moskowitz, (2005). "The 100 Best Companies to Work For."

3.39 "Qualcomm Community Involvement–Corporate Giving." 2005, http://www.qualcomm.com/community/corporate_giving.html on October 23, 2005

3.40 Roth, D. "The $91 Billion Conversation." *Fortune,* October 31, 2005. Retrieved from http://money.cnn.com/magazines/fortune/fortune_archive/2005/10/31/8359156/ on May 18th, 2007.

3.41 Levering and Moskowitz, "In Good Company."

3.42 Barrett, A. "Star Search: How to Recruit, Train, and Hold on to Great People. What Works, What Doesn't." *BusinessWeek,* October 10, 2005, pp. 68–78.

3.43 Kiger, P.J. "Retention on the Brink." *Workforce,* November 2000, pp. 59–65.

3.44 Rusbult, C.E.; D. Farrell; C. Rogers; and A.G. Mainous III. "Impact of Exchange Variables on Exit, Voice, Loyalty, and Neglect: An Integrating Model of Responses to Declining Job Satisfaction." *Academy of Management Journal* 31 (1988), pp. 599–627.

3.45 Farrell, D. "Exit, Voice, Loyalty, and Neglect as Responses to Job Dissatisfaction: A Multidimensional Scaling Study." *Academy of Management Journal* 26 (1983), pp. 596–607.

3.46 Hirschman, A.O. *Exit, Voice, and Loyalty: Responses to Decline in Firms, Organizations, and States.* Cambridge, MA: Harvard University Press, 1970.

3.47 Ibid.

3.48 Farrell, "Exit, Voice, Loyalty, and Neglect."

3.49 Rusbult, Farrell, Rogers, and Mainous, "Impact of Exchange Variables."

3.50 Ibid.

3.51 Griffeth, R.W.; S. Gaertner; and J.K. Sager. "Taxonomic Model of Withdrawal Behaviors: The Adaptive Response Model." *Human Resource Management Review* 9 (1999), pp. 577–90.

3.52 Ibid.

3.53 Ibid.

3.54 Cherrington, D. *The Work Ethic.* New York: AMACOM, 1980.

3.55 Hulin, C.L.; M. Roznowski; and D. Hachiya. "Alternative Opportunities and Withdrawal Decisions: Empirical and Theoretical Discrepancies and an Integration." *Psychological Bulletin* 97 (1985), pp. 233–50.

3.56 Fisher, A. "Turning Clock-Watchers into Stars." *Fortune,* March 22, 2004, p. 60.

3.57 Ibid.

3.58 Hulin, "Adaptation, Persistence, and Commitment."

3.59 Ibid.

3.60 Lim, V.K.G. "The IT Way of Loafing on the Job: Cyberloafing, Neutralizing, and Organizational Justice." *Journal of Organizational Behavior* 23 (2002), pp. 675–94.

3.61 "Does Cyberloafing Undermine Productivity?" *Management Issues News,* 2005, http://www.management-issues.com/display_page.asp?section=research&id=1417 (October 24, 2005).

3.62 "Cyberslacking." *MacMillan English Dictionary,* 2005, http://www.macmillandictionary.com/New-Words/040604-cyberslacking.htm (October 25, 2005).

3.63 Lim, "The IT Way."

3.64 Koslowsky, M.; A. Sagie; M. Krausz; and A.D. Singer. "Correlates of Employee Lateness: Some Theoretical Considerations." *Journal of Applied Psychology* 82 (1997), pp. 79–88.

3.65 Blau, G. "Developing and Testing a Taxonomy of Lateness Behavior." *Journal of Applied Psychology* 79 (1994), pp. 959–70.

3.66 Hamper, B. *Rivethead: Tales from the Assembly Line.* New York: Warner Books, 1991.

3.67 Muchinsky, P.M. "Employee Absenteeism: A Review of the Literature." *Journal of Vocational Behavior* 10 (1977), pp. 316–40.

3.68 Ibid.

3.69 Fichman, M. "Motivational Consequences of Absence and Attendance: Proportional Hazard Estimation of a Dynamic Motivation Model." *Journal of Applied Psychology* 73 (1988), pp. 119–34.

3.70 Martocchio, J.J., and D.I. Jimeno. "Employee Absenteeism as an Affective Event." *Human Resource Management Review* 13 (2003), pp. 227–41.

3.71 Nicholson, N., and G. Johns. "The Absence Climate and the Psychological Contract: Who's in Control of Absence?" *Academy of Management Review* 10 (1985), pp. 397–407.

3.72 Campion, M.A. "Meaning and Measurement of Turnover: Comparison of Alternative Measures and Recommendations for Research." *Journal of Applied Psychology* 76 (1991), pp. 199–212.

3.73 Van Blerkom, M.L. "Class Attendance in Undergraduate Courses." *Journal of Psychology* 126 (1992), pp. 487–94.

3.74 Ibid.

3.75 Devadoss, S., and J. Foltz. "Evaluation of Factors Influencing Student Class Attendance and Performance." *American Journal of Agricultural Economics* 78 (1996), pp. 499–507.

3.76 Shimoff, E., and A. Catania. "Effects of Recording Attendance on Grades in Introductory Psychology." *Teaching of Psychology* 28 (2001), pp. 192–95.

3.77 Devadoss and Foltz, "Evaluation of Factors."

3.78 Lee, T.W., and T.R. Mitchell. "An Alternative Approach: The Unfolding Model of Voluntary Employee Turnover." *Academy of Management Review* 19 (1984), pp. 51–89.

3.79 Mobley, W. "Intermediate Linkages in the Relationship Between Job Satisfaction and Employee Turnover." *Journal of Applied Psychology* 62 (1977), pp. 237–40; Hom, P.W.; R. Griffeth; and C.L. Sellaro. "The Validity of Mobley's (1977) Model of Employee Turnover." *Organizational Behavior and Human Performance* 34 (1984), pp. 141–74.

3.80 Lee and Mitchell, "An Alternative Approach."

3.81 Porter, L.W., and R.M. Steers. "Organizational, Work, and Personal Factors in Employee Turnover and Absenteeism." *Psychological Bulletin* 80 (1973), pp. 151–76.

3.82 Hill, J.M., and E.L. Trist. "Changes in Accidents and Other Absences with Length of Service: A Further Study of Their Incidence and Relation to Each Other in an Iron and Steel Works." *Human Relations* 8 (1955), pp. 121–52.

3.83 Rosse, J.G., and H.E. Miller. "Relationship Between Absenteeism and Other Employee Behaviors." In *Absenteeism: New Approaches to Understanding, Measuring, and Managing Employee Absence,* eds. P.S. Goodman and R. S. Atkin.. San Francisco: Jossey-Bass, 1984, pp. 194–228.

3.84 Hulin, "Adaptation, Persistence, and Commitment."

3.85 Griffeth, R.W.; P.W. Hom; and S. Gaertner. "A Meta-Analysis of Antecedents and Correlates of Employee Turnover: Update, Moderator Tests, and Research Implications for the Next Millennium." *Journal of Management* 26 (2000), pp. 463–88.

3.86 Rosse, J.G. "Relations among Lateness, Absence, and Turnover: Is There a Progression of Withdrawal?" *Human Relations* 41 (1988), pp. 517–31.

3.87 Koslowsky, Sagie, Krausz, and Singer, "Correlates of Employee Lateness."

3.88 U.S. Bureau of Labor Statistics, 2005, http://www.wnjpin.net/OneStopCareerCenter/LaborMarketInformation/lmi03/uslfproj.htm (October 26, 2005).

3.89 Ibid.

3.90 Coy, P. "Old. Smart. Productive." *BusinessWeek,* June 27, 2005, pp. 78–86.

3.91 Fisher, A. "Holding on to Global Talent." *BusinessWeek,* October 31, 2005, p. 202.

3.92 Ibid.

3.93 Reade, C. "Antecedents of Organizational Identification in Multinational Corporations: Fostering Psychological Attachment to the Local Subsidiary and the Global Organization." *International Journal of Human Resource Management* 12 (2001), pp. 1269–91.

3.94 Shaffer, M.A., and D.A. Harrison. "Expatriates' Psychological Withdrawal from International Assignments: Work, Nonwork, and Family Influences." *Personnel Psychology* 51 (1998), pp. 87–118; Hechanova, R.; T.A. Beehr; and N.D. Christiansen. "Antecedents and Consequences of Employees' Adjustment to Overseas Assignment: A Meta-Analytic Review." *Applied Psychology: An International Review* 52 (2003), pp. 213–36.

3.95 Black, J.S.; M. Mendenhall; and G. Oddou. "Toward a Comprehensive Model of International Adjustment: An Integration of Multiple Theoretical Perspectives." *Academy of Management Review* 16 (1991), pp. 291–317.

3.96 Shaffer and Harrison, "Expatriates' Psychological Withdrawal."

3.97 Hechanova, Beehr, and Christiansen, "Antecedents and Consequences of Employees' Adjustment."

3.98 Morris, J.R.; W.F. Cascio; and C.E. Young. "Downsizing after All These Years: Questions and Answers about Who Did It, How Many Did It, and Who Benefited from It." *Organizational Dynamics* 27 (1999), pp. 78–87.

3.99 Ibid.

3.100 Devine, K.; T. Reay; L. Stainton; and R. Collins-Nakai. "Downsizing Outcomes: Better a Victim than a Survivor?" *Human Resource Management* 42 (2003), pp. 109–24.

3.101 Ibid.

3.102 Dessler, G. "How to Earn your Employees' Commitment." *Academy of Management Executive* 13 (1999), pp. 58–67.

3.103 Levering and Moskowitz, "In Good Company."

3.104 Fisher, A. "How You Can Do Better on Diversity." *BusinessWeek,* November 15, 2005, p. 60.; Fisher, "Holding on to Global Talent."

3.105 Shaw, J.D.; J.E. Delery; G.D. Jenkins Jr.; and N. Gupta. "An Organization-Level Analysis of Voluntary and Involuntary Turnover." *Academy of Management Journal* 41 (1998), pp. 511–25.

3.106 Dessler, "How to Earn your Employees' Commitment."

3.107 Levering and Moskowitz, "In Good Company."

3.108 Fisher, "Holding on to Global Talent"; Fisher, A. "How to Keep your Stars from Leaving." *Business-Week,* July 26, 2005, p. 44.

3.109 Cappelli, P. "Managing without Commitment." *Organizational Dynamics* 28 (2000), pp. 11–24.

3.110 Byrnes, "Star Search."

3.111 Ibid.

PART 2

INDIVIDUAL MECHANISMS

CHAPTER 4:
Job Satisfaction

CHAPTER 5:
Stress

CHAPTER 6:
Motivation

CHAPTER 7:
Trust, Justice, and Ethics

CHAPTER 8:
Learning and Decision Making

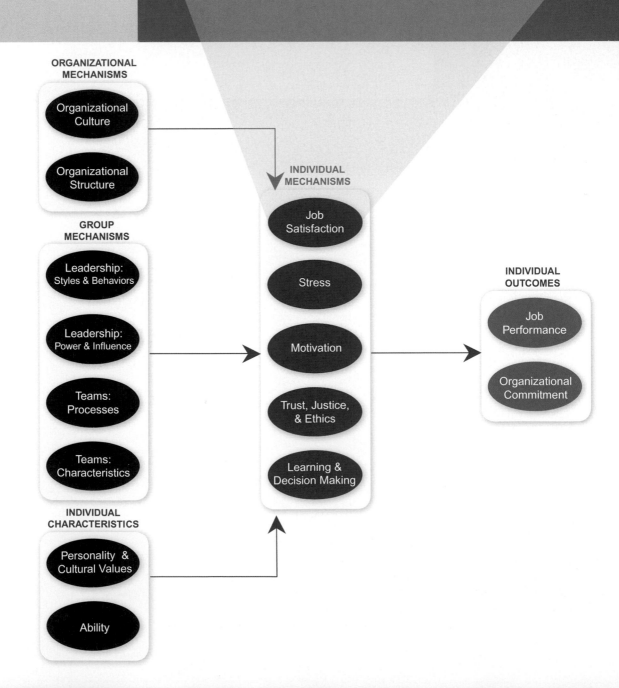

CHAPTER

4

Job Satisfaction

ORGANIZATIONAL
MECHANISMS

Organizational
Culture

Organizational
Structure

GROUP
MECHANISMS

Leadership:
Styles & Behaviors

Leadership:
Power & Influence

Teams:
Processes

Teams:
Characteristics

INDIVIDUAL
CHARACTERISTICS

Personality &
Cultural Values

Ability

INDIVIDUAL
MECHANISMS

Job
Satisfaction

Stress

Motivation

Trust, Justice,
& Ethics

Learning &
Decision Making

INDIVIDUAL
OUTCOMES

Job
Performance

Organizational
Commitment

Wegmans' employee-friendly policies and low job turnover put it high on *Fortune's* list of "100 Best Companies to Work For"—and make it a profitable venture where customers love to shop.

 LEARNING GOALS

After reading this chapter, you should be able to answer the following questions:

4.1 What is job satisfaction?

4.2 What are values, and how do they affect job satisfaction?

4.3 People often evaluate their job satisfaction according to specific facets. What are those facets?

4.4 Which job characteristics can create a sense of satisfaction with the work itself?

4.5 How is job satisfaction affected by day-to-day events?

4.6 What are mood and emotions, and what specific forms do they take?

4.7 How does job satisfaction affect job performance and organizational commitment? How does it affect life satisfaction?

4.8 What steps can organizations take to assess and manage job satisfaction?

WEGMANS FOOD MARKETS

Picture this scenario: You're about to go home for the day, and your spouse or room-mate asks you to stop by the grocery on the way home. "Okay," you say, though the errand doesn't exactly fill you with anticipation or excitement. But it might if you had a Wegmans on your way home. Shopping at Wegmans, a privately owned chain of 67 grocery stores in New York, Pennsylvania, New Jersey, and Virginia, is viewed as a fun event—so much so that the company has received more than 3,000 letters from around the country trying to persuade the chain to expand to new cities.[1] Wegmans understands that successful grocery stores must combat a sobering statistic: 84 percent of consumers believe that all grocery stores are alike. Why travel an extra two blocks to go to a different store? Wegmans has created its own unique identity by offering more of virtually everything, including 500 varieties of cheese, bookstores, child play centers, and dry cleaners on-site. It also stops at nothing to make customers happy, including sending a chef to a customer's home to correct a food order mistake or cooking a family's Thanksgiving turkey at the store because Mom bought one that was too big for her oven.

How does Wegmans create a shopping experience like no other? By being an employer like no other; Wegmans finished first on the list of *Fortune's* "100 Best Companies to Work For" in 2005 and third in 2007.[2] The smiles customers see on the faces of employees at Wegmans are not forced or rehearsed. Instead, they reveal a genuine sense of satisfaction among rank-and-file employees. What makes these employees so satisfied? Well, for one, they make good money, with hourly wages and annual salaries that range toward the high end of the grocery store industry. Wegmans also has shelled out $54 million for college scholarships to full- and part-time employees during the past 20 years and offers profit sharing and medical coverage to its employees. Such employee-friendly policies have resulted in higher labor costs; Wegmans' labor costs run around 16 percent of sales versus 12 percent for its competitors. However, Wegmans enjoys a 6 percent turnover rate instead of the 19 percent rate of competitors, and 20 percent of its employees now have 10 or more years of service. As Chairman Robert Wegman puts it, "I have never given away more than I got back."[3]

The satisfaction felt by Wegmans' employees goes beyond pay and benefits however. The company looks to hire people who have a passion for food and a genuine interest in culinary products, even to the extent that it passes over qualified candidates who lack such feelings. The company sent one of its cheese managers on a 10-day trip through London, Paris, and Italy to learn more about the cheeses Wegmans might offer. Wegmans' employees also have the freedom to do whatever it takes to make a customer happy or improve the store, without having to check with higher-ups. One Wegmans operations chief even noted, only half-jokingly, "We're a $3 billion company run by 16-year-old cashiers."[4] The end result of these philosophies is that employees view their work as very meaningful, with jobs at Wegmans described as "a badge of honor" or "part of the social fabric." Next time you're shopping at your local grocery store, study the employees' faces to see whether they seem to view their work the same way. What emotions do they seem to be feeling, and how do those emotions affect your enjoyment of that particular shopping trip?

JOB SATISFACTION

This chapter takes us to a new portion of our integrative model of organizational behavior. Job satisfaction is one of several individual mechanisms that directly affects job performance and organizational commitment. As shown in the Wegmans example, if employees are very satisfied with their jobs and experience positive emotions while working, they may perform their jobs better and choose to remain with the company for a longer period of time. Think about the worst job that you've held in your life, even if

"You'll enjoy rationalizing working for this company."

Source: Reprinted with permission of Peter Vey.

it was just a summer job or a short-term work assignment. What did you feel during the course of the day? How did those feelings influence the way you behaved, in terms of your time spent on task and citizenship behaviors rather than counterproductive or withdrawal behaviors?

Job satisfaction is defined as a pleasurable emotional state resulting from the appraisal of one's job or job experiences.[5] In other words, it represents how you *feel* about your job and what you *think* about your job. Employees with high job satisfaction experience positive feelings when they think about their duties or take part in task activities. Employees with low job satisfaction experience negative feelings when they think about their duties or take part in their task activities. Unfortunately, workplace surveys suggest that satisfied employees are becoming more and more rare. For example, a recent survey showed that just 49 percent of Americans are satisfied with their jobs, down from 58 percent a decade ago.[6] The survey also revealed that only 20 percent are satisfied with their employer's promotion and reward policies and 33 percent with their pay. Reversing such trends requires a deeper understanding of exactly what drives job satisfaction levels.

4.1
What is job satisfaction?

WHY ARE SOME EMPLOYEES MORE SATISFIED THAN OTHERS?

So what explains why some employees are more satisfied than others? At a general level, employees are satisfied when their job provides the things that they value. **Values** are those things that people consciously or subconsciously want to seek or attain.[7] Think about this question for a few moments: What do you want to attain from your job, that is, what things do you want your job to give you? A good wage? A sense of achievement? Colleagues who are fun to be around? If you had to make a list of the things you value with respect to your job, most or all of them would likely be shown in Table 4-1. This table summarizes the values assessed in the five most popular surveys of work values, broken down into more general categories.[8] Many of those values deal with the things that your work

4.2
What are values, and how do they affect job satisfaction?

TABLE 4-1	Commonly Assessed Work Values
CATEGORIES	**SPECIFIC VALUES**
Pay	High salary Secure salary
Promotions	Frequent promotions Promotions based on ability
Supervision	Good supervisory relations Praise for good work
Coworkers	Enjoyable coworkers Responsible coworkers
Work Itself	Utilization of ability Freedom and independence Intellectual stimulation Creative expression Sense of achievement
Altruism	Helping others Moral causes
Status	Prestige Power over others Fame
Environment	Comfort Safety

Key Question:
Which of these things are *most important* to you?

Source: Adapted from R.V. Dawis, "Vocational Interests, Values, and Preferences," in *Handbook of Industrial and Organizational Psychology,* Vol. 2, eds. M.D. Dunnette and L. M. Hough. (Palo Alto, CA: Consulting Psychologists Press, 1991), pp. 834–71.

can give you, such as good pay or the chance for frequent promotions. Other values pertain to the context that surrounds your work, including whether you have a good boss or good coworkers. Still other values deal with the work itself, like whether your job tasks provide you with freedom or a sense of achievement.

Consider the list of values in Table 4-1. Which would make your "top five" in terms of importance right now, at this stage of your life? Maybe you have a part-time job during college where you value enjoyable coworkers or a comfortable work environment above everything else. Or maybe you're getting established in your career and starting a family, which makes a high salary and frequent promotions especially critical. Or perhaps you're at a point in your career that you feel a need to help others or find an outlet for your creative expression. (In our case, we value fame, which is what led us to write this textbook. We're still waiting for Letterman's call . . . or at least Conan's.) Regardless of your "top five," you can see that different people value different things and that your values may change during the course of your working life.

VALUE FULFILLMENT: VALUE-PERCEPT THEORY

Values play a key role in explaining job satisfaction. **Value-percept theory** argues that job satisfaction depends on whether you *perceive* that your job supplies the things that you *value*.[9] This theory can be summarized with the following equation:

$$\text{Dissatisfaction} = (V_{want} - V_{have}) \times (V_{importance})$$

In this equation, V_{want} reflects how much of a value an employee wants, V_{have} indicates how much of that value the job supplies, and $V_{importance}$ reflects how important the value is to the employee. Big differences between wants and haves create a sense of dissatisfaction, especially when the value in question is important. Note that the difference between V_{want} and V_{have} gets multiplied by importance, so existing discrepancies get magnified for important values and minimized for trivial values. As an example, say that you were evaluating your pay satisfaction. You want to be earning around $70,000 a year but are currently earning $50,000 a year, so there's a $20,000 discrepancy. Does that mean you feel a great deal of pay dissatisfaction? Only if pay is one of the most important values to you from Table 4-1. If pay isn't that important, you likely don't feel much dissatisfaction.

Value-percept theory also suggests that people evaluate job satisfaction according to specific "facets" of the job.[10] After all, a "job" isn't one thing—it's a collection of tasks, relationships, and rewards.[11] The most common facets that employees consider in judging their job satisfaction appear in Figure 4-1. The figure includes the "want vs. have" calculations that drive satisfaction with pay, promotions, supervision, coworkers, and the work itself. The figure also shows how satisfaction with those five facets adds together to create "overall job satisfaction." Figure 4-1 shows that employees might be satisfied for all kinds of reasons. One person may be satisfied because she's in a high-paying job and working for a good boss. Another person may be satisfied because he has good coworkers and enjoyable work tasks. You may have noticed that a few of the values in Table 4-1, such as working for moral causes and gaining fame and prestige, are not represented in Figure 4-1. This omission is because those values are not relevant in all jobs, unlike pay, promotions, and so forth.

4.3

People often evaluate their job satisfaction according to specific facets. What are those facets?

The first facet in Figure 4-1, **pay satisfaction,** refers to employees' feelings about their pay, including whether it is as much as they deserve, secure, and adequate for both normal expenses and luxury items.[12] Similar to the other facets, pay satisfaction is based on a comparison of the pay that employees want and the pay they receive.[13] Although more money is almost always better, most employees base their desired pay on a careful examination of their job duties and the pay given to comparable colleagues.[14] As a result, even non-millionaires can be quite satisfied with their pay (thankfully for most of us!). Take the employees at Bright Horizons, for example. The Massachusetts-based provider of child care and early education programs provides its employees with an average salary of around $50,000 in an industry known for significantly lower wages.[15] Bright Horizons employees experience high pay satisfaction because they make more than comparable colleagues working in the child care area.

The next facet in Figure 4-1, **promotion satisfaction,** refers to employees' feelings about the company's promotion policies and their execution, including whether promotions are frequent, fair, and based on ability.[16] Unlike pay, some employees may not want frequent promotions because promotions bring more responsibility and increased work hours.[17] However, many employees value promotions because they provide opportunities for more personal growth, a better wage, and more prestige. QuikTrip, the Oklahoma-based

FIGURE 4-1   The Value-Percept Theory of Job Satisfaction

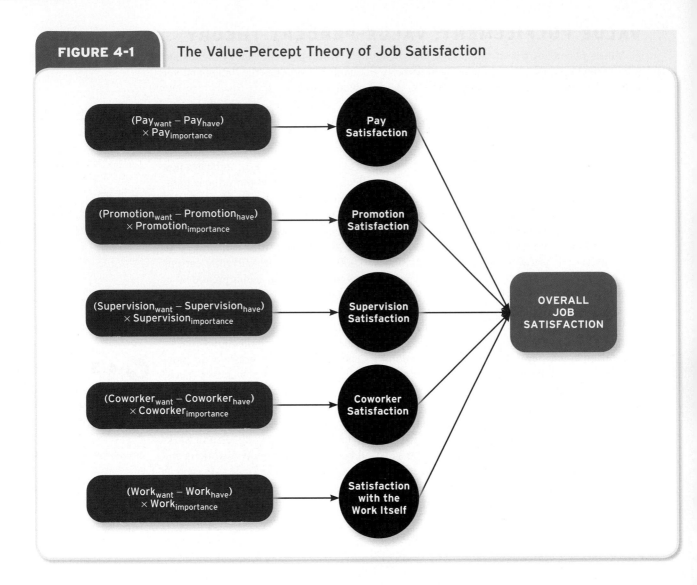

chain of gas and convenience stores, does a good job fostering promotion satisfaction on the part of its employees. "Promote from within" is a key motto in the company, and all 400-plus of its managers worked their way up from entry-level positions.[18]

Supervision satisfaction reflects employees' feelings about their boss, including whether the boss is competent, polite, and a good communicator (rather than lazy, annoying, and too distant).[19] Most employees ask two questions about their supervisors: (1) "Can they help me attain the things that I value?" and (2) "Are they generally likable?"[20] The first question depends on whether supervisors provide rewards for good performance, help employees obtain necessary resources, and protect employees from unnecessary distractions. The second question depends on whether supervisors have good personalities, as well as values and beliefs similar to the employees' philosophies. Valero Energy, the Texas-based oil refiner and gas retailer, works hard to foster a sense of supervision satisfaction. When it comes to receiving bonuses, executives only get theirs when everyone else in the organization has received one.[21] As a result, supervisors work harder to make sure that employees can get their jobs done.

QuikTrip, a chain of gas and convenience stores, excels at providing promotion satisfaction to its employees. Virtually all its managers—over 400 people—were promoted from entry-level jobs.

Coworker satisfaction refers to employees' feelings about their fellow employees, including whether coworkers are smart, responsible, helpful, fun, and interesting as opposed to lazy, gossipy, unpleasant, and boring.[22] Employees ask the same kinds of questions about their coworkers that they do about their supervisors: (1) "Can they help me do my job?" and (2) "Do I enjoy being around them?" The first question is critical because most of us rely, to some extent, on our coworkers when performing job tasks. The second question also is important because we spend just as much time with coworkers as we do members of our own family. Coworkers who are pleasant and fun can make the workweek go much faster, whereas coworkers who are disrespectful and annoying can make even one day seem like an eternity. Arbitron, the New York–based radio market research firm, takes an unusual step to increase coworker satisfaction. Employees can choose to recognize their coworkers' achievements with a $100 American Express gift card, with no restrictions on how many they can give out.[23] Last year, 300 of its 1,400-plus employees received rewards totaling $50,000.

The last facet in Figure 4-1, **satisfaction with the work itself,** reflects employees' feelings about their actual work tasks, including whether those tasks are challenging, interesting, respected, and make use of key skills rather than being dull, repetitive, and uncomfortable.[24] Whereas the previous four facets described the outcomes that result from work (pay, promotions) and the people who surround work (supervisors, coworkers), this facet focuses on what employees actually *do*. After all, even the best boss or most interesting coworkers can't compensate for 40 or 50 hours of complete boredom each week! How can employers instill a sense of satisfaction with the work itself? Valassis, a Michigan-based publisher of newspaper inserts and coupons, gives employees annual skill assessments to get a better feel for what they are good at.[25] It then provides employees with growth opportunities, sometimes even creating new positions to employ special talents.

In summary, value-percept theory suggests that employees will be satisfied when they perceive that their job offers the pay, promotions, supervision, coworkers, and work tasks that they value. Of course, this theory begs the question: Which of those ingredients is most important? In other words, which of the five facets in Figure 4-1 has the strongest influence on overall job satisfaction? Several research studies have examined these issues and come up with the results shown in Figure 4-2. The figure depicts the correlation between each of the five satisfaction facets and an overall index of job satisfaction. (Recall that correlations of .10, .30, and .50 indicate weak, moderate, and strong relationships, respectively.)

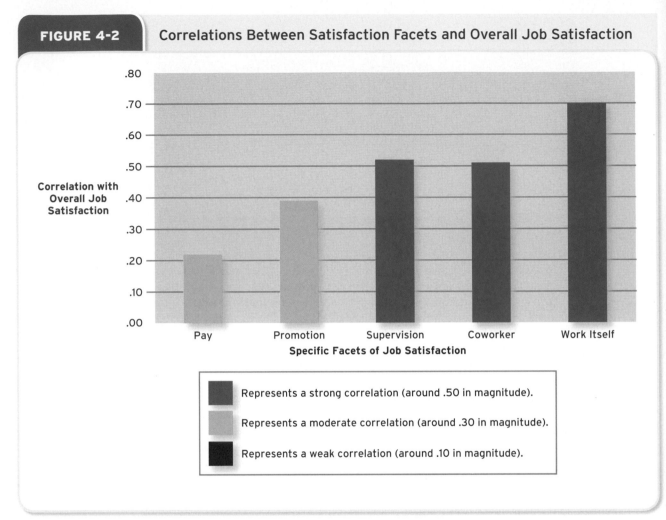

FIGURE 4-2 — Correlations Between Satisfaction Facets and Overall Job Satisfaction

Correlation with Overall Job Satisfaction (y-axis, .00 to .80)

Specific Facets of Job Satisfaction (x-axis: Pay, Promotion, Supervision, Coworker, Work Itself)

Represents a strong correlation (around .50 in magnitude).

Represents a moderate correlation (around .30 in magnitude).

Represents a weak correlation (around .10 in magnitude).

Sources: G.H. Ironson, P.C. Smith, M.T. Brannick, W.M. Gibson, and K.B. Paul, "Construction of a Job in General Scale: A Comparison of Global, Composite, and Specific Measures," *Journal of Applied Psychology* 74 (1989), pp. 193–200; S.S. Russell, C. Spitzmuller, L.F. Lin, J.M. Stanton, P.C. Smith, and G.H. Ironson, "Shorter Can Also Be Better: The Abridged Job in General Scale," *Educational and Psychological Measurement* 64 (2004), pp. 878–93.

Figure 4-2 suggests that satisfaction with the work itself is the single strongest driver of overall job satisfaction.[26] Supervision and coworker satisfaction are also strong drivers, and promotion and pay satisfaction have moderately strong effects. Why is satisfaction with the work itself so critical? Well, consider that a typical workweek contains around 2,400 minutes. How much of that time is spent thinking about how much money you make? 10 minutes? Maybe 20? The same is true for promotions—we may want them, but we don't necessarily spend hours a day thinking about them. We do spend a significant chunk of that time with other people though. Between lunches, meetings, hallway chats, and other conversations, we might easily spend 600 minutes a week with supervisors and coworkers. That leaves almost 1,800 minutes for just us and our work. As a result, it is difficult to be satisfied with your job if you don't like what you actually do. Of course, those of you who are full-time students might wonder what satisfaction means to you. See our **OB for Students** feature for some facets of student satisfaction.

OB FOR STUDENTS

What does satisfaction mean for you as a student? After all, pay, promotions, and supervision are less relevant for full-time students than for full-time employees. One recent study examined the facets of satisfaction for students,[27] including:

• *University satisfaction.* Do students feel good about their university choice and experience, and would they recommend their university to others?
• *Housing satisfaction.* Do students feel good about where they live and the surrounding neighborhood?
• *Leisure satisfaction.* Do students feel good about their social life, their leisure activities, and their friendships?

The results of the study showed that all three facets had moderately strong positive correlations with an index of overall student satisfaction. So students were more satisfied when they liked the university, liked where they lived, and felt that they were having a good time. In addition, the more satisfied the students were, the better they performed in terms of their grade point average (GPA). In other words, happy students tended to be better students.

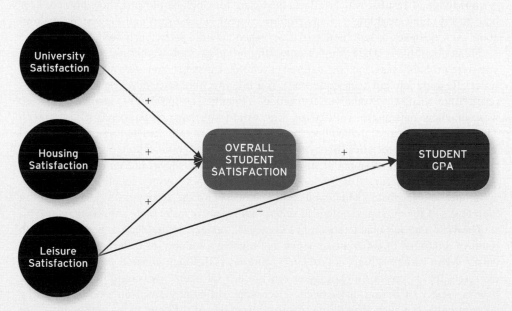

One word of caution, however. Notice the negative path from leisure satisfaction to student GPA. That path indicates that those two variables actually correlate negatively. In other words, having a lot of fun made students more satisfied, but it also made them perform less well in their classes. Moral of the story: You *can* have too much of a good thing!

SATISFACTION WITH THE WORK ITSELF: THE JOB CHARACTERISTICS MODEL

Given how important enjoyable work tasks are to overall job satisfaction, it is worth spending more time describing the kinds of tasks that most people find enjoyable. Researchers began focusing on this question in the 1950s and 1960s, partly in reaction to practices based in the "scientific management" perspective. Scientific management focuses on increasing the efficiency of job tasks by making them more simplified and specialized and using time and motion studies to plan task movements and sequences carefully.[28] The hope was that such steps would increase worker productivity and reduce the breadth of skills required to complete a job, ultimately improving organizational profitability. Instead, the simplified and routine jobs tended to lower job satisfaction while increasing absenteeism and turnover.[29] Put simply: Boring jobs may be easier, but they're not necessarily better.

So what kinds of work tasks are especially satisfying? Research suggests that three "critical psychological states" make work satisfying. The first psychological state is believing in the **meaningfulness of work,** which reflects the degree to which work tasks are viewed as something that "counts" in the employee's system of philosophies and beliefs.[30] Trivial tasks tend to be less satisfying than tasks that make employees feel like they're aiding the organization or society in some meaningful way. The second psychological state is perceiving **responsibility for outcomes,** which captures the degree to which employees feel that they are key drivers of the quality of the unit's work.[31] Sometimes employees feel like their efforts don't really matter, because work outcomes are dictated by effective procedures, efficient technologies, or more influential colleagues. Finally, the third psychological state is **knowledge of results,** which reflects the extent to which employees know how well (or how poorly) they are doing.[32] Many employees work in jobs in which they never find out about their mistakes or have notice of times when they did particularly well.

Think about times when you felt especially proud of a job well done. At that moment, you were probably experiencing all three psychological states. You were aware of the result (after all, some job had been done well). You felt you were somehow responsible for that result (otherwise, why would you feel proud?). Finally, you felt that the result of the work was somehow meaningful (otherwise, why would you have remembered it just now?). The next obvious question then becomes, "What kinds of tasks create these psychological states?" **Job characteristics theory,** which describes the central characteristics of intrinsically satisfying jobs, attempts to answer this question. As shown in Figure 4-3, job characteristics theory argues that five core job characteristics (variety, identity, significance, autonomy, and feedback, which you can remember with the acronym "VISAF") result in high levels of the three psychological states, making work tasks more satisfying.[33]

The first core job characteristic in Figure 4-3, **variety,** is the degree to which the job requires a number of different activities that involve a number of different skills and talents.[34] When variety is high, almost every workday is different in some way, and job holders rarely feel a sense of monotony or repetition.[35] Of course, we could picture jobs that have a variety of boring tasks, such as screwing differently sized nuts onto differently colored bolts, but such jobs do not involve a number of different skills and talents.[36] To provide some examples of low and high job variety, we offer excerpts from Studs Terkel's classic book *Working: People Talk About What They Do All Day and How They Feel About What They Do.*

4.4

Which job characteristics can create a sense of satisfaction with the work itself?

▼**Low Variety: Phil Stallings, Spot-Welder**
I stand in one spot, about two- or three-feet area, all night. The only time a person stops is when the line stops. We do about thirty-two jobs per car, per unit. Forty-eight units an hour, eight hours a day. Thirty-two times forty-eight times eight. Figure it out. That's how many times I push that button . . . . It don't stop. It just goes and goes and goes. I bet there's men who have lived and died out there, never seen the end of that line. And they never will—because it's endless. It's like the serpent. It's just all body, no tail. It can do things to you . . . (Laughs).[37]

▲High Variety: Eugene Russell, Piano Tuner

Every day is different. I work Saturdays and Sundays sometimes. Monday I'm tuning a piano for a record company that had to be done before nine o'clock. When I finish that, I go to another company and do at least four pianos. During that day there's a couple of harpsichords mixed in . . . . I get a big kick out of it, because there are so many facets. Other people go through a routine. At a certain time they punch a clock . . . . Then they're through with it and *then* their life begins. With us the piano business is an integral part of our life. I had a discussion with another tuner, who is a great guitar man. He said "Why are we tuners?" I said, "Because we want to hear good sounds."[38]

FIGURE 4-3 **Job Characteristics Theory**

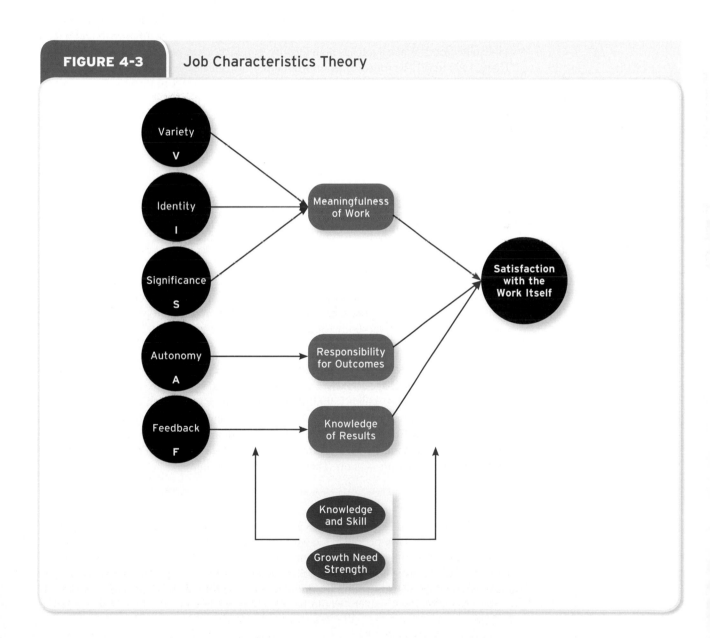

Evidence indicates that our preference for variety is hard-wired into our brains. Research in psychiatry and neuroscience shows that the brain releases a chemical called dopamine whenever a novel stimulus (a new painting, a new meal, a new work challenge) is experienced, and we tend to find this dopamine release quite pleasurable. Unfortunately, the amount of dopamine present in our brains declines over our life spans. One neuroscientist therefore suggests that the best way to protect our dopamine system is through novel, challenging experiences, writing, "The sense of satisfaction after you've successfully handled unexpected tasks or sought out unfamiliar, physically and emotionally demanding activities is your brain's signal that you're doing what nature designed you to do."[39] Something to think about next time you plan to order the same old thing at your favorite restaurant!

The second core job characteristic in Figure 4-3, **identity,** is the degree to which the job requires completing a whole, identifiable, piece of work from beginning to end with a visible outcome.[40] When a job has high identity, employees can point to something and say, "There, I did that." The transformation from inputs to finished product is very visible, and the employee feels a distinct sense of beginning and closure.[41] Think about how you feel when you work for a while on some project but don't quite get it finished—does that lack of closure bug you? If so, identity is an important concern for you. Consider these excerpts from *Working:*

▼Low Identity: Mike Lefevre, Steelworker

It's not just the work. Somebody built the pyramids. Somebody's going to build something. Pyramids, Empire State Building—these things don't just happen. There's hard work behind it. I would like to see a building, say the Empire State, I would like to see on one side of it a foot-wide strip from top to bottom with the name of every bricklayer, the name of every electrician, with all the names. So when a guy walked by, he could take his son and say, "See, that's me over there on the forty-fifth floor. I put the steel beam in." Picasso can point to a painting. What can I point to? A writer can point to a book. Everybody should have something to point to.[42]

▲High Identity: Frank Decker, Interstate Truckdriver

Every load is a challenge and when you finally off-load it, you have a feeling of having completed a job—which I don't think you get in a production line. I pick up a load at the mill, going to Hotpoint in Milwaukee. I take a job and I go through all the process . . . . You feel like your day's work is well done when you're coming back. I used to have problems in the morning, a lot of heartburn, I couldn't eat. But once I off-loaded, the pressure was off. Then I could eat anything.[43]

Significance is the degree to which the job has a substantial impact on the lives of other people, particularly people in the world at large.[44] Virtually any job can be important if it helps put food on the table for a family, send kids to college, or make employees feel like they're doing their part for the working world. That said, significance as a core job characteristic captures something beyond that—the belief that this job *really matters.* If the job was taken away, society would be the worse for it. Consider these excerpts from *Working:*

▼**Low Significance: Louis Hayward, Washroom Attendant**

They come in. They wash their hands after using the service—you hope. (A soft chuckle.) I go through the old brush routine, stand back, expecting a tip. A quarter is what you expect when you hand the guy a towel and a couple of licks of the broom. . . . I'm not particularly proud of what I'm doing. The shine man and I discuss it quite freely. In my own habitat I don't go around saying I'm a washroom attendant at the Palmer House. Outside of my immediate family, very few people know what I do. They do know I work at the Palmer House and let that suffice. You say Palmer House, they automatically assume you're a waiter. . . . The whole thing is obsolete. It's on its way out. This work isn't necessary in the first place. It's so superfluous. It was *never* necessary. (Laughs.)[45]

▲**High Significance: Tom Patrick, Fireman**

Last month there was a second alarm. I was off duty. I ran over there. I'm a bystander. I see these firemen on the roof, with the smoke pouring out around them, and the flames, and they go in . . . . You could see the pride that they were seein'. The f***** world's so f**** up, the country's f**** up. But the firemen, you actually see them produce. You see them put out a fire. You see them come out with babies in their hands. You see them give mouth-to-mouth when a guy's dying. You can't get around that s***. That's real. To me, that's what I want to be.[46]

Autonomy is the degree to which the job provides freedom, independence, and discretion to the individual performing the work.[47] When your job provides autonomy, you view the outcomes of it as the product of your efforts rather than the result of careful instructions from your boss or a well-written manual of procedures.[48] Autonomy comes in multiple forms, including the freedom to control the timing, scheduling, and sequencing of work activities, as well as the procedures and methods used to complete work tasks.[49] To many of us, high levels of autonomy are the difference between "having a long leash" and being "micromanaged." Consider these excerpts from *Working*:

▼**Low Autonomy: Beryl Simpson, Airline Reservationist**

They brought in a computer called Sabre . . . . It has a memory drum and you can retrieve that information forever . . . . With Sabre being so valuable, you were allowed no more than three minutes on the telephone. You had twenty seconds, busy-out time it was called, to put the information into Sabre. Then you had to be available for another phone call. It was almost like a production line. We adjusted to the machine. The casualness, the informality that had been there previously was no longer there . . . . You took thirty minutes for lunch, not thirty-one. If you got a break, you took ten minutes, not eleven . . . . With the airline I had no free will. I was just part of that stupid computer.[50]

▲**High Autonomy: Bud Freeman, Jazz Musician**

I live in absolute freedom. I do what I do because I want to do it. What's wrong with making a living doing something interesting . . . ? The jazz man is expressing freedom in every note he plays. We can only please the audience doing what *we* do. We have to please ourselves first. I want to play for the rest of my life. I don't see any sense in stopping. Were I to live another thirty years—that would make me ninety-five—why not try to play? I can just hear the critics: "Did you hear that wonderful note old man Freeman played last night?" (Laughs.) As Ben Webster says, "I'm going to play this g****** saxophone until they put it on top of me."

Despite the need for discipline and practice, the job of a musician is one with a high degree of autonomy.

The last core job characteristic in Figure 4-3, **feedback,** is the degree to which carrying out the activities required by the job provides the worker with clear information about how well he or she is performing.[51] A critical distinction must be noted: This core characteristic reflects feedback obtained *directly from the job* as opposed to feedback from coworkers or supervisors. Most employees receive formal performance appraisals from their bosses, but that feedback occurs once or maybe twice a year. When the job provides its own feedback, that feedback can be experienced almost every day. Consider these excerpts from *Working:*

▼**Low Feedback: Lilith Reynolds, Government Project Coordinator**
I'm very discouraged about my job right now. . . . I'm to come up with some kind of paper on economic development. It won't be very hard because there's little that can be done. At the end of sixty days I'll present the paper. But because of the reorganization that's come up I'll probably never be asked about the paper.[52]

▲High Feedback: Dolores Dante, Waitress

When somebody says to me, "You're great, how come you're *just* a waitress?" *Just* a waitress. I'd say, "Why, don't you think you deserve to be served by me?" . . . Tips? I feel like Carmen. It's like a gypsy holding out a tambourine and they throw the coin. (Laughs.) . . . People would ask for me. . . . I would like to say to the customer, "Go to so-and-so." But you can't do that, because you feel a sense of loyalty. So you would rush, get to your customers quickly. Some don't care to drink and still they wait for you. That's a compliment.[53]

The passages in this section illustrate the potential importance of each of the five core characteristics. But how important are the core characteristics to satisfaction with the work itself? A meta-analysis of 75 different research studies showed that the five core job characteristics are moderately to strongly related to work satisfaction.[54] However, those results don't mean that *every* employee wants more variety, more autonomy, and so forth. The bottom of Figure 4-3 includes two other variables: **knowledge and skill** and **growth need strength** (which captures whether employees have strong needs for personal accomplishment or developing themselves beyond where they currently are).[55] In the jargon of theory diagrams, these variables are called "moderators." Rather than directly affecting other variables in the diagram, moderators influence the strength of the relationships between variables. If employees lack the required knowledge and skill or lack a desire for growth and development, more variety and autonomy should *not* increase their satisfaction very much.[56] However, when employees are very talented and feel a strong need for growth, the core job characteristics become even more powerful. A graphical depiction of this moderator effect appears in Figure 4-4, where you can see that the relationship between the core job characteristics and satisfaction becomes stronger when growth need strength increases.

| FIGURE 4-4 | Growth Need Strength as a Moderator of Job Characteristic Effects |

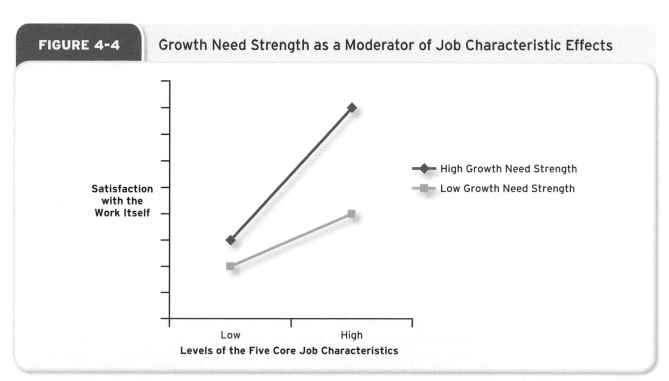

Source: Adapted from B.T. Loher, R.A. Noe, N.L. Moeller, and M.P. Fitzgerald, "A Meta-Analysis of the Relation of Job Characteristics to Job Satisfaction," *Journal of Applied Psychology* 70 (1985), pp. 280–89.

Given how critical the five core job characteristics are to job satisfaction, many organizations have employed job characteristics theory to help improve satisfaction among their employees. The first step in this process is assessing the current level of the characteristics to arrive at a "satisfaction potential score." See our **OB Assessments** feature for more about that step. The organization, together with job design consultants, then attempts to redesign aspects of the job to increase the core job characteristic levels. Often this step results in **job enrichment,** such that the duties and responsibilities associated with a job are expanded to provide more variety, identity, autonomy, and so forth. Research suggests that such enrichment efforts can indeed boost job satisfaction levels.[57] Moreover, enrichment efforts can heighten work accuracy and customer satisfaction, though training and labor costs tend to rise as a result of such changes.[58]

MOOD AND EMOTIONS

4.5

How is job satisfaction affected by day-to-day events?

Let's say you're a satisfied employee, maybe because you get paid well and work for a good boss or because your work tasks provide you with variety and autonomy. Does this mean you'll definitely be satisfied at 11:00 a.m. next Tuesday? Or 2:30 p.m. the following Thursday? Obviously it doesn't. Each employee's satisfaction levels fluctuate over time, rising and falling like some sort of emotional stock market. This fluctuation might seem strange, given that people's pay, supervisors, coworkers, and work tasks don't change from one hour to the next. The key lies in remembering that job satisfaction reflects what you think and feel about your job. So part of it is rational, based on a careful appraisal of the job and the things it supplies. But another part of it is emotional, based on what you feel "in your gut" while you're at work or thinking about work. So a satisfied employee feels good about his or her job *on average,* but things happen during the course of the day to make him or her feel better at some times (and worse at others).

Figure 4-5 illustrates the satisfaction levels for one employee during the course of a workday, from around 9:00 a.m. to 5:00 p.m. You can see that this employee did a number of different things during the day, from answering e-mails to eating lunch with friends to participating in a brainstorming meeting regarding a new project. You can also see that the employee came into the day feeling relatively satisfied, though satisfaction levels had several ebbs and flows during the next eight hours. What's responsible for those ebbs and flows in satisfaction levels? Two related concepts: mood and emotions.

4.6

What are mood and emotions, and what specific forms do they take?

What kind of mood are you in right now? Good? Bad? Somewhere in between? Why are you in that kind of mood? Do you really even know? (If it's a bad mood, we hope it has nothing to do with this book!) **Moods** are states of feeling that are often mild in intensity, last for an extended period of time, and are not explicitly directed at or caused by anything.[59] When people are in a good or bad mood, they don't always know who (or what) deserves the credit or blame; they just happen to be feeling that way for a stretch of their day. Of course, it would be oversimplifying things to call all moods either good or bad. Sometimes we're in a serene mood, and sometimes we're in an enthusiastic mood. Both are "good" but obviously feel quite different. Similarly, sometimes we're in a bored mood, and sometimes we're in a hostile mood. Both are "bad" but, again, feel quite different.

It turns out that there are a number of different moods that we might experience during the workday. Figure 4-6 summarizes the different moods in which people sometimes find themselves. The figure illustrates that moods can be categorized in two ways: **pleasantness** and **engagement.** First, the horizontal axis of the figure reflects whether you feel pleasant (in a "good mood") or unpleasant (in a "bad mood").[60] The figure uses green colors to illustrate pleasant moods and red to illustrate unpleasant moods. Second, the vertical axis of the figure reflects whether you feel engaged, activated, and aroused or disengaged, deactivated, and unaroused.[61] The figure uses darker colors to convey higher levels of engagement and lighter

OB ASSESSMENTS

CORE JOB CHARACTERISTICS

How satisfying are your work tasks? This assessment is designed to measure the five core job characteristics derived from job characteristics theory. Think of your current job or the last job that you held (even if it was a part-time or summer job). Answer each question using the response scale provided. Then subtract your answers to the bold-faced question from 8, with the difference being your new answer for that question. For example, if your original answer for Question 2 was "5," your new answer is "3" (8 − 5). Then use the formula to compute a satisfaction potential score (SPS).

1	2	3	4	5	6	7
VERY INACCURATE	MOSTLY INACCURATE	SLIGHTLY INACCURATE	UNCERTAIN	SLIGHTLY ACCURATE	MOSTLY ACCURATE	VERY ACCURATE

V1. The job requires me to use a number of complex or high-level skills. _____

V2. The job is quite simple and repetitive. _____

I1. The job is arranged so that I can do an entire piece of work from beginning to end. _____

I2. The job provides me the chance to completely finish the pieces of work I begin. _____

S1. This job is one where a lot of other people can be affected by how well the work gets done. _____

S2. The job itself is very significant and important in the broader scheme of things. _____

A1. The job gives me a chance to use my personal initiative and judgment in carrying out the work. _____

A2. The job gives me considerable opportunity for independence and freedom in how I do the work. _____

F1. Just doing the work required by the job provides many chances for me to figure out how well I am doing. _____

F2. After I finish a job, I know whether I performed well. _____

$$SPS = \left| \frac{V1+V2+I1+I2+S1+S2}{6} \right| \times \left| \frac{A1+A2}{2} \right| \times \left| \frac{F1+F2}{2} \right|$$

$$SPS = \left| \frac{}{6} \right| \times \left| \frac{}{2} \right| \times \left| \frac{}{2} \right|$$

$$SPS = \boxed{} \times \boxed{} \times \boxed{} = \boxed{}$$

SCORING

If your score is 150 or above, your work tasks tend to be satisfying and enjoyable. Therefore, you probably view your work as meaningful and feel that you are responsible for (and knowledgeable about) your work outcomes. If your score is less than 150, your work tasks

(Continued)

may not be so satisfying and enjoyable. You might benefit from trying to "enrich" your job by asking your supervisor for more challenging assignments.

Sources: J.R. Hackman and G.R. Oldham, *The Job Diagnostic Survey: An Instrument for the Diagnosis of Jobs and the Evaluation of Job Redesign Projects* (New Haven, CT: Yale University, 1974); J.R. Idaszak and F. Drasgow, "A Revision of the Job Diagnostic Survey: Elimination of a Measurement Artifact," *Journal of Applied Psychology* 72 (1987), pp. 69–74.

colors to convey lower levels. Note that some moods are neither good nor bad. For example, being surprised or astonished (high engagement) and quiet or still (low engagement) are neither pleasant nor unpleasant. As a result, those latter moods are left colorless in Figure 4-6.

Figure 4-6 also illustrates that the most intense positive mood is characterized by feeling enthusiastic, excited, and elated. When employees feel this way, coworkers are likely

FIGURE 4-5   Hour-by-Hour Fluctuations in Job Satisfaction during the Workday

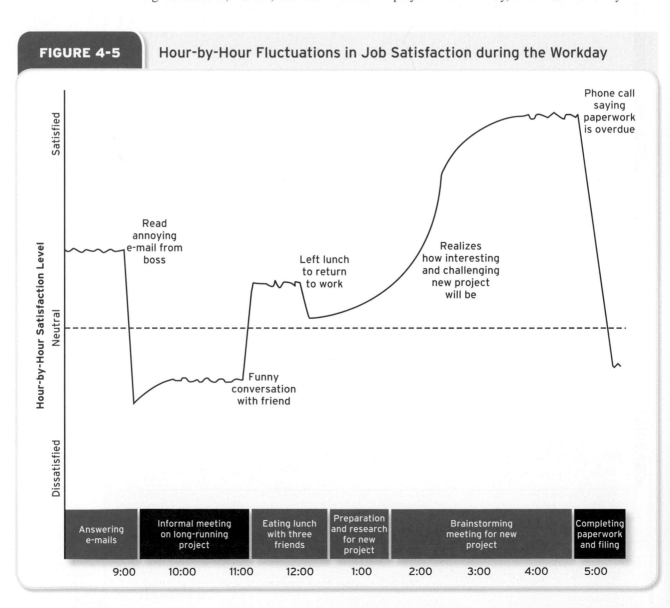

FIGURE 4-6   Different Kinds of Mood

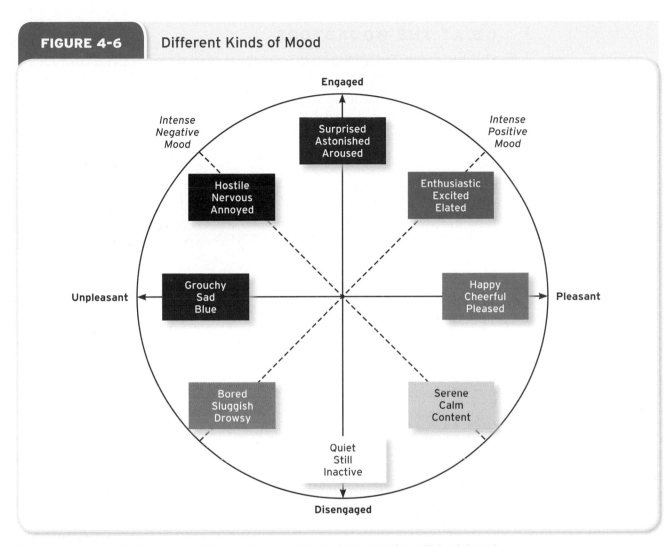

Sources: Adapted from D. Watson and A. Tellegen, "Toward a Consensual Structure of Mood," *Psychological Bulletin* 98 (1985), pp. 219–35; J.A. Russell, "A Circumplex Model of Affect," *Journal of Personality and Social Psychology* 39 (1980), pp. 1161–78; R.J. Larsen and E. Diener, "Promises and Problems with the Circumplex Model of Emotion," in *Review of Personality and Social Psychology: Emotion,* Vol. 13, ed. M.S. Clark (Newbury Park, CA: Sage, 1992), pp. 25–59.

to remark, "Wow, you're sure in a good mood!" In contrast, the most intense negative mood is characterized by feeling hostile, nervous, and annoyed. This kind of mood often triggers the question, "Wow, what's gotten you in such a bad mood?" If we return to our chart of hour-by-hour job satisfaction in Figure 4-5, what kind of mood do you think the employee was in while answering e-mails? Probably a happy, cheerful, and pleased mood. What kind of mood was the employee in during the informal meeting on the long-running project? Probably a grouchy, sad, and blue mood. Finally, what kind of mood do you think the employee was in during the brainstorming meeting for the new project? Clearly, an enthusiastic, excited, and elated mood. This employee would report especially high levels of job satisfaction at this point in time. For an explanation of why the employee might be feeling this way, see the **OB at the Bookstore** feature.

Some organizations take creative steps to foster positive moods among their employees. For example, the SAS Institute, the North Carolina–based maker of statistical software

OB AT THE BOOKSTORE

FINDING FLOW: THE PSYCHOLOGY OF ENGAGEMENT WITH EVERYDAY LIFE
by Mihaly Csikszentmihalyi (New York: Basic Books, 1997).

A typical day is full of anxiety and boredom. Flow experiences provide the flashes of intensive living against this dull background.

With those words, Mihaly Csikszentmihalyi (pronounced CHICK-sent-me-high-ee) describes what makes "flow" so special. Flow occurs when our complete attention is focused on some challenging activity—one that we possess the skills needed to conquer. Our attention gets so focused that we lose track of time and completely ignore the distractions around us. Athletes refer to it as being "in the zone." You can probably remember flow experiences when doing active leisure activities, such as playing sports, making music, or playing chess or poker. But flow can also be experienced at work. The author defines flow using the following diagram:

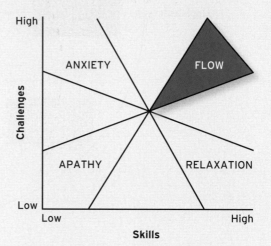

Source: From *Finding Flow: The Psychology of Engagement with Everyday Life* by Mihaly Csikszentmihalyi, Basic Books. Copyright © 1997. Reprinted with permission of Basic Books, a member of Perseus Books Group.

The diagram reveals that flow has a lot in common with the intense positive mood in Figure 4-6. In fact, it's a good bet that the employee in Figure 4-5 achieved flow during that afternoon brainstorming meeting. The flow concept also echoes parts of job characteristics theory. Specifically, the intersection of high skills and high challenges is similar to the intersection of high levels of core job characteristics and high levels of knowledge and skill.

Interestingly, Csikszentmihalyi argues that we experience flow more often at work than we do during leisure for two reasons. First, he argues that much of our leisure time is spent in passive recreation (watching TV, socializing), during which flow is unlikely to develop. Second, he suggests that work tasks can provide a match between skills and challenges and can require high levels of concentration. The flow concept therefore provides another explanation for why high levels of satisfaction with the work itself can be so rewarding.

packages, has an on-site gym with a pool, billiards, volleyball courts, soccer fields, tennis courts, ping-pong tables, and a putting green.[62] Sometimes a good game of ping-pong is all it takes to make a grouchy mood turn cheerful! Griffin Hospital, based in Connecticut, offers its employees (and patients) family-style kitchens, strolling musicians, non-fluorescent lighting, and chair massages.[63] Such perks may not rival the importance of pay, promotions, supervision, coworkers, and the work itself as far as job satisfaction is concerned, but they can help boost employees' moods during a particular workday.

Let's return to our chart of hour-by-hour job satisfaction in Figure 4-5. Although it's fairly easy to see the different moods that occur during the day, it also is obvious that there are events that trigger sudden changes in mood. Why does this occur? Because specific events at work cause positive and negative emotions. **Emotions** are states of feeling that are often intense, last for only a few minutes, and are clearly directed at (and caused by) someone or some circumstance. The difference between moods and emotions becomes clear in the way we describe them to others. We describe moods by saying, "I'm feeling grouchy," but we describe emotions by saying, "I'm feeling angry *at my boss.*"[64] Emotions arc always *about something.*

People experience a variety of different emotions during their daily lives. Table 4-2 provides a summary of many of the most important.[65] **Positive emotions** include joy, pride, relief, hope, love, and compassion. **Negative emotions** include anger, anxiety, fear, guilt, shame, sadness, envy, and disgust. What emotion do you think the employee experienced in

TABLE 4-2	Different Kinds of Emotions
Positive Emotions	**Description**
Joy	A feeling of great pleasure
Pride	Enhancement of identity by taking credit for achievement
Relief	A distressing condition has changed for the better
Hope	Fearing the worst but wanting better
Love	Desiring or participating in affection
Compassion	Being moved by another's situation
Negative Emotions	
Anger	A demeaning offense against me and mine
Anxiety	Facing an uncertain or vague threat
Fear	Facing an immediate and concrete danger
Guilt	Having broken a moral code
Shame	Failing to live up to your ideal self
Sadness	Having experienced an irreversible loss
Envy	Wanting what someone else has
Disgust	Revulsion aroused by something offensive

Source: Adapted from R.S. Lazarus, *Emotion and Adaptation* (New York: Oxford University, 1991).

OB ON SCREEN

THE ISLAND

I wish that there was more . . . more than just waiting to go to the Island.

With those words, Lincoln Six Echo (Ewan McGregor) sums up his monotonous existence in *The Island* (Dir.: Michael Bay, DreamWorks, 2005). He gets up each morning, puts on his white jumpsuit, and goes through life within the boundaries of a sealed complex, designed to protect the survivors of "the contamination" from the pathogens that have destroyed the outside world. Life within the complex is dedicated to keeping its occupants alive and healthy over the long term, as the survivors slowly begin to repopulate the damaged planet.

Unfortunately for Lincoln, the complex seems dedicated to keeping its occupants in a relatively disengaged mood at all times: quiet, still, calm, and serene. Expressing annoyance at any little thing brings a visit from one of the security personnel. So does getting too cozy with any of the other occupants, as when Lincoln receives a "proximity warning" for touching the arm of Jordan Two Delta (Scarlett Johansson). The repeating message over the loudspeaker says it all: "Be polite, pleasant, and peaceful. A healthy person is a happy person."

Things aren't much better at Lincoln's job, where he monitors a set of thin tubes day in and day out, without even knowing where the tubes go or what's flowing through them. As he says to his friend, Jones Three Echo (Ethan Phillips), "Jones, do you ever get bored doing this . . . this boring job. . . . I mean, what are we doing here anyway?" His job is clearly low on every conceivable core job characteristic.

The only emotion that is encouraged in the complex is hope. Every day a lottery occurs in which one lucky soul wins a one-way ticket to "the island"—nature's last remaining pathogen-free zone. Each night, those who don't win the lottery are left to cling to this motto: "Your time will come." Unfortunately, things are not what they seem, and the island may not be the paradise it's made out to be. Suffice it to say that a trip to the island won't exactly result in feelings of serenity and contentment!

Figure 4-5 when reading a disrespectful e-mail from the boss? Probably anger. What emotion do you think that same employee enjoyed during a funny conversation with a friend? Possibly joy, or maybe relief that lunch had arrived and a somewhat bad day was halfway over. Leaving lunch to return to work might have triggered either anxiety (because the bad day might resume) or sadness (because the fun time with friends had ended). Luckily, the employee's sense of joy at taking on a new project that was interesting and challenging was right around the corner. The day did end on a down note, however, as the phone call signaling overdue paperwork was likely met with some mix of anger, fear, guilt, or even disgust (no one likes paperwork!).

Of course, just because employees *feel* many of the emotions in Table 4-2 during the workday doesn't mean they're supposed to *show* those emotions. Some jobs demand that employees live up to the adage "never let 'em see you sweat." In particular, service jobs in which employees make direct contact with customers often require those employees to hide any anger, anxiety, sadness, or disgust that they may feel. Such jobs are high in what is called **emotional labor,** or the need to manage emotions to complete job duties successfully.[66] Flight attendants are trained to "put on a happy face" in front of passengers, retail salespeople are trained to suppress any annoyance with customers, and restaurant servers are trained to act like they're having fun on their job even when they're not.

Is it a good idea to require emotional labor on the part of employees? Research on **emotional contagion** shows that one person can "catch" or "be infected by" the emotions of another person.[67] If a customer service representative is angry or sad, those negative emotions can be transferred to a customer (like a cold or disease). If that transfer occurs, it becomes less likely that customers view the experience favorably and spend more money, which potentially harms the bottom line. From this perspective, emotional labor seems like a vital part of good customer service. Unfortunately, other evidence suggests that emotional labor places great strain on employees and that their "bottled up" emotions may end up bubbling over, sometimes resulting in angry outbursts against customers or emotional exhaustion and burnout on the part of employees.[68] For more on managing emotions, see our **OB on Screen** feature.

SUMMARY: WHY ARE SOME EMPLOYEES MORE SATISFIED THAN OTHERS?

So what explains why some employees are more satisfied than others? As we show in Figure 4-7, answering that question requires paying attention to the more rational appraisals people make about their job and the things it supplies for them, such as pay, promotions, supervision, coworkers, and the work itself. Satisfaction with the work itself, in turn, is affected by the five core job characteristics: variety, identity, significance, autonomy, and feedback. However, answering this question also requires paying attention to daily fluctuations in how people feel, in terms of their positive and negative moods and positive and negative emotions. In this way, a generally satisfied employee may act unhappy at a given moment, just as a generally dissatisfied employee may act happy at a given moment. Understanding those sorts of fluctuations can help managers separate long-term problems (boring tasks, incompetent coworkers) from more short-lived issues (a bad meeting, an annoying interaction).

HOW IMPORTANT IS JOB SATISFACTION?

Several factors influence an employee's job satisfaction, from pay to coworkers to job tasks to day-to-day moods and emotions. Of course, the most obvious remaining question is, "Does job satisfaction really matter?" More precisely, does job satisfaction have a

FIGURE 4-7   **Why Are Some Employees More Satisfied than Others?**

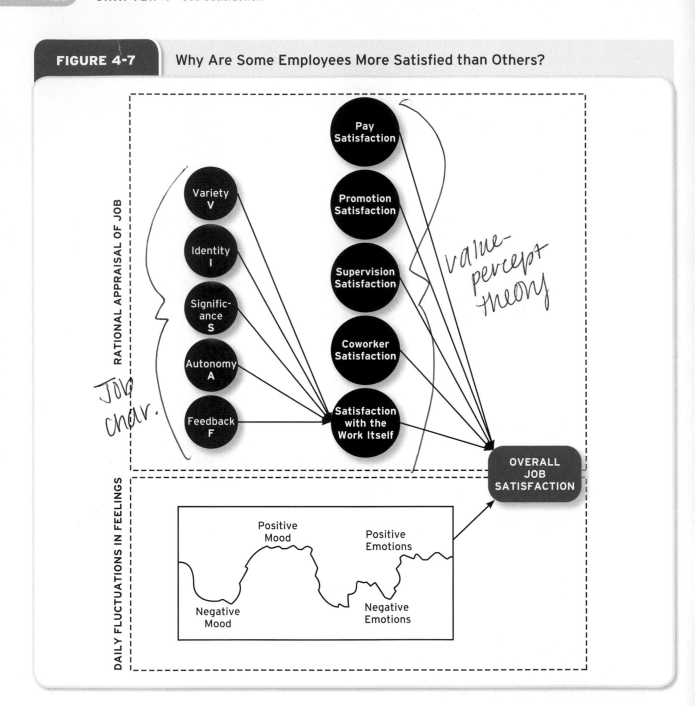

significant impact on job performance and organizational commitment—the two primary outcomes in our integrative model of OB? Figure 4-8 summarizes the research evidence linking job satisfaction to job performance and organizational commitment. This same sort of figure will appear in each of the remaining chapters of this book, so that you can get a better feel for which of the concepts in our integrative model has the strongest impact on performance and commitment.

FIGURE 4-8   Effects of Job Satisfaction on Performance and Commitment

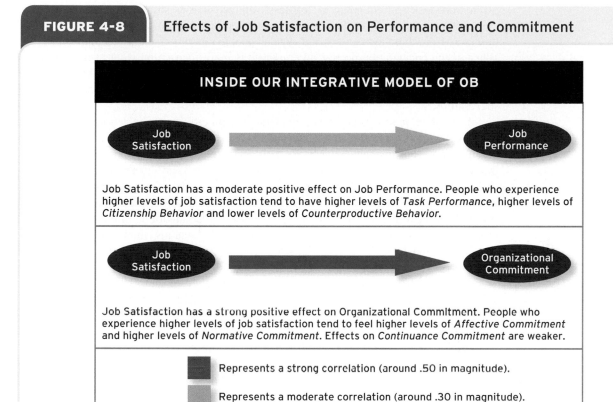

Sources: A. Cooper-Hakim and C. Viswesvaran, "The Construct of Work Commitment: Testing an Integrative Framework," *Psychological Bulletin* 131 (2005), pp. 241–59; R.S. Dalal, "A Meta-Analysis of the Relationship Between Organizational Citizenship Behavior and Counterproductive Work Behavior," *Journal of Applied Psychology* 90 (2005), pp. 1241–55; D.A. Harrison, D.A. Newman, and P.L. Roth, "How Important are Job Attitudes? Meta-Analytic Comparisons of Integrative Behavioral Outcomes and Time Sequences," *Academy of Management Journal* 49 (2006), pp. 305–25; T.A. Judge, C.J. Thoreson, J.E. Bono, and G.K. Patton, "The Job Satisfaction–Job Performance Relationship: A Qualitative and Quantitative Review," *Psychological Bulletin* 127 (2001), pp. 376–407; J.A. LePine, A. Erez, and D.E. Johnson, "The Nature and Dimensionality of Organizational Citizenship Behavior: A Critical Review and Meta-Analysis," *Journal of Applied Psychology* 87 (2002), pp. 52–65; J.P. Meyer, D.J. Stanley, L. Herscovitch, and L. Topolnytsky, "Affective, Continuance, and Normative Commitment to the Organization: A Meta-Analysis of Antecedents, Correlates, and Consequences," *Journal of Vocational Behavior* 61 (2002), pp. 20–52.

Figure 4-8 reveals that job satisfaction does influence job performance. Why? One reason is that job satisfaction is moderately correlated with task performance. Satisfied employees do a better job of fulfilling the duties described in their job descriptions,[69] and evidence suggests that positive feelings improve creativity, problem solving, and decision making[70] and enhance memory and recall of certain kinds of information.[71] Positive feelings also improve general activity and energy levels.[72] Apart from these sorts of findings, the benefits of job satisfaction for task performance might be explained on an hour-by-hour basis. At any given moment, employees wage a war between paying attention to a

 4.7

How does job satisfaction affect job performance and organizational commitment? How does it affect life satisfaction?

given work task and attending to "off-task" things, such as stray thoughts, distractions, interruptions, and so forth. Positive feelings when working on job tasks can pull attention away from those distractions and channel people's attention to task accomplishment.[73] When such concentration occurs, an employee is more focused on work at a given point in time. Of course, the relationship between satisfaction and task performance can work in reverse to some extent, such that people tend to enjoy jobs that they can perform more successfully.[74]

Job satisfaction also is correlated moderately with citizenship behavior. Satisfied employees engage in more frequent "extra mile" behaviors to help their coworkers and their organization.[75] Positive feelings increase their desire to interact with others and often result in spontaneous acts of helping, because employees seek to behave in a manner that matches their current mood.[76] In addition, job satisfaction has a moderate negative correlation with counterproductive behavior. Satisfied employees engage in fewer intentionally destructive actions that could harm their workplace.[77] Intense dissatisfaction is often the trigger that prompts an employee to "lash out" by engaging in rule breaking, theft, sabotage, or other retaliatory behaviors.[78] The more satisfied employees are, the less likely they will feel those sorts of temptations.

Figure 4-8 also reveals that job satisfaction influences organizational commitment. Why? Job satisfaction is strongly correlated with affective commitment, so satisfied employees are more likely to want to stay with the organization.[79] After all, why would employees want to leave a place where they're happy? Another reason is that job satisfaction is strongly correlated with normative commitment. Satisfied employees are more likely to feel an obligation to remain with their firm[80] and a need to "repay" the organization for whatever it is that makes them so satisfied, whether good pay, interesting job tasks, or effective supervision. However, job satisfaction is uncorrelated with continuance commitment, because satisfaction does not create a cost-based need to remain with the organization. Still, when taken together, these commitment effects become more apparent when you consider the kinds of employees who withdraw from the organization. In many cases, dissatisfied employees are those who sit daydreaming at their desks, come in late, are frequently absent, and eventually decide to quit their jobs.

LIFE SATISFACTION

Of course, job satisfaction is important for other reasons as well—reasons that have little to do with job performance or organizational commitment. For example, job satisfaction is strongly related to **life satisfaction,** or the degree to which employees feel a sense of happiness with their lives. Research shows that job satisfaction is one of the strongest predictors of life satisfaction. Put simply, people feel better about their lives when they feel better about their jobs.[81] This link makes sense when you realize how much of our identity is wrapped up in our jobs. What's the first question that people ask one another after being introduced? That's right—"What do you do?" If you feel bad about your answer to that question, it's hard to feel good about your life.

The connection between job satisfaction and life satisfaction also makes sense given how much of our lives are spent at work. Table 4-3 presents the results of one study examining time spent on daily activities, along with reported levels of positive and negative feelings during the course of those activities.[82] The participants in the study spent most of their day at work. Unfortunately, that time resulted in the highest levels of negative feelings and the second-lowest levels of positive feelings (behind only commuting). Home and leisure activities (e.g., socializing, relaxing, exercising, intimate relations) were deemed much more satisfying but took up a much smaller portion of the day. The

TABLE 4-3   How We Spend Our Days

ACTIVITY	AVERAGE HOURS PER DAY	POSITIVE FEELINGS	NEGATIVE FEELINGS
Working	6.9	3.62	**0.97**
On the phone	2.5	3.92	**0.85**
Socializing	2.3	4.59	**0.57**
Eating	2.2	4.34	**0.59**
Relaxing	2.2	4.42	**0.51**
Watching TV	2.2	4.19	**0.58**
Computer/e-mail/Internet	1.9	3.81	**0.80**
Commuting	1.6	3.45	**0.89**
Housework	1.1	3.73	**0.77**
Interacting with kids	1.1	3.86	**0.91**
Napping	0.9	3.87	**0.60**
Praying/meditating	0.4	4.35	**0.59**
Exercising	0.2	4.31	**0.50**
Intimate relations	0.2	5.10	**0.36**

Notes: Positive and negative feelings measured using a scale of 0 (not at all) to 6 (very much).
Source: D. Kahneman, A.B. Krueger, D.A. Schkade, N. Schwarz, and A.A. Stone, "A Survey Method for Characterizing Daily Life Experience: The Day Reconstruction Method," *Science* 306 (2004), pp. 1776–80.

implication is clear: If we want to feel better about our days, we need to find a way to be more satisfied with our jobs.

Increases in job satisfaction have a stronger impact on life satisfaction than do increases in salary or income. As the old adage goes, "money can't buy happiness." This finding may seem surprising, given that pay satisfaction is one facet of overall job satisfaction (see Figure 4-1). However, you might recall that pay satisfaction is a weaker driver of overall job satisfaction than other facets, such as the work itself, supervision, or coworkers (see Figure 4-2). We should also note that pay satisfaction depends less on absolute salary levels and more on relative salary levels (i.e., how your salary compares to your circle of peers). As the writer H.L. Mencken once remarked, "A wealthy man is one who earns $100 a year more than his wife's sister's husband."[83] For more on the relationship between money and happiness, see our **OB Internationally** feature.

"Researchers say I'm not happier for being richer, but do you know how much researchers make?"

Source: © The New Yorker Collection 2001 Pat Byrnes from cartoonbank.com. All rights reserved.

OB INTERNATIONALLY

The "money can't buy happiness" adage can even be supported using national-level data. For example, survey data in the United States, Britain, and Japan show that people are no happier today than they were 50 years ago, even though average incomes have more than doubled during that span.[84] Another way of examining this issue explores the connection between national wealth and average happiness: Do wealthier nations have citizens with higher levels of life satisfaction? The figure below provides a representation of the relationship between average income per citizen for a nation and the percentage of respondents who describe themselves as happy, according to population surveys.[85]

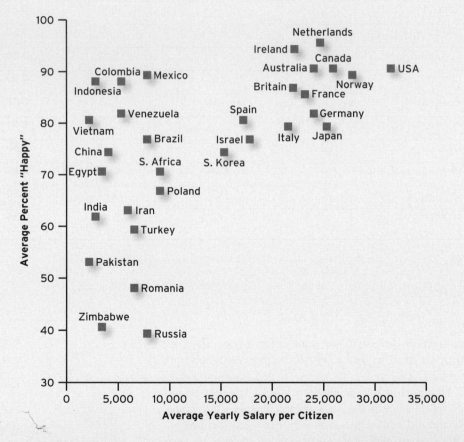

Comparing countries reveals that nations above the poverty line are indeed happier than nations below the poverty line. However, for countries with an average income of $20,000 or more, additional income is not associated with higher levels of life satisfaction.[86] For example, the United States is the richest country on Earth, but it trails nations like the Netherlands and Ireland in life satisfaction. Understanding differences in life satisfaction across nations is important to organizations for two reasons. First, such differences may influence how receptive a given nation is to the company's products. Second, such differences may affect the kinds of policies and practices an organization needs to use when employing individuals in that nation.

APPLICATION: TRACKING SATISFACTION

Because job satisfaction seems to be a key driver of job performance, organizational commitment, and life satisfaction, it's important for managers to understand just how satisfied their employees are. Gauging satisfaction is vital for organizations like Wegmans, whose employees have direct customer contact, but it can be important in other organizations as well. Several methods assess the job satisfaction of rank-and-file employees, including focus groups, interviews, and attitude surveys. Of those three choices, attitude surveys are often the most accurate and most effective.[87] Attitude surveys can provide a "snapshot" of how satisfied the workforce is and, if repeated over time, reveal trends in satisfaction levels. They also can explore the effectiveness of major job changes by comparing attitude survey results before and after a change.

Although organizations are often tempted to design their own attitude surveys, there are benefits to using existing surveys that are already in wide use. One of the most widely administered job satisfaction surveys is the Job Descriptive Index (JDI). The JDI assesses all five satisfaction facets in Figure 4-1: pay satisfaction, promotion satisfaction, supervisor satisfaction, coworker satisfaction, and satisfaction with the work itself. The JDI also has been subjected to a great deal of research attention that, by and large, supports its accuracy.[88] Furthermore, the JDI includes a companion survey—the Job in General (JIG) scale—that assesses overall job satisfaction.[89] Excerpts from the JDI and JIG appear in Table 4-4.[90] One strength of the JDI is that the questions are written in a very simple and straightforward fashion so that they can be easily understood by most employees.

4.8

What steps can organizations take to assess and manage job satisfaction?

The developers of the JDI offer several suggestions regarding its administration.[91] For example, they recommend surveying as much of the company as possible because any unsurveyed employees might feel that their feelings are less important. They also recommend that surveys be anonymous so that employees can be as honest as possible without worrying about being punished for any critical comments about the organization. Therefore, companies must be careful in collecting demographic information on the surveys. Some demographic information is vital for comparing satisfaction levels across relevant groups, but too much information will make employees feel like they could be identified. Finally, the developers suggest that the survey should be administered by the firm's human resources group or an outside consulting agency. This structure will help employees feel that their anonymity is more protected.

Once JDI data have been collected, a number of interesting questions can be explored.[92] First, the data can indicate whether the organization is satisfied or dissatisfied by comparing average scores for each facet with the JDI's "neutral levels" for those facets (the "neutral levels" are available in the JDI manual). Second, it becomes possible to compare the organization's scores with national norms to provide some context for the firm's satisfaction levels. The JDI manual also provides national norms for all facets and breaks down those norms according to relevant demographic groups (e.g., managers vs. nonmanagers, new vs. senior employees, gender, education). Third, the JDI allows for within-organization comparisons to determine which departments have the highest satisfaction levels and which have the lowest.

The results of attitude survey efforts should then be fed back to employees so that they feel involved in the process. Of course, attitude surveys ideally should be a catalyst for some kind of improvement effort.[93] Surveys that never lead to any kind of on-the-job change eventually may be viewed as a waste of time. As a result, the organization should be prepared to react to the survey results with specific goals and action steps. For example, an organization with low pay satisfaction may react by conducting additional benchmarking

TABLE 4-4	Excerpts from the Job Descriptive Index and the Job in General Scale

Think of the work you do at present. How well does each of the following words or phrases describe your work? In the blank beside each word or phrase below, write

_Y_ for "Yes" if it describes your work
_N_ for "No" if it does NOT describe it
_?_ for "?" if you cannot decide

Pay Satisfaction[a]	**Coworker Satisfaction**[a]
___ Well paid	___ Stimulating
___ Bad	___ Smart
___ Barely live on income	___ Unpleasant
Promotion Satisfaction[a]	**Satisfaction with Work Itself**[a]
___ Regular promotions	___ Fascinating
___ Promotion on ability	___ Pleasant
___ Opportunities somewhat limited	___ Can see my results
Supervision Satisfaction[a]	**OVERALL JOB SATISFACTION**[b]
___ Knows job well	___ Better than most
___ Around when needed	___ Worthwhile
___ Doesn't supervise enough	___ Worse than most

[a]The Job Descriptive Index, © Bowling Green State University (1975, 1985, 1997).
[b]The Job in General Scale, © Bowling Green State University (1982, 1985).
Source: W.K. Balzer, J.A. Kihn, P.C. Smith, J.L. Irwin, P.D. Bachiochi, C. Robie, E.F. Sinar, and L.F. Parra, "Users' Manual for the Job Descriptive Index (JDI; 1997 version) and the Job in General Scales," in *Electronic Resources for the JDI and JIG,* eds. J.M. Stanton and C.D. Crossley (Bowling Green, OH: Bowling Green State University, 2000). Reprinted with permission.

to see whether compensation levels are trailing those of competitors. An organization with low promotion satisfaction might react by revising its system for assessing performance. Finally, an organization that struggles with satisfaction with the work itself could attempt to redesign key job tasks or, if that proves too costly, train supervisors in strategies for increasing the five core job characteristics on a more informal basis.

TAKEAWAYS

4.1 Job satisfaction is a pleasurable emotional state resulting from the appraisal of one's job or job experiences. It represents how you feel about your job and what you think about your job.

4.2 Values are things that people consciously or subconsciously want to seek or attain. According to value-percept theory, job satisfaction depends on whether you perceive that your job supplies those things that you value.

4.3 People often appraise their job satisfaction according to more specific facets of their job. These satisfaction facets include pay satisfaction, promotion satisfaction, supervision satisfaction, coworker satisfaction, and satisfaction with the work itself.

4.4   Job characteristics theory suggests that five "core characteristics"—variety, identity, significance, autonomy, and feedback—combine to result in particularly high levels of satisfaction with the work itself.

4.5   Apart from the influence of supervision, coworkers, pay, and the work itself, job satisfaction levels fluctuate during the course of the day. Rises and falls in job satisfaction are triggered by positive and negative events that are experienced. Those events trigger changes in emotions that eventually give way to changes in mood.

4.6   Moods are states of feeling that are often mild in intensity, last for an extended period of time, and are not explicitly directed at anything. Intense positive moods include being enthusiastic, excited, and elated. Intense negative moods include being hostile, nervous, and annoyed. Emotions are states of feeling that are often intense, last only for a few minutes, and are clearly directed at someone or some circumstance. Positive emotions include joy, pride, relief, hope, love, and compassion. Negative emotions include anger, anxiety, fear, guilt, shame, sadness, envy, and disgust.

4.7   Job satisfaction has a moderately positive relationship with job performance and a strong positive relationship with organizational commitment. It also has a strong positive relationship with life satisfaction.

4.8   Organizations can assess and manage job satisfaction using attitude surveys such as the Job Descriptive Index (JDI), which assesses pay satisfaction, promotion satisfaction, supervisor satisfaction, coworker satisfaction, and satisfaction with the work itself. It can be used to assess the levels of job satisfaction experienced by employees, and its specific facet scores can identify particular interventions that would be effective.

KEY TERMS

- Job satisfaction — *p. 105*
- Values — *p. 105*
- Value-percept theory — *p. 107*
- Pay satisfaction — *p. 107*
- Promotion satisfaction — *p. 107*
- Supervision satisfaction — *p. 108*
- Coworker satisfaction — *p. 109*
- Satisfaction with the work itself — *p. 109*
- Meaningfulness of work — *p. 112*
- Responsibility for outcomes — *p. 112*
- Knowledge of results — *p. 112*
- Job characteristics theory — *p. 112*
- Variety — *p. 112*
- Identity — *p. 114*
- Significance — *p. 114*
- Autonomy — *p. 115*
- Feedback — *p. 116*
- Knowledge and skill — *p. 117*
- Growth need strength — *p. 117*
- Job enrichment — *p. 118*
- Moods — *p. 118*
- Pleasantness — *p. 118*
- Engagement — *p. 118*
- Emotions — *p. 123*
- Positive emotions — *p. 123*
- Negative emotions — *p. 123*
- Emotional labor — *p. 125*
- Emotional contagion — *p. 125*
- Life satisfaction — *p. 128*

DISCUSSION QUESTIONS

4.1 Which of the values in Table 4-1 do you think are the most important to employees in general? Are there times when the values in the last three categories (altruism, status, and environment) become more important than the values in the first five categories (pay, promotions, supervision, coworkers, the work itself)?

4.2 What steps can organizations take to improve promotion satisfaction, supervision satisfaction, and coworker satisfaction?

4.3 Consider the five core job characteristics (variety, identity, significance, autonomy, and feedback). Do you think that any one of those characteristics is more important than the other four? Is it possible to have too much of some job characteristics?

4.4 We sometimes describe colleagues or friends as "moody." What do you think it means to be "moody" from the perspective of Figure 4-6?

4.5 Consider the list of positive and negative emotions in Table 4-2. Which of these emotions are most frequently experienced at work? What causes them?

CASE   WEGMANS FOOD MARKETS

If you have ever entered Wegmans Food Markets, you likely noticed that the store is in a league of its own. Wegmans Food Markets offer customers more than 60,000 products, market cafes, patisseries, natural foods, and kids' fun centers, just to name a few. The amenities offered to consumers may seem unbelievable, but the high level of customer service is even more remarkable. Wegmans Food Markets has managed the impossible: It has differentiated itself from the overabundance of supermarkets.

In addition to being named to *Fortune's* list of the "100 Best Companies to Work For" for 10 consecutive years, Wegmans Food Markets in 2007 ranked fifth on *BusinessWeek's* first ever listing of the 25 customer service champs. Wegmans describes its approach as "knowledge-based service." To support its approach, the company reorganized its operations, moving some work offsite and retraining the employees to help customers rather than being tied to a counter or backroom operations. Obviously, the top customer satisfaction accolades cannot come without employee satisfaction. The company also has received recognition for being one of the "World's Most Ethical Companies" by *Ethisphere* magazine. Danny Wegman, CEO of Wegmans Food Markets, believes his company's success is due to his people. Wegman offers employees a premium wage, great benefits, and scholarship opportunities. In addition, employees get the rare opportunity to be empowered in the supermarket. It does not matter what your level in the organization, your input is considered, and if accepted, it could affect the entire company. Employees' high levels of job satisfaction equate with an 89-year-old food store chain that continuously outperforms the competition in a fiercely competitive industry.

4.1 What factors cause employees at Wegmans Food Markets to have a high level of job satisfaction? Explain.

4.2 What differentiates Wegmans Food Markets from other grocery stores? Explain.

Sources: "100 Best Companies to Work For," Fortune, January 22, 2007; "Customer Service Champs," Business-Week, March 5, 2007; "Wegmans Food Markets, Inc.: An Overview," 2007, www.wegmans.com; "Wegmans Named to 'World's Most Ethical Companies' List by *Ethisphere* Magazine," 2007, www.wegmans.com; "What Makes an Organization the #1 Company to Work For?" www.astd.org.

EXERCISE JOB SATISFACTION ACROSS JOBS

The purpose of this exercise is to examine satisfaction with the work itself across jobs. This exercise uses groups of six participants, so your instructor will either assign you to a group of six or ask you to create your own group of six. The exercise has the following steps:

1. Use the OB Assessment for Chapter 4 to calculate the Satisfaction Potential Score (SPS) for the following four jobs:

   a. A lobster fisherman who runs his own boat with his son.
   b. A standup comedian.
   c. A computer programmer whose assignment is to replace "98" with "1998" in thousands of lines of computer code.
   d. A president of the United States.

2. Which job has the highest SPS? Which core job characteristics best explain why some jobs have high scores and other jobs have low scores? Write down the scores for the four jobs in an Excel file on the classroom computer or on the chalkboard.

3. Class discussion (whether in groups or as a class) should center on two questions. First, is the job that scored the highest really the one that would be the most enjoyable on a day-in, day-out basis? Second, does that mean it would be the job that you would pick if you could snap your fingers and magically attain one of the jobs on the list? Why or why not? What other job satisfaction theory is relevant to this issue?

ENDNOTES

4.1 Levering, R., and M. Moskowitz. "The 100 Best Companies to Work For." *Fortune,* January 24, 2005; pp. 64–68.Levering, R., and M. Moskowitz. "In Good Company." *Fortune,* January 22, 2007.pp. 94–114.

4.2 Levering and Moskowitz, "The 100 Best."

4.3 Ibid.

4.4 Ibid.

4.5 Locke, E.A. "The Nature and Causes of Job Satisfaction." In *Handbook of Industrial and Organizational Psychology,* ed. M. Dunnette. Chicago, IL: Rand McNally, 1976, pp. 1297–1350.

4.6 Koretz, G. "Hate Your Job? Join the Club." *BusinessWeek,* October 6, 2003.p. 40.

4.7 Locke, "The Nature and Causes."

4.8 Dawis, R.V. "Vocational Interests, Values, and Preferences." In *Handbook of Industrial and Organizational Psychology,* Vol. 2, eds. M.D. Dunnette and L.M. Hough Palo Alto, CA: Consulting Psychologists Press, 1991, pp. 834–71.

4.9 Locke, "The Nature and Causes."

4.10 Judge, T.A., and A.H. Church. "Job Satisfaction: Research and Practice." In *Industrial and Organizational Psychology: Linking Theory with Practice,* eds. C.L. Cooper and E.A. Locke. Oxford, UK: Blackwell, 2000, pp. 166–98.

4.11 Locke, "The Nature and Causes."

4.12 Smith, P.C.; L.M. Kendall; and C.L. Hulin. *The Measurement of Satisfaction in Work and Retirement.* Chicago: Rand McNally, 1969.

4.13 Lawler, E.E. *Pay and Organizational Effectiveness: A Psychological View.* New York: McGraw-Hill, 1971.

4.14 Locke, "The Nature and Causes."

4.15 Levering and Moskowitz, "The 100 Best."

4.16 Smith, Kendall, and Hulin, "The Measurement of Satisfaction."

4.17 Locke, "The Nature and Causes."

4.18 Levering and Moskowitz, "The 100 Best."

4.19 Smith, Kendall, and Hulin, "The measurement of satisfaction."

4.20 Locke, "The Nature and Causes."

4.21 Levering and Moskowitz, "The 100 Best."

4.22 Smith, Kendall, and Hulin, "The Measurement of Satisfaction."

4.23 Levering and Moskowitz, "The 100 Best."

4.24 Smith, Kendall, and Hulin, "The Measurement of Satisfaction."

4.25 Levering and Moskowitz, "The 100 Best."

4.26 Ironson, G.H.; P.C. Smith; M.T. Brannick; W.M. Gibson; and K.B. Paul. "Construction of a Job in General Scale: A Comparison of Global, Composite, and Specific Measures." *Journal of Applied Psychology* 74 (1989), pp. 193–200; Russell, S.S.; C. Spitzmuller; L.F. Lin; J.M. Stanton; P.C. Smith; and G.H. Ironson. "Shorter Can Also Be Better: The Abridged Job in General Scale." *Educational and Psychological Measurement* 64 (2004), pp. 878–93.

4.27 Rode, J.C.; M.L. Arthaud-Day; C.H. Mooney; J.P. Near; T.T. Baldwin; W.H. Bommer; and R.S. Rubin. "Life Satisfaction and Student Performance." *Academy of Management Learning and Education* 4 (2005), pp. 421–33.

4.28 Taylor, F.W. *The Principles of Scientific Management.* New York: Wiley, 1911; Gilbreth, F.B. *Motion Study: A Method for Increasing the Efficiency of the Workman.* New York: Van Nostrand, 1911.

4.29 Hackman, J.R.; and E.E. Lawler III. (1971)"Employee Reactions to Job Characteristics." *Journal of Applied Psychology* 55(), pp. 259–86.

4.30 Hackman, J.R., and G.R. Oldham. *Work Redesign.* Reading, MA: Addison-Wesley, 1980.

4.31 Ibid.

4.32 Ibid.

4.33 Hackman, J.R., and G.R. Oldham. "Motivation through the Design of Work: Test of a Theory." *Organizational Behavior and Human Decision Processes* 16 (1976), pp. 250–79.

4.34 Hackman and Oldham, *Work Redesign.*

4.35 Turner, A.N., and P.R. Lawrence. *Industrial Jobs and the Worker.* Boston: Harvard University Graduate School of Business Administration, 1965.

4.36 Hackman and Lawler, "Employee Reactions."

4.37 Terkel, S. *Working: People Talk About What They Do All Day and How They Feel About What They Do.* New York: Pantheon Books, 1974, pp. 159–60.

4.38 Ibid., pp. 318–21.

4.39 Berns, G. *Satisfaction: The Science of Finding True Fulfillment.* New York: Henry Holt and Company, 2005, p. xiv.

4.40 Hackman and Oldham, *Work Redesign.*

4.41 Turner and Lawrence, *Industrial Jobs.*

4.42 Terkel, *Working,* p. xxxii.

4.43 Ibid., pp. 213–14.

4.44 Hackman and Oldham, *Work Redesign.*

4.45 Terkel, *Working,* pp. 107–109.

4.46 Ibid., p. 589.

4.47 Hackman and Oldham, *Work Redesign.*

4.48 Turner and Lawrence, *Industrial Jobs.*

4.49 Breaugh, J.A. "The Measurement of Work Autonomy. *Human Relations* 38 (1985), pp. 551–70.

4.50 Terkel, *Working,* pp. 49–50.

4.51 Hackman and Oldham, *Work Redesign.*

4.52 Terkel, *Working,* p. 346.

4.53 Ibid., pp. 295–96.

4.54 Fried, Y., and G.R. Ferris. "The Validity of the Job Characteristics Model: A Review and Meta-Analysis." *Personnel Psychology* 40 (1987), pp. 287–322.

4.55 Hackman and Oldham, *Work Redesign.*

4.56 Loher, B.T.; R.A. Noe; N.L. Moeller; and M.P. Fitzgerald. "A Meta-Analysis of the Relation of Job Characteristics to Job Satisfaction." *Journal of Applied Psychology* 70 (1985), pp. 280–89.

4.57 Campion, M.A., and C.L. McClelland. "Interdisciplinary Examination of the Costs and Benefits of Enlarged Jobs: A Job Design Quasi-Experiment." *Journal of Applied Psychology* 76 (1991), pp. 186–98.

4.58 Ibid.

4.59 Morris, W.N. *Mood: The Frame of Mind.* New York: Springer-Verlag, 1989.

4.60 Watson, D., and A. Tellegen. "Toward a Consensual Structure of Mood." *Psychological Bulletin* 98 (1985), pp. 219–35; Russell, J.A. "A Circumplex Model of Affect." *Journal of Personality and Social Psychology* 39 (1980), pp. 1161–78; Larsen, R.J., and E. Diener. "Promises and Problems with the Circumplex Model of Emotion." In *Review of Personality and Social Psychology: Emotion,* Vol. 13, ed. M.S.

Clark. Newbury Park, CA: Sage, 1992, pp. 25–59.

4.61 Ibid.

4.62 Levering and Moskowitz, "The 100 Best."

4.63 Ibid.

4.64 Weiss, H.M., and K.E. Kurek. "Dispositional Influences on Affective Experiences at Work." In *Personality and Work: Reconsidering the Role of Personality in Organizations,* eds. M.R. Barrick and A.M. Ryan. San Francisco: Jossey-Bass, 2003, pp. 121–49.

4.65 Lazarus, R.S. *Emotion and Adaptation.* New York: Oxford University, 1991.

4.66 Hochschild, A.R. *The Managed Heart: Commercialization of Human Feeling.* Berkeley, CA: University of California Press, 1983; Rafaeli, A., and R.I. Sutton. "The Expression of Emotion in Organizational Life." *Research in Organizational Behavior* 11 (1989), pp. 1–42.

4.67 Hatfield, E.; J.T. Cacioppo; and R.L. Rapson. *Emotional Contagion.* New York: Cambridge University Press, 1994.

4.68 Ashkanasy, N.M.; C.E.J. Hartel; and C.S. Daus. "Diversity and Emotion: The New Frontiers in Organizational Behavior Research." *Journal of Management* 28 (2002), pp. 307–38.

4.69 Judge, T.A.; C.J. Thoreson; J.E. Bono; and G.K Patton. "The Job Satisfaction–Job Performance Relationship: A Qualitative and Quantitative Review." *Psychological Bulletin* 127 (2001), pp. 376–407.

4.70 Brief, A.P., and H.M. Weiss. "Organizational Behavior: Affect in the Workplace." *Annual Review of Psychology* 53 (2002), pp. 279–307.

4.71 Isen, A.M., and R.A. Baron. "Positive Affect as a Factor in Organizational Behavior." *Research in Organizational Behavior* 13 (1991), pp. 1–53.

4.72 Lucas, R.E., and E. Diener. "The Happy Worker: Hypotheses about the Role of Positive Affect in Worker Satisfaction." In *Personality and Work: Reconsidering the Role of Personality in Organizations,* eds. M.R. Barrick and A.M. Ryan. San Francisco: Jossey-Bass, 2003, pp. 30–59.

4.73 Beal, D.J.; H.M. Weiss; E. Barros; and S.M. MacDermid. "An Episodic Process Model of Affective Influences on Performance." *Journal of Applied Psychology* 90 (2005), pp. 1054–68.

4.74 Locke, "The Nature and Causes."

4.75 LePine, J.A.; A. Erez; and D.E. Johnson. "The Nature and Dimensionality of Organizational Citizenship Behavior: A Critical Review and Meta-Analysis." *Journal of Applied Psychology* 87 (2002), pp. 52–65.

4.76 George, J.M. "Trait and State Affect." In *Individual Differences and Behavior in Organizations,* ed. K.R. Murphy. San Francisco: Jossey-Bass, 1996, pp. 145–71.

4.77 Dalal, R.S. "A Meta-Analysis of the Relationship Between Organizational Citizenship Behavior and Counterproductive Work Behavior." *Journal of Applied Psychology* 90 (2005), pp. 1241–55.

4.78 Sackett, P.R., and C.J. DeVore. "Counterproductive Behaviors at Work." In *Handbook of Industrial, Work, and Organizational Psychology,* Vol. 1, eds. N. Anderson, D.S. Ones, H.K. Sinangil, and C. Viswesvaran. Thousand Oaks, CA: Sage, 2001, pp. 145–51.

4.79 Cooper-Hakim, A., and C. Viswes-varan. "The Construct of Work Commitment: Testing an Integrative Framework." *Psychological Bulletin* 131 (2005), pp. 241–59; Harrison, D.A.; D. Newman; and P.L. Roth. "How Important Are Job Attitudes? Meta-Analytic Comparisons of Integrative Behavioral Outcomes and Time Sequences." *Academy of Management Journal* 49 (2006), pp. 305–25; Meyer, J.P.; D.J. Stanley; L. Herscovitch; and L. Topolnytsky. "Affective, Continuance, and Normative Commitment to the Organization: A Meta-Analysis of Antecedents, Correlates, and Consequences." *Journal of Vocational Behavior* 61 (2002), pp. 20–52.

4.80 Ibid.

4.81 Tait, M.; M.Y. Padgett; and T.T. Baldwin. "Job and Life Satisfaction: A Reexamination of the Strength of the Relationship and Gender Effects as a Function of the Date of the Study." *Journal of Applied Psychology* 74 (1989), pp. 502–507; Judge, T.A., and S. Watanabe. "Another Look at the Job Satisfaction–Life Satisfaction Relationship." *Journal of Applied Psychology* 78 (1993), pp. 939–48.

4.82 Kahneman, D.; A.B. Krueger; D.A. Schkade; N. Schwarz; and A.A. Stone. "A Survey Method for Characterizing Daily Life Experience: The Day Reconstruction Method." *Science* 306 (2004), pp. 1776–80.

4.83 Layard, R. *Happiness.* New York: Penguin Press, 2005, p. 41.

4.84 Ibid.

4.85 R. Layard, qtd. in Diener, E., and E. Suh. "National Differences in Subjective Well-Being." In *Well-Being: The Foundations of Hedonic Psychology,* eds. D. Kahneman, E. Diener, and N. Schwarz. New York: Russell Sage Foundation, 1999.

4.86 Layard, *Happiness.*

4.87 Saari, L.M., and T.A. Judge. "Employee Attitudes and Job Satisfaction." *Human Resource Management* 43 (2004), pp. 395–407.

4.88 Kinicki, A.J.; F.M. McKee-Ryan; C.A. Schriesheim; and K.P. Carson. "Assessing the Construct Validity of the Job Descriptive Index: A Review and Meta-Analysis." *Journal of Applied Psychology* 87 (2002), pp. 14–32; Hanisch, K.A. "The Job Descriptive Index Revisited: Questions about the Question Mark." *Journal of Applied Psychology* 77 (1992), pp. 377–82; Jung, K.G.; A. Dalessio; and S.M. Johnson. "Stability of the Factor Structure of the Job Descriptive Index." *Academy of Management Journal* 29 (1986), pp. 609–16.

4.89 Ironson, Smith, Brannick, Gibson, and Paul, "Construction"; Russell, Spitzmuller, Lin, Stanton, Smith, and Ironson, "Shorter Can also Be Better."

4.90 Balzer, W.K.; J.A. Kihn; P.C. Smith; J.L. Irwin; P.D. Bachiochi; C. Robie; E.F. Sinar; and LF. Parra. "Users' Manual for the Job Descriptive Index (JDI; 1997 version) and the Job in General Scales." In *Electronic Resources for the JDI and JIG,* eds. J.M. Stanton and C.D. Crossley. Bowling Green, OH: Bowling Green State University, 2000.

4.91 Ibid.

4.92 Ibid.

4.93 Saari and Judge, "Employee Attitudes."

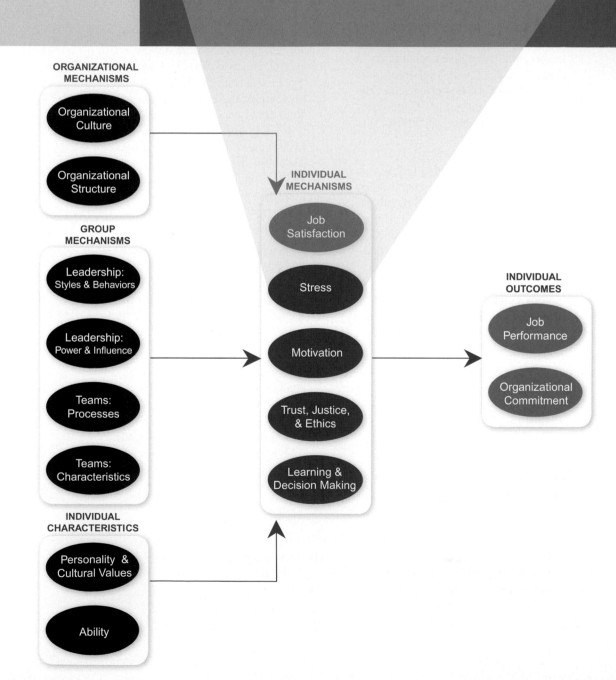

ORGANIZATIONAL
MECHANISMS

Organizational
Culture

Organizational
Structure

GROUP
MECHANISMS

Leadership:
Styles & Behaviors

Leadership:
Power & Influence

Teams:
Processes

Teams:
Characteristics

INDIVIDUAL
CHARACTERISTICS

Personality &
Cultural Values

Ability

INDIVIDUAL
MECHANISMS

Job
Satisfaction

Stress

Motivation

Trust, Justice,
& Ethics

Learning &
Decision Making

INDIVIDUAL
OUTCOMES

Job
Performance

Organizational
Commitment

Financial services provider Capital One understands the need for employees to release a little stress during the workday and offers exercise and relaxation facilities among its benefits.

 LEARNING GOALS

After reading this chapter, you should be able to answer the following questions:

5.1 What is stress? What are stressors and strains, and how are these concepts different than stress?

5.2 What are the four main types of work stressors?

5.3 How do individual employees cope with stress?

5.4 How do the Type A Behavior Pattern and social support influence the stress process?

5.5 How does stress affect job performance and organizational commitment?

5.6 What steps can organizations take to manage employee stress?

CAPITAL ONE

How often do feel like you need to blow off some steam at the end of a pressure-filled day? Imagine how great it would be to walk from your office to a nearby state-of-the-art fitness facility that included basketball courts, racquetball courts, lighted tennis and sand volleyball courts, softball fields, exercise floors, strength training and cardiovascular equipment, and a locker room. Or think abut how convenient it would be if that same nearby facility had nature-based walking trails and a Tai-Chi garden that you could use whenever you felt the need. You could have all of this as part of your benefits package if you were an employee of Capital One, one of the fastest growing and most admired financial services providers in the world today.

Although not all of you have a Capital One credit card, most of you probably are familiar with the company's name and slogan, "What's in your wallet?" So how did Capital One grow from nothing in 1995 to #206 on the *Fortune* 500 by 2005? Capital One's phenomenal growth and success has been attributed, in part, to its corporate values, which include investing in employees' professional and personal growth and encouraging healthy stress management.[1] Capital One's belief regarding the linkage between employee well-being and the company's success was summed up nicely by Dr. Steven Noeldner, senior manager of health and productivity at Capital One: "I think all the great visionaries for business in America are saying that in the 21st century, the most valuable asset that any company has, or will have, is its human capital. And companies don't think twice about investing in maintaining their trucks that deliver their products. . . . If they give that same kind of thought to their most valuable asset—the human capital—then this is almost a no-brainer."[2]

Consistent with the value it places on the health and well-being of employees, Capital One invested millions of dollars in world-class fitness centers at many of their locations to help employees manage stress. It also collected data to assess whether participation rates in those centers were associated with benefits to the company. According to Larry Ebert, vice president of real estate for Capital One, the investment in first-class fitness centers and other amenities that create a more positive work environment appears to have paid off in increases in productivity and reductions in health care costs.[3] Those increases match scientific research showing that participation in fitness activities reduces stress levels, the risk of coronary heart disease, and memory loss.[4]

STRESS

Stress is an OB topic that is probably quite familiar to you. Even if you don't have a lot of work experience, consider how you feel toward the end of a semester when you have to cram for several final exams and finish a couple of term projects. At the same time, you might have also been looking for a job or planning a trip with friends or family. Although some people might be able to deal with all of these demands without becoming too frazzled, most people would say that this type of scenario causes them to feel "stressed out." This stressed-out feeling might even be accompanied by headaches, stomach upsets, backaches, or sleeping difficulties. Although you might believe your stress will diminish once you graduate and settle down, high stress on the job is more prevalent than it has ever been before.[5] The Federal Government's National Institute for Occupational Safety and Health (NIOSH) summarized findings from several sources that indicated that up to 40 percent of U.S. workers feel their jobs are "very stressful" or "extremely stressful."[6] Unfortunately, high stress is even more prevalent in the types of jobs that most of you are likely to have after you graduate, because managers are approximately 21 percent more likely than the average worker to describe their jobs as stressful.[7] Table 5-1 provides a listing of where several jobs rank on the list of least to most stressful.

Stress is defined as a psychological response to demands for which there is something at stake and coping with those demands taxes or exceeds a person's capacity or

5.1

What is stress? What are stressors and strains, and how are these concepts different than stress?

TABLE 5-1   Jobs Rated from Least Stressful (1) to Most Stressful (250)

LEAST STRESSFUL JOBS	STRESS LEVEL	MOST STRESSFUL JOBS	STRESS LEVEL
1. Musical instrument repairer	18.77	212. Registered nurse	62.14
2. Florist	18.80	220. Attorney	64.33
4. Actuary	20.18	223. Newspaper reporter	65.26
6. Appliance repairer	21.12	226. Architect	66.92
8. Librarian	21.40	228. Lumberjack	67.60
10. File clerk	21.71	229. Fisherman	69.82
11. Piano tuner	22.29	230. Stockbroker	71.65
12. Janitor	22.44	231. U.S. Congressperson	72.05
16. Vending machine repairer	23.47	233. Real estate agent	73.06
18. Barber	23.62	234. Advertising account exec	74.55
24. Mathematician	24.67	238. Public relations exec	78.52
29. Cashier	25.11	240. Air traffic controller	83.13
30. Dishwasher	25.32	241. Airline pilot	85.35
32. Pharmacist	25.87	243. Police officer	93.89
40. Biologist	26.94	244. Astronaut	99.34
44. Computer programmer	27.00	245. Surgeon	99.46
50. Astronomer	28.06	246. Taxi driver	100.49
56. Historian	28.41	248. Senior corporate exec	108.62
67. Bank teller	30.12	249. Firefighter	110.93
78. Accountant	31.13	250. U.S. President	176.55

Source: Adapted from L. Krantz, *Jobs Rated Almanac,* 6th ed.(Fort Lee, NJ: Barricade Books, Inc., 2002)
The stress level score is calculated by summing points in 21 categories, including deadlines, competitiveness, environmental conditions, speed required, precision required, initiative required, physical demands, and hazards encountered.

resources.[8] The particular demands that cause people to experience stress are called **stressors.** The negative consequences that occur when demands tax or exceed one's capacity or resources are called **strains.** Our definition of stress illustrates that it depends on both the nature of the demand and the person who confronts it. People differ in terms of how they evaluate stressors and the way they cope with them. As a result, they may experience different levels of stress even when confronted with the exact same situations.

WHY ARE SOME EMPLOYEES MORE "STRESSED" THAN OTHERS?

To fully understand what it means to feel "stressed," it is necessary to describe, in more detail, how stressors are perceived and appraised. When people first encounter stressors, the process of **primary appraisal** is triggered.[9] As described in Figure 5-1, primary appraisal occurs as people evaluate the significance and the meaning of the stressors they are confronting. Here, people first consider whether a demand causes them to feel stressed, and if it does, they consider the implications of the stressor in terms of their personal goals and overall well-being.

As an example of a primary appraisal, consider the job of a cashier at a well-run convenience store. In this store, cashiers engage in routine sales transactions with customers. Customers walk in the store and select merchandise, and the cashier on duty rings up the sale and collects the money. Under normal day-to-day circumstances at this store, a well-trained cashier would not likely feel that these transactions are overly taxing or exceeding his or her capacity, so that cashier would not likely appraise these job demands as stressful. Job demands that tend not to be appraised as stressful are called **benign job demands.**

However, consider how convenience store cashiers would react in a different store in which the cash register and credit card machine break down often and without warning. The cashiers who work at this store would likely view their job as more stressful because they would have to diagnose and fix problems with equipment while dealing with customers who are growing more and more impatient. Furthermore, the cashiers in this store might appraise the stressful situation as one that unnecessarily prevents them from achieving their goal of being viewed as an effective employee in the eyes of the customers and the store manager.

| FIGURE 5-1 | Stressors and Their Appraisal |

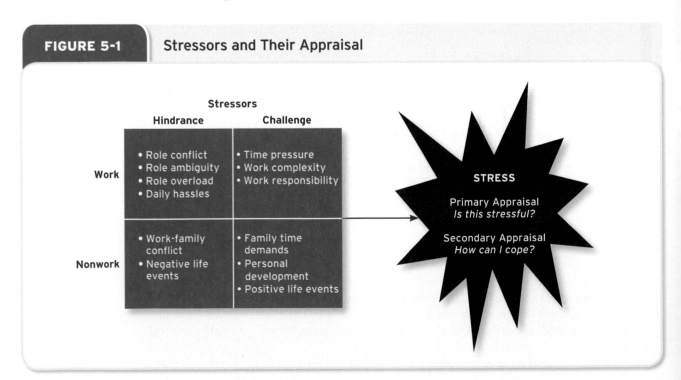

Finally, consider a third convenience store in which the cashier's workload is higher due to additional responsibilities that include receiving merchandise from vendors, taking physical inventory, and training new employees. In this store, the cashiers may appraise their jobs as stressful because of the higher workload and need to balance different priorities. However, in contrast to the cashiers in the previous example, cashiers in this store might appraise these demands as providing an opportunity to learn and demonstrate the type of competence that often is rewarded with satisfying promotions and pay raises.

TYPES OF STRESSORS

In the previous two examples, the cashiers were confronted with demands that a primary appraisal would label as "stressful." However, the specific demands in the two examples have an important difference. Dealing with equipment breakdowns or unhappy customers has little to no benefit to the employee in the long term. These kinds of stressors are called **hindrance stressors**—stressful demands that are perceived as hindering progress toward personal accomplishments or goal attainment.[10] Hindrance stressors tend to trigger negative emotions such as anger and anxiety. In contrast, managing additional responsibilities or higher workloads has a long-term benefit, in that it helps build the employee's skills. These kinds of stressors are called **challenge stressors**—stressful demands that are perceived as opportunities for learning, growth, and achievement. Although challenge stressors can be exhausting, they often trigger positive emotions such as pride and enthusiasm. Figure 5-1 lists a number of hindrance and challenge stressors, some of which are experienced at work and some of which are experienced outside work.[11]

WORK HINDRANCE STRESSORS. One type of work-related hindrance stressor is **role conflict,** which refers to conflicting expectations that other people may have of us. As an example of role conflict that occurs from incompatible demands within a single role that a person may hold, consider the job of a call center operator. People holding these jobs are generally expected to contact as many people as possible over a given time period, which means spending as little time as possible with each person who is contacted. At the same time however, call center operators are also expected to be responsive to the questions and concerns raised by the people they contact. Because effectiveness in this aspect of the job may require a great deal of time, the call center operator is put in a position in which he or she simply cannot meet both types of expectations.

5.2

What are the four main types of work stressors?

Hindrance stressors like irritable customers trigger unhelpful emotions like anger and anxiety.

Role ambiguity refers to the lack of information regarding what needs to be done in a role, as well as unpredictability regarding the consequences of performance in that role.[12] Employees are sometimes asked to work on projects for which they are given very few instructions or guidelines about how things are supposed to be done. In these cases, employees may not know how much money they can spend on the project, how long it's supposed to take, or what exactly the finished product is supposed to look like. Role ambiguity is often experienced among new employees who haven't been around long enough to receive instructions from supervisors or observe and model the role behaviors of more senior colleagues. Students sometimes experience role ambiguity when professors remain vague about particular course requirements or how grading is going to be performed. In such cases, the class becomes stressful because it's not quite clear what it takes to get a good grade.

Role overload occurs when the number of demanding roles a person holds is so high that the person simply cannot perform some or all of the roles very effectively. Role overload as a source of stress is becoming very prevalent for employees in many different industries. For example, the workload for executives and managers who work in investment banking, consulting, and law is so high that 80-hour workweeks are becoming the norm. Although this trend may not be surprising to some of you, people holding these jobs also indicate that they would not be able to complete most of the work that is required of them, even if they worked twice as many hours.[13] If employees actually put in enough time to meet those sorts of role demands, they might forget what life was like outside of their offices or cubicles!

One final type of work-related hindrance stressor, **daily hassles,** reflects the relatively minor day-to-day demands that get in the way of accomplishing the things that we really want to accomplish. Examples of hassles include having to deal with unnecessary paperwork, office equipment malfunctions, conflict with abrasive coworkers, and useless communications. Although these examples of daily hassles may seem relatively minor, taken together, they can be extremely time consuming and stressful. Indeed, according to one survey, 40 percent of executives spend somewhere between a half day and a full day each week on communications that are not useful or necessary.[14] Our **OB at the Bookstore** feature describes a book that focuses on the effects of stressful hassles and what you can do to manage them effectively.

WORK CHALLENGE STRESSORS. One type of work-related challenge stressor is **time pressure**—a strong sense that the amount of time you have to do a task is just not quite enough. Although most people appraise situations with high time pressure as rather stressful, they also tend to appraise these situations as more challenging than hindering. This is because time pressure demands tend to be viewed as something to strive for given that success in meeting such demands can be satisfying. As an example of this positive effect of high time pressure, consider Michael Jones, an architect at a top New York firm. His job involves overseeing multiple projects with tight deadlines, and as a result, he has to work at a hectic pace. Although Jones readily acknowledges that his job is stressful,

"Some of the poor wretches eventually become unable to leave the safety of their cubicles."

OB AT THE BOOKSTORE

DON'T SWEAT THE SMALL STUFF AT WORK
by Richard Carlson (New York: Hyperion, 1998).

. . . if you can learn to treat the smaller hassles with more perspective, wisdom, patience, and with a better sense of humor, you'll begin to bring out the best in yourself as well as others.

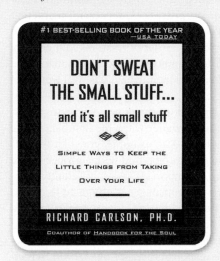

According to Richard Carlson, a stress consultant and bestselling author, we tend to treat the daily hassles we encounter at work as if it were "big stuff," causing us to become overwhelmed and frustrated. With those words, Carlson emphasizes that we can deal with stress better if we recognize that small stuff is inevitable. Frequent interruptions, disappointments, incompetent people, bureaucracy, and so forth will happen most days.

Throughout the book, Carlson draws from behavioral–cognitive techniques to offer specific suggestions about how best to handle the typical hassles of work and life. For example, one chapter focuses on "almost finished syndrome." He notes that having several incomplete tasks hanging over your head can be stressful. He also notes that if you move on to another project when the original one is only 99 percent complete, it often takes as long to complete that last 1 percent as it did to complete the initial 99 percent. To avoid this problem, Carlson offers the very simple suggestion of committing to completing a project before moving on to the next one.

In other chapters, Carlson suggests that people should make allowances for those things they can't control but that are otherwise predictable. He illustrates his point by noting that incompetence is a fact of life—there will always be a certain number of people who will make you wonder how they manage to keep their job. So rather than getting burned out when we have to deal with someone who is incompetent, Carlson suggests that we need to anticipate and plan for this inevitable part of our lives.

Toward the end of the book, Carlson suggests that the majority of our day-to-day stress originates within us. We engage in "thought attacks" by blowing things out of proportion, overanalyzing our lives and exaggerating our problems. He suggests that the hardest part of managing our own stress is admitting that a majority of our stress is self-induced. As an example, he describes a research study someone conducted that interviewed drivers on a busy freeway on-ramp. This study showed that a percentage of the drivers were so incensed by the traffic that they actually yelled and cursed at the interviewer. Other drivers, however, used the time to listen to audiotapes or talk on the phone. Some even said it was their favorite time of day because they could slow down and relax. Carlson suggests that these diverse reactions illustrate that you have a choice in how you respond to circumstances. You can choose to be frustrated, or you can deal with the circumstance in a positive way.

he also believes that the outcome of having all the stress is satisfying. Jones is able to see the product of his labor over the Manhattan skyline, which makes him feel like he is a part of something.[15]

Work complexity refers to the degree to which the requirements of the work, in terms of knowledge, skills, and abilities, tax or exceed the capabilities of the person who is responsible for performing the work. As an example of work complexity, consider the nature of employee development practices that organizations use to train future executives and organizational leaders. In many cases, these practices involve giving people jobs that require skills and knowledge that the people do not yet possess. A successful marketing manager who is being groomed for an executive level position may, for example, be asked to manage a poorly performing production facility with poor labor relations in a country halfway around the world. Although these types of developmental experiences tend to be quite stressful, managers report that being stretched beyond their capacity is well worth the associated discomfort.[16]

Work responsibility refers to the nature of the obligations that a person has to others. Generally speaking, the level of responsibility in a job is higher when the number, scope, and importance of the obligations in that job are higher. As an example, consider the difference in responsibility levels of a grocery store manager compared with a grocery store bagger. Although the bagger is obligated to perform an important task—efficiently placing items in bags so as not to damage the items—the store manager is obligated to ensure that the store is profitable, the customers are satisfied, and the employees are happy and safe. As with people's reactions to time pressure and work complexity, people tend to evaluate demands associated with high responsibility as both stressful and potentially positive. For an example of exceptionally high work responsibility, see our **OB on Screen** feature.

NONWORK HINDRANCE STRESSORS. Although in the United States the majority of people spend more time at the office than anywhere else,[17] there are a number of stressful demands outside of work that have implications for managing behavior in organizations. In essence, stressors experienced outside of work may have effects that "spill over" to affect the employee at work.[18] One example of nonwork hindrance stressors is **work–family conflict,** a special form of role conflict in which the demands of a work role hinder the fulfillment of the demands in a family role (or vice versa). We most often think of cases in which work demands hinder family role performance, termed "work to family conflict." For example, employees who have to deal with lots of hindrances at work may have trouble switching off the frustration after they get home, and as a consequence, they may become irritable and impatient with family and friends. However, work–family conflict can occur in the other direction as well. For example, "family to work conflict" would occur if a salesperson who is experiencing the stress of marital conflict comes to work harboring emotional pain and negative feelings, which makes it difficult to interact with customers effectively.

Nonwork hindrance stressors also come in the form of **negative life events.** Research has revealed that a number of life events are perceived as quite stressful, particularly when they result in significant changes to a person's life.[19] Table 5-2 provides a listing of some commonly experienced life events, along with a score that estimates how stressful each event is perceived to be. As the table reveals, many of the most stressful life events do not occur at work. Rather, they include family events such as the death of a spouse or close family member, a divorce or marital separation, a jail term, or a personal illness. These events would be classified as hindrance stressors because they hinder the ability to achieve life goals and are associated with negative emotions.

OB ON SCREEN

PUSHING TIN

This job can be a little bit STRESS-ful!

With those words, the employees of New York's TRACON Center (Terminal Rader Approach Control) summarize what it means to be an air traffic controller in *Pushing Tin* (Dir. Mike Newell, 20th Century Fox, 1999). The TRACON employees guide 7,000 aircraft a day around the Kennedy, LaGuardia, and Newark airports, the nation's most congested airspace.

From the action depicted in the opening scenes in the movie, you should be able to appreciate that one of the most obvious stressors in the job of an air traffic controller is the high workload. Controllers sit in a darkened room trying to keep track of hundreds of blips and other pieces of information on their radar scopes, all while talking to the pilots of several aircraft. In the opening scene, for example, Nick Falzone (John Cusack) says something along the lines of, "Continental 981, 8 miles from the outer marker, turn left heading 080, maintain 2,000, until intercepting localizer, cleared ILS runway 4 right approach." Although you might be able to bark this command in less than 6 seconds, like Nick did in this scene, consider that air traffic controllers are typically responsible for directing several aircraft at the same time, each moving in different directions at speeds of up to 300 miles per hour.

A second key stressor for air traffic controllers is the responsibility they have for tens of thousands of lives every day. Although controller errors that result in midair collisions are extremely rare, the possibility weighs heavily on the minds of controllers, especially after they lose "the picture" (controller speak for the mental representation of an assigned airspace and all the aircraft within it) because of extreme workload, loss of concentration, or equipment malfunctions. As an example, a scene in the movie depicts the facility manager giving a tour to several elementary school children. He tells them, "Did you youngsters know that an air traffic controller is responsible for more lives in a single shift than a surgeon is in his entire life?" A young boy responds by saying, "It looks like a computer game"—to which the manager responds, "This is no game young man, I'll tell you that. If you make a mistake here, there's no reset button."

(Continued)

In fact, it is not unusual for air traffic controllers to experience emotional and physical strains because of the on-the-job stress they face. As one of the kids stated during the tour, "I hear that air traffic controllers have the highest rates of clinical depression, nervous breakdowns, heart attacks, and alcoholism of any profession." With statements like that, you'd probably guess that the TRACON employees view student tour groups as a hindrance stressor.

NONWORK CHALLENGE STRESSORS. Of course, the nonwork domain can be a source of challenge stressors as well. **Family time demands** reflect the time that a person commits to participate in an array of family activities and responsibilities. Specific examples of family time demands include time spent involved in family pursuits such as traveling, attending social events and organized activities, hosting parties, and planning and making home improvements. Examples of **personal development** activities include participation in formal education programs, music lessons, sports-related training, hobby-related self-education, participation in local government, or volunteer work. Finally, Table 5-2 includes some **positive life events** that are sources of nonwork challenge stressors. For example, marriage, pregnancy, the addition of a new family member, and ending school are all stressful in their own way. However, each is associated with some positive, rather than negative, emotions.

TABLE 5-2		Stressful Life Events	
LIFE EVENT	**STRESS SCORE**	**LIFE EVENT**	**STRESS SCORE**
Death of a spouse	100	Trouble with in-laws	29
Divorce	73	Outstanding achievement	28
Marital separation	65	Begin or end school	26
Jail term	63	Change in living conditions	25
Death of close family member	63	Trouble with boss	23
Personal illness	53	Change in work hours	20
Marriage	50	Change in residence	20
Fired at work	47	Change in schools	20
Marital reconciliation	45	Change in social activities	18
Retirement	45	Change in sleeping habits	16
Pregnancy	40	Change in family get-togethers	15
Gain of new family member	39	Change in eating habits	15
Death of close friend	37	Vacations	13
Change in occupation	36	The holiday season	12
Child leaving home	29	Minor violations of the law	11

Source: Adapted from T.H. Holmes and R.H. Rahe, "The Social Re-Adjustment Rating Scale," *Journal of Psychosomatic Research* 11 (1967), pp. 213–18.

HOW DO PEOPLE COPE WITH STRESSORS?

After people appraise a stressful demand, they ask themselves, "What *should* I do" and "What *can* I do" to deal with this situation? These questions, which reflect the **secondary appraisal** shown in Figure 5-1, center on the issue of how people cope with the various stressors that they face.[20] **Coping** refers to the behaviors and thoughts that people use to manage both the stressful demands that they face and the emotions associated with those stressful demands.[21] As Table 5-3 illustrates, coping can involve many different types of activities, and these activities can be grouped into four broad categories based on two dimensions.[22] The first dimension refers to the method of coping (behavioral versus cognitive), and the second dimension refers to the focus of coping (problem solving versus regulation of emotions).

The first part of our coping definition highlights the idea that methods of coping can be categorized on the basis of whether they involve behaviors or cognitions. **Behavioral coping** involves the set of physical activities that are used to deal with a stressful situation. In one example of behavioral coping, a person who is confronted with a lot of time pressure at work might chose to cope by working faster. In another example of behavioral coping, an employee who has several daily hassles might cope by avoiding work—coming in late, leaving early, or even staying home. As a final example of behavioral coping, employees often cope with the stress of an international assignment by returning home from the assignment prematurely. As our **OB Internationally** feature illustrates, international assignments are becoming increasingly prevalent, and the costs of these early returns to organizations can be extraordinary.

In contrast to behavioral coping, **cognitive coping** refers to the thoughts that are involved in trying to deal with a stressful situation. For example, the person who is confronted with an increase in time pressure might cope by thinking about different ways of accomplishing the work more efficiently. As another example of cognitive coping, the employee who is confronted with daily hassles might try to convince him- or herself that the hassles are not that bad after all.

Whereas the first part of our coping definition refers to the method of coping, the second part refers to the focus of coping—that is, does the coping attempt to address the stressful demand or the emotions triggered by the demand?[27] **Problem-focused coping** refers to behaviors and cognitions intended to manage the stressful situation itself. To understand problem-focused coping, consider how the people in the previous two paragraphs coped

5.3

How do individual employees cope with stress?

TABLE 5-3	Examples of Coping Strategies	
	PROBLEM-FOCUSED	**EMOTION-FOCUSED**
Behavioral Methods	Working harder Seeking assistance Acquiring additional resources	Engaging in alternative activities Seeking support Venting anger
Cognitive Methods	Strategizing Self-motivation Changing priorities	Avoiding, distancing, and ignoring Looking for the positive in the negative Reappraising

Source: Adapted from J.C. Latack and S.J. Havlovic, "Coping with Job Stress: A Conceptual Evaluation Framework for Coping Measures," *Journal of Organizational Behavior* 13 (1992), pp. 479–508.

OB INTERNATIONALLY

Due to the trend of increased globalization of business organizations, the number of employees who are sent abroad to work for their organization has increased recently. In one recent survey of global relocation data and trends, for example, 47 percent of the companies reported an increase in the number of expatriate assignments over the previous year, and 54 percent projected increases in these assignments in the following year. This survey also indicated that more than half of all employees sent abroad expected their assignment to last between one and three years.[23]

Unfortunately, a significant number of those expatriate assignments do not succeed because the employee returns home earlier than planned. In fact, up to 40 percent of all American expatriates return home early, and it has been estimated that each early return costs the host organization approximately $100,000.[24] A second important way that international assignments fail is that expatriates often fail to perform their roles effectively. Given that expatriate assignments are both extremely expensive and crucially important to the success of many businesses today, there has been a strong interest in identifying factors that influence expatriate success, in terms of both early returns and role effectiveness.

One of the key drivers of expatriate effectiveness is how they handle the overwhelming stress of being abroad.[25] Expatriates who experience more stress as a result of cultural, interpersonal, or job factors tend to be less satisfied with their job, more likely to think about leaving the assignment early, and more likely to perform at subpar levels. In light of such findings, organizations should consider implementing practices targeted directly at managing expatriate stress levels. One practice that could prove useful is cross-cultural training, which focuses on helping people appreciate cultural differences and interact more comfortably with the host country nationals. Although cross-cultural training seems like a good stress management practice, it isn't offered as frequently as you might think.[26] Surveys suggest that many U.S. companies offer no formal cross-cultural training at all. Even when training is offered, it tends to focus more on language acquisition than on cultural understanding and interaction skills. In addition, training tends to occur only on a pre-departure basis, with little follow-up once the employee is abroad. It seems clear that organizations should emphasize this particular stress-management program to a greater degree if they wish to improve the success of their expatriates.

with time pressure. In the first example, the person attempted to address the time pressure by working harder, whereas in the second example, the person focused on how to accomplish the work more efficiently. Although the specific coping methods differed, both of these people reacted to the time pressure similarly, in that they focused their effort on meeting the demand rather than trying to avoid it.

In contrast to problem-focused coping, **emotion-focused coping** refers to the various ways in which people manage their own emotional reactions to stressful demands. The reactions to the daily hassles that we described previously illustrated two types of emotion-focused coping. In the first example, the employee used avoidance and distancing behaviors to reduce the emotional distress caused by the stressful situation. In the second example, the employee reappraised the demand to make it seem less stressful and threatening. Although people may be successful at changing the way different situations are construed to avoid feeling unpleasant emotions, the demand or problem that initially triggered the appraisal process remains.

It might be obvious to you by now that the choice of a coping strategy has important implications for how effectively people can meet or adapt to the different stressors that they face. In the work context, for example, a manager would most likely want subordinates to cope with the stress of a heavy workload by using a problem-focused strategy—working harder—rather than an emotion-focused strategy—drinking two saki bombs at lunch to create distance from the stressor. Of course, there are some situations in which emotion-focused coping may be functional for the person. As an example, consider a person who repeatedly fails to make it through the auditions for *American Idol,* despite years of voice lessons and countless hours of practice. At some point, if this person did not have the capability to cope emotionally—perhaps by lowering her aspirations, or at least ignoring Simon Cowell's sarcastic barbs—this person's self-concept could be damaged, which could translate into reduced effectiveness in other roles that she fills.

What coping strategy do you use to keep track of all your assignments, exams, and deadlines for your classes?

How do people choose a particular coping strategy? One factor that influences this choice is the set of beliefs that people have about how well different coping strategies can address different demands. In essence, people are likely to choose the coping strategy that they believe has the highest likelihood of meeting the demand that they face. For example, a student may come to understand that the likelihood of effectively coping with a demanding final exam is higher if she studies hard rather than trying to escape from the situation by going out until 3:00 a.m. The choice also depends on the degree to which a person believes that he or she has what it takes to execute the coping strategy effectively. Returning to the previous example, if the student had already failed the first two exams in the course, despite trying hard, she may come to believe that a problem-focused coping strategy will not work. In this situation, because the student may feel helpless to address the demand directly, an emotion-focused coping strategy would be most likely.

One critical factor that determines coping strategy choice is the degree to which people believe that a particular strategy gives them some degree of control over the stressor or how they feel about it. If a person believes that a demand can be addressed with a problem-focused coping strategy, and the person also has confidence that he can use that problem-focused strategy effectively, then he will feel some control over the situation and likely use a problem-focused strategy. If a person believes that a demand cannot be addressed with a problem-focused strategy or does not believe she can effectively enact that strategy, then she likely will feel a lack of control over the situation and tend to use an emotion-focused coping strategy to decrease emotional discomfort.

So what determines how people develop a sense of control? It appears that one important factor is the nature of the stressful demand itself. In particular, people are likely to feel less control over a stressor when they appraise it as a hindrance rather than a challenge. Consider one of the life events in Table 5-2: "Trouble with boss." This event would be categorized as a hindrance stressor because it hinders goal achievement and triggers negative emotions. If you're like most people, you would want to change the behavior of your boss so that the trouble would stop and you could go on with your work. However, it's also likely that you would feel like you have little control over this situation because bosses are in a position of power and complaining to your boss's boss might not be an option for you. The anxiety and hopelessness triggered by the situation would further erode any sense of control over the situation, likely leading to emotion-focused coping.[28]

THE EXPERIENCE OF STRAIN

Earlier in this chapter, we defined strains as the negative consequences associated with stress. How exactly does stress cause strain? Consider the case of Naomi Henderson, the CEO of RIVA, a small market-research firm in Rockville, Maryland. The job of CEO is quite demanding, and Henderson found herself working 120 hours a week to cope with the heavy workload. One night she woke up to go to the bathroom and found that she literally could not move—she was paralyzed. After being rushed to the emergency room, Henderson, along with her husband, was told by the doctor that the diagnosis was stress. The doctor recommended rest in bed for 14 hours a day for six weeks.[29] Although this example may seem extreme to you, the demands of many managerial and executive level jobs are often excessive,[30] and the negative health consequences that result are fairly predictable. In fact, if you've ever been in a situation in which you've experienced heavy stress for more than a couple of days, you can probably appreciate the toll that stress can take on you. Although people react to stress differently, you may have felt unusually exhausted, irritable, and achy. What might be surprising to you is that the mechanism within your body that gives you the ability to function effectively in the face of stressful demands is the same mechanism that ends up causing you these problems. So what is this mechanism?

Medical researchers who study stress have spent years examining the body's response to different sorts of stressful demands.[31] Many of these findings have been summarized in a theory called the **general adaptation syndrome (GAS),** which is illustrated in Figure 5-2.[32] In a nutshell, GAS suggests that the body has a set of responses that allow it to adapt and function effectively in the face of stressful demands. However, when stressful demands do not ramp down or the demands occur too frequently, the body's adaptive responses become toxic. To better understand GAS, let's consider what occurs after a person is confronted with a stressful demand.

The first stage of the GAS is the alarm reaction. Upon being confronted with a stressor, there is a relatively brief period of time in which resistance to the stressor is temporarily lowered. At this point the body and mind haven't reacted yet—in essence, the stressor simply "sinks in." Immediately thereafter, the body activates several defense mechanisms to resist and counteract the stressor. At this point in the alarm reaction stage, the body (actually, the adrenal medulla and the postganglionic fibers of the sympathetic nervous system, for any future doctors in the class) begins to secrete chemical compounds (catecholamines

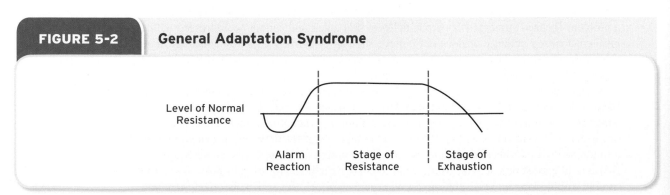

FIGURE 5-2   **General Adaptation Syndrome**

Source: Adapted from H. Seyle, *The Stress of Life*, revised ed. (New York: McGraw Hill, 1976), p. 111.

such as adrenaline, noradrenaline, and dopamine—don't worry, these aren't in the "Key Terms" section) that circulate in the blood.[33] These chemical compounds cause increases in heart rate and blood pressure, and blood is redirected away from organs such as the spleen to the brain and skeletal muscles.

The changes that occur in the alarm stage prepare the mind and body for "fight or flight."[34] After this point, the person is in the second stage of the GAS, the stage of resistance. Here, the increased arousal of his or her mind and body caused by the secretion of chemicals helps the person respond and adapt to the demand. Unfortunately, if the chemicals in the blood remain elevated because of prolonged or repeated exposure to the stressor, the body begins to break down, and exhaustion and even death may occur. This last stage is the stage of exhaustion. Although the GAS might sound like a theory that describes reactions to extreme types of stressors—being chased through a jungle by a hungry tiger, for example—research suggests that most types of stressors evoke the same sequence of physiological events. Therefore, negative consequences to the body occur even with the more mundane stressors that most of us face in our lives. As shown in Figure 5-3, those negative consequences come in three varieties: physiological strains, psychological strains, and behavioral strains.[35]

Physiological strains that result from stressors occur in at least four systems of the human body. First, stressors can reduce the effectiveness of the body's immune system, which makes it more difficult for the body to ward off illness and infection. Have you ever noticed that you're more likely to catch a cold during or immediately after final exam week? Second, stressors can harm the body's cardiovascular system, cause the heart to race, increase blood pressure, and create coronary artery disease. Third, stressors can cause problems in the body's musculoskeletal system. Tension headaches, tight shoulders, and back pain have all been linked to a variety of stressors. Fourth, stressors cause gastrointestinal system problems. Symptoms of this type of strain include stomachaches, indigestion, diarrhea, and constipation.[36]

Although you might be tempted to dismiss the importance of physiological strains because the base rate for serious illness and disease is low for people in their 20s and 30s, research shows that dismissal may be a mistake. For example, high-pressure work deadlines increase the chance of heart attack within the next 24 hours by a factor of six.[37] So, even though the likelihood of suffering a heart attack may be low for the young, who would want to increase their risk by 600 percent? Perhaps more important, the negative physiological effects of stress persist over time and may not become manifest until far into the future. One study showed that eye problems, allergic complaints, and chronic diseases could be attributed to stress measured eight years earlier.[38]

Psychological strains that result from stressors include depression, anxiety, anger, hostility, reduced self-confidence, irritability, inability to think clearly, forgetfulness, lack of creativity, memory loss, and (not surprising, given the rest of this list) a loss of sense of humor.[39] Although these strains are less obviously connected to GAS than the physical strains that we described in the previous paragraph, each is likely to be a symptom of **burnout.** The concept of burnout has been studied extensively by researchers, though there is not yet a complete consensus on its definition. We define it here as the emotional, mental, and physical exhaustion that results from having to cope with stressful demands on an ongoing basis.[40]

Relative to physiological and psychological strains, **behavioral strains** are the least connected to GAS. In fact, unhealthy behaviors such as grinding one's teeth at night, being overly critical and bossy, excessive smoking, compulsive gum chewing, overuse of alcohol, and compulsive eating[41] can be thought of as the behavioral symptoms of the other types of strains.

FIGURE 5-3   **Examples of Strain**

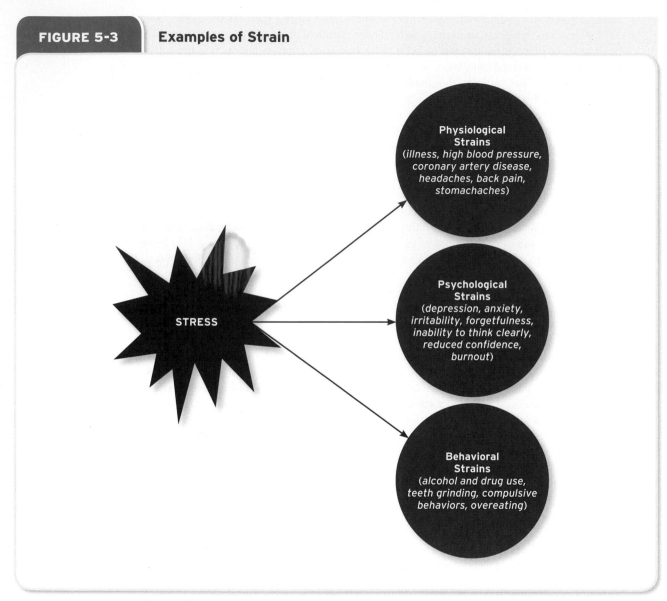

Source: M.E. Burke, "2005 Benefits Survey Report," *Society of Human Resource Management.* Reprinted with permission.

ACCOUNTING FOR INDIVIDUALS IN THE STRESS PROCESS

So far in this chapter, we've discussed how the typical or average person reacts to different sorts of stressors. Of course, people differ in terms of how they typically react to stressful demands. One way that people differ in their reaction to stress depends on whether they exhibit the **Type A Behavior Pattern.** "Type A" people have a strong sense of time urgency and tend to be impatient, hard-driving, competitive, controlling, aggressive, and even hostile[42] If you walk, talk, and eat at a quick pace, and if you find yourself constantly annoyed with people who do things too slowly, chances are that you're a Type A person. With that said, one way to tell for sure is to fill out the Type A questionnaire in our **OB Assessments** feature.

5.4

How do the Type A Behavior Pattern and social support influence the stress process?

OB ASSESSMENTS

TYPE A BEHAVIOR PATTERN

Do you think that you are especially sensitive to stress? This assessment is designed to measure the extent to which you're a Type A person—someone who typically engages in hard-driving, competitive, and aggressive behavior. Answer each question using the response scale provided. Then subtract your answers to the bold-faced questions from 8, with the difference being your new answers for those questions. For example, if your original answer for Question 3 was "2", your new answer is "6" (8 − 2). Then sum your answers for the twelve questions.

1	2	3	4	5	6	7
STRONGLY DISAGREE	DISAGREE	SLIGHTLY DISAGREE	NEUTRAL	SLIGHTLY AGREE	AGREE	STRONGLY AGREE

1. Having work to complete "stirs me into action" more than other people. _____

2. When a person is talking and takes too long to come to the point, I frequently feel like hurrying the person along. _____

3. **Nowadays, I consider myself to be relaxed and easygoing.** _____

4. Typically, I get irritated extremely easily. _____

5. My best friends would rate my general activity level as very high. _____

6. I definitely tend to do most things in a hurry. _____

7. I take my work much more seriously than most. _____

8. **I seldom get angry.** _____

9. I often set deadlines for myself work-wise. _____

10. I feel very impatient when I have to wait in line. _____

11. I put much more effort into my work than other people do. _____

12. **Compared with others, I approach life much less seriously.** _____

SCORING

If your scores sum up to 53 or above, you would be considered a Type A person, which means that you may perceive higher stress levels in your life and be more sensitive to that stress. If your scores sum up to 52 or below, you would be considered a Type B person. This means that you sense less stress in your life and are less sensitive to the stress that is experienced.

Source: C. D. Jenkins, S. J. Zyzanski, and R. H. Rosenman. "Progress Toward Validation of a Computer Scored Test for the Type A Coronary Prone Behavior Pattern," *Psychosomatic Medicine,* 33, 193, 202 (1971). Reprinted with permission of Lippincott, Williams & Wilkins.

In the context of this chapter, the Type A Behavior Pattern is important because it can influence each variable in our general model of stress. First, the Type A Behavior Pattern may have a direct influence on the level of stressors that a person confronts. To understand why this connection might be true, consider that Type A persons tend to be hard-driving and have a strong desire to achieve. Because the behaviors that reflect these tendencies are valued by the organization, Type A individuals receive "rewards" in the form of increases in the amount and level of work required. In addition, because Type A people tend to be aggressive and competitive, they may be more prone to interpersonal conflict. We're sure that most of you would agree that conflict with peers and coworkers is an important stressor.

Second, in addition to the effect on stressors, the Type A Behavior Pattern is important because it influences the stress process itself.[43] This effect of the Type A Behavior Pattern is easy to understand if you consider that hard-driving competitiveness makes people hypersensitive to demands that could potentially affect their progress toward their goal attainment. In essence, Type A individuals are simply more likely to appraise demands as being stressful rather than being benign.

Third, and perhaps most important, the Type A Behavior Pattern has been directly linked to coronary heart disease[44] and other physiological, psychological, and behavioral strains.[45] The size of the relationship between the Type A Behavior Pattern and these strains is not so strong as to suggest that if you're a Type A person, you should immediately call 911. However, the linkage is strong enough to suggest that the risk of these problems is significantly higher for people who typically engage in Type A behaviors.

Another individual factor that affects the way people manage stress is the degree of **social support** that they receive. Social support refers to the help that people receive when they are confronted with stressful demands, and there are at least two major types.[46] One type of social support is called **instrumental support,** which refers to the help people receive that can be used to address the stressful demand directly. For example, if a person is overloaded with work, a coworker could provide instrumental support by taking over some of the work or offering suggestions about how to do the work more efficiently. A second type of social support is called **emotional support.** This type of support refers to the help people receive in addressing the emotional distress that accompanies stressful demands. As an example, the supervisor of the individual who is overloaded with work might provide emotional support by showing interest in the employee's situation and appearing to be understanding and empathetic. As alluded to in these examples, social support may come

Social support from friends, coworkers, and family can be a big help in managing stress, even though it usually occurs outside the stress-causing environment.

from coworkers as well as from supervisors. However, social support also may be provided by family members and friends outside the context of the stressful demand.[47]

Similar to the Type A Behavior Pattern, social support has the potential to influence the stress process in several different ways. However, most research on social support focuses on the ways that social support buffers the relationship between stressors and strains. According to this research, high levels of social support provide a person with instrumental or emotional resources that are useful for coping with the stressor, which tends to reduce the harmful consequences of the stressor to that individual. With low levels of social support, the person does not have extra coping resources available, so the stressor tends to have effects that are more harmful. In essence, this perspective casts social support as a moderator of the relationship between stressors and strains (moderators are variables that affect the strength of the relationship between two other variables). In this particular case, the relationship between stress and strain tends to be weaker at higher levels of social support and stronger at lower levels of social support. Although not every research study has found support for the buffering effect of social support,[48] the majority of research evidence has been supportive.[49]

SUMMARY: WHY ARE SOME EMPLOYEES MORE "STRESSED" THAN OTHERS?

So what explains why some employees are more stressed than others? As shown in Figure 5-4, answering that question requires paying attention to the particular stressors

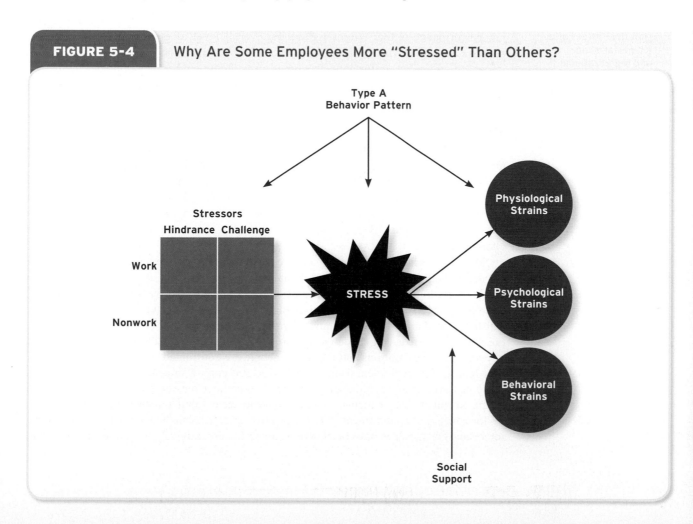

FIGURE 5-4   Why Are Some Employees More "Stressed" Than Others?

the employee is experiencing, including hindrance and challenge stressors originating in both the work and nonwork domains. However, it also depends on how those stressors are appraised and coped with, which determines whether physiological, psychological, and behavioral strains are experienced. Finally, answering the question depends on whether the employee is "Type A" or "Type B" and whether the employee has a high or low amount of social support. Understanding all of these factors can help explain why some people can shoulder stressful circumstances for weeks at a time, whereas others seem to be "at the end of their rope" when faced with even relatively minor job demands.

HOW IMPORTANT IS STRESS?

In the previous sections, we described how stressors and the stress process influence strains and, ultimately, people's health and well-being. Although these effects are important, you're probably curious about the impact that strains have on job performance and organizational commitment, the two outcomes in our integrative model of OB. Figure 5-5 summarizes the research evidence linking strains to job performance and organizational commitment.

5.5

How does stress affect job performance and organizational commitment?

Figure 5-5 reveals that strains have a moderately negative effect on job performance.[50] A general explanation for this negative relationship between strains and job performance is that strains reduce the overall level of energy and attention that people could otherwise bring to their job duties.[51] In fact, the reason for the negative impact of strains on performance becomes quite obvious when you consider the nature of the individual strains that we mentioned in the previous section. Certainly, you would agree that physiological, psychological, and behavioral strains in the form of illnesses, exhaustion, and drunkenness would detract from employee effectiveness in almost any job context.

Figure 5-5 also reveals that strains have a strong negative effect on organizational commitment.[52] Why might this be? Well, strains are generally dissatisfying to people, and as we discussed in the previous chapter, satisfaction has a strong impact on the degree to which people feel committed to their organization.[53] People who work at jobs that they know are causing them to feel constantly sick and exhausted will likely be dissatisfied with their jobs and feel less desire to stay with the organization and more desire to consider alternatives.

So in this discussion and Figure 5-5, we portray stress as something that has a negative impact on both job performance and organizational commitment. But this is not quite the whole story. In fact, though all types of stressors are positively associated with strains, certain types of stressors have positive relationships with performance and commitment. But how can that be? To understand why this complexity might be true, recall from our previous discussions that challenge stressors such as time pressure and responsibility tend to evoke positive emotions and that when people are confronted with challenge stressors, they tend to deal with them using problem-focused coping strategies. The net benefits of those positive emotions and coping strategies sometimes outweigh the costs of the added strain, meaning that challenge stressors tend to have small positive relationships with performance and commitment.[54] These positive effects of challenge stressors on several important job variables have been demonstrated for executives,[55] as well as employees in

FIGURE 5-5 Effects of Strains on Performance and Commitment

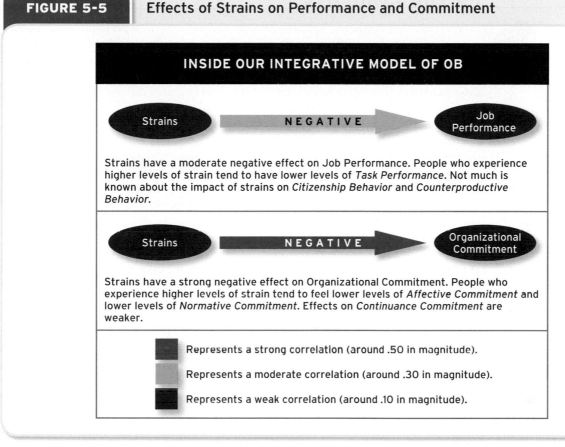

Sources: J.A. LePine, N.P. Podsakoff, and M.A. LePine, "A Meta-Analytic Test of the Challenge Stressor–Hindrance Stressor Framework: An Explanation for Inconsistent Relationships Among Stressors and Performance," *Academy of Management Journal* 48 (2005), pp. 764–75; N.P. Podsakoff, J.A. LePine, and M.A. LePine, "Differential Challenge Stressor–Hindrance Stressor Relationships with Job Attitudes, Turnover Intentions, Turnover, and Withdrawal Behavior: A Meta-Analysis," *Journal of Applied Psychology* 92 (2007). pp. 438–454.

lower-level jobs,[56] and as our **OB for Students** feature illustrates, the positive effect of challenge stressors applies to students as well.[57]

APPLICATION: STRESS MANAGEMENT

Previously, we described how employee stress results in strains that cost organizations in terms of reduced employee performance and commitment. However, there are other important costs to consider that relate to employee health. Most organizations provide some sort of health care benefits for their employees,[59] and all but the smallest organizations pay worker's compensation insurance, the rates for which are determined, in part, by the nature of the job and the organization's history of work-related injuries and illnesses. So what role does stress play in these costs?

OB FOR STUDENTS

You might be wondering how the concepts and theories of stress apply in the context of your role as a student. Well, one recent study found that students face a number of hindrance stressors and challenge stressors in an academic context. Although the presence of different sorts of stressors might not surprise you, these researchers also found that these two types of stressors significantly affected the grades of the students but in different directions.[58]

Hindrance stressors included demands such as the amount of time spent on busywork for your classes, the degree to which favoritism affects final grades in your classes, and the amount of hassles you need to go through to get projects/assignments done. Challenge stressors included demands such as the difficulty of the work required in your classes, the volume of coursework that must be completed in your classes, and the time pressures experienced for completing work required in your classes. So how did these two types of stressors affect students' grades?

On the one hand, students who experienced higher levels of hindrance stressors tended to have lower grades. One reason is that coping with hindrance stressors was exhausting, and feeling this way made it more difficult to put forth the energy to study. A second reason is that hindrance stressors decreased students' motivation to learn. Students who faced a lot of hindrance stressors apparently did not believe that studying hard would result in good grades, and accordingly, they did not put forth the necessary effort.

On the other hand, students who experienced higher levels of challenge stressors tended to have higher grades. The authors' explanation for this effect was that challenge stressors motivated students to invest more effort in their learning. Although students felt that coping with challenge stressors was exhausting, the positive force of motivation was significantly more powerful. In essence, challenge stressors motivated students to work hard in spite of feeling extremely tired. So what can you do with this information?

One option might be to try and change the situation by taking action to decrease the level of hindrance stressors you experience. Although this approach might be possible with some hindrances—asking professors to provide clarifying instruction for example—the approach may be more difficult with others—such as asking the professor to reduce the amount of busywork. A second option would be to try to think of hindrances as challenges. Although it might be difficult to convince yourself that coping with hindrances such as busywork and favoritism is beneficial to your growth and learning, the research findings suggest that the effort might be worthwhile.

Well, it turns out that these health-related costs are driven to a great extent by employee stress. Estimates are that between 60 percent and 90 percent of all doctor visits can be attributed to stress-related causes,[60] and the cost of providing health care to people who experience high levels of stress appears to be approximately 50 percent higher than that for those who experience lower levels of stress.[61] Statistics from jobs in different industries indicate that the frequency of worker's compensation claims is dramatically higher when the level of stress on the job is high. As one example, the frequency of claims was more than 800 percent higher for a copy machine distributor when the level of stress at the job site was high.[62] So what do all these costs mean to you as a student of organizational behavior or as a manager?

For one thing, the relationship between stress and health care costs means that there may be huge dividends for organizations that learn how to manage stress more effectively.

As the opening of this chapter illustrated, companies such as Capital One recognize the potential for a positive return on their investment in practices aimed at reducing employee stress. In fact, surveys indicate that the vast majority of companies in the United States provide benefits, in one form or another, that are intended to help employees cope with stressful demands and reduce the associated strains.[63] Next, we describe some approaches that organizations use to manage employee stress.

 5.6

What steps can organizations take to manage employee stress?

ASSESSMENT

The first step in managing stress is to assess the level and sources of stress in the workplace. Although there are many ways to accomplish this type of evaluation, often referred to as a **stress audit**, managers can begin by asking themselves questions about the nature of the jobs in their organization to estimate whether high stress levels may be a problem.[64] The first category of questions might involve the degree to which the organization is going through change that would likely increase uncertainty among employees. As an example, a merger between two companies might increase employees' uncertainty about their job security and possible career paths. As another example, employees in an organization that has transitioned to team-based work might be concerned about how their individual performance contributions will be recognized and rewarded. A second category of questions might center on the work itself. These questions typically focus on the level and types of stressors experienced by the employees. The third category of questions could involve the quality of relationships between not only employees but also employees and the organization. Here, an important question to consider is whether organizational politics play a large role in administrative decisions.

REDUCING STRESSORS

Once a stress audit reveals that stress may be a problem, the next step is to consider alternative courses of action. One general course of action involves managing stressors, which may be accomplished in one of two ways. First, organizations could try to eliminate or significantly reduce stressful demands. As an example of this approach, 19 percent of organizations in one recent survey used **job sharing** to reduce role overload and foster work–life balance.[65] Job sharing does not mean splitting one job into two but rather indicates that two people share the responsibilities of a single job, as if the two people were a single performing unit. The assumption underlying the practice is that "although businesses are becoming 24/7, people don't."[66]

You might be tempted to believe that job sharing would be most appropriate in lower-level jobs, where responsibilities and tasks are limited in number and relatively easy to divide. In actuality, job sharing is being used even at the highest levels in organizations. At Boston-based Fleet Bank, for example, two women shared the position of vice president for global markets and foreign exchange for six years until their department was dissolved when Fleet was acquired by Bank of America. During this time, they had one desk, one chair, one computer, one telephone, one voicemail account, one set of goals, and one performance review. They each worked 20–25 hours a week and performed the role effectively and seamlessly.[67]

PROVIDING RESOURCES

Although reducing stressors may reduce the overall level of stress that a person experiences, this approach is likely to be most beneficial when the focus of the effort is on hindrance stressors rather than challenge stressors.[68] Hindrance stressors such as role ambiguity, conflict, and politics not only cause strains but also decrease commitment and job performance. In contrast, though challenge stressors such as time pressure and responsibility cause strains, they also tend to be motivating and satisfying, and as a consequence, they generally are positively related to commitment and performance.

So as a supplement to reducing stressors, organizations can provide resources that help employees cope with stressful demands.[69] One way that organizations provide resources to employees is through **training interventions** aimed at increasing job-related competencies and skills. Employees who possess more competencies and skills can handle more demands rather than appraise the demands as overly taxing or exceeding their capacity. Training that increases employee competencies and skills is also beneficial to the extent that it promotes a sense that the demands are more controllable, and as we discussed in a previous section, a sense of control promotes problem-focused coping strategies.

A second way that organizations provide resources to employees so that they can cope more effectively is though **supportive practices** that help employees manage and balance the demands that exist in the different roles they have. Although we only have room in this chapter to describe a few of these practices, Table 5-4 lists many examples, as well as the percentage of organizations that were found to use them in a recent survey of almost 400 organizations.[70]

The first supportive practice example is flextime, which was used by 56 percent of the organizations in the survey. Organizations that use flextime give employees some

TABLE 5-4	Examples of Supportive Practices Used by Organizations			
PRACTICE	**% OF 370 ORGANIZATIONS**	**% OF SMALL ORGANIZATIONS**	**% OF MEDIUM ORGANIZATIONS**	**% OF LARGE ORGANIZATIONS**
Flextime	56%	57%	56%	56%
Part-time telecommuting	37	36	33	43
Compressed workweek	33	27	30	41
Bring child to work if needed	27	43	25	18
Full-time telecommuting	19	14	18	24
Lactation program	19	8	20	28
On-site child care	6	1	3	13
Company supported child care center	4	0	1	11

Source: M.E. Burke, *2005 Benefits Survey Report* (Alexandria, VA: Society of Human Resource Management Research Department, 2005). Reprinted with permission.

degree of latitude in terms of which hours they need to be present at the workplace. Flexible working hours give employees the ability to cope with demands away from work, so they don't have to worry about these demands while they're at work. As another example of a supportive practice, 37 percent of the organizations in the survey allowed telecommuting on a part-time basis. By providing the opportunity to work at home or some other location with computer access, employees are put in a better position to cope with demands that might be impossible to cope with otherwise. As a final supportive practice example, approximately one-third of all companies in the survey allowed for compressed workweeks, in which full-time employees work additional hours on some days and have shorter days or time off on other days. As with flextime and telecommuting, compressed workweeks give employees the ability to manage both work and nonwork role demands. We should also note that practices such as flextime, telecommuting, and compressed workweeks not only facilitate stress management but also appear to have other benefits. At companies such as Xerox, Corning, and United Parcel Services, implementing these types of practices resulted in improvements in productivity, innovation, absenteeism, and turnover.[71]

REDUCING STRAINS

As an alternative to managing stressors, many organizations use practices that reduce strains.[72] One type of strain-reducing practice involves **relaxation techniques,** such as progressive muscle relaxation, meditation, and miscellaneous calming activities like taking walks, writing in a journal, and deep breathing.[73] Although these relaxation techniques differ, the basic idea is the same—they teach people how to counteract the effects of stressors by engaging in activities that slow the heart rate, breathing rate, and blood pressure.[74] As an example of a relatively simple relaxation technique, consider the recommendation of Herbert Benson, a physician and president of the Mind/Body Medical Institute in Boston. He suggests that people under stress should repeat a word, sound, prayer, phrase, or motion for 10–20 minutes once or twice a day and, during that time, try to completely ignore other thoughts that may come to mind.[75] As another example, recall the case of Naomi Henderson, the market research firm CEO who literally became paralyzed by all the stress in her job. Well, we're happy to say that Henderson got better, but she was able to do so only after being treated by a physician who helped her learn how to reduce her own strains by doing "mental aerobics." Those exercises involved taking breaks every hour to stretch and do deep breathing, taking short naps to replenish energy, and learning how to say no politely to unreasonable demands.[76]

A second general category of strain-reducing practices involves **cognitive–behavioral techniques.** In general, these techniques attempt to help people appraise and cope with stressors in a more rational manner.[77] To understand what these techniques involve, think of someone you know who not only exaggerates the level and importance of stressful demands but also predicts doom and disaster after quickly concluding that the demands simply cannot be met. If you know someone like this, you might recommend cognitive–behavioral training that involves "self-talk," a technique in which people learn to say things about stressful demands that reflect rationality and optimism. So, when confronted with a stressful demand, this person might be trained to say, "This demand isn't so tough; if I work hard I can accomplish it." In addition, cognitive–behavioral training typically involves instruction about tools that foster effective coping. So, in addition to the self-talk, the person might be trained on how to prioritize demands, manage time, communicate needs, and seek support.[78]

A third category of strain-reducing practices involves **health and wellness programs.** For example, almost three-quarters of the organizations in one survey reported having employee assistance programs intended to help people with personal problems such as alcoholism and other addictions. More than 60 percent of organizations in this survey provided employees with wellness programs and resources. The nature of these programs and resources vary a great deal from organization to organization, but in general, they are comprehensive efforts that include health screening (blood pressure, cholesterol levels, pulmonary functioning) and health-related courses and information. Other examples of health and wellness programs intended to reduce strain include smoking cessation programs, on-site fitness centers or fitness center memberships, and weight loss and nutrition programs.[79]

TAKEAWAYS

5.1   Stress refers to the psychological response to demands when there is something at stake for the individual and coping with these demands would tax or exceed the individual's capacity or resources. Stressors are the demands that cause the stress response, and strains are the negative consequences of the stress response.

5.2   Stressors come in two general forms: challenge stressors, which are perceived as opportunities for growth and achievement, and hindrance stressors, which are perceived as hurdles to goal achievement. These two stressors can be found in both work and nonwork domains.

5.3   Coping with stress involves thoughts and behaviors that address one of two goals: addressing the stressful demand or decreasing the emotional discomfort associated with the demand.

5.4   Individual differences in the Type A Behavior Pattern affect how people experience stress in three ways. Type A people tend to experience more stressors, appraise more demands as stressful, and be prone to experiencing more strains. Individual differences in social support influence the strength of the stress–strain relationship, such that more support acts as a buffer that prevents the onset of strain.

5.5   Although the body tries to adapt to different sorts of stressors, along the lines of what is described by the general adaptation syndrome (GAS), over time, this adaptive response wears out the body, and exhaustion and collapse may occur. The resulting strain has a moderate negative relationship with job performance and a strong negative relationship with organizational commitment.

5.6   Because of the high costs associated with employee stress, organizations assess and manage stress using a number of different practices. In general, these practices focus on reducing or eliminating stressors, providing resources that employees can use to cope with stressors, or trying to reduce the strains.

KEY TERMS

- Stress   *p. 142*
- Stressors   *p. 143*
- Strains   *p. 143*
- Primary appraisal   *p. 144*
- Benign job demands   *p. 144*
- Hindrance stressors   *p. 145*
- Challenge stressors   *p. 145*
- Role conflict   *p. 145*
- Role ambiguity   *p. 146*
- Role overload   *p. 146*
- Daily hassles   *p. 146*
- Time pressure   *p. 146*
- Work complexity   *p. 148*
- Work responsibility   *p. 148*
- Work–family conflict   *p. 148*
- Negative life events   *p. 148*
- Family time demands   *p. 150*
- Personal development   *p. 150*
- Positive life events   *p. 150*
- Secondary appraisal   *p. 151*
- Coping   *p. 151*
- Behavioral coping   *p. 151*
- Cognitive coping   *p. 151*
- Problem-focused coping   *p. 151*
- Emotion-focused coping   *p. 152*
- General adaptation syndrome (GAS) *p. 154*
- Physiological strains   *p. 155*
- Psychological strains   *p. 155*
- Burnout   *p. 155*
- Behavioral strains   *p. 155*
- Type A Behavior Pattern   *p. 156*
- Social support   *p. 158*
- Instrumental support   *p. 158*
- Emotional support   *p. 158*
- Stress audit   *p. 163*
- Job sharing   *p. 163*
- Training interventions   *p. 164*
- Supportive practices   *p. 164*
- Relaxation techniques   *p. 165*
- Cognitive–behavioral techniques *p. 165*
- Health and wellness programs *p. 166*

DISCUSSION QUESTIONS

5.1 Prior to reading this chapter, how did you define stress? Did your definition of stress reflect stressors, the stress process, strains, or some combination?

5.2 Describe your dream job and then provide a list of the types of stressors that you would expect to be present. Is the list dominated by challenge stressors or hindrance stressors? Why do you think this is?

5.3 Think about the dream job that you described in the previous question. How much of your salary, if any at all, would you give up to eliminate the most important hindrance stressors? Why?

5.4 If you had several job offers after graduating, to what degree would the level of challenge stressors in the different jobs influence your choice of which job to take? Why?

5.5 How would you assess your ability to handle stress? Given the information provided in this chapter, what could you do to improve your effectiveness in this area?

5.6 If you managed people in an organization in which there were lots of hindrance stressors, what actions would you take to help ensure that your employees coped with the stressors using a problem-focused as opposed to an emotion-focused coping strategy?

CASE CAPITAL ONE

Stress is a problem that occurs on a daily basis, no matter where you work. Capital One has been in a state of constant change during the past several years, trying to keep up with its rapid growth. Employees within the company are accustomed to change, but their morale dropped to a record low during 2002. The human resources managers at the company conducted a "stress audit" to establish the cost of stress to the company in terms of productivity and attrition. Capital One has since attempted to reduce stress strategically throughout the organization.

Capital One has established three types of intervention to help employees reduce stress. Each employee experiences stressors differently and has different responses to those stressors, so Capital One devised a plan of action to address a diverse workforce. First, management looked at the causes of stress in various departments and put into place policies and procedures to help remove stressors. Second, Capital One established programs to help employees find the best way for them to cope with their personal stress. Third, on-site counseling is available to employees who are already suffering from signs of stress. The results of these three interventions have been phenomenal—lower absenteeism, higher employee retention, and increased productivity. Capital One is leading the way in the field of strategic stress management.

5.1 Do you view Capital One's approach to stress as effective? What other aspects would you add? Explain.

5.2 What can other companies learn from Capital One's decision to reduce stress throughout the organization? How can they incorporate this change? Explain.

Sources: D. Doke, "Happy Talking," *Occupational Health,* April 2004; L. Johnson, "Rapid Onboarding at Capital One," *Harvard Management Update,* September 2006; "Strategic Stress Management," http://www.ceridian.co.uk/hr/downloads/CapitalOne10371.pdf (June 20, 2007).

EXERCISE MANAGING STRESS

The purpose of this exercise is to explore ways of managing stress to reduce strain. This exercise uses groups of six participants, so your instructor will either assign you to a group of six or ask you to create your own group of six. The exercise has the following steps:

1. One method of managing stress is finding a way to reduce the hindrance stressors encountered on the job. In groups of 4–6 students, describe the hindrance stressors that you currently are experiencing. Each student should describe the 2 to 3 most important stressors. Other students should then offer strategies for reducing or alleviating the stressors.

HINDRANCE STRESSORS EXPERIENCED	STRATEGIES FOR MANAGING STRESSORS
Role Conflict:	
Role Ambiguity:	
Role Overload:	
Daily Hassles:	

2. Another method of managing stress is to improve work–life balance. The circle below represents how "waking hours" are divided among five types of activities: school, work, personal relaxation, time with friends, and time with family. Draw two versions of your own circle: your waking hours as they currently are, and your waking hours as you wish them to be. Other students should then offer strategies for making the necessary life changes.

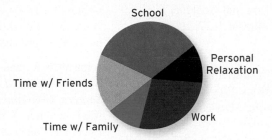

3. A third method of managing stress is improving *hardiness*—a sort of mental and physical health that can act as a buffer, preventing stress from resulting in strain. The table below lists a number of questions that can help diagnose your hardiness. Discuss your answers for each question, then with the help of other students, brainstorm ways to increase that hardiness factor.

HARDINESS FACTOR	STRATEGIES FOR IMPROVING FACTOR
Relaxation: Do you spend enough time reading, listening to music, meditating, or pursuing your hobbies?	
Exercise: Do you spend enough time doing cardiovascular, strength, and flexibility sorts of exercises?	
Diet: Do you manage your diet adequately by eating healthily and avoiding foods high in fat?	

4. Class discussion (whether in groups or as a class) should center on two issues. First, many of the stress-managing factors, especially in Steps 2 and 3, take up precious time. Does this make them an ineffective strategy for managing stress? Why or why not? Second, consider your Type A score in the OB Assessments for this chapter. If you are high on Type A, does that make these strategies more or less important?

ENDNOTES

5.1 Hunnicutt, D., and S. Noeldner. "A WELCOA Expert Interview . . . Capitalizing on Fitness." *2003 Wellness Councils of America.* http://www.davidhunnicutt.com/pdf/Noeldner_INTERVIEW.pdf (March 27, 2007).

5.2 Ibid.

5.3 Kozlowski, D. "The Facility Factor: Can Buildings Boost Productivity?" *Building Operating Management* 51, no. 8 (August 2004), pp. 24–30, www.ProQuest.com (March 27, 2007).

5.4 "Workplace Wellbeing: A Positive Touch," *Employee Benefits Magazine* June 2004, www.ProQuest.com, (March 27, 2007); Gebhardt, D.L., and C.E. Crump. "Employee Fitness and Wellness Programs in the Workplace." *American Psychologist* 45 (1990), pp. 262–72; Jacobson, B. H., and S.G. Aldana. "Relationship Between Frequency of Aerobic Activity and Illness-Related Absenteeism in a Large Employee Sample." *Journal of Occupational and Environmental Medicine* 43 (2001), pp. 1019–25; Parker-Pope, T. "Personal Health (Special Report); The Secrets of Successful Aging: What Science Tells Us about Growing Older—and Staying Healthy." *The Wall Street Journal* June 20, 2005, p. R1, www.ProQuest.com, (March 27, 2007).

5.5 Miller, J., and M. Miller. "Get a Life!" *Fortune* 152, no. 11 (November 28, 2005), pp. 109–124, www.ProQuest.com, (March 27, 2007).

5.6 Sauter, S.; L. Murphy; M. Colligan; N. Swanson; J. Hurrell Jr.; F. Scharf Jr.; R. Sinclair; P. Grubb; L. Goldenhar; T. Alterman; J. Johnston; A. Hamilton; and J. Tisdale. *Stress at Work,* DHHS (NIOSH) Publication No. 99-101 (Cincinnati, OH: U.S. Department of Health and Human Services, Public Health Service, Centers for Disease Control and Prevention, National Institute for Occupational Safety and Health, 1999).

5.7 Johnson, S.R., and L.D. Eldridge. *Employee-Related Stress on the Job: Sources, Consequences, and What's Next,* Technical Report #003 (Rochester, NY: Genesee Survey Services, Inc., 2004).

5.8 Lazarus, R.S., and S. Folkman. *Stress, Appraisal, and Coping* (New York: Springer Publishing Company, Inc., 1984).

5.9 Ibid.

5.10 LePine, J.A.; M.A. LePine; and C.L. Jackson. "Challenge and Hindrance Stress: Relationships with Exhaustion, Motivation to Learn, and Learning Performance." *Journal of Applied Psychology* 89 (2004), pp. 883–91; LePine, J.A.; N.P. Podsakoff; and M.A. LePine. "A Meta-Analytic Test of the Challenge Stressor–Hindrance Stressor Framework: An Explanation for Inconsistent Relationships among Stressors and Performance." *Academy of Management Journal* 48 (2005), pp. 764–75; Podsakoff, N.P.; J.A. LePine; M.A. LePine. "Differential Challenge Stressor–Hindrance Stressor Relationships with Job Attitudes, Turnover Intentions, Turnover, and Withdrawal Behavior: A Meta-Analysis." *Journal of Applied Psychology* 92 (2007), pp. 438–54.

5.11 LePine, J.A.; M.A. LePine; and J.R. Saul. "Relationships among Work and Non-Work Challenge and Hindrance Stressors and Non-Work and Work Criteria: A Theory of Cross-Domain Stressor Effects." In *Research in Occupational Stress and Well Being,* ed. P.L. Perrewé and D.C. Ganster (San Diego: JAI Press/Elsevier, 6) pp. 35–72.

5.12 Kahn, R.; D. Wolfe; R. Quinn; J.. Snoek; and R.A. Rosenthal. *Organizational Stress: Studies in Role Conflict and Ambiguity* (New York: John Wiley, 1964); Pearce, J. "Bringing Some Clarity to Role Ambiguity Research." *Academy of Management Review* 6 (1981), pp. 665–74.

5.13 Miller and Miller, "Get a Life!"

5.14 Mandel, M. "The Real Reasons You're Working So Hard . . . and What You Can Do about It." *BusinessWeek* 3953 (October 3, 2005), pp. 60–67, www.ProQuest.com (March 27, 2007).

5.15 O'Connor, A. "Cracking under Pressure? It's Just the Opposite for Some; Sick of Work—Last of Three Articles: Thriving under Stress." *The New York Times,* Section A, Column 5 (September 10, 2004), p. 1, www.ProQuest.com (March 27, 2007).

5.16 McCall, M.W.; M.M. Lombardo; and A.M. Morrison. *The Lessons of Experience: How Successful Executives Develop on the Job* (Lexington, MA: Lexington Books, 1988).

5.17 Neufeld, S. *Work-Related Stress: What You Need to Know,* (n.d.)http://healthyplace.healthology.com/focus_article.asp?f=mentalhealth&c=work_related_stress (October 27, 2005); http://www.breastcancerfocus.com/focus_article.asp?b=healthology&f=mentalhealth&c=work_related_stress&pg=1 (March 27, 2007).

5.18 Crouter, A. "Spillover from Family to Work: The Neglected Side of the Work–Family Interface." *Human Relations* 37 (1984), pp. 425–42; Rice, R.W.; M.R. Frone; and D.B. McFarlin. "Work and Nonwork Conflict and the Perceived Quality of Life." *Journal of Organizational Behavior* 13 (1992), pp. 155–68.

5.19 Holmes, T.H., and R.H. Rahe. "The Social Readjustment Rating Scale." *Journal of Psychosomatic Research* 11 (1967), pp. 213–18; U.S. Department of Health and Human Services. *Mental Health: A Report of the Surgeon General* (Rockville, MD: U.S. Department of Health and Human Services, Substance Abuse and Mental Health Services, National Institutes of Health Services Administration, Center for Health, National Institute of Mental Health, 1999), Ch. 4.

5.20 Lazarus and Folkman, *Stress, Appraisal, and Coping.*

5.21 Folkman, S.; R.S. Lazarus; C. Dunkel-Schetter; A. Delongis; and R.J. Gruen. "Dynamics of a Stressful Encounter: Cognitive Appraisal, Coping, and Encounter Outcomes." *Journal of Personality and Social Psychology* 50 (1986), pp. 992–1003.

5.22 Latack, J.C., and S.J. Havlovic. "Coping with Job Stress: A Conceptual Evaluation Framework for Coping Measures." *Journal of Organizational Behavior* 13 (1992), pp. 479–508.

5.23 *Global Relocation Trends, 2005 Survey Report.* (Woodridge, IL: GMAC Global Relocation Services, 2006), http://www.gmacglobalrelocation.com/insight_support/global_relocation.asp (March 27, 2007).

5.24 Black, J.S.; M. Mendenhall; and G. Oddou. "Toward a Comprehensive Model of International Adjustment: An Integration of Multiple Theoretical Perspectives." *Academy of Management Review* 16 (1991), pp. 291–317.

5.25 Bhaskar-Shrinivas, P.; D.A. Harrison; M.A. Shaffer; and D.M. Luk. "Input-Based and Time-Based Models of International Adjustment: Meta-Analytic Evidence and Theoretical Extensions." *Academy of Management Journal* 48 (2005), pp. 257–81.

5.26 Mendenhall, M.E.; T.M. Kulmann; G.K. Stahl; and J.S. Osland. "Employee Development and Expatriate Assignments." In *Blackwell Handbook of Cross-Cultural Management,* eds. M.J. Gannon and K.L. Newman. Malden, MA: Blackwell, 2002, pp. 155–84.

5.27 Kahn et al. *Organizational Stress;* Lazarus and Folkman, *Stress, Appraisal, and Coping.*

5.28 Lazarus, R.S. "Progress on a Cognitive–Motivational–Relational Theory of Emotion." *American Psychologist* 46 (1991), pp. 819–34.

5.29 Daniels, C. "The Last Taboo: It's Not Sex. It's Not Drinking. It's Stress—and It's Soaring." *Fortune* 146, no. 8 (2002), pp. 136–44, www.ProQuest.com (March 27, 2007).

5.30 Miller and Miller, "Get a Life!"

5.31 Selye, H. *The Stress of Life.* (New York: McGraw-Hill, 1976).

5.32 Ibid.

5.33 Goldstein, D.L. *Stress, Catecholamines, & Cardiovascular Disease.* (New York: Oxford University Press, 1995).

5.34 Cannon, W.B. "Stresses and Strains of Homeostasis." *American Journal of Medical Science* 189 (1935), pp. 1–14.

5.35 Kahn, R.L., and P. Byosiere. "Stress in Organizations." In *Handbook of Industrial and Organizational Psychology,* Vol. 4. ed. M.D. Dunette, J.M.R. Hough, and H.C. Triandis. Palo Alto, CA: Consulting Psychologists Press, 1992), pp. 517–650.

5.36 Defrank, R.S., and J.M. Ivancevich. "Stress on the Job: An Executive Update." *Academy of Management Executive* 12 (1998), pp. 55–66; Haran, C. "Do You Know Your Early Warning Stress Signals?," 2005, http://abcnews.go.com/Health/Healthology/story?id=421825 (October 27, 2005).

5.37 Stöppler, M.C. "High Pressure Work Deadlines Raise Heart Attack Risk," http://stress.about.com/od/heartdissease/a/deadline.htm (October 1, 2005)., http

5.38 Leitner, K., and M.G. Resch. "Do the Effects of Job Stressors on Health Persist over Time? A Longitudinal Study with Observational Stress Measures." *Journal of Occupational Health Psychology* 10 (2005), pp. 18–30.

5.39 Defrank and Ivancevich, "Stress on the Job"; Haran, *Do You Know?*

5.40 Pines, A., and D. Kafry. (1978), "Occupational Tedium in the Social Services." *Social Work* 23, no. 6 (1978), pp. 499–507.

5.41 Defrank and Ivancevich, "Stress on the Job."

5.42 Friedman, M., and R.H. Rosenman. *Type A Behavior and Your Heart.* (New York: Knopf, 1974).

5.43 Ganster, D.C. "Type A Behavior and Occupational Stress. Job Stress: From Theory to Suggestion. *Journal of Organizational Behavior Management* 8 (Special issue, 1987), pp. 61–84.

5.44 Friedman and Rosenman, *Type A Behavior;* Yarnold, P.R., and F.B. Bryant. "A Note on Measurement Issues in Type A Research: Let's Not Throw Out the Baby with the Bath Water." *Journal of Personality Assessment* 52 (1988), pp. 410–19.

5.45 Abush, R., and E.J. Burkhead. "Job Stress in Midlife Working Women:

Relationships among Personality Type, Job Characteristics, and Job Tension." *Journal of Counseling Psychology* 31 (1984), pp. 36–44; Dearborn, M.J., and J.E. Hastings. "Type A Personality as a Mediator of Stress and Strain in Employed Women." *Journal of Human Stress* 13 (1987), pp. 53–60; Howard, J.H.; D.A. Cunningham; and P.A. Rechnitzer. "Role Ambiguity, Type A Behavior, and Job Satisfaction: Moderating Effects on Cardiovascular and Biochemical Responses Associated with Coronary Risk." *Journal of Applied Psychology* 71 (1986), pp. 95–101.

5.46 Cooper, C.L.; P.J. Dewe; and M.P. O'Driscoll. *Organizational Stress.* Thousand Oaks, CA: Sage Publications, 2001.

5.47 Fusilier, M.R.; D.C. Ganster; and B.T. Mayes. "Effects of Social Support, Role Stress, and Locus of Control on Health. *Journal of Management* 13 (1987), pp. 517–28.

5.48 Jayaratne, S.; T. Tripodi; and W.A. Chess. "Perceptions of Emotional Support, Stress, and Strain by Male and Female Social Workers." *Social Work Research and Abstracts* 19 (1983), pp. 19–27; Kobasa, S. "Commitment and Coping in Stress among Lawyers." *Journal of Personality and Social Psychology* 42 (1982), pp. 707–17; LaRocco, J.M., and A.P. Jones. "Co-Worker and Leader Support as Moderators of Stress–Strain Relationships in Work Situations." *Journal of Applied Psychology* 63 (1978), pp. 629–34.

5.49 Kahn and Byosiere, "Stress in Organizations."

5.50 LePine et al., "A Meta-Analytic Test."

5.51 Cohen, S. "After Effects of Stress on Human Performance and Social Behavior: A Review of Research and Theory." *Psychological Bulletin* 88 (1980), pp. 82–108.

5.52 Podsakoff et al., "Differential Challenge Stressor–Hindrance Stressor Relationships."

5.53 Bedeian, A.G., and A. Armenakis. "A Path-Analytic Study of the Consequences of Role Conflict and Ambiguity." *Academy of Management Journal* 24 (1981), pp. 417–24; Schaubroeck, J.; J.L. Cotton; and K.R. Jennings. "Antecedents and Consequences of Role Stress: A Covariance Structure Analysis." *Journal of Organizational Behavior* 10 (1989), pp. 35–58.

5.54 LePine et al., "A Meta-Analytic Test"; Podsakoff et al., "Differential Challenge Stressor–Hindrance Stressor Relationships."

5.55 Cavanaugh, M.A.; W.R. Boswell; M.V. Roehling; and J.W. Boudreau." An Empirical Examination of Self-Reported Work Stress among U.S. Managers." *Journal of Applied Psychology* 85 (2000), pp. 65–74.

5.56 Boswell, W.R.; J.B. Olson-Buchanan; and M.A. LePine. "The Relationship Between Work-Related Stress and Work Outcomes: The Role of Felt-Challenge and Psychological Strain." *Journal of Vocational Behavior* 64 (2004), pp. 165–81.

5.57 LePine et al., "Challenge and Hindrance Stress."

5.58 Ibid.

5.59 Burke, M.E. "2005 Benefits Survey Report." Alexandria, VA: Society of Human Resource Management Research Department, 2005.

5.60 Perkins, A. "Medical Costs: Saving Money by Reducing Stress." *Harvard Business Review* 72, no. 6 (1994), p. 12.

5.61 Sauter, S.; L. Murphy; M. Colligan; N. Swanson; J. Hurrell Jr.; F. Scharf

Jr.; R. Sinclair; P. Grubb; L. Goldenhar; T. Alterman; J. Johnston; A. Hamilton; and J. Tisdale. *Is Your Boss Making You Sick?* http://abcnews.go.com/GMA/Careers/story?id=1251346&gma=true (October 27, 2005).

5.62 Defrank and Ivancevich, "Stress on the Job."

5.63 Noyce, J. "Help Employees Manage Stress to Prevent Absenteeism, Errors. *Minneapolis/St. Paul The Business Journal.* August 22, 2003. http://twincities.bizjournals.com/twincities/stories/2003/08/25/smallb2.html (March 27, 2007); Burke, "2005 Benefits Survey Report."

5.64 Defrank and Ivancevich, "Stress on the Job"; Cooper, C.L. "The Costs of Stress at Work. *The Safety & Health Practitioner* 19 (2001), pp. 24–26.

5.65 Burke, "2005 Benefits Survey Report."

5.66 Miller and Miller, "Get a Life!"

5.67 Ibid.; Cunningham, C.R., and S.S. Murray. "Two Executives, One Career." *Harvard Business Review* 83, no. 2 (February 2005), pp. 125–31.

5.68 LePine et al., "A Meta-Analytic Test"; Podsakoff et al., "Differential Challenge Stressor–Hindrance Stress Relationships."

5.69 Sonnentag, S., and M. Frese. "Stress in Organizations." In *Comprehensive Handbook of Psychology: Vol. 12. Industrial and Organizational Psychology,* eds. W.C. Borman, D.R. Ilgen, and R.J. Klimoski. New York: Wiley, 2003, pp. 453–91.

5.70 Burke, "2005 Benefits Survey Report."

5.71 Defrank and Ivancevich, "Stress on the Job"; Austin, N.K. "Work–Life Paradox." *Incentive* 178 (2004), p. 18.

5.72 Murphy, L.R. "Stress Management in Work Settings: A Critical Review of Health Effects." *American Journal of Health Promotion* 11 (1996), pp. 112–35.

5.73 Neufeld, *Work-Related Stress.*

5.74 Haran, *Do You Know?*

5.75 Ibid.

5.76 Daniels, "The Last Taboo."

5.77 Sonnentag and Frese, "Stress in Organizations."

5.78 Neufeld, *Work-Related Stress.*

5.79 Neufeld, *Work-Related Stress;* Burke, "2005 Benefits Survey Report."

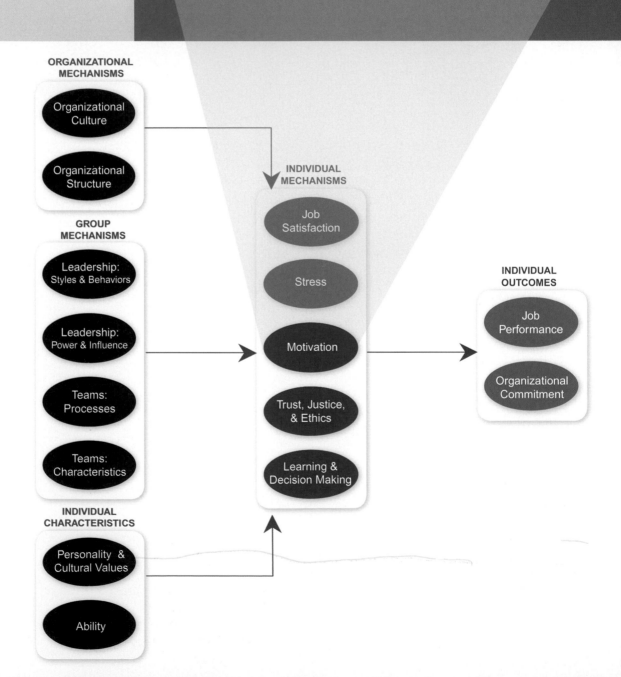

CHAPTER

6

Motivation

ORGANIZATIONAL MECHANISMS

- Organizational Culture
- Organizational Structure

GROUP MECHANISMS

- Leadership: Styles & Behaviors
- Leadership: Power & Influence
- Teams: Processes
- Teams: Characteristics

INDIVIDUAL CHARACTERISTICS

- Personality & Cultural Values
- Ability

INDIVIDUAL MECHANISMS

- Job Satisfaction
- Stress
- Motivation
- Trust, Justice, & Ethics
- Learning & Decision Making

INDIVIDUAL OUTCOMES

- Job Performance
- Organizational Commitment

Nucor Steel motivates its employees with bonuses tied to both profits and quality that can triple their pay.

 LEARNING GOALS

After reading this chapter, you should be able to answer the following questions:

6.1 What is motivation?

6.2 What is expectancy theory, and what are the three beliefs that help determine how work effort is directed?

6.3 What is goal setting theory? What two qualities make goals strong predictors of task performance? How and when do those effects occur?

6.4 What does it mean for rewards to be "equitable," and how are perceptions of equity determined? How do employees respond when they feel a sense of inequity?

6.5 What is psychological empowerment? What four beliefs help create a sense of empowerment among employees?

6.6 How does motivation affect job performance and organizational commitment?

6.7 What steps can organizations take to increase employee motivation?

NUCOR STEEL

Have you ever been in this situation? It's 3:00 p.m. on a Thursday, it's been a long, hard day, and you're tempted to just "go through the motions" for the next two hours. Not work quite as hard, not pay attention quite as closely—just finish out the day and go home. What would keep you motivated to continue working your hardest right up to 5:00 p.m.? Nucor Steel, the nation's largest steel producer and steel recycler, uses a variety of strategies to maximize employee motivation. Nucor is a "minimill" steel-maker, meaning that it melts scrap steel for automobiles, household appliances, and mobile homes in an electric arc furnace to make new steel.[1] Nucor has almost 12,000 employees working in mills in Indiana, North Carolina, Nebraska, Wisconsin, and New York, among other states.[2]

What exactly does Nucor do to motivate its employees? For starters, Nucor employees get paid more when they (and the company) perform better. Department managers' base salary is 10–25 percent lower than the industry average, but they can earn bonuses of 75–90 percent of their salary if their plant does well.[3] James Coblin, Nucor's vice president of human resources, sums up the strategy this way: "In average-to-bad years, we earn less than our peers in other companies. That's supposed to teach us that we don't want to be average or bad. We want to be good."[4] The same sort of accountability is in place for the steelworkers. Their base pay is around $10 an hour, relative to $16 to 21 as the industry average, but a bonus tied to the production of defect-free steel during an employee's entire shift can triple those earnings. The steelworkers also receive profit-sharing bonuses that further reward them in good times. The end result is that Nucor steelworkers took home an average of $99,000 in 2005, versus a $70,000 average take-home for their peers at U.S. Steel.[5]

Of course, there's more to motivation than yearly earnings, and Nucor also strives to make work seem intrinsically rewarding to its employees. For example, plant managers set up contests in which shifts receive specific goals related to safety, efficiency, and output.[6] These contests bring an element of fun and competition to the workday, as one shift tries to outdo the others. Nucor employees also enjoy more decision-making responsibility than steelworkers at other companies. When new plants are acquired, the new employees are asked to inspect existing plants to suggest improvements, just as Nucor veterans are asked to inspect the acquired plant. These and other responsibilities are designed to make each employee feel like a "mini-CEO." One symbol of that philosophy is that the name of every single Nucor employee gets put on the cover of the company's annual report.[7]

MOTIVATION

Few OB topics matter more to employees and managers than motivation. How many times have you wondered to yourself, "Why can't I get myself going today?" Or how many times have you looked at a friend or coworker and wondered, "Why are they working so slowly right now?" Both of these questions are asking about "motivation," which is a derivation of the Latin word for movement, *movere*.[8] Those Latin roots nicely capture the meaning of motivation, as motivated employees simply move faster and longer than unmotivated employees. More formally, **motivation** is defined as a set of energetic forces that originates both within and outside an employee, initiates work-related effort, and determines its direction, intensity, and persistence.[9] Motivation is a critical consideration because job performance is largely a function of two factors: motivation and ability (see Chapter 10 on Ability for more discussion of such issues).[10]

6.1

What is motivation?

The first part of the motivation definition illustrates that motivation is not one thing but rather a set of distinct forces. Some of those forces are internal to the employee, such as a sense of self-confidence, whereas others are external to the employee, such as the goals an employee is given. The next part of that definition illustrates that motivation determines a number of facets of an employee's work effort, as summarized in Figure 6-1 which depicts a scenario where your boss has given you an assignment to work on. Motivation determines *what* employees do at a given moment—the direction in which their effort is channeled. Every moment of the workday offers choices between task and citizenship sorts of actions or withdrawal and counterproductive sorts of actions. When it's 3:00 p.m. on a Thursday, do you keep working on the assignment your boss gave you, or do you launch Internet Explorer and start browsing for a while? Once the direction of effort has been decided, motivation goes on to determine *how hard* an employee works—the intensity of effort—and *for how long*—the persistence of effort. We all have friends or coworkers who work extremely hard for . . . say . . . 5 minutes. We also have friends or coworkers who work extremely long hours but always seem to be functioning at half-speed. Neither of those groups of people would be described as extremely motivated.

FIGURE 6-1   **Motivation and Effort**

MOTIVATION DETERMINES THE . . .

DIRECTION of Effort:	INTENSITY of Effort:	PERSISTENCE of Effort:
What are you going to do right now?	*How hard are you going to work on it?*	*How long are you going to work on it?*
The assignment your boss gave you yesterday?	As hard as you can, or only at half-speed?	For five hours or five minutes?

Or are you going to send e-mails to your friends . . .

. . . or surf the Web for a while?

WHY ARE SOME EMPLOYEES MORE MOTIVATED THAN OTHERS?

There are a number of theories and concepts that attempt to explain why some employees are more motivated than others. The sections that follow review those theories and concepts in some detail. Most of them are relevant to each of the three motivation components described in Figure 6-1. However, some of them are uniquely suited to explaining the direction of effort, whereas others do a better job of explaining the intensity and persistence of effort.

EXPECTANCY THEORY

6.2

What is expectancy theory, and what are the three beliefs that help determine how work effort is directed?

What makes you decide to direct your effort to work assignments rather than taking a break or wasting time? Or what makes you decide to be a "good citizen" by helping out a colleague or attending some optional company function? **Expectancy theory** describes the cognitive process that employees go through to make choices among different voluntary responses.[11] Drawing on earlier models from psychology, expectancy theory argues that employee behavior is directed toward pleasure and away from pain or, more generally, toward certain outcomes and away from others.[12] How do employees make the choices that take them in the "right direction"? The theory suggests that our choices depend on three specific beliefs that are based in our past learning and experience: expectancy, instrumentality, and valence. These three beliefs are summarized in Figure 6-2, and we review each of them in turn.

EXPECTANCY. Expectancy represents the belief that exerting a high level of effort will result in the successful performance of some task. More technically, expectancy is a subjective probability, ranging from 0 (no chance!) to 1 (a mortal lock!) that a specific amount of effort will result in a specific level of performance (abbreviated E → P). Think of a task at which you're not particularly good, such as writing romantic poetry. You may not be very motivated to write romantic poetry because you don't believe that your effort, no matter how hard you try, will result in a poem that "moves" your significant other. As another example, you'll be more motivated to work on the assignment described in Figure 6-1 if you're confident that trying hard will allow you to complete it successfully.

What factors shape our expectancy for a particular task? One of the most critical factors is **self-efficacy,** defined as the belief that a person has the capabilities needed to execute the behaviors required for task success.[13] Think of self-efficacy as a kind of self-confidence or a task-specific version of self-esteem.[14] Employees who feel more "efficacious" (that is, self-confident) for a particular task will tend to perceive higher levels of expectancy—and therefore be more likely to choose to exert high levels of effort. Why do some employees have higher self-efficacy for a given task than other employees? Figure 6-3 can help explain such differences.

When employees consider efficacy levels for a given task, they first consider their **past accomplishments**—the degree to which they have succeeded or failed in similar sorts of tasks in the past.[15] They also consider **vicarious experiences** by taking into account their observations and discussions with others who have performed such tasks.[16] Self-efficacy is also dictated by **verbal persuasion,** because friends, coworkers, and leaders can persuade employees that they can "get the job done." Finally, efficacy is dictated by **emotional cues,** in that feelings of fear or anxiety can create doubts about task accomplishment, whereas pride and enthusiasm can bolster confidence levels.[17] Taken together, these

FIGURE 6-2 | Expectancy Theory

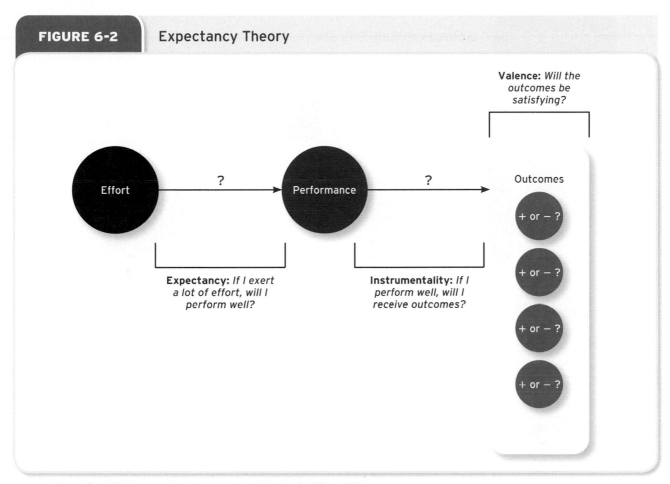

Source: Adapted from V.H. Vroom, *Work and Motivation* (New York: Wiley, 1964).

efficacy sources shape analyses of how difficult the task requirements are and how adequate an employee's personal and situational resources will prove to be.[18] They also explain the content of most "halftime speeches" offered by coaches during sporting events; such speeches commonly include references to past comebacks or victories (past accomplishments), pep talks about how good the team is (verbal persuasion), and cheers to rally the troops (emotional cues).

INSTRUMENTALITY. **Instrumentality** represents the belief that successful performance will result in some outcome(s).[19] More technically, instrumentality is a set of subjective probabilities, each ranging from 0 (no chance!) to 1 (a mortal lock!) that successful performance will bring a set of outcomes (abbreviated P → O). The term "instrumentality" makes sense when you consider the meaning of the adjective "instrumental." We say something is "instrumental" when it helps attain something else—for example, reading this chapter is instrumental for getting a good grade in an OB class (at least, we hope so!).[20] The compensation policies used by Nucor Steel are designed to create a sense of instrumentality among employees, because creating defect-free steel (successful performance) results in a bonus (outcome).

Unfortunately, evidence indicates that many employees don't perceive high levels of instrumentality in their workplace. One survey of more than 10,000 employees in 2005 revealed that 60 percent viewed seniority as the key determinant of their pay.[21] Those that

| FIGURE 6-3 | Sources of Self-Efficacy |

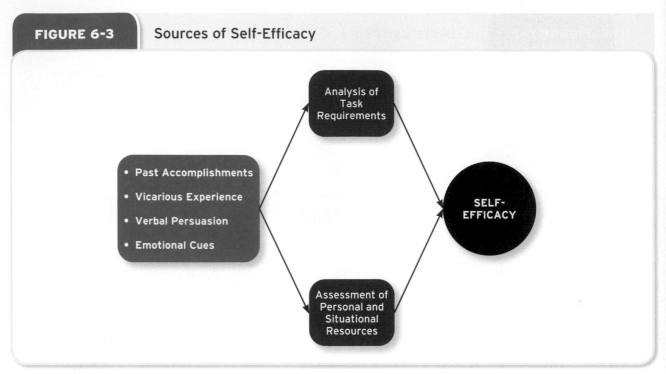

Source: Adapted from A. Bandura, "Self-Efficacy: Toward a Unifying Theory of Behavioral Change," *Psychological Review* 84 (1977), pp. 191–215; M.E. Gist and T.R. Mitchell, "Self-Efficacy: A Theoretical Analysis of its Determinants and Malleability," *Academy of Management Review* 17 (1992), pp. 183–211.

viewed successful performance as the key driver: only 35 percent. A similar survey one year later suggested that instrumentality perceptions vary by organizational level. When asked whether their last raise was based on their job performance, 46 percent of managers agreed, but only 29 percent of nonmanagers agreed.[22] Such low numbers reveal that some organizations consider factors other than performance when making pay decisions.

VALENCE. Valence reflects the anticipated value of the outcomes associated with performance (abbreviated V).[23] Valences can be positive ("I would prefer *having* outcome X to not having it"), negative ("I would prefer *not having* outcome X to having it"), or zero ("I'm bored . . . are we still talking about outcome X?"). Salary increases, bonuses, and more informal rewards are typical examples of "positively valenced" outcomes, whereas disciplinary actions, demotions, and terminations are typical examples of "negatively valenced" outcomes.[24] In this way, employees are more motivated when successful performance helps them attain attractive outcomes, such as bonuses, while helping them avoid unattractive outcomes, such as termination.

What exactly makes some outcomes more "positively valenced" than others? In general, outcomes are deemed more attractive when they help satisfy needs. **Needs** can be defined as cognitive groupings or clusters of outcomes that are viewed as having critical psychological or physiological consequences.[25] Although scholars once suggested that certain needs are "universal" across people,[26] it is likely that different people have different "need hierarchies" that they use to evaluate potential outcomes. Table 6-1 describes many of the needs that are commonly studied in OB.[27] The terms and labels assigned to those needs often vary, so the table includes our labels as well as alternative labels that might sometimes be encountered.

TABLE 6-1	Commonly Studied Needs in OB	
NEED LABEL	ALTERNATIVE LABELS	DESCRIPTION
Existence	Physiological, Safety	The need for the food, shelter, safety, and protection required for human existence.
Relatedness	Love, Belongingness	The need to create and maintain lasting, positive, interpersonal relationships.
Control	Autonomy, Responsibility	The need to be able to predict and control one's future.
Esteem	Self-regard, Growth	The need to hold a high evaluation of oneself and to feel effective and respected by others.
Meaning	Self-actualization	The need to perform tasks that one cares about and that appeal to one's ideals and sense of purpose.

Sources: Adapted from A.H. Maslow, "A Theory of Human Motivation," *Psychological Review* 50 (1943), pp. 370–96; C.P. Alderfer, "An Empirical Test of a New Theory of Human Needs," *Organizational Behavior and Human Performance* 4 (1969), pp. 142–75; E.L. Deci and R.M Ryan, "The 'What' and 'Why' of Goal Pursuits: Human Needs and the Self Determination of Behavior," *Psychological Inquiry* 11 (2000), pp. 227–68; R. Cropanzano, Z.S. Byrne, D.R. Bobocel, and D.R. Rupp, "Moral Virtues, Fairness Heuristics, Social Entities, and Other Denizens of Organizational Justice," *Journal of Vocational Behavior* 58 (2001), pp. 164–209; K.D. Williams, "Social Ostracism," in *Aversive Interpersonal Behaviors,* ed. R.M. Kowalski (New York: Plenum Press, 1997), pp. 133–70.

Table 6-2 lists some of the most commonly considered outcomes in studies of motivation. Outcomes that are deemed particularly attractive are likely to satisfy a number of different needs. For example, praise can signal that interpersonal bonds are strong (satisfying relatedness needs) while also signaling competence (satisfying esteem needs). Note also that some of the outcomes in Table 6-2 result from other people acknowledging successful performance, whereas others are self-generated, originating in task performance itself. The former set creates **extrinsic motivation**—motivation that is controlled by some contingency that depends on task performance.[28] The latter set creates **intrinsic motivation**—motivation that is felt when task performance serves as its own reward.[29] Extrinsic and intrinsic motivation together represent an employee's "total motivation" level. For more on the distinction between intrinsic and extrinsic motivation, see our **OB on Screen** feature.

You might wonder which of the outcomes in the table are most attractive to employees. That's a difficult question to answer, given that different employees emphasize different needs, but two things are clear. First, the attractiveness of outcomes varies across cultures. For example, good performance on a project in an American company might earn a "spot award," such as an expensive watch or a trip to Las Vegas. However, a moped would likely be deemed more attractive in congested areas like India or China, and trips to alcohol- and gambling-intensive areas are taboo in parts of Asia or the Middle East.[30] Second, research suggests that employees underestimate how powerful a motivator pay is to them.[31] When employees rank the importance of outcomes like those in Table 6-2, they often put pay in

TABLE 6-2	Extrinsic and Intrinsic Outcomes	
EXTRINSIC OUTCOMES	**INTRINSIC OUTCOMES**	
Pay	Enjoyment	
Bonuses	Interestingness	
Promotions	Accomplishment	
Benefits and perks	Knowledge gain	
Spot awards	Skill development	
Praise	Personal expression	
Job security	(Lack of) Boredom	
Support	(Lack of) Anxiety	
Free time	(Lack of) Frustration	
(Lack of) Disciplinary actions		
(Lack of) Demotions		
(Lack of) Terminations		

Sources: Adapted from E.E. Lawler III and J.L. Suttle, "Expectancy Theory and Job Behavior," *Organizational Behavior and Human Performance* 9 (1973), pp. 482–503; J. Galbraith and L.L. Cummings, "An Empirical Investigation of the Motivational Determinants of Task Performance: Interactive Effects Between Instrumentality–Valence and Motivation–Ability," *Organizational Behavior and Human Performance* 2 (1967), pp. 237–57; E. McAuley, S. Wraith, and T.E. Duncan, "Self-Efficacy, Perceptions of Success, and Intrinsic Motivation for Exercise," *Journal of Applied Social Psychology* 21 (1991), pp. 139–55; A.S. Waterman, S.J. Schwartz, E. Goldbacher, H. Green, C. Miller, and S. Philip, "Predicting the Subjective Experience of Intrinsic Motivation: The Roles of Self-Determination, the Balance of Challenges and Skills, and Self-Realization Values," *Personality and Social Psychology Bulletin* 29 (2003), pp. 1447–58.

fifth or sixth place. However, research studies show that financial incentives almost always have a stronger impact on motivation than other sorts of outcomes.[32]

Why can pay and bonuses be so motivational? One reason is that money, like many of the outcomes in Table 6-2, is relevant to multiple needs. For example, money can help satisfy existence needs by helping employees buy food, afford a house, and save for retirement. However, money also conveys a sense of esteem, as raises signal that employees are competent and well-regarded.[33] In fact, research suggests that people differ in how they view the **meaning of money**—the degree to which they view money as having symbolic, not just economic, value.[34] The symbolic value of money can be summarized in at least three dimensions: achievement (i.e., money symbolizes success), respect (i.e., money brings respect in one's community), and freedom (i.e., money provides opportunity).[35]

Who is more likely to view money from these more symbolic perspectives? Some research suggests that men are more likely to view money as representing achievement, respect, and freedom than are women.[36] Research also suggests that employees with higher salaries are more likely to view money in achievement-related terms.[37] Younger employees are less likely to view money in a positive light, relative to older employees.[38] Differences

OB ON SCREEN

TALLADEGA NIGHTS: THE BALLAD OF RICKY BOBBY

It's because it's what you love, Ricky. It is who you were born to be. And here you sit. Thinking. Well, Ricky Bobby is not a thinker. Ricky Bobby is a driver. He is a doer, and that's what you need to do. You don't need to think . . . you need to drive. . . . When the fear rises up in your belly, you use it. And you know that fear is power-ful, because it has been there for billions of years. And it is good. And you use it . . . and then you win, Ricky. You WIN! And you don't win for anybody else. You win for you. . . .

With those words, Susan (Amy Adams) tries to motivate Ricky Bobby (Will Ferrell) to return to the NASCAR circuit in *Talladega Nights* (Dir. Adam McKay, Sony Pictures, 2006). A few months earlier, no motivational speech would have been needed, as Ricky Bobby was one of the most successful drivers in all of NASCAR. At that point in his career, Ricky Bobby's motivation was based on winning and the extrinsic rewards that winning brought with it. He adopted his father's mantra: "If you ain't first, you're last!"

He also opened every meal with a long list of the things he was thankful for—things that winning had brought him.

All that changed after a serious accident during a race. Ricky Bobby lost his self-efficacy in the weeks following the accident, then lost his sponsor, his house, and his wife. To add insult to injury, his dad admitted that the "If you ain't first, you're last!" philosophy had been nonsense all along. Lacking any motivation to return to NASCAR, Ricky Bobby settled for delivering pizza on a bicycle while waiting for his application to MTV's *The Real World* to be processed.

It took his former assistant, Susan, to awaken Ricky Bobby from his malaise. Her speech reminded him that he chose to become a driver in the first place for one reason and one reason only: He wanted to go fast. Driving a race car used to be intrinsically motivating for him, providing him with enjoyment and personal expression rather than the boredom that his current life possessed. Without giving away the ending, Susan's words inspired Ricky to return to NASCAR, armed with a deeper sense of intrinsic motivation for driving fast.

in education do not appear to impact the meaning of money, however.[39] How do you view the meaning of money? See our **OB Assessments** feature to find out.

MOTIVATIONAL FORCE. According to expectancy theory, the direction of effort is dictated by three beliefs: expectancy (E → P), instrumentality (P → O), and valence (V). More specifically, the theory suggests that the total "motivational force" to perform a given action can be described using the following formula:[40]

$$\text{Motivational Force} = \boxed{E \rightarrow P} \times \boxed{\Sigma[(P \rightarrow O) \times V]}$$

The Σ symbol in the equation signifies that instrumentalities and valences are judged with various outcomes in mind, and motivation increases as successful performance is linked to more and more attractive outcomes. Note the significance of the multiplication signs in the formula: Motivational force equals zero if any one of the three beliefs is zero. In other words, it doesn't matter how confident you are if performance doesn't result in any outcomes. Similarly, it doesn't matter how well performance is evaluated and rewarded if you don't believe you can perform well.

GOAL SETTING THEORY

So, returning to the choice shown in Figure 6-1, let's say that you feel confident you can perform well on the assignment your boss gave you and that you also believe successful performance will bring valued outcomes. Now that you've chosen to direct your effort to that assignment, two critical questions remain: How hard will you work, and for how long? To shed some more light on these questions, you stop by your boss's office and ask her, "So, when exactly do you need this done?" After thinking about it for a while, she concludes, "Just do your best." After returning to your desk, you realize that you're still not sure how much to focus on the assignment, or how long you should work on it before turning to something else.

6.3

What is goal setting theory? What two qualities make goals strong predictors of task performance? How and when do those effects occur?

Goal setting theory views goals as the primary drivers of the intensity and persistence of effort.[41] Goals are defined as the objective or aim of an action and typically refer to attaining a specific standard of proficiency, often within a specified time limit.[42] More specifically, the theory argues that assigning employees **specific and difficult goals** will result in higher levels of performance than assigning no goals, easy goals, or "do-your-best" goals.[43] Why are specific and difficult goals more effective than do-your-best ones? After all, doesn't "your best" imply the highest possible levels of effort? The reason is that few people know what their "best" is (and even fewer managers can tell whether employees are truly doing their "best"). Assigning specific and difficult goals gives people a number to shoot for—a "measuring stick" that can be used to tell them how hard they need to work and for how long. So if your boss had said, "Have the assignment on my desk by 10:30 a.m. on Tuesday, with no more than two mistakes," you would have known exactly how hard to work and for how long.

Of course, a key question then becomes, "What's a difficult goal?" Figure 6-4 illustrates the predicted relationship between goal difficulty and task performance. When goals are easy, there's no reason to work your hardest or your longest, so task effort is lower. As goals move from moderate to difficult, the intensity and persistence of effort become maximized. At some point, however, the limits of a person's ability get reached, and self-efficacy begins to diminish. At that point, goals move from difficult to impossible, and employees feel somewhat helpless when attempting to achieve them. At that point, effort and performance inevitably decline. So a difficult goal is one that stretches an employee to perform at his or her maximum level while still staying within the boundaries of his or her ability.

OB ASSESSMENTS

THE MEANING OF MONEY

How do you view money—what meaning do you attach to it? This assessment will tell you where you stand on the three facets of the meaning of money—money as achievement, money as respect, and money as freedom. Answer each question using the response scale provided. Then follow the instructions below to score yourself.

1	2	3	4	5	6	7
STRONGLY DISAGREE	DISAGREE	SLIGHTLY DISAGREE	NEUTRAL	SLIGHTLY AGREE	AGREE	STRONGLY AGREE

1. Money represents one's achievement. _____

2. Money is a symbol of success. _____

3. Money is the most important goal in my life. _____

4. Money can buy everything. _____

5. Money makes people respect you in the community. _____

6. Money will help you express your competence and abilities. _____

7. Money can bring you many friends. _____

8. Money is honorable. _____

9. Money gives you autonomy and freedom. _____

10. Money can give you the opportunity to be what you want to be. _____

11. Money in the bank is a sign of security. _____

12. Money means power. _____

SCORING

Money as Achievement: Sum up items 1–4. _____
Money as Respect: Sum up items 5–8. _____
Money as Freedom: Sum up items 9–12. _____

INTERPRETATION

Money as Achievement: High = 13 or above. Low = 12 or below.
Money as Respect: High = 15 or above. Low = 14 or below.
Money as Freedom: High = 20 or above. Low = 19 or below.

If you scored high on all three dimensions, then you view money as having multiple, noneconomic meanings. This result means that money is likely a powerful motivator for you.

Source: Adapted from T.L. Tang, "The Meaning of Money Revisited," *Journal of Organizational Behavior* 13 (1982), pp. 197–202.

FIGURE 6-4   Goal Difficulty and Task Performance

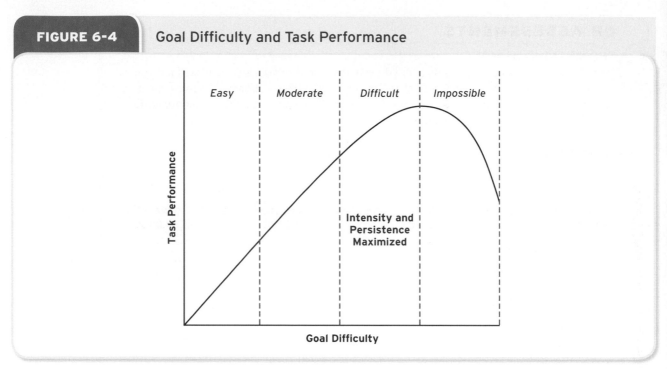

Source: Adapted from E.A. Locke and G.P. Latham, *A Theory of Goal Setting and Task Performance* (Englewood Cliffs, NJ: Prentice Hall, 1990).

The effects of specific and difficult goals on task performance have been tested in several hundred studies using many kinds of settings and tasks. A sampling of those settings and tasks is shown in Table 6-3.[44] Overall, around 90 percent of the goal setting studies support the beneficial effects of specific and difficult goals on task performance.[45] Although some of the settings and tasks shown in the table are unlikely to be major parts of your career (archery, handball, Lego construction), others should be very relevant to the readers (and authors!) of this book (managing and supervision, studying, faculty research). Then again, who wouldn't want a career in Lego construction?

Why exactly do specific and difficult goals have such positive effects? Figure 6-5 presents goal setting theory in more detail to understand that question better.[46] First, the assignment of a specific and difficult goal shapes people's own **self-set goals**—the internalized goals that people use to monitor their own task progress.[47] In the absence of an assigned goal, employees may not even consider what their own goals are, or they may self-set relatively easy goals that they are certain to meet. As a self-set goal becomes more difficult, the intensity of effort increases, and the persistence of effort gets extended. However, goals have another effect; they trigger the creation of **task strategies,** defined as learning plans and problem-solving approaches used to achieve successful performance.[48] In the absence of a goal, it's easy to rely on trial-and-error to figure out how best to do a task. Under the pressure of a measuring stick, however, it becomes more effective to plan out the next move.

Figure 6-5 also includes three variables that specify when assigned goals will have stronger or weaker effects on task performance. In the jargon of theory diagrams, these variables are called "moderators." Rather than directly affecting other variables in the diagram, moderators affect the strength of the relationships between variables. One moderator is **feedback,** which consists of updates on employee progress toward goal attainment.[49] Imagine being challenged to beat a friend's score on the *Halo 3* video game but

TABLE 6-3   Settings and Tasks Used in Goal Setting Research

SETTINGS AND TASKS

Air traffic control	Management training
Archery	Marine recruit performance
Arithmetic	Maze learning
Beverage consumption	Mining
Can collecting	Nursing
Chess	Proofreading
Computer games	Production and manufacturing
Course work	Puzzles
Drilling	Reading
Driving	Returning surveys
Energy conservation	Safety behaviors
Exercise	Sales
Faculty research	Scientific and R&D work
Handball	Sewing
Juggling	Sit-ups
Lego construction	Studying
Logging	Weight lifting
Managing and supervision	Weight loss

Source: Adapted from E.A. Locke and G.P. Latham, *A Theory of Goal Setting and Task Performance* (Englewood Cliffs, NJ: Prentice Hall, 1990).

then not being told what exactly your score was as you were playing. How would you know how hard to try? Another moderator is **task complexity,** which reflects how complicated the information and actions involved in a task are, as well as how much the task changes.[50] In general, the effects of specific and difficult goals are almost twice as strong on simple tasks as on complex tasks, though the effects of goals remain beneficial even in complex cases.[51] Goal setting at Wyeth, the New Jersey–based

As the new chief of research and development at Wyeth, Inc., a pharmaceutical company, Robert Ruffolo offered company scientists a bonus for discovering 12 new drug compounds every year. They've done it every year and are now reaching for a new goal of 15.

pharmaceuticals company, illustrates the value of goals for complex tasks (after all, what's more complicated than chemistry?).[52] When Robert Ruffolo was appointed the new chief

FIGURE 6-5   Goal Setting Theory

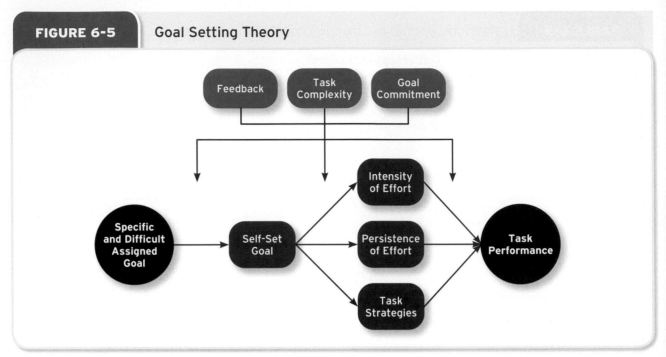

Sources: Adapted from E.A. Locke and G.P. Latham, *A Theory of Goal Setting and Task Performance* (Englewood Cliffs, NJ: Prentice Hall, 1990); E.A. Locke and G.P. Latham, "Building a Practically Useful Theory of Goal Setting and Task Motivation: A 35-Year Odyssey," *American Psychologist* 57 (2002), pp. 705–17; G.P. Latham, "Motivate Employee Performance through Goal-Setting," in *Blackwell Handbook of Principles of Organizational Behavior,* ed. E.A. Locke (Malden, MA: Blackwell, 2000), pp. 107–19.

of R&D six years ago, he was concerned about the low number of new drug compounds being generated by Wyeth's labs. His solution? He gave scientists a goal of discovering 12 new drug compounds every year, up from the 4 compounds they were previously averaging, with bonuses contingent on reaching the goals. Wyeth's scientists have reached the goal every year since, and the goal was upped to 15 compounds in 2006.

The final moderator shown in Figure 6-5 is **goal commitment,** defined as the degree to which a person accepts a goal and is determined to try to reach it.[53] When goal commitment is high, assigning specific and difficult goals will have significant benefits for task performance. However, when goal commitment is low, those effects become much weaker.[54] The importance of goal commitment raises the question of how best to foster commitment when assigning goals to employees. Table 6-4 summarizes some of the most powerful strategies for fostering goal commitment, which range from rewards to supervisory support to employee participation.[55]

Microsoft recently revised its use of goal setting principles in an effort to boost goal commitment and task performance.[56] The company had become concerned that employees viewed their goals as objectives they *hoped* to meet rather than objectives they were *committed* to meeting. Moreover, approximately 25–40 percent of employees were working under goals that were either not specific enough or not measurable enough to offer feedback. To combat these trends, managers are now trained to identify five to seven **S. M.A.R.T. goals** for each employee (S.M.A.R.T. stands for **S**pecific, **M**easurable, **A**chievable, **R**esults-Based, and **T**ime-Sensitive), with rewards directly linked to goal achievement.

TABLE 6-4	Strategies for Fostering Goal Commitment
STRATEGY	**DESCRIPTION**
Rewards	Tie goal achievement to the receipt of monetary or nonmonetary rewards.
Publicity	Publicize the goal to significant others and coworkers to create some social pressure to attain it.
Support	Provide supportive supervision to aid employees if they struggle to attain the goal.
Participation	Collaborate on setting the specific proficiency level and due date for a goal, so that the employee feels a sense of ownership over the goal.
Resources	Provide the resources needed to attain the goal and remove any constraints that could hold back task efforts.

Sources: Adapted from J.R. Hollenbeck and H.J. Klein, "Goal Commitment and the Goal-Setting Process: Problems, Prospects, and Proposals for Future Research," *Journal of Applied Psychology* 72 (1987), pp. 212–20; H.J. Klein, M.J. Wesson, J.R. Hollenbeck, and B.J. Alge, "Goal Commitment and the Goal-Setting Process: Conceptual Clarification and Empirical Synthesis," *Journal of Applied Psychology* 84 (1999), pp. 885–96; E.A. Locke, G.P. Latham, and M. Erez, "The Determinants of Goal Commitment," *Academy of Management Review* 13 (1988), pp. 23–29; G.P. Latham, "The Motivational Benefits of Goal-Setting," *Academy of Management Executive* 18 (2004), pp. 126–29.

Managers and employees participate jointly in the goal setting process, and managers offer support by suggesting task strategies that employees can use to achieve the goals. In this way, managers and employees come to understand the "how" of achievement, not just the "what."[57] For insights into how goal setting operates across cultures, see our **OB Internationally** feature.

EQUITY THEORY

Returning to our running example in Figure 6-1, imagine that at this point, you've decided to work on the assignment your boss gave you, and you've been told that it is due by Tuesday at 10:30 a.m. and cannot have any more than two mistakes in it. That's a specific and difficult goal, so Internet Explorer hasn't been launched in a while, and you haven't even thought about checking your e-mail. In short, you've been working very hard for a few hours, until the guy from across the hall pops his head in. You tell him what you're working on, and he nods sympathetically, saying, "Yeah, the boss gave me a similar assignment that sounds just as tough. I think she realized how tough it was though, because she said I could use the company's playoff tickets if I finish it on time." Playoff tickets? Playoff tickets?? Looks like it's time to check that e-mail after all. . . .

Unlike the first two theories, **equity theory** acknowledges that motivation doesn't just depend on your own beliefs and circumstances but also on what happens to *other people*.[63] More specifically, equity theory suggests that employees create a "mental ledger" of the outcomes (or rewards) they get from their job duties.[64] What outcomes might be part of your mental ledger? That's completely up to you and depends on what you find valuable,

6.4

What does it mean for rewards to be "equitable," and how are perceptions of equity determined? How do employees respond when they feel a sense of inequity?

OB INTERNATIONALLY

Research in cross-cultural OB suggests that there are some "universals" when it comes to motivation. For example, interesting work, pay, achievement, and growth are billed as motivating forces whose importance does not vary across cultures.[58] Of course, some motivation principles do vary in their effectiveness across cultures, including some of the strategies for fostering goal commitment.

Types of Goals. Should goals be given on an individual or a groupwide basis? Employees in the United States usually prefer to be given individual goals. In contrast, employees in other countries, including China and Japan, prefer to receive team goals.[59] This difference likely reflects the stronger emphasis on collective responsibility and cooperation in those cultures.

Rewards. Rewards tend to increase goal commitment across cultures, but cultures vary in the types of rewards that they value. Employees in the United States prefer to have rewards allocated according to merit. In contrast, employees in other countries, including China, Japan, and Sweden, prefer that rewards be allocated equally across members of the work unit.[60] Employees in India prefer a third allocation strategy—doling out rewards according to need. These cultural differences show that nations differ in how they prioritize individual achievement, collective solidarity, and the welfare of others.

Participation. National culture also affects the importance of participation in setting goals. Research suggests that employees in the United States are likely to accept assigned goals because the culture emphasizes hierarchical authority. In contrast, employees in Israel, which lacks a cultural emphasis on hierarchy, do not respond as well to assigned goals.[61] Instead, employees in Israel place a premium on participation in goal setting.

Feedback. Culture also influences how individuals respond when they receive feedback regarding goal progress. As with participation, research suggests that employees in the United States are more likely to accept feedback because they are comfortable with hierarchical authority relationships and have a strong desire to reduce uncertainty.[62] Other cultures, like England, place less value on reducing uncertainty, making feedback less critical to them.

though Table 6-5 provides a listing of some commonly considered outcomes. Equity theory further suggests that employees create a mental ledger of the inputs (or contributions and investments) they put into their job duties.[65] Again, the composition of your mental ledger is completely specific to you, but Table 6-5 provides a listing of some inputs that seem to matter to most employees.

So what exactly do you do with these mental tallies of outcomes and inputs? Equity theory argues that you compare your ratio of outcomes and inputs to the ratio of some **comparison other**—some person who seems to provide an intuitive frame of reference for judging equity.[66] There are three general possibilities that can result from this "cognitive calculus," as shown in Figure 6-6. The first possibility is that the ratio of outcomes to inputs is balanced between you and your comparison other. In this case, you feel a sense of equity, and you're likely to maintain the intensity and persistence of your effort. This situation would have occurred if you have been offered playoff tickets, just like your colleague.

TABLE 6-5	Some Outcomes and Inputs Considered by Equity Theory	
OUTCOMES	**INPUTS**	
Pay	Effort	
Seniority benefits	Performance	
Fringe benefits	Skills and abilities	
Status symbols	Education	
Satisfying supervision	Experience	
Workplace perks	Training	
Intrinsic rewards	Seniority	

Sources: Adapted from J.S. Adams, "Inequity in Social Exchange," in *Advances in Experimental Social Psychology,* Vol. 2, ed. L. Berkowitz (New York: Academic Press, 1965), pp. 267–99.

The second possibility is that your ratio of outcomes to inputs is less than your comparison other's ratio. According to equity theory, any imbalance in ratios triggers **equity distress**—an internal tension that can only be alleviated by restoring balance to the ratios.[67] In an underreward case, the equity distress likely takes the form of negative emotions such as anger or envy. One way to stop feeling those emotions is to try to restore the balance in some way; Figure 6-6 reveals two methods for doing so. You could be constructive and proactive by talking to your boss and explaining why you deserve better outcomes. Such actions would result in the growth of your outcomes, restoring balance to the ratio. Of course, anger often results in actions that are destructive rather than constructive, and research shows that feelings of underreward inequity are among the strongest predictors of counterproductive behaviors, such as employee theft (see Chapter 7 on Trust, Justice, and Ethics for more on this issue).[68] More relevant to this chapter, another means of restoring balance is to shrink your inputs by lowering the intensity and persistence of effort. Remember, it's not the total outcomes or inputs that matter in equity theory—it's only the ratio.

The third possibility is that your ratio of outcomes to inputs is greater than your comparison other's ratio. Equity distress again gets experienced, and the tension likely creates negative emotions such as guilt or anxiety. Balance could be restored by shrinking your outcomes (taking less money, giving something back to the comparison other), but the theory acknowledges that such actions are unlikely in most cases.[69] Instead, the more likely solution is to increase your inputs in some way. You could increase the intensity and persistence of your task effort or decide to engage in more "extra mile" citizenship behaviors. At some point though, there may not be enough hours in the day to increase your inputs any further. An alternative (and less labor-intensive) means of increasing your inputs is to simply rethink them—to reexamine your mental ledger to see if you may have "undersold" your true contributions. On second thought, maybe your education or seniority is more critical than you realized, or maybe your skills and abilities are more vital to the organization. This **cognitive distortion** allows you to restore balance mentally, without altering your behavior in any way.

There is one other way of restoring balance, regardless of underreward or overreward circumstances, that is not depicted in Figure 6-6: Change your comparison other. After all,

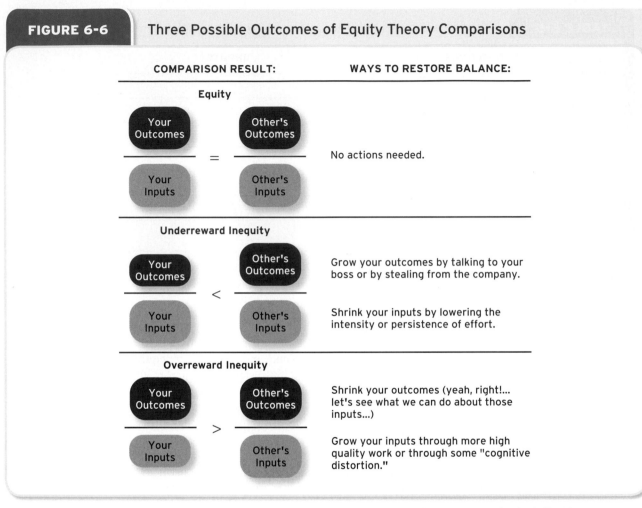

FIGURE 6-6   Three Possible Outcomes of Equity Theory Comparisons

COMPARISON RESULT: WAYS TO RESTORE BALANCE:

Source: Adapted from Adams, J.S. (1965). "Inequity in Social Exchange." In L. Berkowitz (Ed.), *Advances in Experimental Social Psychology* (Vol. 2, pp. 267–299). New York: Academic Press.

we compare our "lots in life" to a variety of other individuals. Table 6-6 summarizes the different kinds of comparison others that can be used.[70] Some of those comparisons are **internal comparisons**, meaning they are made using someone in the same company.[71] Others are **external comparisons**, meaning that they are made using someone in a different company. If a given comparison results in high levels of anger and envy or high levels of guilt and anxiety, the frame of reference may be shifted. In fact, research suggests that employees don't just compare themselves to one other person; instead, they make multiple comparisons to a variety of different others.[72] Although it may be possible to create a sort of "overall equity" judgment, research shows that people draw distinctions between the various equity comparisons shown in the table. For example, one study shows that job equity is the most powerful driver of citizenship behaviors, whereas occupational equity is the most powerful driver of employee withdrawal.[73]

These mechanisms make it clear that judging equity is a very subjective process. Recent data from a Salary.com report highlight that very subjectivity. A survey of 1,500 employees revealed that 65 percent of the respondents planned to look for a new job in the next three months, with 57 percent doing so because they felt underpaid. However, Salary.com estimated that only 19 percent of those workers really were underpaid, taking into account their relevant inputs and the current market conditions. In fact, it was estimated that 17 percent were actually being overpaid by their companies! On the one hand, that subjectivity is likely to be frustrating to most managers in charge of compensation. On the other hand, it is important to realize that the intensity and persistence of employees' effort is driven by their own equity perceptions, not anyone else's.

Perhaps many employees feel they are underpaid because they compare their earnings with their CEO's. Just consider the total pay of *BusinessWeek*'s 10 Highest-Paid CEOs in 2005, with the numbers representing millions of dollars: Former CEO Terry Semel of Yahoo ($120.1), Lew Frankfort of Coach ($58.7), C. John Wilder of TXU ($54.9), Ray Irani of Occidental Petroleum ($37.8), Paul Evanson of Allegheny Energy ($37.5), former CEO Robert Nardelli of Home Depot ($36.7), Robert Toll of Toll Brothers ($36.4), Bruce

TABLE 6-6	Judging Equity with Different Comparison Others
COMPARISON TYPE	**DESCRIPTION AND SAMPLE SURVEY ITEM**
Job Equity	Compare with others doing the same job in the same organization. Sample survey item: *Compared with others doing the same job as me in my company with similar education, seniority, and effort, I earn about:*
Company Equity	Compare with others in the same organization doing substantially different jobs. Sample survey item: *Compared with others in my company on other jobs doing work that is similar in responsibility, skill, effort, education, and working condition required, I earn about:*
Occupational Equity	Compare with others doing essentially the same job in other organizations. Sample survey item: *Compared with others doing my job in other companies in the area with similar education, seniority, and effort, I earn about:*
Educational Equity	Compare with others who have attained the same education level. Sample survey item: *Compared with people I know with similar education and responsibility as me, I earn about:*
Age Equity	Compare with others of the same age. Sample survey item: *Compared with those of my age, I earn about:*

40% less	30% less	20% less	10% less	About the same	10% more	20% more	30% more	40% more

Source: R.W. Scholl, E.A. Cooper, and J.F. McKenna, "Referent Selection in Determining Equity Perceptions: Differential Effects on Behavioral and Attitudinal Outcomes," *Personnel Psychology* 40 (1987), pp. 113–24. Reprinted with permission of Blackwell Publishing.

"This is sloth—greed is on the top floor."

Karatz of KB Home ($34.5), James Cayne of Bear Sterns ($32.6), and Edward Zander of Motorola ($32.3).[74] That total pay includes salary and bonuses, the value of company stock options granted, and other forms of long-term compensation.

Those statistics reflect the growing disconnect between what CEOs make and what the typical employee makes.[75] In 1980, the median compensation for CEOs was 33 times that of the average worker. In 2004, that ratio had climbed to 104 times the average worker's compensation. In fact, the top 10 percent of CEOs made 350 times more than rank-and-file employees in 2004. Why do the boards of directors grant such large compensation packages to CEOs? Although there are many reasons, some have speculated that the pay packages are viewed as status symbols, and many CEOs view themselves in celebrity terms, along the lines of professional athletes.[76] Alternatively, CEO pay packages may be viewed as rewards for years of climbing the corporate ladder and as insurance policies against the short term of office for most CEOs.

Can such high pay totals ever be viewed as equitable in an equity theory sense? Performance is a key input in any equity theory calculation, and it should be noted that the 10 most highly paid CEOs produced an average shareholder return of 57 percent for their companies. In addition, CEOs likely have unusually high levels of many other inputs, including effort, skills and abilities, education, experience, training, and seniority. Furthermore, CEOs likely use other CEOs as their comparison others—not rank-and-file employees—making them less likely to feel a sense of overreward inequity. Of course, that choice doesn't stop the rank-and-file employees from comparing their pay to their CEOs. Possibly for that reason, some CEOs have been lauded for what they *don't* make. Warren Buffett of Berkshire Hathaway ($308,000), Charles Jenkins Jr. of Publix Supermarkets ($564,000), and Steve Ballmer of Microsoft ($871,000) are some of the more recognizable names who didn't even crack a million dollars in total compensation in 2003.[77]

Some organizations grapple with concerns about equity by emphasizing pay secrecy (though that doesn't help with CEO comparisons, given that the Securities and Exchange Commission demands the disclosure of CEO pay for all publicly traded companies). One survey indicated that 36 percent of companies explicitly discourage employees from discussing pay with their colleagues, and surveys also indicate that most employees approve of pay secrecy.[78] Is pay secrecy a good idea? Although it has not been the subject of much research, there appear to be pluses and minuses associated with pay secrecy. On the plus side, such policies may reduce conflict between employees while appealing to concerns about personal privacy. On the minus side, employees may respond to a lack of accurate information by guessing at equity levels, possibly perceiving more underpayment inequity than truly exists. In addition, the insistence on secrecy might cause employees to view the company with a sense of distrust (see Chapter 7 on Trust, Justice, and Ethics for more on this issue).[79] How might these sorts of secrecy policies affect you as a student? See our **OB for Students** feature for a discussion of grade secrecy.

PSYCHOLOGICAL EMPOWERMENT

Now we return, for one last time, to our running example in Figure 6-1. When last we checked in, your motivation levels had suffered because you learned your coworker was offered the company's playoff tickets for successfully completing a similar assignment. As

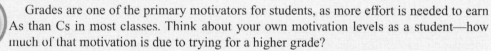

OB FOR STUDENTS

Grades are one of the primary motivators for students, as more effort is needed to earn As than Cs in most classes. Think about your own motivation levels as a student—how much of that motivation is due to trying for a higher grade?

Now here's the question we want you to consider: What would happen to your motivation to learn if your grades *became secret,* or more specifically, if your school adopted a policy that prohibited you or your university from disclosing grades to recruiters? Four of the nation's top business schools, including Harvard University, Stanford University, and the University of Chicago, have implemented just such a policy.[80] Students at those schools are forbidden from sharing grades with recruiters, even if that means jeopardizing a potential job offer. The rationale for grade secrecy policies is twofold. First, grade secrecy is believed to reduce competitiveness between students, fostering a more cohesive atmosphere within student cohorts. Second, grade secrecy is meant to allow students to take tougher, more challenging electives without worrying about their GPA.

So what would happen to your motivation levels if grade secrecy was instituted at your school? The more salient norm of secrecy might discourage you from sharing grades with your classmates, making it more difficult to judge the equity of your grades relative to those received by other students. Grade secrecy might also reduce the valence of the grades themselves, with an A losing some of its anticipated value relative to a B or C. If those effects occurred, then motivation to learn would decline under a grade secrecy system.

Faculty at the University of Pennsylvania's Wharton School believe that grade secrecy has had that sort of negative impact in their MBA program. As a result, they are pushing to relax their nondisclosure policy. At Wharton, undergraduates who are not affected by the grade secrecy policy are outperforming MBAs in the same courses. Meanwhile, student surveys reveal that the time spent on academics has fallen by 22 percent for MBA students over the past four years. For their part, recruiters have had to resort to testing applicants' quantitative skills, because grades in technical classes are no longer available. Still, the MBA students at Wharton remain firmly in support of the grade secrecy policy. Which side would you take in this debate?

you browse the Web in total "time-wasting mode," you begin thinking about all the reasons you hate working on this assignment. Even aside from the issue of goals and rewards, you keep coming back to this issue: You would never have taken on this project *by choice.* More specifically, the project itself doesn't seem very meaningful, and you doubt that it will have any real impact on the functioning of the organization.

6.5

What is psychological empowerment? What four beliefs help create a sense of empowerment among employees?

Those sentiments signal a low level of **psychological empowerment,** which reflects an energy rooted in the belief that work tasks contribute to some larger purpose.[81] Psychological empowerment represents a form of intrinsic motivation, in that merely performing the work tasks serves as its own reward and supplies many of the intrinsic outcomes shown in Table 6-2. The concept of psychological empowerment has much in common with our discussion of "satisfaction with the work itself" in Chapter 4 on Job Satisfaction. That discussion illustrated that jobs with high levels of variety, significance, and autonomy can be intrinsically satisfying.[82] Models of psychological empowerment argue that a similar set of concepts can make work tasks intrinsically motivating. Four concepts are particularly important: meaningfulness, self-determination, competence, and impact.

Meaningfulness captures the value of a work goal or purpose, relative to a person's own ideals and passions.[83] When a task is relevant to a meaningful purpose, it becomes easier to concentrate on the task and get excited about it. You might even find yourself cutting other tasks short so you can devote more time to the meaningful one or thinking about the task outside of work hours.[84] In contrast, working on tasks that are not meaningful brings with it a sense of emptiness and detachment. As a result, you might need to mentally force yourself to keep working on the task. Managers can instill a sense of meaningfulness by articulating an exciting vision or purpose and fostering a noncynical climate in which employees are free to express idealism and passion without criticism.[85] For their part, employees can build their own sense of meaningfulness by identifying and clarifying their own passions. What exactly makes them excited and fulfilled at work, and how can they seek out more opportunities to feel that way?

Self-determination reflects a sense of choice in the initiation and continuation of work tasks. Employees with high levels of self-determination can choose what tasks to work on, how to structure those tasks, and how long to pursue those tasks. That sense of self-determination is a strong driver of intrinsic motivation, because it allows employees to pursue activities that they themselves find meaningful and interesting.[86] Managers can instill a sense of self-determination in their employees by delegating work tasks, rather than micromanaging them, and by trusting

"Really, I'm fine. It was just a fleeting sense of purpose—I'm sure it will pass."

Source: © The New Yorker Collection 2000 Tom Cheney from cartoonbank.com. All rights reserved.

employees to come up with their own approach to certain tasks.[87] For their part, employees can gain more self-determination by earning the trust of their bosses and negotiating for the latitude that comes with that increased trust.

Competence captures a person's belief in his or her capability to perform work tasks successfully.[88] Competence is identical to the self-efficacy concept reviewed previously in this chapter; employees with a strong sense of competence (or self-efficacy) believe they can execute the particular behaviors needed to achieve success at work. Competence brings with it a sense of pride and mastery that is itself intrinsically motivating. Managers can instill a sense of competence in their employees by providing opportunities for training and knowledge gain, expressing positive feedback, and providing challenges that are an appropriate match for employees' skill levels.[89] Employees can build their own competence by engaging in self-directed learning, seeking out feedback from their managers, and managing their own workloads.

Impact reflects the sense that a person's actions "make a difference"—that progress is being made toward fulfilling some important purpose.[90] Phrases such as "moving forward," "being on track," and "getting there" convey a sense of impact.[91] The polar opposite of impact is "learned helplessness"—the sense that it doesn't matter what a person does, nothing will make a difference. Here, phrases such as "stuck in a rut," "at a standstill," or "going nowhere" become more relevant. Managers can instill a sense of impact by celebrating milestones along the journey to task accomplishment, particularly for tasks that span a long time frame.[92] Employees can attain a deeper sense of impact by building the collaborative relationships needed to speed task progress and initiating their own celebrations of "small wins" along the way.

In summary, psychologically empowered employees believe their work has a meaningful purpose, that they have chosen to pursue that purpose in the way they see fit, that they are capable of succeeding in their work tasks, and that they are making progress toward achieving their work goals. Many of Nucor Steel's initiatives could serve as a "how-to guide" for creating psychological empowerment. Nucor's supportive, close-knit culture allows employees to express their passion and ideals, and the increased decision-making responsibility instills a sense of self-determination and impact among the rank-and-file employees.[93] Nucor also stresses competence through extensive cross-training of team

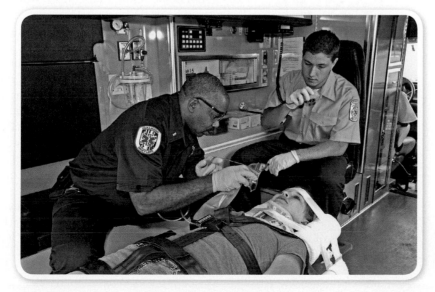

The belief that your work makes a difference, or has impact, is psychologically empowering.

members and intensive examinations of newly acquired plants to see what can be learned from their practices. For an example of another company that has embraced the principles of psychological empowerment, see our **OB at the Bookstore** feature.

SUMMARY: WHY ARE SOME EMPLOYEES MORE MOTIVATED THAN OTHERS?

So what explains why some employees are more motivated than others? As shown in Figure 6-7, answering that question requires considering all the energetic forces that

OB AT THE BOOKSTORE

FISH! A REMARKABLE WAY TO BOOST MORALE AND IMPROVE RESULTS
by Stephen Lundin, Harry Paul, and John Christensen (New York: Hyperion, 2000).

There is always a choice about the way you do your work, even if there is not a choice about the work itself. That was the biggest lesson we learned in building the world famous Pike Place fish market. We can choose the attitude we bring to our work.

With those words, Lonnie, a fictional fishmonger in the Fish! parable, explains one of the key tenets of psychological empowerment to Mary Jane, a manager at nearby First Guarantee Financial. Mary Jane's work unit had been described as a "toxic waste dump," and she had been charged with cleaning things up. Little did she know that a stroll to a local fish market—famous for flinging fish and shipping them worldwide—would provide her with the inspiration to do just that.

As Mary Jane listened to Lonnie during her lunch hour, she protested, "But, we don't have anything to throw! We have boring work to do." Lonnie's quote highlights that

employees do have self-determination for the *way* they work, even when they can't choose their work tasks. This insight became the first of Mary Jane's rules for reviving her unit: *Choose your attitude*. As Lonnie himself admitted, "Working in a fish market is cold, wet, smelly, sloppy, difficult work. But we have a choice about our attitude while we are doing that work."

Mary Jane's other rules echoed other facets of psychological empowerment. The employees in Mary Jane's unit didn't see the meaningfulness in their work. After noting how the fishmongers resolved to "make their customer's day" and "be present" when interacting with customers, Mary Jane's employees realized their work was important to First Guarantee. As they began to view their work in more meaningful terms, Mary Jane's employees began to perceive that they could make a difference in ways they never expected, increasing their feelings of impact. The "toxic waste dump" had been replaced by a psychologically empowered unit . . . without throwing a thing.

FIGURE 6-7 — Why Are Some Employees More Motivated Than Others?

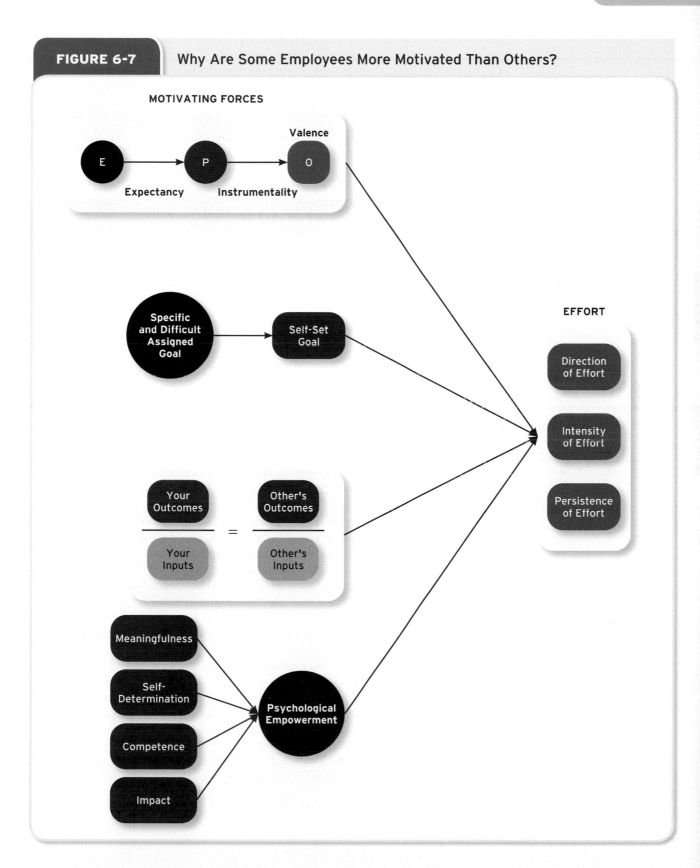

initiate work-related effort, including expectancy theory concepts (expectancy, instrumentality, valence), the existence (or absence) of specific and difficult goals, perceptions of equity, and feelings of psychological empowerment. Unmotivated employees may simply lack confidence due to a lack of expectancy or competence or the assignment of an unachievable goal. Such employees may feel their performance is not properly rewarded due to a lack of instrumentality, a lack of valence, or feelings of inequity. Finally, it may be that their work simply isn't challenging or intrinsically rewarding due to the assignment of easy or abstract goals or the absence of meaningfulness, self-determination, and impact.

HOW IMPORTANT IS MOTIVATION?

6.6

How does motivation affect job performance and organizational commitment?

Does motivation have a significant impact on the two primary outcomes in our integrative model of OB—does it correlate with job performance and organizational commitment? Answering that question is somewhat complicated, because motivation is not just one thing but rather a set of energetic forces. Figure 6-8 summarizes the research evidence linking motivation to job performance and organizational commitment. The figure expresses the likely combined impact of all those energetic forces on the two outcomes in our OB model.

Turning first to job performance, literally thousands of studies support the relationships between the various motivating forces and task performance. The motivating force with the strongest performance effect is self-efficacy/competence, because people who feel a sense of internal self-confidence tend to outperform those who doubt their capabilities.[94] Difficult goals are the second most powerful motivating force; people who receive such goals outperform the recipients of easy goals.[95] The motivational force created by high levels of valence, instrumentality, and expectancy is the next most powerful motivational variable for task performance.[96] Finally, perceptions of equity have a somewhat weaker effect on task performance.[97]

Less attention has been devoted to the linkages between motivation variables and citizenship and counterproductive behavior. With respect to the former, employees who engage in more work-related effort would seem more likely to perform "extra-mile" sorts of actions, because those actions themselves require extra effort. The best evidence in support of that claim comes from research on equity. Specifically, employees who feel a sense of equity on the job are more likely to engage in citizenship behaviors, particularly when those behaviors aid the organization.[98] The same employees are less likely to engage in counterproductive behaviors, because such behaviors often serve as a retaliation against perceived inequities.[99]

As with citizenship behaviors, the relationship between motivation and organizational commitment seems straightforward. After all, the psychological and physical forms of withdrawal that characterize less committed employees are themselves evidence of low levels of motivation. Clearly employees who are daydreaming, coming in late, and taking longer breaks are struggling to put forth consistently high levels of work effort. Research on equity and organizational commitment offers the clearest insights into the motivation–commitment relationship. Specifically, employees who feel a sense of equity are more emotionally attached to their firms and feel a stronger sense of obligation to remain.[100]

| FIGURE 6-8 | Effects of Motivation on Performance and Commitment |

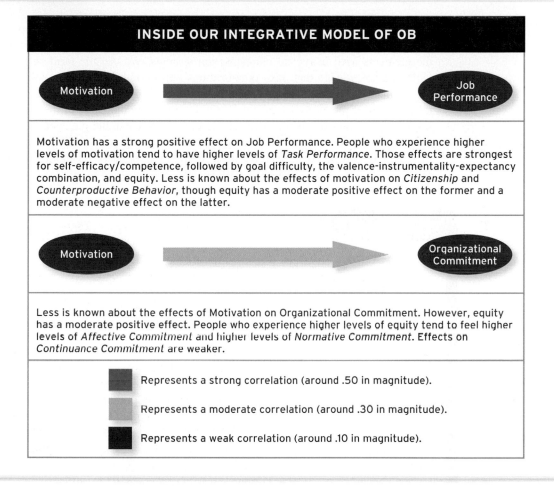

INSIDE OUR INTEGRATIVE MODEL OF OB

Motivation → Job Performance

Motivation has a strong positive effect on Job Performance. People who experience higher levels of motivation tend to have higher levels of *Task Performance*. Those effects are strongest for self-efficacy/competence, followed by goal difficulty, the valence-instrumentality-expectancy combination, and equity. Less is known about the effects of motivation on *Citizenship* and *Counterproductive Behavior*, though equity has a moderate positive effect on the former and a moderate negative effect on the latter.

Motivation → Organizational Commitment

Less is known about the effects of Motivation on Organizational Commitment. However, equity has a moderate positive effect. People who experience higher levels of equity tend to feel higher levels of *Affective Commitment* and higher levels of *Normative Commitment*. Effects on *Continuance Commitment* are weaker.

Represents a strong correlation (around .50 in magnitude).

Represents a moderate correlation (around .30 in magnitude).

Represents a weak correlation (around .10 in magnitude).

Sources: Y. Cohen-Charash and P.E. Spector, "The Role of Justice in Organizations: A Meta-Analysis," *Organizational Behavior and Human Decision Processes* 86 (2001), pp. 287–321; J.A. Colquitt, D.E. Conlon, M.J. Wesson, C.O.L.H. Porter, and K.Y. Ng, "Justice at the Millennium: A Meta-Analytic Review of 25 Years of Organizational Justice Research," *Journal of Applied Psychology* 86 (2001), pp. 425–45; J.P. Meyer, D.J. Stanley, L. Herscovitch, and L. Topolnytsky, "Affective, Continuance, and Normative Commitment to the Organization: A Meta-Analysis of Antecedents, Correlates, and Consequences," *Journal of Vocational Behavior* 61 (2002), pp. 20–52; A.D. Stajkovic and F. Luthans, "Self-Efficacy and Work-Related Performance: A Meta-Analysis," *Psychological Bulletin* 124 (1998), pp. 240–61; W. Van Eerde and H. Thierry, "Vroom's Expectancy Models and Work-Related Criteria: A Meta-Analysis," *Journal of Applied Psychology* 81 (1996), pp. 575–86; R.E. Wood, A.J. Mento, and E.A. Locke, "Task Complexity as a Moderator of Goal Effects: A Meta-Analysis," *Journal of Applied Psychology* 72 (1987), pp. 416–25.

APPLICATION: COMPENSATION SYSTEMS

The most important area in which motivation concepts are applied in organizations is in the design of compensation systems. Table 6-7 provides an overview of many of the elements used in typical compensation systems. We use the term "element" in the table to acknowledge that most organizations use a combination of multiple approaches to compensate their employees. Two points must be noted about Table 6-7. First, the descriptions of the elements are simplistic; the reality is that each of the elements can be implemented and executed in a variety of ways.[101] Second, the elements are designed to do more than just motivate. For example, plans that put pay "at risk" rather than creating increases in base salary are geared toward control of labor costs. As another example, plans that reward unit or organizational performance are designed to reinforce collaboration,

TABLE 6-7	Compensation Plan Elements
ELEMENT	**DESCRIPTION**
Individual-Focused	
Piece-Rate	A specified rate is paid for each unit produced, each unit sold, or each service provided.
Merit Pay	An increase to base salary is made in accordance with performance evaluation ratings.
Lump-Sum Bonuses	A bonus is received for meeting individual goals but no change is made to base salary. The potential bonus represents "at risk" pay that must be re-earned each year. Base salary may be lower in cases in which potential bonuses may be large.
Recognition Awards	Tangible awards (gift cards, merchandise, trips, special events, time off, plaques) or intangible awards (praise) are given on an impromptu basis to recognize achievement.
Unit-Focused	
Gainsharing	A bonus is received for meeting unit goals (department goals, plant goals, business unit goals) for criteria controllable by employees (labor costs, use of materials, quality). No change is made to base salary. The potential bonus represents "at risk" pay that must be re-earned each year. Base salary may be lower in cases in which potential bonuses may be large.
Organization-Focused	
Profit Sharing	A bonus is received when the publicly reported earnings of a company exceed some minimum level, with the magnitude of the bonus contingent on the magnitude of the profits. No change is made to base salary. The potential bonus represents "at risk" pay that must be re-earned each year. Base salary may be lower in cases in which potential bonuses may be large.

information sharing, and monitoring among employees, regardless of their impact on motivation levels.

One way of judging the motivational impact of compensation plan elements is to consider whether the elements provide difficult and specific goals for channeling work effort. Merit pay and profit sharing offer little in the way of difficult and specific goals, because both essentially challenge employees to make next year as good (or better) than this year. In contrast, lump-sum bonuses and gainsharing provide a forum for assigning difficult and specific goals; the former does so at the individual level and the latter at the unit level. Partly for this reason, both types of plans have been credited with improvements in employee productivity.[102]

6.7

What steps can organizations take to increase employee motivation?

Another way of judging the motivational impact of the compensation plan elements is to consider the correspondence between individual performance levels and individual monetary outcomes. After all, that correspondence influences perceptions of both instrumentality and equity. Profit sharing, for example, is unlikely to have strong motivational consequences because an individual employee can do little to improve the profitability of the company, regardless of his or her job performance.[103] Instrumentality and equity are more achievable with gainsharing, because the relevant unit is smaller and the relevant outcomes are more controllable. Still, the highest instrumentality and equity levels will typically be achieved through individual-focused compensation elements. Piece-rate plans can create stronger performance–outcome contingencies but are difficult to apply outside of manufacturing, sales, and service contexts. Merit pay represents the most common element of organizational compensation plans, yet the pay increase for top performers (5.6 percent on average) is only modestly greater than the pay increase for poor performers (2.5 percent on average).[104]

One factor that hinders merit pay is the accuracy of the performance evaluations that feed into the compensation decision. Think of all the times you've been evaluated by someone else, whether in school or in the workplace. How many times have you reacted by thinking, "Where did that rating come from?" or "I think I'm being evaluated on the wrong things!" Performance evaluation experts suggest that employees should be evaluated on behaviors that are controllable by the employees (see Chapter 2 on Job Performance for more discussion of this issue), observable by managers, and critical to the implementation of the firm's strategy.[105] The managers who conduct evaluations also need to be trained in how to conduct them, which typically involves gaining knowledge of the relevant behaviors ahead of time and being taught to keep records of employee behavior between evaluation sessions.[106]

Even if employees are evaluated on the right things by a boss who has a good handle on their performance, it's important to understand the context in which performance ratings occur. Some managers might knowingly give inaccurate evaluations due to workplace politics and a desire to not "make waves." In particular, it's tempting for managers to be very lenient in their performance evaluations so that everyone "goes home happy." Unfortunately, such practices only serve to damage instrumentality and equity because they fail to separate star employees from struggling employees. To ensure that such separation occurs, Yahoo, the California-based Internet company, has instituted a "stacked ranking" system to determine compensation, in which managers rank all the employees within their unit from top to bottom.[107] Employees at the top end of those rankings then receive higher bonuses than employees at the bottom end. Although such practices raise concerns about employee morale and excessive competitiveness, research suggests that such forced distribution systems can boost the performance of a company's workforce, especially for the first few years after their implementation.[108]

TAKEAWAYS

6.1 Motivation is defined as a set of energetic forces that originates both within and outside an employee, initiates work-related effort, and determines its direction, intensity, and persistence.

6.2 Expectancy theory describes the cognitive process that employees go through to make choices among different voluntary behaviors. Effort is directed toward behaviors when effort is believed to result in performance (expectancy), performance is believed to result in outcomes (instrumentality), and those outcomes are anticipated to be valuable (valence).

6.3 Goal setting theory describes the impact of assigned goals on the intensity and persistence of effort. Goals become strong drivers of motivation and performance when they are difficult and specific. Specific and difficult goals affect performance by increasing self-set goals and task strategies. Those effects occur more frequently when employees are given feedback, tasks are not too complex, and goal commitment is high.

6.4 Rewards are equitable when a person's ratio of outcomes to inputs matches those of some relevant comparison other. A sense of inequity triggers equity distress. Underreward inequity typically results in lower levels of motivation or higher levels of counterproductive behavior. Overreward inequity typically results in cognitive distortion, in which inputs are reevaluated in a more positive light.

6.5 Psychological empowerment reflects an energy rooted in the belief that tasks are contributing to some larger purpose. Psychological empowerment is fostered when work goals appeal to employees' passions (meaningfulness), employees have a sense of choice regarding work tasks (self-determination), employees feel capable of performing successfully (competence), and employees feel they are making progress toward fulfilling their purpose (impact).

6.6 Motivation has a strong positive relationship with job performance and a moderate positive relationship with organizational commitment. Of all the energetic forces subsumed by motivation, self-efficacy/competence has the strongest relationship with performance.

6.7 Organizations use compensation practices to increase motivation. Those practices may include individual-focused elements (piece-rate, merit pay, lump-sum bonuses, recognition awards), unit-focused elements (gainsharing), or organization-focused elements (profit sharing).

KEY TERMS

• Motivation	*p. 178*	• Emotional cues	*p. 180*
• Expectancy theory	*p. 180*	• Instrumentality	*p. 181*
• Expectancy	*p. 180*	• Valence	*p. 182*
• Self-efficacy	*p. 180*	• Needs	*p. 182*
• Past accomplishments	*p. 180*	• Extrinsic motivation	*p. 183*
• Vicarious experiences	*p. 180*	• Intrinsic motivation	*p. 183*
• Verbal persuasion	*p. 180*	• Meaning of money	*p. 184*

- Goal setting theory *p. 186*
- Specific and difficult goals *p. 186*
- Self-set goals *p. 188*
- Task strategies *p. 188*
- Feedback *p. 188*
- Task complexity *p. 189*
- Goal commitment *p. 190*
- S.M.A.R.T. goals *p. 190*
- Equity theory *p. 191*
- Comparison other *p. 192*
- Equity distress *p. 193*
- Cognitive distortion *p. 193*
- Internal comparisons *p. 194*
- External comparisons *p. 194*
- Psychological empowerment *p. 198*
- Meaningfulness *p. 198*
- Self-determination *p. 198*
- Competence *p. 199*
- Impact *p. 199*

DISCUSSION QUESTIONS

6.1 Which of the outcomes in Table 6-2 are most appealing to you? Are you more attracted to extrinsic outcomes or intrinsic outcomes? Do you think that your preferences will change as you get older?

6.2 Assume that you were working on a group project and that one of your teammates was nervous about speaking in front of the class during the presentation. Drawing on Figure 6-3, what exactly could you do to make your classmate feel more confident?

6.3 Consider the five strategies for fostering goal commitment (rewards, publicity, support, participation, and resources). Which of those strategies do you think is most effective? Can you picture any of them having potential drawbacks?

6.4 How do you tend to respond when you experience overreward and underreward inequity? Why do you respond that way rather than with some other combination in Figure 6-6?

6.5 Think about a job that you've held in which you felt very low levels of psychological empowerment. What could the organization have done to increase empowerment levels?

CASE NUCOR STEEL

Nucor Steel is a unique organization that lives or dies by its employees' passion for teamwork. Nucor has a compensation plan that rewards employees for successful teamwork. Employees are very conscientious about teamwork, because if they cannot create synergy among their teams, they will not earn as much as employees at other steel companies. There are no upper limits on the bonuses a team can earn, but they generally are in the range of 100–220 percent of an employees' base salary. You may be thinking that Nucor is only interested in the quantity its employees produce, but there is also an incentive plan to improve quality.

The employees at Nucor Steel are not the typical worker bees you might expect at a steel plant. Nucor Steel has cultivated an engaged workforce that enables the organization to use a flattened organizational hierarchy. The organizational structure at Nucor empowers employees to make decisions that actually affect the entire organization. Even if an employee's idea fails after implementation, the company remains adamant about listening to new ideas. Nucor Steel's incentives have created a motivated workforce that has delivered unbelievable returns to shareholders. With a seven-year tenure as CEO, Daniel R. DiMicco was voted one of the top 10 best performing bosses by *Forbes* in 2007. In fiscal year 2006, the revenues of the company increased by 16 percent to $14.8 billion, and profits went up by 34 percent to $1.8 billion. No doubt, all were winners: the employees, the managers, and the shareholders.

6.1 Nucor Steel employees are motivated by financial incentives only. Do you agree? Explain.

6.2 Do you believe Nucor's employee incentives give it a competitive advantage in the industry? Explain.

Sources: M. Bolch, "Rewarding the Team," *HR Magazine,* February 2007; "By the Numbers: America's Best Performing Bosses," Forbes, May 3, 2007; "The Art of Motivation," *BusinessWeek,* May 1, 2006.

EXERCISE   GEORGE LUMBER

The purpose of this exercise is to demonstrate how compensation can be used to influence motivation. This exercise uses groups of six participants, so your instructor will either assign you to a group of six or ask you to create your own group of six. George Lumber is a small, family-owned business, run by Angelo George and his father Ira. Business has been good—until last year, as seen in the chart below.

YEAR	NUMBER OF EMPLOYEES	PROFIT
2007	52	$300,000
2006	47	$700,000
2005	40	$500,000
2004	25	$300,000
2003	5	$100,000

After a careful analysis of new building starts, the cost of raw materials, taxes, and other business conditions, Angelo and Ira have come to the conclusion that the decline in profits is due to a decline in sales revenue from their weekend sales shift. The 10 weekend employees tend to be the newest salespeople hired at the company. Many of them are working part-time and either going to school during the week or holding down another job. Few of them see a position at George Lumber as a career goal, but recently, Ira has had two people from the weekend shift approach him to see if weekday work might be available. Because weekend employees are part-time, they are not generally offered benefits, though Angelo has studied the possibility. Frankly, he is not sure that these employees would even want the same benefits. How is it possible that Tina, who is 18 years of age and hoping for a career as an architect when she finishes college, might want the same things as Oscar, who is 69 years old and works to get extra money to pay for his prescription drugs every month?

Over dinner one night, Angelo and Ira brainstormed ways to motivate their employees. They came up with several ideas, including (1) giving a monthly bonus to the employee with the highest sales for that month; (2) offering a "cafeteria-style" benefits package, from which employees could select the types of benefits that would best fit their needs, up to a cost of $300 per month; (3) setting up a training program for weekend employees; (4) initiating an "on the spot" bonus of $50 for the employees who get "caught" giving superior customer service; and (5) offering to promote the employee with the highest sales at the end of the summer to a full-time position.

1. Evaluate the advantages and disadvantages of each of these motivational options from the perspective of expectancy theory, goal setting theory, and equity theory.
2. Develop a compensation plan using the elements of expectancy theory, goal setting theory, and equity theory. How would you sell your plan to Angelo and Ira?

ENDNOTES

6.1 Byrnes, N. "The Art of Motivation: What You Can Learn from a Company that Treats Workers Like Owners. Inside the Surprising Performance Culture of Steelmaker Nucor." *BusinessWeek,* October 6, 2006, pp. 57–62.

6.2 "About Us." http://www.nucor.com/indexinner.aspx?finpage=aboutus (September 1, 2006).

6.3 Byrnes, "The Art of Motivation."

6.4 Ibid.

6.5 Ibid.

6.6 Ibid.

6.7 Ibid.

6.8 Steers, R.M.; R.T. Mowday; and D. Shapiro. "The Future of Work Motivation." *Academy of Management Review* 29 (2004), pp. 379–87. See also Latham, G.P. *Work Motivation: History, Theory, Research, and Practice.* Thousand Oaks, CA: Sage, 2006.

6.9 Latham, G.P., and C.C. Pinder. "Work Motivation Theory and Research at the Dawn of the Twenty-First Century." *Annual Review of Psychology* 56 (2005), pp. 485–516.

6.10 Maier, N.R.F. *Psychology in Industry.* 2nd ed. Boston: Houghton-Mifflin, 1955.

6.11 Vroom, V.H. *Work and Motivation.* New York: Wiley, 1964.

6.12 Ibid.; see also Thorndike, E.L. "The Law of Effect." *American Journal of Psychology* 39 (1964), pp. 212–22; Hull, C.L. *Essentials of Behavior.* New Haven: Yale University Press, 1951; Postman, L. "The History and Present Status of the Law of Effect." *Psychological Bulletin* 44 (1947), pp. 489–563.

6.13 Bandura, A. "Self-Efficacy: Toward a Unifying Theory of Behavioral Change." *Psychological Review* 84 (1977), pp. 191–215.

6.14 Brockner, J. *Self-Esteem at Work.* Lexington, MA: Lexington Books, 1988.

6.15 Bandura, "Self-Efficacy."

6.16 Ibid.

6.17 Ibid.

6.18 Gist, M.E., and T.R. Mitchell. "Self-Efficacy: A Theoretical Analysis of its Determinants and Malleability." *Academy of Management Review* 17 (1992), pp. 183–211.

6.19 Vroom, *Work and Motivation.*

6.20 Pinder, C.C. *Work Motivation.* Glenview, IL: Scott, Foresman, 1984.

6.21 Stillings, J., and L. Snyder. "Up Front: The Stat." *BusinessWeek,* July 4 ,2005, p. 12.

6.22 Stead, D. "Up Front: The Big Picture." *BusinessWeek,* May 29, 2006, p. 11.

6.23 Vroom, *Work and Motivation.*

6.24 Pinder, *Work Motivation.*

6.25 Landy, F.J., and W.S. Becker. "Motivation Theory Reconsidered." In *Research in Organizational Behavior,* Vol. 9, ed. B.M. Staw and L.L. Cummings. Greenwich, CT: JAI Press, 1987, pp. 1–38; Naylor, J.C.; D.R. Pritchard; and D.R. Ilgen. *A Theory of Behavior in Organizations.* New York: Academic Press, 1980.

6.26 Maslow, A.H. "A Theory of Human Motivation." *Psychological Review* 50 (1943), pp. 370–96; Alderfer, C.P. "An Empirical Test of a New Theory of Human Needs." *Organizational Behavior and Human Performance* 4 (1969), pp. 142–75.

6.27 Ibid.; see also Deci, E.L., and R.M. Ryan. "The 'What' and 'Why' of Goal Pursuits: Human Needs and the Self-Determination of Behavior." *Psychological Inquiry* 11 (2000), pp. 227–68; Cropanzano, R.; Z.S. Byrne; D.R. Bobocel; and D.R. Rupp. "Moral Virtues, Fairness Heuristics, Social Entities, and Other Denizens of Organizational Justice." *Journal of Vocational Behavior* 58

(2001), pp. 164–209; Williams, K.D. "Social Ostracism." In *Aversive Interpersonal Behaviors,* ed. R.M. Kowalski. New York: Plenum Press, 1997, pp. 133–70; Thomas, K.W., and B.A. Velthouse. "Cognitive Elements of Empowerment: An 'Interpretive' Model of Intrinsic Task Motivation." *Academy of Management Review* 15 (1990), pp. 666–81.

6.28 Deci and Ryan, "The 'What' and 'Why';" Naylor, Pritchard, and Ilgen, *A Theory of Behavior in Organizations.*

6.29 Ibid.

6.30 Speizer, I. "Incentives Catch on Overseas, but Value of Awards Can Too Easily Get Lost in Translation." *Workforce,* November 21, 2005, pp. 46–49.

6.31 Rynes, S.L.; B. Gerhart; and K.A. Minette. "The Importance of Pay in Employee Motivation: Discrepancies Between What People Say and What They Do." *Human Resource Management* 43 (2004), pp. 381–394; Rynes, S.L.; K.G. Brown; and A.E. Colbert. "Seven Common Misconceptions about Human Resource Practices: Research Findings Versus Practitioner Beliefs." *Academy of Management Executive* 16 (2002), pp. 92–102.

6.32 Rynes, Gerhart, and Minette, "The Importance of Pay."

6.33 Ibid.

6.34 Mitchell, T.R., and A.E. Mickel. "The Meaning of Money: An Individual Differences Perspective." *Academy of Management Review* 24 (1999), pp. 568–78.

6.35 Tang, T.L. "The Meaning of Money Revisited." *Journal of Organizational Behavior* 13 (1992), pp. 197–202.

6.36 Tang, T.L. "The Development of a Short Money Ethic Scale: Attitudes Toward Money and Pay Satisfaction Revisited." *Personality and Individual Differences* 19 (1995), pp. 809–16.

6.37 Tang, "The Meaning of Money Revisited."

6.38 Tang, "The Meaning of Money Revisited"; Tang, "The Development of a Short Money Ethic Scale."

6.39 Tang, "The Development of a Short Money Ethic Scale."

6.40 Vroom, *Work and Motivation.* Lawler E.E. III, and J.L. Suttle. "Expectancy Theory and Job Behavior." *Organizational Behavior and Human Performance* 9 (1973), pp. 482–503.

6.41 Locke, E.A. "Toward a Theory of Task Motivation and Incentives." *Organizational Behavior and Human Performance* 3 (1968), pp. 157–89.

6.42 Locke, E.A.; K.N. Shaw; L.M. Saari; and G.P. Latham. "Goal Setting and Task Performance: 1969–1980." *Psychological Bulletin* 90 (1981), pp. 125–52.

6.43 Locke, E.A., and G.P. Latham. *A Theory of Goal Setting and Task Performance.* Englewood Cliffs, NJ: Prentice Hall, 1990.

6.44 Ibid.

6.45 Ibid.

6.46 Ibid.; see also Locke, E.A., and G.P. Latham. "Building a Practically Useful Theory of Goal Setting and Task Motivation: A 35-Year Odyssey." *American Psychologist* 57 (2002), pp. 705–17; Latham, G.P. "Motivate Employee Performance through Goal-Setting." In *Blackwell Handbook of Principles of Organizational Behavior,* ed. E.A. Locke.

Malden, MA: Blackwell, 2000, pp. 107–19.

6.47 Locke and Latham, *A Theory of Goal Setting.*

6.48 Locke et al., "Goal Setting and Task Performance."

6.49 Ibid.; Locke and Latham, *A Theory of Goal Setting;* Locke and Latham, "Building a Practically Useful Theory."

6.50 Wood, R.E.; A.J. Mento; and E.A. Locke. "Task Complexity as a Moderator of Goal Effects: A Meta-Analysis." *Journal of Applied Psychology* 72 (1987), pp. 416–25.

6.51 Ibid.

6.52 Barrett, A. "Cracking the Whip at Wyeth." *BusinessWeek,* February 6, 2006, pp. 70–71.

6.53 Hollenbeck, J.R., and H.J. Klein. "Goal Commitment and the Goal-Setting Process: Problems, Prospects, and Proposal for Future Research." *Journal of Applied Psychology* 72 (1987), pp. 212–20; see also Locke et al., "Goal Setting and Task Performance."

6.54 Klein, H.J.; M.J. Wesson; J.R. Hollenbeck; and B.J. Alge. "Goal Commitment and the Goal-Setting Process: Conceptual Clarification and Empirical Synthesis." *Journal of Applied Psychology* 84 (1999), pp. 885–96; Donovan, J.J., and D.J. Radosevich. "The Moderating Role of Goal Commitment on the Goal Difficulty–Performance Relationship. A Meta-Analytic Review and Critical Reanalysis." *Journal of Applied Psychology* 83 (1998), pp. 308–15.

6.55 Hollenbeck and Klein, "Goal Commitment and the Goal-Setting Process"; Klein et al., "Goal Commitment;" Locke, E.A.; G.P Latham;

and M. Erez. "The Determinants of Goal Commitment." *Academy of Management Review* 13 (1988), pp. 23–29; Latham, G.P. "The Motivational Benefits of Goal-Setting." *Academy of Management Executive* 18 (2004), pp. 126–29.

6.56 Shaw, K.N. "Changing the Goal Setting Process at Microsoft." *Academy of Management Executive* (2004), 18, 139–142.

6.57 Ibid.

6.58 Aguinis, H., and C.A. Henle. "The Search for Universals in Cross-Cultural Organizational Behavior." In *Organizational Behavior: The State of the Science,* ed. J. Greenberg. Mahwah, NJ: Erlbaum, 2003, 373–411.

6.59 Earley, P.C., and C.B Gibson. "Taking Stock in our Progress on Individualism–Collectivism: 100 Years of Solidarity and Community." *Journal of Management* 24 (1998), pp. 265–304.

6.60 Erez, M. "A Culture-Based Model of Work Motivation." *New Perspectives on International Industrial/Organizational Psychology,* ed. P.C. Earley and M. Erez. , 1997, pp. 193–242. San Francisco: New Lexington Press.

6.61 Erez, M., and P.C. Earley. "Comparative Analysis of Goal-Setting Strategies Across Cultures." *Journal of Applied Psychology* 72 (1987), pp. 658–65.

6.62 Audia, P.G., and S. Tams. "Goal Setting, Performance Appraisal, and Feedback Across Cultures." In *Blackwell Handbook of Cross-Cultural Management,* ed. M.J. Gannon and K.L. Newman. Malden, MA: Blackwell, 2002, pp. 142–54.

6.63 Adams, J.S., and W.B. Rosenbaum. "The Relationship of Worker Productivity to Cognitive Dissonance about Wage Inequities." *Journal of Applied Psychology* 46 (1962), pp. 161–64.

6.64 Adams, J.S. "Inequity in Social Exchange." In *Advances in Experimental Social Psychology,* Vol. 2, ed. L. Berkowitz. New York: Academic Press, 1965, pp. 267–99; see also Homans, G.C. *Social Behaviour: Its Elementary Forms.* London: Routledge & Kegan Paul, 1961.

6.65 Ibid.

6.66 Adams, "Inequality in Social Exchange."

6.67 Ibid.

6.68 Greenberg, J. "Employee Theft as a Reaction to Underpayment Inequity: The Hidden Cost of Paycuts." *Journal of Applied Psychology* 75 (1990), pp. 561–68; Greenberg, J. "Stealing in the Name of Justice: Informational and Interpersonal Moderators of Theft Reactions to Underpayment Inequity." *Organizational Behavior and Human Decision Processes* 54 (1993), pp. 81–103.

6.69 Adams, "Inequality in Social Exchange."

6.70 Scholl, R.W.; E.A. Cooper; and J.F. McKenna. "Referent Selection in Determining Equity Perceptions: Differential Effects on Behavioral and Attitudinal Outcomes." *Personnel Psychology* 40 (1987), pp. 113–24.

6.71 Ibid.

6.72 Ibid.; see also Finn, R.H., and S.M. Lee. "Salary Equity: Its Determination, Analysis, and Correlates." *Journal of Applied Psychology* 56 (1972), pp. 283–92.

6.73 Scholl, Cooper, and McKenna, "Referent Selection."

6.74 Lavelle, L. "A Payday for Performance: Compensation Is Less Outrageous this Year, Except for CEOs Who Delivered." *BusinessWeek,* April 18, 2005, pp. 78–80.

6.75 Kirkland, R. "The Real CEO." *Fortune,* July 10, 2006, pp. 78–92.

6.76 Sulkowicz, K. "CEO Pay: The Prestige, the Peril." *BusinessWeek,* November 20, 2006, p. 18.

6.77 Corio, P. "When Will They Stop?" *Fortune,* May 3, 2004, pp. 123–128.

6.78 Colella, A.; R.L. Paetzold; A. Zardkoohi; and M. Wesson. "Exposing Pay Secrecy." *Academy of Management Review.*(2007), 32, 55–71.

6.79 Ibid.

6.80 Gloeckler, G. "Campus Confidential." *BusinessWeek,* September 12, 2005, pp. 75–76.

6.81 Thomas, K.W., and B.A. Velthouse. "Cognitive Elements of Empowerment: An 'Interpretive' Model of Intrinsic Task Motivation." *Academy of Management Review* 15 (1990), pp. 666–81.

6.82 Hackman, J.R., and G.R. Oldham. *Work Redesign.* Reading, MA: Addison-Wesley, 1980.

6.83 Thomas and Velthouse, "Cognitive Elements of Empowerment"; Spreitzer, G.M. "Psychological Empowerment in the Workplace: Dimensions, Measurement, and Validation." *Academy of Management Journal* 38 (1995), pp. 1442–65; Deci, E.L., and R.M. Ryan. *Intrinsic Motivation and Self-Determination in Human Behavior.* New York: Plenum, 1985; Hackman and Oldham, *Work Redesign.*

6.84 Thomas, K.W. *Intrinsic Motivation at Work: Building Energy and Commitment.* San Francisco, CA: Berrett-Koehler Publishers, 2000.

6.85 Ibid.

6.86 Thomas and Velthouse, "Cognitive Elements of Empowerment"; Spreitzer, "Psychological Empowerment."

6.87 Thomas, *Intrinsic Motivation at Work.*

6.88 Thomas and Velthouse, "Cognitive Elements of Empowerment"; Spreitzer, "Psychological Empowerment."

6.89 Thomas, *Intrinsic Motivation at Work.*

6.90 Thomas and Velthouse, "Cognitive Elements of Empowerment."

6.91 Thomas, *Intrinsic Motivation at Work.*

6.92 Ibid.

6.93 Byrnes, "The Art of Motivation."

6.94 Stajkovic, A.D., and F. Luthans. "Self-Efficacy and Work-Related Performance: A Meta-Analysis." *Psychological Bulletin* 124 (1998), pp. 240–61.

6.95 Wood, Mento, and Locke, "Task Complexity as a Moderator."

6.96 Van Eerde, W., and H. Thierry. "Vroom's Expectancy Models and Work-Related Criteria: A Meta-Analysis." *Journal of Applied Psychology* 81 (1996), pp. 575–86.

6.97 Cohen-Charash, Y., and P.E. Spector. "The Role of Justice in Organizations: A Meta-Analysis." *Organizational Behavior and Human Decision Processes* 86 (2001), pp. 287–321; Colquitt, J.A.; D.E. Conlon; M.J. Wesson; C.O.L.H. Porter; and K.Y. Ng. "Justice at the Millennium: A Meta-Analytic Review of 25 Years of Organizational Justice Research." *Journal of Applied Psychology* 86 (2001), pp. 425–45.

6.98 Ibid.

6.99 Ibid.

6.100 Ibid.

6.101 Lawler, E.E., III. *Rewarding Excellence: Pay Strategies for the New Economy.* San Francisco, CA: Jossey-Bass, 2000.

6.102 Ibid.; see also Durham, C.C., and K.M. Bartol. "Pay for Performance." In *Handbook of Principles of Organizational Behavior,* ed. E.A. Locke. Malden, MA: Blackwell, 2000, pp. 150–65; Gerhart, B.; H.B. Minkoff; and R.N. Olsen. "Employee Compensation: Theory, Practice, and Evidence." In *Handbook of Human Resource Management,* ed. G.R. Ferris, S.D. Rosen, and D.T. Barnum. Malden, MA: Blackwell, 1995, pp. 528–47

6.103 Ibid.

6.104 Hansen, F. "Pushing Performance Management." *Workforce,* November 21, 2005. p. 22.

6.105 Latham, G., and S. Latham. "Overlooking Theory and Research in Performance Appraisal at One's Peril: Much Done, More to Do." In *Industrial and Organizational Psychology: Linking Theory with Practice,* ed. C.L. Cooper and E.A. Locke. Oxford, UK: Blackwell, 2000, pp. 199–215.

6.106 Ibid.

6.107 McGregor, J. "The Struggle to Measure Performance." *BusinessWeek,* January 9, 2006, pp. 26–28.

6.108 Scullen, S.E.; P.K. Bergey; and L. Aiman-Smith. "Forced Distribution Rating Systems and the Improvement of Workforce Potential: A Baseline Simulation." *Personnel Psychology* 58 (2005), pp. 1–32.

CHAPTER

7

Trust, Justice, and Ethics

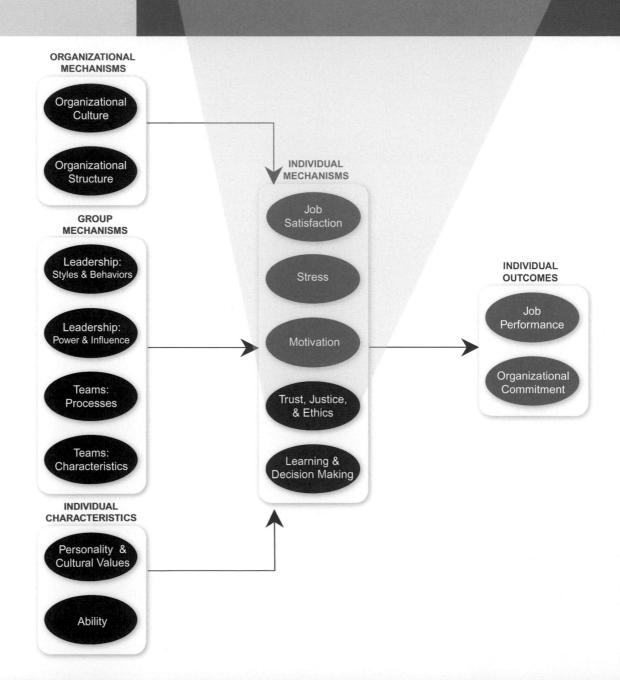

Wal-Mart has long enjoyed success with its famously low prices. But it faces an ethical crisis in the wake of reports of low wages and benefits, discrimination, and tax evasion and fraud by top management.

 LEARNING GOALS

After reading this chapter, you should be able to answer the following questions:

7.1 What is trust? What are justice and ethics?

7.2 In what three sources can trust be rooted? What dimensions can be used to describe how trustworthy an authority is?

7.3 Employees judge the fairness of an authority's decision making along four dimensions. What are those dimensions?

7.4 What is the four-component model of ethical decision making?

7.5 How does trust affect job performance and organizational commitment?

7.6 What steps can organizations take to become more trustworthy?

WAL-MART

What two words pop into your head when you hear "Wal-Mart"? For many people, "low prices" would be the answer. From this perspective, Wal-Mart is viewed as an American success story—the company founded in Bentonville, Arkansas, by a folksy entrepreneur who built a brilliant distribution system to bring products to customers at lower costs.[1] Those prices are critical to many shoppers and families, especially those who live on tight monthly budgets. As Wal-Mart describes it, the company's mission is to "lower the world's cost of living," with one estimate suggesting that the company saves consumers $20 billion a year.[2] Indeed, we could argue that Wal-Mart represents the single most powerful force against inflation in the country. That low-price formula has proven so successful that Wal-Mart stands as the largest company in the history of the world,[3] with 1.8 million people on the payroll as of 2005.[4] That size has brought about incredible market dominance, as Wal-Mart's 3,811 U.S. stores—more than one for every county in the country—control 45 percent of general merchandise sales.[5]

Other people, however, think of different words when they hear "Wal-Mart"—words like "evil empire." Those low prices often force local shops out of business, one reason the potential construction of new Wal-Mart stores has been met with stiff resistance in California, Illinois, and New York.[6] Wal-Mart is also accused of forcing its suppliers to cut corners to meet its price demands, using its leverage to buy products more cheaply than its competing retailers.[7] Wal-Mart also had to pay a record $11 million settlement to U.S. Immigration and Customs Enforcement because it hired hundreds of illegal immigrants to clean floors at 60 of its stores.[8] There have also been missteps among its top management, as Tom Coughlin, the former number 2 executive, is currently serving a 27-month house arrest sentence on charges of tax evasion, fraud, and embezzlement of company funds.[9]

Many of the most fervent criticisms of Wal-Mart, however, center on how it treats its employees. Critics argue that the "always low prices" goal is built on an "always low wages" reality, with Wal-Mart offering pay and benefits that cannot be considered a living wage.[10] Critics note that Wal-Mart employees are paid so little—$9.68 per hour on average—that the only store they can afford to shop at is Wal-Mart![11] Health benefits are also a point of contention, with Wal-Mart spending 30 percent less on average than its retail peers.[12] Apart from general concerns about its compensation, Wal-Mart has come under fire for illegal actions. For example, the company was recently forced to pay $78 million to 185,000 employees who claimed they were denied breaks and forced to work off the clock.[13] That $78 million pales in comparison to the class action lawsuit brought against the company by 1.5 million current and former female employees.[14] That suit, the largest of its kind in the nation's history, alleges that women get paid less than men for the same jobs and that men are promoted more frequently than women within the company. Analysts suggest that settling this discrimination case could wind up costing Wal-Mart $8 billion.[15]

One spokeswoman for the company worries that shoppers could start feeling guilty about going to Wal-Mart,[16] and one report suggests that 14 percent of the Americans living within range of a Wal-Mart store could be categorized as "conscientious objectors" to the company's practices.[17] In response to such pressures, Wal-Mart has undertaken some important reform efforts. For example, the company hired 300 new human resources managers to work out in the field in an effort to improve the company's hiring and communication practices, along with employee morale and job behaviors.[18] Wal-Mart's CEO, Lee Scott, seems to understand the situation he's facing. At a recent company gathering, Scott noted, "We have to remember that any bad incident that occurs is not only a reflection on the individual who did it but on all of us here."[19] He went on to suggest that any Wal-Mart employee who does something unfair or unethical is "getting ready to take out the paint brush and put a big black mark across Wal-Mart Stores."

TRUST, JUSTICE, AND ETHICS

When describing Wal-Mart's recent missteps, one market researcher noted, "Their reputation in the area of trust has been slipping, and trust was probably their greatest asset."[20] **Trust** is defined as the willingness to be vulnerable to an authority based on positive expectations about the authority's actions and intentions.[21] When we trust, we become willing to "put ourselves out there," even though that choice could be met with disappointment. This definition can be used to highlight the important distinction between "trust" and "risk." Actually making oneself vulnerable to an authority is a risk; trust reflects the willingness to take that risk. This definition also illustrates where trust comes from, as it is based on an assessment of how a given authority is likely to behave in a particular situation.

7.1

What is trust? What are justice and ethics?

Who is the authority referenced in the trust definition? Sometimes that authority is person-based, as when you trust a specific Wal-Mart manager to be honest about a product's shortcomings. Sometimes that authority is organization-based, as when you trust that Wal-Mart, as a company, will treat your cousin fairly when he accepts a job. Because we don't usually have direct knowledge about the company as a whole, an organization-based version of trust depends largely on a company's reputation. Table 7-1 summarizes organizations with good reputations, based on *Fortune*'s list of "America's Most Admired Companies."[22] Although Wal-Mart makes the list at #19, it should be noted that the company ranked #1 as recently as 2004.

Issues of trust are intertwined with two related concepts. **Justice** reflects the perceived fairness of an authority's decision making.[23] When employees perceive high levels of justice, they believe that decision outcomes are fair and that decision-making processes are designed and implemented in a fair manner. Justice concepts can be used to explain why employees judge some authorities as more trustworthy than others.[24] **Ethics** reflects the degree to which the behaviors of an authority are in accordance with generally accepted moral norms.[25] When employees perceive high levels of ethics, they believe that things are being done the way they "should be" or "ought to be" done. Ethics concepts can be used to explain why authorities decide to act in a trustworthy or untrustworthy manner.

TABLE 7-1	"America's Most Admired Companies"
1. General Electric	11. Goldman Sachs
2. Starbucks	12. Microsoft
3. Toyota Motor	13. Target
4. Berkshire Hathaway	14. 3M
5. Southwest Airlines	15. Nordstrom
6. FedEx	16. United Parcel Service
7. Apple	17. American Express
8. Google	18. Costco Wholesale
9. Johnson & Johnson	19. PepsiCo (tie)
10. Procter & Gamble	19. Wal-Mart (tie)

Source: A. Fisher, "America's Most Admired Companies," *Fortune*, March 19, 2007, pp. 88–112. Copyright © 2004 Time Inc. All rights reserved.

WHY ARE SOME AUTHORITIES MORE TRUSTED THAN OTHERS?

Think about a particular boss or instructor—one whom you've spent a significant amount of time around. Do you trust that person? Would you be willing to let that person have significant influence over your professional or educational future? For example, would you be willing to let that person serve as a reference for you or write you a letter of recommendation, even though you'd have no way of monitoring what he or she said about you? When you think about the level of trust you feel for that particular authority, what exactly makes you feel that way? This question speaks to the factors that drive trust—the factors that help inspire a willingness to be vulnerable.

TRUST

As shown in Figure 7-1, trust is rooted in different kinds of factors. Sometimes trust is **disposition-based,** meaning that your personality traits include a general propensity

FIGURE 7-1   Factors That Influence Trust Levels

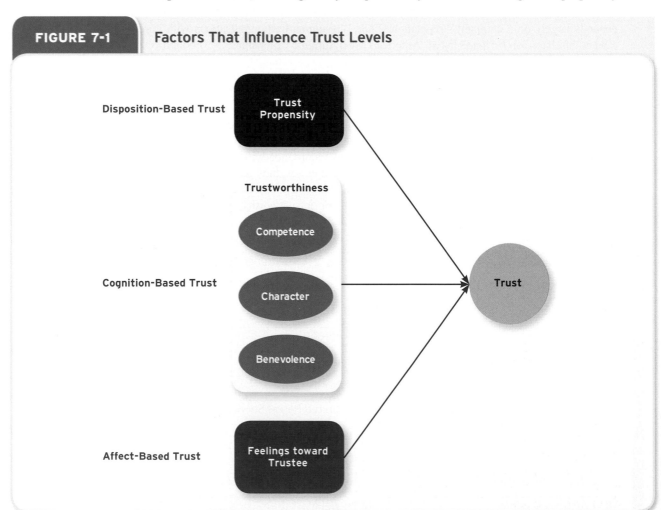

Sources: Adapted from R.C. Mayer, J.H. Davis, and F.D. Schoorman, "An Integrative Model of Organizational Trust," *Academy of Management Review* 20 (1995), pp. 709–34; D.J. McAllister, "Affect- and Cognition-Based Trust as Foundations for Interpersonal Cooperation in Organizations," *Academy of Management Journal* 38 (1995), pp. 24–59.

to trust others. Sometimes trust is **cognition-based,** meaning that it is rooted in a rational assessment of the authority's trustworthiness.[26] Sometimes trust is **affect-based,** meaning that it depends on feelings toward the authority that go beyond any rational assessment.[27] The sections that follow describe each of these trust forms in more detail.

DISPOSITION-BASED TRUST. Disposition-based trust has less to do with the authority and more to do with the trustor. Some trustors are high in **trust propensity**—a general expectation that the words, promises, and statements of individuals and groups can be relied upon.[28] Some have argued that trust propensity represents a sort of "faith in human nature," in that trusting people view others in more favorable terms than do suspicious people.[29] The importance of trust propensity is most obvious in interactions with strangers, in which any acceptance of vulnerability would amount to "blind trust."[30] On the one hand, people who are high in trust propensity may be fooled into trusting others who are not worthy of it.[31] On the other hand, those who are low in trust propensity may be fooled by not trusting someone who is actually deserving of it. Both situations can be damaging; as one scholar noted, "We are doomed if we trust all and equally doomed if we trust none."[32] Where do you stack up on trust propensity? See our **OB Assessments** feature to find out.

Where does our trust propensity come from? As with all traits, trust propensity is a product of both nature and nurture (see Chapter 9 on Personality and Cultural Values for more discussion of these issues). If our parents are dispositionally suspicious, we may either inherit that tendency genetically or model it as we watch them exhibit distrust in their day-to-day lives. Research also suggests that trust propensity is shaped by early childhood experiences.[33] In fact, trust propensity may be one of the first personality traits to develop, because infants must immediately learn to trust their parents to meet their needs. The more our needs are met as children, the more trusting we become; the more we are disappointed as children, the less trusting we become. Our propensities continue to be shaped later in life as we gain experiences with friends, schools, churches, local government authorities, and other relevant groups.[34]

The nation in which we live also affects our trust propensity. Research by the World Values Study Group examines differences between nations on various attitudes and perceptions. The study group collects interview data from 45 different societies with a total sample size of more than 90,000 participants. One of the questions asked by the study group measures trust propensity. Specifically, participants are asked, "Generally speaking, would you say that most people can be trusted or that you can't be too careful in dealing with people?" Figure 7-2 shows the percentage of participants who answered "Most people can be trusted" for this question, as opposed to "Can't be too careful," for several of the nations included in the study. The results reveal that trust propensity levels are actually relatively high in the United States, especially in relation to countries in Europe and South America.

COGNITION-BASED TRUST. Disposition-based trust guides us in cases when we don't yet have data about a particular authority. However, eventually we gain enough knowledge to gauge the authority's **trustworthiness,** defined as the characteristics or attributes of a trustee that inspire trust.[35] At that point, our trust begins to be based on cognitions we've developed about the authority, as opposed to our own personality or disposition. In this way, cognition-based trust is driven by the

7.2

In what three sources can trust be rooted? What dimensions can be used to describe how trustworthy an authority is?

Children whose needs are generally met tend to grow into trusting adults.

OB ASSESSMENTS

TRUST PROPENSITY

Are you a trusting person or a suspicious person by nature? This assessment is designed to measure trust propensity—a dispositional willingness to trust other people. Answer each question using the response scale provided. Then subtract your answers to the bold-faced questions from 6, with the difference being your new answers for those questions. For example, if your original answer for question 4 was "4," your new answer is "2" (6–4). Then sum up your answers for the eight questions.

1	2	3	4	5
STRONGLY DISAGREE	DISAGREE	NEUTRAL	AGREE	STRONGLY AGREE

1. **One should be very cautious with strangers.** _____

2. Most experts tell the truth about the limits of their knowledge. _____

3. Most people can be counted on to do what they say they will do. _____

4. **These days, you must be alert or someone is likely to take advantage of you.** _____

5. Most salespeople are honest in describing their products. _____

6. Most repair people will not overcharge people who are ignorant of their specialty. _____

7. Most people answer public opinion polls honestly. _____

8. Most adults are competent at their jobs. _____

SCORING

If your scores sum up to 21 or above, you tend to be trusting of other people, which means you are often willing to accept some vulnerability to others under conditions of risk. If your scores sum up to 20 or below, you tend to be suspicious of other people, which means you are rarely willing to accept some vulnerability to others under conditions of risk.

Sources: R.C. Mayer and J.H. Davis, "The Effect of the Performance Appraisal System on Trust for Management: A Field Quasi-Experiment," *Journal of Applied Psychology* 84 (1999), pp. 123–36. Copyright © 1999 by the American Psychological Associated. Adapted with permission. No further reproduction or distribution is permitted without written permission from the American Psychological Association; F.D. Schoorman, R.C. Mayer, C. Roger, and J.H. Davis. "Empowerment in Veterinary Clinics: The Role of Trust in Delegation." Presented in a Symposium on Trust at the 11th Annual Conference, Society for Industrial and Organizational Psychology (SIOP), (April 1996), San Diego.

authority's "track record."[36] If that track record has shown the authority to be trustworthy, then vulnerability to the authority can be accepted. If that track record is spotty however, then trust may not be warranted. Research suggests that we gauge the track record of an authority along three dimensions: competence, character, and benevolence.[37]

FIGURE 7-2	**Trust Propensities by Nation**

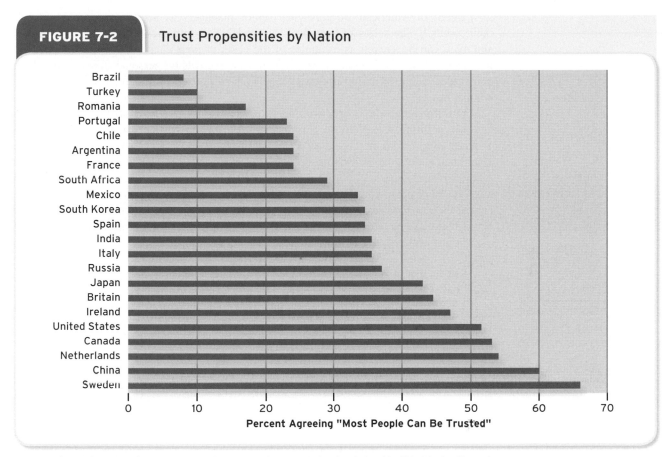

Source: Adapted from J.J. Johnson and J.B. Cullen, "Trust in Cross-Cultural Relationships," in *Blackwell Handbook of Cross-Cultural Management,* eds. M.J. Gannon and K.L. Newman (Malden, MA: Blackwell, 2002), pp. 335–60.

The first dimension of trustworthiness is **competence,** defined as the skills, abilities, and areas of expertise that enable an authority to be successful in some specific area (see Chapter 10 on Ability for more discussion of these issues).[38] Think about the decision-making process that you go through when choosing a doctor, lawyer, or mechanic. Clearly one of the first things you consider is competence, because you're not going to trust them if they don't know a scalpel from a retractor, a tort from a writ, or a camshaft from a crankshaft. Of course, listing a specific area is a key component of the competence definition; you wouldn't trust a mechanic to perform surgery, nor would you trust a doctor to fix your car! The competence of business authorities may be considered on a number of levels. For example, a manager may be judged according to the functional expertise of a particular industry or vocation but also according to his or her leadership skills and general business sense.[39]

The second dimension of trustworthiness is **character,** defined as the perception that the authority adheres to a set of values and principles that the trustor finds acceptable.[40] When authorities are perceived to be of sound character, it means that they have integrity— that they have honest motives and intentions. Character also conveys an alignment between words and deeds—a sense that authorities keep their promises, "walk the talk," and "do what they say they will do."[41] Unfortunately, a recent survey indicated that only around

20 percent of American workers view senior managers as acting in accordance with their words.[42] The series of high-profile scandals at companies like Enron, WorldCom, and Tyco can be viewed as examples of the costs of poor character. In those cases, top management hid debt, misstated earnings, and used profits for personal gain—all of which constituted dishonest actions that went against the espoused values and principles of those companies.

The third dimension of trustworthiness is **benevolence,** defined as the belief that the authority wants to do good for the trustor, apart from any selfish or profit-centered motives.[43] When authorities are perceived as benevolent, it means that they care for employees, are concerned about their well-being, and feel a sense of loyalty to them. The mentor–protégé relationship provides a good example of benevolence at work.[44] The best mentors would never do anything to hurt their protégés. They go out of their way to be helpful, even at the cost of their own personal productivity and in the absence of any financial reward. Clearly benevolence, along with competence and character, provides a set of good reasons to trust a particular authority.[45] For more on how these three trustworthiness facets can be used to gauge trust, see our **OB on Screen** feature.

AFFECT-BASED TRUST. Although competence, character, and benevolence provide three good reasons to trust an authority, the third form of trust isn't really rooted in reason at all. Affect-based trust is more emotional than rational. With affect-based trust, we trust because we have feelings for the person in question; we really like them and have a fondness for them. Those feelings are what prompt us to accept vulnerability to another person. Put simply, we trust them because we like them.

Affect-based trust acts as a supplement to the types of trust discussed previously.[47] Figure 7-3 describes how the various forms of trust can build on one another over time. In new relationships, trust depends solely on our own trust propensity. In most relationships, that propensity eventually gets supplemented by knowledge about competence, character, or benevolence, at which point cognition-based trust develops. In a select few of those relationships, an emotional bond develops, and our feelings for the trustee further increase our willingness to accept vulnerability. These relationships are characterized by a mutual investment of time and energy, a sense of deep attachment, and the realization that both parties would feel a sense of loss if the relationship were dissolved.[48]

SUMMARY. Taken together, disposition-based trust, cognition-based trust, and affect-based trust provide three completely different sources of trust in a particular authority. In the case of disposition-based trust, our willingness to be vulnerable has little to do with the authority and more to do with our genes and our early life experiences. In the case of affect-based trust, our willingness to be vulnerable has little to do with a rational assessment of the authority's merits and more to do with our emotional fondness for the authority. Only in the case of cognition-based trust do we rationally evaluate the pluses and minuses of an authority, in terms of its competence, character, and benevolence. But how exactly do we gauge those trustworthiness forms? One way is to consider whether authorities adhere to rules of justice.

JUSTICE

It's often difficult to assess the competence, character, and benevolence of authorities accurately, particularly early in a working relationship. What employees need in such circumstances is some sort of observable behavioral evidence that an authority might be trustworthy. Justice provides that sort of behavioral evidence, because authorities who

OB ON SCREEN

PIRATES OF THE CARIBBEAN: THE CURSE OF THE BLACK PEARL

May I ask you something? Have I ever given you reason not to trust me?

With those words, Captain Jack Sparrow (Johnny Depp) poses a difficult question in *Pirates of the Caribbean: The Curse of the Black Pearl* (Dir. Gore Verbinski, Disney, 2003). There are a whole host of reasons not to trust Jack. The most obvious comes during a sword-fight between Jack and young Will Turner (Orlando Bloom), when Jack breaks the rules of engagement by pulling his gun. "You cheated," Will pleads. "Pirate," Jack answers.

From a competence perspective, Jack actually does a lot to inspire trust. His skills at hatching a plan belie his crazy demeanor. He also happens to be a good swordsman and a remarkably good escape artist. So when Jack suggests a course of action, you're tempted to follow it. Indeed, early in the film, after Jack steals a ship from Britain's Port Royal, one of the British soldiers remarks that Jack must be the best pirate he's ever seen.

As with any pirate, however, Jack struggles with character. In addition to the afore-mentioned gun incident, Jack lies, steals, and rarely does exactly what he says he'd do. Although he appears to hold firmly to the "pirate's code," most pirates view the code more as a set of guidelines than actual rules. And that code includes such lofty sayings as, "Any-one who falls behind is left behind."

From a benevolence perspective, Jack does seem to care sincerely for Will and Elizabeth (Keira Knightly), the British Governor's daughter for whom Will is secretly carrying a torch. In fact, Jack routinely risks his own life to save one or both of them throughout the film. But does he do so merely to further his own profit-driven motives?

Jack's nemesis, Captain Barbossa (Geoffrey Rush), sums up the uncertainty about Jack's trustworthiness, saying, "I must admit Jack, I thought I had you figured, but it turns out you're a hard man to predict." Jack's reply: "Me? I'm dishonest, and a dishonest man you can always trust to be dishonest … honestly." That answer doesn't really clear things up, does it? As Elizabeth asks near the climax of the film, "Whose side is Jack on?" Will's answer: "At the moment?"

FIGURE 7-3 | Types of Trust Over Time

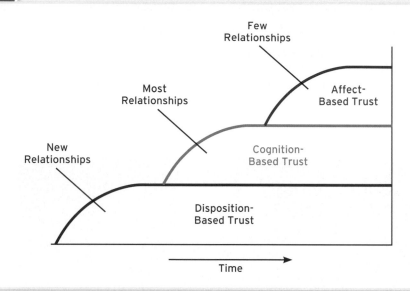

Sources: Adapted from R.J. Lewicki and B.B. Bunker, "Developing and Maintaining Trust in Work Relationships," in *Trust in Organizations: Frontiers of Theory and Research,* eds. R.M. Kramer and T.R. Tyler (Thousand Oaks, CA: Sage, 1996), pp. 114–39; R.C. Mayer, J.H. Davis, and F.D. Schoorman, "An Integrative Model of Organizational Trust," *Academy of Management Review* 20 (1995), pp. 709–34.

treat employees more fairly are usually judged to be more trustworthy.[49] As shown in Table 7-2, employees can judge the fairness of an authority's decision making along four dimensions: distributive justice, procedural justice, interpersonal justice, and informational justice.

DISTRIBUTIVE JUSTICE. Distributive justice reflects the perceived fairness of decision-making outcomes.[50] Employees gauge distributive justice by asking whether decision outcomes, such as pay, rewards, evaluations, promotions, and work assignments, are allocated using proper norms. In most business situations, the proper norm is equity, with more outcomes allocated to those who contribute more inputs (see Chapter 6 on Motivation for more discussion of equity). The equity norm is typically judged to be the fairest choice in situations in which the goal is to maximize the productivity of individual employees.[51]

However, other allocation norms become appropriate in situations in which other goals are critical. In team-based work, building harmony and solidarity in work groups can become just as important as individual productivity. In such cases, an equality norm may be judged more fair, such that all team members receive the same amount of relevant rewards.[52] The equality norm is typically used in student project groups, in which all group members receive exactly the same grade on a project, regardless of their individual productivity levels. In cases in which the welfare of a particular employee is the critical concern, a need norm may be judged more fair. For example, PricewaterhouseCoopers, the New York–based accounting firm, wired $4,000 to 43 employees who were affected by Hurricane Katrina.[53] The company also gave those employees food, lodging, and transportation for a three-month period.

PROCEDURAL JUSTICE. In addition to judging the fairness of a decision outcome, employees may consider the process that led to that outcome. **Procedural justice** reflects

 7.3

Employees judge the fairness of an authority's decision making along four dimensions. What are those dimensions?

TABLE 7-2	The Four Dimensions of Justice

Distributive Justice Rules	Description
Equity vs. equality vs. need	Are rewards allocated according to the proper norm?
Procedural Justice Rules	
Voice	Do employees get to provide input into procedures?
Correctability	Do procedures build in mechanisms for appeals?
Consistency	Are procedures consistent across people and time?
Bias Suppression	Are procedures neutral and unbiased?
Representativeness	Do procedures consider the needs of all groups?
Accuracy	Are procedures based on accurate information?
Interpersonal Justice Rules	
Respect	Do authorities treat employees with sincerity?
Propriety	Do authorities refrain from improper remarks?
Informational Justice Rules	
Justification	Do authorities explain procedures thoroughly?
Truthfulness	Are those explanations honest?

Sources: J.S. Adams, "Inequity in Social Exchange," in *Advances in Experimental Social Psychology,* Vol. 2, ed. L. Berkowitz (New York: Academic Press, 1965), pp. 267–99; R.J. Bies and J.F. Moag, "Interactional Justice: Communication Criteria of Fairness," in *Research on Negotiations in Organizations,* Vol. 1, eds. R.J. Lewicki, B.H. Sheppard, and M.H. Bazerman (Greenwich, CT: JAI Press, 1986), pp. 43–55; G.S. Leventhal, "The Distribution of Rewards and Resources in Groups and Organizations," in *Advances in Experimental Social Psychology,* Vol. 9, eds. L. Berkowitz and W. Walster (New York: Academic Press, 1976), pp. 91–131; G.S. Leventhal, "What Should Be Done with Equity Theory? New Approaches to the Study of Fairness in Social Relationships," in *Social Exchange: Advances in Theory and Research,* eds. K. Gergen, M. Greenberg, and R. Willis (New York: Plenum Press, 1980), pp. 27–55; J. Thibaut and L. Walker, *Procedural Justice: A Psychological Analysis* (Hillsdale, NJ: Erlbaum, 1975).

the perceived fairness of decision-making processes.[54] Procedural justice is fostered when authorities adhere to rules of fair process. One of those rules is voice, which concerns giving employees a chance to express their opinions and views during the course of decision making.[55] A related rule is correctability, which provides employees with a chance to request an appeal when a procedure seems to have worked ineffectively. Research suggests that voice improves employees reactions to decisions,[56] largely because it gives employees a sense of ownership over the decisions that occur at work. In fact, employees value voice even when it doesn't always result in the outcomes they want or when their appeals don't always reverse the decisions that were made.[57] Why? Because employees like to be heard—the expression of opinions is a valued end, in-and-of-itself, as long as employees feel those opinions were truly considered.

Aside from voice and correctability, procedural justice is fostered when authorities adhere to four rules that serve to create equal employment opportunity. The consistency, bias suppression, representativeness, and accuracy rules help ensure that procedures are neutral and objective, as opposed to biased and discriminatory. These sorts of procedural rules are relevant in many areas of working life. As one example, the rules can be used to make hiring practices more fair by ensuring that interview questions are unbiased and asked in the same manner across applications. As another example, the rules can be used to make compensation practices more fair by ensuring that accurate measures of job performance are used to provide input for merit raises.

These sorts of procedural justice rules are critical because employment data suggest that gender and race continue to have significant impacts on organizational decision making. Compensation data suggest that women almost always earn less than men for doing the same job. More specifically, women and men earn roughly the same in jobs that pay $25,000–$30,000 a year, but the gap widens as the salary increases.[58] Female psychologists earn 83 percent of what males earn, female college professors earn 75 percent of what males earn, and female lawyers and judges earn 69 percent of what males earn. As a result, sex discrimination cases have risen dramatically in recent years, with each victory adding weight to existing concerns about unfairness. As one employment lawyer put it, "Employees already mistrust employers. So each time a case reveals a secret that was never told, employees think, 'Aha! They really *are* paying men more than women.'"[59]

Compensation data also suggest that African American men only earn 76 percent of what Caucasian men earn.[60] Education differences don't explain the gap, because Caucasian high school dropouts are twice as likely to find jobs as African American dropouts. Such differences are likely due to procedural injustice in some form, with procedures functioning in an inconsistent, biased, and inaccurate manner across Caucasian and African American applicants. Of course, some companies seem to do a better job of treating minorities fairly. Table 7-3 provides the list of *Fortune*'s "50 Best Companies for Minorities," a list that is based on hiring, promotion, and retention rates for minority employees. Now you have two reasons to eat at McDonald's: tasty fries and procedural justice!

If you're a college football fan, you hear procedural justice issues discussed every Monday of the fall. That's because the Bowl Championship Series (BCS) standings are released on Mondays, starting a few weeks into the football season. Unlike other college sports, football does not have a season-ending playoff to crown its champion. Instead, a procedure is used to rank teams week-in and week-out, with the top two teams in the season-ending rankings squaring off for the national championship. The BCS rankings are (more or less) an average of three types of rankings: (1) the *USA Today* College Coaches Poll, whose rankings depend on 63 Division 1-A football coaches; (2) the Harris Interactive Poll, whose rankings come from 114 former coaches, players, and administrators, along with members of the media; and (3) computer polls, which determine rankings by averaging together six completely different sets of computer rankings.[61]

The Monday release of the BCS standings typically brings a wave of complaints to local sports talk radio programs. Why? Often because the process seems unfair. The bias suppression rule is violated because coaches are free to vote for their own team or teams in their conference, and the members of the Harris Interactive Poll also have conference affiliations that could color their voting. The accuracy rule is violated because it's a good bet that the East Coast coaches and Harris Poll members are in bed before the big Oregon versus Washington State game kicks off at 10:15 p.m. Eastern time. The correctability rule is violated because when things go wrong with the polls, they can't be "tweaked" until the next off-season. Finally, the representativeness rule is violated because schools from smaller conferences face an uphill climb, even when they keep winning their games. That's because the computer polls consider "strength of schedule" in their rankings, and smaller schools almost always have a weaker strength of schedule. Even if Fresno State wants to play Ohio State, it's a good bet the Buckeyes will only agree to play the game if it's in Columbus.

You might be wondering, "Does procedural justice really matter—don't people just care about the outcomes that they receive?" In the case of the BCS, don't fans just care where they end up in the rankings, not how they got there? Research suggests that distributive justice and procedural justice combine to influence employee reactions, as shown in

TABLE 7-3	The "50 Best Companies for Minorities"
1. McDonald's	26. Coca-Cola
2. Fannie Mae	27. Nordstrom
3. Sempra Energy	28. Avon Products
4. Union Bank of California	29. Abbott Laboratories
5. Denny's	30. Knight-Ridder
6. U.S. Postal Service	31. Golden West Financial
7. PepsiCo	32. Starwood Hotels
8. Southern California Edison	33. Darden Restaurants
9. Freddie Mac	34. Safeway
10. PNM Resources	35. Wyndham International
11. PG&E Corporation	36. Levi Strauss
12. SBC Communications	37. Pepco Holdings
13. Hilton Hotels	38. Citigroup
14. Verizon Communications	39. Prudential Financial
15. Yum Brands	40. Schering-Plough
16. Colgate-Palmolive	41. American Express
17. Xerox	42. MGM Mirage
18. Hyatt	43. JPMorgan Chase
19. Washington Mutual	44. Pitney Bowes
20. TIAA-CREF	45. Procter & Gamble
21. Applied Materials	46. General Motors
22. Consolidated Edison	47. Eastman Kodak
23. United Parcel Service	48. Merck
24. DTE Energy	49. AT&T
25. BellSouth	50. Bank of America

Source: C. Daniels, "50 Best Companies for Minorities," *Fortune,* June 28, 2004, pp. 136–56. Copyright © 2004 Time Inc. All rights reserved.

Figure 7-4.[62] It's true that when outcomes are good, people don't spend as much time worrying about how fair the process was, as illustrated by the green line in the figure, which shows that procedural justice has little impact on reactions when distributive justice is high. Those of us at the University of Florida didn't much care about the fairness of the BCS ranking process at the end of the 2006–2007 season, because we found ourselves

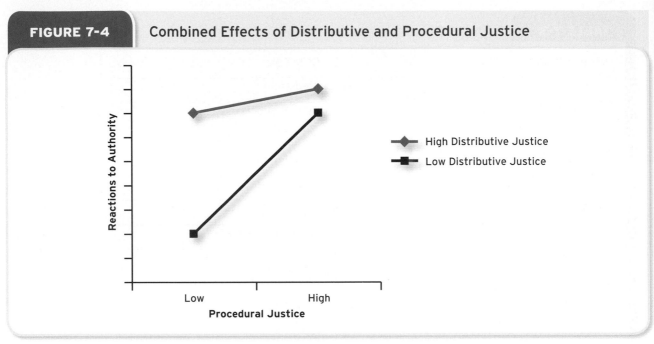

FIGURE 7-4   Combined Effects of Distributive and Procedural Justice

Source: Adapted from J. Brockner and B.M. Wiesenfeld, "An Integrative Framework for Explaining Reactions to Decisions: Interactive Effects of Outcomes and Procedures," *Psychological Bulletin* 120 (1996), pp. 189–208.

in the national championship game. However, when outcomes are bad, procedural justice becomes enormously important. Research shows that negative or unexpected events trigger a thorough examination of process issues, making adherence to rules like consistency, bias suppression, and accuracy much more vital.[63] Folks at the University of Michigan did care about the fairness of the BCS ranking process at the end of that same season, because they found themselves out of the championship game despite being ranked #2 for much of the season.

In fact, research shows that procedural justice tends to be a stronger driver of reactions to authorities than distributive justice. For example, a meta-analysis of 183 studies showed that procedural justice was a stronger predictor of satisfaction with supervision, overall job satisfaction, and organizational commitment than distributive justice.[64] Why does the decision-making process sometimes matter more than the decision-making outcome? Likely because employees understand that outcomes come and go—some may be in your favor while others may be a bit disappointing. Procedures, however, are more long-lasting and stay in place until the organization redesigns them or a new leader arrives to revise them.

INTERPERSONAL JUSTICE. In addition to judging the fairness of decision outcomes and processes, employees might consider how authorities treat them as the procedures are implemented. **Interpersonal justice** reflects the perceived fairness of the treatment received by employees from authorities.[65] Interpersonal justice is fostered when authorities adhere to two particular rules. The respect rule pertains to whether authorities treat employees in a dignified and sincere manner, and the propriety rule reflects whether authorities refrain from making improper or offensive remarks. From this perspective, interpersonal *injustice* occurs when authorities bad-mouth employees; criticize, berate, embarrass, or humiliate them in public; or refer to them with racist or sexist labels.[66]

How common are instances of interpersonal injustice? A survey of nearly 5,000 employees found that 36 percent reported persistent hostility from authorities and coworkers, when persistent hostility was defined as experiencing one abusive act at least weekly for a period of one year.[67] How damaging are such acts? One study asked 41 employees to complete a survey on interactions with authorities and coworkers four times a day for 2 to 3 weeks using a palmtop computer.[68] Two kinds of interactions were coded—positive experiences and negative experiences—and participants also reported on their current mood (e.g., happy, pleased, sad, blue, unhappy). The results of the study showed that positive interactions were more common than negative interactions, but the effects of negative interactions on mood were five times stronger than the effects of positive interactions. Such findings suggest that violations of the respect and propriety rules loom much larger than adherence to such rules.[69] Indeed, research suggests that violations of interpersonal justice rules reduce employees' job satisfaction, life satisfaction, and organizational commitment while increasing feelings of depression, anxiety, and burnout.[70]

INFORMATIONAL JUSTICE. Finally, employees may consider the kind of information that authorities provide during the course of organizational decision making. **Informational justice** reflects the perceived fairness of the communications provided to employees from authorities.[71] Informational justice is fostered when authorities adhere to two particular rules. The justification rule mandates that authorities explain decision-making procedures and outcomes in a comprehensive and reasonable manner, and the truthfulness rule requires that those communications be honest and candid. Although it seems like common sense that organizations would explain decisions in a comprehensive and adequate manner, that's often not the case. For example, RadioShack, the Texas-based home electronics retailer, was recently criticized for firing 400 employees via e-mail.[72] Employees at the Fort Worth headquarters received messages on a Tuesday morning saying: "The work force reduction notification is currently in progress. Unfortunately your position is one that has been eliminated." After receiving the 18-word message, employees had 30 minutes to make phone calls and say goodbye to fellow employees, before packing up their belongings in boxes and plastic bags.

These sorts of informational injustices are all too common, for a variety of reasons. One reason is that sharing bad news is the worst part of the job for most managers, leading them to distance themselves when it's time to play messenger.[73] Another reason is that managers worry about triggering a lawsuit if they comprehensively and honestly explain the real reasons for a layoff, a poor evaluation, or a missed promotion. Ironically, that defense mechanism is typically counterproductive, because research suggests that honest and adequate explanations are actually a powerful strategy for reducing retaliation responses against the organization.[74] In fact, low levels of informational justice can come back to haunt the organization if a wrongful termination claim is actually filed. How? Because the organization typically needs to provide performance evaluations for the terminated employee over the past few years, to show that the employee was fired for poor performance.[75] If

RadioShack recently violated the norms of informational justice by laying off 400 employees in Fort Worth via a curt e-mail of 18 words.

managers refrained from offering candid and honest explanations on those evaluations, then the organization can't offer anything to justify the termination.

One study provides a particularly effective demonstration of the power of informational justice (and interpersonal justice). The study occurred in three plants of a Midwestern manufacturing company that specialized in small mechanical parts for the aerospace and automotive industries.[76] The company had recently lost two of its largest contracts and was forced to cut wages by 15 percent in two of the three plants. The company was planning to offer a short, impersonal explanation for the pay cut to both of the affected plants. However, as part of a research study, the company was convinced to offer a longer, more sincere explanation at one of the plants. Theft levels were then tracked before, during, and after the 10-week pay cut using the company's standard accounting formulas for inventory "shrinkage."

The results of the study are shown in Figure 7-5. In the plant without the pay cut, no change in theft levels occurred over the 10-week period. In the plant with the short, impersonal explanation, theft rose dramatically during the pay cut, likely as a means of retaliating for perceived inequity, before falling to previous levels once the cut had passed. Importantly, in the plant with the long, sincere explanation, the rise in theft was much less significant during the pay cut, with theft levels again falling back to normal levels once the cut had ended. Clearly, the higher levels of informational and interpersonal justice were worth it from a cost-savings perspective. The difference in theft across the two plants is remarkable, given that the long, sincere explanation was only 143 words longer than the short, impersonal explanation. What's an extra 45 seconds if it can save a few thousand dollars?

SUMMARY. Taken together, distributive, procedural, interpersonal, and informational justice can be used to describe how fairly employees are treated by authorities. When

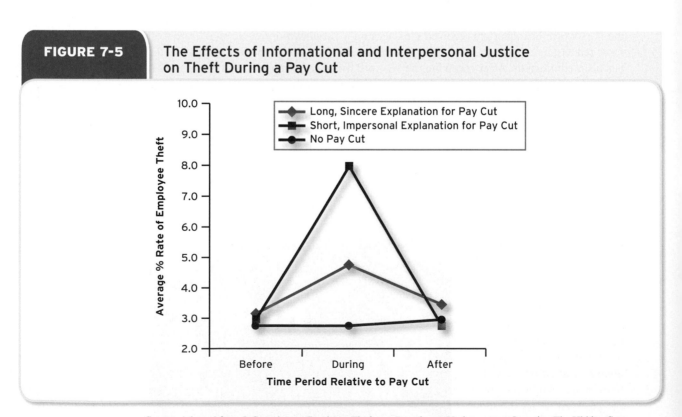

FIGURE 7-5   The Effects of Informational and Interpersonal Justice on Theft During a Pay Cut

Source: Adapted from J. Greenberg, "Employee Theft as a Reaction to Underpayment Inequity: The Hidden Cost of Paycuts," *Journal of Applied Psychology* 75 (1990), pp. 561–68.

an authority adheres to the justice rules in Table 7-2, it provides behavioral data that the authority might be trustworthy. Studies show that all four justice forms have strong correlations with employee trust levels.[77] All else being equal, employees trust authorities who allocate outcomes fairly; make decisions in a consistent, unbiased, and accurate way; and communicate decision-making details in a respectful, comprehensive, and honest manner. Which authorities are most likely to adhere to these sorts of rules? Research on ethics can provide some answers.

ETHICS

Research on ethics seeks to explain why people behave in a manner consistent with generally accepted norms of morality, and why they sometimes violate those norms.[78] Some ethics studies focus on behaviors that exceed minimum standards of morality, such as charitable giving or **whistle-blowing,** which occurs when employees expose illegal actions by their employer. Other studies focus on behaviors that fall below minimum standards of morality, such as lying and cheating. Still other studies focus on behaviors that merely reach minimum standards of morality, such as obeying the law. Regardless of the particular area of focus, such research continues to be a critical area of OB because unethical acts are so common in organizations. For example, recent surveys suggest that 76 percent of employees have observed illegal or unethical conduct on the job within the past 12 months.[79] Those base rates may be even higher in some countries, as described in our **OB Internationally** feature.

How can we explain exactly why an authority would choose to act in an unethical manner? One set of answers can be derived from research in social psychology. As shown in Figure 7-6, the four-component model of ethical decision making argues that ethical

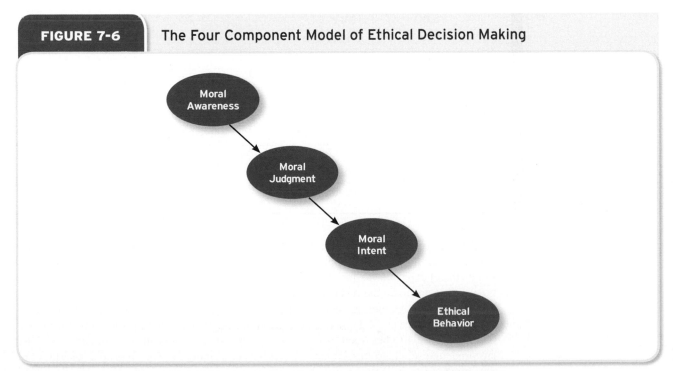

FIGURE 7-6   The Four Component Model of Ethical Decision Making

Source: Adapted from J.R. Rest, *Moral Development: Advances in Research and Theory* (New York: Praeger, 1986).

OB INTERNATIONALLY

Unethical actions can be defined as behaviors that fall below minimum standards of morality. For multinational corporations, however, the relevant question becomes "Whose standards of morality?" Research on business ethics across cultures reveals that different countries have very different baseline levels of unethical actions. Transparency International is an organization that monitors unethical practices in countries around the world. Using data from businesspeople, risk analysts, investigative journalists, country experts, and public citizens, the organization rates countries on a scale of 1 (unethical) to 10 (ethical).[80] Here are some of the scores from the 1999 version of the rankings:

SCORE	COUNTRY	SCORE	COUNTRY
10.0	Denmark	3.8	Lithuania
9.8	Finland	3.8	South Korea
9.4	Sweden	3.6	Philippines
9.2	Canada	3.6	Turkey
9.0	Netherlands	3.4	China
8.7	Australia	3.4	Mexico
8.6	Germany	3.3	Egypt
7.7	Hong Kong	3.3	Romania
7.7	Ireland	3.2	Thailand
7.5	United States	3.0	Argentina
6.8	Israel	2.9	Colombia
6.6	France	2.9	India
6.0	Japan	2.6	Ukraine
5.6	Taiwan	2.6	Venezuela
5.3	Belgium	2.6	Vietnam
5.1	Costa Rica	2.4	Russia
4.9	Greece	2.3	Kazakhstan
4.7	Italy	2.2	Pakistan
4.6	Czech Republic	2.0	Kenya
4.1	Brazil	1.6	Nigeria
3.8	Jamaica	1.5	Cameroon

These rankings reveal the challenges involved for any multinational corporation that does business in areas at the top and bottom of the rankings. Should the company have the same ethical expectations for employees in all countries, regardless of ethical norms? For now, that seems to be the most common position. For example, the Coca-Cola Company's Code of Business Conduct "applies to all the Company's business worldwide and to all Company employees."[81] The code is given to all employees along with a letter from the CEO and covers topics such as conflicts of interest, dealing with government officials, customer and supplier interactions, and political contributions. The code also describes the disciplinary actions associated with any violations of the code.

behaviors result from a multistage sequence beginning with moral awareness, continuing on to moral judgment, and then moral intent and ethical behavior.[82] The sections that follow review the components of this model in more detail.

MORAL AWARENESS. The first step needed to explain why an authority acts ethically is **moral awareness,** which occurs when an authority recognizes that a moral issue exists in a situation or that an ethical standard or principle is relevant to the circumstance.[83] Ethical issues rarely come equipped with "red flags" that mark them as morally sensitive—something is needed to make moral standards salient.[84] As an example, assume you worked for a videogame company whose most popular game involves assuming the role of a criminal in a big city and taking part in multiple storylines involving a variety of illegal activities, such as carjacking, bank robbery, assassination, and the killing of law enforcement personnel and innocent bystanders. A member of this game's development team has suggested embedding hidden sex scenes into the game, which is currently rated "mature" by the Entertainment Software Rating Board.

Is there an ethical issue at play here? On the one hand, you might be tempted to say that the game is already rated "mature" and that such hidden scenes are only extending the already less-than-wholesome nature of the game. Besides, "Easter eggs"—hidden objects in movies, DVDs, or computer and video games—have a long history in the entertainment industry. On the other hand, the hidden scenes constitute deception of the rating board, the customer, and potentially the customer's parents. And that deception issue stands apart from any moral issues raised by the actual content of the hidden scenes. If this story sounds familiar to you, it's because it actually happened with *Grand Theft Auto: San Andreas,* a game manufactured by a division of Take Two Interactive Software.[85] The hidden scenes, which began with the invitation, "How 'bout some coffee?" could be accessed using software available on the Internet. Take Two contends that the code for the scenes was put into early drafts of the game but was supposed to be removed before the game went to market.

Moral awareness depends in part on the characteristics of the authority involved. An authority's **ethical sensitivity** reflects the ability to recognize that a particular decision has ethical content.[86] Ethical sensitivity can be measured by giving people a business case to read that includes a number of somewhat subtle ethical issues, along with a number of other sorts of issues (work sequencing challenges, organizing challenges, specific technical issues). Participants describe the issues that are raised in the case in an open-ended fashion, with ethical sensitivity captured by the number of ethical issues spotted within the case. In the Take Two example, it may be that the employees in charge of the *Grand Theft Auto* game weren't sensitive enough to recognize that the hidden scenes represented an ethical issue. That premise makes some sense, given that Take Two has had other ethical struggles, including having to settle charges of fraudulent accounting with the Securities and Exchange Commission.

7.4

What is the four-component model of ethical decision making?

The programmers of *Grand Theft Auto* appeared to lack moral awareness when it was discovered that a hidden portion of the popular computer game, which could be easily accessed with free software, contained sex scenes.

Moral awareness also depends on the characteristics of the issue itself. **Moral intensity** captures the degree to which the issue has ethical urgency.[87] Moral intensity is driven by six factors, summarized in Table 7-4. A particular issue is high in moral intensity if the magnitude of its consequences are high, there is strong social consensus about the act, the probability of the act occurring and having the predicted consequences is high, those consequences will occur soon, the decision makers are close to those who will be affected, and the consequences are not concentrated on a select few. In the case of the *Grand Theft Auto* hidden scenes, it may be that Take Two felt that the consequences of the act would be minor, the scenes might not be discovered, or the people who would be adversely affected are very different in a psychological sense.

TABLE 7-4	The Six Facets of Moral Intensity
Facet	**Description**
Magnitude of consequences	How much harm (or benefit) would be done to other people?
Social consensus	How much agreement is there that the proposed act would be evil (or good)?
Probability of effect	How likely is it that the act will actually occur and that the assumed consequences will match predictions?
Temporal immediacy	How much time will pass between the act and the onset of its consequences?
Proximity	How near (in a psychological or physical sense) is the authority to those who will be affected?
Concentration of effect	Will the consequences be concentrated on a limited set of people, or will they be more far reaching?

Source: Adapted from T.M. Jones, "Ethical Decision Making by Individuals in Organizations: An Issue-Contingent Model." *Academy of Management Review* 16 (1991), pp. 366–95.

MORAL JUDGMENT. Assuming an authority recognizes that a moral issue exists in a situation, the next step is **moral judgment,** which is when the authority accurately identifies the morally "right" course of action.[88] What factors affect moral judgment? One factor is moral development, as described by Kohlberg's theory of **cognitive moral development.**[89] This theory argues that as people age and mature, they move through several stages of moral development—each more mature and sophisticated than the prior one. These stages are shown in Figure 7-7. Research suggests that most children are at the preconventional level, so their actions are motivated by the avoidance of punishment (Stage 1) and the maintaining of "You scratch my back, I'll scratch yours" sorts of relationships (Stage 2). Most adults, in contrast, are at the conventional level, with their ethical thinking influenced by the opinions of relevant authorities (Stage 3), along with more formal rules and standards (Stage 4).[90] That positioning is relevant for organizations because it suggests that the ethical decisions of employees can be influenced by organizational norms, practices, and reward systems.

Research suggests that fewer than 20 percent of Americans reach the principled (sometimes called "postconventional") level.[91] The principles those individuals utilize during

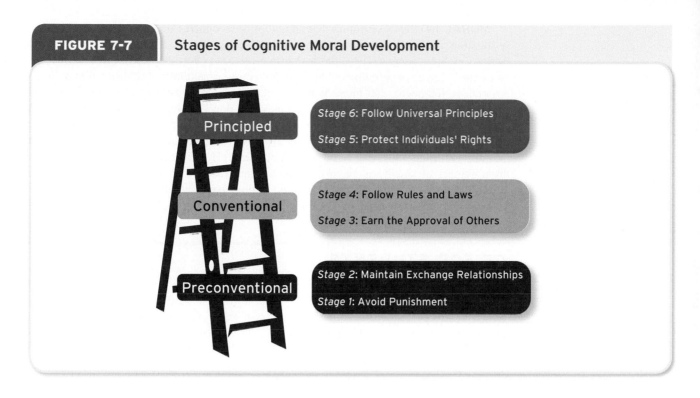

FIGURE 7-7 Stages of Cognitive Moral Development

Principled
- *Stage 6:* Follow Universal Principles
- *Stage 5:* Protect Individuals' Rights

Conventional
- *Stage 4:* Follow Rules and Laws
- *Stage 3:* Earn the Approval of Others

Preconventional
- *Stage 2:* Maintain Exchange Relationships
- *Stage 1:* Avoid Punishment

ethical decision making are called **ethical ideologies.**[92] Those in Stage 5 may be more likely to adopt a **relativism** ideology and reject the notion of universal moral rules.[93] Relativists agree with statements like, "Whether a lie is judged to be moral or immoral depends upon the circumstances surrounding the decision."[94] Such people may also be more likely to adopt a **utilitarianism** ideology where ethical actions are defined as those that achieve the most valuable ends.[95] When asked to describe the character traits that are most impor-

tant to them, utilitarians prioritize traits such as "resourceful," "effective," "productive," and "winner."[96] In contrast, those in Stage 6 should be more likely to adopt an **idealism** ideology and embrace the notion of universal moral rules.[97] Idealists agree with statements like, "The existence of potential harm to others is always wrong, irrespective of the benefits to be gained."[98] Such people also may be more likely to adopt a **formalism** ideology where ethical actions are defined using a set of guiding principles.[99] When asked to describe the character traits that are most important to them, formalists prioritize traits like "trustworthy," "honest," "principled," and "dependable."[100]

"Miss Dugan, will you send someone in here who can distinguish right from wrong?"

MORAL INTENT. Assuming that an authority recognizes that a moral issue exists in a situation and possesses the cognitive moral development to choose the right course of action, one step remains: The authority has to *want* to act ethically. **Moral intent** reflects an authority's degree of commitment to the moral course of action.[101] The distinction between awareness, judgment, and intent is important, because many unethical people know and understand that what they do is wrong—they just don't really care. One driver of moral intent is **moral identity**—the degree to which a person sees him- or herself as a "moral person."[102] Having a strong moral identity increases ethical behaviors because failing to act morally will trigger a strong sense of guilt or shame. However, moral intent is also driven by a number of situational factors, including the existence of on-the-job pressures, role conflict, and rewards and incentives that can be more easily attained by unethical means.[103] See our **OB for Students** feature for more on these issues.

OB FOR STUDENTS

The most relevant form of unethical behavior for students is cheating on exams and assignments. How common is cheating? One survey of almost 50,000 students at 69 schools found that 26 percent of undergraduate business majors admitted to serious cheating on exams, with 54 percent admitting to cheating on written assignments (including plagiarism or using a friend's homework).[104] And the problem is not confined to undergraduate business students. In April 2007, the Dean of the Duke Business School announced that almost 10 percent of the MBA class of 2008 had been caught cheating on a take-home final exam.[105]

Why do students cheat? One likely reason is that grade pressures reduce moral intent—even when students recognize that cheating is a moral issue and that the right decision is not to cheat, they do it anyway. Some support for this notion comes from a recent study of cheating among 5,331 students at 54 colleges.[106] The students filled out anonymous surveys measuring 13 different cheating behaviors, along with four potential predictors of cheating: (1) understanding of academic integrity policies, (2) likelihood of being reported by a peer if caught cheating, (3) perceived severity of cheating penalties, and (4) how often they had observed another student cheating. Of those four potential predictors, which do you think had the strongest effect? That's right—observing another student cheating. In fact, none of the other three factors had any statistical relationship with cheating behaviors. It may be that seeing others cheat creates a sort of peer pressure to "keep up with one's classmates," particularly when classes are graded on a curve.

Another possible reason for cheating is that students' moral judgments about the act have changed. In reflecting on the Duke incident, observers noted that the cheaters were all of the "cut and paste" or "Napster" generation, many of whom had worked in technology jobs in which open source code was championed and technological collaboration was vital to job success.[107] From this perspective, cheating may simply be viewed as an extension of that sort of collaboration. Regardless, schools need to gain a much deeper understanding of why students cheat if such unethical behaviors are to be curbed.

SUMMARY: WHY ARE SOME AUTHORITIES MORE TRUSTED THAN OTHERS?

So what explains why some authorities are more trusted than others? As shown in Figure 7-8, answering that question requires understanding the different sources in which trust can be based, including dispositions, cognitions, and affect. Disposition-based trust

FIGURE 7-8 Why Are Some Authorities More Trusted Than Others?

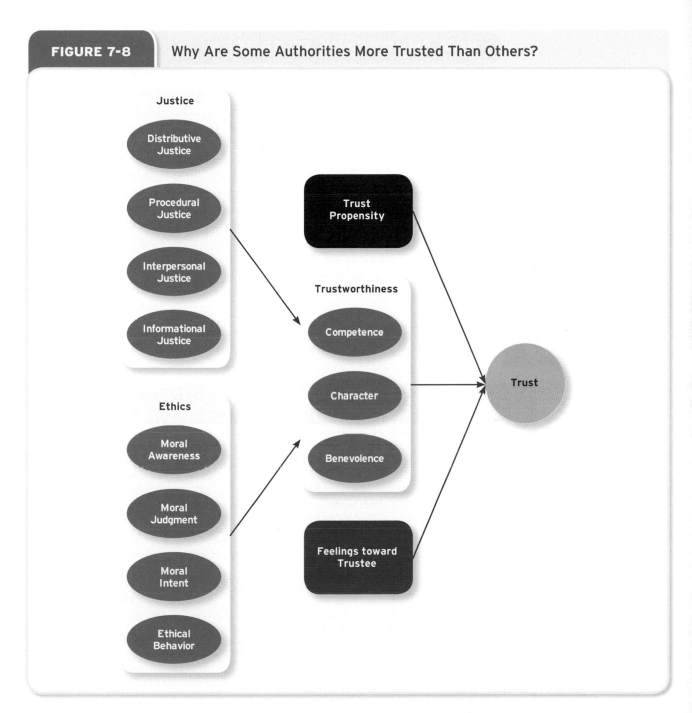

is rooted in an individual's trust propensity, whereas affect-based trust is rooted in a fondness for the authority. Cognition-based trust is driven by perceptions of trustworthiness, as employees attempt to assess the competence, character, and benevolence of authorities. Unfortunately, it is often difficult to gauge trustworthiness accurately, so employees instead look to more observable behaviors that can be used as indirect evidence of trustworthiness. Those behaviors may center on the justice of authorities, with employees considering the distributive, procedural, interpersonal, and informational justice experienced at work. The ethical behaviors of authorities, which are driven by their moral awareness, their moral judgment, and their moral intent, are also relevant to trustworthiness.

HOW IMPORTANT IS TRUST?

7.5

How does trust affect job performance and organizational commitment?

Does trust have a significant impact on the two primary outcomes in our integrative model of OB—does it correlate with job performance and organizational commitment? Figure 7-9 summarizes the research evidence linking trust to job performance and organizational commitment. The figure reveals that trust does affect job performance. Why? One reason is that trust is moderately correlated with task performance. A study of employees in eight plants of a tool manufacturing company sheds some light on why trust benefits task performance.[108] The study gave employees survey measures of their trust in two different authorities: their plant's manager and the company's top management team. Both trust measures were significant predictors of employees' **ability to focus,** which reflects the degree to which employees can devote their attention to work, as opposed to "covering their backside," "playing politics," and "keeping an eye on the boss." The ability to focus is clearly vital to task performance in many jobs, particularly when job duties become more complex.

FIGURE 7-9   Effects of Trust on Performance and Commitment

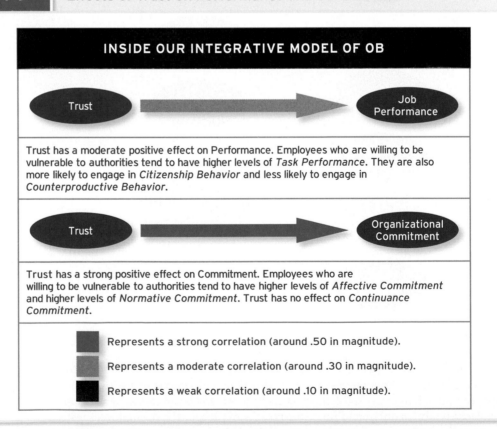

Sources: K.T. Dirks and D.L. Ferrin, "Trust in Leadership: Meta-Analytic Findings and Implications for Research and Practice," *Journal of Applied Psychology* 87 (2002), pp. 611–28; J.A. Colquitt, B.A. Scott, and J.A. LePine, "Trust, Trustworthiness, and Trust Propensity: A Meta-Analytic Test of their Unique Relationships with Risk Taking and Job Performance," *Journal of Applied Psychology* 92 (2007), pp. 909–27.

Trust also influences citizenship behavior and counterproductive behavior. Why? One reason is that the willingness to accept vulnerability changes the nature of the employee–employer relationship. Employees who don't trust their authorities have **economic exchange** relationships that are based on narrowly defined, quid pro quo obligations that are specified in advance and have an explicit repayment schedule.[109] Economic exchanges are impersonal and resemble contractual agreements, such that employees agree to fulfill the duties in their job description in exchange for financial compensation. As trust increases, **social exchange** relationships develop that are based on vaguely defined obligations that are open-ended and long term in their repayment schedule.[110] Social exchanges are characterized by mutual investment, such that employees agree to go above and beyond their duties in exchange for fair and proper treatment by authorities. In social exchange contexts, employees are willing to engage in beneficial behaviors because they trust that those efforts will eventually be rewarded.

Figure 7-9 also reveals that trust affects organizational commitment. Why? One reason is that trusting an authority increases the likelihood that an emotional bond will develop,[111] particularly if that trust is rooted in positive feelings for the authority. Trusting an authority also makes it more likely that a sense of obligation will develop, because employees feel more confident that the authority deserves that obligation. When negative events occur, employees who trust the authority are willing to accept the vulnerability that comes with continued employment,[112] remaining confident in their belief that the situation will eventually improve. For more discussion of the importance of trust in the workplace, see our **OB at the Bookstore** feature.

APPLICATION: SOCIAL RESPONSIBILITY

Now that you understand the factors that drive trust in authorities and the importance of trust levels to performance and commitment, we turn our attention to a very practical question: "How can organizations become more trustworthy?" In the case of Wal-Mart, how can it reverse its negative reputational momentum and be viewed, once again, as an organization worthy of trust? Certainly that's a big question with no single answer. However, one start is to focus the organization's attention on **corporate social responsibility,** a perspective that acknowledges that the responsibility of a business encompasses the economic, legal, ethical, and citizenship expectations of society.[113] This perspective maintains the belief that the foundation of any business is profitability, because organizations must fulfill their economic responsibilities to their employees and shareholders. However, the social responsibility lens supplements that belief by arguing that the company's obligations do not end with profit maximization.

The legal component of corporate social responsibility argues that the law represents society's codification of right and wrong and must therefore be followed.[114] Fulfilling this component speaks to the character of the organization and suggests that it has reached conventional levels of moral development. Wal-Mart's legal problems signal a breach of this component, and any attempts to repair the organization's trustworthiness will likely require an end to its legal troubles. What steps can organizations take to promote legal compliance? Computer Associates International, the New York–based maker of computer security software, is one of a number of companies with a new breed of compliance officer.[115] As part of a series of reforms to avoid a trial over accounting fraud, the company gave its new compliance officer, who was a former chief trial attorney for the U.S. Navy, unprecedented power. The officer has direct access to the CEO, can go over the CEO's

7.6

What steps can organizations take to become more trustworthy?

OB AT THE BOOKSTORE

THE SPEED OF TRUST: THE ONE THING THAT CHANGES EVERYTHING
by Stephen M. R. Covey (New York: The Free Press, 2006).

There is one thing that is common to every individual, relationship, team, family, organization, nation, economy, and civilization throughout the world—one thing which, if removed, will destroy the most powerful government, the most successful business, the most thriving economy, the most influential leadership, the greatest friendship, the strongest character, the deepest love . . . That one thing is trust.

With those words, Covey summarizes the central premise of his book: Trust is vital within and outside organizations. Covey summarizes the importance of trust with one simple formula:

$$\downarrow \text{Trust} = \downarrow \text{Speed} \uparrow \text{Cost}$$

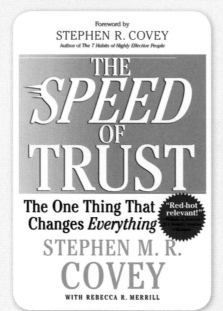

He uses an example to illustrate the formula. The Sarbanes-Oxley Act was passed in response to the accounting scandals at Enron, WorldCom, and others. The act's many regulations are an expression of distrust. Chief financial officers report that compliance with the act requires an enormous amount of time, reducing the speed of company operations. Costs, in turn, increase, with one study suggesting that compliance with the Sarbanes-Oxley Act costs $35 billion.

Covey conveys the same sort of premise in another way by describing what could be called a *distrust tax*. Every time you work with someone whom you distrust, you spend some portion of your time monitoring and checking up on them. That distrust mimics a tax, reducing your productivity by 10 percent, 20 percent, or even 30 percent. Similarly, every time you work with people who distrust you, they spend time performing the same sorts of behaviors. Their distrust acts as the same sort of tax, reducing the overall productivity of the unit. That distrust tax can be contrasted with what Covey terms the *trust dividend,* where high trust amplifies the gains derived from employee skills and effort. As Covey describes it, "High trust is like the leaven in bread, which lifts everything around it."

head if need be, and has the authority to fire managers and employees who violate company guidelines.

The ethical component of corporate social responsibility argues that organizations have an obligation to do what is right, just, and fair and to avoid harm.[116] Fulfilling this component is relevant to the character and benevolence of the organization and suggests that it has reached one of the principled levels of moral development. Regardless of its legal implications, the way Wal-Mart treats its employees speaks to the ethical makeup of its culture. What can organizations do to improve that culture? J.M. Smuckers, the Ohio-based food and beverage maker, requires all of its 3,500 employees to attend training sessions on moral awareness and moral judgment.[117] Employees go through programs every 3–5 years and sign a nine-page ethics statement annually. That statement, which the company treats as a living document, spells out the values and ethical ideologies that Smuckers employees can use to navigate moral dilemmas.

The citizenship component of corporate social responsibility argues that organizations should contribute resources to improve the quality of life in the communities in which they work.[118] Sometimes this component involves philanthropic efforts, in which cash donations are given to charitable groups. Wal-Mart, for example, contributed $188 million in cash donations in fiscal year 2004, as compared with $108 million for Target.[119] However, the citizenship component may also involve efforts geared toward environmental sustainability. Several notable companies, including Nike, Dupont, and Bayer, have been lauded for their efforts to address concerns about climate change.[120] For his part, Lee Scott is spearheading an effort to make Wal-Mart's operations more environmentally sustainable by increasing efficiency, reducing energy usage, and lowering waste. Those are important goals for a company that is the nation's largest private user of electricity and the owner of the second-largest fleet of trucks.[121]

TAKEAWAYS

7.1 Trust is the willingness to be vulnerable to an authority based on positive expectations about the authority's actions and intentions. Justice reflects the perceived fairness of an authority's decision making and can be used to explain why employees judge some authorities as more trustworthy than others. Ethics reflects the degree to which the behaviors of an authority are in accordance with generally accepted moral norms and can be used to explain why authorities choose to act in a trustworthy manner.

7.2 Trust can be disposition-based, meaning that one's personality includes a general propensity to trust others. Trust can also be cognition-based, meaning that it's rooted in a rational assessment of the authority's trustworthiness. Finally, trust can be affect-based, meaning that it's rooted in feelings toward the authority that go beyond any rational assessment of trustworthiness. Trustworthiness is judged along three dimensions: competence, character, and benevolence.

7.3 The fairness of an authority's decision making can be judged along four dimensions. Distributive justice reflects the perceived fairness of decision-making outcomes. Procedural justice reflects the perceived fairness of decision-making processes. Interpersonal justice reflects the perceived fairness of the treatment received by employees from authorities. Informational justice reflects the perceived fairness of the communications provided to employees from authorities.

7.4 The four-component model of ethical decision making argues that ethical behavior depends on three concepts. Moral awareness reflects whether an authority recognizes that a moral issue exists in a situation. Moral judgment reflects whether the authority can accurately identify the "right" course of action. Moral intent reflects an authority's degree of commitment to the moral course of action.

7.5 Trust has a moderate positive relationship with job performance and a strong positive relationship with organizational commitment.

7.6 Organizations can become more trustworthy by emphasizing corporate social responsibility, a perspective that acknowledges that the responsibility of a business encompasses the economic, legal, ethical, and citizenship expectations of society.

KEY TERMS

• Trust	*p. 219*	• Moral awareness	*p. 235*
• Justice	*p. 219*	• Ethical sensitivity	*p. 235*
• Ethics	*p. 219*	• Moral intensity	*p. 236*
• Disposition-based trust	*p. 220*	• Moral judgment	*p. 236*
• Cognition-based trust	*p. 221*	• Cognitive moral development	*p. 236*
• Affect-based trust	*p. 221*	• Ethical ideology	*p. 237*
• Trust propensity	*p. 221*	• Relativism	*p. 237*
• Trustworthiness	*p. 221*	• Utilitarianism	*p. 237*
• Competence	*p. 223*	• Idealism	*p. 237*
• Character	*p. 223*	• Formalism	*p. 237*
• Benevolence	*p. 224*	• Moral intent	*p. 238*
• Distributive justice	*p. 226*	• Moral identity	*p. 238*
• Procedural justice	*p. 226*	• Ability to focus	*p. 240*
• Interpersonal justice	*p. 230*	• Economic exchange	*p. 241*
• Informational justice	*p. 231*	• Social exchange	*p. 241*
• Whistle-blowing	*p. 233*	• Corporate social responsibility	*p. 241*

DISCUSSION QUESTIONS

7.1 Were you aware of the ethical criticisms that Wal-Mart has received? Do those criticisms affect your likelihood of shopping there? Why or why not?

7.2 Consider the three dimensions of trustworthiness (competence, character, and benevolence). Which of those dimensions would be most important when deciding whether to trust your boss? What about when deciding whether to trust a friend? If your two answers differ, why do they?

7.3 Putting yourself in the shoes of a manager, which of the four justice dimensions (distributive, procedural, interpersonal, informational) would you find it most difficult to maximize? Which would be the easiest to maximize?

7.4 Which component of ethical decision making do you believe best explains student cheating: moral awareness, moral judgment, or moral intent? Why do you feel that way?

7.5 Assume you were applying for a job at a company known for its corporate social responsibility. How important would that be to you when deciding whether to accept a job offer?

CASE   WAL-MART

Wal-Mart has a rich history dating back to its founding in Arkansas in 1962. The company has always been proud of having one of the strictest and most stringent ethics policies in the industry. Every employee in the company is encouraged to report suspicions of unethical activities. However, in recent years, Wal-Mart's business tactics have come under constant scrutiny from critics. A report by McKinsey & Co. discovered that as early as 2004, 8 percent of the company's customers had stopped shopping there due to its negative media attention.

The consumer backlash against Wal-Mart's new negative image has adversely influenced the company's bottom line. Consumers have stopped shopping at Wal-Mart stores because the company is perceived as unfair to workers or bad for the economy. State governments, such as in Maryland, now require Wal-Mart to provide a minimum level of employee health care. In the past seven years, the company's shares have returned −3.4 percent annually. Consumers are wary about shopping at Wal-Mart, and investors want bigger returns.

In an attempt to win back consumers, Wal-Mart has hired several public relations professionals, which is more than a defensive tactic by the company. The intent is to increase the public's awareness of the good the company has done for local communities and its entire workforce. But when Wal-Mart hired former Atlanta Mayor Andrew Young, its plan backfired. Young stated in a newspaper interview that ethnic store owners sold spoiled food to Atlanta's inner city residents. Wal-Mart is now fighting an uphill battle to regain its reputation. Is it too late to salvage it?

7.1   How has Wal-Mart's trustworthiness been affected? Can Wal-Mart recover from so many negative events and publicity? Explain.

7.2   Poor ethics do not hinder the performance of a large corporation like Wal-Mart. Do you agree? Explain.

Sources: M. Boyle, "Wal-Mart: Desperately Seeking Ethics," *Fortune,* March 7, 2006; P. Gogoi, "Wal-Mart's Latest Ethics Controversy," *BusinessWeek,* June 13, 2007; P. Gogoi, "Wal-Mart: A Reputation Crisis," *Business Week,* October 31, 2006; P. Gogoi, "Wal-Mart's Political Payouts," *BusinessWeek,* September 29, 2006, www. businessweek.com; N. Vardi, "Would Sam Be Proud?" *Forbes,* May 3, 2007.

EXERCISE   TRUSTWORTHINESS AND TRUST

The purpose of this exercise is to explore the factors that lead one person to trust another. This exercise uses groups of six participants, so your instructor will either assign you to a group of six or ask you to create your own group of six. The exercise has the following steps:

1. Individually, read the following paragraphs that describe three people *who might work for you.* For each, how comfortable would you be turning over to him or her a project that was very important to you if you could not monitor what he or she did? (1 = *petrified;* 10 – *completely comfortable*).

> J.B. was promoted to his/her current position shortly before you were transferred in as head of the department. On paper, J.B. is qualified, but you have some serious doubts about his/her skills. J.B. has an MBA from a well-respected university and has been in the current position for over a year.

During that time, you have found some very surprising mistakes and oversights in J.B.'s work. J.B. doesn't seem to have a grasp of how the company operates and what his/her role is supposed to be. When you have tried to explain these things, J.B. claims to understand. However, J.B.'s work doesn't seem to show it. J.B. really likes you and bends over backward to help you out whenever possible. All of J.B.'s peers seem to like him/her, and J.B. has gained a bit of a reputation among them and the customers for being very fair.

Sandy has been with your company for a long time and has worked for you for about a year. Inasmuch as Sandy's job is fairly technical, Sandy has continued to attend seminars and read technical journals to keep up to date. Sandy's work is always careful and complete. Sandy has on a number of occasions shown great loyalty to you, the boss. For example, just last month, Sandy blocked information from getting to your boss that would have made you look bad. On several occasions, Sandy has misled people in other departments to keep them from taking resources away from your department.

Pat recently transferred to your division from the company's East Coast division. Pat wanted to get back closer to family. Pat's former department head had tried unsuccessfully to block Pat's leaving, arguing that Pat was "just too important" to let him/her go. The quality of Pat's work appears to justify the former manager's reluctance to let Pat leave. Pat does not seem to have trouble making friends and is quite popular but has refused all of your attempts to get to know him/her. When you have gone to lunch together, Pat mostly listened to what you had to say and didn't say much. Pat often seems to have his/her guard up when talking with you. In dealings with other employees and with customers, Pat is fair and honest.

Based on your ratings, whom would you trust the most? In your groups, explain your ratings. What factors were most critical to your trust assessments?

2. Individually, read the following paragraphs that describe three people for *whom you might work.* For each, how comfortable would you be turning over to this manager control over *your destiny in the company* if you could not monitor what he or she did? (1 = petrified; 10 = completely comfortable).

In dealing with you, Terry is a no-nonsense kind of manager. Terry has always acted on the up-and-up from everything you've seen and heard. Terry always gets things done well and is respected by all. Your attempts to go to lunch, socialize, and build a relationship have always been politely refused. Terry has a number of friends at work, but you do not seem to be one of them.

You've worked for Taylor for several years. Taylor has always been honest with you and shown a genuine concern for others, as well as for the profitability of the business. Taylor has always been particularly good to you, and it's clear that Taylor likes and respects you. Taylor frequently has problems getting the bills paid and customers served on time and does not seem to manage the company's finances very well. Taylor does not seem to have clear objectives about what things are important for the operation of the business.

You have always found your manager, Jesse, to have strong skills. Jesse is on the phone with another manager. You hear Jesse commit to getting a report done by Friday. Once off the phone, Jesse makes a snappy remark about hell freezing over and continues your performance review. You can recall a number of other occasions when Jesse told someone one thing and turned around and told you something entirely different. Jesse has always been nice to you and seems to like you. Jesse tells you you're meeting all your goals and should expect a promotion and pay increase within the next six months to a year.

Based on your ratings, whom would you trust most? In your groups, explain your ratings. What factors were most critical to your trust assessments?

3. Class discussion, whether in groups or as a class, should center on this question: What factors caused you to trust one person more than the others in the two sets of scenarios? Do the relevant factors vary when trust refers to a subordinate compared with when trust refers to a supervisor? How?

Source: Adapted from R.C. Mayer and P.M. Norman, "Exploring Attributes of Trustworthiness: A Classroom Exercise," *Journal of Management Education* 28 (2004), pp. 224–49.

ENDNOTES

7.1 Useem, J. "Should We Admire Wal-Mart?" *Fortune,* March 8, 2004, pp. 118–20.

7.2 Ibid.

7.3 Fishman, C. *The Wal-Mart Effect.* New York: Penguin Books, 2006.

7.4 Serwer, A. "Bruised in Bentonville." *Fortune,* April 18, 2005, pp. 84–89.

7.5 Fishman, *The Wal-Mart Effect;* Bianco, A. "Wal-Mart's Midlife Crisis." *BusinessWeek,* April 30, 2007, pp. 46–56.

7.6 Gunther, M. "The Green Machine." *Fortune,* August 7, 2006, pp. 42–57.

7.7 Useem, "Should We Admire Wal-Mart?"

7.8 Serwer, "Bruised in Bentonville."

7.9 Bianco, "Wal-Mart's Midlife Crisis."

7.10 Serwer, "Bruised in Bentonville."

7.11 Ibid.; Gunther, "The Green Machine."

7.12 Gunther, "The Green Machine."

7.13 Birger, J. "The Unending Woes of Lee Scott." *Fortune,* January 22, 2007, pp. 118–22.

7.14 Bernstein, A. "Wal-Mart vs. Class Actions." *BusinessWeek,* March 21, 2005, pp. 73–74.

7.15 Daniels, C. "Wal-Mart's Women Problem." *Fortune,* July 12, 2004, p. 28.

7.16 Useem, "Should We Admire Wal-Mart?"

7.17 Bianco, "Wal-Mart's Midlife Crisis."

7.18 Marquez, J. "Wal-Mart Puts on a New Face." *Workforce,* August 14, 2006, pp. 29–34.

7.19 Schlender, B. "Wal-Mart's $288 Billion Meeting." *Fortune,* April 18, 2005, pp. 90–106.

7.20 Berner, R. "Can Wal-Mart Fit into a White Hat?" *BusinessWeek,* October 3, 2005, pp. 94–96.

7.21 Mayer, R.C.; J.H. Davis; and F.D. Schoorman. "An Integrative Model of Organizational Trust." *Academy of Management Review* 20 (1995), pp. 709–34; Rousseau, D.M.; S.B. Sitkin; R.S. Burt; and C. Camerer. "Not So Different After All: A Cross-Discipline View of Trust." *Academy of Management Review* 23 (1998), pp. 393–404.

7.22 Fisher, A. "America's Most Admired Companies." *Fortune,* March 19, 2007, pp. 88–112.

7.23 Greenberg, J. "A Taxonomy of Organizational Justice Theories."

Academy of Management Review 12 (1987), pp. 9–22.

7.24 Lind, E.A. "Fairness Heuristic Theory: Justice Judgments as Pivotal Cognitions in Organizational Relations." In *Advances in Organizational Justice,* eds. J. Greenberg and R. Cropanzano. Stanford, CA: Stanford University Press, 2001, pp. 56–88; Van den Bos, K. "Fairness Heuristic Theory: Assessing the Information to Which People Are Reacting Has a Pivotal Role in Understanding Organizational Justice." In *Theoretical and Cultural Perspectives on Organizational Justice,* eds. S. Gilliland, D. Steiner, and D. Skarlicki. Greenwich, CT: Information Age Publishing, 2001, pp. 63–84; Van den Bos, K.; E.A. Lind; and H.A.M. Wilke. "The Psychology of Procedural and Distributive Justice Viewed from the Perspective of Fairness Heuristic Theory." In *Justice in the Workplace,* Vol. 2, ed. R. Cropanzano. Mahwah, NJ: Erlbaum, 2001, pp. 49–66.

7.25 Trevino, L.K.; G.R. Weaver; and S.J. Reynolds. "Behavioral Ethics in Organizations: A Review." *Journal of Management* 32 (2006), pp. 951–90.

7.26 McAllister, D.J. "Affect- and Cognition-Based Trust as Foundations for Interpersonal Cooperation in Organizations." *Academy of Management Journal* 38 (1995), pp. 24–59.

7.27 Ibid.

7.28 Mayer et al., "An Integrative Model"; Rotter, J.B. "A New Scale for the Measurement of Interpersonal Trust." *Journal of Personality* 35 (1967), pp. 651–65; Rotter, J.B. "Generalized Expectancies for Interpersonal Trust." *American Psychologist* 26 (1971), pp. 443–52; Rotter, J.B. "Interpersonal Trust, Trustworthiness, and Gullibility."

American Psychologist 35 (1980), pp. 1–7.

7.29 Rosenberg, M. "Misanthropy and Political Ideology." *American Sociological Review* 21 (1956), pp. 690–95; Wrightsman, L.S. Jr. "Measurement of Philosophies of Human Nature." *Psychological Reports* 14 (1964), pp. 743–51.

7.30 Mayer et al., "An Integrative Model."

7.31 Jones, W.H.; L.L. Couch; and S. Scott. "Trust and Betrayal: The Psychology of Getting Along and Getting Ahead." In *Handbook of Personality Psychology,* eds. R. Hogan, J.S. Johnson, and S.R. Briggs. San Diego, CA: Academic Press, 1997, pp. 465–82.

7.32 Stack, L.C. "Trust." In *Dimensionality of Personality,* eds. H. London and J.E. Exner, Jr. New York: Wiley, 1978, pp. 561–99.

7.33 Webb, W.M., and P. Worchel. "Trust and Distrust." In *Psychology of Intergroup Relations,* eds. S. Worchel and W.G. Austin. Chicago: Nelson-Hall, 1986, pp. 213–28; Erickson, E.H. *Childhood and Society.* 2nd ed. New York: Norton, 1963.

7.34 Stack, "Trust."

7.35 Mayer et al., "An Integrative Model."

7.36 McAllister, D.J. "Affect- and Cognition-Based Trust as Foundations for Interpersonal Cooperation in Organizations." *Academy of Management Journal* 38 (1995), pp. 24–59; Lewicki, R.J.; and B.B. Bunker. "Developing and Maintaining Trust in Work Relationships." In *Trust in Organizations: Frontiers of Theory and Research,* eds. R.M. Kramer and T.R. Tyler. Thousand Oaks, CA: Sage, 1996, pp. 114–39.

7.37 Mayer et al., "An Integrative Model."

7.38 Ibid.; Gabarro, J.J. "The Development of Trust, Influence, and Expectations." In A *Interpersonal Behavior: Communication and Understanding in Relationships,* eds. G. Athos and J.J. Gabarro. Englewood Cliffs, NJ: Prentice-Hall, 1978, pp. 290–303.

7.39 Gabarro, "The Development."

7.40 Mayer et al., "An Integrative Model"; Gabarro, "The Development."

7.41 Mayer et al., "An Integrative Model;" Simons, T. "Behavioral Integrity: The Perceived Alignment Between Managers' Words and Deeds as a Research Focus." *Organization Science* 13 (2002), pp. 18–35; Dineen, B.R.; R.J. Lewicki; and E.C. Tomlinson. "Supervisory Guidance and Behavioral Integrity: Relationships with Employee Citizenship and Deviant Behavior." *Journal of Applied Psychology* 91 (2006), pp. 622–35.

7.42 Dineen et al. "Supervisory Guidance"; Bates, S. "Poll: Employees Skeptical about Management Actions." *HR Magazine,* June 2002, p. 12.

7.43 Mayer et al., "An Integrative Model."

7.44 Ibid.

7.45 Lewis, J.D., and A. Weigert. "Trust as a Social Reality." *Social Forces* 63 (1985), pp. 967–85.

7.46 Becker, L.C. "Trust as Noncognitive Security about Motives." *Ethics* 107 (1996), pp. 43–61.

7.47 McAllister, "Affect- and Cognition-Based Trust"; Lewicki and Bunker, "Developing and Maintaining Trust"; Lewis and Weigert, "Trust as Noncognitive Security."

7.48 McAllister, "Affect- and Cognition-Based Trust."

7.49 Lind, "Fairness Heuristic Theory: Assessing"; Van den Bos, "Fairness Heuristic Theory: Justice"; Van den Bos et al., "The Psychology of Procedural and Distributive Justice."

7.50 Adams, J.S. "Inequity in Social Exchange." In *Advances in Experimental Social Psychology,* Vol. 2, ed. L. Berkowitz. New York: Academic Press, 1965, pp. 267–99; Leventhal, G.S. "The Distribution of Rewards and Resources in Groups and Organizations." In *Advances in Experimental Social Psychology,* Vol. 9, eds. L. Berkowitz and W. Walster. New York: Academic Press, 1976, pp. 91–131.

7.51 Leventhal, "The Distribution of Rewards."

7.52 Ibid.

7.53 Levering, R., and M. Moskowitz. "In Good Company." *Fortune,* January 22, 2007, pp. 94–114.

7.54 Leventhal, G.S. "What Should Be Done with Equity Theory? New Approaches to the Study of Fairness in Social Relationships." In *Social Exchange: Advances in Theory and Research,* eds. K. Gergen, M. Greenberg, and R. Willis. New York: Plenum Press, 1980, pp. 27–55; Thibaut, J., and L. Walker. *Procedural Justice: A Psychological Analysis.* Hillsdale, NJ: Erlbaum, 1975.

7.55 Folger, R. "Distributive and Procedural Justice: Combined Impact of 'Voice' and improvement on experienced inequity." *Journal of Personality and Social Psychology* 35 (1977), pp. 108–19.

7.56 Colquitt, J.A.; D.E. Conlon; M.J. Wesson; C.O.L.H. Porter; and K.Y.

Ng. "Justice at the Millennium: A Meta-Analytic Review of 25 Years of Organizational Justice Research." *Journal of Applied Psychology* 86 (2001), pp. 425–45.

7.57 Tyler, T.R.; K.A. Rasinski; and N. Spodick. "Influence of Voice on Satisfaction with Leaders: Exploring the Meaning of Process Control." *Journal of Personality and Social Psychology* 48 (1985), pp. 72–81; Earley, P.C.; and E.A. Lind. "Procedural Justice and Participation in Task Selection: The Role of Control in Mediating Justice Judgments." *Journal of Personality and Social Psychology* 52 (1987), pp. 1148–60; Lind, E.A.; R. Kanfer; and P.C. Earley. "Voice, Control, and Procedural Justice: Instrumental and Noninstrumental Concerns in Fairness Judgments." *Journal of Personality and Social Psychology* 59 (1990), pp. 952–59; Korsgaard, M.A., and L. Roberson. "Procedural Justice in Performance Evaluation: The Role of Instrumental and Non-Instrumental Voice in Performance Appraisal Discussions." *Journal of Management* 21 (1995), pp. 657–69.

7.58 Morris, B. "How Corporate America Is Betraying Women." *Fortune,* January 10, 2005, pp. 64–74.

7.59 Ibid.

7.60 Hansen, F. "Race and Gender Still Matter." *Workforce,* September 11, 2006, p. 12.

7.61 BCS Standings, 2007, http://www.bcsfootball.org/bcsfb/standings (May 27, 2007).

7.62 Brockner, J., and B.M. Wiesenfeld. "An Integrative Framework for Explaining Reactions to Decisions: Interactive Effects of Outcomes and Procedures." *Psychological Bulletin* 120 (1996), pp. 189–208.

7.63 Ibid.

7.64 Colquitt et al., "Justice at the Millennium"; Cohen-Charash, Y.; and P.E. Spector. "The Role of Justice in Organizations: A Meta-Analysis." *Organizational Behavior and Human Decision Processes* 86 (2001), pp. 278–321.

7.65 Bics, R.J., and J.F. Moag. "Interactional Justice: Communication Criteria of Fairness." In *Research on Negotiations in Organizations,* Vol. 1, eds. R.J. Lewicki, B.H. Sheppard, and M.H. Bazerman. Greenwich, CT: JAI Press, 1986, pp. 43–55; Greenberg, J. "The Social Side of Fairness: Interpersonal and Informational Classes of Organizational Justice." In *Justice in the Workplace: Approaching Fairness in Human Resource Management,* ed. R. Cropanzano. Hillsdale, NJ: Erlbaum, 1993, pp. 79–103.

7.66 Bies, R.J. "Interactional (In)justice: The Sacred and the Profane." In *Advances in Organizational Justice,* eds. J. Greenberg and R. Cropanzano. Stanford, CA: Stanford University Press, 2001, pp. 85–108.

7.67 Sutton, R.I. *The No Asshole Rule.* New York: Warner Business Books, 2007.

7.68 Miner, A.G.; T.M. Glomb; and C. Hulin. "Experience Sampling Mode and Its Correlates at Work." *Journal of Occupational and Organizational Psychology* 78 (2005), pp. 171–93.

7.69 Gilliland, S.W.; L. Benson; and D.H. Schepers. "A Rejection Threshold in Justice Evaluations: Effects on Judgment and Decision-Making." *Organizational Behavior and Human Decision Processes* 76 (1998), pp. 113–31.

7.70 Tepper, B.J. "Consequences of Abusive Supervision." *Academy of Management Journal* 43 (2000), pp. 178–90.

7.71 Bies and Moag, "Interactional Justice"; Greenberg, "The Social Side of Fairness."

7.72 "RadioShack Fires 400 Employees by Email," http://abcnews.go.com/Technology/wireStory?id=2374917&CMPOTC-RSSFeeds0312 (May 28, 2007).

7.73 Folger, R., and D.P. Skarlicki. "Fairness as a Dependent Variable: Why Tough Times Can Lead to Bad Management." In *Justice in the Workplace: From Theory to Practice,* ed. R. Cropanzano. Mahwah, NJ: Erlbaum, 2001, pp. 97–118.

7.74 Shaw, J.C.; R.E. Wild; and J.A. Colquitt. "To Justify or Excuse?: A Meta-Analysis of the Effects of Explanations." *Journal of Applied Psychology* 88 (2003), pp. 444–58.

7.75 Orey, M. "Fear of Firing." *BusinessWeek,* April 23, 2007, pp. 52–62.

7.76 Greenberg, J. "Employee Theft as a Reaction to Underpayment Inequity: The Hidden Cost of Paycuts." *Journal of Applied Psychology* 75 (1990), pp. 561–68.

7.77 Colquitt et al., "Justice at the Millennium"; Cohen-Charash and Spector, "The Role of Justice."

7.78 Trevino et al., "Behavioral Ethics."

7.79 Covey, S.M.R. *The Speed of Trust: The One Thing that Changes Everything.* New York: The Free Press, 2006.

7.80 Robertson, D.C. "Business Ethics Across Cultures." In *The Blackwell Handbook of Cross-Cultural Management,* eds. M.J. Gannon and K.L. Newman. Malden, MA: Blackwell, 2002, pp. 361–92.

7.81 Robertson, "Business Ethics Across Cultures."

7.82 Trevino et al., "Behavioral Ethics"; Rest, J.R. *Moral Development:*

Advances in Research and Theory. New York: Praeger, 2006; Butterfield, K.D.; L.K. Trevino; and G.R. Weaver. "Moral Awareness in Business Organizations: Influences of Issue-Related and Social Context Factors." *Human Relations* 53 (2000), pp. 981–1018.

7.83 Trevino et al., "Behavioral Ethics"; Rest, *Moral Development.*

7.84 Butterfield et al., "Moral Awareness."

7.85 McLean, B. "Sex, Lies, and Videogames." *Fortune,* August 22, 2005, pp. 66–70.

7.86 Sparks, J.R., and S.D. Hunt. "Marketing Research Ethical Sensitivity: Conceptualization, Measurement, and Exploratory Investigation." *Journal of Marketing* 62 (1998), pp. 92–109.

7.87 Jones, T.M. "Ethical Decision Making by Individuals in Organizations: An Issue-Contingent Model." *Academy of Management Review* 16 (1991), pp. 366–95; Butterfield et al., "Moral Awareness."

7.88 Trevino et al., "Behavioral Ethics"; Rest, *Moral Development.*

7.89 Kohlberg, L. "Stage and Sequence: The Cognitive Developmental Approach to Socialization." In *Handbook of Socialization Theory,* ed. D.A. Goslin. Chicago: Rand McNally, 1969, pp. 347–480; Kohlberg, L. "The Claim to Moral Adequacy of a Highest Stage of Moral Judgment." *Journal of Philosophy* 70 (1973), pp. 630–46.

7.90 Trevino et al., "Behavioral Ethics."

7.91 Ibid.; Rest, J.; D. Narvaez; M.J. Bebeau; and S.J. Thoma. *Postconventional Moral Thinking: A Neo-Kohlbergian Approach.* Mahwah, NJ: Lawrence Erlbaum, 1999.

7.92   Forsyth, D.R. "A Taxonomy of Ethical Ideologies." *Journal of Personality and Social Psychology* 39 (1980), pp. 175–84.

7.93   Ibid.

7.94   Ibid.

7.95   Schminke, M.; M.L. Ambrose; and T.W. Noel. "The Effect of Ethical Frameworks on Perceptions of Organizational Justice." *Academy of Management Journal* 40 (1997), pp. 1190–1207; Brady, F.N., and G.E. Wheeler. "An Empirical Study of Ethical Predispositions." *Journal of Business Ethics* 15 (1996), pp. 927–40.

7.96   Ibid.

7.97   Forsyth, "A Taxonomy of Ethical Ideologies."

7.98   Ibid.

7.99   Schminke et al., "The Effect of Ethical Frameworks"; Brady and Wheeler, "An Empirical Study of Ethical Predispositions."

7.100   Ibid.

7.101   Trevino et al., "Behavioral Ethics"; Rest, *Moral Development.*

7.102   Bergman, R. "Identity as Motivation: Toward a Theory of the Moral Self." In *Moral Development, Self and Identity,* eds. D.K. Lapsley and D. Narvaez. Mahwah, NJ: Lawrence Erlbaum, 2004, pp. 21–46.

7.103   Trevino et al., "Behavioral Ethics"; Schweitzer, M.E.; L. Ordonez; and B. Douma. "Goal Setting as a Motivator of Unethical Behavior." *Academy of Management Journal* 47 (2004), pp. 422–32.

7.104   Oh, H. "Biz Majors Get an F for Honesty." *BusinessWeek,* February 6, 2006, p. 14.

7.105   Conlin, M. "Cheating—or Postmodern Learning?" *BusinessWeek,* May 14, 2007, p. 42.

7.106   McCabe, D.L. "Academic Dishonesty in Graduate Business Programs: Prevalence, Causes, and Proposed Action." *Academy of Management Learning and Education* 5 (2006), pp. 294–305.

7.107   Conlin, "Cheating—or Postmodern Learning?"

7.108   Mayer, R.C., and M.B. Gavin. "Trust in Management and Performance: Who Minds the Shop While the Employees Watch the Boss?" *Academy of Management Journal* 48 (2005), pp. 874–88.

7.109   Blau, P. *Exchange and Power in Social Life.* New York: Wiley, 1964; Shore, L.M.; L.E. Tetrick; P. Lynch; and K. Barksdale. "Social and Economic Exchange: Construct Development and Validation." *Journal of Applied Social Psychology* 36 (2006), pp. 837–67.

7.110   Ibid.

7.111   Dirks, K.T., and D.L. Ferrin. "Trust in Leadership: Meta-Analytic Findings and Implications for Research and Practice." *Journal of Applied Psychology* 87 (2002), pp. 611–28.

7.112   Ibid.

7.113   Carroll, A.B. "A Three-Dimensional Model of Corporate Social Performance." *Academy of Management Review* 4 (1979), pp. 497–505; Carroll, A.B. "The Pyramid of Corporate Social Responsibility: Toward the Moral Management of Organizational Stakeholders." *Business Horizons* 34 (1991), pp. 39–48; Carroll, A.B. "The Four Faces of Corporate Citizenship." *Business and Society Review* 100 (1998), pp. 1–7; Carroll, A.B. "Corporate Social Responsibility—Evolution of a Definitional Construct." *Business and Society* 38 (1999), pp. 268–95.

7.114 Carroll, "The Pyramid."

7.115 Weber, J. "The New Ethics Enforcers." *BusinessWeek,* February 13, 2006, pp. 76–77.

7.116 Carroll, "The Pyramid."

7.117 Schoeff, M., Jr. "J. M. Smuckers Co." *Workforce,* March 13, 2006, p. 19.

7.118 Carroll, "The Pyramid."

7.119 Byrnes, N. "Smarter Corporate Giving." *BusinessWeek,* November 28, 2005, pp. 68–76.

7.120 Aston, A., and B. Helm. "The Race Against Climate Change." *BusinessWeek,* December 12, 2005, pp. 58–66; Holmes, S. "Nike Goes for the Green." *BusinessWeek,* September 25, 2006, pp. 106–108.

7.121 Gunther, "The Green Machine."

Learning and Decision Making

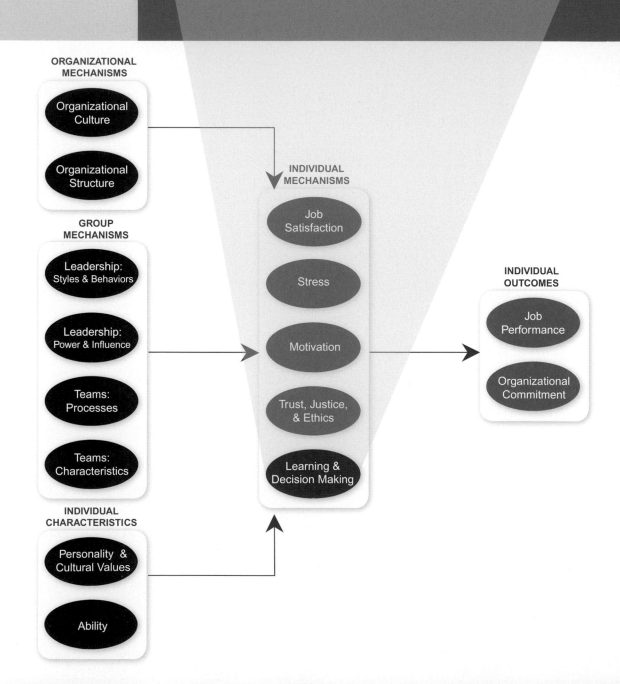

ORGANIZATIONAL
MECHANISMS

Organizational
Culture

Organizational
Structure

GROUP
MECHANISMS

Leadership:
Styles & Behaviors

Leadership:
Power & Influence

Teams:
Processes

Teams:
Characteristics

INDIVIDUAL
CHARACTERISTICS

Personality &
Cultural Values

Ability

INDIVIDUAL
MECHANISMS

Job
Satisfaction

Stress

Motivation

Trust, Justice,
& Ethics

Learning &
Decision Making

INDIVIDUAL
OUTCOMES

Job
Performance

Organizational
Commitment

Pictured here are Nuclear Engineers Butch Woodley (left) and Dave Stinson, who are part of a mentoring program where older engineers are paired with younger ones. The Tennessee Valley Authority grasped the value of learning quickly, if belatedly, when it realized a few years ago that more than half its employees could be looking to retire at about the same time. Who would replace the depth of knowledge they took with them?

LEARNING GOALS

After reading this chapter, you should be able to answer the following questions:

8.1 What is learning? What is decision making?

8.2 What types of knowledge can employees gain as they learn and build expertise?

8.3 What are the methods by which employees learn in organizations?

8.4 What two methods can employees use to make decisions?

8.5 What decision-making problems can prevent employees from translating their learning into accurate decisions?

8.6 How does learning affect job performance and organizational commitment?

8.7 What steps can organizations take to foster learning?

TENNESSEE VALLEY AUTHORITY

The Tennessee Valley Authority (TVA) is the largest public power company in the United States.[1] The TVA, along with many other U.S. companies, is facing the consequences of having a workforce that is rapidly approaching retirement. In 1998, TVA's workforce of 13,000 employees had an average age of 48 years.[2] Given this average age, more than half of its employee population potentially could have left the company during the past 10 years. But having an aging workforce is not only a TVA concern. Surveys show that 70–80 percent of executives are concerned about the effect of the aging workforce on their companies. However, fewer than 20 percent report that they have begun to do anything about it.[3]

Once TVA got over the shock, it began to look at the consequences the massive number of retirements would have on its ability to operate. It would have to find a way to not only replace many of these workers with new employees but also retain the knowledge these future retirees possessed. Similar to workers at other companies, TVA employees both perform tasks based on certain skills they might learn through training or education and possess unique knowledge that can be learned only through experience. This knowledge allows them to perform their jobs more effectively and make decisions with which others would struggle. For example, one TVA worker could detect corrosion in water pipes by banging his wrench against the pipe and listening to the sound it made.[4] You aren't going to find that in a manual somewhere!

The TVA is approaching this "brain drain" in a unique way that other companies, such as John Deere, Siemens, Delta Airlines, and World Bank, are trying to copy.[5] The company developed a system designed to highlight where it should put its focus in regard to retaining knowledge. First, it asked employees to provide a nonbinding estimate of when they were planning to retire. Second, it had each line manager assign a "position risk factor" to each employee by asking questions such as, "What knowledge is likely to be lost when this employee leaves?" and "What are the consequences to the company of losing that knowledge?" Each supervisor also came up with ideas on how to prevent that knowledge loss. By multiplying the "critical knowledge score" with when the employee was planning to retire, TVA was able to recognize its most immediate problem areas.[6] At that point, TVA's goals became finding a way to capture and retain as much of that knowledge as possible before the employee left. How can such knowledge be retained, especially when asking the "experts" to write down what they know and how they know it is often impractical? The TVA and other companies have started "shadowing" or apprenticeship programs that allow younger workers to watch more experienced workers in order to gain their knowledge.

LEARNING AND DECISION MAKING

8.1

What is learning? What is decision making?

The TVA is so concerned about its impending "brain drain" problem because learning and decision making are so important in organizations. **Learning** reflects relatively permanent changes in an employee's knowledge or skill that result from experience.[7] The more employees learn, the more they bring to the table when they come to work. Why is learning so important? Because it has a significant impact on **decision making**, which refers to the process of generating and choosing from a set of alternatives to solve a problem. The more knowledge and skills employees possess, the more likely they are to make accurate and sound decisions. The risk, at TVA and other organizations, is that less experienced employees will lack the knowledge base needed to make the right decisions when stepping into new roles.

One reason inexperience can be so problematic is that learning is not necessarily easy. Have you ever watched "experts" perform their jobs? How is it that someone becomes an expert? How did that employee in the TVA example learn to detect corrosion in a pipe by banging a wrench against it? It takes a significant amount of time to become proficient at most complex jobs. It takes most employees anywhere from three months to a year to perform at a satisfactory level.[8] To develop high levels of expertise takes significantly longer. This difficulty makes it even more important for companies to find a way to improve learning and decision making by their employees.

WHY DO SOME EMPLOYEES LEARN TO MAKE DECISIONS BETTER THAN OTHERS?

Bill Buford, a journalist interested in becoming a chef, was hired by Mario Batali's world-renowned restaurant Babbo in New York. At some point early in his tenure in the kitchen, he realized he was in over his head while he stood and watched other, more experienced cooks work at an unbelievably frantic pace. He knew right then that he had a decision to make:

> "I was at a go-forward-or-backward moment. If I went backward, I'd be saying, 'Thanks for the visit, very interesting, that's sure not me.' But how to go forward? There was no place for me. These people were at a higher level of labor. They didn't think. Their skills were so deeply inculcated they were available to them as instincts. I didn't have skills of that kind and couldn't imagine how you'd learn them. I was aware of being poised on the verge of something: a long, arduous, confidence-bashing, profoundly humiliating experience."[9]

In this situation, Buford realized that his coworkers had more expertise than he did. **Expertise** refers to the knowledge and skills that distinguish experts from novices and less experienced people.[10] Research shows that the differences between experts and novices is almost always a function of learning as opposed to the more popular view that intelligence or other innate differences make the difference.[11] Although learning cannot be directly seen or observed, we can tell when people have learned by observing their behaviors. It is those behaviors that can be used to tell experts from novices, and it is changes in those behaviors that can be used to show that learners are gaining knowledge. Although it's sometimes easy for employees to mimic a behavior once or twice, or get lucky with a few key decisions, true learning only occurs when changes in behavior become relatively permanent and are repeated over time. Understanding why some employees prove better at this than others requires understanding what exactly employees learn and how they do it.

TYPES OF KNOWLEDGE

Employees learn two basic types of knowledge, both of which have important implications for organizations. **Explicit knowledge** is the kind of information you are likely to think about when you picture someone sitting down at a desk to learn. It's information that is relatively easily communicated and a large part of what companies teach during training sessions. Think about it this way: If you can put the information or knowledge in a manual or write it down for someone else, chances are good you're talking about explicit knowledge. As you read this textbook, we're doing our best to communicate explicit knowledge to you that will be useful to you in your future job. Although such information is necessary to perform well, it winds up being a relatively minor portion of all that you need to know.

8.2

What types of knowledge can employees gain as they learn and build expertise?

Expertise is the accumulation of superior knowledge and skills in a field that separates experts from everyone else.

Tacit knowledge, in contrast, is what employees can typically learn only through experience.[12] It's not easily communicated but could very well be the most important aspect of what we learn in organizations.[13] In fact, it's been argued that up to 90 percent of the knowledge contained in organizations occurs in tacit form.[14] Did you ever get to be so good at something that you had the ability to do it but couldn't really explain it to someone else? That's a common way to explain tacit knowledge. It's been described as the "know-how," "know-what," and "know who" acquired solely through experience.[15] Others have used terms such as intuition, skills, insight, beliefs, mental models, and practical intelligence.[16] Table 8–1 lists the qualities that help explain the differences between explicit and tacit knowledge. Some would go as far as to say that explicit knowledge is what everyone can find and use, but tacit knowledge is what separates experts from common people.[17]

TABLE 8-1	Characteristics of Explicit and Tacit Knowledge	
EXPLICIT KNOWLEDGE	**TACIT KNOWLEDGE**
Easily transferred through written or verbal communication	Very difficult, if not impossible, to articulate to others
Readily available to most	Highly personal in nature
Can be learned through books	Based on experience
Always conscious and accessible information	Sometimes holders don't even recognize that they possess it
General information	Typically job- and/or situation-specific

Source: Adapted from R. McAdam, B. Mason, and J. McCrory, "Exploring the Dichotomies within the Tacit Knowledge Literature: Towards a Process of Tacit Knowing in Organizations," *Journal of Knowledge Management* 11 (2007), pp. 43–59.

METHODS OF LEARNING

8.3

What are the methods by which employees learn in organizations?

Tacit and explicit knowledge are extremely important to employees and organizations. As an employee, it's hard to build a high level of tacit knowledge without some level of explicit knowledge to build off of. From an organization's perspective, the tacit knowledge its employees accumulate may be the single most important strategic asset a company possesses.[18] The question then becomes: How do employees learn these types of knowledge? The short answer is that we learn through reinforcement (rewards and punishment), observation, and experience.

REINFORCEMENT. We've known for a long time that managers use various methods of reinforcement to induce desirable or reduce undesirable behaviors by their employees. Originally known as operant conditioning, B.F. Skinner was the first to pioneer the notion that we learn by observing the link between our voluntary behavior and the consequences that follow it. Research has continually demonstrated that people will exhibit specific behaviors if they are rewarded for doing so. Not surprisingly, we have a tendency to repeat behaviors that result in consequences that we like and to not exhibit behaviors that result in consequences we don't like. Figure 8-1 shows this operant conditioning process.

In that model, you can see that there are antecedents or events that precede or signal certain behaviors, which are then followed by consequences. Antecedents in organizations are typically goals, rules, instructions, or other types of information that help show employees what

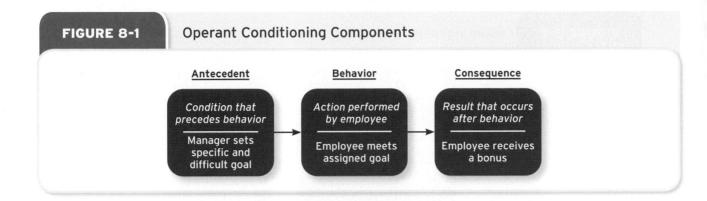

FIGURE 8-1   Operant Conditioning Components

Antecedent

Condition that precedes behavior

Manager sets specific and difficult goal

Behavior

Action performed by employee

Employee meets assigned goal

Consequence

Result that occurs after behavior

Employee receives a bonus

is expected of them. Although antecedents are useful for motivational reasons, it is primarily the consequences of actions that drive behavior. This entire process of reinforcement is a continuous cycle, and the repetition of behaviors is strengthened to the degree that reinforcement continues to occur. There are four specific consequences typically used by organizations to modify employee behavior, known as the **contingencies of reinforcement.**[19] Figure 8-2 summarizes these contingencies. It's important to separate these contingencies into what they are designed to do, namely, increase desired behaviors or decrease unwanted behaviors.

Two contingencies of reinforcement are used to increase desired behaviors. **Positive reinforcement** occurs when a positive outcome follows a desired behavior. It is perhaps the most common type of reinforcement and the type we think of when an employee receives some type of "reward." Increased pay, promotions, praise from a manager or coworkers, and public recognition would all be considered positive reinforcement when given as a result of an employee exhibiting wanted behaviors. For positive reinforcement to be successful, an employee needs to see a direct link between his or her behavior and the desired outcome (see Chapter 6 on Motivation for more discussion of these issues). If the consequence isn't realized until long after a specific behavior, then the odds that the employee will link the two is minimized. **Negative reinforcement** occurs when an unwanted outcome is removed following a desired behavior. Have you ever performed a task for the specific reason of not getting yelled at? If so, you learned to perform certain behaviors through the use of negative reinforcement. Perhaps there are some tasks your job requires that you don't enjoy. If your manager removes these responsibilities specifically because you perform well at another aspect of your job, then this could also be seen as negative reinforcement. It is important to remember that even though the word "negative" has a sour connotation to it, it is designed to *increase* desired behaviors.

The next two contingencies of reinforcement are designed to decrease undesired behaviors. **Punishment** occurs when an unwanted outcome follows an unwanted behavior. Punishment is exactly what it sounds like. In other words, the employee is given something he or she doesn't like as a result of performing a behavior that the organization

Positive reinforcement like public recognition both encourages employees and helps ensure that desirable behaviors will be imitated and repeated.

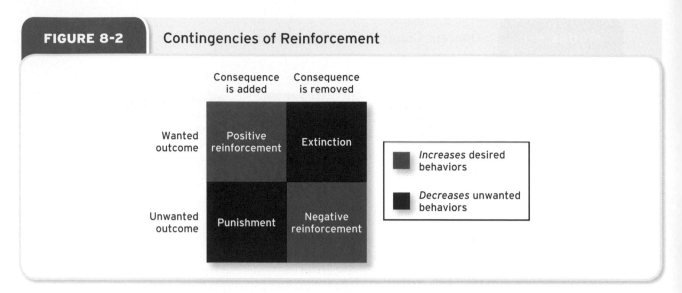

FIGURE 8-2   Contingencies of Reinforcement

doesn't like. Suspending an employee for showing up to work late, assigning job tasks generally seen as demeaning for not following safety procedures, or even firing an employee for gross misconduct are all examples of punishment. **Extinction** occurs when there is the removal of a consequence following an unwanted behavior. The use of extinction to reinforce behavior can be purposeful or accidental. Perhaps an employee receives attention from coworkers when he or she acts in ways that are somewhat childish at work. Finding a way to remove the attention would be a purposeful act of extinction. Similarly though, perhaps an employee works late every now and then to finish up job tasks when work gets busy, but his or her manager stops acknowledging that hard work. Desired behavior that is not reinforced will diminish over time. In this way, a manager who does nothing to reinforce good behavior is actually decreasing the odds that it will be repeated!

In general, positive reinforcement and extinction should be the most common forms of reinforcement used by managers to create learning among their employees. Positive reinforcement doesn't have to be in the form of material rewards to be effective. There are many ways for managers to encourage wanted behaviors. Offering praise, providing feedback, public recognition, and small celebrations are all ways to encourage employees and increase the chances they will continue to exhibit desired behaviors. At the same time, extinction is an effective way to stop unwanted behaviors. Both of these contingencies deliver their intended results, but perhaps more important, they do so without creating feelings of animosity and conflict. Although punishment and negative reinforcement will work, they tend to bring other, detrimental consequences along with them.

Whereas the type of reinforcement used to modify behavior is important, research also shows that the timing of reinforcement is equally important.[20] Therefore, it's important to examine the timing of when the contingencies are applied, referred to as **schedules of reinforcement.** Table 8-2 provides a summary of the five schedules of reinforcement. **Continuous reinforcement** is the simplest schedule of reinforcement and happens when a specific consequence follows each and every occurrence of a desired behavior. For most jobs, continuous reinforcement is impractical. As a manager, can you imagine providing positive reinforcement every time someone exhibits a desired behavior? It's a good thing that research also shows that under many circumstances, continuous reinforcement might be considered the least long-lasting, because as soon as the consequence stops, the desired behavior stops along with it.[21]

TABLE 8-2	Schedules of Reinforcement		
REINFORCEMENT SCHEDULE	REWARD GIVEN FOLLOWING	POTENTIAL LEVEL OF PERFORMANCE	EXAMPLE
Continuous	Every desired behavior	High, but difficult to maintain	Praise
Fixed Interval	Fixed time periods	Average	Paycheck
Variable Interval	Variable time periods	Moderately high	Supervisor walk-by
Fixed Ratio	Fixed number of desired behaviors	High	Piece-rate pay
Variable Ratio	Variable number of desired behaviors	Very high	Commission pay

The other four schedules differ in terms of their variability and the basis of the consequences. Two schedules are interval based; that is, they distribute reinforcement based on the amount of time that passes. A **fixed interval schedule** is probably the single most common form of reinforcement schedule. With this schedule, workers are rewarded after a certain amount of time, and the length of time between reinforcement periods stays the same. Every time an employee gets a paycheck after a predetermined period of time, he or she is being reinforced on a fixed interval schedule. **Variable interval schedules** are designed to reinforce behavior at more random points in time. A supervisor walking around at different points of time every day is a good example of a variable interval schedule. If that supervisor walked around at the same exact time every day, do you think workers would be more or less prone to exhibit good behaviors throughout the day?

The other two reinforcement schedules are based on actual behaviors. **Fixed ratio schedules** reinforce behaviors after a certain number of them have been exhibited. Some manufacturing plants have created piece-rate pay systems in which workers are paid according to the number of items they produce. Employees know ahead of time how many items they have to produce to be reinforced. **Variable ratio schedules** reward people after a varying number of exhibited behaviors. Salespeople, for example, are often compensated based on commission because they receive extra pay every time they sell an item. However, a car salesman doesn't make a sale every time someone walks in the door of the dealership. Sometimes it takes exhibiting good sales behaviors to 8 or 9 customers to make a sale. Take a slot machine as an example. The machine doesn't reward you for every lever pull or even every 10 lever pulls—you never know when the next winning pull will be. Would you say that slot machines do a good job of reinforcing the behavior that casinos would like you to have? You bet!

On the whole, research has consistently shown that variable schedules lead to higher levels of performance than fixed schedules. Think about it this way: Do you study more consistently in a class that gives pop quizzes or one that simply tests you three set times a semester? Research also shows that desired behaviors tend to disappear much more quickly when reinforcement is discontinued under fixed plans. However, variable schedules are not always appropriate for some types of reinforcement. How would you like it if your employer decided to give you your paychecks on a variable schedule? Sorry, you're not getting a paycheck this week—maybe next week! Moreover, studies suggest that

"Oh, not bad. The light comes on, I press the bar, they write me a check. How about you?"

continuous or fixed schedules can be better for reinforcing new behaviors or behaviors that don't occur on a frequent basis.

OBSERVATION. In addition to learning through reinforcement, **social learning theory** argues that people in organizations have the ability to learn through the observation of others.[22] In fact, many would argue that social learning is the primary way by which employees gain knowledge in organizations.[23] Think about where you are most likely to get your cues while working in an organization. When possible, chances are good you'll look around at other employees to figure out the appropriate behaviors on your job. Not only do employees have the ability to see the link between their own behaviors and their consequences, they can also observe the behaviors and consequences of others.[24] When employees observe the actions of others, learn from what they observe, and then repeat the observed behavior, they are engaging in **behavioral modeling.**

For behavior modeling to occur successfully, a number of processes have to take place. These steps are shown in Figure 8-3. First, the learner must focus attention on

---

FIGURE 8-3   The Modeling Process

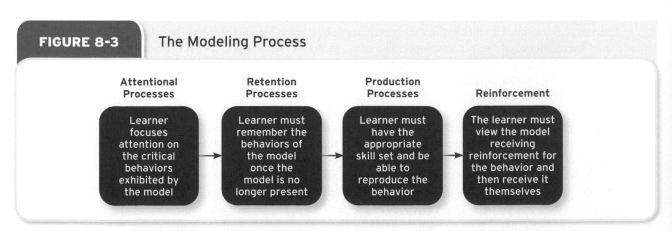

Attentional Processes	Retention Processes	Production Processes	Reinforcement
Learner focuses attention on the critical behaviors exhibited by the model	Learner must remember the behaviors of the model once the model is no longer present	Learner must have the appropriate skill set and be able to reproduce the behavior	The learner must view the model receiving reinforcement for the behavior and then receive it themselves

Source: Adapted from H.M. Weiss, "Learning Theory and Industrial and Organizational Psychology," in *Handbook of Industrial and Organizational Psychology,* eds. M.D. Dunnette and L.M. Hough. (Consulting Psychologists Press: Palo Alto, CA, 1990), pp. 75–169.

David Mackay was provided an unusual opportunity to learn by observation and behavioral modeling before becoming CEO of Kellogg's. He "shadowed" his predecessor for two years to gain insider experience before taking the helm.

an appropriate model and accurately perceive the critical behavior the model exhibits. That model might be a supervisor, a coworker, or even a subordinate. Some organizations go out of their way to supply role models for newcomers or inexperienced workers to watch and learn from. In our opening vignette, TVA was assigning younger workers to follow and model older workers in the hopes of capturing the tacit knowledge they had acquired. In fact, because tacit knowledge is so difficult to communicate, modeling might be the single best way to acquire it. For that reason, modeling is a continual process that is used at all levels of many organizations. Kellogg's, the Michigan-based cereal company, groomed current CEO David Mackay for two years by allowing him to observe and model an interim, experienced CEO prior to taking over the helm. Mackay shadowed the CEO and observed boardroom proceedings to gain the insider experience that the Kellogg's board felt he was lacking.[25] Needless to say, choosing a good model is important, and not all models are good ones. Salomon Brothers, the New York–based investment bank, learned this lesson the hard way when employees began to model the unethical behaviors of their managers and leaders.[26]

Second, the learner actually needs to remember exactly what the model's behavior was and how they did it. This step is easier said than done when watching experts perform their job, because so much of what they do remains unspoken and can occur at a rapid pace. Third, the learner must undertake production processes, or actually be able to reproduce what the model did. Not only must the learner have the requisite knowledge and physical skills to be able to perform the task; now he or she must translate what he or she has observed into action. Do you remember the first time you drove a car? Chances are good you'd been watching other drivers for many years, picking up bits and pieces of how to do it through observation. However, things became different when you were behind the wheel for the first time. All of a sudden, there was a lot of information to process, and years and years of observation had to be put into action.

Fourth, the last step of behavior modeling is reinforcement. This reinforcement can come from observation, direct experience, or both. The learner can observe the consequences of the model having exhibited the behavior (positive reinforcement or punishment), which in itself will help ingrain the desirability of performing the behavior. In addition, it's important for the learner to receive reinforcement after replicating the behavior. If the newly acquired behaviors are positively reinforced, the likelihood of continued behavior increases.

OB ASSESSMENTS

GOAL ORIENTATION

What does your goal orientation look like? This assessment is designed to measure all three dimensions of goal orientation. Please write a number next to each statement that indicates the extent to which it accurately describes your attitude toward work while you are on the job. Answer each question using the response scale provided. Then sum up your answers for each of the three dimensions.

1	2	3	4	5
STRONGLY DISAGREE	DISAGREE	NEUTRAL	AGREE	STRONGLY AGREE

1. I am willing to select challenging assignments that I can learn a lot from. _____

2. I often look for opportunities to develop new skills and knowledge. _____

3. I enjoy challenging and difficult tasks where I'll learn new skills. _____

4. For me, development of my ability is important enough to take risks. _____

5. I prefer to work in situations that require a high level of ability and talent. _____

6. I like to show that I can perform better than my coworkers. _____

7. I try to figure out what it takes to prove my ability to others at work. _____

8. I enjoy it when others at work are aware of how well I am doing. _____

9. I prefer to work on projects where I can prove my ability to others. _____

10. I would avoid taking on a new task if there was a chance that I would appear incompetent to others. _____

11. Avoiding a show of low ability is more important to me than learning a new skill. _____

12. I'm concerned about taking on a task at work if my performance would reveal that I had low ability. _____

13. I prefer to avoid situations at work where I might perform poorly. _____

SCORING AND INTERPRETATION:

Learning Orientation: Sum up items 1–5.
Performance-Prove Orientation: Sum up items 6–9.
Performance-Avoid Orientation: Sum up items 10–13.

For learning orientation, scores of 20 or more are above average, and scores of 19 or less are below average. For the two performance orientations, scores of 15 or more are above average, and scores of 14 or less are below average.

Source: Adapted from J.F. Brett and D. VandeWalle, "Goal Orientation and Goal Content as Predictors of Performance in a Training Program," *Journal of Applied Psychology* 84 (1999), pp. 863–73.

GOAL ORIENTATION. Before we leave this section, it's important to recognize that people learn somewhat differently according to their predispositions or attitudes toward learning and performance. These differences are reflected in different "goal orientations" that capture the kinds of activities and goals that they prioritize. Some people have what is known as a **learning orientation,** where building competence is deemed more important than demonstrating competence. "Learning-oriented" persons enjoy working on new kinds of tasks, even if they fail during their early experiences. Such people view failure in positive terms—as a means of increasing knowledge and skills in the long run.[27]

For others, the demonstration of competence is deemed a more important goal than the building of competence. That demonstration of competence can be motivated by two different thought processes. Those with a **performance-prove orientation** focus on demonstrating their competence so that others think favorably of them. Those with a **performance-avoid orientation** focus on demonstrating their competence so that others will not think poorly of them. In either case, "performance-oriented" people tend to work mainly on tasks at which they're already good, preventing them from failing in front of others. Such individuals view failure in negative terms—as an indictment of their ability and competence.

Research has shown that a learning goal orientation improves self-confidence, feedback-seeking behavior, learning strategy development, and learning performance.[28] Research on the two performance orientations is more mixed. Although it would seem that focusing on performance should improve performance-based outcomes, research shows that isn't necessarily the case. On the whole, a performance-prove orientation tends to be a mixed bag, producing varying levels of performance and outcomes. What is more clear are the detrimental effects of having a performance-avoid orientation. Employees who enter learning situations with a fear of looking bad in front of others tend to learn less and have substantially higher levels of anxiety.[29] What kind of orientation do you tend to exhibit? See our **OB Assessments** feature to find out.

METHODS OF DECISION MAKING

How do employees take explicit and tacit knowledge, however it's gained, and turn that knowledge into effective decision making? Sometimes that process is very straightforward. **Programmed decisions** are decisions that become somewhat automatic because a person's knowledge allows him or her to recognize and identify a situation and the course of action that needs to be taken. As shown in Figure 8-4, experts often respond to an identified problem by realizing that they've dealt with it before. That realization triggers a programmed decision that is implemented and then evaluated according to its ability to deliver the expected outcome. For experts who possess high levels of explicit and tacit knowledge, many decisions they face are of this programmed variety. That's not to say that the decisions are necessarily easy. It simply means that their experience and knowledge allows them to see the problems more easily and recognize and implement solutions more quickly.

To experts, this kind of decision making sometimes comes across as intuition or a "gut feeling." **Intuition** can be described as emotionally charged judgments that arise through quick, nonconscious, and holistic associations.[30] Because of their tacit knowledge, experts sometimes cannot put into words why they know that a problem exists, why a solution will work, or how they accomplished a task. They just "know." Of course, the difficulty arises in knowing when to trust that "gut instinct" and when not to.[31] As a general rule of thumb, you should probably ask yourself how much expertise you have in that on which you are making a judgment. In other words, don't go laying down your life savings on a spin of the roulette wheel in Vegas because your intuition tells you "red"! Effective intuition results when people have a certain amount of tacit knowledge. For more discussion of such issues, see our **OB at the Bookstore** feature.

 8.4

What two methods can employees use to make decisions?

FIGURE 8-4   Programmed and Nonprogrammed Decisions

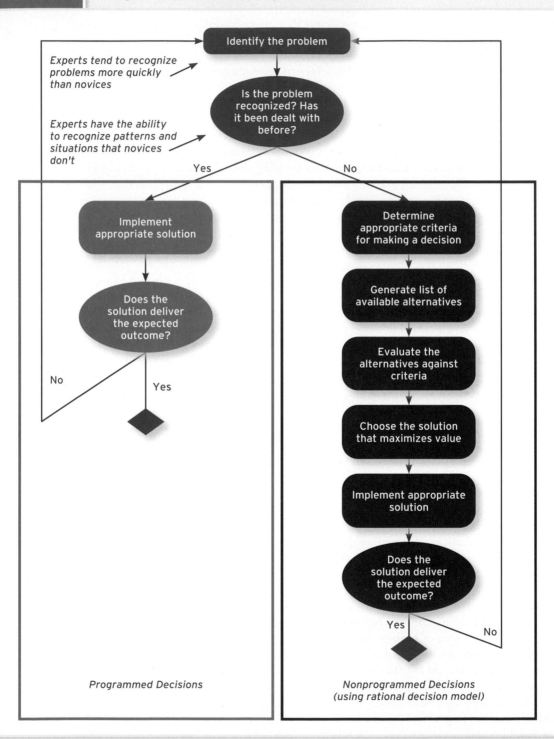

OB AT THE BOOKSTORE

BLINK: THE POWER OF THINKING WITHOUT THINKING
by Malcolm Gladwell (New York: Little, Brown & Co., 2005).

Decisions made very quickly can be every bit as good as decisions made cautiously and deliberately.

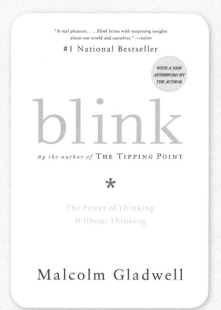

With those words, Malcolm Gladwell summarizes his book's take on decision making. The book opens with a story about a rare, ancient, Greek statue under consideration for purchase by the J. Paul Getty Museum in California. Due diligence had been performed on the statue, its papers seemed to be in order, and numerous, detailed scientific analyses had been performed by a geologist to confirm its authenticity. After purchasing this extraordinary statue and publicizing its purchase to the outside world, the museum subsequently began to show it to numerous art experts. Expert after expert told the museum that there was something wrong with the piece. They couldn't put their finger on why they knew it was a fake, they just knew. The fingernails weren't right, the statue was too fresh, it just felt wrong. These experts were able to come to a conclusion simply based off a quick first impression. The experts turned out to be right, and the statue was uncovered as a fraud after considerable expense and embarrassment to the museum.

The book goes on to describe numerous experts (doctors, salespeople, marriage experts) who had the ability to take a quick snapshot of a situation (what Gladwell calls "thin-slicing") and make judgments and decisions on the basis of what appeared to be limited information. Unfortunately for most of us, we don't always possess that kind of expertise for the decisions that we need to make. Indeed, Gladwell switches gears halfway through the book and details numerous examples in which quick decisions are ineffective. In essence, Gladwell tells us that most of our first impressions are wrong. This shift gives the book a duality that can be frustrating for some readers. On the one hand, some people have the ability to make quick accurate decisions. On the other hand, many of us can't do that, and the reasons for those differences aren't fully explained.

Of course, it's clearly true that some people have the ability to make immediate and accurate decisions based on snap judgments. However, in every example in the book in which someone has the ability to do so, it is important to note that they are *experts* on the topic at hand. These experts have spent years and years developing knowledge and skill through practice, repetition, and experience. To the nonexpert, it seems like these decisions are "intuition" or "snap judgments," but in reality, the processing time for these experts in gathering pertinent information has been so automatized that it only seems that way. They bring a great deal of tacit knowledge to these specific situations, and many times, in a point noted by Gladwell, they are unable to verbalize exactly why it is they make the decisions they do.

When a situation arises that is new, complex and not recognized, it calls for a **nonprogrammed decision** on the part of the employee. Organizations are complex and changing environments, and many workers are faced with uncertainty on a daily basis. In these instances, employees have to make sense of their environment, understand the problems they are faced with, and come up with solutions to overcome them. As a general rule of thumb, as employees move up the corporate ladder, a larger percentage of their decisions become less and less programmed. How should decision making proceed in such contexts? The **rational decision-making model** offers a step-by-step approach to making decisions that maximize outcomes by examining all available alternatives. As shown in Figure 8-4, this model becomes relevant when people don't recognize a problem as one they have dealt with before.

The first step in the rational decision-making model is to identify the criteria that are important in making the decision, taking into account all involved parties. The second step is to generate a list of all available alternatives that might be potential solutions to the problem. At this point, evaluating the alternatives is not necessary. The responsibility simply lies in coming up with as many potential solutions as possible. The third step in the model is the evaluation of those alternatives against the criteria laid out in step one. Does it matter how much the alternative costs? What exactly will happen as a result of various choices? What will the side effects of the alternative be? The fourth step is to select the alternative that results in the best outcome. That is, given the costs and benefits of each alternative, which alternative provides us with the most value? The fifth step is to implement the alternative.

The rational decision-making model assumes that people are, of course, perfectly rational. However, problems immediately arise when we start to examine some of the assumptions the model makes about human decision makers.[32] The model assumes there is a clear and definite problem to solve and that people have the ability to identify what that exact problem is. It also assumes that decision makers have perfect information—that they know and are able to identify the available alternatives and the outcomes that would be associated with those alternatives. The model further assumes that time and money are generally not issues when it comes to making a decision, that decision makers always choose the solution that maximizes value, and that they will act in the best interests of the organization. Given all these assumptions, perhaps we shouldn't label the model as "rational" after all! For an example of one decision maker who can follow the tenets of the rational decision-making model, see our **OB on Screen** feature.

DECISION-MAKING PROBLEMS

8.5

What decision-making problems can prevent employees from translating their learning into accurate decisions?

Because employees don't always make rational decisions, it's easy to second-guess decisions after the fact. Many decisions made inside organizations look good at the time and were made with perfectly good justifications to support them but turn out to have what are perceived as "bad results." The reality, however, is that it's a lot easier to question decisions in hindsight. As Warren Buffet, CEO of Berkshire Hathaway, is often quoted as saying, "In the business world, the rearview mirror is always clearer than the windshield."[33] Our responsibility here is not to rehash all the poor decisions employees and managers have made (and there are many of them!) but rather to detail some of the most common reasons for bad decision making—in other words, when are people most likely to falter in terms of the rational decision-making model and why?

LIMITED INFORMATION. Although most employees perceive themselves as rational decision makers, the reality is that they are all subject to **bounded rationality.** Bounded rationality is the notion that decision makers simply do not have the ability or resources to process all available information and alternatives to make an optimal decision.[34] A comparison

OB ON SCREEN

STAR TREK: FIRST CONTACT

Data: *Captain, I believe I am feeling . . . anxiety. It is an intriguing sensation. A most distracting—*

Picard: *(Interrupting) Data, I am sure it is a fascinating experience, but perhaps you should deactivate your emotion chip for now.*

Data: *Good idea sir. (click) Done.*

Picard: *Data, there are times when I envy you.*

With these words, Captain Jean-Luc Picard (Patrick Stewart) tells Data (Brent Spiner) that he wished he had Data's ability to do what all of us would like to be able to do from time to time: make perfectly rational decisions. You see, Data is an android (a robot made to resemble a human) who serves as the chief operations officer aboard the USS Enterprise in *Star Trek: First Contact* (Dir. Jonathan Frakes, Paramount Pictures, 1996). Data, with his extremely advanced computer for a brain, is able to make close to perfect decisions by calculating probabilities with all possible available information. His brain works so quickly that a decision lasting .63 seconds feels "like an eternity" to him. Wouldn't we all like to have that ability?

Throughout the newer generation of *Star Trek* episodes and movies, Data exhibits an overwhelming desire to become more "human" in order to understand his shipmates. As an android with no emotions, he lacks the ability to understand why humans make the irrational mistakes they sometimes do. He doesn't comprehend humor, selfish desires, or making decisions for reasons other than achieving the optimal solution.

In a prior *Star Trek* movie, Data's creator provides him with an "emotion chip" that allows him to be distracted by the emotions and feelings that we're faced with every day. In the scene shown, Data and Captain Picard are about to enter what is an extremely dangerous, life-and-death situation. Needless to say, Captain Picard prefers that Data enter the situation with the enviable ability to turn off his emotions and make rational decisions. While Data strives to feel emotion in his quest to understand human behavior, employees and managers often wish they had the ability to make decisions free from the distractions of emotion. However, as long as we are "human," all we can do is strive to make decisions in as rational a manner as possible.

of bounded rationality and rational decision making is presented in Table 8-3. This limit results in two major problems for making decisions. First, people have to filter and simplify information to make sense of their complex environment and the myriad of potential choices they face.[35] This simplification leads them to miss information when perceiving problems, generating and evaluating alternatives, or judging the results. Second, because people cannot possibly consider every single alternative when making a decision, they satisfice. **Satisficing** results when decision makers select the first acceptable alternative considered.[36]

TABLE 8-3	Rational Decision Making vs. Bounded Rationality	
TO BE RATIONAL DECISION MAKERS, WE *SHOULD*...	**BOUNDED RATIONALITY SAYS WE *ARE LIKELY TO*...**
Identify the problem by thoroughly examining the situation and considering all interested parties.	Boil the problem down to something that is easily understood.
Develop an exhaustive list of alternatives to consider as solutions.	Come up with a few solutions that tend to be straightforward, familiar, and similar to what is currently being done.
Evaluate all the alternatives simultaneously.	Evaluate each alternative as soon as we think of it.
Use accurate information to evaluate alternatives.	Use distorted and inaccurate information during the evaluation process.
Pick the alternative that maximizes value.	Pick the first acceptable alternative (satisfice).

Sources: Adapted from H.A. Simon, "Rational Decision Making in Organizations," *American Economic Review* 69 (1979), pp. 493–513; D. Kahneman, "Maps of Bounded Rationality: Psychology for Behavioral Economics," *The American Economic Review* 93 (2003), pp. 1449–75; S.W. Williams, *Making Better Business Decisions* (Thousand Oaks, CA: Sage Publications, 2002).

In addition to choosing the first acceptable alternative, decision makers tend to come up with alternatives that are straightforward, familiar, and not that different from what they're already doing. When you and another person are deciding where to go out for dinner tonight, will you sit down and list every restaurant available to you within a certain mile limit? Of course not. You'll start listing off alternatives, generally starting with the closest and most familiar, until both parties arrive at a restaurant that is acceptable to them. Making decisions this way is no big deal when it comes to deciding where to go for dinner, because the consequences of a poor decision are minimal. However, many managers make decisions that have critical consequences for their employees and their customers. In those cases, making a decision without thoroughly looking into the alternatives becomes a problem!

FAULTY PERCEPTIONS. As decision makers, employees are forced to rely on their perceptions to make decisions. Perception is the process of selecting, organizing, storing, and retrieving information about the environment. Although perceptions can be very useful, because they help us to make sense of the environment around us, they can often become distorted versions of reality. Perceptions can be dangerous in decision making, because we tend to make assumptions or evaluations on the basis of them. **Selective perception** is the tendency for people to see their environment only as it affects them and as it is consistent with their expectations. Has someone ever told you, "You only see what you want to see"? If a relative, spouse, or significant other said that to you, chances are good it probably wasn't the best experience. That person was likely upset that you did not perceive the environment (or what was important to them) the same way they did. Selective perception affects our ability to identify problems, generate and evaluate alternatives, and judge outcomes. In other words, we take "shortcuts" when we process information. In the following paragraphs, we'll discuss some of the ways in which we take perceptual shortcuts when dealing with people and situations.

One false assumption people tend to make when it comes to other people is the belief that others think, feel, and act the same way they do. This assumption is known as a **projection bias.** That is, people project their own thoughts, attitudes, and motives onto other people. "I would never do that—that's unethical" equates to "They would never do that—that's unethical." Projection bias causes problems in decision making because it limits our ability to develop appropriate criteria for a decision and evaluate decisions carefully. The bias causes people to assume that everyone's criteria will be just like theirs and that everyone will react to the decision just as they did.

Another example of faulty perceptions is caused by the way we cognitively organize people into groups. **Social identity theory** holds that people identify themselves by the groups to which they belong and perceive and judge others by their group memberships.[37] There is a substantial amount of research that shows that we like to categorize people on the basis of the groups to which they belong.[38] These groups could be based on demographic information (gender, race, religion, hair color), occupational information (scientists, engineers, accountants), where they work (GE, Halliburton, Microsoft), what country they are from (Americans, French, Chinese), or any other subgroup that makes sense to the perceiver. You might categorize students on campus by whether they are a member of a fraternity or sorority. Those inside the Greek system categorize people by which fraternity or sorority they belong to. And people within a certain fraternity might group their own members on the basis of whom they hang out with the most. There is practically no end to the number of subgroups that people can come up with.

A **stereotype** occurs when assumptions are made about others on the basis of their membership in a social group.[39] Although not all stereotypes are bad per se, our decision-making process becomes faulty when we make inaccurate generalizations. Many companies work hard to help their employees avoid stereotyping, because doing so can lead to illegal discrimination in the workplace. Ortho-McNeil Pharmaceutical, Wells Fargo, Kaiser Permanente, and Microsoft (just to name a few) have developed extensive diversity training programs to help their employees overcome specific cultural, racial, and gender stereotypes in the workplace.[40]

When confronted with situations of uncertainty that require a decision on our part, we often use **heuristics**—simple, efficient, rules of thumb that allow us to make decisions more easily. In general, heuristics are not bad. In fact, they lead to correct decisions more often than not.[41] However, heuristics can also bias us toward inaccurate decisions at times. Consider this example from one of the earliest studies on decision-making heuristics: "Consider the letter R. Is R more likely to appear in the first position of a word or the third position of a word?"[42] If your answer was the first position of a word, you answered incorrectly and fell victim to one of the most frequently talked about heuristics. The **availability bias** is the tendency for people to base their judgments on information that is easier to recall. It is significantly easier for almost everyone to remember words in which R is the first letter as opposed to the third. The availability bias is why more people are afraid to fly than statistics would support. Every single plane crash is plastered all over the news, making plane crashes more available in memory than successful plane landings.

Aside from the availability bias, there are many other biases that affect the way we make decisions. Table 8-4 describes 15 of the most well-researched decision-making biases. After reading all of them, you might wonder how we ever make accurate decisions at all! The answer is that we do our best to think rationally through our most important decisions prior to

TABLE 8-4	Decision-Making Biases
NAME OF BIAS	**DESCRIPTION**
Anchoring	The tendency to rely too heavily, or "anchor," on one trait or piece of information when making decisions.
Availability bias	A biased prediction, due to the tendency to focus on the most salient and emotionally charged outcome.
Bandwagon effect	The tendency to do (or believe) things because many other people do (or believe) the same.
Choice-supportive bias	The tendency to remember one's choices as better than they actually were.
Confirmation bias	The tendency to search for or interpret information in a way that confirms one's preconceptions.
Contrast effect	The enhancement or diminishment of a weight or other measurement when compared with recently observed contrasting object.
False consensus effect	The tendency for people to overestimate the degree to which others agree with them.
Gambler's fallacy	The tendency to assume that individual random events are influenced by previous random events. For example, "I've flipped heads with this coin so many times that tails is bound to come up sooner or later."
Halo effect	The tendency for a person's positive or negative traits to "spill over" from one area of their personality to another in others' perceptions of them.
Hindsight bias	Sometimes called the "I-knew-it-all-along" effect, the inclination to see past events as being predictable.
Illusion of control	The tendency for human beings to believe they can control or at least influence outcomes that they clearly cannot.
Primacy effect	The tendency to weigh initial events more than subsequent events.
Projection bias	The tendency to unconsciously assume that others share the same or similar thoughts, beliefs, values, or positions.
Recency effect	The tendency to weigh recent events more than earlier events.
Self-fulfilling prophecy	The tendency to engage in behaviors that elicit results that will (consciously or subconsciously) confirm our beliefs.

Sources: J. Baron, *Thinking and Deciding* (3rd ed.). Cambridge, UK: Cambridge University Press, 2000; R.E. Nisbett, L. Ross, *Human inference: Strategies and shortcomings of social judgment.* Englewood Cliffs, N.J.: Prentice-Hall, 1980; D.G. Meyers, *Social Psychology.* Boston, MA: McGraw-Hill, 2005; G. Gigerenzer, P.M. Todd, ABC Research Group, *Simple Heuristics That Make Us Smart.* New York, NY, Oxford University Press, 1999; D. Kahneman, A. Tversky, & P. Slovic, *Judgment under Uncertainty: Heuristics & Biases,* Cambridge, UK: Cambridge University Press, 1982.

making them and tend to use heuristics for decisions that are less important or that need to be made more quickly. Regardless of how often we fall victim to the biases, being aware of potential decision errors can help us make them less frequently.

FAULTY ATTRIBUTIONS. Another category of decision-making problems centers on how we explain the actions and events that occur around us. Research on attributions suggests that when people witness a behavior or outcome, they make a judgment about whether it was internally or externally caused. For example, when a coworker of yours named Joe shows up late to work and misses an important group presentation, you'll almost certainly make a judgment about why that happened. You might attribute Joe's outcome to internal factors—for example, suggesting that he is lazy or has a poor work ethic. Or you might attribute Joe's outcome to external factors—for example, suggesting that there was unusually bad traffic that day or that other factors prevented him from arriving on time.

The **fundamental attribution error** argues that people have a tendency to judge others' behaviors as due to internal factors.[43] This error suggests that you would likely judge Joe as having low motivation, poor organizational skills, or some other negative internal attribute. What if you yourself had showed up late? It turns out that we're less harsh when judging ourselves. The **self-serving bias** occurs when we attribute our own failures to external factors and our own successes to internal factors. Interestingly, evidence suggests that attributions across cultures doesn't always work the same way; see our **OB Internationally** feature for more discussion of this issue.

OB INTERNATIONALLY

Any time a major accident occurs in a company, or any time a significant breach of ethics occurs, a company is expected to respond accordingly. One of the natural reactions of employees, customers, and other observers is to attribute the cause of the negative event to someone. Who this blame gets placed on might be very different, depending on the part of the world in which the company is operating. A culture such as the United States tends to blame the particular individuals most responsible for the event, whereas East Asian (China, Korea, Japan) cultures tend to blame the organization itself.[44] For example, when scandals within organizations occur (e.g., "rogue trading" in an investment bank), newspapers in the United States often publish the name of the employee and discuss the individual worker involved, whereas East Asian newspapers refer to the organization itself.[45]

Interestingly, these biases place different responsibilities on the leaders of organizations in these countries. In East Asian cultures, it's typical for the leader of an organization to take the blame for accidents, regardless of whether he or she had direct responsibility for them.[46] For example, in 2002, the director of a hospital in Tokyo was forced to resign when the cover-up of a medical accident was discovered, even though the director didn't start his job until after the cover-up took place! Similar events are common, such as the resignation of the CEO of Japan Airlines after a jet crashed, killing 500 people. In the United States, in contrast, CEOs rarely take the same level of blame. When Joseph Hazelwood crashed the Exxon Valdez into the Alaskan coastline, there were no calls for the Exxon CEO to resign. It was simply assumed by the American public that he had nothing to do with the accident.

Much of the reasoning for such differences has to do with the way the cultures view individuals and groups. East Asian cultures tend to treat groups as entities and not as individuals, whereas the culture in the United States tends to see individuals acting of their own accord.[47] This difference means that organizational leaders should be very cognizant of how to handle crises, depending on the country in which the negative event occurs. An apology offered by a senior leader is likely to be seen by East Asians as the company taking responsibility, whereas in the United States, it's more likely to be taken as an admission of personal guilt.[48]

One model of attribution processes suggests that when people have a level of familiarity with the person being judged, they'll use a more detailed decision framework. This model is illustrated in Figure 8–5.[49] To return to our previous example, if we want to explore why Joe arrived late to work, we can ask three kinds of questions:

Consensus: Did others act the same way under similar situations? In other words, did others arrive late on the same day?

Distinctiveness: Does this person tend to act differently in other circumstances? In other words, is Joe responsible when it comes to personal appointments, not just work appointments?

Consistency: Does this person always do this when performing this task? In other words, has Joe arrived late for work before?

The way in which these questions are answered will determine if an internal or external attribution is made. An internal attribution, such as laziness or low motivation for Joe, will occur if there is low consensus (others arrived on time), low distinctiveness (Joe is irresponsible with other commitments as well), and high consistency (Joe has arrived late before). An external attribution, such as bad traffic or a power outage, will occur if there is high consensus (others arrived late), high distinctiveness (Joe is responsible with other commitments), and low consistency (Joe has never come late to work before).

FIGURE 8-5   Consensus, Distinctiveness, and Consistency

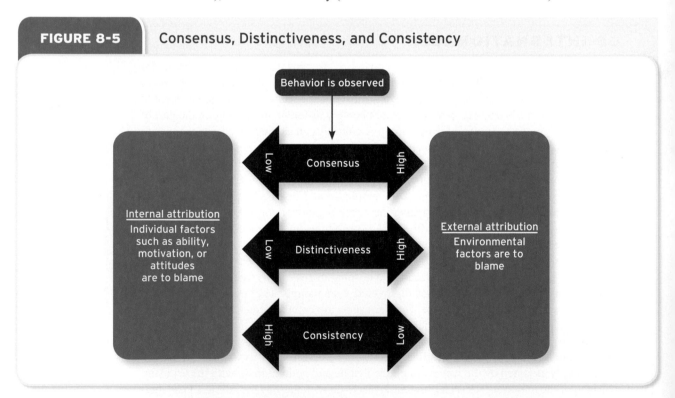

ESCALATION OF COMMITMENT. Our last category of decision-making problems centers on what happens as a decision begins to go wrong. **Escalation of commitment** refers to the decision to continue to follow a failing course of action.[50] The expression "throwing good money after bad" captures this common decision-making error. An enormous amount of research shows that people have a tendency, when presented with a series of decisions, to escalate their commitment to previous decisions, even in the face of

United Airlines took 10 years to finally abandon an expensive but faulty baggage handling system at Denver International Airport, illustrating the power of escalation of commitment.

obvious failures.[51] Why do decision makers fall victim to this sort of error? They may feel an obligation to stick with their decision to avoid looking incompetent. They may also want to avoid admitting that they made a mistake. Those escalation tendencies become particularly strong when decision makers have invested a lot of money into the decision and when the project in question seems quite close to completion.[52]

One recent example of escalation of commitment is United Airlines' abandonment of the automated baggage handling system at the Denver International Airport. When it opened in 1995 (after a two-year delay), the baggage handling system with 26 miles of track designed to haul baggage across three terminals was supposed to be the single most advanced baggage handling system in the world. However, originally scheduled to cost $186 million dollars, a series of delays and technological problems caused the cost of the system to skyrocket by $1 million per day. Because of a series of technological issues, the system never really worked very well. In fact, United was the only airline in the airport willing to use it. It took 10 years and many mangled and lost suitcases before United finally "cut its losses," saving itself $1 million a month in maintenance fees.[53]

SUMMARY: WHY DO SOME EMPLOYEES LEARN TO MAKE DECISIONS BETTER THAN OTHERS?

So what explains why some employees learn to make better decisions than others? As shown in Figure 8-6, answering that question requires understanding how employees learn, what kind of knowledge they gain, and how they use that knowledge to make decisions. Employees learn from a combination of reinforcement and observation, and that learning depends in part on whether they are learning-oriented or performance-oriented. Some of that learning results in increases in explicit knowledge, and some of that learning results in increases in tacit knowledge. Those two forms of knowledge, which combine to form an employee's expertise, are then used in decision making. If a given problem has been encountered before, decision making occurs in a more automatic, programmed fashion. If the problem is new or unfamiliar, nonprogrammed decision making occurs, hopefully following the rational decision-making model. Unfortunately, a number of decision-making problems can hinder the effectiveness of such decisions, including limited information, faulty perceptions, faulty attributions, and escalation of commitment.

FIGURE 8-6   Why Do Some Employees Learn to Make Decisions Better Than Others?

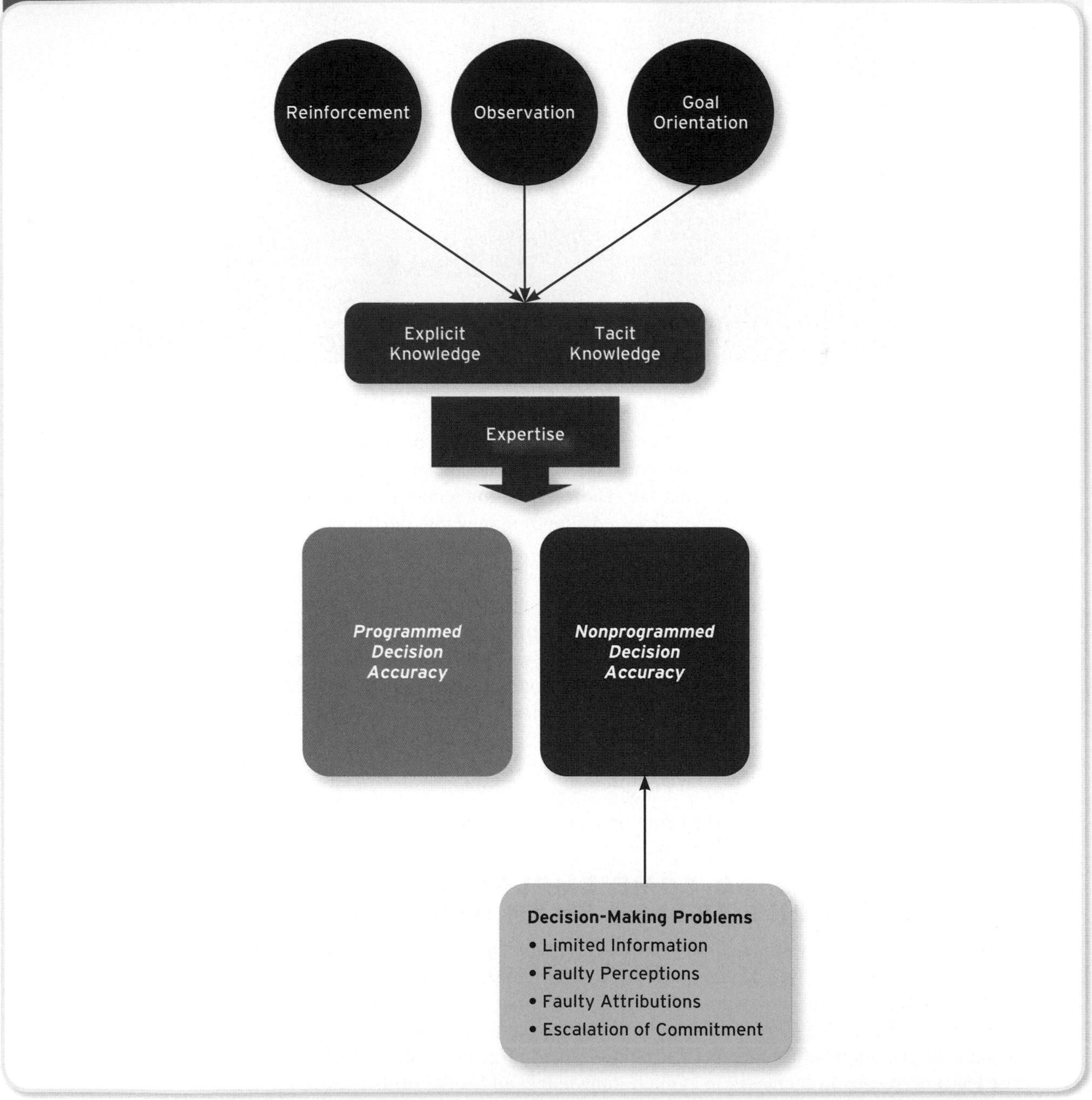

HOW IMPORTANT IS LEARNING?

Does learning have a significant impact on the two primary outcomes in our integrative model of OB—does it correlate with job performance and organizational commitment? Figure 8-7 summarizes the research evidence linking learning to job performance

| FIGURE 8-7 | Effects of Learning on Performance and Commitment |

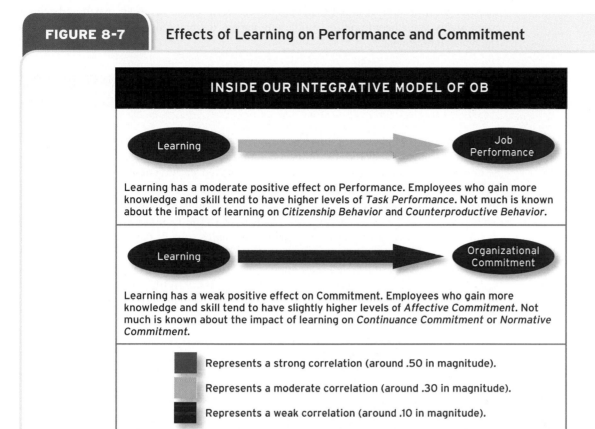

INSIDE OUR INTEGRATIVE MODEL OF OB

Learning → Job Performance

Learning has a moderate positive effect on Performance. Employees who gain more knowledge and skill tend to have higher levels of *Task Performance*. Not much is known about the impact of learning on *Citizenship Behavior* and *Counterproductive Behavior*.

Learning → Organizational Commitment

Learning has a weak positive effect on Commitment. Employees who gain more knowledge and skill tend to have slightly higher levels of *Affective Commitment*. Not much is known about the impact of learning on *Continuance Commitment* or *Normative Commitment*.

Represents a strong correlation (around .50 in magnitude).

Represents a moderate correlation (around .30 in magnitude).

Represents a weak correlation (around .10 in magnitude).

Sources: G.M. Alliger, S.I. Tannenbaum, W. Bennett Jr., H. Traver, and A. Shotland, "A Meta-Analysis of the Relations among Training Criteria," *Personnel Psychology* 50 (1997), pp. 341–58; J.A. Colquitt, J.A. Lepine, and R.A. Noe, "Toward an Integrative Theory of Training Motivation: A Meta-Analytic Path Analysis of 20 Years of Research," *Journal of Applied Psychology* 85 (2000), pp. 678–707; J.P. Meyer, D.J. Stanley, L. Herscovitch, and L. Topolnytsky, "Affective, Continuance, and Normative Commitment to the Organization: A Meta-Analysis of Antecedents, Correlates, and Consequences," *Journal of Vocational Behavior* 61 (2002), pp. 20–52.

and organizational commitment. The figure reveals that learning does influence job performance. Why? The primary reason is that learning is moderately correlated with task performance. It's difficult to fulfill one's job duties if the employee doesn't possess adequate levels of job knowledge. In fact, there are reasons to suggest that the moderate correlation depicted in the figure is actually an underestimate of learning's importance. That's because most of the research linking learning to task performance focuses on explicit learning, which is more practical to measure. It's difficult to measure tacit knowledge because of its unspoken nature, but clearly such knowledge is relevant to task performance. Learning seems less relevant to citizenship behavior and counterproductive behavior however, given that those behaviors are often less dependent on knowledge and expertise.

Figure 8-7 also reveals that learning is only weakly related to organizational commitment.[54] In general, having higher levels of job knowledge is associated with slight increases in emotional attachment to the firm. It is true that companies that have a reputation as organizations that value learning tend to receive higher-quality applicants for jobs.[55] However, there is an important distinction between organizations that offer learning opportunities and employees who take advantage of those opportunities to actually gain

8.6

How does learning affect job performance and organizational commitment?

knowledge. Moreover, it may be that employees with higher levels of expertise become more highly valued commodities on the job market, thereby reducing their levels of continuance commitment.

APPLICATION: TRAINING

8.7

What steps can organizations take to foster learning?

How can organizations improve learning in an effort to boost employee expertise and, ultimately, improve decision making? One approach is to rely on **training,** which represents a systematic effort by organizations to facilitate the learning of job-related knowledge and behavior. Organizations spent over $55.8 billion and approximately $1,273 per learner on formal training and development costs in 2006.[56] Estimates suggest that organizations spend three to six times that amount on informal, observational, and on-the-job training.[57] A full discussion of all the types of training companies offer is beyond the scope of this section, but suffice it to say that companies are using many different methods to help their employees acquire explicit and tacit knowledge. Technological changes are altering the way those methods are delivered, as instructor-led classroom training has declined while online self-study programs have increased.[58] As described in our **OB for Students** section,

OB FOR STUDENTS

What does learning and training have to do with you as a student? We hope this is a reasonably clear question for you already! However, there are some changes on the way in terms of how you might get taught in the future by both companies and universities. Technology and the changing marketplace (that includes you!) are forcing universities to incorporate online education as part of their ongoing strategies.[59] Online courses are growing by leaps and bounds across campuses all over the United States and internationally. If you're not already experiencing virtual content in some form, chances are good many of you will have the opportunity to receive it in the not-too-distant future. Overall, higher education enrollment in the United States is relatively stable, but enrollment in online courses is increasing exponentially.[60] For example, going into the 2007 academic school year, Penn State University had 5,691 students participating in online classes, and the University of Massachusetts had almost double that number.[61]

One of the reasons universities have been slow to incorporate online education is the belief by many faculty members that the same level of knowledge cannot be transmitted online. However, a recent meta-analysis suggests that this belief is unfounded! Research shows no difference between online and regular classroom instruction in terms of the measured learning of explicit knowledge. Interestingly enough though, the study found that the highest levels of learning occurred when the two methods were mixed (part of the class online, part in the classroom).[62] It may be that two different learning strategies are used under such scenarios, which allows different kinds of learners to take advantage of what suits them best.[63] At the moment, companies are well ahead of the curve at delivering effective online classes. Intuit, the maker of personal and small business software including Quicken and TurboTax, has been using the mixed method of training for quite a while. It employs face-to-face training to establish relationships prior to moving into a virtual classroom.[64] Such corporate efforts will likely help establish a blueprint for universities to follow as they expand their online offerings.

these technological changes are occurring on university campuses as well. Indeed, some of you may be working in a virtual classroom right now!

In addition to traditional training experiences, companies are also heavily focused on **knowledge transfer** from their older, experienced workers to their younger employees. As illustrated by the Tennessee Valley Authority example, companies are using variations of **behavior modeling training** to ensure that employees have the ability to observe and learn from those in the company with significant amounts of tacit knowledge. For example, Raytheon, the Massachusetts-based defense and aerospace supplier, has created a training program called "Leave-a-Legacy" that pairs employees holding vital knowledge with high-potential subordinates. Raytheon's program is not one of those "have lunch once a month" mentor programs—it's a relatively regimented program in which younger workers follow older workers around for extended periods of time, ensuring adequate opportunities for observation. Each pair of employees is also assigned a third-party coach that helps the knowledge transfer take place.[65]

Another form of knowledge transfer that's being used by companies more frequently is communities of practice. **Communities of practice** are groups of employees who work together and learn from one another by collaborating over an extended period of time.[66] A large number of companies are utilizing this newer form of informal social learning. John Deere, the Illinois-based manufacturer of agricultural equipment, implemented an informal training process in 2002 and now has a network of more than 300 communities dealing with issues such as mergers and acquisitions and its Deere Production System.[67] Communities of practice introduce their own unique complications, but the potential of their ability to transfer knowledge through employees is significant.[68]

The success of these programs, as well as more traditional types of training, hinges on transfer of training. **Transfer of training** occurs when the knowledge, skills, and behaviors used on the job are maintained by the learner once training ends and generalized to the workplace once the learner returns to the job.[69] Transfer of training can be fostered if organizations create a **climate for transfer**—an environment that can support the use of new skills. There are a variety of factors that can help organizations foster such a climate. The degree to which the trainee's manager supports the importance of the newly acquired knowledge and skills and stresses its application to the job is perhaps the most important factor. Peer support is helpful, because having multiple trainees learning the same material reduces anxiety and allows the trainees to share concerns and work through problems. Opportunities to use the learned knowledge are also crucial, because practice and repetition are key components of learning. Because companies have a huge stake in increasing and transferring knowledge within their employee base, creating a climate for the transfer of that knowledge is imperative to the success of formal learning systems.[70]

TAKEAWAYS

8.1 Learning is a relatively permanent change in an employee's knowledge or skill that results from experience. Decision making refers to the process of generating and choosing from a set of alternatives to solve a problem.

8.2 Employees gain both explicit and tacit knowledge as they build expertise. Explicit knowledge is easily communicated and available to everyone. Tacit knowledge, however, is something employees can only learn through experience.

8.3 Employees learn new knowledge through reinforcement and observation of others. That learning also depends on whether the employees are learning-oriented or performance-oriented.

8.4 Programmed decisions are decisions that become somewhat automatic because a person's knowledge allows him or her to recognize and identify a situation and the course of action that needs to be taken. Many task-related decisions made by experts are programmed decisions. Nonprogrammed decisions are made when a problem is new, complex, or not recognized. Ideally, such decisions are made by following the steps in the rational decision-making model.

8.5 Employees are less able to translate their learning into accurate decisions when they struggle with limited information, faulty perceptions, faulty attributions, and escalation of commitment.

8.6 Learning has a moderate positive relationship with job performance and a weak positive relationship with organizational commitment.

8.7 Through various forms of training, companies can give employees more knowledge and a wider array of experiences that they can use to make decisions.

KEY TERMS

- Learning • p. 256
- Decision making • p. 256
- Expertise • p. 257
- Explicit knowledge • p. 257
- Tacit knowledge • p. 258
- Contingencies of reinforcement • p. 259
- Positive reinforcement • p. 259
- Negative reinforcement • p. 259
- Punishment • p. 259
- Extinction • p. 260
- Schedules of reinforcement • p. 260
- Continuous reinforcement • p. 260
- Fixed interval schedule • p. 261
- Variable interval schedule • p. 261
- Fixed ratio schedule • p. 261
- Variable ratio schedule • p. 261
- Social learning theory • p. 262
- Behavioral modeling • p. 262
- Learning orientation • p. 265
- Performance-prove orientation • p. 265
- Performance-avoid orientation • p. 265
- Programmed decision • p. 265
- Intuition • p. 265
- Nonprogrammed decision • p. 268
- Rational decision-making model • p. 268
- Bounded rationality • p. 268
- Satisficing • p. 270
- Selective perception • p. 270
- Projection bias • p. 271
- Social identity theory • p. 271
- Stereotype • p. 271
- Heuristics • p. 271
- Availability bias • p. 271
- Fundamental attribution error • p. 273
- Self-serving bias • p. 273
- Consensus • p. 274
- Distinctiveness • p. 274
- Consistency • p. 274
- Escalation of commitment • p. 274
- Training • p. 278
- Knowledge transfer • p. 279
- Behavior modeling training • p. 279
- Communities of practice • p. 279
- Transfer of training • p. 279
- Climate for transfer • p. 279

DISCUSSION QUESTIONS

8.1 In your current or past workplaces, what types of tacit knowledge did experienced workers possess? What did this knowledge allow them to do?

8.2 Companies rely on employees with substantial amounts of tacit knowledge. Why do companies struggle when these employees leave the organization unexpectedly? What can companies do to help ensure that they retain tacit knowledge?

8.3 What does the term "expert" mean to you? What exactly do experts do that novices don't?

8.4 Given your occupational choice, how do you expect to learn what you need to know when you start working? Do you expect the company to provide you with these opportunities, or will you have to seek them out on your own?

8.5 Do you consider yourself a "rational" decision maker? For what types of decisions are you determined to be the most rational? What types of decisions are likely to cause you to behave irrationally?

8.6 Given your background, which of the decision-making biases listed in the chapter do you most struggle with? What could you do to overcome those biases to make more accurate decisions?

CASE   TENNESSEE VALLEY AUTHORITY

Preserving the knowledge of employees in the face of the retirement of the Baby Boomer generation is a serious problem faced by the Tennessee Valley Authority (TVA). This problem is not unique to TVA, but its timely solution to the problem is worth highlighting. The human resources department engaged in an interview process to determine the critical skills needed to be retained by employees in various jobs. This process was welcomed by employees who recognized the need to transfer critical job-related skills to future employees.

The Tennessee Valley Authority also is actively seeking qualified college graduates to combat its brain drain. Some companies are making the mistake of hiring graduates to replace seasoned engineers; instead, TVA has developed a progression program to allow new graduates to develop into seasoned engineers in four to six years. The nurturing of these new employees ensures that the company will have enough qualified engineers to take over the roles of veteran employees who will be retiring in the near future. The future of the TVA looks bright, thanks to the company's decision to transfer critical skills to the new generation of employees entering the company.

8.1 Can tacit knowledge be transferred to new Tennessee Valley Authority employees through its progression program? Explain.

8.2 Will critical job skills be lost without a formal system in place to record them? Explain.

Sources: G. George, "Electricity Recruiting Around the World," *Transmission & Distribution World,* January 2004; D. Hall, "Let's Invest in People," *Transmission & Distribution World,* May 2005; B. Leonard, "Taking HR to the Next Level," *HR Magazine,* July 2003.

EXERCISE   DECISION-MAKING BIAS[1]

The purpose of this exercise is to illustrate how decision making can be influenced by decision heuristics, availability bias, and escalation of commitment. This exercise uses groups of six participants, so your instructor will either assign you to a group of six or ask you to create your own group of six. The exercise has the following steps:

1. Answer each of the problems below.

   A. A certain town is served by two hospitals. In the larger hospital, about 45 babies are born each day, and in the smaller hospital, about 15 babies are born each day. Although the overall proportion of boys is about 50 percent, the actual proportion at either hospital may be greater or less than 50 percent on any given day. At the end of a year, which hospital will have the greater number of days on which more than 60 percent of the babies born were boys?
      a. The large hospital.
      b. The small hospital.
      c. Neither–the number of days will be about the same (within 5 percent of each other).

   B. Linda is 31, single, outspoken, and very bright. She majored in philosophy in college. As a student, she was deeply concerned with discrimination and other social issues and participated in antinuclear demonstrations. Which statement is more likely:
      a. Linda is a bank teller.
      b. Linda is a bank teller and active in the feminist movement.

   C. A cab was involved in a hit-and-run accident. Two cab companies serve the city: the Green, which operates 85 percent of the cabs, and the Blue, which operates the remaining 15 percent. A witness identifies the hit-and-run cab as Blue. When the court tests the reliability of the witness under circumstances similar to those on the night of the accident, he correctly identifies the color of the cab 80 percent of the time and misidentifies it the other 20 percent. What's the probability that the cab involved in the accident was Blue, as the witness stated?

   D. Imagine that you face this pair of concurrent decisions. Examine these decisions, then indicate which choices you prefer.
      Decision I: Choose between:
      a. a sure gain of $240 and
      b. a 25 percent chance of winning $1,000 and a 75 percent chance of winning nothing.

      Decision II: Choose between:
      a. a sure loss of $750 and
      b. a 75 percent chance of losing $1,000 and a 25 percent chance of losing nothing.

[1]This exercise originally appeared in *Organizational Behavior and Management* (7th ed.) by Ivancevich, Konopaske, and Matteson (New York: McGraw-Hill, 2005); used with permission. Original exercises are based on: (1) A. Tversky and D. Kahneman, "Rational Choice and the Framing of Decisions," *Journal of Business* 59 (1986), pp. 251–78; (2) A. Tversky and D. Kahneman, "The Framing of Decisions and the Psychology of Choice," *Science* 211 (1981), pp. 453–58; (3) A. Tversky and D. Kahneman, "Extensional vs. Intuitive Reasoning: The Conjunction Fallacy in Probability Judgment," *Psychological Review* 90 (1983), pp. 293–315; and (4) K. McKean, "Decisions, Decisions," *Discovery Magazine,* June 1985.

Decision III: Choose between:
a. a sure loss of $3,000 and
b. an 80 percent chance of losing $4,000 and a 20 percent chance of losing nothing.

E. a. You've decided to see a Broadway play and have bought a $40 ticket. As you enter the theater, you realize you've lost your ticket. You can't remember the seat number, so you can't prove to the management that you bought a ticket. Would you spend $40 for a new ticket?

b. You've reserved a seat for a Broadway play, for which the ticket price is $40. As you enter the theater to buy your ticket, you discover you've lost $40 from your pocket. Would you still buy the ticket? (Assume you have enough cash left to do so.)

F. Imagine you have operable lung cancer and must choose between two treatments: surgery and radiation. Of 100 people having surgery, 10 die during the operation, 32 (including those original 10) are dead after 1 year, and 66 are dead after 5 years. Of 100 people having radiation therapy, none dies during treatment, 23 are dead after one year, and 78 after 5 years. Which treatment would you prefer?

2. Your instructor will give you the correct answer to each problem.

3. Class discussion, whether in groups or as a class, should focus on the following questions: How accurate were the descriptions you reached? What decision-making problems were evident in the decisions you reached? Consider especially where decision heuristics, availability, and escalation of commitment may have influenced your decisions. How could you improve your decision making to make it more accurate?

ENDNOTES

8.1 http://www.tva.com. Accessed May 22, 2007.

8.2 De Long, D.W., and T. Davenport. "Better Practices for Retaining Organizational Knowledge: Lessons from the Leading Edge." *Employment Relations Today* 30 (2003), pp. 51–63.

8.3 Fisher, A. "Retain Your Brains." *Fortune,* July 24, 2006, pp. 49–50.

8.4 Ibid.

8.5 De Long and Davenport, "Better Practices."

8.6 Fisher, "Retain your Brains."

8.7 Weiss, H.M. "Learning Theory and Industrial and Organizational Psychology." In *Handbook of Industrial and Organizational Psychology,* eds. M.D. Dunnette and L.M. Hough. Palo Alto, CA: Consulting Psychologists Press, 1990, pp. 75–169.

8.8 Tai, B., and N.R. Lockwood. "Organizational Entry: Onboarding, Orientation, and Socialization." *SHRM Research Paper.* www.shrm.org. Accessed June 4, 2007.

8.9 Buford, B. *Heat.* New York: Knopf, 2006, pp. 49–50.

8.10 Ericsson, K.A. "An Introduction to *Cambridge Handbook of Expertise and Expert Performance:* Its Development, Organization, and Content." In *The Cambridge Handbook of Expertise and Expert Performance,* eds. K.A. Ericsson, N. Charness, P.J. Feltovich, and R.R. Hoffman. New York: Cambridge University Press, 2006, pp. 3–19.

8.11 Ericsson, K.A., and A.C. Lehmann. "Experts and Exceptional Performance: Evidence of Maximal Adaptation to Task Constraints." *Annual Review of Psychology* 47 (1996), pp. 273–305.

8.12 Brockmann, E.N., and W.P. Anthony. "Tacit Knowledge and Strategic Decision Making." *Group & Organizational Management* 27 (December 2002), pp. 436–55.

8.13 Wagner, R.K., and R.J. Sternberg. "Practical Intelligence in Real-World Pursuits: The Role of Tacit Knowledge." *Journal of Personality and Social Psychology* 4 (1985), pp. 436–58.

8.14 Wah, L. "Making Knowledge Stick." *Management Review* 88 (1999), pp. 24–33.

8.15 Eucker, T.R. "Understanding the Impact of Tacit Knowledge Loss." *Knowledge Management Review* March 2007, pp. 10–13.

8.16 McAdam, R.; B. Mason; and J. McCrory. "Exploring the Dichotomies Within the Tacit Knowledge Literature: Towards a Process of Tacit Knowing in Organizations." *Journal of Knowledge Management* 11 (2007), pp. 43–59.

8.17 Lawson, C., and E. Lorenzi. "Collective Learning, Tacit Knowledge, and Regional Innovative Capacity." *Regional Studies* 21 (1999), pp. 487–513.

8.18 Nonaka, I. "The Knowledge-Creating Company." *Harvard Business Review* 69 (1991), pp. 96–104; Nonaka, I. "A Dynamic Theory of Organizational Knowledge Creation." *Organizational Science* 5 (1994), pp. 14–37.

8.19 Luthans, F., and R. Kreitner. *Organizational Behavior Modification and Beyond.* Glenview, IL: Scott, Foresman, 1985.

8.20 Latham, G.P.; and V.L. Huber. "Schedules of Reinforcement: Lessons from the Past and Issues for Future." *Journal of Organizational Behavior Management* 13 (1992), pp. 125–49.

8.21 Luthans and Kreitner, *Organizational Behavior Modification.*

8.22 Bandura, A. *Social Foundations of Thought and Action: A Social Cognitive Theory.* Englewood Cliffs, NJ: Prentice Hall, 1986.

8.23 Weiss, "Learning Theory."

8.24 Pescuric, A., and W.C. Byham. "The New Look of Behavior Modeling." *Training & Development* 50 (July 1996), pp. 24–30.

8.25 Weber, J. "The Accidental CEO." *BusinessWeek* April 23, 2007, pp. 64–72.

8.26 Sims, R.R., and J. Brinkmann. "Leaders as Moral Role Models: The Case of John Gutfreund at Salomon Brothers." *Journal of Business Ethics* 35 (2002), pp. 327–40.

8.27 VandeWalle, D. "Development and Validation of a Work Domain Goal Orientation Instrument." *Educational and Psychological Measurement* 8 (1997), pp. 995–1015.

8.28 Payne, S.C.; S. Youngcourt; and J.M. Beaubien. "A Meta-Analytic Examination of the Goal Orientation Nomological Net." *Journal of*

Applied Psychology 92 (2007), pp. 128–50.

8.29 Ibid.

8.30 Dane, E., and M.G. Pratt. "Exploring Intuition and Its Role in Managerial Decision Making." *Academy of Management Review,* 32 (2007), pp. 33–54. Hayashi, A.M. "When to Trust your Gut." *Harvard Business Review,* February 2001, pp. 59–65.

8.31 March, J.G. *A Primer on Decision Making.* New York: The Free Press, 1994.

8.32 http://www.quotationspage.com/quote/25953.html (April 2007).

8.33 Simon, H.A. "A Behavioral Model of Rational Choice." *Quarterly Journal of Economics* 69 (1955), pp. 99–118.

8.34 Simon, H.A. "Rational Decision Making in Organizations." *American Economic Review* 69 (1979), pp. 493–513.

8.35 March, J.G., and H.A. Simon. *Organizations.* New York: Wiley, 1958.

8.36 Hogg, M.A., and D.J. Terry. "Social Identity and Self-Categorization Process in Organizational Contexts." *Academy of Management Review* 25 (January 2000), pp. 121–40.

8.37 Judd, C.M., and B. Park. "Definition and Assessment of Accuracy in Social Stereotypes." *Psychological Review* 100 (January 1993), pp. 109–28.

8.38 Ashforth, B.E., and F. Mael. "Social Identity Theory and the Organization." *Academy of Management Review* 14 (1989), pp. 20–39; Howard, J.A. "Social Psychology of Identities." *Annual Review of Sociology* 26 (2000), pp. 367–93.

8.39 Society for Human Resource Management. "Diversity Training." 2006, www.shrm.org/diversity. Accessed June 1, 2007.

8.40 Kahneman, D.; P. Slovic; and A. Tversky, eds. *Judgment under Uncertainty: Heuristics and Biases.* Cambridge, UK: Cambridge University Press, 1982.

8.41 Kahneman, D., and A. Tversky. "On the Psychology of Prediction." *Psychological Review* 80 (1973), pp. 237–51.

8.42 Ross, L. "The Intuitive Psychologist and His Shortcomings: Distortions in the Attribution Process." In *Advances in Experimental Social Psychology,* ed. L. Berkowitz. New York: Academic Press, 1977, pp. 173–220. See also Jones, E.E., and V.A. Harris. "The Attribution of Attitudes." *Journal of Experimental Social Psychology* 3 (1967), pp. 1–24.

8.43 Zemba, Y.; M.I. Young; and M.W. Morris. "Blaming Leaders for Organizational Accidents: Proxy Logic in Collective versus Individual-Agency Cultures." *Organizational Behavior and Human Decision Processes* 101 (2006), pp. 36–51.

8.44 Menon, T.; M.W. Morris; C. Chiu; and Y. Hong. "Culture and the Construal of Agency: Attribution to Individual Versus Group Dispositions." *Journal of Personality and Social Psychology* 76 (1999), pp. 701–17.

8.45 Zemba et al., "Blaming Leaders."

8.46 Chiu, C.; M.W. Morris; Y. Hong; and T. Menon. "Motivated Cultural Cognition: The Impact of Implicit Cultural Theories on Dispositional Attribution Varies as a Function of Need for Closure." *Journal of Personality and Social Psychology* 78 (2000), pp. 247–59.

8.47 Zemba et al., "Blaming Leaders."

8.48 Kelley, H.H. "The Processes of Casual Attribution." *American Psychologist* 28 (1973), pp. 107–28; Kelley, H.H. "Attribution in Social Interaction." In *Attribution: Perceiving the Causes of Behavior,* ed. E. Jones. Morristown, NJ: General Learning Press, 1972.

8.49 Staw, B.M., and J. Ross. "Behavior in Escalation Situations: Antecedents, Prototypes, and Solutions." In *Research in Organizational Behavior,* Vol. 9, eds. L.L. Cummings and B.M. Staw. Greenwich, CT: JAI Press, 1987, pp. 39–78; Staw, B.M. "Knee-Deep in the Big Muddy: A Study of Escalating Commitment to a Chosen Course of Action." *Organizational Behavior and Human Performance* 16 (1976), pp. 27–44.

8.50 Brockner, J. "The Escalation of Commitment to a Failing Course of Action: Toward Theoretical Progress." *Academy of Management Review* 17 (1992), pp. 39–61; Staw, B.M. "The Escalation of Commitment: An Update and Appraisal." In *Organizational Decision Making,* ed. Z. Shapira. New York: Cambridge University Press, 1997.

8.51 Conlon, D.E., and H. Garland. "The Role of Project Completion Information in Resource Allocation Decisions." *Academy of Management Journal* 36 (1993), pp. 402–13; Moon, H. "Looking Forward and Looking Back: Integrating Completion and Sunk-Cost Effects within an Escalation of Commitment Progress Decision."*Journal of Applied Psychology* 86 (2001), pp. 104–13.

8.52 Johnson, K. "Denver Airport to Mangle Last Bag." *The New York Times,* August 27, 2005.

8.53 Alliger, G.M.; S.I. Tannenbaum; W. Bennett Jr.; H. Traver; and A. Shotland. "A Meta-Analysis of the Relations Among Training Criteria." *Personnel Psychology* 50 (1997), pp. 341–58; Colquitt, J.A.; J.A. Lepine; and R..A. Noe. "Toward an Integrative Theory of Training Motivation: A Meta-Analytic Path Analysis of 20 Years of Research." *Journal of Applied Psychology* 85 (2000), pp. 678–707; Meyer, J.P.; D.J. Stanley; L. Herscovitch, and L. Topolnytsky. "Affective, Continuance, and Normative Commitment to the Organization: A Meta-Analysis of Antecedents, Correlates, and Consequences." *Journal of Vocational Behavior* 61 (2002), pp. 20–52.

8.54 Averbrook, J. "Connecting CLO's with the Recruiting Process." *Chief Learning Officer* 4 (2005), pp. 24–27.

8.55 "Spending on Learning and Training Is Increasing: ASTD Report. *HR Focus* 83 (2006), p. 9.

8.56 Carnevale, A.P. "The Learning Enterprise." *Training and Development Journal,* February 1989, pp. 26–37.

8.57 "$56 Billion Budgeted for Formal Training." *Training* 43, 2006 pp. 20–32.

8.58 Folkers, D. "Competing in the Marketspace: Incorporating Online Education into Higher Education–An Organizational Perspective." *Information Resources Management Journal* 18 (2005), pp. 61–77.

8.59 Golden, D. "Degrees@StateU; Online University Enrollment Soars as Quality Improves; Tuition Funds Other Projects." *The Wall Street Journal,* May 9, 2006, p. B1.

8.60 Ibid.

8.61 Sitzman, T.; K. Kraiger; D. Stewart; and R. Wisher. "The Comparative Effectiveness of Web-Based and Classroom Instruction: A Meta-Analysis." *Personnel Psychology* 59 (2006), pp. 623–64. See also Zhao,

Y.; J. Lei; B.Y.C. Lai; and H.S. Tan. "What Makes the Difference? A Practical Analysis of Research on the Effectiveness of Distance Education." *Teachers College Record* 107 (2005), pp. 1836–84.

8.62 Arbaugh, J.B. "Is There an Optimal Design for On-Line MBA Courses?" *Academy of Management Learning and Education* 4 (2005), pp. 135–49.

8.63 Clark, R.C. "Harnessing the Virtual Classroom." *T + D* 59(2005), pp. 40–45.

8.64 Tyler, K. "Training Revs Up." *HRMagazine,* 50 (2005), pp. 58–63.

8.65 Stamps, D. "Communities of Practice." *Training,* February 1997, pp. 35–42.

8.66 Sauve, E. "Informal Knowledge Transfer." *T + D* 61 (2007), pp. 22–24.

8.67 Allan, B., and D. Lewis. "Virtual Learning Communities as a Vehicle for Workforce Development: A Case Study." *Journal of Workplace Learning* 18 (2006), pp. 367–83.

8.68 Noe, R.A. *Employee Training and Development.* Burr Ridge, IL: Irwin/McGraw-Hill, 1999.

8.69 Tracey, J.B.; S.I. Tannenbaum; and M.J. Kavanaugh. "Applying Trained Skills on the Job: The Importance of the Work Environment." *Journal of Applied Psychology* 80 (1995), pp. 239–52.

INDIVIDUAL CHARACTERISTICS

CHAPTER 9:
Personality and Cultural Values

CHAPTER 10:
Ability

Personality and Cultural Values

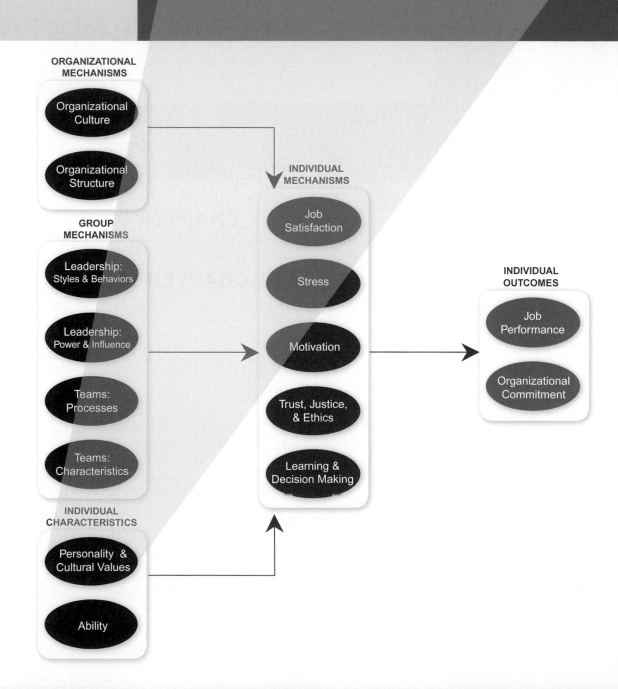

ORGANIZATIONAL MECHANISMS
- Organizational Culture
- Organizational Structure

GROUP MECHANISMS
- Leadership: Styles & Behaviors
- Leadership: Power & Influence
- Teams: Processes
- Teams: Characteristics

INDIVIDUAL CHARACTERISTICS
- Personality & Cultural Values
- Ability

INDIVIDUAL MECHANISMS
- Job Satisfaction
- Stress
- Motivation
- Trust, Justice, & Ethics
- Learning & Decision Making

INDIVIDUAL OUTCOMES
- Job Performance
- Organizational Commitment

The Teach for America volunteer program screens recruits using a rigorous process to assess personality traits that could contribute to effectiveness in the classroom.

LEARNING GOALS

After reading this chapter, you should be able to answer the following questions:

9.1 What is personality, and how can it be distinguished from ability? What are cultural values?

9.2 Is personality driven by nature or by nurture? How can we tell?

9.3 What are the "Big Five?" Are there other taxonomies that can be used to describe personality other than the Big Five?

9.4 What are Hofstede's dimensions of cultural values?

9.5 How does personality affect job performance and organizational commitment?

9.6 Are personality tests useful tools for organizational hiring?

TEACH FOR AMERICA

What are (or were) your plans for the year after college graduation? Going straight into the working world? Moving on to graduate school? Taking a year off to recharge? How about teaching sixth graders in one of America's most troubled and impoverished school systems? Nineteen thousand graduating seniors chose that option in 2006 by applying to Teach for America, a Peace Corps-style program that has become one of the largest hirers of college seniors.[1] Teach for America requires its hires to make a two-year commitment to teaching at some of the nation's toughest public schools. Those

2006 applicants included 10 percent of the senior classes at Yale and Dartmouth, 9 percent at Columbia, and 8 percent at the University of Chicago.

Teach for America uses a rigorous screening process to examine the qualifications of its applicants, eventually hiring 2,400 of the 19,000 individuals who applied in 2006. That process includes hours of interviews and tests to measure a number of traits, including achievement, personal responsibility, critical thinking, organizational skills, motivational skills, respect for others, and commitment to teaching.[2] Those traits are vital, given the challenges faced by Teach for America recruits. Most work 80–90 hours a week, which includes a 7:00 a.m. to 6:00 p.m. weekday schedule, along with hours of outside tutoring and preparation. One recruit summarized his experiences at a low-income high school in the Bronx, noting, "I was expecting it to be very hard, but it's harder than I thought it would be, and in a way I've never experienced before."[3]

The traits possessed by Teach for America (TFA) recruits have made them especially popular in New York City, where 8 percent of the city's new hires in 2006 came from the program.[4] The chancellor of New York City schools captured the appeal of the program, noting that "Generally, the TFA teachers are much less excuse-bound and more entrepreneurial and creative." Companies such as JP Morgan, Goldman Sachs, and Amgen have even begun partnering with Teach for America, with some offering job deferrals for people who want to teach for two years before joining their firms. Although studies are split about whether students taught by Teach for America recruits perform better than those taught by other uncertified instructors,[5] it seems clear that the program excels in identifying those people who are willing to "go the extra mile" in their classrooms.[6] As the program's founder, Wendy Kopp, notes, "We look for people with certain personalities."[7]

PERSONALITY AND CULTURAL VALUES

It seems clear from the opening example that Teach for America focuses a great deal on personality when deciding whom to accept into its program. **Personality** refers to the structures and propensities inside a person that explain his or her characteristic patterns of thought, emotion, and behavior.[8] Personality creates a person's social reputation—the way he or she is perceived by friends, family, coworkers, and supervisors.[9] In this way, personality captures *what people are like,* in contrast to ability (the subject of Chapter 10), which captures *what people can do.* The interviews and tests used by Teach for America are trying to gauge whether a given recruit "is like" the profile of past recruits who have proven successful in their schools.

9.1

What is personality, and how can it be distinguished from ability? What are cultural values?

Even though we sometimes describe people as having "a good personality," personality is actually a collection of multiple specific traits. **Traits** are defined as recurring regularities or trends in people's responses to their environment.[10] Adjectives such as responsible, critical, organized, or achievement-oriented are all examples of traits. As we describe later, traits are a function of your genes and your environment. One important environmental factor is the culture in which you were raised. **Cultural values,** defined as shared beliefs about desirable end states or modes of conduct in a given culture,[11] influence the expression of a person's traits. In this way, an achievement-oriented middle school teacher in Tokyo may act very differently than an achievement-oriented middle school teacher in New York.[12] Teach for America recruits bring with them a set of distinctly American cultural values, and those values likely influence their reactions and behaviors in the classroom.

HOW CAN WE DESCRIBE WHAT EMPLOYEES ARE LIKE?

We can use personality traits and cultural values to describe what employees are like. For example, how would you describe your first college roommate to one of your classmates? You'd start off using certain adjectives—maybe the roommate was funny and outgoing, or maybe polite and organized. Of course, it would take more than a few adjectives to describe your roommate fully. You could probably go on listing traits for several minutes, maybe even coming up with 100 traits or more. Although 100 traits may sound like a lot, personality researchers note that the third edition of Webster's Unabridged Dictionary contains 1,710 adjectives that can be used to describe someone's traits![13] Was your roommate abrasive, adulterous, agitable, alarmable, antisocial, arbitrative, arrogant, asocial, audacious, aweless, and awkward? We hope not!

THE BIG FIVE TAXONOMY

With 1,710 adjectives, you might be worrying about the length of this chapter (or the difficulty of your next exam!). Fortunately, it turns out that most adjectives are variations of five broad "factors" or "dimensions" that can be used to summarize our personalities.[14] Those five personality dimensions include **conscientiousness, agreeableness, neuroticism, openness to experience,** and **extraversion.** Collectively, these dimensions have been dubbed the **Big Five.**[15] Figure 9-1 lists the traits that can be found within each of the

FIGURE 9-1	Trait Adjectives Associated with the Big Five

C	A	N	O	E
Conscientiousness	**Agreeableness**	**Neuroticism**	**Openness**	**Extraversion**
• Dependable • Organized • Reliable • Ambitious • Hardworking • Persevering	• Kind • Cooperative • Sympathetic • Helpful • Courteous • Warm	• Nervous • Moody • Emotional • Insecure • Jealous • Unstable	• Curious • Imaginative • Creative • Complex • Refined • Sophisticated	• Talkative • Sociable • Passionate • Assertive • Bold • Dominant
NOT	NOT	NOT	NOT	NOT
• Careless • Sloppy • Inefficient • Negligent • Lazy • Irresponsible	• Critical • Antagonistic • Callous • Selfish • Rude • Cold	• Calm • Steady • Relaxed • At ease • Secure • Contented	• Uninquisitive • Conventional • Conforming • Simple • Unartistic • Traditional	• Quiet • Shy • Inhibited • Bashful • Reserved • Submissive

Sources: G. Saucier, "Mini-Markers: A Brief Version of Goldberg's Unipolar Big-Five Markers," *Journal of Personality Assessment* 63 (1994), pp. 506–516; L.R. Goldberg, "The Development of Markers for the Big-Five Factor Structure," *Psychological Assessment* 4 (1992), pp. 26–42; R.R. McCrae and P.T. Costa Jr., "Validation of the Five-Factor Model of Personality across Instruments and Observers," *Journal of Personality and Social Psychology* 52 (1987), pp. 81–90.

Big Five dimensions. We acknowledge that it can be hard to remember the particular labels for the Big Five dimensions, and we only wish there was some acronym that could make the process easier. . . .

Would you like to see what your Big Five profile looks like? Our **OB Assessments** feature will show you where you stand on each of the five dimensions. After you've gotten a feel for your personality profile, you might be wondering about some of the following questions: How does personality develop? Why do people have the traits that they possess? Will those traits change over time? All of these questions are variations on the "nature vs. nurture" debate: Is personality a function of our genes, or is it something that we develop as a function of our experiences and surroundings? As you might guess, it's sometimes difficult to tease apart the impact of nature and nurture on personality. Let's assume for a moment that you're especially extraverted and so are your parents. Does this mean you've inherited their "extraversion gene"? Or does it mean that you observed and copied their extraverted behavior during your childhood (and were rewarded with praise for doing so)? It's impossible to know, because the effects of nature and nurture are acting in combination in this example.

9.2

Is personality driven by nature or by nurture? How can we tell?

One method of separating nature and nurture effects is to study identical twins who have been adopted by different sets of parents at birth. For example, the University of Minnesota has been conducting studies of pairs of identical twins reared apart for several decades.[16] Such studies find, for example, that extraversion scores tend to be significantly correlated across pairs of identical twins.[17] Such findings can clearly be attributed to "nature," because identical twins share 100 percent of their genetic material, but cannot be explained by "nurture," because the twins were raised in different environments. A review of several different twin studies concludes that genes have a significant impact on people's Big Five profile. More specifically, 49 percent of the variation in extraversion is accounted for by genetic differences.[18] The genetic impact is somewhat smaller for the rest of the Big Five: 45 percent for openness, 41 percent for neuroticism, 38 percent for conscientiousness, and 35 percent for agreeableness.

Another method of examining the genetic basis of personality is to examine changes in personality traits over time. Longitudinal studies require participants to complete personality assessments at multiple time periods, often separated by several years. If personality has a strong genetic component, then people's Big Five profiles at, say, age 21 should be very similar to their profiles at age 50. Figure 9-2 summarizes the results of 92 studies that assess personality changes in more than 50,000 people.[19] The figure notes personality changes across seven time periods, including teenage years (age 10–18), college years (18–22), and people's 20s, 30s, 40s, 50s, and 60s. The y-axis expresses changes in personality in standard deviation terms, ranging from +1 (one standard deviation increase on a given dimension) to −1 (one standard deviation decrease on a given dimension). In standard deviation terms, a change of .20 is generally considered small, a change of .50 is generally considered medium, and a change of .80 is generally considered large.[20]

Figure 9-2 reveals that extraversion typically remains quite stable throughout a person's life. Openness to experience also remains stable, after

Many personality traits, like extraversion, are similar across twins even if they're reared apart.

OB ASSESSMENTS

THE BIG FIVE

What does your personality profile look like? This assessment is designed to measure the five major dimensions of personality: conscientiousness (C), agreeableness (A), neuroticism (N), openness to experience (O), and extraversion (E). Listed below are phrases describing people's behaviors. Please write a number next to each statement that indicates the extent to which it accurately describes you. Answer each question using the response scale provided. Then subtract your answers to the bold-faced questions from 6, with the difference being your new answer for those questions. For example, if your original answer for question 6 was "2," your new answer is "4" (6 − 2).

1	2	3	4	5
VERY INACCURATE	MODERATELY INACCURATE	NEITHER INACCURATE NOR ACCURATE	MODERATELY ACCURATE	VERY ACCURATE

1. I am the life of the party. _____

2. I sympathize with others' feelings. _____

3. I get chores done right away. _____

4. I have frequent mood swings. _____

5. I have a vivid imagination. _____

6. I don't talk a lot. _____

7. I am not interested in other people's problems. _____

8. I often forget to put things back in their proper place. _____

9. I am relaxed most of the time. _____

10. I am not interested in abstract ideas. _____

11. I talk to a lot of different people at parties. _____

12. I feel others' emotions. _____

13. I like order. _____

14. I get upset easily. _____

15. I have difficulty understanding abstract ideas. _____

16. I keep in the background. _____

17. I am not really interested in others. _____

18. I make a mess of things. _____

19. I seldom feel blue. _____

20. I do not have a good imagination. _____

SCORING AND INTERPRETATION:

Conscientiousness: Sum up items 3, 8, 13, and 18.

Agreeableness: Sum up items 2, 7, 12, and 17.

Neuroticism: Sum up items 4, 9, 14, and 19.

Openness to Experience: Sum up items 5, 10, 15, and 20.

Extraversion: Sum up items 1, 6, 11, and 16.

Now chart your scores in the figure below to see whether you are above or below the norm for each dimension.

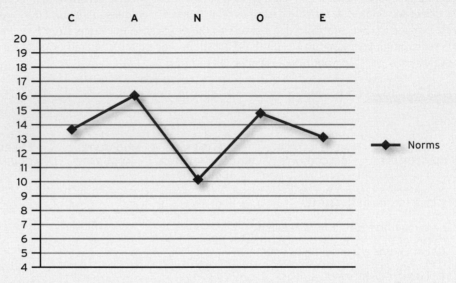

Source: M.B. Donnellan, F.L. Oswald, B.M. Baird, and R.E. Lucas, "The Mini-IPIP Scales: Tiny-Yet-Effective Measures of the Big Five Factors of Personality," *Psychological Assessment* 18 (2006), pp. 192–203. Copyright © 2006 by the American Psychological Association. Adopted with permission. No further reproduction or distribution is permitted without written permission from the American Psychological Association.

a sharp increase from the teenage years to college age. The stability of those two dimensions makes sense because extraversion and openness are most dependent on genes.[21] The other three dimensions, however, change quite significantly over a person's life span. Figure 9-2 shows that people get more conscientious, more agreeable, and less neurotic from their teenage years into their 40s, 50s, and 60s. Although those changes may be encouraging if you dislike your own personal Big Five profile, it is important to realize that any changes in personality are very gradual. Consider this question: Can you detect any personality changes in your closest friends? Chances are you can't, unless you've known those friends for a period of several years. That long-term lens is needed to spot gradual fluctuations in Big Five levels. The sections that follow provide more detail about each of the Big Five dimensions.

CONSCIENTIOUSNESS. As shown in Figure 9-1, conscientious people are dependable, organized, reliable, ambitious, hardworking, and persevering.[22] It's difficult, if not impossible, to envision a job in which those traits will not be beneficial.[23] That's not a claim we make about all of the Big Five, because some jobs require high levels of agreeableness, extraversion, or openness, while others demand low levels of those same traits. We don't want to spoil the "how important is personality?" discussion that concludes this chapter, but suffice it to say that conscientiousness has the biggest influence on job performance of any of the Big Five. Of course, the key question therefore becomes: Why is conscientiousness so valuable?

| FIGURE 9-2 | Changes in Big Five Dimensions over the Life Span |

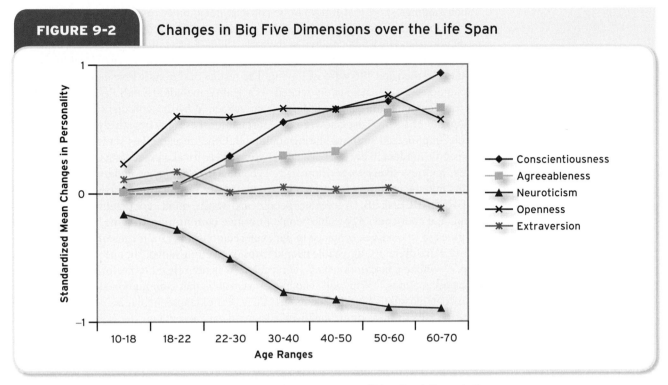

Source: Adapted from B.W. Roberts, K.E. Walton, and W. Viechtbauer, "Patterns of Mean-Level Change in Personality Traits across the Life Course: A Meta-Analysis of Longitudinal Studies," *Psychological Bulletin* 132 (2006), pp. 1–25.

One reason can be found in the general goals that people prioritize in their working life. Conscientious employees prioritize **accomplishment striving,** which reflects a strong desire to accomplish task-related goals as a means of expressing personality.[24] People who are "accomplishment strivers" have a built-in desire to finish work tasks, channel a high proportion of their efforts toward those tasks, and work harder and longer on task assignments. As evidence of their accomplishment-striving nature, one research study showed that conscientious salespeople set higher sales goals for themselves than unconscientious salespeople and were more committed to meeting those goals.[25] Another study of salespeople showed that conscientious salespeople's organizational skills were particularly valuable during their first year of employment, and their ambitious nature became more critical as they gained tenure and experience.[26]

A third research study provides particularly compelling evidence regarding the benefits of conscientiousness.[27] The study used data from the University of California, Berkeley's Intergenerational Studies, which collected data about a set of children in the late 1920s and early 1930s. Those researchers gathered personality data using interviews and assessments of the children by trained psychologists. Follow-up studies collected data on the same sample as they reached early adulthood, middle age, and late adulthood. This last time period included assessments of career success, which included ratings of annual income and occupational prestige. The results of the study showed that childhood conscientiousness was strongly correlated with ratings of career success five decades later! In fact, those conscientiousness effects were roughly twice as strong as the effects of the other Big Five dimensions.

Such findings show that it pays to be conscientious; other research even suggests that conscientiousness is good for your health. For example, one study gathered data about the conscientiousness of 1,528 children in the early 1920s.[28] Data on health-relevant behaviors were then gathered in 1950 for 1,215 of the original participants. By 1986, 419 of the participants had died and 796 were still living. The results of the study revealed that childhood conscientiousness was negatively related to mortality, including death from injuries, death from cardiovascular disease, and death from cancer. Why did conscientious participants live longer? The study also showed that conscientiousness was negatively related to alcohol consumption and smoking during adulthood. Other research has shown that conscientious people are less likely to abuse drugs, more likely to take preventative steps to remain healthy, and less likely to perform risky behaviors as a driver or pedestrian.[29] For more insights into the benefits of conscientiousness, see our **OB on Screen** feature.

AGREEABLENESS. Agreeable people are warm, kind, cooperative, sympathetic, helpful, and courteous. Agreeable people prioritize **communion striving,** which reflects a strong desire to obtain acceptance in personal relationships as a means of expressing personality. Put differently, agreeable people focus on "getting along," not necessarily "getting ahead."[32] Unlike conscientiousness, agreeableness is not related to performance across all jobs or occupations.[33] Why not? The biggest reason is that communion striving is beneficial in some positions but detrimental in others. For example, managers often need to prioritize the effectiveness of the unit over a desire to gain acceptance. In such cases, effective job performance may demand being disagreeable in the face of unreasonable requests or demands.

Of course, there are some jobs in which agreeableness can be beneficial. The most obvious example is service jobs—jobs in which the employee has direct, face-to-face, or verbal contact with a customer. How many times have you encountered a customer service person who is cold, rude, or antagonistic? Did you tend to buy the company's product after such experiences? Research suggests that agreeable employees have stronger customer service skills.[34] One reason for their effectiveness in customer service environments is that they are reluctant to react to conflict with criticism, threats, or manipulation.[35] Instead, they tend to react to conflict by walking away, adopting a "wait-and-see" attitude, or giving in to the other person.

One study provides unique insights into the effects of agreeableness. The study used a variation of "lived day analysis," where a portion of a participant's daily routine is recorded and analyzed.[36] Ninety-six undergraduates completed assessments of the Big Five personality dimensions before being fitted with a digital recorder and an electronic microphone that could be clipped to their shirt collar. The microphone recorded 30 seconds of footage at 12-minute intervals over the course of two weekdays, with participants unable to track when footage was actually being recorded. Trained coders then rated the sounds and conversations recorded on the microphone. The results of the study revealed a number of interesting expressions of agreeableness. Agreeable participants were significantly less likely to be at home in their apartment during recordings; instead, they spent more time in public places. They were also less likely to use swear words and more likely to use words that conveyed personal rapport during conversations.

EXTRAVERSION. Extraverted people are talkative, sociable, passionate, assertive, bold, and dominant (in contrast to introverts, who are quiet, shy, and reserved). Of the Big Five, extraversion is the easiest to judge in **zero acquaintance** situations—situations in which two people have only just met. Consider times when you've been around a stranger in a doctor's office, in line at a grocery store, or in an airport terminal. It only takes about 5 minutes to figure out whether that stranger is extraverted or introverted.[37] Extraversion is also the Big Five dimension that you knew your standing on, even before taking our self-assessment. People rarely consider how open they are to new experiences or how agreeable they are, but almost everyone already self-identifies as an "extravert" or "introvert."

OB ON SCREEN

THE BREAK-UP

> Brooke: *You know what Gary? I asked you to do one thing today, one very simple thing—to bring me 12 lemons—and you brought me 3.*

> Gary: *If I knew that it was gonna be this much trouble, I would've brought home 24 lemons, even 100 lemons. You know what I wish? I wish everyone that was at that table had their own little private bag of lemons!*

> Brooke: *It's not about the lemons. . . . I'm just saying it'd be nice if you did things that I asked. It would be even nicer if you did things without me having to ask you!*

With those words, Gary (Vince Vaughn) and Brooke (Jennifer Aniston) reveal one of the biggest stumbling blocks in their relationship in *The Break-Up* (Dir.: Adam McKay, Sony Pictures, 2006). From Brooke's perspective, Gary isn't very conscientious. She put together a dinner party for their families and gave Gary one assignment: Bring home 12 lemons for a centerpiece. He brought 3. After the party was over, she had one additional request—to help her do the dishes. Gary wanted to play a video game instead, noting that they could do the dishes in the morning.

Brooke isn't the only one who complains about Gary's lack of conscientiousness. Gary's brother, who co-owns their tour guide company, is constantly pleading with Gary to get his tour logs done so he can keep the company's books straight. But Gary always has an excuse for putting off his paperwork, to the point that he's three months behind on his logs.

If Brooke and Gary decide to remain broken up, what could Brooke do to find a more conscientious boyfriend the next time around? One approach might be to turn to dating Web sites that use personality tests to assess conscientiousness. For example, eHarmony requires members to spend 45 minutes filling out a 436-question personality test that assesses 29 different personality dimensions.[30] Two of those dimensions—"industry" and "ambition"—clearly represent conscientiousness.[31] As another option, Brooke could bring a copy of this chapter's OB Assessments with her to her next social gathering. After all, it makes a great ice breaker!

Like agreeableness, extraversion is not necessarily related to performance across all jobs or occupations. However, extraverted people prioritize **status striving,** which reflects a strong desire to obtain power and influence within a social structure as a means of expressing personality.[38] Extraverts care a lot about being successful and influential and direct their work efforts toward "moving up" and developing a strong reputation. Indeed, research suggests that extraverts are more likely to emerge as leaders in social and task-related groups.[39] They also tend to be rated as more effective in a leadership role by the people who are following them.[40] One potential reason for these findings is that people tend to view extraverts, who are more energetic and outgoing, as more "leaderlike" than introverts.

In addition to being related to leadership emergence and effectiveness, research suggests that extraverts tend to be happier with their jobs. You may recall from Chapter 4 on Job Satisfaction that people's day-to-day moods can be categorized along two dimensions: pleasantness and engagement. As illustrated in Figure 9-3, extraverted employees tend to be high in what's called **positive affectivity**—a dispositional tendency to experience pleasant, engaging moods such as enthusiasm, excitement, and elation.[41] That tendency to

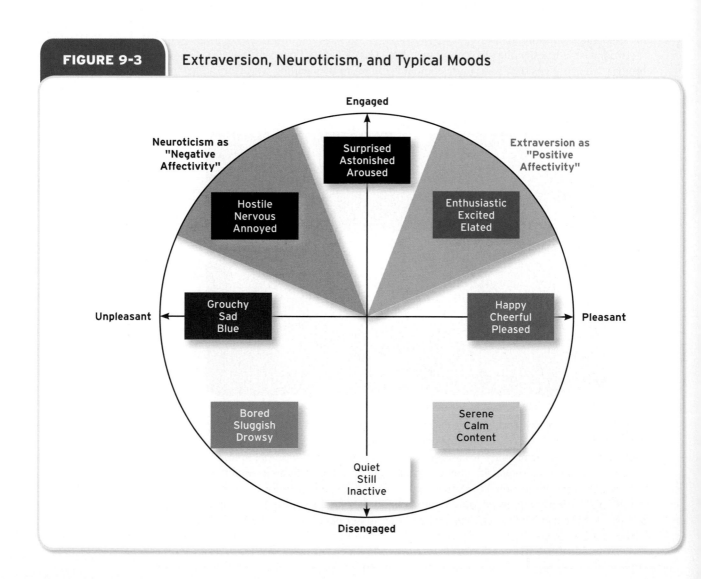

FIGURE 9-3 Extraversion, Neuroticism, and Typical Moods

Engaged

Neuroticism as "Negative Affectivity"

Extraversion as "Positive Affectivity"

Surprised Astonished Aroused

Hostile Nervous Annoyed

Enthusiastic Excited Elated

Unpleasant

Grouchy Sad Blue

Happy Cheerful Pleased

Pleasant

Bored Sluggish Drowsy

Serene Calm Content

Quiet Still Inactive

Disengaged

"I could cry when I think of the years I wasted accumulating money, only to learn that my cheerful disposition is genetic."

experience positive moods across situations explains why extraverts tend to be more satisfied with their jobs.[42] Research now acknowledges that employees' genes have a significant impact on their job satisfaction and that much of that genetic influence is due to extraversion (and neuroticism, as discussed next). For example, one study of identical twins reared apart showed that twins' job satisfaction levels were significantly correlated, even when the twins held jobs that were quite different in terms of their duties, their complexity, and their working conditions.[43] In fact, this study suggested that around 30 percent of the variation in job satisfaction is due to genetic factors such as personality.

Other research suggests that extraverts have more to be happy about than just their jobs. One study asked students to complete a "life event checklist" by indicating whether various events had happened to them in the preceding four years.[44] The results showed that extraversion was associated with more positive events, such as joining a club or athletic team, going on vacation with friends, getting a raise at work, receiving an award for nonacademic reasons, and getting married or engaged. Other studies have linked extraversion to the number of same-sex peers, number of dating partners, frequency of alcohol consumption, and frequency of attending parties.[45] However, extraverts spend so much time doing those things that they wind up having less frequent interactions with their family.[46] Even parents of extraverts enjoy a phone call home now and again!

NEUROTICISM. Neurotic people are nervous, moody, emotional, insecure, and jealous. Occasionally you may see this Big Five dimension called by its flip side: "Emotional Stability" or "Emotional Adjustment." If conscientiousness is the most important of the Big Five from the perspective of job performance, neuroticism is the second most important.[47] There are few jobs for which the traits associated with neuroticism are beneficial to on-the-job behaviors. Instead, most jobs benefit from employees who are calm, steady, and secure.

Whereas extraversion is synonymous with positive affectivity, neuroticism is synonymous with **negative affectivity**—a dispositional tendency to experience unpleasant moods such as hostility, nervousness, and annoyance (see Figure 9-3).[48] That tendency to experience negative moods explains why neurotic employees often experience lower levels of job satisfaction than their less neurotic counterparts.[49] Along with extraversion, neuroticism explains much of the impact of genetic factors on job satisfaction. Research suggests that the negative affectivity associated with neuroticism even influences more general life satisfaction, such that neurotic people tend to be less happy with their lives in general.[50] In fact, one method of assessing neuroticism (or negative affectivity) is to determine how unhappy people are with everyday objects and things. This "gripe index" is shown in Table 9-1. If you find yourself dissatisfied with several of the objects in that table, then you probably experience negative moods quite frequently.

TABLE 9-1	The Neutral Objects Questionnaire (a.k.a. The "Gripe Index")

Instructions: The following questions ask about your degree of satisfaction with several items. Consider each item carefully. Circle the numbered response that best represents your feelings about the corresponding item. Then sum up your score.

	DISSATISFIED	NEUTRAL	SATISFIED
Your telephone number	1	2	3
8½ × 11 paper	1	2	3
Popular music	1	2	3
Modern art	1	2	3
Your first name	1	2	3
Restaurant food	1	2	3
Public transportation	1	2	3
Telephone service	1	2	3
The way you were raised	1	2	3
Advertising	1	2	3
The way people drive	1	2	3
Local speed limits	1	2	3
Television programs	1	2	3
The people you know	1	2	3
Yourself	1	2	3
Your relaxation time	1	2	3
Local newspapers	1	2	3
Today's cars	1	2	3
The quality of food you buy	1	2	3
The movies being produced today	1	2	3
The climate where you live	1	2	3
The high school you attended	1	2	3
The neighbors you have	1	2	3
The residence where you live	1	2	3
The city in which you live	1	2	3

Interpretation: If you scored below a 50, you tend to be less satisfied with everyday objects than the typical respondent. Such a score may indicate negative affectivity, a tendency to feel negative emotional states frequently. (Or perhaps you should change your phone number!)

Sources: Adapted from T.A. Judge, "Does Affective Disposition Moderate the Relationship Between Job Satisfaction and Voluntary Turnover?" *Journal of Applied Psychology* 78 (1993), pp. 395–401; J. Weitz, "A Neglected Concept in the Study of Job Satisfaction," *Personnel Psychology* 5 (1952), pp. 201–205.

Neuroticism also influences the way that people deal with stressful situations. Specifically, neuroticism is associated with a **differential exposure** to stressors, meaning that neurotic people are more likely to appraise day-to-day situations as stressful (and therefore feel like they are exposed to stressors more frequently).[51] Neuroticism is also associated with a **differential reactivity** to stressors, meaning that neurotic people are less likely to believe they can cope with the stressors that they experience.[52] Neuroticism is largely responsible for the Type A Behavior Pattern that has been shown to affect employees' health and ability to manage stressful environments.[53] That is, neurotic people are much more likely to be "Type As," whereas less neurotic individuals are much more likely to be "Type Bs" (see Chapter 5 on Stress for more discussion of these issues).

Neuroticism is also strongly related to **locus of control,** which reflects whether people attribute the causes of events to themselves or to the external environment.[54] Neurotic people tend to hold an *external* locus of control, meaning that they often believe that the events that occur around them are driven by luck, chance, or fate. Less neurotic people tend to hold an *internal* locus of control, meaning that they believe that their own behavior dictates events. Table 9-2 provides more detail about the external versus internal distinction. The table includes a number of beliefs that are representative of an external or internal viewpoint, including beliefs about life in general, work, school, politics, and relationships. If you tend to agree more strongly with the beliefs in the left column, then you have a more external locus of control. If you tend to agree more with the right column, your locus is more internal.

How important is locus of control? One meta-analysis of 135 different research studies showed that an internal locus of control was associated with higher levels of job satisfaction and job performance.[55] A second meta-analysis of 222 different research studies showed that people with an internal locus of control enjoyed better health, including higher self-reported mental well-being, fewer self-reported physical symptoms, lower blood pressure, and lower stress hormone secretion.[56] Internals also enjoyed more social support at

TABLE 9-2	External and Internal Locus of Control	
PEOPLE WITH AN EXTERNAL LOCUS OF CONTROL TEND TO BELIEVE:	**PEOPLE WITH AN INTERNAL LOCUS OF CONTROL TEND TO BELIEVE:**
Many of the unhappy things in people's lives are partly due to bad luck.	People's misfortunes result from the mistakes they make.
Getting a good job depends mainly on being in the right place at the right time.	Becoming a success is a matter of hard work; luck has little or nothing to do with it.
Many times exam questions tend to be so unrelated to course work that studying is really useless.	In the case of the well-prepared student, there is rarely if ever such a thing as an unfair test.
This world is run by the few people in power, and there is not much the little guy can do about it.	The average citizen can have an influence in government decisions.
There's not much use in trying too hard to please people; if they like you, they like you.	People are lonely because they don't try to be friendly.

Source: Adapted from J.B. Rotter, "Generalized Expectancies for Internal versus External Control of Reinforcement," *Psychological Monographs* 80 (1966), pp. 1–28.

People who are open to new experiences tend to do well in situations that offer frequent opportunities to learn new things, such as teaching.

work than externals and sensed that they had a stronger relationship with their supervisors. They viewed their jobs as having more beneficial characteristics, such as autonomy and significance, and fewer negative characteristics, such as conflict and ambiguity. In addition, those with an internal locus of control earned a higher salary than those with an external locus.

OPENNESS TO EXPERIENCE. The final dimension of the Big Five is openness to experience. Open people are curious, imaginative, creative, complex, refined, and sophisticated. Of all the Big Five, openness to experience has the most alternative labels. Sometimes it's called "Inquisitiveness" or "Intellectualness" or even "Culture" (not in the national culture sense—rather, in the "high culture" sense of knowing fine wine, art, and classical music). Much like agreeableness and extraversion, the traits associated with openness are beneficial in some jobs but not others.

As a result, openness is not related to job performance across all occupations.

What jobs benefit from high levels of openness? Generally speaking, jobs that are very fluid and dynamic, with rapid changes in job demands. Research shows that open employees excel in learning and training environments, because their curiosity gives them a built-in desire to learn new things.[57] They also tend to be more adaptable and quick to identify when the "old way of doing things" is no longer effective, excelling at the search for a new and better approach.[58] In fact, conscientious employees are sometimes less effective than open employees in such environments, because their persevering nature sometimes prevents them from abandoning "tried-and-true" task strategies.

Openness to experience is also more likely to be valuable in jobs that require high levels of **creativity,** defined as the capacity to generate novel and useful ideas and solutions.[59] The relationship between openness and creativity can be seen in Figure 9-4. Together with cognitive ability (discussed in Chapter 10 on Ability), openness to experience is a key driver of creative thought, as smart and open people excel at the style of thinking

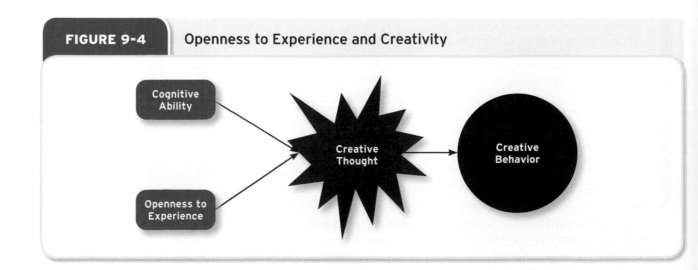

FIGURE 9-4 **Openness to Experience and Creativity**

demanded by creativity. How good are you at creative thinking? See Figure 9-5 to find out. Creative thought then results in creative behavior when people come up with new ideas, create fresh approaches to problems, or suggest new innovations that can help improve the workplace.[60] The creativity benefits of openness likely explain why highly open individuals are more likely to migrate into artistic and scientific fields, in which novel and original products are so critical.[61]

FIGURE 9-5	Tests of Creative Thinking

Instructions: Do you consider yourself to be a creative thinker? See if you can solve the problems below. If you need help, the answers can be found in the Takeaways section of this chapter.

1. What gets wetter as it dries?

2. A woman had two sons who were born on the same hour of the same day of the same year. But they were not twins. How could this be so?

3. What occurs once in June, once in July, and twice in August?

4. Make this mathematical expression true by drawing only a single straight line:

$$5+5+5 = 550$$

5. Join all nine of the dots below using only four (or fewer) straight lines, without lifting your pen from the paper and without retracing the lines.

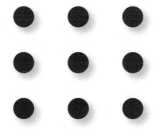

Source: http://home.swipnet.se/~w-19502/puzzles.htm; http://www.mycoted.com/Category:Puzzles

BMW, the German automaker, seems to understand the importance of openness to experience, along with several of the other Big Five dimensions. BMW has worked hard to create a culture of innovation in which there is never a penalty for proposing new and outlandish ways of improving its cars.[62] Those proposed improvements include a "smart card" that can be taken out of your own BMW and plugged into a rented one, passing along your music, podcast, and comfort settings to the new vehicle. Openness is needed to foster such creative thought, but agreeableness is also key to BMW's culture. Stefan Krause, BMW's chief financial officer, summarizes how to push a creative idea successfully: "You can go into fighting mode or you can ask permission and get everyone to support you. If you do it without building ties, you will be blocked."

BMW employees also draw on their conscientiousness in those critical times when a new technology is introduced or production volume is expanded. During those time periods, employees from other factories may move into temporary housing far from home to put in extra hours on another plant's line. Why are employees so devoted? For one thing, no one at BMW can remember a layoff—something that is incredibly unique in the auto industry. That's part of the reason BMW's human resources group receives more than 200,000 applications annually. Those fortunate enough to make it to the interview stage participate in elaborate, day-long drills in teams to make sure that their personalities provide a good match for the company.

The cafeteria at BMW's Leipzig facility, where the assembly line moves above to give employees a feel for the rhythm of the plant.

OTHER TAXONOMIES OF PERSONALITY

9.3

What are the "Big Five?" Are there other taxonomies that can be used to describe personality other than the Big Five?

Although the Big Five is the dominant lens for examining personality, it's not the only framework with which you might be familiar. One of the most widely administered personality measures in organizations is the **Myers-Briggs Type Indicator** (or MBTI).[63] This instrument was originally created to test a theory of psychological types advanced by the noted psychologist Carl Jung.[64] The MBTI evaluates individuals on the basis of four types of preferences:[65]

• Extraversion (being energized by people and social interactions) versus Introversion (being energized by private time and reflection).
• Sensing (preferring clear and concrete facts and data) versus Intuition (preferring hunches and speculations based on theory and imagination).
• Thinking (approaching decisions with logic and critical analysis) versus Feeling (approaching decisions with an emphasis on others' needs and feelings).
• Judging (approaching tasks by planning and setting goals) versus Perceiving (preferring to have flexibility and spontaneity when performing tasks).

The MBTI categorizes people into one of 16 different types on the basis of their preferences. For example, an "ISTJ" has a preference for Introversion, Sensing, Thinking, and Judging. Research on the MBTI suggests that managers are more likely to be "TJs" than the general population.[66] Moreover, the different personality types seem to approach decision-making tasks with differing emphases on facts, logic, and plans. That said, there is little evidence that the MBTI is a useful tool for predicting the job satisfaction, motivation, performance, or commitment of employees across jobs.[67] Indeed, one of the reasons the MBTI is so widely used is that there really isn't a "bad type"—no one who gets their profile is receiving negative news. As a result, the most appropriate use of the MBTI is in a team-building context, to help different members understand their varying approaches to accomplishing tasks. Using the MBTI as any kind of hiring or selection tool does not appear to be warranted, based on existing research.

A second alternative to the Big Five is offered by research on vocational interests.[68] **Interests** are expressions of personality that influence behavior through preferences for certain environments and activities.[69] Interests reflect stable and enduring likes and dislikes that can explain why people are drawn toward some careers and away from others.[70] Holland's **RIASEC model** suggests that interests can be summarized by six different personality types:[71]

- Realistic: Enjoy practical, hands-on, real-world tasks. Tend to be frank, practical, determined, and rugged.
- Investigative: Enjoy abstract, analytical, theory-oriented tasks. Tend to be analytical, intellectual, reserved, and scholarly.
- Artistic: Enjoy entertaining and fascinating others using imagination. Tend to be original, independent, impulsive, and creative.
- Social: Enjoy helping, serving, or assisting others. Tend to be helpful, inspiring, informative, and empathic.
- Enterprising: Enjoy persuading, leading, or outperforming others. Tend to be energetic, sociable, ambitious, and risk-taking.
- Conventional: Enjoy organizing, counting, or regulating people or things. Tend to be careful, conservative, self-controlled, and structured.

As shown in Figure 9-6, the RIASEC model further suggests that the personality types can be classified along two dimensions: the degree to which employees prefer to work with data versus ideas and the degree to which they prefer to work with people versus things. For example, those with a Realistic personality prefer to work with things and data more than people and ideas. The model arranges the personality types in a hexagonal fashion, with types adjacent to one another being more similar than types that are more distant. The central premise of the RIASEC model is that employees have more career satisfaction and longevity in occupations that match their personality type.[72] For example, Realistic people should be happier as craftspeople than as counselors because a craftsperson's duties provide a good match to their personality. One of the most common applications of the RIASEC model is interest inventories, which provide people their scores on relevant personality dimensions, along with a list of occupations that could provide a good match for that profile.[73]

CULTURAL VALUES

Now that we've described a number of personality traits, we turn our attention to the cultural values that can affect the expression of those traits.[74] To some extent, cultural values provide countries with their own distinct personalities. For example, we can say that Australian people, on average, value the traits associated with extraversion more than Chinese people.[75] We can also say that Swiss people, on average, value the traits associated with openness more than Irish people. Such statements are based on research that reveals consistent between-nation differences on various personality traits. Of course, that doesn't mean that all Australian, Chinese, Swiss, and Irish citizens have exactly the same personality—merely that certain cultures tend to have higher levels of certain traits.

FIGURE 9-6   Holland's RIASEC Model

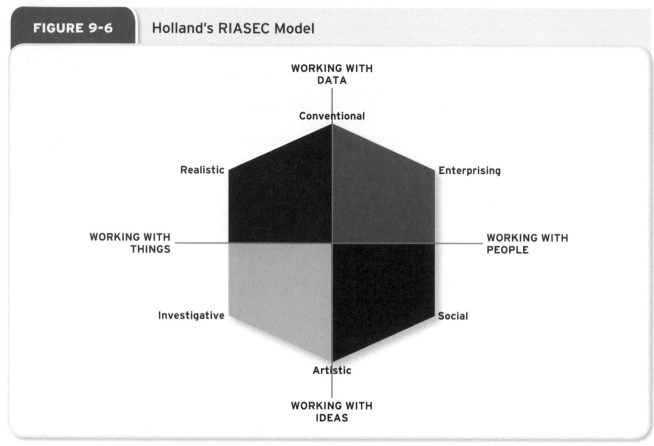

Sources: Adapted from J.L. Holland, *Making Vocational Choices: A Theory of Careers* (Englewood Cliffs, NJ: Prentice-Hall, 1973).

Although it's possible to describe nations on values relevant to the Big Five, as we just did, there are other values that are more commonly used to categorize nations. Many of those values are derived from a landmark study in the late 1960s and early 1970s by Geert Hofstede, who analyzed data about 88,000 IBM employees from 72 countries in 20 languages.[76] His research showed that employees working in different countries tended to prioritize different values, and those values clustered into several distinct dimensions. Those dimensions are summarized in Table 9-3 and include **individualism–collectivism, power distance, uncertainty avoidance, masculinity–femininity,** and **short-term vs. long-term orientation.** The table also includes cultures that tend to be high on a given dimension.

9.4

What are Hofstede's dimensions of cultural values?

The table reveals that citizens of the United States tend to be high on individualism, low on power distance, low on uncertainty avoidance, high on masculinity, and high on short-term orientation. Why is this description important to know? Because it illustrates the adjustments that American employees and American businesses may need to make when doing business in other cultures. Differences in cultural values can create differences in reactions to change, conflict management styles, negotiation approaches, and reward preferences.[77] Failing to understand those differences can compromise the effectiveness of multinational groups and organizations. Such problems are particularly likely if employees are high in **ethnocentrism,** defined as a propensity to view one's own cultural values as

TABLE 9-3	Hofstede's Dimensions of Cultural Values

Individualism-Collectivism

INDIVIDUALISM	COLLECTIVISM
The culture is a loosely knit social framework in which people take care of themselves and their immediate family.	The culture is a tight social framework in which people take care of the members of a broader ingroup and act loyal to it.
United States, the Netherlands, France	*Indonesia, China, West Africa*

Power Distance

LOW	HIGH
The culture prefers that power be distributed uniformly where possible, in a more egalitarian fashion.	The culture accepts the fact that power is usually distributed unequally within organizations.
United States, Germany, the Netherlands	*Russia, China, Indonesia*

Uncertainty Avoidance

LOW	HIGH
The culture tolerates uncertain and ambiguous situations and values unusual ideas and behaviors.	The culture feels threatened by uncertain and ambiguous situations and relies on formal rules to create stability.
United States, Indonesia, the Netherlands	*Japan, Russia, France*

Masculinity-Femininity

MASCULINITY	FEMININITY
The culture values stereotypically male traits such as assertiveness and the acquisition of money and things.	The culture values stereotypically female traits such as caring for others and caring about quality of life.
United States, Japan, Germany	*The Netherlands, Russia, France*

Short-Term vs. Long-Term Orientation

SHORT TERM	LONG TERM
The culture stresses values that are more past- and present-oriented, such as respect for tradition and fulfilling obligations.	The culture stresses values that are more future-oriented, such as persistence, prudence, and thrift.
United States, Russia, West Africa	*China, Japan, the Netherlands*

Sources: G. Hofstede, *Culture's Consequences: International Differences in Work Related Values* (Beverly Hills, CA: Sage, 1980); G. Hofstede, "Cultural Constraints in Management Theories," *Academy of Management Executive* 7 (1993), pp. 81–94; G. Hofstede and M.H. Bond, "The Confucius Connection: From Cultural Roots to Economic Growth," *Organizational Dynamics* 16 (1988), pp. 5–21; B.L. Kirkman, K.B. Lowe, and C.B. Gibson, "A Quarter Century of *Culture's Consequences:* A Review of Empirical Research Incorporating Hofstede's Cultural Values Framework," *Journal of International Business Studies* 37 (2006), pp. 285–320.

"right" and those of other cultures as "wrong."[78] For more discussion of this issue, see our **OB Internationally** feature.

Of Hofstede's five dimensions, individualism–collectivism has received the most research attention, by a wide margin.[81] Much of this research has focused on the individualism–collectivism of individual people rather than nations, sometimes referred to as "psychological individualism" or "psychological collectivism."[82] This focus on individuals rather

OB INTERNATIONALLY

Research suggests that ethnocentrism hinders the effectiveness of expatriates, who are employees working full-time in other countries. Ethnocentrism makes expatriates less likely to adjust to a new culture, less likely to fulfill the duties required of their international assignment, and more likely to withdraw from that assignment. So how can organizations identify employees with the right personalities to serve as expatriates?

One potentially useful tool is the *multicultural personality questionnaire,* which assesses five personality dimensions that can maximize the satisfaction, commitment, and performance of expatriates.[79] Those dimensions are listed below, along with some sample items for each.

Cultural Empathy. A tendency to empathize with the feelings, thoughts, and behaviors of individuals with different cultural values.

- I understand other people's feelings.
- I take other people's habits into consideration.

Open-mindedness. A tendency to have an open and unprejudiced attitude toward other cultural values and norms.

- I get involved in other cultures.
- I find other religions interesting.

Emotional Stability. A tendency to remain calm in the kinds of stressful situations that can be encountered in foreign environments.

- I can put setbacks in perspective.
- I take it for granted that things will turn out right.

Social Initiative. A tendency to be proactive when approaching social situations, which aids in building connections.

- I easily approach other people.
- I am often the driving force behind things.

Flexibility. A tendency to regard new situations as a challenge and to adjust behaviors to meet that challenge.

- I could start a new life easily.
- I feel comfortable in different cultures.

Research has linked these five personality traits to a number of expatriate success factors. For example, individuals with a "multicultural personality" are more likely to aspire to international positions, more likely to gain international experience, more likely to adjust to new assignments, and more likely to be happy with their lives during those assignments.[80] In fact, research even suggests that expatriates who fit this profile are actually healthier, both physically and mentally.

than nations is understandable, given that some experts estimate that only 60 percent of the citizens in a collective culture actually hold collective cultural values themselves.[83] Studies of psychological collectivism have revealed that collective employees identify deeply with relevant ingroups, such as family members, close friends, or work teams. They prefer to interact with those ingroups, care for the members of those ingroups, and accept and prioritize ingroup norms and goals.[84] If you serve as a member of any student project teams, see our **OB for Students** feature to find out how psychological collectivism could benefit you.

SUMMARY: HOW CAN WE DESCRIBE WHAT EMPLOYEES ARE LIKE?

So how can we explain what employees are like? As shown in Figure 9-7, many of the thousands of adjectives we use to describe people can be boiled down into the Big Five dimensions of personality. Conscientiousness reflects the reliability, perseverance, and ambition of employees. Agreeableness captures their tendency to cooperate with others in a warm and sympathetic fashion. Neuroticism reflects the tendency to experience negative moods and emotions frequently on a day-to-day basis. Individuals who are high on openness to experience are creative, imaginative, and curious. Finally, extraverts are

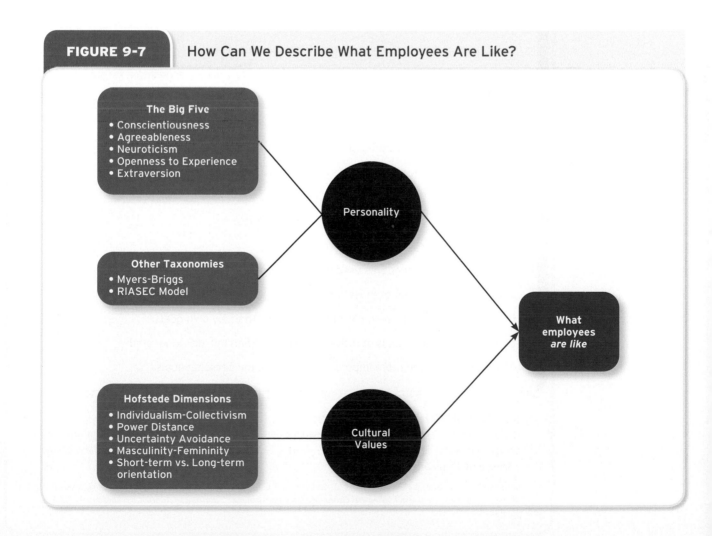

FIGURE 9-7 How Can We Describe What Employees Are Like?

The Big Five
- Conscientiousness
- Agreeableness
- Neuroticism
- Openness to Experience
- Extraversion

Other Taxonomies
- Myers-Briggs
- RIASEC Model

Personality

Hofstede Dimensions
- Individualism-Collectivism
- Power Distance
- Uncertainty Avoidance
- Masculinity-Femininity
- Short-term vs. Long-term orientation

Cultural Values

What employees are like

OB FOR STUDENTS

Are you psychologically collective (or are some of your fellow group members)? Past research suggests that people who hold collective values are more self-confident in group settings, are more cooperative by nature, and prefer to be evaluated and rewarded on a groupwide basis (as when student group members all receive the same grade on a class project).[85] Collective group members also perform their group duties at a higher level, engage in more citizenship behavior, and refrain from counterproductive behaviors that could harm the group.[86] To assess your psychological collectivism, think about the work groups to which you currently belong and have belonged to in the past. The items below ask about your relationship with, and thoughts about, *those particular groups.* Respond to the following questions as honestly as possible using the response scale provided. Then sum up your scores.

1	2	3	4	5
STRONGLY DISAGREE	DISAGREE	NEUTRAL	AGREE	STRONGLY AGREE

1. I preferred to work in those groups rather than working alone. _____

2. Working in those groups was better than working alone. _____

3. I wanted to work with those groups as opposed to working alone. _____

4. I felt comfortable counting on group members to do their part. _____

5. I was not bothered by the need to rely on group members. _____

6. I felt comfortable trusting group members to handle their tasks. _____

7. The health of those groups was important to me. _____

8. I cared about the well-being of those groups. _____

9. I was concerned about the needs of those groups. _____

10. I followed the norms of those groups. _____

11. I followed the procedures used by those groups. _____

12. I accepted the rules of those groups. _____

13. I cared more about the goals of those groups than my own goals. _____

14. I emphasized the goals of those groups more than my individual goals. _____

15. Group goals were more important to me than my personal goals. _____

SCORING AND INTERPRETATION:

If you scored a 53 or above, you hold collectivistic work values, which means that you prioritize the needs and well-being of the groups to which you belong, and you adhere to the norms and goals of those groups.

Source: C. L. Jackson; J. A. Colquitt; M. J. Wesson; and C. P. Zapata-Phelan, "Psychological Collectivism: A Measurement Validation and Linkage to Group Member Performance." *Journal of Applied Psychology* 91 (2006), pp. 884–99.

talkative, sociable, and assertive and typically experience positive moods and emotions. Other personality taxonomies, like the MBTI or the RIASEC model, can also capture many employee traits. Beyond personality, however, what employees are like also depends on the culture in which they were raised. Cultural values like individualism–collectivism, power distance, uncertainty avoidance, masculinity–femininity, and short-term vs. long-term orientation influence employees' thoughts, emotions, and behaviors.

HOW IMPORTANT ARE PERSONALITY AND CULTURAL VALUES?

We've already described a number of reasons why the Big Five should be important considerations, particularly in the case of conscientiousness. What if we focus specifically on the two outcomes in our integrative model of OB, performance and commitment? Figure 9-8 summarizes the research evidence linking conscientiousness to those two outcomes. The figure reveals that conscientiousness affects job performance. Of the Big Five, conscientiousness has the strongest effect on task performance,[87] partly because conscientious employees have higher levels of *motivation* than other employees.[88] They are more self-confident, perceive a clearer linkage between their effort and their performance, and are more likely to set goals and commit to them. For these reasons, conscientiousness is a key driver of what's referred to as **typical performance,** reflecting performance in the routine conditions that surround daily job tasks.[89] An employee's ability, in contrast, is a key driver of **maximum performance,** reflecting performance in brief, special circumstances that demand a person's best effort.

Conscientious employees are also more likely to engage in citizenship behaviors.[90] Why? One reason is that conscientious employees are so punctual and have such good work attendance that they are simply more available to offer "extra mile" sorts of contributions. Another reason is that they engage in so much more work-related effort that they have more energy to devote to citizenship behaviors.[91] Finally, conscientious employees are less likely to engage in counterproductive behaviors,[92] for two major reasons. First, they tend to have higher levels of *job satisfaction,*[93] making it less likely that they'll feel a need to retaliate against their organization. Second, even if they do perceive some slight or injustice, their dependable and reliable nature should prevent them from violating organizational norms by engaging in negative actions.[94]

9.5

How does personality affect job performance and organizational commitment?

Figure 9-8 also reveals that conscientious employees tend to be more committed to their organization.[95] They are less likely to engage in day-to-day psychological and physical withdrawal behaviors because such actions go against their work habits. They are also significantly less likely to voluntarily leave the organization.[96] Why? One reason is that the persevering nature of conscientious employees prompts them to persist in a given course of action for long periods of time. That persistence can be seen in their daily work effort, but it extends to a sense of commitment to the organization as well.[97] Another reason is that conscientious employees are better at managing *stress,* perceiving lower levels of key stressors, and being less affected by them at work.[98]

In some respects, Figure 9-8 understates the importance of conscientiousness (and personality, more generally). Why? Because personality becomes more important in some contexts than in others. The principle of **situational strength** suggests that "strong situations" have clear behavioral expectations, incentives, or instructions that make differences between individuals less important, whereas "weak situations" lack those cues.[99] Personality variables tend to be more significant drivers of behavior in weak situations than in strong situations.[100] Similarly, the principle of **trait activation** suggests that some

| FIGURE 9-8 | Effects of Personality on Performance and Commitment |

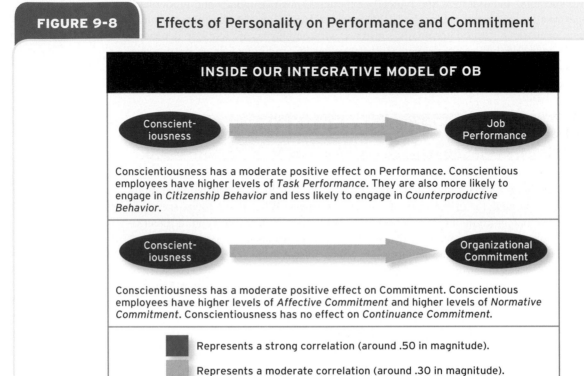

INSIDE OUR INTEGRATIVE MODEL OF OB

Conscientiousness → Job Performance

Conscientiousness has a moderate positive effect on Performance. Conscientious employees have higher levels of *Task Performance*. They are also more likely to engage in *Citizenship Behavior* and less likely to engage in *Counterproductive Behavior*.

Conscientiousness → Organizational Commitment

Conscientiousness has a moderate positive effect on Commitment. Conscientious employees have higher levels of *Affective Commitment* and higher levels of *Normative Commitment*. Conscientiousness has no effect on *Continuance Commitment*.

Represents a strong correlation (around .50 in magnitude).

Represents a moderate correlation (around .30 in magnitude).

Represents a weak correlation (around .10 in magnitude).

Sources: M.R. Barrick, M.K. Mount, and T.A. Judge, "Personality and Performance at the Beginning of the New Millennium: What Do We Know and Where Do We Go Next?" *International Journal of Selection and Assessment* 9 (2001), pp. 9–30; C.M. Berry, D.S. Ones, and P.R. Sackett, "Interpersonal Deviance, Organizational Deviance, and Their Common Correlates: A Review and Meta-Analysis," *Journal of Applied Psychology* 92 (2007), pp. 410–24; A. Cooper-Hakim and C. Viswesvaran, "The Construct of Work Commitment: Testing an Integrative Framework," *Psychological Bulletin* 131 (2005), pp. 241–59; L.M. Hough and A. Furnham, "Use of Personality Variables in Work Settings," in *Handbook of Psychology*, Vol. 12, eds. W.C. Borman, D.R. Ilgen, and R.J. Klimoski (Hoboken, NJ: Wiley, 2003), pp. 131–69; J.E. Mathieu and D.M. Zajac, "A Review and Meta-Analysis of the Antecedents, Correlates, and Consequences of Organizational Commitment," *Psychological Bulletin* 108 (1990), pp. 171–94; J.F. Salgado, "The Big Five Personality Dimensions and Counterproductive Behaviors," *International Journal of Selection and Assessment* 10 (2002), pp. 117–25.

situations provide cues that trigger the expression of a given trait.[101] For example, a cry for help provides a cue that can trigger the expression of empathy. Personality variables tend to be more significant drivers of behaviors in situations that provide relevant cues than in situations in which those cues are lacking. For more discussion of the importance of the situation, see our **OB at the Bookstore** feature.

APPLICATION: PERSONALITY TESTS

Given how important personality traits can be to job performance and organizational commitment, it's not surprising that many organizations attempt to gauge the personality of job applicants, as in our opening example of Teach for America. But what's the best

OB AT THE BOOKSTORE

NOW, DISCOVER YOUR STRENGTHS
by Marcus Buckingham and Donald O. Clifton (Free Press: New York, 2001).

To excel in your chosen field and to find lasting satisfaction in doing so, you will need to understand your unique patterns. You will need to become an expert at finding and describing and applying and practicing and refining your strengths.

With those words, the authors emphasize the importance of discovering your strengths in their best-selling sequel to *First, Break all the Rules*.[102] According to the authors, individuals' strengths are dictated by three things: knowledge, skills, and talents. Talents, in turn, are defined as naturally recurring and relatively enduring patterns of thought, feeling, or behavior. The book provides an overview of 34 different "talent themes" and includes a link to an online assessment for discovering your top five themes. Although the authors draw a distinction between talents and personality, it seems clear that many of the talent themes are related to the Big Five. Listed below are some of the talents discussed by the authors and where they might fit within the Big Five:

- *Conscientiousness:* May underlie talents such as Achiever, Arranger, Deliberative, Focus, and Responsibility.
- *Agreeableness:* May underlie talents such as Empathy, Harmony, Includer, and Relator.
- *Neuroticism:* Low neuroticism may underlie talents such as Connectedness, Maximizer, and Self-Assurance.
- *Openness to Experience:* May underlie talents such as Adaptability, Ideation, Input, Intellection, and Learner.
- *Extraversion:* May underlie talents such as Command, Communication, Positivity, and Woo.

The central thesis of the book is that people will be more successful if they "play to their strengths" as opposed to focusing on improving their weaknesses. To provide support for this premise, the authors review research by The Gallup Organization that asked 198,000 employees the following question: "At work do you have the opportunity to do what you do best every day?" When employees answered "strongly agree" to this question, they were 38 percent more likely to work in a unit with high performance and 50 percent more likely to work in a unit with low turnover. That's the good news. What's the bad news? Only 20 percent of the respondents actually felt that they were given the opportunity to use their talents on a daily basis. Instead, they were "miscast" in jobs, assignments, or roles that weren't well-suited to them. The lesson is clear: To make the most of your talents and personality traits, you need to place yourself in situations where they can benefit you.

way to do that? Many organizations try to assess personality through interviews by looking for cues that an applicant is conscientious or agreeable or has high levels of some other relevant personality dimension. Can you see a potential problem with this approach? Here's a hint: When was the last time you went into an interview and acted careless, sloppy, moody, or insecure? It's probably been a while. In fact, most interview preparation courses and books train applicants to exhibit the very personality traits that many employers are looking for!

To examine whether interviewers can gauge the Big Five, one study asked 26 interviewers, all of whom were human resources practitioners with more than 12 years of hiring experience, to assess the personalities of undergraduate business students who were on the job market.[103] The interviewers met with an average of three students for 30 minutes and were instructed to follow the interview protocols used in their own organizations. Once the interviews had concluded, the study gathered multiple ratings of the Big Five, including ratings from the interviewer, the student, and a close friend of the student. The results of the study showed that the interviewers' ratings of extraversion, agreeableness, and openness were fairly consistent with the students' own ratings, as well as their friends' ratings. In contrast, interviewers' ratings of conscientiousness and neuroticism were only weakly related to the students' and friends' ratings. This study therefore shows that interviewers are unable to gauge the two Big Five dimensions that are most highly related to job performance.

9.6

Are personality tests useful tools for organizational hiring?

Rather than using interviews to assess personality, more and more companies are relying on paper-and-pencil "personality tests" like the kind shown in our OB Assessments. A recent survey of *Fortune* 1000 firms suggests that around one-third of those organizations rely on, or plan to implement, some form of personality testing.[104] If you've ever applied for an hourly position at Best Buy, Blockbuster, Target, Toys "R" Us, Marriott, Bennigan's, Universal Studios, Sports Authority, CVS Pharmacy, Albertson's, or the Fresh Market, you may have been asked to take a personality test at a computer kiosk as part of your application.[105] That test was designed by Unicru, the market leader in personality tests for hourly positions, based in Beaverton, Oregon (Unicru was recently acquired by Kronos, a company specializing in human resource management software systems).[106] Unicru's test includes 50 questions, many of which are clearly tapping the Big Five:

- You do things carefully so you don't make mistakes.[107] (high conscientiousness)
- You can easily cheer up and forget a problem.[108] (low neuroticism)
- You don't act polite when you don't want to.[109] (low agreeableness)
- You'd rather blend into the crowd than stand out.[110] (low extraversion)

Ten minutes after an applicant completes the personality test at the kiosk, the hiring manager receives an e-mailed or faxed report that identifies the applicant with a "green light," "yellow light," or "red light."[111] Green lights earn an automatic follow-up interview, yellow lights require some managerial discretion, and red lights are excused from the hiring process. The report also includes some recommended interview questions to follow up on any concerns that might have arisen from the personality responses. Unicru has built a database of 370,000 employee personality profiles, together with the actual job results for those employees, which enables it to look for profiles of effective and committed employees. Unicru also encourages employers to save the data from the personality tests for several years, to verify that responses correlate with performance evaluations and turnover over time.

Of course, personality testing is not without controversy. Privacy advocates worry about the security of the personality profiles that are stored in large databases.[112] There's also no guarantee that the personality tests used by a company are actually valid assessments, because few of them have been subject to scientific investigation.[113] For example, we are not aware of any scientific studies in peer-reviewed journals that have comprehensively validated Unicru's personality test. One leading personality researcher estimates that there are 2,500 personality test publishers in the United States, only a few of which pay close enough attention to the accuracy of their instruments. Because the industry is not regulated, the best bet for companies that are thinking about using personality tests is to start with the tests that have been comprehensively validated in scientific journals. Table 9-4 provides a list of some of the most well-validated measures of the Big Five personality dimensions. The vendors that own these measures typically offer software and services for scoring the instruments, interpreting the data against relevant population norms, and creating feedback sheets.

One particular subset of personality tests is particularly controversial. **Integrity tests,** sometimes also called "honesty tests," are personality tests that focus specifically on a predisposition to engage in theft and other counterproductive behaviors.[114] Integrity tests were created, in part, as a reaction to Congress's decision to make polygraph (or "lie detector") tests illegal as a tool for organizational hiring. Integrity tests typically come in two general varieties. **Clear purpose tests** ask applicants about their attitudes toward dishonesty, beliefs about the frequency of dishonesty, endorsements of common rationalizations for dishonesty, desire to punish dishonesty, and confessions of past dishonesty.[115] **Veiled purpose tests** do not reference dishonesty explicitly but instead assess more general personality traits that are associated with dishonest acts. Table 9-5 provides sample items for both types of integrity tests. You might notice that the veiled purpose items resemble some of the items in our OB Assessment for the Big Five. Most integrity tests actually assess, in large part, a combination of high conscientiousness, high agreeableness, and low neuroticism.[116]

Do integrity tests actually work? One study examined the effectiveness of integrity tests in a sample of convenience store clerks.[117] The chain had been struggling with inventory "shrinkage" due to theft and began using a clear purpose integrity test to combat that trend. The study compared the integrity test scores for employees who were fired for theft-related reasons (e.g., taking merchandise, mishandling cash, having frequent cash register shortages) with a sample of demographically similar employees in good standing. The results of the study revealed that employees who were terminated for theft had scored significantly lower on the integrity test than employees who were not terminated. These sorts of results are not unusual; a meta-analysis of 443 studies including more than 500,000 employees has shown that integrity test scores have a moderately strong, negative correlation with counterproductive behaviors such as theft.[118] In fact, integrity test scores are actually more strongly related to job performance than conscientiousness scores, largely because integrity tests sample a blend of multiple Big Five dimensions.[119]

TABLE 9-4	A Sampling of Well-Validated Measures of the Big Five	
NAME OF INSTRUMENT	**VENDOR**	**TIME REQUIRED**
NEO Five-Factor Inventory (NEO-FFI)	Sigma Assessment Systems	15 minutes
Personal Characteristics Inventory (PCI)	Wonderlic	20 minutes
Personality Research Form (PRF)	Sigma Assessment Systems	45 minutes
Hogan Personality Inventory (HPI)	Hogan Assessment Systems	15 minutes
Big Five Inventory (BFI)	TestMaster	10 minutes

TABLE 9-5	Sample Integrity Test Items
TYPE OF TEST	**SAMPLE ITEMS**
Clear Purpose	• Did you ever think about taking money from where you worked, but didn't go through with it? • Have you ever borrowed something from work without telling anyone? • Is it OK to get around the law if you don't break it? • If you were sent an extra item with an order, would you send it back? • Do most employees take small items from work? • What dollar value would a worker have to steal before you would fire them?
Veiled Purpose	• I like to plan things carefully ahead of time. • I often act quickly without stopping to think things through. • I've never hurt anyone's feelings. • I have a feeling someone is out to get me. • I don't feel I've had control over my life.

Source: J.E. Wanek, P.R. Sackett, and D.S. Ones, "Towards an Understanding of Integrity Test Similarities and Differences: An Item-Level Analysis of Seven Tests," *Personnel Psychology* 56 (2003), pp. 873–94. Reprinted with permission of Blackwell Publishing.

"Remember when I said I was going to be honest with you, Jeff? That was a big, fat lie."

You might find it surprising that integrity tests (or personality tests in general) can be so effective. After all, don't applicants just lie on the test? Before we answer that question, consider what you would do if you applied for a job and had to answer questions on a 1 (Strongly Disagree) to 5 (Strongly Agree) scale that were obviously measuring integrity. If a response of 5 indicated high integrity, how would you answer? You probably wouldn't answer all 5s because it would be clear that you were **faking**—exaggerating your responses to a personality test in a socially desirable fashion. You might worry that the computers that score the test have some ability to "flag" faked responses (indeed, the scoring procedures for many personality tests do flag applicants with an unusual pattern of responses).[120]

So how would you answer? Chances are, you'd allow your answers to have "a grain of truth"—you'd just exaggerate that true response a bit to make yourself look better. Figure 9-9 summarizes what this sort of faking might look like, with red circles representing

FIGURE 9-9 The Effects of Faking on Correlations with Integrity Tests

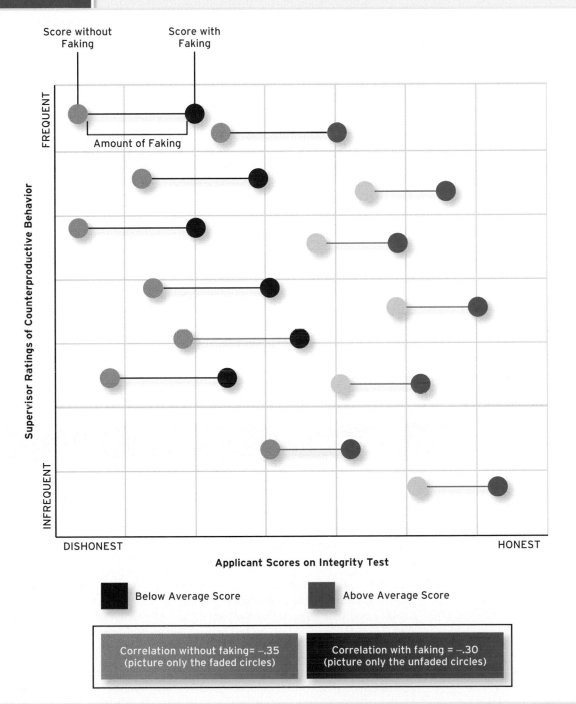

below-average scores on an integrity test and green circles representing above-average scores. Research on personality testing suggests that virtually everyone fakes their responses to some degree, as evidenced in the difference between the faded circles (which represent the "true" responses) and the unfaded circles (which represent the exaggerated responses).[121] Do dishonest people fake more? To some degree. Figure 9-9 reveals that applicants who scored below average on the test faked a bit more than applicants who scored above average on the test. But the disparity in the amount of faking is not large, likely because dishonest people tend to view their behavior as perfectly normal—they believe everyone feels and acts just like they do.

The figure reveals that it could be dangerous to set some artificial cutoff score for making hiring decisions, because it's possible for someone to "fake their way" across that cutoff (note that two of the individuals in the figure went from a below-average score to an above-average score by faking). With that caution in mind, here's the critical point illustrated by Figure 9-9: *Because everyone fakes to some degree, correlations with outcomes like theft or other counterproductive behaviors are relatively unaffected.*[122] Picture the scatterplot in the figure with just the faded circles—what does the correlation between integrity test scores and supervisor ratings of counterproductive behavior look like? Now picture the scatterplot with just the unfaded circles—what does that correlation look like? About the same, right? The tendency to fake doesn't really alter the rank order in scores from most dishonest to most honest, so the test is still useful as a tool for predicting counterproductive behavior. In fact, experts on personnel selection agree that personality and integrity tests are among the most useful tools for hiring—more useful even than the typical version of the employment interview.[123] One of the only tools that's more useful than a personality test is an ability test—as noted in our next chapter.[124]

TAKEAWAYS

9.1 Personality refers to the structures and propensities inside a person that explain his or her characteristic patterns of thought, emotion, and behavior. It also refers to a person's social reputation—the way he or she is perceived by others. In this way, personality captures *what people are like* (unlike ability, which reflects *what people can do*). Cultural values are shared beliefs about desirable end states or modes of conduct in a given culture that influence the expression of traits.

9.2 Although both nature and nurture are important, personality is affected significantly by genetic factors. Studies of identical twins reared apart and studies of personality stability over time suggest that between 35 and 45 percent of the variation in personality is genetic. Personality can be changed, but such changes are only apparent over the course of several years.

9.3 The "Big Five" includes conscientiousness (e.g., dependable, organized, reliable), agreeableness (e.g., warm, kind, cooperative), neuroticism (e.g., nervous, moody, emotional), openness to experience (e.g., curious, imaginative, creative), and extraversion (e.g., talkative, sociable, passionate). Although the Big Five is the dominant taxonomy of personality, other taxonomies include the Myers-Briggs Type Inventory and Holland's RIASEC model.

9.4 Hofstede's dimensions of cultural values include individualism–collectivism, power distance, uncertainty avoidance, masculinity–femininity, and short-term vs. long-term orientation.

9.5 Conscientiousness has a moderate positive relationship with job performance and a moderate positive relationship with organizational commitment. It has stronger effects on these outcomes than the rest of the Big Five.

9.6 Personality tests are useful tools for organizational hiring. Research suggests that applicants do "fake" to some degree on the tests, but faking does not significantly lower the correlation between test scores and the relevant outcomes.

Here are the answers to the tests of creative thinking in Figure 9-5: (1) A towel. (2) They were triplets. (3) The letter U. (4) Draw a line to turn the + into a 4. (5) Solving this puzzle literally requires you to "think outside the box" (yes, that's where it came from!) Nowhere in the instructions did it state that you needed to keep the lines inside the square formed by the dots. Connect the dots using the four lines shown below:

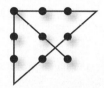

KEY TERMS

- Personality — p. 292
- Traits — p. 292
- Cultural values — p. 292
- Conscientiousness — p. 293
- Agreeableness — p. 293
- Neuroticism — p. 293
- Openness to experience — p. 293
- Extraversion — p. 293
- Big Five — p. 293
- Accomplishment striving — p. 297
- Communion striving — p. 298
- Zero acquaintance — p. 298
- Status striving — p. 300
- Positive affectivity — p. 300
- Negative affectivity — p. 301
- Differential exposure — p. 303
- Differential reactivity — p. 303
- Locus of control — p. 303
- Creativity — p. 304
- Myers-Briggs Type Indicator — p. 306
- Interests — p. 307
- RIASEC model — p. 307
- Individualism–collectivism — p. 308
- Power distance — p. 308
- Uncertainty avoidance — p. 308
- Masculinity–femininity — p. 308
- Short-term vs. long-term orientation — p. 308
- Ethnocentrism — p. 308
- Typical performance — p. 313
- Maximum performance — p. 313
- Situational strength — p. 313
- Trait activation — p. 313
- Integrity tests — p. 317
- Clear purpose tests — p. 317
- Veiled purpose tests — p. 317
- Faking — p. 318

DISCUSSION QUESTIONS

9.1 Assume that you were accepted into the Teach for America program and found yourself teaching in a troubled and impoverished school system. Rank in order the Big Five dimensions from most important to least important in terms of their ability to help you succeed in that environment. Why did you rank them that way?

9.2 Research on genetic influences on personality suggests that more than half of the variation in personality is due to nurture—to life experiences. What life experiences could make someone more conscientious? More agreeable? More neurotic? More extraverted? More open to new experiences?

9.3 Consider the personality dimensions included in the Myers-Briggs Type Inventory and the RIASEC model. If you had to "slot" those dimensions into the Big Five, would you be able to? Which dimensions don't seem to fit?

9.4 Consider the profile of the United States on Hofstede's cultural values, as shown in Table 9-3. Do you personally feel like you fit the United States profile, or do your values differ in some respects? If you served as an expatriate, meaning you were working in another country, which cultural value differences would be most difficult for you to deal with?

9.5 If you owned your own business and had a problem with employee theft, would you use an integrity test? Why or why not?

CASE TEACH FOR AMERICA

The job market for college graduates is strong, but one of the hottest recruiters is Teach for America (TFA). This organization seems like an unlikely candidate for job seekers, because TFA offers a low salary and promises a strenuous work schedule. So why is this job so appealing to college graduates? High-achieving college students appreciate the program for the challenge it represents.

Teach for America, a creative program intended to help solve the teacher shortage epidemic in the United States, recruits the best and brightest college students to share their expertise in some of the most challenging public schools across the country. Teachers who complete the program then use their experiences to make positive social changes in their lifetime.

What qualifications does a candidate need to be accepted into this program? A stringent screening process evaluates the personalities and capabilities of each candidate. Students accepted into the program must have shown their ability to succeed in the classroom and in leadership roles in campus organizations. The alumni of Teach for America make positive impacts in society, whether it be in education or public office. Do you have the personality for Teach for America?

9.1 Which of the Big Five personality dimensions are evident in Teach for America candidates? Explain.

9.2 If you were recruiting college students to enter the Teach for America program, what personality type would you chose from Holland's RIASEC model?

Sources: W. Kopp, "The Young Can Be Agents of Change," *Global Agenda,* January 2005; J. Pope, "Teach for America Surging in Popularity," *Boston Globe,* June 18, 2006; M. Raymond and S. Fletcher, "Teach for America," *Education Next,* Hoover Institution, 2002.

EXERCISE   LEADER PERSONALITY

The purpose of this exercise is to use the Big 5 personality characteristics (conscientious-ness, agreeableness, neuroticism, openness to experience, and extraversion) to describe a leader's personality. This exercise uses groups of six participants, so your instructor will either assign you to a group of six or ask you to create your own group of six. The exer-cise has the following steps:

1. Read the following information about Jerry Yang:

   When Yahoo announced that CEO Terry Semel was leaving, to be replaced by Yahoo founder Jerry Yang, Mark Evans, a newspaper journalist and blogger, said, "Yang has never given the impression he's CEO material. While he's certainly well-respected, Yang doesn't ooze with charisma, personality or leadership, which makes him an interesting choice as CEO."[125] So who is Jerry Yang? Is he CEO material?

   In 2000, *Fortune* Magazine called Jerry Yang "the quintessential self-taught entre-preneur of his generation."[126] He and his partner, David Filo, were both in the PhD engineering program at Stanford University when they decided to start their own busi-ness. As he says, "We both thought we'd rather be technical people at a small company than just another researcher at a big corporate lab."[127] Although he was studying com-puter assisted design (CAD), Yang started looking at the Internet because he wanted to keep up with other things that might be cool. When asked how he moved from the technical side of things to starting a real company, Yang said that he "instinctively" knew where the product was going and how to develop it. Now, Yang is trying to make the company grow—he talks about his long-term ambition to create a company that will grow and outlive him.[128]

   Although Yang says that he and his partner Filo are perfectionists, they reach out to everyone in the organization for ideas. This trait is one of the things that kept people with the company when it was small and enabled it to rebound from the difficult times that followed the 2001 technology bust in Silicon Valley.[129] Libby Sartain, Yahoo's head of Human Resources, says that Yang is focused on culture—whether he knows it or not.[130]

   Yang never finished his doctoral program. Even after Yahoo started and Yang was worth millions of dollars, he said that not finishing bothered him.[131] In his own words, "I'm not a quitter."[132] But he also explains that even if he had finished his thesis, his work would have influenced very few people, whereas Yahoo is used by millions everyday. He says knowing that he is going to impact all those lives is "sort of like a drug."[133]

2. Individually, describe Jerry Yang's personality. Is he high or low on conscientiousness, agreeableness, neuroticism, openness to experience, and extraversion? Be sure to cite specific information from the description to justify your answer.

3. Working in your groups, compare your profile of Jerry Yang with the profiles created by your fellow group members. How are they the same? Different?

4. Create an "ideal profile" of a high-tech leader. How do you think the profile of a great high-tech leader might differ from the profile of CEOs in other industries?

5. Design an experiment to test your profile of a great high-tech executive. How could you prove that your version of "what it takes" is correct? Be specific; describe how you would measure whether or not people fit your profile, along with how you would test to see if people with your profile really are better high-tech CEOs.

ENDNOTES

9.1 Sellers, P. "The Recruiter." *Fortune,* November 27, 2006, pp. 87–89.

9.2 Decker, P.T.; D.P. Mayer; and S. Glazerman. *The Effects of Teach for America on Students: Findings from a National Evaluation.* Mathematic Policy Research, Inc. http://www.teachforamerica.org/assets/documents/mathematica_results_6.9.04.pdf (February 23, 2007).

9.3 Gillers, G. "Learning Curve." *Current Magazine,* April 10, 2006, http://www.msnbc.msn.com/id/12206029/site/newsweek/ (February 23, 2007).

9.4 Sellers, "The Recruiter."

9.5 Decker, Mayer, and Glazerman, *The Effects of Teach for America;* Laczko-Kerr, I., and D.C. Berliner. "The Effectiveness of 'Teach for America' and Other Under-Certified Teachers on Student Academic Achievement: A Case of Harmful Public Policy." *Education Policy Analysis Archives* 10, no. 37 2002), http://epaa.asu.edu/epaa/v10n37/ (February 23, 2007).

9.6 Gillers, "Learning Curve."

9.7 Ibid.

9.8 Funder, D.C. "Personality." *Annual Review of Psychology* 52 (2001), pp. 197–221; Hogan, R.T. "Personality and Personality Measurement." *Handbook of Industrial and Organizational Psychology,* Vol. 2, eds. M.D. Dunnette and L.M. Hough. Palo Alto, CA: Consulting Psychologists Press, 1991, pp. 873–919.

9.9 Hogan, "Personality and Personality Measurement."

9.10 Ibid.

9.11 Rokeach, M. *The Nature of Human Values.* New York: Free Press, 1973; Steers, R.M., and C.J. Sanchez-Runde. "Culture, Motivation, and Work Behavior." In *Blackwell Handbook of Cross-Cultural Management,* eds. M.J. Gannon and K.L. Newman. Malden, MA: Blackwell, 2002, pp. 190–213.

9.12 McAdams, D.P., and J.L. Pals. "A New Big Five: Fundamental Principles for an Integrative Science of Personality." *American Psychologist* 61 (2006), pp. 204–17.

9.13 Goldberg, L.R. "From Ace to Zombie: Some Explorations in the Language of Personality." In *Advances in Personality Assessment,* Vol. 1, eds. C.D. Spielberger and J.N. Butcher. Hillsdale, NJ: Erlbaum, 1982, pp. 203–34. See also Allport, G.W., and H.S. Odbert. "Trait-Names: A Psycho-Lexical Study." *Psychological Monographs* 47, no. 1 (1936), Whole No. 211; Norman, W.T. *2800 Personality Trait Descriptors: Normative Operating Characteristics for a University Population.* Ann Arbor, MI: University of Michigan Department of Psychology, 1967.

9.14 Tupes, E.C., and R.E. Christal. *Recurrent Personality Factors Based on Trait Ratings.* USAF ASD Technical Report No. 61–97, Lackland Air Force Base, TX: United States Air Force, 1961; reprinted in *Journal of Personality* 60, pp. 225–51; Norman, W.T. "Toward an Adequate Taxonomy of Personality Attributes: Replicated Factor Structure in Peer Nomination Personality Ratings." *Journal of Abnormal and Social Psychology* 66 (1963), pp. 574–83; Digman, J.M., and N.K. Takemoto-Chock. "Factors in the Natural Language of Personality: Re-Analysis, Comparison, and Interpretation of

Six Major Studies." *Multivariate Behavioral Research* 16 (1981), pp. 149–70; McCrae, R.R., and P.T. Costa Jr. "Updating Norman's 'Adequate Taxonomy': Intelligence and Personality Dimensions in Natural Language and in Questionnaires." *Journal of Personality and Social Psychology* 49 (1985), pp. 710–21; Goldberg, L.R. "An Alternative 'Description of Personality': The Big-Five Factor Structure." *Journal of Personality and Social Psychology* 59 (1990), pp. 1216–29.

9.15 Goldberg, L.R. "Language and Individual Differences: The Search for Universals in Personality Lexicons." In *Review of Personality and Social Psychology,* Vol. 2, ed. L. Wheeler. Beverly Hills, CA: Sage, 1981, pp. 141–65.

9.16 Arvey, R.D., and T.J. Bouchard Jr. "Genetics, Twins, and Organizational Behavior." In *Research in Organizational Behavior,* Vol. 16, eds. B.M. Staw and L.L. Cummings. Greenwich, CT: JAI Press, 1994, pp. 47–82.

9.17 Loehlin, J.C. *Genes and Environment in Personality Development.* Newbury Park, CA: Sage, 1992.

9.18 Ibid.

9.19 Roberts, B.W.; K.E. Walton; and W. Viechtbauer. "Patterns of Mean-Level Change in Personality Traits across the Life Course: A Meta-Analysis of Longitudinal Studies." *Psychological Bulletin* 132 (2006), pp. 1–25.

9.20 Cohen, J. *Statistical Power Analysis for Behavioral Sciences,* 2nd ed. Hillsdale, NJ: Erlbaum, 1988.

9.21 Loehlin, *Genes and Environment.*

9.22 Saucier, G. "Mini-Markers: A Brief Version of Goldberg's Unipolar Big-Five Markers." *Journal of*

Personality Assessment 63 (1994), pp. 506–16; Goldberg, L.R. "The Development of Markers for the Big-Five Factor Structure." *Psychological Assessment* 4 (1992), pp. 26–42; McCrae, R.R., and P.T. Costa Jr. "Validation of the Five-Factor Model of Personality Across Instruments and Observers." *Journal of Personality and Social Psychology* 52 (1987), pp. 81–90.

9.23 Barrick, M.R., and M.K. Mount. "The Big Five Personality Dimensions and Job Performance: A Meta-Analysis." *Personnel Psychology* 44 (1991), pp. 1–26.

9.24 Barrick, M.R.; G.L. Stewart; and M. Piotrowski. "Personality and Job Performance: Test of the Mediating Effects of Motivation among Sales Representatives." *Journal of Applied Psychology* 87 (2002), pp. 43–51.

9.25 Barrick, M.R.; M.K. Mount; and J.P. Strauss. "Conscientiousness and Performance of Sales Representatives: Test of the Mediating Effects of Goal Setting." *Journal of Applied Psychology* 78 (1993), pp. 715–22.

9.26 Stewart, G.L. "Trait Bandwidth and Stages of Job Performance: Assessing Differential Effects for Conscientiousness and its Subtraits." *Journal of Applied Psychology* 84 (1999), pp. 959–68.

9.27 Judge, T.A.; C.A. Higgins; C.J. Thoreson; and M.R. Barrick. "The Big Five Personality Traits, General Mental Ability, and Career Success across the Life Span." *Personnel Psychology* 52 (1999), pp. 621–52.

9.28 Friedman, H.S.; J.S. Tucker; J.E. Schwartz; L.R. Martin; C. Tomlinson-Keasey; D.L. Wingard; and M.H. Criqui. "Childhood Conscientiousness and Longevity: Health Behaviors and Cause of Death." *Journal of Personality and Social Psychology* 68 (1995), pp. 696–703.

9.29 Roberts, B.W.; O.S. Chernyshenko; S. Stark; and L.R. Goldberg. "The Structure of Conscientiousness: An Empirical Investigation Based on Seven Major Personality Dimensions." *Personnel Psychology* 58 (2005), pp. 103–39.

9.30 Palmeri, D. "Dr. Warren's Lonely Hearts Club." *BusinessWeek,* February 20, 2006, pp. 82–84.

9.31 "What Are the 29 Dimensions?" http:// www.eharmony.com/singles/servlet/ about/dimensions (January 6, 2007).

9.32 Hogan, J., and B. Holland. "Using Theory to Evaluate Personality and Job-Performance Relations: A Socioanalytic Perspective." *Journal of Applied Psychology* 88 (2003), pp. 100–12.

9.33 Barrick and Mount, "The Big Five Personality Dimensions."

9.34 Frei, R.L., and M.A. McDaniel. "Validity of Customer Service Measures in Personnel Selection: A Review of Criterion and Construct Evidence." *Human Performance* 11 (1998), pp. 1–27.

9.35 Graziano, W.G.; L.A. Jensen-Campbell; and E.C. Hair. "Perceiving Interpersonal Conflict and Reacting to It: The Case for Agreeableness." *Journal of Personality and Social Psychology* 70 (1996), pp. 820–35.

9.36 Mehl, M.R.; S.D. Gosling; and J.W. Pennebaker. "Personality in Its Natural Habitat: Manifestations and Implicit Folk Theories of Personality in Daily Life." *Journal of Personality and Social Psychology* 90 (2006), pp. 862–77.

9.37 Albright, L.; D.A. Kenny; and T.E. Malloy. "Consensus in Personality Judgments at Zero Acquaintance." *Journal of Personality and Social Psychology* 55 (1988), pp. 387–95;

Levesque, M.J., and D.A. Kenny. "Accuracy of Behavioral Predictions at Zero Acquaintance: A Social Relations Analysis." *Journal of Personality and Social Psychology* 65 (1993), pp. 1178–87.

9.38 Barrick, M.R.; G.L. Stewart; and M. Piotrowski. "Personality and Job Performance: Test of the Mediating Effects of Motivation among Sales Representatives." *Journal of Applied Psychology* 87 (2002), pp. 43–51.

9.39 Judge, T.A.; J.E. Bono; R. Ilies; and M.W. Gerhardt. "Personality and Leadership: A Qualitative and Quantitative Review." *Journal of Applied Psychology* 87 (2002), pp. 765–80.

9.40 Ibid.

9.41 Thoreson, C.J.; S.A. Kaplan; A.P. Barsky; C.R. Warren; and K. de Chermont. "The Affective Underpinnings of Job Perceptions and Attitudes: A Meta-Analytic Review and Integration." *Psychological Bulletin* 129 (2003), pp. 914–45.

9.42 Ibid; Judge, T.A.; D. Heller; and M.K. Mount. "Five-Factor Model of Personality and Job Satisfaction: A Meta-Analysis." *Journal of Applied Psychology* 87 (2003), pp. 530–41.

9.43 Arvey, R.D.; T.J. Bouchard; N.L. Segal; and L.M. Abraham. Job Satisfaction: Environmental and Genetic Components. *Journal of Applied Psychology* 74 (1989), pp. 187–92.

9.44 Magnus, K.; E. Diener; F. Fujita; and W. Pavot. "Extraversion and Neuroticism as Predictors of Objective Life Events: A Longitudinal Analysis." *Journal of Personality and Social Psychology* 65 (1992), pp. 1046–53.

9.45 Paunonen, S.V. "Big Five Predictors of Personality and Replicated Predictions of Behavior." *Journal of Personality and Social Psychology* 84 (2003), pp. 411–24; Asendorpf, J.B., and S. Wilpers. "Personality

Effects on Social Relationships."
Journal of Personality and Social Psychology 74 (1998), pp. 1531–44.

9.46 Asendorpf and Wilpers, "Personality Effects on Social Relationships."

9.47 Barrick, M.R., and M.K. Mount. "Select on Conscientiousness and Emotional Stability." In *Blackwell Handbook of Principles of Organizational Behavior,* ed. E.A. Locke. Malden, MA: Blackwell, 2000, pp. 15–28.

9.48 Thoreson et al., "The Affective Underpinnings."

9.49 Ibid.

9.50 DeNeve, K.M., and H. Cooper. "The Happy Personality: A Meta-Analysis of 137 Personality Traits and Subjective Well-Being." *Psychological Bulletin* 124 (1998), pp. 197–229.

9.51 Bolger, N., and A. Zuckerman. "A Framework for Studying Personality in the Stress Process." *Journal of Personality and Social Psychology* 69 (1995), pp. 890–902.

9.52 Ibid.

9.53 Friedman, M., and R.H. Rosenman. *Type A Behavior and Your Heart.* New York: Knopf, 1974.

9.54 Rotter, J.B. "Generalized Expectancies for Internal versus External Control of Reinforcement." *Psychological Monographs* 80 (1966), pp. 1–28.

9.55 Judge, T.A., and J.E. Bono. "Relationship of Core Self-Evaluations Traits—Self-Esteem, Generalized Self-Efficacy, Locus of Control, and Emotional Stability—with Job Satisfaction and Job Performance: A Meta-Analysis." *Journal of Applied Psychology* 86 (2001), pp. 80–92.

9.56 Ng, T.W.H.; K.L. Sorensen; and L.T. Eby. "Locus of Control at Work:

A Meta-Analysis." *Journal of Organizational Behavior* 27 (2006), pp. 1057–87.

9.57 Barrick and Mount, "The Big Five Personality Dimensions"; Cellar, D.F.; M.L. Miller; D.D. Doverspike; and J.D. Klawsky. "Comparison of Factor Structures and Criterion-Related Validity Coefficients for Two Measures of Personality Based on the Five Factor Model." *Journal of Applied Psychology* 81 (1996), pp. 694–704.

9.58 LePine, J.A.; J.A. Colquitt; and A. Erez. "Adaptability to Changing Task Contexts: Effects of General Cognitive Ability, Conscientiousness, and Openness to Experience." *Personnel Psychology* 53 (2000), pp. 563–93; Thoreson, C.J.; J.C. Bradley; P.D. Bliese; and J.D. Thoreson. "The Big Five Personality Traits and Individual Job Performance Growth Trajectories in Maintenance and Transitional Job Stages." *Journal of Applied Psychology* 89 (2004), pp. 835–53.

9.59 Shalley, C.E.; J. Zhou; and G.R. Oldham. "The Effects of Personal and Contextual Characteristics on Creativity: Where Should We Go from Here?" *Journal of Management* 30 (2004), pp. 933–58.

9.60 Zhou, J., and J.M. George. "When Job Dissatisfaction Leads to Creativity: Encouraging the Expression of Voice." *Academy of Management Journal* 44 (2001), pp. 682–96.

9.61 Feist, G.J. "A Meta-Analysis of Personality in Scientific and Artistic Creativity." *Personality and Social Psychology Review* 2 (1998), pp. 290–309.

9.62 Edmondson, G. "BMW's Dream Factory." *BusinessWeek,* October 16, 2006, pp. 70–80.

9.63 Myers, I.B., and M.H. McCaulley. *Manual: A Guide to the Development and Use of the Myers-Briggs Type Indicator.* Palo Alto, CA: Consulting Psychologists Press, 1985.

9.64 Jung, C.G. *The Collected Works of C. G. Jung, Vol. 6: Psychological Types,* trans. H.G. Baynes, ed. R. F. Hull. Princeton, NJ: Princeton University Press, 1971.

9.65 Gardner, W.L., and M.J. Martinko. "Using the Myers-Briggs Type Indicator to Study Managers: A Literature Review and Research Agenda." *Journal of Management* 22 (1996), pp. 45–83; "What Is Your Myers Briggs Personality Type?" http://www.personalitypathways .com/type_inventory.html (March 18, 2007).

9.66 Gardner and Martinko, "Using the Myers-Briggs Type Indicator."

9.67 Ibid.

9.68 Holland, J.L. "A Theory of Vocational Choice." *Journal of Counseling Psychology* 6 (1959), pp. 35–45; Holland, J.L. *Making Vocational Choices: A Theory of Vocational Personalities and Work Environments,* 3rd ed. Odessa, FL: Psychological Assessment Resources, 1997.

9.69 Mount, M.K.; M.R. Barrick; S.M. Scullen; and J. Rounds. "Higher-Order Dimensions of the Big Five Personality Traits and the Big Six Vocational Interests." *Personnel Psychology* 58 (2005), pp. 447–78.

9.70 Strong, E.K. "An 18-Year Longitudinal Report on Interests." In *The Strong Vocational Interest Blank: Research and Uses,* ed. W.L. Layton. Minneapolis, MN: University of Minnesota Press, 1960.

9.71 Holland, J.L. *Making Vocational Choices: A Theory of Careers.*

Englewood Cliffs, NJ: Prentice-Hall, 1973; "Providing Holland Code Resources Worldwide." Hollandcodes.com, http://www. hollandcodes.com/holland_occupational_codes.html (March 18, 2007).

9.72 Muchinsky, P.M. "Applications of Holland's Theory in Industrial and Organizational Settings." *Journal of Vocational Behavior* 55 (1999), pp. 127–35.

9.73 Campbell, D.P., and F.H. Borgen. "Holland's Theory and the Development of Interest Inventories." *Journal of Vocational Behavior* 55 (1999), pp. 86–101; Rayman, J., and L. Atanasoff. "Holland's Theory of Career Intervention: The Power of the Hexagon." *Journal of Vocational Behavior* 55 (1999), pp. 114–26.

9.74 McAdams and Pals, "A New Big Five."

9.75 McCrae, R.R., and A. Terracciano, et al. "Personality Profiles of Cultures: Aggregate Personality Traits." *Journal of Personality and Social Psychology* 89 (2005), pp. 407–25.

9.76 Hofstede, G. *Culture's Consequences: International Differences in Work Related Values.* Beverly Hills, CA: Sage, 1980; Kirkman, B.L.; K.B. Lowe; and C.B. Gibson. "A Quarter Century of *Culture's Consequences:* A Review of Empirical Research Incorporating Hofstede's Cultural Values Framework." *Journal of International Business Studies* 37 (2006), pp. 285–320.

9.77 Kirkman, Lowe, and Gibson, "A Quarter Century."

9.78 Black, J.S. "The Relationship of Personal Characteristics with the Adjustment of Japanese Expatriate Managers." *Management International Review* 30 (1990), pp. 119–34.

9.79   Van der Zee, K.I., and J.P. Van Oudenhoven. "The Multicultural Personality Questionnaire: Reliability and Validity of Self- and Other Ratings of Multicultural Effectiveness." *Journal of Research in Personality* 35 (2001), pp. 278–88.

9.80   Van der Zee, K.I., and U. Brinkmann. "Construct Validity Evidence for the Intercultural Readiness Check Against the Multicultural Personality Questionnaire." *International Journal of Selection and Assessment* 12 (2004), pp. 285–90; Van Oudenhoven, J.P., and K.I. Van der Zee. "Predicting Multicultural Effectiveness of International Students: The Multicultural Personality Questionnaire." *International Journal of Intercultural Relations* 26 (2002), pp. 679–94; Van Oudenhoven, J.P.; S. Mol; and K.I. Van der Zee. "Study of the Adjustment of Western Expatriates in Taiwan ROC with the Multicultural Personality Questionnaire." *Asian Journal of Social Psychology* 6 (2003), pp. 159–70.

9.81   Oyserman, D.; H.M. Coon; and M. Kemmelmeier. "Rethinking Individualism and Collectivism: Evaluation of Theoretical Assumptions and Meta-Analyses." *Psychological Bulletin* 128 (2002), pp. 3–72.

9.82   Jackson, C.L.; J.A. Colquitt; M.J. Wesson; and C.P. Zapata-Phelan. "Psychological Collectivism: A Measurement Validation and Linkage to Group Member Performance." *Journal of Applied Psychology* 91 (2006), pp. 884–99.

9.83   Triandis, H.C., and E.M. Suh. "Cultural Influences on Personality." *Annual Review of Psychology* 53 (2002), pp. 133–60.

9.84   Jackson et al., "Psychological Collectivism."

9.85   Cox, T.H.; S.A. Lobel; and P.L. McLeod. "Effects of Ethnic Group Cultural Differences on Cooperative and Competitive Behavior on a Group Task." *Academy of Management Journal* 34 (1991), pp. 827–47; Eby, L.T., and G.H. Dobbins. "Collectivistic Orientation in Teams: An Individual and Group-Level Analysis." *Journal of Organizational Behavior* 18 (1997), pp. 275–95; Ramamoorthy, N., and S.J. Carroll. "Individualism/Collectivism Orientations and Reactions Toward Alternative Human Resource Management Practices." *Human Relations* 51 (1998), pp. 571–88.

9.86   Jackson et al., "Psychological Collectivism."

9.87   Barrick, M.R.; M.K. Mount; and T.A. Judge. "Personality and Performance at the Beginning of the New Millennium: What Do We Know and Where Do We Go Next?" *International Journal of Selection and Assessment* 9 (2001), pp. 9–30; Hough, L.M., and A. Furnham. "Use of Personality Variables in Work Settings." In *Handbook of Psychology,* Vol. 12, eds. W.C. Borman, D.R. Ilgen, and R.J. Klimoski. Hoboken, NJ: Wiley, 2003, pp. 131–69.

9.88   Judge, T. A., and Ilies, R. "Relationship of Personality to Performance Motivation: A Meta-Analysis." *Journal of Applied Psychology,* 87 (2002), pp. 797–807.

9.89   Sackett, P.R.; S. Zedeck; and L. Fogli. "Relations Between Measures of Typical and Maximum Job Performance." *Journal of Applied Psychology* 73 (1988), pp. 482–86.

9.90   Hough and Furnham, "Use of Personality Variables in Work Settings."

9.91   Mount, M. K., and Barrick, M. R. "The Big Five Personality

Dimensions: Implications for Research and Practice in Human Resources Management." In G. R. Ferris, ed. *Research in Personnel and Human Resource Management* (1995), pp. 153–200. Greenwich, CT: JAI Press.

9.92 Salgado, J.F. "The Big Five Personality Dimensions and Counterproductive Behaviors." *International Journal of Selection and Assessment* 10 (2002), pp. 117–25.

9.93 Judge, Heller, and Mount, "Five Factor Model."

9.94 Cullen, M.J., and P. Sackett. "Personality and Counterproductive Work Behavior." In *Personality and Work,* eds. M.A. Barrick and A.M. Ryan. San Francisco: Jossey-Bass, 2003, pp. 150–82.

9.95 Cooper-Hakim, A., and C. Viswesvaran. "The Construct of Work Commitment: Testing an Integrative Framework." *Psychological Bulletin* 131 (2005), pp. 241–59; Mathieu, J.E., and D.M. Zajac. "A Review and Meta-Analysis of the Antecedents, Correlates, and Consequences of Organizational Commitment." *Psychological Bulletin* 108 (1990), pp. 171–94.

9.96 Salgado, "The Big Five Personality Dimensions."

9.97 Cooper-Hakim and Viswesvaran, "The Construct of Work Commitment."

9.98 Grant, S., and J. Langan-Fox. "Personality and Occupational Stressor–Strain Relationships: The Role of the Big Five." *Journal of Occupational Health Psychology* 12 (2007), pp. 20–33.

9.99 Mischel, W. "The Interaction of Person and Situation." In *Personality at the Crossroads: Current Issues in Interactional Psychology,* eds. D. Magnusson and N.S. Endler. Hillsdale, NJ: Erlbaum, 1977,

pp. 333–52; Weiss, H.M., and S. Adler. "Personality and Organizational Behavior." In *Research in Organizational Behavior,* Vol. 6, eds. B.M. Staw and L.L. Cummings. Greenwich, CT: JAI Press, 1984, pp. 1–50.

9.100 Barrick, M.R., and M.K. Mount. "Autonomy as a Moderator of the Relationship Between the Big Five Personality Dimensions and Job Performance." *Journal of Applied Psychology* 78 (1993), pp. 111–18.

9.101 Tett, R.P., and D.D. Burnett. "A Personality Trait-Based Interactionist Model of Job Performance." *Journal of Applied Psychology* 88 (2003), pp. 500–17.

9.102 Buckingham, M., and C. Coffman. *First, Break All the Rules.* New York: Pocket Books, 1999.

9.103 Barrick, M.R.; G.K. Patton; and S.N. Haugland. "Accuracy of Interviewer Judgments of Job Applicant Personality Traits." *Personnel Psychology* 53 (2000), pp. 925–51.

9.104 Piotrowski, C., and T. Armstrong. "Current Recruitment and Selection Practices: A National Survey of *Fortune* 1000 Firms." *North American Journal of Psychology* 8 (2006), pp. 489–96.

9.105 Frauenheim, E. "The (Would-Be) King of HR Software." *Workforce,* August 14, 2006. pp. 34–39; Frauenheim, E. "Unicru Beefs Up Data in Latest Screening Tool." *Workforce,* March 13, 2006, pp. 9–10; Overholt, A. "True or False: You're Hiring the Right People." *Fast Company* 55 (January 2002), p. 110; Dixon, P. "Employment Application Kiosks and Sites. Excerpted from the 2003 Job Search Privacy Study: Job Searching in the Networked Environment: Consumer Privacy Benchmarks." *World Privacy Forum,* November 11, 2003, http://www.

worldprivacyforum.org (February 24, 2006).

9.106 Frauenheim, "The (Would-Be) King."

9.107 Overholt, "True or False."

9.108 Ibid.

9.109 Frauenheim, "Unicru Beefs Up Data."

9.110 Gellar, A. "Hiring by Computer." http://jobboomcc.canoe.ca/News/2004/06/09/1225576-sun.html (February 24, 2006).

9.111 Overholt, "True or False."

9.112 Dixon, "Employment Application Kiosks and Sites."

9.113 Frauenheim, "The (Would-Be) King."

9.114 Sackett, P.R., and M.M. Harris. "Honesty Testing for Personnel Selection: A Review and Critique." *Personnel Psychology* 37 (1984), pp. 221–45; Sackett, P.R.; L.R. Burris; and C. Callahan. "Integrity Testing for Personnel Selection: An Update." *Personnel Psychology* 42 (1989), pp. 491–528; Sackett, P.R., and J.E. Wanek. "New Developments in the Use of Measures of Honesty, Integrity, Conscientiousness, Dependability, Trustworthiness, and Reliability for Personnel Selection." *Personnel Psychology* 49 (1996), pp. 787–829; Miner, J.B., and M.H. Capps. *How Honesty Testing Works.* Westport, CT: Quorum Books, 1996.

9.115 Sackett, Burris, Callahan, "Integrity Testing"; Ones, D.S.; C. Viswesvaran, and F.L. Schmidt. "Comprehensive Meta-Analysis of Integrity Test Validities: Findings and Implications for Personnel Selection and Theories of Job Performance." *Journal of Applied Psychology* 78 (1993), pp. 679–703.

9.116 Wanek, J.E.; P.R. Sackett; and D.S. Ones. "Towards an Understanding of Integrity Test Similarities and Differences: An Item-Level Analysis of Seven Tests." *Personnel Psychology* 56 (2003), pp. 873–94; Marcus, B.; S. Hoft; and M. Riediger. "Integrity Tests and the Five-Factor Model of Personality: A Review and Empirical Test of Two Alternative Positions." *International Journal of Selection and Assessment* 14 (2006), pp. 113–30.

9.117 Bernardin, H.J., and D.K. Cooke. "Validity of an Honesty Test in Predicting Theft among Convenience Store Employees." *Academy of Management Journal* 36 (1993), pp. 1097–1108.

9.118 Ones, Viswesvaran, and Schmidt, "A Comprehensive Meta-Analysis."

9.119 Ibid.

9.120 Goffin, R.D., and N.D. Christiansen. "Correcting Personality Tests for Faking: A Review of Popular Personality Tests and an Initial Survey of Researchers." *International Journal of Selection and Assessment* 11 (2003), pp. 340–44.

9.121 Birkeland, S.A.; T.M. Manson; J.L. Kisamore; M.T. Brannick; and M.A. Smith. "A Meta-Analytic Investigation of Job Applicant Faking on Personality Measures." *International Journal of Selection and Assessment* 14 (2006), pp. 317–35; Viswesvaran, C., and D.S. Ones. "Meta-Analysis of Fakability Estimates: Implications for Personality Measurement." *Educational and Psychological Measurement* 59 (1999), pp. 197–210.

9.122 Miner and Capps, *How Honesty Testing Works;*. Cunningham, M.R.; D.T. Wong; and A.P. Barbee. "Self-Presentation Dynamics on Overt Integrity Tests: Experimental Studies of the Reid Report." *Journal of*

Applied Psychology 79 (1994), pp. 643–58; Ones, D.S., and C. Viswesvaran. "The Effects of Social Desirability and Faking on Personality and Integrity Assessment for Personnel Selection." *Human Performance* 11 (1998), pp. 245–69.

9.123 Cortina, J.M.; N.B. Goldstein; S.C. Payne; H.K. Davison; and S.W. Gilliland. "The Incremental Validity of Interview Scores over and above Cognitive Ability and Conscientiousness Scores." *Personnel Psychology* 53 (2000), pp. 325–51.

9.124 Schmidt, F.L., and J.E. Hunter. "Select on Intelligence." In *Blackwell Handbook of Principles of Organizational Behavior,* ed. E.A. Locke. Malden, MA: Blackwell, 2000, pp. 3–14.

9.125 Evans, M. "Jerry Yang: Yahoo CEO: Wow." http://markevanstech .com/2007/06/19/jerry-yang-yahoo-ceo-wow/ (July 1, 2007).

9.126 Schlender, B. "The Customer Is the Decision Maker." Fortune 141, No. 5 (March 6, 2000), pp. 84–86.

9.127 Ibid., p. 84.

9.128 Ibid.

9.129 Ibid.

9.130 Breen, B. "She's Helping Yahoo Act Normal." Fast Company, April 2003, p. 92.

9.131 Yang, J. "Turn On, Type In and Drop Out." Forbes 160 (December 1, 1997), pp. 50–51.

9.132 Ibid.

9.133 Ibid.

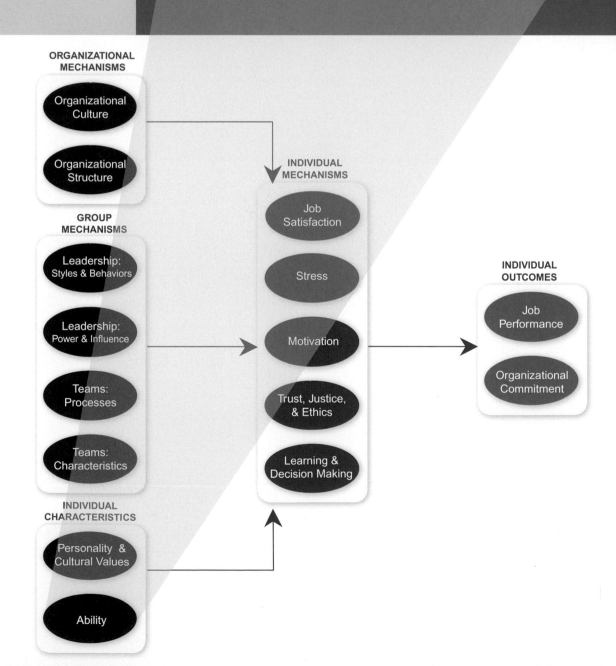

ORGANIZATIONAL MECHANISMS

Organizational Culture

Organizational Structure

GROUP MECHANISMS

Leadership: Styles & Behaviors

Leadership: Power & Influence

Teams: Processes

Teams: Characteristics

INDIVIDUAL CHARACTERISTICS

Personality & Cultural Values

Ability

INDIVIDUAL MECHANISMS

Job Satisfaction

Stress

Motivation

Trust, Justice, & Ethics

Learning & Decision Making

INDIVIDUAL OUTCOMES

Job Performance

Organizational Commitment

Considered one of the best places to work in the United States, Google uses billboards like this one to catch the eye of smart and talented recruits.

 LEARNING GOALS

After reading this chapter, you should be able to answer the following questions:

10.1 What is ability, and where do individual differences in ability come from?

10.2 What are the various types of cognitive ability?

10.3 What are the various types of emotional ability?

10.4 What are the various types of physical ability?

10.5 How does cognitive ability affect job performance and organizational commitment?

10.6 What steps can organizations take to hire people with high levels of cognitive ability?

GOOGLE

How long has it been since you last used Google to do a search on the Internet or navigate the Web? If you've worked on your computer today, chances are it hasn't been more than a few hours. In fact, Google has more than 300 million users across the globe[1] and is by far and away the most popular Internet search engine.[2] With all this popularity has come staggering financial success. Google's revenues increased from $86.4 million in 2001 to $6.14 billion in 2006, when the company had a market value of over $115 billion. To put this in perspective, $115 billion is almost 50 percent higher than the *combined* market value of the "big three" automakers in Detroit.

So how did Google become so wildly successful? Well, for one thing, cofounders Larry Page and Sergey Brin developed and patented an algorithm that made Internet searches much more efficient and user friendly than what was previously available. However, another key factor that has allowed Google to achieve continued success is its strategy of hiring employees who are extremely intelligent. How does Google go about hiring the best and the brightest? The company has used a number of innovative techniques to attract and recruit a huge pool of really smart people. For example, Google placed billboards in Silicon Valley and Harvard Square with the brainteaser, "first 10-digit prime found in consecutive digits of *e*.com." (Confused? See the Takeaways at the end of the chapter for the solution.) People who solved the brainteaser were taken to a Web site with a more difficult brainteaser. Solving that one resulted in Google asking for the person's resume.[3]

As another example, Google developed something called the *Google Labs Aptitude Test* (GLAT for short) and published it in magazines that smart techies might read. The GLAT is similar to the SAT and includes questions such as, "How many different ways can you color an icosahedron with one of three colors on each face?" and "On an infinite, two-dimensional, rectangular lattice of 1-ohm resistors, what is the resistance between two nodes that are a knight's move away?" The GLAT also includes questions for which there are no correct answers per se, but instead require originality. For example, one question asks, "Write a haiku describing methods for predicting search traffic seasonality." Another notes, "This space is intentionally left blank. Please fill it with something that improves upon emptiness."

Google used the GLAT as a public relations tool to attract people who are smart and who are interested in the types of problems in the test. As noted on the Official Google Blog, where the test is available, "We enjoyed writing it, and if you're our kind of uber-geek, you'll enjoy taking it, and maybe you'd enjoy life as a Googler."[4] How effective are practices like these in generating a large pool of potential Googlers? On average, Google hires about 9 people a day from the 150,000 resumes received each month—a very selective ratio.[5] The people who are brought in for an interview typically face 10-person interview panels who ask very difficult questions. For example, someone who applies for a technical job might be asked to solve math algorithms and answer technical questions about software and computer networking.[6] Clearly Google understands the need to hire smart people.[7] It also understands that if Google is not successful in beating out rivals like Yahoo and Microsoft for the best and brightest, odds are the company will go the way of AltaVista and Inktomi, two of the previous leaders in the Internet search business.

ABILITY

The topic of ability is probably already familiar to you. One reason is because "ability" is an everyday word in our language, and we've all developed a pretty good understanding of our own abilities. So if the topic is so familiar to you already, why would we write an entire chapter on it for this textbook? Well for one thing, there are many different types of abilities, some of which are important but might not be as familiar to you. Another reason we included a chapter on abilities is that though it might seem obvious that abilities are highly related to effectiveness in jobs, this relationship is truer in some circumstances than in others. Finally, it may be useful to understand how organizations use information about people's abilities to make good managerial decisions. Our chapter is organized around these three issues.

Ability refers to the relatively stable capabilities people have to perform a particular range of different but related activities.[8] In contrast to skills, which can be improved over time with training and experience, ability is relatively stable. Although abilities can change slowly over time with repeated practice and repetition, the level of a given ability generally limits how much a person can improve, even with the best training in the world. One reason for this stability relates to the "nature vs. nurture" question, an issue that has been much debated in OB (see Chapter 9 on Personality for more discussion of this issue). Are abilities a function of our genes, or are they something we develop as a function of our experiences and surroundings? As our **OB on Screen** feature illustrates, the answer to this question has important individual, organizational, and public policy implications.

As it turns out, abilities are a function of both genes and the environment, and the amount attributable to each source depends somewhat on the nature of the ability. Consider physical abilities for a moment. Although training that involves weightlifting, dancing, and swimming can improve a person's strength, equilibrium, and endurance, there are limits to how much improvement is possible with such training. As an example, you would likely agree that no matter how much he trained, someone like Napoleon Dynamite would have a difficult time earning a contract with a team in the National Football League. From looking at his picture, you might agree that he would likely be unable to compete with people who are more genetically gifted in the types of physical abilities that matter in professional football. As another example, if you've seen the TV show *My Name is Earl,* you are likely familiar with the character Randy, played by Ethan Suplee. Randy is softhearted but somewhat dimwitted, and many of the episodes depict him making silly but costly mistakes in various jobs and then getting fired. Even if he went to the best schools in the world, it would be hard to imagine Randy being especially successful at any sort of job that required much brainpower.

For cognitive abilities, it appears that genes and the environment play roughly equal roles.[9] However, differences in cognitive abilities due to the environment become less apparent as people get older, which may be especially true for the effect of the family environment.[10] As an example, though neglect, abuse, and deprivation may have a negative impact on how children fare on standardized intelligence tests, that negative impact does not tend to carry over into adulthood. Beyond the family situation, what are some other factors in the environment that affect

The character Napoleon Dynamite (played by Jon Heder in the film of the same name) is someone obviously lacking in outstanding physical abilities.

10.1

What is ability, and where do individual differences in ability come from?

OB ON SCREEN

GATTACA

I belonged to a new underclass, no longer determined by social status or the color of your skin. No, we now have discrimination down to a science.

With those words, Vincent (Ethan Hawke) sums up what it's like to live in the not-too-distant future.

Gattaca (Dir. Andrew Niccol, Columbia Pictures, 1997) is a futuristic film that illustrates a society in which genetic information is used to sort people into different social classes. The film depicts the upper class, or "valids," as comprising people who were genetically engineered to be attractive, healthy, and superior with respect to their physical and cognitive abilities. The lower class in the film consists of the "invalids," or people who were conceived the old-fashioned way. People in this class are more susceptible to diseases and generally have inferior physical and cognitive abilities.

There are several aspects of the film that illustrate concepts related to abilities. First and most obviously, the film clearly depicts abilities as being attributable, at least in part, to genes. Immediately following his birth, Vincent was given a DNA test that revealed to his parents that he would suffer from nearsightedness and a congenital heart defect that would not only make him physically weak but would also limit his life expectancy to 30 years. In contrast, Vincent's brother Anton was genetically engineered, and as a result of this process, he was healthy and physically strong.

Second, the film illustrates the idea that abilities play an important role in determining the potential to be effective in job settings and that organizations take abilities into account when selecting people for jobs. Vincent wanted to attend astronaut training at Gattaca Aerospace Corporation; however, admittance was limited to those who possessed superior abilities.

Third, and perhaps most important, the film illustrates that though physical and cognitive abilities may have a strong impact on effectiveness in different tasks and jobs, there are additional factors that play an important role. Early in the film, for example, younger brother Anton easily defeats Vincent in swimming challenges in the ocean. Later however, Vincent relies on his sheer drive to succeed to surpass Anton in these challenges. In fact, Vincent uses that same drive throughout the film to succeed in contexts in which others who possess superior abilities fall short. Vincent's drive may be evidence of important emotional abilities, or it may point to the existence of some important and effective personality traits.

cognitive abilities? First, the quantity of schooling may be important because it provides opportunities for people to develop knowledge and critical thinking skills.[11] Second, there is evidence that our choice of occupations may influence our cognitive abilities. It appears that complex work develops and exercises our minds, which promotes higher performance on intelligence tests.[12] Third, biological factors are known to affect cognitive abilities negatively during childhood. Examples include malnutrition, exposure to toxins such as lead, and prenatal exposure to alcohol.

WHAT DOES IT MEAN FOR AN EMPLOYEE TO BE "ABLE"?

As the examples in the previous paragraph imply, there are different types of ability. Whereas the Napoleon Dynamite example refers to physical ability, the Randy example refers to cognitive ability. In fact, there are many different facets of ability, and they can be grouped into subsets by considering similarities in the nature of the activities involved. As detailed in the sections to follow, abilities can be grouped into three general categories: cognitive, emotional, and physical. Taken together, these abilities capture *what people can do.* That's in contrast to personality (the subject of Chapter 9), which captures *what people are like.* As with personality, organizational personnel and hiring systems focus on finding an applicant whose abilities match the requirements of a given job.

"I'm going to need to speak to someone from either personnel or maintenance."

Source: © The New Yorker Collection 2006 Christopher Weyant from cartoonbank.com. All rights reserved.

COGNITIVE ABILITY

Cognitive abilities are capabilities related to the acquisition and application of knowledge in problem solving.[13] Cognitive abilities are very relevant in the jobs most of you will be involved with—that is, work involving the use of information to make decisions and solve problems. Chances are good that your cognitive abilities have been tested several times throughout your life. For example, almost all children in the United States take standardized tests of intelligence at some point during elementary school. Although you might not remember taking one of these, you probably remember taking the Scholastic Assessment Test (SAT). And though you probably only thought about the SAT as a test that would have a major impact on where you could and could not go to college, the SAT is actually a test of cognitive ability.

You might also remember that the SAT included a variety of different questions; some tested your ability to do math problems, whereas other questions assessed your ability to complete sentences and make analogies. The different types of questions reflect that there are several specific types of cognitive ability that contribute to effectiveness on intellectual tasks. Table 10-1 lists many of these cognitive ability types, along with their specific facets and some jobs in which they are thought to be important.

VERBAL ABILITY. Verbal ability refers to various capabilities associated with understanding and expressing oral and written communication. **Oral comprehension** is the

10.2

What are the various types of cognitive ability?

TABLE 10-1	Types and Facets of Cognitive Ability	
TYPE	**MORE SPECIFIC FACET**	**JOBS WHERE RELEVANT**
Verbal	*Oral* and *Written Comprehension:* Understanding written and spoken words and sentences *Oral* and *Written Expression:* Communicating ideas by speaking or writing so that others can understand	Business executives; police, fire, and ambulance dispatchers; clinical psychologists
Quantitative	*Number Facility:* Performing basic math operations quickly and correctly *Mathematical Reasoning:* Selecting the right method or formula to solve a problem	Treasurers; financial managers; mathematical technicians; statisticians
Reasoning	*Problem Sensitivity:* Understanding when there is a problem or when something may go wrong *Deductive Reasoning:* Applying general rules to specific problems *Inductive Reasoning:* Combining specific information to form general conclusions *Originality:* Developing new ideas	Anesthesiologists; surgeons; business executives; fire inspectors; judges; police detectives; forensic scientists; cartoonists; designers
Spatial	*Spatial Orientation:* Knowing where one is relative to objects in the environment *Visualization:* Imagining how something will look after it has been rearranged	Pilots; drivers; boat captains; photographers; set designers; sketch artists
Perceptual	*Speed and Flexibility of Closure:* Making sense of information and finding patterns *Perceptual Speed:* Comparing information or objects with remembered information or objects	Musicians; fire fighters; police officers; pilots; mail clerks; inspectors

Source: Adapted from E.A. Fleishman, D.P. Costanza, and J. Marshall-Mies, " Abilities," in *An Occupational Information System for the 21st Century: The Development of O*NET,* eds. N.G. Peterson, M.D. Mumford, W.C. Borman, P.R. Jeanneret, and E.A. Fleishman (Washington DC: American Psychological Association, 1999), pp. 175–95.

ability to understand spoken words and sentences, and **written comprehension** is the ability to understand written words and sentences. Although these two aspects of verbal ability would seem highly related—that is, people who have high oral comprehension would tend to have high written comprehensive, and vice versa—it is not difficult to think of people who might be high on one ability but low on the other. As an example, it has been reported that as a result of his dyslexia, Tom Cruise has poor written comprehension and can only learn his lines after listening to them on tape.[14]

Because of his dyslexia, Tom Cruise struggles with written comprehension. He learns the lines for his movies by listening to them on tape.

Two other verbal abilities are **oral expression,** which refers to the ability to communicate ideas by speaking, and **written expression,** which refers to the ability to communicate ideas in writing. Again, though it might seem that these abilities should be highly related, they are not necessarily. You may have taken a class with a professor who has published several well-regarded books and articles but had a very difficult time expressing concepts and theories to students effectively. Although there could be many reasons, one possible explanation is that the professor had high ability in terms of written expression but low ability in terms of oral expression.

Generally speaking, verbal abilities are most important in jobs in which effectiveness depends on understanding and communicating ideas and information to others. The effectiveness of business executives depends on their ability to consider information from reports and other executives and staff, as well as their ability to articulate a vision and strategy that promotes employee understanding. As another example, consider how important the verbal abilities of a 9-1-1 dispatcher might be if a loved one suddenly became ill and stopped breathing one evening.

QUANTITATIVE ABILITY. Quantitative ability refers to two types of mathematical capabilities. The first is **number facility,** which is the capability to do simple math operations (adding, subtracting, multiplying, and dividing). The second is **mathematical reasoning,** which refers to the ability to choose and apply formulas to solve problems that involve numbers. If you think back to the SAT, you can probably remember problems such as the following: "There were two trains 800 miles apart, and they were traveling toward each other on the same track. The first train began traveling at noon and averaged 45 miles per hour. The second train started off two hours later. At what speed did the second train average if the two trains smashed into each other at 10:00 p.m. of the same day"?

Although number facility may be necessary to solve this problem, mathematical reasoning is crucial because the test taker needs to know which formulas to apply. Although most of us wish that problems like this would be limited to test-taking contexts (especially this particular problem), there are countless situations in which quantitative abilities are important. For example, consider the importance of quantitative ability in jobs involving statistics, accounting, and engineering. Quantitative abilities may be important in less complex, lower-level jobs as well. Have you ever been at a fast-food restaurant or convenience store when the cash register wasn't working and the clerk couldn't manage to count out change correctly or quickly? If you have, you witnessed a very good example of low quantitative ability, and perhaps some very annoyed customers.

REASONING ABILITY. Reasoning ability is actually a diverse set of abilities associated with sensing and solving problems using insight, rules, and logic. The first reasoning ability, **problem sensitivity,** is the ability to sense that there's a problem right now or likely to be one in the near future. Anesthesiology is a great example of a job for which problem sensitivity is crucial. Before surgeries, anesthesiologists give drugs to patients so that surgical procedures can take place without the patients experiencing pain. However, during the surgery, patients can have negative reactions to the drugs that might result in the loss of life. So the ability of the anesthesiologist to sense when something is wrong even before the problem is fully apparent can be a life-or-death matter.

The second type of reasoning ability is called **deductive reasoning.** This ability, which refers to the use of general rules to solve problems, is important in any job in which people are presented with a set of facts that need to be applied to make effective decisions. The job of a judge requires deductive reasoning because it centers on making decisions by applying the rules of law to make verdicts. In contrast, **inductive reasoning** refers to the ability to consider several specific pieces of information and then reach a more general conclusion regarding how those pieces are related. Every episode of the CBS show *CSI* is filled with inductive reasoning. Crime scene investigators, like Gil Grissom, are experts at considering things like the blood splatter patterns, bruises, abrasions, DNA, fibers, and fingerprints to reach conclusions about causes of death and possible perpetrators.

Finally, **originality** refers to the ability to develop clever and novel ways to solve problems. Larry Page and Sergey Brin, the two founders of Google, provide good examples of originality. They not only developed the search software that gave Google a competitive advantage, but they also created the first completely new advertising medium in nearly half a century. They also refuse to follow conventional wisdom when it comes to managerial practices and business decisions.[15] Clearly, originality is important in a wide variety of occupations, but in some jobs, originality is the most critical ability. For example, a cartoonist, designer, writer, or advertising executive without originality would find it difficult to be successful.

SPATIAL ABILITY. There are two main types of spatial abilities. The first is called **spatial orientation,** which refers to having a good understanding of where one is relative to other things in the environment. A tourist with high spatial organization would have no trouble finding her way back to her hotel on foot after a long day of sightseeing, even without a map or help from anyone on the street. The second spatial ability is called **visualization,** which is the ability to imagine how separate things will look if they were put together in a particular way. If you're good at imagining how a room would look if it were rearranged, or if your friends are impressed that you can buy things that go together well, chances are that you would score high on visualization.

PERCEPTUAL ABILITY. Perceptual abilities generally refer to being able to perceive, understand, and recall patterns of information. More specifically, **speed and flexibility of closure** refers to being able to pick out a pattern of information quickly in the presence of distracting information, even without all the information present. This ability is easy to understand if you've ever seen the CBS show *Numb3rs.* In the show, Charlie Eppes helps the FBI solve crimes by using his genius to discover patterns in data and information. In the series premiere, for example, Charlie used the metaphor of a sprinkler to describe his unique ability, noting, "Say I couldn't see the sprinkler; from the pattern of the drops, I could calculate its precise location." Related to this ability is **perceptual speed,** which refers to being able to examine and compare numbers, letters, and objects quickly. If you can go into the produce section of a supermarket and choose the best tomatoes faster than the people around you, chances are you have high perceptual speed. Effectiveness in jobs in which people need to proofread documents, sort things, or categorize objects depends a lot on perceptual speed.

GENERAL MENTAL ABILITY. If you've read the preceding sections thoughtfully, you probably thought about where you stand on the different types of cognitive abilities. In doing so, you may have also reached the conclusion that you are higher on some of these abilities and lower on others. Maybe you think of yourself as being smart in verbal abilities but not as smart in quantitative abilities. In fact, most people score more similarly across their cognitive abilities than they realize. People who are high on verbal abilities also tend to be high on reasoning, quantitative, spatial, and perceptual abilities, and people who are low on verbal abilities tend to be low on the other abilities. Although this consistency might not apply to everyone, it applies often enough that researchers have been trying to understand why this occurs for well over 100 years.[16]

The most popular explanation for the similarity in the levels of different cognitive abilities within people is that there is a **general mental ability**—sometimes called *g* or the *g factor*—that underlies or causes all of the more specific cognitive abilities we have discussed so far.[17] To understand what this ability means more clearly, consider the diagram in Figure 10-1 that depicts general mental ability as the area in common across the more specific cognitive abilities that we have discussed. This overlap exists because each of the specific abilities depends somewhat on the brain's ability to process information effectively. So, because some brains are capable of processing information more effectively than others, some people tend to score higher across the specific abilities, whereas others tend to score lower.

You are probably familiar with the intelligence quotient, which is known as IQ. IQ was something originally used in educational contexts to diagnose learning disabilities, and accordingly, tests to measure IQ were developed using questions with which disabled students might struggle. IQ tests were then scaled as a percentage that indicated a person's mental age relative to his or her chronological age. IQ scores lower than 100 were interpreted as indicating a potential learning or educational deficiency, whereas scores higher than 100 were interpreted as indicating that someone was particularly bright for their age. However, it turns out that IQ tests and tests of general mental ability are often quite similar in terms of the types of questions included, and more important, scores on the two types of tests say pretty much the same thing about the people who take them. Does a high IQ boost managerial effectiveness? We'll discuss that later. For now, see our **OB at the Bookstore** feature for a discussion of the types of abilities that some writers believe executives need most.

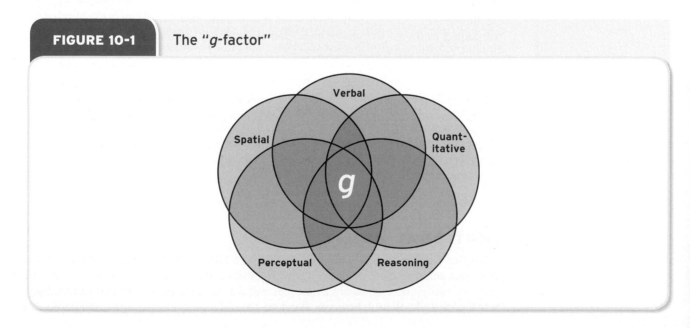

FIGURE 10-1   The "*g*-factor"

OB AT THE BOOKSTORE

EXECUTIVE INTELLIGENCE: WHAT ALL GREAT LEADERS HAVE
by Justin Menkes (New York: Collins, 2005).

Just as one's proficiency in math is in part determined by one's ability to add, sub-tract, multiply, and divide, there are specific cognitive skills that determine a person's success within each of the "subjects" of executive work (p. 55).

What All
Great Leaders Have

EXECUTIVE INTELLIGENCE

JUSTIN MENKES

*"Executive Intelligence is a breakthrough. Packed with
useful concepts and case illustrations, this book shows
what it takes to be a successful leader in any organization."*
—Noel M. Tichy, professor, the Ross School,
University of Michigan, and author of *The Cycle of Leadership*

In his book *Executive Intelligence: What All Great Leaders Have,* Justin Menkes presents a case for the importance of executive intelligence as a key factor that determines whether business leaders succeed or fail. In the first section of the book, Menkes describes and defines executive intelligence as a set of aptitudes that involve accomplishing tasks, working with and through other people, and evaluating oneself and adapting one's behavior to meet the demands of the situation. Menkes emphasizes that effectiveness in these areas requires a special kind of critical thinking, that is, being able to tailor solutions to specific problems by applying the right information and ignoring all the wrong information. In this first section, Menkes illustrates these ideas using vivid examples of executives at companies such as Avon, Boeing, Dell, General Motors, Lucent, and Rubbermaid.

In the second and third sections of the book, Menkes discusses why high executive intelligence is so rare and how executive intelligence differs from cognitive intelligence and personality. In the chapters that constitute these two sections, Menkes clearly outlines his position that though cognitive intelligence and personality may affect an executive's performance, executive intelligence matters more. Although Menkes provides a reasonable case for his position and supports it with some excellent examples, we are not aware of much scientific research that actually compares the relative importance of executive intelligence with characteristics such as general cognitive ability and personality.

In the end, the idea that there is a specific type of intelligence relevant to executives is interesting and intuitively appealing. The book is also chockfull of examples of well-known executives that have demonstrated various levels of executive intelligence. Finally, though the usefulness of executive intelligence needs further scientific evaluation, the framework Menkes offers is somewhat consistent with the scientific research on multiple intelligences.[18]

EMOTIONAL ABILITY

Michael Scott, who is played by Steve Carell on NBC's *The Office,* believes that he's a great boss, multitalented, and super funny. He also believes that he's a people person—he thinks he really understands his employees and that his employees like and respect him. Unbeknownst to Michael, however, he comes across to all but one of his employees as

"I don't have to be smart, because someday I'll just hire lots of smart people to work for me."

insensitive and incompetent to the point of being pathetic. Although entertaining to TV viewers, it shouldn't be too hard to imagine how a lack of self-awareness and an inability to read others' emotions could result in significant problems for bosses and employees. In this section of the chapter, we describe the concept of emotional abilities—precisely the type of ability that Michael Scott appears to lack.

So how are emotional abilities different than cognitive abilities? Most of us know someone who is very smart from a "cognitive ability" or IQ standpoint, but at the same time, the person just can't manage to be effective in real-world situations that involve other people. As an example, you may have played *Trivial Pursuit* with a group of friends and found someone at the table who could not only answer the majority of the questions correctly but also managed to say odd or inappropriate things throughout the game. You may also know someone who doesn't seem very "book smart" but always seems able to get things done and says the right things at the right time. In the context of the same *Trivial Pursuit* game, such a person might have answered most of the game questions incorrectly, but sensing how uncomfortable and angry people were becoming with the annoying player, made jokes to lighten things up.

In fact, for several decades now, researchers have been investigating whether there is a type of ability that influences the degree to which people tend to be effective in social situations, regardless of their level of other cognitive abilities.[19] Although there has been some debate among these researchers,[20] many believe that there is a human ability that affects social functioning, called **emotional intelligence.**[21] Emotional intelligence is defined in terms of four different but related abilities.[22]

SELF-AWARENESS. The first type of emotional intelligence is **self-awareness,** or the appraisal and expression of emotions in oneself. This facet refers to the ability of an individual to understand the types of emotions he or she is experiencing, the willingness to acknowledge them, and the capability to express them naturally.[23] As an example, someone who is low in this aspect of emotional intelligence might not admit to himself or show anyone else that he is feeling somewhat anxious during the first few days of a new job. These types of emotions are perfectly natural in this job context, and ignoring them might increase the stress of the situation. Ignoring those emotions might also send the wrong signal to new colleagues, who might wonder, "Why isn't the new hire more excited about his new job?"

OTHER AWARENESS. The second facet of emotional intelligence is called **other awareness,** or the appraisal and recognition of emotion in others.[24] As the name of this facet implies, it refers to a person's ability to recognize and understand the emotions that other people are feeling. People who are high in this aspect of emotional intelligence are not

10.3

What are the various types of emotional ability?

"Other awareness" is one aspect of emotional intelligence that allows us to empathize with others and understand their feelings.

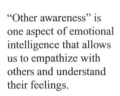

only sensitive to the feelings of others but also can anticipate the emotions that people will experience in different situations. In contrast, people who are low in this aspect of emotional intelligence do not effectively sense the emotions that others are experiencing, and if the emotions are negative, this inability could result in the person doing something that worsens the situation. As a specific example, have you ever had a professor who could not sense that students in class did not understand the material being presented in a lecture? When that professor continued to press on with the overheads, oblivious to the fact that the students were becoming even more confused, it was poor other awareness in action.

EMOTION REGULATION. The third facet of emotional intelligence, **emotion regulation,** refers to being able to recover quickly from emotional experiences.[25] As an example of this aspect of emotional intelligence, consider the possible responses of someone who is listening to NPR while driving his brand new Saturn to work and is cut off by an aggressive driver who, as she passes by, throws a beer can and shouts an obscenity. If this person is able to regulate his emotions effectively, he would be able to recover quickly from the initial anger and shock of the encounter. He would be able to get back to whatever he was listening to on the radio, and by the time he got to work, the incident would likely be all but forgotten. However, if this person was not able to regulate his emotions effectively, he might lose his temper, tailgate the aggressive driver, and then ram into her rusted-out 1968 Ford pickup at the next stoplight. We hope it is obvious to you that the former response is much more appropriate than the latter, which could prove quite costly to the individual. Although this example highlights the importance of regulating negative emotions, we should also point out that this aspect of emotional intelligence applies to positive emotions. Consider the response of someone who is told that she is about to receive a significant pay raise. If this person is unable to regulate her own emotions effectively, she might feel joyous and giddy the rest of the day and, as a consequence, not be able to accomplish any more work.

USE OF EMOTIONS. The fourth aspect of emotional intelligence is the **use of emotions.**[26] This capability reflects the degree to which people can harness emotions and employ them to improve their chances of being successful in whatever they are seeking to do. To understand this facet of emotional intelligence, consider a writer who is struggling to finish a book but is under a serious time crunch because of the contract with the publisher. If the writer was high in this aspect of emotional intelligence, she would likely psych herself up for the challenge and encourage herself to work hard through any bouts of writer's block. In contrast, if the writer is low in this aspect of emotional intelligence, she might begin to doubt her competence as a writer and think about different things she could do with her life. Because these behaviors will slow progress on the book even further, the number and intensity of self-defeating thoughts might increase, and ultimately, the writer might withdraw from the task entirely.

APPLYING EMOTIONAL INTELLIGENCE. Although you may appreciate how emotional intelligence can be relevant to effectiveness in a variety of interpersonal situations, you might be wondering whether knowledge of emotional intelligence can be useful to managers in their quest to make their organizations more effective. It turns out there is growing evidence that the answer to this questions is "yes."[27] In fact, the U.S. Air Force studied recruiters and found that those recruiters who were high in some aspects of emotional intelligence were three times more likely to meet recruiting quotas than recruiters who scored lower in the same aspects of emotional intelligence.[28] Recruiters with high emotional intelligence were more effective because they projected positive emotions and could quickly sense and appropriately respond to recruits' concerns. Because these capabilities made recruiting easier, there was less pressure to meet performance quotas, which translated into fewer hours at the office, higher satisfaction, and ultimately higher retention. In fact, after the Air Force began requiring new recruiters to pass an emotional intelligence test, turnover among new recruiters dropped from 25 percent to 2 percent. Given that, on average, it costs about $30,000 to train a new recruiter, this lower turnover translated into about $2.75 million in savings a year.

As a second example, in the early 1990s, executives at IDS Life Insurance, a subsidiary of American Express, began experimenting with emotional intelligence training to increase the sales performance of their financial service advisors.[29] The executives believed that the most effective advisors had high emotional intelligence—they could easily put themselves in the shoes of prospective clients to build solid client–advisor relationships, they could better motivate themselves to sell insurance, and they could effectively manage their emotions in the face of all the disappointment that comes with trying to make sales. Apparently the IDS executives were correct, because in one early assessment of the training program involving only a small number of advisors, the increase in revenues attributable to the training amounted to tens of millions of dollars. To date, thousands of financial service advisors and other personnel at IDS and American Express have taken courses in emotional intelligence that range from a few hours to several days.

Although the two previous examples illustrate the usefulness of staffing and training practices based on emotional intelligence, there is some evidence that emotional intelligence may have a significantly stronger impact on the job performance of some people rather than others. One recent study, for example, found that emotional intelligence is a more important determinant of job performance for people with lower levels of cognitive intelligence.[30] The explanation for this relationship is easy to understand if you consider that, in many circumstances, high emotional intelligence can compensate somewhat for low cognitive intelligence. In other words, exceptional "people smarts" can, to some extent, make up for deficiencies in "book smarts." Finally, as the **OB Internationally** insert box discusses, emotional intelligence is the foundation for cultural intelligence, a type of intelligence that enables people to be effective in contexts in which they interact with people from different cultures.[31]

ASSESSING EMOTIONAL INTELLIGENCE. As we discussed previously, cognitive abilities are typically assessed using measures with questions such as those included in SAT or IQ tests. So how is emotional intelligence assessed? One type of emotional intelligence assessment is similar to a SAT-style test, because questions are scored as correct or incorrect. As the example items in Figure 10-2 illustrate, test takers are asked to describe the emotions of people depicted in pictures, predict emotional responses to different situations, and identify appropriate and inappropriate emotional responses. After a person takes the test, it is sent back to the test publisher to be scored.

Another type of assessment asks people about their behaviors and preferences, thought to reflect emotional intelligence. One of the first tests of this type, the "Emotional Quotient Inventory (EQ-i),"[35] includes 133 such questions. Although the EQ-i has been used by many organizations in an attempt to improve managerial practices and organizational effectiveness, it has been criticized for measuring personality traits more than actual abilities.[36] More recently, a group of researchers published a very short and easy-to-score measure specifically designed to assess each of the four facets of emotional intelligence described

OB INTERNATIONALLY

Employees in today's organizations need to work effectively with individuals from different cultures, and there are three reasons why. First, the U.S. workforce is becoming increasingly diverse with respect to cultural backgrounds, and as a result, most people in organizations work with others whose culture is different than theirs. Second, many organizations use teams that are intentionally composed of individuals from different cultures to accomplish work or make decisions that leverage knowledge and perspectives from different cultures. Third, most large organizations send employees on international assignments to carry out work or conduct business. With these three trends in mind, the key question for a student of OB must be: What makes some people more or less effective in culturally diverse contexts? According to some, the answer to this question turns out to be cultural intelligence, a type of ability closely related to emotional intelligence.[32]

Cultural intelligence refers to the ability to discern differences among people that are due to culture and understand what these differences mean in terms of the way people tend to think and behave in different situations. There are three sources of cultural intelligence that correspond to the "head," "body," and "heart."[33] The source of cultural intelligence that corresponds to the head is called *cognitive cultural intelligence.* This concept refers to the ability to sense differences among people due to culture and use this knowledge in planning how to interact with others in anticipation of a cross-cultural encounter. The source of cultural intelligence that corresponds to the body is called *physical cultural intelligence,* which refers to the ability to adapt one's behavior when a cultural encounter requires it. Finally, the source of cultural intelligence that corresponds to the heart is called *emotional cultural intelligence.* This concept refers to the level of effort and persistence an individual exerts when trying to understand and adapt to new cultures.

An understanding of the concept of cultural intelligence may be quite useful because it is an ability that can be improved through training experiences.[34] Although such training could take many forms, many programs would begin with an assessment of individual trainees with respect to the sources of cultural intelligence to identify which areas are particularly weak. Consider, for example, an individual who was very knowledgeable about the customs and norms of another culture and was very willing to learn more but who just could not alter her body language and eye contact so that it was appropriate for the other culture. In this particular case, the aim of the training would be to improve physical cultural intelligence. The individual might be asked to study video that contrasts correct and incorrect body language and eye contact. The individual might also be asked to engage in role playing exercises to model the appropriate behavior and receive feedback from an expert. Finally, the individual might be asked to take acting classes. Although such training may seem to be quite involved and expensive, the costs of poor performance in cross-cultural contexts can be devastating for both the employee and the organization.

in this section.[37] Although this assessment is similar in format to the EQ-i, the items do not appear to overlap as much with aspects of personality. You can take the test yourself in our **OB Assessments** feature to see where you stand in terms of emotional intelligence.

PHYSICAL ABILITIES

Physical abilities are likely very familiar to you because many of you took physical education classes early in your school career. Maybe you were evaluated on whether you could climb a rope to the ceiling of a gymnasium, run around a track several times, or kick a ball

FIGURE 10-2   Sample Items from the Mayer-Salovey-Caruso Emotional Intelligence Test

1. **Indicate how much of each emotion is expressed by this face:**

	None				Very Much
a) Happiness	1	2	3	4	5
b) Anger	1	2	3	4	5
c) Fear	1	2	3	4	5
d) Excitement	1	2	3	4	5
e) Surprise	1	2	3	4	5

2. **What mood(s) might be helpful to feel when meeting in-laws for the very first time?**

	Not Useful				Useful
a) Slight Tension	1	2	3	4	5
b) Surprise	1	2	3	4	5
c) Joy	1	2	3	4	5

3. **Tom felt anxious, and became a bit stressed when he thought about all the work he needed to do. When his supervisor brought him an additional project, he felt _____. (Select the best choice.)**

   a) Overwhelmed
   b) Depressed
   c) Ashamed
   d) Self-conscious
   e) Jittery

4. **Debbie just came back from vacation. She was feeling peaceful and content. How well would each action preserve her mood?**

   Action 1: She started to make a list of things at home that she needed to do.
        Very Ineffective   1........2........3........4........5   Very Effective
   Action 2: She began thinking about where and when she would go on her next vacation.
        Very Ineffective   1........2........3........4........5   Very Effective
   Action 3: She decided it was best to ignore the feeling since it wouldn't last anyway.
        Very Ineffective   1........2........3........4........5   Very Effective

Source: Copyright © 2006 J. Mayer, P. Salovey, and D. Caruso. Reprinted with permission.
Note that the photo in item 1 does not appear in the test published by Multi-Health Systems.

OB ASSESSMENTS

EMOTIONAL INTELLIGENCE

How high is your emotional intelligence? This assessment will tell you where you stand on the four facets of emotional intelligence discussed in this chapter—self-awareness, other awareness, emotion regulation, and emotion use. Answer each question using the response scale provided. Remember, there are no right or wrong answers, so for this test to be useful to you, you need to answer honestly. Then follow the instructions below to score yourself.

1	2	3	4	5	6	7
TOTALLY DISAGREE	DISAGREE	SOMEWHAT DISAGREE	NEUTRAL	SOMEWHAT AGREE	AGREE	TOTALLY AGREE

1. I have a good sense of why I have certain feelings most of the time. _____

2. I have a good understanding of my own emotions. _____

3. I really understand what I feel. _____

4. I always know whether or not I am happy. _____

5. I am a good observer of others' emotions. _____

6. I always know my friends' emotions from their behavior. _____

7. I am sensitive to the feelings and emotions of others. _____

8. I have a good understanding of the emotions of people around me. _____

9. I always set goals for myself and then try my best to achieve them. _____

10. I always tell myself I am a competent person. _____

11. I am a self-motivating person. _____

12. I would always encourage myself to try my best. _____

13. I am able to control my temper so that I can handle difficulties rationally. _____

14. I am quite capable of controlling my own emotions. _____

15. I can always calm down quickly when I am very angry. _____

16. I have good control over my own emotions. _____

SCORING AND INTERPRETATION:

Self-Awareness: Sum up items 1–4.

Other Awareness: Sum up items 5–8.

Emotion Use: Sum up items 9–12.

Emotion Regulation: Sum up items 13–16.

If you scored 19 or above, then you are above average on a particular dimension. If you scored 18 or below, then you are below average on a particular dimension.

Sources: K.S. Law, C.S. Wong, and L.J. Song, "The Construct and Criterion Validity of Emotional Intelligence and its Potential Utility for Management Studies," *Journal of Applied Psychology* 89 (2004), pp. 483–96; C.S. Wong and K.S. Law, "The Effects of Leader and Follower Emotional Intelligence on Performance and Attitude," *The Leadership Quarterly* 13 (2002), pp. 243–74.

to a teammate who was running full stride. Or maybe you've applied for a job and had to take a test that assessed your ability to manipulate and assemble small mechanical parts. As a final example, and the one likely to be most familiar, you've probably been subject to tests that measure the quality of your vision and hearing. Although these examples may not seem to be related, each refers to a different type of physical ability. In this section, we review a few important types of physical abilities, which are illustrated in Table 10-2.[38]

STRENGTH. Although strength generally refers to the degree to which the body is capable of exerting force, there are actually several different types of strength that are important, depending on the job. **Static strength** refers to the ability to lift, push, or pull very heavy objects using the hands, arms, legs, shoulder, or back. Static strength is involved in jobs in which people need to lift objects like boxes, equipment, machine parts, and heavy tools. With **explosive strength,** the person exerts short bursts of energy to move him- or herself or an object. Employees who are required to run, jump, or throw things at work depend on their explosive strength to be effective. The final type of strength, **dynamic strength,** refers to the ability to exert force for a prolonged period of time without becoming overly fatigued and giving out. Dynamic strength is involved in jobs in which the person has to climb ropes or ladders or pull him- or herself up onto platforms. Although jobs requiring physical strength may vary as to which category is important, there are also many jobs that require all three categories. Firefighters, for example, must typically pass grueling tests of strength before being hired. In Dublin, California, one part of the firefighter strength test involves climbing a long flight of stairs under time constraints without touching the rails while wearing a 50-pound vest and carrying another 25 pounds of equipment. Another part of the test involves safely moving a 165-pound dummy out of harm's way.[39]

STAMINA. Stamina refers to the ability of a person's lungs and circulatory system to work efficiently while he or she is engaging in prolonged physical activity. Stamina may be important in jobs that require running, swimming, and climbing. In fact, stamina is involved whenever the nature of the physical activity causes the heart rate to climb and the depth and rate of breathing to increase for prolonged periods of time. As you can imagine, the firefighter test described in the previous paragraph assesses stamina as well as strength.

FLEXIBILITY AND COORDINATION. Generally speaking, flexibility refers to the ability to bend, stretch, twist, or reach. When a job requires extreme ranges of motion— for example, when people need to work in a cramped compartment or an awkward position—the type of flexibility involved is called **extent flexibility.** If you've ever watched a person working inside the trunk of a car installing speakers, you've seen extent flexibility. When a job requires repeated and somewhat quick bends, stretches, twists, or reaches, the type of flexibility involved is called **dynamic flexibility.** To understand what dynamic flexibility involves, picture a house painter on a ladder trying to paint some trim just within reach.

As with flexibility, there are two types of coordination that may be important in some jobs. **Gross body coordination** refers to the ability to synchronize the movements of the body, arms, and legs to do something while the whole body is in motion. In contrast, **gross body equilibrium** involves the ability to maintain the balance of the body in unstable contexts or when the person has to change directions. Jumping rope effectively requires gross body coordination; walking on a balance beam requires gross body equilibrium. Both types of coordination are important in contexts that involve quick movements. However, gross body equilibrium is more important when the work environment is artificially elevated and inherently unstable.

TABLE 10-2	Physical Abilities	
TYPE	**MORE SPECIFIC FACET**	**JOBS WHERE RELEVANT**
Strength	*Static:* Lifting, pushing, pulling heavy objects *Explosive:* Exerting short burst of muscular force to move oneself or objects *Dynamic:* Exerting muscular force repeatedly or continuously	Structural iron and steel workers; tractor trailer and heavy truck drivers; farm workers; firefighters
Stamina	Exerting oneself over a period of time without circulatory system giving out	Athletes; dancers; commercial divers; firefighters
Flexibility & Coordination	*Extent Flexibility:* Degree of bending, stretching, twisting of body, arms, legs *Dynamic Flexibility:* Speed of bending, stretching, twisting of body, arms, legs *Gross Body Coordination:* Coordinating movement of body, arms, and legs in activities that involve all three together *Gross Body Equilibrium:* Ability to regain balance in contexts where balance is upset	Athletes; dancers; riggers; industrial machinery mechanics; choreographers; commercial divers; structural iron and steel workers
Psychomotor	*Fine Manipulative Abilities:* Keeping hand and arm steady while grasping, manipulating, and assembling small objects *Control Movement Abilities:* Making quick, precise adjustments to a machine while operating it *Response Orientation:* Quickly choosing among appropriate alternative movements *Reaction Time:* Quickly responding to signals with body movements	Fabric menders; potters; timing device assemblers; jewelers; construction drillers; agricultural equipment operators; photographers; highway patrol pilots; athletes
Sensory	*Near and Far Vision:* Seeing details of an object up close or at a distance *Night Vision:* Seeing well in low light *Visual Color Discrimination:* Detecting difference in colors and shades *Depth Perception:* Judging relative distances *Hearing Sensitivity:* Hearing difference in sounds that vary in terms of pitch and loudness *Auditory Attention:* Focusing on a source of sound in the presence of other sources *Speech Recognition:* Identifying and understanding speech of others	Electronic testers and inspectors; highway patrol pilots; tractor trailer, truck, and bus drivers; airline pilots; photographers; musicians and composers; industrial machine mechanics; speech pathologists

Source: Adapted from E.A. Fleishman, D.P. Costanza, and J. Marshall-Mies, "Abilities," in *An Occupational Information System for the 21st Century: The Development of O*NET,* eds. N.G. Peterson, M.D. Mumford, W.C. Borman, P.R. Jeanneret, and E.A. Fleishman (Washington DC: American Psychological Association, 1999), pp. 175–95.

PSYCHOMOTOR ABILITIES. There are several different examples of psychomotor abilities, which generally refer to the capacity to manipulate and control objects. **Fine manipulative abilities** refer to the ability to keep the arms and hands steady while using the hands to do precise work, generally on small or delicate objects such as arteries, nerves, gems, and watches. **Control movement abilities** are important in tasks for which people have to make different precise adjustments using machinery to complete the work effectively. Anyone who drills things for a living, whether it be wood, concrete, or teeth, needs this type of ability. The ability to choose the right action quickly in response to several different signals is called **response orientation.** It shouldn't be too difficult to imagine the importance of response orientation for an airline pilot who responds to the flashing lights, buzzers, and verbal information triggered during an in-flight emergency. The final psychomotor ability we describe is called **response time.** This ability reflects how quickly an individual responds to signaling information after it occurs. Returning to the previous example, most of us would feel more secure if our airline pilot had both a fast response orientation and a quick response time. After all, making the right decision may not be useful in this context if the decision is made too late!

SENSORY ABILITIES. Sensory abilities refer to capabilities associated with vision and hearing. Examples of important visual abilities include the ability to see things up close and at a distance (**near and far vision**) or in low light contexts (**night vision**), as well as the ability to perceive colors and judge relative distances between things accurately (**visual color discrimination** and **depth perception**). There are many different jobs that emphasize only one or two of these visual abilities. For example, whereas effectiveness as a watch repairer depends on good near vision, effectiveness as an interior designer depends on visual color discrimination. However, there are other jobs in which effectiveness might depend on almost all categories of visual abilities. A fighter pilot needs near vision to read instruments and checklists, far vision and depth perception to see enemy targets and landmarks, night vision to conduct operations in low light, and visual color discrimination to interpret information from warning lights and computer readouts correctly.

Abilities related to hearing, also referred to as auditory abilities, include the capability to hear and discriminate sounds that vary in terms of loudness and pitch (**hearing sensitivity**), being able to focus on a single sound in the presence of many other sounds (**auditory attention**), and the ability to identify and understand the speech of another person (**speech recognition**). Per-

haps the most obvious jobs for which auditory abilities would be important are musicians and composers (yes, we are going to ignore exceptions like Beethoven, who was deaf at the time he wrote his Ninth Symphony). However, with these jobs, the emphasis would likely be on hearing sensitivity and auditory attention rather than speech recognition (who listens to lyrics these days?). Another job for which auditory abilities might be crucially important is bartending, especially if the bar is crowded and

Marin Alsop is the music director of the Baltimore Symphony, a job in which auditory abilities like the capacity to hear and discriminate different sounds and focus on one among many are critical.

noisy. In this context, a bartender needs auditory attention and speech recognition to be able to isolate and understand the words of a single patron against the backdrop of the loud chatter.

SUMMARY: WHAT DOES IT MEAN FOR AN EMPLOYEE TO BE "ABLE"?

Thus far in the chapter, we have presented you with a fairly detailed description of the domain of human abilities, which are summarized in Figure 10-3. Although the list of abilities included in the figure may seem somewhat daunting, we hope that you can appreciate that this set of abilities describes each and every one of us. Moreover, as we have alluded to throughout the chapter, these abilities play an important role in determining how effective we can be at different tasks and jobs.

| **FIGURE 10-3** | What Does It Mean For An Employee To Be "Able?" |

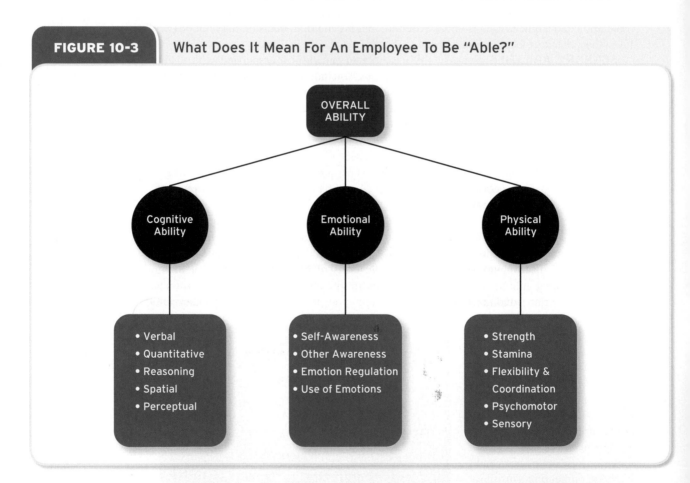

HOW IMPORTANT IS ABILITY?

So, now that you know what ability is and where it comes from, let's turn to the next important question: Does ability really matter? That is, does ability have a significant impact on job performance and organizational commitment—the two primary outcomes in our integrative model of OB? The answer to this question depends on what type of ability you are referring to—cognitive, emotional, or physical. We focus our discussion on cognitive ability because it's the most relevant form of ability across all jobs and is likely to be important in the kinds of positions that students in an OB course will be pursuing. As it turns out, there is a huge body of research linking general cognitive ability to job performance, as summarized in Figure 10-4.[40]

The figure reveals that cognitive ability is a strong predictor of job performance—in particular, the task performance aspect. Across all jobs, smarter employees fulfill the requirements of their job descriptions more effectively than do less smart employees. In fact, of all the variables discussed in this book, none has a stronger correlation with task performance than general cognitive ability. Thousands of organizations, and many that are quite well known, assess cognitive ability in an effort to select the best candidates available for specific jobs.[41] The use of cognitive ability tests for this purpose appears to be reasonable, given that scores on such tests have a strong positive

10.5

How does cognitive ability affect job performance and organizational commitment?

FIGURE 10-4   Effects of General Cognitive Ability on Performance and Commitment

INSIDE OUR INTEGRATIVE MODEL OF OB

Cognitive Ability ⟶ Job Performance

General cognitive ability has a strong positive effect on *Task Performance*. However, the correlation is higher for jobs that are more complex than average and lower for jobs that are less complex than average. The effects of general cognitive ability are near zero for *Citizenship Behavior* and *Counterproductive Behavior*.

Cognitive Ability ⟶ Organizational Commitment

General cognitive ability has no effect on *Affective Commitment*, *Continuance Commitment*, or *Normative Commitment*. Smarter employees are no more, or no less, likely to want to remain members of the organization.

Represents a strong correlation (around .50 in magnitude).

Represents a moderate correlation (around .30 in magnitude).

Represents a weak correlation (around .10 in magnitude).

Sources: J.W. Boudreau, W.R. Boswell, T.A. Judge, and R.D Bretz, "Personality and Cognitive Ability as Predictors of Job Search Among Employed Managers," *Personnel Psychology* 54 (2001), pp. 25–50; S.M. Colarelli, R.A. Dean, and C. Konstans, "Comparative Effects of Personal and Situational Influences on Job Outcomes of New Professionals," *Journal of Applied Psychology* 72 (1987), pp. 558–66; D.N. Dickter, M. Roznowski, and D.A. Harrison, "Temporal Tempering: An Event History Analysis of the Process of Voluntary Turnover," *Journal of Applied Psychology* 81 (1996), pp. 705–16; F.L. Schmidt and J. Hunter, "General Mental Ability in the World of Work: Occupational Attainment and Job Performance," *Journal of Personality and Social Psychology* 86 (2004), pp. 162–73.

correlation with measures of performance across different types of jobs.[42] In fact, as our **OB for Students** feature suggests, this relationship holds even for performance in academic contexts.

OB FOR STUDENTS

We mentioned the Scholastic Assessment Test, or the SAT, several times in this chapter because it's likely to be quite familiar to you. Most colleges and universities in the United States take these scores into account when deciding which students to admit, and you may have studied hard to make sure you got a score that was acceptable to the schools you were interested in. Was it worth it?

As we noted previously, the SAT includes sections that assess verbal and math (quantitative) abilities, and when considered together, the scores indicate general cognitive ability.[43] In fact, the SAT now consists of two parts. The three-hour SAT I is the test we just referred to. The SAT II, which is now used by some schools for admission decisions, consists of one-hour tests (22 in all) that measure knowledge in specific subject areas such as English, history, mathematics, science, and foreign languages.[44] Although the intent of the SAT II was to assess academic achievement rather than cognitive ability, scores on the tests correlate very strongly to performance on the SAT I, and there is not much evidence that the SAT II is much more useful than the SAT I in helping schools make decisions about which students to admit.[45]

But does the SAT really relate to how well someone does in college? Many of you are likely to be skeptical because you probably know someone who did extremely well on the SAT but performed poorly as a college student. Similarly, you probably know someone who didn't do that well on the SAT but who performed well as a college student. As it turns out, the SAT is actually fairly good at predicting college performance. Students with higher SAT scores tend to perform much better in their first year of college, end up with a higher cumulative grade point average, and have a higher likelihood of graduating.[46]

Another question you may have is whether information about the SAT is useful beyond information about high school grade point averages. After all, it's reasonable that a student who was effective in high school would also be effective in college. In fact, research shows that though high school grade point averages predict college performance, SAT scores add significantly to the prediction.[47] Consider for a moment the results from a study that examined the college graduation rate for students with different levels of high school grade point averages and SAT scores.[48] For "A" students in high school, the rate of college graduation was 28 percent for students who scored less than 700 on their SAT and 80 percent for students who scored more than 1300. Interestingly, however, the SAT was not as useful in predicting the graduation rates for students who performed poorly in high school. For C+ students, for example, the rate of college graduation ranged from 17 to 28 percent across the full spectrum of SAT scores.

So what explains why general cognitive ability relates to task performance? People who have higher general cognitive ability tend to be better at *learning and decision making*. They are able to gain more knowledge from their experiences at a faster rate, and as a result, they develop a bigger pool of knowledge regarding how to do their jobs effectively.[49]

There are however three important caveats that we should mention. First, cognitive ability tends to be more strongly correlated with task performance than citizenship behavior or counterproductive behavior.[50] An increased amount of job knowledge helps an employee complete job tasks, but it does not necessarily affect the choice to help a coworker or refrain from breaking an important rule. Second, the positive correlation between cognitive ability and performance is even stronger in jobs that are complex or situations that demand adaptability.[51] Third, people may do poorly on a test of general cognitive ability for reasons other than a lack of cognitive ability. As an example, people who come from economically disadvantaged backgrounds may do poorly on such tests, not because they lack the underlying cognitive ability but because they may not have had the learning opportunities needed to provide the appropriate responses,

In contrast to relationships with job performance, research has not supported a significant linkage between cognitive ability and organizational commitment.[52] On the one hand, we might expect a positive relationship with commitment because people with higher cognitive ability tend to perform more effectively, and therefore, they might feel they fit well with their job. On the other hand, we might expect to see a negative relationship with commitment because people with higher cognitive ability possess more job knowledge, which increases their value on the job market, and in turn the likelihood that they would leave for another job.[53] In the end, knowing how smart an employee is tells us very little about the likelihood that he or she will remain a member of the organization.

APPLICATION: THE WONDERLIC

Given the strong relationship between general cognitive ability and job performance, it isn't surprising that many organizations apply the content of this chapter by using ability tests to hire new employees. One of the most widely used tests is the **Wonderlic Personnel Test,** a 12-minute test of general cognitive ability that consists of 50 questions. It has been in use for several decades now and given to more than 120 million people by thousands of organizations.[54] From the example items that appear in Figure 10-5, you should be able to see how the items correspond with many of the cognitive abilities that we described previously.

People who take the test receive one point for each correct response, and those points are summed to give a total score that can be used as a basis for selecting people for different jobs. The Wonderlic User's Manual offers recommendations for minimum passing scores for different job families, some of which are included in Table 10-3. For example, a score of 17 is the minimum suggested score for unskilled laborer, a score of 21—which is the average for high school graduates, and which corresponds to an IQ of approximately 100—is the minimum suggested score for a firefighter. A score of 28 is the minimum suggested score for upper-level managerial and executive work and is around the average for all college graduates.

You'll hear about the Wonderlic Personnel Test every March and April, because NFL football teams take Wonderlic scores into account when drafting college players. One question that people always debate during this time is whether scores on a test of cognitive ability are relevant to a football player's performance on the field. Although supporters of the Wonderlic's use in the NFL argue that cognitive ability is necessary to remember plays and learn complex offensive and defensive systems, many people wonder how the ability

10.6
What steps can organizations take to hire people with high levels of cognitive ability?

FIGURE 10-5   Sample Wonderlic Questions

1. Which of the following is the earliest date?

    A) Jan. 16, 1898   B) Feb. 21, 1889   C) Feb. 2, 1898   D) Jan. 7, 1898   E) Jan. 30, 1889

2. **LOW** is to **HIGH** as **EASY** is to ___?___ .

    J) **SUCCESSFUL**   K) **PURE**   L) **TALL**   M) **INTERESTING**   N) **DIFFICULT**

3. A featured product from an Internet retailer generated 27, 99, 80, 115 and 213 orders over a 5-hour period. Which graph below best represents this trend?

    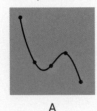   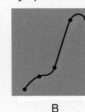         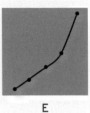

    A   B   C   D   E

4. What is the next number in the series?   29   41   53   65   77   ___?___

    J) 75   K) 88   L) 89   M) 98   N) 99

5. *One word below appears in color. What is the OPPOSITE of that word?*
   She gave a complex answer to the question and we all agreed with her.

    A) long   B) better   C) simple   D) wrong   E) kind

6. Jose's monthly parking fee for April was $150; for May it was $10 more than April; and for June $40 more than May. His average monthly parking fee was ___?___ for these 3 months.

    J) $66   K)$160   L) $166   M) $170   N) $200

7. *If the first two statements are true, is the final statement true?*

    Sandra is responsible for ordering all office supplies.

    Notebooks are office supplies.

    Sandra is responsible for ordering notebooks.

    A) yes   B) no   C) uncertain

8. Which THREE choices are needed to create the figure on the left? Only pieces of the same color may overlap.

    J   K   L   M   N

9. Which THREE of the following words have similar meanings?

    A) observable   B) manifest   C) hypothetical   D) indefinite   E) theoretical

10. Last year, 12 out of 600 employees at a service organization were rewarded for their excellence in customer service, which was ___?___ of the employees.

    J) 1%   K) 2%   L) 3%   M) 4%   N) 6%

Answers:

    1. E,   2. N,   3. D,   4. L,   5. C,   6. M,   7. A,   8. KLM,   9. CDE,   10. K

TABLE 10-3	Suggested Minimum Wonderlic Scores for Various Jobs

JOB	AVERAGE SCORES
Mechanical Engineer	30
Attorney	29
Executive	28
Teacher	27
Nurse	26
Office Manager	25
Advertising Sales	24
Manager/Supervisor	23
Police Officer	22
Firefighter	21
Cashier	20
Hospital Orderly	19
Machine Operator	18
Unskilled Laborer	17
Maid-Matron	16

Source: *Wonderlic Personnel Test and Scholastic Level Exam: User's Manual* (Libertyville, IL: Wonderlic Personnel Test, Inc., 1992), pp. 28–29. Reprinted with permission of Wonderlic, Inc.

to answer questions like those listed in Figure 10-5 relates to a player's ability to complete a pass, run for a touchdown, tackle an opponent, or kick a field goal. Moreover, detractors of the Wonderlic wonder why a poor score should overshadow a record of superior accomplishments on the playing field.

Nevertheless, it appears that teams do take these scores seriously. As an example, after directing his Texas Longhorns to the National Championship over the University of Southern California, quarterback Vince Young was one of the hottest players coming into the 2006 NFL draft. Before the draft, however, reports began circulating that he scored a 6 on the Wonderlic, a score thought to be too low for an NFL quarterback. Sportswriters then began to project that Young would end up being drafted after players with clearly inferior records of accomplishments on the field.[55] Later, Young retook the test and scored a 16. Although the score was considered low for quarterback prospects (which averaged 25.5 in 2005), this score was enough of an improvement for the Tennessee Titans, who drafted him third overall that year. Someone on the Tennessee staff may have recalled that Dan Marino also scored a 16 on the way to his Hall of Fame–worthy career.[56]

TAKEAWAYS

10.1 Ability refers to the relatively stable capabilities of people to perform a particular range of different but related activities. Differences in ability are a function of both genes and the environment.

10.2 Cognitive abilities include verbal ability, quantitative ability, reasoning ability, spatial ability, and perceptual ability. General mental ability, or *g,* underlies all of these more specific cognitive abilities.

10.3 Emotional intelligence includes four specific kinds of emotional skills: self-awareness, other awareness, emotion regulation, and use of emotions.

10.4 Physical abilities include strength, stamina, flexibility and coordination, psychomotor abilities, and sensory abilities.

10.5 General cognitive ability has a strong positive relationship with job performance, due primarily to its effects on task performance. In contrast, general cognitive ability is not related to organizational commitment.

10.6 Many organizations use cognitive ability tests to hire applicants with high levels of general mental ability. One of the most commonly used tests is the Wonderlic Personnel Test.

Looking for the answer to the Google brainteaser? The "*e*" in the question refers to the transcendental number used as the basis for natural logarithms. Here is *e* to 150 decimal places: 2.718281828459045235360287471352662497757247093699959574966967627724076630353547594571382178525166427427466391932003059921817413596629043572900334295260. The first 10-digit prime number in *e*'s decimal string is 7427466391. Going to 7427466391.com used to take potential Googlers to an even more difficult brainteaser.

KEY TERMS

- Ability   *p. 337*
- Cognitive abilities   *p. 339*
- Oral comprehension   *p. 340*
- Written comprehension   *p. 341*
- Oral expression   *p. 341*
- Written expression   *p. 341*
- Number facility   *p. 341*
- Mathematical reasoning   *p. 341*
- Problem sensitivity   *p. 342*
- Deductive reasoning   *p. 342*
- Inductive reasoning   *p. 342*
- Originality   *p. 342*
- Spatial orientation   *p. 342*
- Visualization   *p. 342*
- Speed & flexibility of closure   *p. 342*
- Perceptual speed   *p. 342*
- General mental ability   *p. 343*

- Emotional intelligence   *p. 345*
- Self-awareness   *p. 345*
- Other awareness   *p. 345*
- Emotion regulation   *p. 346*
- Use of emotions   *p. 346*
- Static strength   *p. 351*
- Explosive strength   *p. 351*
- Dynamic strength   *p. 351*
- Stamina   *p. 351*
- Extent flexibility   *p. 351*
- Dynamic flexibility   *p. 351*
- Gross body coordination   *p. 351*
- Gross body equilibrium   *p. 351*
- Fine manipulative abilities   *p. 353*
- Control movement abilities   *p. 353*
- Response orientation   *p. 353*
- Response time   *p. 353*

- Near and far vision   *p. 353*
- Night vision   *p. 353*
- Visual color discrimination *p. 353*
- Depth perception   *p. 353*
- Hearing sensitivity   *p. 353*
- Auditory attention   *p. 353*
- Speech recognition   *p. 353*
- Wonderlic Personnel Test   *p. 357*

DISCUSSION QUESTIONS

10.1 What roles do learning, education, and other experiences play in determining a person's abilities? For which type of ability—cognitive, emotional, or physical—do these factors play the largest role?

10.2 Think of a job that requires very high levels of certain cognitive abilities. Can you think of a way to redesign that job so that people who lack those abilities could still perform the job effectively? Now respond to the same question with regard to emotional and physical abilities.

10.3 Consider your responses to the previous questions. Are cognitive, emotional, and physical abilities different in the degree to which jobs can be redesigned to accommodate people who lack relevant abilities? What are the implications of this difference, if there is one?

10.4 Think of experiences you've had with people who demonstrated unusually high or low levels of emotional intelligence. Then consider how you would rate them in terms of their cognitive abilities. Do you think that emotional intelligence "bleeds over" to affect people's perceptions of cognitive ability?

10.5 What combination of abilities is appropriate for the job of your dreams? Do you possess those abilities? If you fall short on any of these abilities, what could you do to improve?

CASE GOOGLE

Google's strong magnetism has turned the technology company into the Mecca for talented intellects across the world. Talented individuals from academia and respected technology companies are jumping to Google to join its unique culture and flex their intellectual power. The culture at Google encourages top talent to pursue innovative entrepreneurial projects. For example, engineers may work on their own projects for the company one day a week. For this reason, Google has attracted tech gurus such as Rob Pike, one of the creators of the Unix operating system.

In 2006, *BusinessWeek* named Google the thirteenth best place to launch a career. It offers many appeals for smart employees who choose to pursue a career path with the search engine behemoth. Some are attracted to the opportunity to solve enormous, unsolved technical challenges, which could benefit millions of people daily. Others are drawn to the company to get the chance to work with tech gurus who have already revolutionized the industry. Whatever the reason, Google is accumulating the most intelligent human capital in the world.

10.1 Does Google's success rely on its ability to attract and retain the most talented employees? Explain.

10.2 Can a company have too much intellectual human capital? Explain.

Sources: "Google Faces Brain Drain as Anniversaries Hit," April 11, 2007, http://www.redorbit.com/news/technology/898498/google_faces_brain_drain_as_anniversaries_hit/index.html# (June 20, 2007); K. Hafner, "New Incentive for Google Employees: Awards Worth Millions," *The New York Times,* February 1, 2005; "Revenge of the Nerds–Again," *BusinessWeek,* August 8, 2005; "The Best Places to Launch a Career," *BusinessWeek,* September 18, 2006.

EXERCISE   EMOTIONAL INTELLIGENCE

The purpose of this exercise is to help you become more aware of your emotions and the emotions of others, as well as to see how emotions can be regulated and used in your daily life. This exercise uses groups of six participants, so your instructor will either assign you to a group of six or ask you to create your own group of six. The exercise has the following steps:

1. Think about situations in which you've experienced each of the following four emotions:
   - Joy
   - Anxiety
   - Sadness
   - Indignation

2. In writing or in group discussion, answer the following questions about each situation:

   a. What, exactly, triggered your emotion in this situation?
   b. What impact did your emotions have on the outcome of the situation? Consider how your emotions affected you, others, and the general outcome of the situation. (Was it positive or negative?)
   c. What strategies did you use to deal with the emotion?
   d. What other strategies could you have used to deal with the emotion?

   For example, one student noted: "I always get anxious when I take tests. Last week, I was supposed to have a midterm in Accounting, and sure enough, the upcoming test triggered my anxiety. Because I was anxious, I put off studying, and I tried to get some friends to go out to a club with me. We all had a good time that night, but the next day I got a D on my Accounting test, and two of my friends failed their Management midterms. I was using procrastination and avoidance as strategies for dealing with my anxiety. Another strategy I could have used was to face the anxiety head on by talking to my professor to get a better understanding of the material that was going to be on the test, or by getting a group of my friends together to form a study group for Accounting."

3. Compare your responses with the responses of your fellow group members. As a group, answer the following questions:

   a. What emotional triggers do you share? In what ways are your emotional triggers different?

b. Are there some strategies for dealing with emotions that seem especially helpful? Unhelpful?

c. According to the stories told by the group, are there times when emotions actually help get a task done or a goal accomplished? How might you harness your emotions to help you achieve specific outcomes in the future?

Source: Adapted from material in M.A. Brackett and N.A. Katulak, "Emotional Intelligence in the Classroom: Skill-Based Training for Teachers and Students," in *Improving Emotional Intelligence: A Practitioner's Guide,* eds. J. Ciarrochi and J.D. Mayer (New York: Psychology Press/Taylor & Francis, 2006), pp. 1–27.

ENDNOTES

10.1 Ferguson, C.H. "What's Next for Google?" *Technology Review* 108, no. 1 (January 2005), pp. 38–46.

10.2 Elgin, B. "Google's Leap May Slow Rival's Growth." *BusinessWeek* 3943, no. 45 (July 18, 2005). ProQuest database (May 14, 2007).

10.3 "Brain Teasers Help Google Recruit Workers." *CNN.com Technology.* November 4, 2004, www.topcoder.com/pressroom/cnn_110404.pdf (June 2, 2006).

10.4 Eustace, A. "Pencils Down, People." *Google Blog.* September 30, 2004, http://googleblog.blogspot.com/soo4/09/pencils-down-people.html (May 12, 2006).

10.5 Kopytoff, V. "How Google Woos the Best and Brightest." *San Francisco Chronicle,* December 18, 2005, A1. Lexis Nexis Academic database (May 12, 2006).

10.6 Ibid.

10.7 Ibid.

10.8 Fleishman, E.A.; D.P. Costanza; and J. Marshall-Mies. "Abilities." In *An Occupational Information System for the 21st Century: The Development of O*NET,* eds. N.G. Peterson, M.D. Mumford, W.C. Borman, P.R. Jeanneret, and E.A. Fleishman. Washington, DC: American Psychological Association, 1999, pp. 175–95.

10.9 Neisser, U.; G. Boodoo; T.J. Bouchard; A.W. Boykin; N. Brody; S.J. Ceci; D.F. Halpern; J.C. Loehlin; R. Perloff; R.J. Sternberg; and S. Urbina. "Intelligence: Knowns and Unknowns." *American Psychologist* 51 (1996), pp. 77–101.

10.10 McCartney, K.; M.J. Harris; and F. Bernieri. "Growing Up and Growing Apart: A Developmental Meta-Analysis of Twin Studies." *Psychological Bulletin* 107 (1990), pp. 226–37.

10.11 Ceci, S.J. "How Much Does Schooling Influence General Intelligence and its Cognitive Components? A Reassessment of the Evidence." *Developmental Psychology* 27 (1991), pp. 703–22.

10.12 Kohn, M.L., and C. Schooler. "Occupational Experience and Psychological Functioning: An Assessment of Reciprocal Effects." *American Sociological Review* 38 (1973), pp. 97–118; Kohn, M.L., and C. Schooler. *Work and Personality: An Inquiry into the Impact of Social Stratification.* Norwood, NJ: Ablex, 1983; Neisser et al., "Intelligence."

10.13 O*Net Online, http://online.onet-center.org/find/descriptor/browse/Abilities/#cur (June 5, 2006).

10.14 *Disability Fact Sheet Handbook* University of California, Irvine. http://www.disability.uci.edu/

disability_handbook/famous_people. htm (June 9, 2006).

10.15 Vogelstein, F. "Google @ $165: Are These Guys for Real? *Fortune* 150, no. 12 (December 13, 2004), p. 98. ProQuest database (May 14, 2007).

10.16 Carroll, J.B. *Human Cognitive Abilities: A Survey of Factor-Analytic Studies.* New York: Cambridge University Press, 1993; Cattell, R.B. "The Measurement of Adult Intelligence. *Psychological Bulletin* 40 (1943), pp. 153–93; Galton, F. *Inquire into Human Faculty and its Development.* London: Macmillan, 1883; Spearman, C. "General Intelligence, Objectively Determined and Measured." *American Journal of Psychology* 15 (1904), pp. 201–93; Thurstone, L.L. "Primary Mental Abilities." *Psychometric Monographs* (Whole No. 1, 1938); Vernon, P.E. *The Structure of Human Abilities.* London: Methuen, 1950.

10.17 Spearman, "General Intelligence"; Spearman, C. *The Abilities of Man: Their Nature and Measurement.* New York: MacMillan, 1927.

10.18 Gardner, H. *Frames of Mind: The Theory of Multiple Intelligences.* New York: Basic Books, 1983; Sternberg, R.J. *Beyond IQ: A Triarchic Theory of Human Intelligence.* New York: Cambridge University Press, 1985.

10.19 Bar-On, R. *Development of the Bar-On EQ-i: A Measure of Emotional Intelligence and Social Intelligence.* Toronto: Multi-Health Systems, 1997; Gardner, H. *The Shattered Mind.* New York: Knopf, 1975; Goleman, D. *Emotional Intelligence: Why It Can Matter More than IQ.* New York: Bantam Books, 1995; Thorndike, R.K. "Intelligence and Its Uses." *Harper's Magazine* 140 (1920), pp. 227–335.

10.20 Matthews, G.; A.K. Emo; R.D. Roberts; and M. Zeidner. "What Is This Thing Called Emotional Intelligence?" In *A Critique of Emotional Intelligence: What Are the Problems and How Can They Be Fixed?* Ed. K.R. Murphy. Mahwah, NJ: Lawrence Erlbaum Associates, 2006, pp. 3–36.

10.21 Salovey, P., and J.D. Mayer. "Emotional Intelligence." *Imagination, Cognition, and Personality* 9 (1990), pp. 185–211.

10.22 Davies, M.; L. Stankov; and R.D. Roberts. "Emotional Intelligence: In Search of an Elusive Construct." *Journal of Personality and Social Psychology* 75 (1998), pp. 989–1015.

10.23 Davies et al., "Emotional Intelligence"; Law, K.S.; C.S. Wong; and L.J. Song. "The Construct and Criterion Validity of Emotional Intelligence and Its Potential Utility for Management Studies." *Journal of Applied Psychology* 89 (2004), pp. 483–96.

10.24 Ibid.

10.25 Ibid.

10.26 Ibid.

10.27 Cherniss, C. "The Business Case for Emotional Intelligence." *Consortium for Research on Emotional Intelligence in Organizations.* 2004. http:// www.eiconsortium.org/research/ business_case_for_ei.htm (July 7, 2006); Cote, S., and C.T.H. Miners. "Emotional Intelligence, Cognitive Intelligence, and Job Performance." *Administrative Science Quarterly* 51 (2006), pp. 1–28; Fisher, A. "Success Secret: A High Emotional IQ. *Fortune* 138, no. 8 (October 26, 1998), p. 293. ProQuest database (May 14, 2007); Kendell, J. "Can't We All Just Get Along?; 'Emotional Intelligence,' or EI, May Sound like a

Squishy Management Concept—But It Gets Results." *BusinessWeek* 3702 (October 9, 2000), p. F18. ProQuest database (May 14, 2007); Schwartz, T. "How Do You Feel?" *Fast Company* 35 (June 2000), p. 296. http://pf.fastcompany.com/magazine/35/emotion.html (June 28, 2006).

10.28 Cherniss, "The Business Case"; Schwartz, "How Do You Feel?"

10.29 Schwartz, "How Do You Feel?"

10.30 Cote and Miners, "Emotional Intelligence."

10.31 Earley, P.C., and E. Mosakowski. "Cultural Intelligence." *Harvard Business Review* 82 (2004), pp. 139–46.

10.32 Earley, P.C., and S. Ang. *Cultural Intelligence: Individual Interactions across Cultures.* Stanford, CA: Stanford University Press, 2003.

10.33 Earley and Mosakowski, "Cultural Intelligence."

10.34 Ibid.

10.35 Bar-On, *Development of the Bar-On EQ-i.*

10.36 Conte, J.M., and M.A. Dean. Can Emotional Intelligence Be Measured? In *A Critique of Emotional Intelligence: What Are the Problems and How Can They Be Fixed?* Ed. K.R. Murphy. Mahwah, NJ: Lawrence Erlbaum Associates, 2006, pp. 54–81.

10.37 Law et al., "The Construct and Criterion Validity."

10.38 Fleishman, E.A. "Human Abilities and the Acquisition of Skill." In *Acquisition of Skill,* ed. E.A. Bilodeau. New York: Academic Press, 1966, pp. 147–67; Fleishman et al., "Abilities"; Fleishman, E.A., and M.E. Reilly. *Handbook of Human Abilities: Definitions, Measurements, and Job Task Requirements.* Palo Alto, CA:

Consulting Psychologists Press, Inc., 1992.

10.39 Kazmi, S. "Firefighters Put Through Paces in One-Stop Testing." *Knight Ridder Tribune Business News,* August 18, 2005, p. 1. ProQuest database (May 13, 2006).

10.40 Lubinski, D. "Introduction to the Special Section on Cognitive Abilities: 100 years after Spearman's (1904) 'General Intelligence,' 'objectively determined and measured'." *Journal of Personality and Social Psychology* 86 (2004), pp. 96–111.

10.41 Frey, M.C., and D.K. Detterman. "Scholastic Assessment of *g*? The Relationship Between the Scholastic Assessment Test and General Cognitive Ability." *Psychological Science* 15 (2004), pp. 373–78.

10.42 Korbin, J.L.; W.J. Camara; and G.B. Milewski. "The Utility of the SAT I and SAT II for Admissions Decisions in California and the Nation." *The College Board, Research Report No. 2002–6.* New York. College Entrance Examination Board, 2002.

10.43 Ibid.

10.44 Ibid.

10.45 Camara, W.J., and G. Echternacht. "The SAT I and High School Grades: Utility in Predicting Success in College." *The College Board, Research Note RN-10.* New York: The College Entrance Examination Board, July 2000.

10.46 Austin, A.; L. Tsui; and J. Avalos. *Degree Attainment at American Colleges and Universities: Effect of Race, Gender, and Institutional Type.* Washington, DC: American Council on Education, 1996.

10.47 Seligman, D. "Brains in the Office." *Fortune* 135, no. 1 (January 13, 1997), p. 38. ProQuest database (May 14, 2007).

10.48 Schmidt, F.L., and J.E. Hunter. "Select on Intelligence." In *Blackwell Handbook of Principles of Organizational Behavior,* ed. E.A. Locke. Malden, MA: Blackwell Publishers, Inc., 2000, pp. 3–14.

10.49 Hunter, J.E., and F.L. Schmidt. "Intelligence and Job Performance: Economic and Social Implications." *Psychology, Public Policy, and Law* 2 (1996), pp. 447–72; Schmidt, F.L.; J.E. Hunter; A.N. Outerbridge; and S. Goff. "The Joint Relations of Experience and Ability with Job Performance: A Test of Three Hypotheses." *Journal of Applied Psychology* 73 (1988), pp. 46–57.

10.50 Motowidlo, S.J.; W.S. Borman; and M.J. Schmit. "A Theory of Individual Differences in Task and Contextual Performance." *Human Performance* 10 (1997), pp. 71–83.

10.51 LePine, J.A.; J.A. Colquitt; and A. Erez. "Adaptability to Changing Task Contexts: Effects of General Cognitive Ability, Conscientiousness, and Openness to Experience." *Personnel Psychology* 53 (2000), pp. 563–93; Schmidt and Hunter, "Select on Intelligence."

10.52 Boudreau, J.W.; W.R. Boswell; T.A. Judge; and R.D. Bretz. "Personality and Cognitive Ability as Predictors of Job Search among Employed Managers." *Personnel Psychology* 54 (2001), pp. 25–50; Colarelli, S.M.; R.A. Dean; and C. Konstans. "Comparative Effects of Personal and Situational Influences on Job Outcomes of New Professionals." *Journal of Applied Psychology* 72 (1987), pp. 558–66; Dickter, D.N.; M. Roznowski; and D.A. Harrison. "Temporal Tempering: An Event History Analysis of the Process of Voluntary Turnover." *Journal of Applied Psychology* 81 (1996), pp. 705–16.

10.53 Boudreau et al., "Personality and Cognitive Ability."

10.54 Wonderlic Web site, http://www.wonderlic.com/Products/product.asp?prod_id=4 (July 12, 2006).

10.55 Dougherty, P., and J. Wyatt. "Will Wonderlic Cause Teams to Wonder about Young?" *USA Today,* March 1, 2006. http://www.usatoday.com/sports/football/draft/2006-03-01-young-wonderlic_x.htm (July 12, 2006).

10.56 Barra, A. "Do These NFL Scores Count for Anything?" *The Wall Street Journal,* April 25, 2006, p. D-6. ProQuest database (May 14, 2007).

GROUP MECHANISMS

CHAPTER 11:
Teams: Characteristics

CHAPTER 12:
Teams: Processes

CHAPTER 13:
Leadership: Power and Influence

CHAPTER 14:
Leadership: Styles and Behaviors

Teams: Characteristics

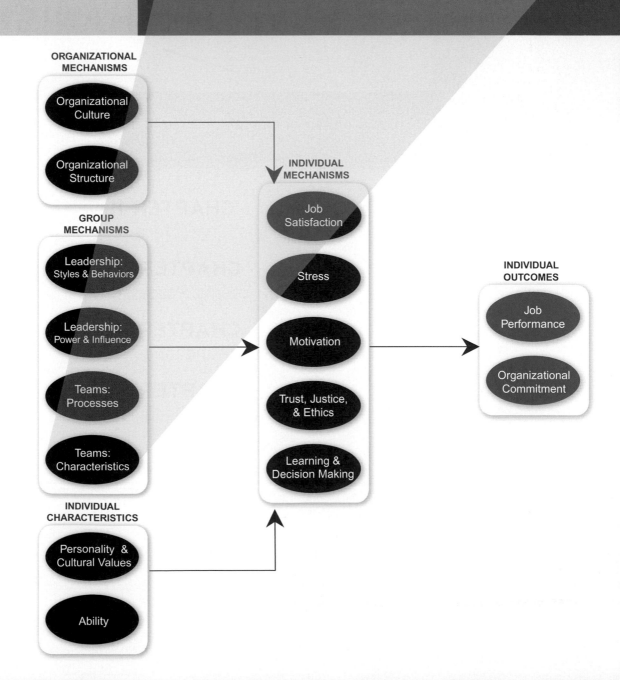

ORGANIZATIONAL MECHANISMS

- Organizational Culture
- Organizational Structure

GROUP MECHANISMS

- Leadership: Styles & Behaviors
- Leadership: Power & Influence
- Teams: Processes
- Teams: Characteristics

INDIVIDUAL CHARACTERISTICS

- Personality & Cultural Values
- Ability

INDIVIDUAL MECHANISMS

- Job Satisfaction
- Stress
- Motivation
- Trust, Justice, & Ethics
- Learning & Decision Making

INDIVIDUAL OUTCOMES

- Job Performance
- Organizational Commitment

Teams are responsible for many elements of Pixar's success, including its production of innovative animation like the hit film *Finding Nemo.*

 LEARNING GOALS

After reading this chapter, you should be able to answer the following questions:

11.1 What is a team, and how are teams different than groups?

11.2 What are the five general team types, how are those team types distinct from one another, and what factors make it difficult to provide an exact team classification?

11.3 What are the three general types of team interdependence?

11.4 What factors are involved in team composition?

11.5 How do team characteristics influence team effectiveness?

11.6 How can team compensation be used to manage team effectiveness?

PIXAR

Chances are you've seen one of the following animated movies over the past decade or so: *Toy Story, Toy Story 2, A Bug's Life, Monster's Inc., Finding Nemo, The Incredibles,* or *Cars.* If you have, you're not alone. These critically acclaimed films, produced by Pixar, were huge hits at the box office. *Finding Nemo,* for example, grossed over $865 million as of late 2006 and stands as one of the ten highest grossing films of all time.[1] All this success led Disney to acquire Pixar for over $7 billion dollars—not a bad price for a 20-year-old company.[2] But how did Pixar achieve so much success in such a short period of time? The most obvious factor is that Pixar developed highly innovative computer graphics and production software for filmmaking, bringing a vibrancy and richness to its movies that had never been seen before.

A less obvious contributor to Pixar's success is that the company is built around talented people who work in highly effective teams. Perhaps the best example is the team at the top of the company: Ed Catmull, John Lasseter, and Steve Jobs.[3] Catmull dreamed up the idea of making computer-animated films and is the member most responsible for the majority of Pixar's technical achievements. Lasseter, originally a Disney animator, is the "artist" of the team. He personally directed Pixar's first three films and is the company's creative force. Finally, there is Steve Jobs. He's the CEO of Pixar and the member most responsible for the business decisions that allowed the company to grow into a multibillion dollar enterprise in less than two decades.

Even apart from its top managers, there are a number of characteristics that make the teams at Pixar effective. For example, Pixar's teams are composed of members with very different sources of expertise and knowledge, who collaborate closely with one another on most aspects of the filmmaking enterprise.[4] For example, artists directly consult with engineers to request new types of visual effects. Engineers communicate ideas for new visual effects directly to producers. This sort of direct communication between people with different functional backgrounds helps the teams cope with the sheer complexity of making animated films. It also helps Pixar's teams produce highly innovative films, which is one key to their box office success.

Another factor that makes Pixar's teams so effective is that the majority of the members have stayed together throughout the company's relatively brief history. This practice stands in stark contrast to the norm in the film industry of assembling a new set of actors, producers, technicians, and support personnel for each new project.[5] Why has keeping the teams together been so effective for Pixar? For one thing, it enabled team members to develop a solid understanding of how other members' knowledge and skills can help them accomplish their own tasks. Moreover, when entering new projects, team members already have a sense of everyone's strengths, weaknesses, and personality quirks. As a result, the team is more capable of avoiding the kinds of misunderstandings that can distract teams from their work.

TEAM CHARACTERISTICS

The topic of teams is likely familiar to almost anyone who might be reading this book. In fact, you've probably had first-hand experience with several different types of teams at different points in your life. As an example, most of you have played a team sport or two (yes, playing kickball in gym class counts). Most of you have also worked in student teams to complete projects or assignments for a course. Or perhaps you've worked closely with a small group of people to accomplish a task that was important to you—planning an event, raising money for a charity, or starting and running a small cash business. Finally, some of you have been members of organizational teams responsible for making a product, providing a service, or generating recommendations for solving company problems.

A **team** consists of two or more people who work interdependently over some time period to accomplish common goals related to some task-oriented purpose.[6] You can think of teams as a subset of the more general term "group," where groups are just a collection of two or more people. Teams differ from groups in two primary respects. First, the interactions within teams revolve around a deeper dependence on one another than the interactions within groups. Second, the interactions within teams occur with a specific task-related purpose in mind. Although the members of a friendship group may engage in small talk, gossip, or in-depth conversations on a frequent basis, the members of a team depend on one another for critical information, materials, and actions that are needed to accomplish their purpose.

11.1

What is a team, and how are teams different than groups?

The use of teams in today's organizations is widespread. National surveys indicate that teams are used in the majority of organizations in the United States, and this is true regardless of whether the organization is large or small.[7] In fact, some researchers suggest that almost all major U.S. companies are currently using teams or planning to implement them and that up to 50 percent of all employees in the United States work in a team as part of their job.[8] Thus, whereas the use of teams was limited to pioneers such as Procter & Gamble in the 1960s, teams are currently used in all types of industries to accomplish all the types of work necessary to make organizations run effectively.[9]

Why have teams become so widespread? The most obvious reason is that the nature of the work needed to be done requires them. As work has become more complex, interaction among multiple team members has become more vital because it allows the team to pool complementary knowledge and skill. As an example, surgical teams consist of individuals who receive specialized training in the activities needed to conduct surgical procedures safely. The team consists of a surgeon who received training for the procedure in question, an anesthesiologist who received training necessary to manage patient pain, and an operating room nurse who was trained on how to provide overall care for the patient. As our **OB at the Bookstore** feature illustrates, teams may be much more effective than individuals in work contexts in which complex decisions need to be made, especially when the teams are designed with certain characteristics in mind.

WHAT CHARACTERISTICS CAN BE USED TO DESCRIBE TEAMS?

This is the first of two chapters on teams. This chapter focuses on team characteristics—the task, unit, and member qualities that can be used to describe teams. Team characteristics provide a means of categorizing and examining teams, which is important because teams come in so many shapes and sizes. Chapter 12 will focus on team processes—the specific actions and behaviors that teams can engage in to achieve synergy. The concepts in that chapter will help explain why some teams are more or less effective than their characteristics would suggest they should be. For now, however, we turn our attention to this question: "What characteristics can be used to describe teams?"

TEAM TYPES

One way to describe teams is to take advantage of existing taxonomies that place teams into various types. One such taxonomy is illustrated in Table 11-1. The table illustrates that there are five general types of teams and that each is associated with a number of defining characteristics.[10] The most notable characteristics include the team's purpose, the length of the team's existence, and the amount of time involvement the team requires of its individual members. The sections to follow review these types of teams in turn.

OB AT THE BOOKSTORE

THE WISDOM OF CROWDS
by James Surowiecki (New York: Doubleday, 2004).

One of the striking things about the wisdom of crowds is that even though its effects are all around us, it's easy to miss, and, even when it's seen, it can be hard to accept. Most of us, whether as voters or investors or consumers or managers, believe that valuable knowledge is concentrated in a very few hands (or rather, in a very few heads) . . . . The argument of this book is that chasing the expert is a mistake, and a costly one at that.

With those words, Surowiecki presents a compelling case that under the right conditions, groups of people (or "crowds") make better decisions than the most knowledgeable person in the group could by him- or herself. Although this might seem straightforward, what is surprising is Suroweicki's claim that it is even true in circumstances in which the group is dominated by people who are not particularly well-informed or rational.

Early in the book, Surowiecki discusses the types of decision-making situations for which groups are particularly well suited, and he provides several interesting examples of methods that have been used to capitalize on group wisdom. As one example, he describes how group wisdom is built into the algorithm that Google uses to find the links that are most relevant to you. Its PageRank system assigns "votes" to Internet pages on the basis of how many people have pages linked to it and weighs the votes on the basis of the importance of the pages that cast the votes. As another example, Surowiecki describes how the Iowa Electronic Market (IEM) is used to predict election outcomes. People who participate in this group buy and sell a sort of stock according to how well they think candidates will do in a given election, and the final price of the stock translates into the odds of winning. The outcome of this process tends to be a much better prediction of election outcomes than major national polls.

Surowiecki notes, however, that for groups to have wisdom, three conditions need to be present. The first condition is that there needs to be diversity. Although he doesn't mention which characteristics the diversity should be based on, he argues that the diversity should lead to a diverse set of solutions. He notes that diversity increases not only the range of alternative solutions but also the probability that members will share their solutions with others. The second condition for wisdom is that the group needs to have independent thinkers who rely on their own data and intuition. This condition makes it more likely that new information enters the group that calls into question the existing wisdom. Finally, there needs to be decentralization, or the empowerment of individual members to make decisions based on their own local knowledge. When enough people make informed decisions, the group becomes a system capable of collective wisdom.

TABLE 11-1	Types of Teams			
TYPE OF TEAM	**PURPOSE AND ACTIVITIES**	**LIFE SPAN**	**MEMBER INVOLVEMENT**	**SPECIFIC EXAMPLES**
Work Team	Produce goods or provide services.	Long	High	Self-managed work team Production team Maintenance team Sales team
Management Team	Integrate activities of subunits across business functions.	Long	Moderate	Top management team
Parallel Team	Provide recommenda-tions and resolve issues.	Varies	Low	Quality circle Advisory council Committee
Project Team	Produce a one-time out-put (product, service, plan, design, etc.).	Varies	Varies	Product design team Research group Planning team
Action Team	Perform complex tasks that vary in duration and take place in highly visible or challenging circumstances.	Varies	Varies	Surgical team Musical group Expedition team Sports team

Sources: S.G. Cohen and D.E. Bailey, "What Makes Teams Work: Group Effectiveness Research from the Shop Floor to the Executive Suite," *Journal of Management* 27 (1997), pp. 239–90; E. Sundstrom, K.P. De Meuse, and D. Futrell, "Work Teams: Applications and Effectiveness." *American Psychologist* 45 (1990), pp. 120–33.

WORK TEAMS. Work teams are designed to be relatively permanent. Their purpose is to produce goods or provide services, and they generally require a full-time commitment from their members. Although all work teams have these defining characteristics, they can vary a great deal across organizations in other important ways. One way that work teams vary is in the degree to which members have autonomy in defining their roles and decision making. In traditional work teams, members have very specific sets of job duties, and their decision making is confined to the activities required by those duties. Members of self-managed work teams, in contrast, are not locked into specific jobs. Instead, they jointly decide how to organize themselves and carry out the team's work.

MANAGEMENT TEAMS. Management teams are similar to work teams in that they are designed to be relatively permanent; however, they are also distinct in a number of important ways. Whereas work teams focus on the accomplishment of core operational-level production and service tasks, management teams participate in managerial-level tasks that affect the entire organization. Specifically, management teams are responsible for coordinating the activities of organizational subunits—typically departments or func-tional areas—to help the organization achieve its long-term goals. Top management teams, for example, consist of senior-level executives who meet to make decisions about the stra-tegic direction of the organization. It may also be worth mentioning that because members of management teams are typically heads of departments, their commitment to the man-agement team is offset somewhat by the responsibilities they have in leading their unit.

 11.2

What are the five general team types, how are those team types distinct from one another, and what factors make it difficult to provide an exact team classification?

PARALLEL TEAMS. Parallel teams are composed of members from various jobs who provide recommendations to managers about important issues that run "parallel" to the organization's production process.[11] Parallel teams require only part-time commitment from members, and they can be permanent or temporary, depending on their aim. Quality circles, for example, consist of individuals who normally perform core production tasks but also meet regularly to identify production-related problems and opportunities for improvement. As an example of a more temporary parallel team, committees often form to deal with unique issues or issues that arise only periodically.

PROJECT TEAMS. Project teams are formed to take on "one-time" tasks that are generally complex and require a lot of input from members with different types of training and expertise.[12] Although project teams only exist as long as it takes to finish a project, some projects are quite complex and can take years to complete. Members of some project teams work full-time, whereas other teams only demand a part-time commitment. A planning team comprised of engineers, architects, designers, and builders, charged with designing a suburban town center, might work together full-time for a year or more. In contrast, the engineers and artists who constitute a design team responsible for creating an electric toothbrush might work together for a month on the project while also serving on other project teams.

ACTION TEAMS. Action teams perform tasks that are normally limited in duration. However, those tasks are quite complex and take place in contexts that are either highly visible to an audience or of a highly challenging nature.[13] Some types of action teams work together for an extended period of time. For example, sports teams remain intact for at least one season, and musical groups like the Rolling Stones may stick together for decades. Other types of action teams stay together only as long as the task takes to complete. Surgical teams and aircraft flight crews may only work together as a unit for a single two-hour surgery or flight.

SUMMARY. Figure 11-1 summarizes the five types of teams. How easy is it to classify teams into one of the types? Well, it turns out that teams often fit into more than one category. Take the teams that produce films at Pixar, for example. On the one hand, because the key members of Pixar's teams have stuck together for each film the company has produced, it might seem like Pixar uses work teams. On the other hand, because the creation of each film can be viewed as a project, and because members are likely involved in multiple

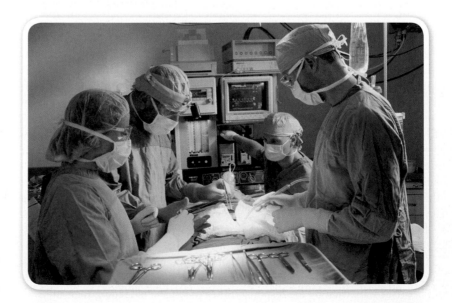

An action team like a surgical team often performs tasks that are complex in execution but of limited duration.

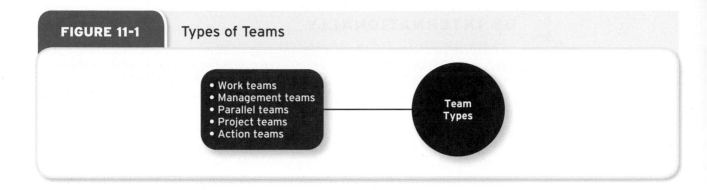

FIGURE 11-1   Types of Teams

- Work teams
- Management teams
- Parallel teams
- Project teams
- Action teams

Team Types

ongoing projects, it might seem reasonable to say that Pixar uses project teams. It's probably most appropriate to say that Pixar teams have characteristics of both work teams and project teams.

VARIATIONS WITHIN TEAM TYPES

Even knowing whether a team is a project team, an action team, or some other type of team doesn't tell you the whole story. Often there are important variations within those categories that are needed to understand a team's functioning. For example, **virtual teams** are teams in which the members are geographically dispersed, and interdependent activity occurs through electronic communications—primarily e-mail, instant messaging, and Web conferencing. Although communications and group networking software is far from perfect, it has advanced to the point that it's possible for teams doing all sorts of work to function virtually. In fact, recent estimates suggest that there are tens of millions of virtual teams operating today. As our **OB Internationally** feature illustrates, virtual teams are not just an efficient way to accomplish work when members are geographically separated. They may also be used to make continuous progress on work tasks without members having to work 24/7.

In addition to varying in their "virtuality," teams of any type can differ in the amount of experience they have working together. One way to understand this point is to consider what occurs in teams at different stages of their development as they progress from a newly formed to a well-established team. According to the most well-known theory of team development, teams go through a progression of four stages shown in the top panel of Figure 11-2.[19] In the first stage, called **forming,** members orient themselves by trying to understand the boundaries in the team. Members try to get a feel for what is expected of them, what types of behaviors are out of bounds, and who's in charge. In the next stage, called **storming,** members remain committed to ideas they bring with them to the team. This initial unwillingness to accommodate others' ideas triggers conflict that negatively affects some interpersonal relationships and harms the team's progress. During the next stage, **norming,** members realize that they need to work together to accomplish team goals, and consequently, they begin to cooperate with one another. Feelings of solidarity develop as members work toward team goals. Over time, norms and expectations develop regarding what different members are responsible for doing. In the final stage of team development, which is called **performing,** members are comfortable working within their roles, and the team makes progress toward goals.

But does this sequence of forming, storming, norming, and performing apply to the development of all types of teams? Chances are that you've had some experience with teams that would lead you to answer this question with a "no." One situation in which this

OB INTERNATIONALLY

Two trends are changing the way work is accomplished in organizations today. First, businesses are increasingly conducting operations on a global basis, and as a consequence, they often employ people who live in countries around the world to perform important aspects of work. Second, communications technology has advanced to the point that it is relatively easy to communicate with groups of people located almost anywhere. Taken together, these trends have resulted in tremendous growth in the number of global virtual teams—teams of globally dispersed individuals who interact primarily through electronic communications.

Although the use of communications technology has reduced physical distance as a barrier to teamwork, differences in time zones remain a significant challenge to global virtual teams.[14] Consider the example of how Logitech developed and manufactured its flagship mouse, the Revolution. Product design and mechanical engineering took place in Ireland, electrical engineering took place in Switzerland, tooling took place in Taiwan, manufacturing took place in China, and software engineering and quality assurance took place in California.[15] Beyond obvious language issues, just imagine how difficult it must be for members of this sort of dispersed team to find convenient times to communicate with one another. If a team member in California needs to meet virtually with the team on Friday at noon (Pacific Standard Time), it would be 8:00 p.m. Friday evening in Ireland and 4:00 a.m. Friday morning in Taiwan.

Although time zone differences have been considered a hindrance to virtual teams, organizations such as IBM, Electronic Data Systems, and Logitech have begun to use them as a means of gaining a competitive advantage. In these organizations, the team's work simply *follows the sun*.[16] That is, work is accomplished continuously because members of a team who are finishing their workday in one country hand off the work to team members in another country who have just arrived at the office. Because hand-offs can occur continuously, product development and other work can be completed much more quickly.

Although "follow the sun" practices are gaining attention in many companies that operate globally, there are some issues that need to be considered.[17] As one example, language and cultural differences can create misunderstandings that prevent work from being accomplished effectively after it has been handed off. Systems that teams use to hand off work therefore need to be detailed and well understood by all team members, and members need to be willing to ask for clarification if they have questions. In addition, there are more general concerns that such "follow the sun" practices will prompt companies like IBM to ship more white collar jobs overseas.[18]

developmental sequence is less applicable is when teams are formed with clear expectations regarding what is expected from the team and its members. With action teams, for example, there are established rules and standard operating procedures that guide team members' behavior and their interactions with one another. As a specific example, an aircraft flight crew does not have to go through the forming, storming, norming, and performing stages to figure out that the pilot flies the plane and the flight attendant serves the beverages.

A second situation in which the development sequence is less applicable may be in certain types of project teams that follow a pattern of development called **punctuated equilibrium**.[20] This sequence appears in the bottom panel of Figure 11-2. At the initial team meeting, members make assumptions and establish a pattern of behavior that lasts for the first half of its life. That pattern of behavior continues to dominate the team's behavior as

FIGURE 11-2 | Two Models of Team Development

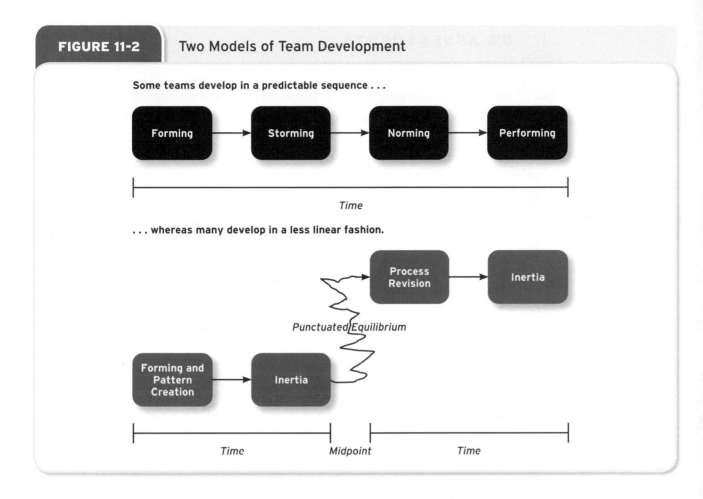

Some teams develop in a predictable sequence...

Forming → Storming → Norming → Performing

Time

...whereas many develop in a less linear fashion.

Forming and Pattern Creation → Inertia

Punctuated Equilibrium

Process Revision → Inertia

Time | Midpoint | Time

it settles into a sort of inertia. At the midway point of the project—and this is true regardless of the length of the project—something remarkable happens. Members realize that they have to change their task paradigm fundamentally to complete it on time. Teams that take this opportunity to plan a new approach during this transition tend to do well, and the new framework dominates their behavior until task completion. However, teams that do not take the opportunity to change their approach tend to persist with their original pattern and may "go down with a sinking ship."

TEAM INTERDEPENDENCE

In addition to taxonomies of team types, we can describe teams by talking about the interdependence that governs connections among team members. In a general sense, you can think of interdependence as the way in which the members of a team are linked to one another. That linkage between members is most often thought of in terms of the interactions that take place as the team accomplishes its work. However, linkages among team members also exist with respect to their goals and rewards. In fact, you can find out where your student project team stands on different aspects of interdependence using our **OB Assessments** feature.

TASK INTERDEPENDENCE. Task interdependence refers the degree to which team members interact with and rely on other team members for the information, materials, and resources needed to accomplish work for the team.[21] As Figure 11-3 illustrates,

11.3

What are the three general types of team interdependence?

OB ASSESSMENTS

INTERDEPENDENCE

How interdependent is your student project team? This assessment is designed to measure three types of interdependence: task interdependence, goal interdependence, and outcome interdependence. Read each of the following questions with a relevant student team in mind. Answer each question using the response scale provided. Then follow the instructions below to score yourself.

1	2	3	4	5	6	7
TOTALLY DISAGREE	DISAGREE	SOMEWHAT DISAGREE	NEUTRAL	SOMEWHAT AGREE	AGREE	TOTALLY AGREE

1. I cannot accomplish my tasks without information or materials from other members of my team. _____
2. Other members of my team depend on me for information or materials needed to perform their tasks. _____
3. Within my team, jobs performed by team members are related to one another. _____
4. My work goals come directly from the goals of my team. _____
5. My work activities on any given day are determined by my team's goals for that day. _____
6. I do very few activities on my job that are not related to the goals of my team. _____
7. Feedback about how well I am doing my job comes primarily from information about how well the entire team is doing. _____
8. Evaluations of my performance are strongly influenced by how well my team performs. _____
9. Many rewards from my work (e.g., pay, grades) are determined in large part by my contributions as a team member. _____

SCORING AND INTERPRETATION

Task Interdependence: Sum up items 1–3. _____
Goal Interdependence: Sum up items 4–6. _____
Outcome Interdependence: Sum up items 7–9. _____

If you scored 14 or above, then you are above average on a particular dimension. If you scored 13 or below, then your team is below average on a particular dimension.

Source: M.A. Campion, E.M. Papper, and G.J. Medsker, "Relations Between Work Team Characteristics and Effectiveness: A Replication and Extension," *Personnel Psychology* 49 (1996), pp. 429–52. Reprinted with permission of Blackwell Publishing.

there are four primary types of task interdependence, and each requires a different degree of interaction and coordination.[22]

The type of task interdependence with the lowest degree of required coordination is **pooled interdependence.**[23] With this type of interdependence, group members complete

FIGURE 11-3	Task Interdependence and Coordination Requirements

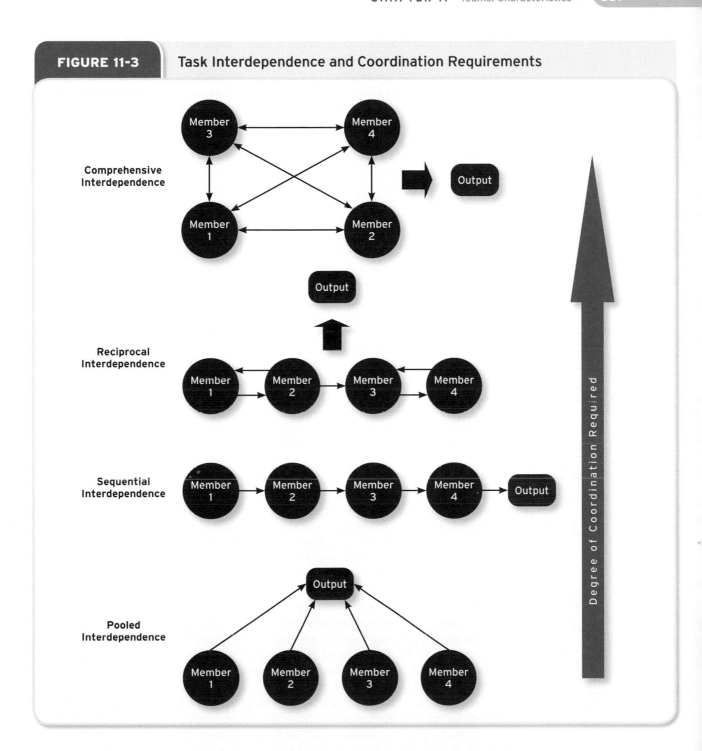

their work assignments independently, and then this work is simply "piled up" to represent the group's output. Consider what pooled interdependence would be like on a fishing boat. Each fisherman would bait his or her own pole, drop the baited line into the water, reel the fish in, remove the fish from the hook, and, finally, throw the fish into a tank filled with ice and other fish. At the end of the day, the boat's production would be the weight of the total fish that were caught.

The next type of task interdependence is called **sequential interdependence.**[24] With this type of interdependence, different tasks are done in a prescribed order, and the group is structured such that the members specialize in these tasks. Although members in groups with sequential interdependence interact to carry out their work, the interaction only occurs between members who perform tasks that are next to each other in the sequence. Moreover, the member performing the task in the latter part of the sequence depends on the member performing the task in the earlier part of the sequence, but not the other way around. The classic assembly line in manufacturing contexts provides an excellent example of this type of interdependence. In this context, an employee attaches a part to the unit being built, and once this is accomplished, the unit moves on to another employee who adds another part. The process typically ends with the unit being inspected and then packaged for shipping.

Reciprocal interdependence is the next type of task interdependence.[25] Similar to sequential interdependence, members are specialized to perform specific tasks. However, instead of a strict sequence of activities, members interact with a subset of other members to complete the team's work. To understand reciprocal interdependence, consider a team of people who are involved in a business that designs custom homes for wealthy clients. After meeting with a client, the salesperson would provide general criteria, structural and aesthetic details, and some rough sketches to an architect who would work up some initial plans and elevations. The architect then would submit the initial plans to the salesperson, who would review the plans with the customer. Typically, the plans need to be revised by the architect several times, and during this process, customers have questions and requests that require the architect to consult with other members of the team. For example, the architect and structural engineer may have to interact to decide where to locate support beams and load-bearing walls. The architect and construction supervisor might also have to meet to discuss revisions to a design feature that turns out to be too costly. As a final example, the salesperson might have to interact with the designers to assist the customer in the selection of additional features, materials, and colors, which would then need to be included in a revision of the plan by the architect.

Finally, **comprehensive interdependence** requires the highest level of interaction and coordination among members as they try to accomplish work.[26] In groups with comprehensive interdependence, each member has a great deal of discretion in terms of what they do and with whom they interact in the course of the collaboration involved in accomplishing the team's work. Teams at IDEO, arguably the world's most successful product design firm, function with comprehensive interdependence. These teams are composed of individuals from very diverse backgrounds, and they meet as a team quite often to share knowledge and ideas to solve problems related to their design projects.[27]

It is important to note that there is no one right way to design teams with respect to task interdependence. However, it is also important to recognize the trade-offs associated with the different types. On the one hand, as the level of task interdependence increases, members must spend increasing amounts of time communicating and coordinating with other members to complete tasks. This type of coordination can result in decreases in productivity, which is the ratio of work completed per the amount of time worked. On the other hand, increases in task interdependence increase the ability of the team to adapt to new situations. The more members interact and communicate with other members, the more likely it is that the team will be able to devise solutions to novel problems it may face.

GOAL INTERDEPENDENCE. In addition to being linked to one another by task activities, members may be linked by their goals.[28] A high degree of **goal interdependence** exists when team members have a shared vision of the team's goal and align their individual goals with that vision as a result.[29] To understand the power of goal interdependence, visualize a row boat with several people on board, each with a paddle.[30] If each person on

Aligning the goals of everyone on the team is a big part of the job of coach. That's what creates goal interdependence.

the boat wants to go to the exact same place on the other side of a lake, they will all row in the same direction, and the boat will arrive at the desired location. If, however, each person believes the boat should go someplace different, each person will row in a different direction, and the boat will have major problems getting anywhere.

So how do you create high levels of goal interdependence? One thing to do would be to ensure that the team has a formalized mission statement that members buy in to. Mission statements can take a variety of forms, but good ones clearly describe what the team is trying to accomplish in a way that creates a sense of commitment and urgency among team members.[31] Mission statements can come directly from the organization or team leaders, but in many circumstances, it makes more sense for teams to go through the process of developing their own mission statements. This process not only helps members better understand what the team needs to do but also increases feelings of ownership toward the mission statement itself. Table 11-2 describes a set of recommended steps that teams can take to develop their own mission statements.[32]

Although you might believe that the mission or goal in some team tasks is very obvious, all too often this isn't the case. In sports teams, for example, you would expect that the obvious goal in the minds of the team members would be to win or defeat the opponent. However, it's often the case that team members have individual goals that are drastically different. Some players might have the goal of impressing fans and thus do things to show off their own skills to the detriment of the team. Other players might have the goal of avoiding injury and thus fail to exert maximum effort in the game. Finally, others might be thinking of future goals—maybe winning a championship or making it to the hall of fame. As a consequence, their minds are not focused completely on the game they're currently playing. The bottom line is that goal interdependence should not be taken for granted even in situations in which the goal seems self-evident.

OUTCOME INTERDEPENDENCE. The final type of interdependence relates to how members are linked to one another in terms of the feedback and outcomes they receive as a consequence of working in the team.[33] A high degree of **outcome interdependence** exists when team members share in the rewards that the team earns, with reward examples including pay, bonuses, formal feedback and recognition, pats on the back, extra time off, and continued team survival. Of course, because team achievement depends on the

TABLE 11-2	The Mission Statement Development Process

STEPS IN MISSION STATEMENT DEVELOPMENT

1. The team should meet in a room where there can be uninterrupted discussion for 1-3 hours.

2. A facilitator should describe the purpose of a mission statement, along with important details that members of the team should consider. Those details may include the products, outcomes, or services that the team is responsible for providing, as well as relevant time constraints.

3. The team should brainstorm to identify potential phrases or elements to include in the mission statement.

4. If the team is large enough, subgroups should be formed to create "first draft" mission statements. Those mission statements should include action verbs and be no more than four sentences.

5. The subgroups should share the first drafts with one another.

6. The team should then try to integrate the best ideas into a single mission statement.

7. The resulting mission statement should be evaluated using the following criteria:
   Clarity—It should focus clearly on a single key purpose.
   Relevance—It should focus on something that is desired by the team members.
   Significance—If achieved, there are benefits that excite the members.
   Believability—It reflects something that members believe they can achieve.
   Urgency—It creates a sense of challenge and commitment.

8. The team should then revise any weak areas of the mission statement. The team should continue to work on the mission statement until there is consensus that it inspires dedication and commitment among members toward a common purpose.

Source: P.S. MacMillan, *The Performance Factor: Unlocking the Secrets of Teamwork* (Nashville, Broadman & Holman Publishers, 2001), pp. 51–53. This material is used by permission of the publisher.

performance of each team member, high outcome interdependence also implies that team members depend on the performance of other team members for the rewards that they receive. In contrast, low outcome interdependence exists in teams in which individual members receive rewards and punishments on the basis of their own performance, without regard to the performance of the team. As we will discuss in the Application section at the end of this chapter, the way a team is designed with respect to outcome interdependence has important implications for the level of cooperation and motivation in the team. See our **OB for Students** feature for more discussion of outcome interdependence.

TEAM COMPOSITION

You probably already agree that team effectiveness hinges on **team composition**—or the mix of people who make up the team. If you've been a member of a particularly effective team, you may have noticed that the team seemed to have the right mix of abilities and personalities. Team members were not only capable of performing their role responsibilities effectively, but they also cooperated and got along fairly well together. In this section, we identify the most important characteristics to consider in team composition,

OB FOR STUDENTS

You probably work in a team in at least some of your courses (if you don't now, you probably will at some point in the future). So, assuming that you want to perform well in your courses and want a satisfying academic experience, you should be interested in knowing whether there are certain characteristics of student teams that make them more effective and satisfying. In fact, a recent research study indicates that student teams should be designed with at least two characteristics in mind.[34]

The first characteristic of effective student teams is rotating leadership responsibilities among members across different assignments. Although you might think that it isn't necessary to assign a formal leader for projects—because students don't have any formal authority over other students—that might be a mistake. By formally assigning leadership responsibilities, the team has someone who can make sure that the team stays on schedule and that important parts of the project don't "slip through the cracks." By rotating leadership responsibilities across projects, members understand that they will at some point have the leader role, and as a consequence, they will be more likely to go out of their way to help whoever the current leader is. As you might imagine, this ultimately helps the team perform better in the long run. In the research study, teams that rotated leadership had members who spoke up more often with ideas and suggestions to help their team. In addition, members of teams with rotated leadership were more cooperative, and those teams wound up scoring higher on course projects.

The second characteristic of effective student teams is using peer evaluations that are tied to grades. When members understand that they will be evaluated by their peers with respect to being cooperative, dependable, and sharing equally in the work, they tend to feel more accountable to one another. As a result, members engage in more frequent positive teamwork behaviors. In fact, the study revealed that the use of peer evaluations that could influence 10 percent of a student's final grade resulted in members who were more cooperative and shared the work more equally. Ultimately, those benefits resulted in higher scores on team projects and members who were more satisfied with their team experience.

and we describe how these elements combine to influence team functioning and effectiveness. As shown in Figure 11-4, five aspects of team composition are crucial: roles, ability, personality, diversity, and size.

MEMBER ROLES. A **role** is defined as the behavior a person is expected to display in a given context. In a team setting, there are a variety of roles that members can take or develop, and depending on the specific situation, the presence or absence of members who possess these roles may have a strong impact on team effectiveness. One obvious way to distinguish roles is to consider the role of the leader and the role of members. In **leader–staff teams,** the leader makes decisions for the team and provides direction and control over members who perform assigned tasks, so this distinction makes sense in that the responsibilities of the leader and the rest of the team are distinct.[35] Typically, however, team members have some latitude with respect to the behaviors they exhibit. In these situations, team roles can be described in terms of the three rather broad categories, which are shown in Table 11-3: team task roles, team building roles, and individualistic roles.[36]

Team task roles refer to behaviors that directly facilitate the accomplishment of team tasks. Examples include the orienter who establishes the direction for the team, the devil's advocate who offers constructive challenges to the team's status quo, and the energizer

11.4

What factors are involved in team composition?

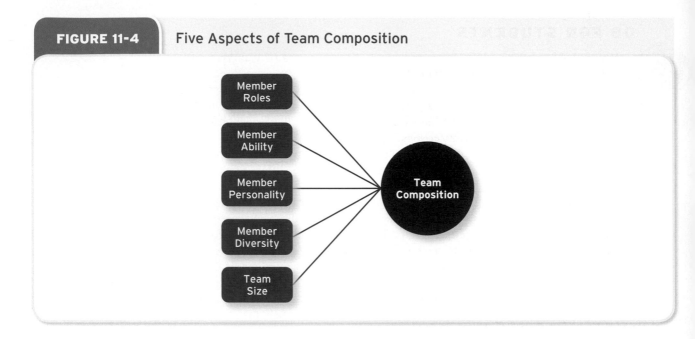

FIGURE 11-4   Five Aspects of Team Composition

who motivates team members to work harder toward team goals. As you may have realized, the importance of specific task-oriented roles depends on the nature of the work in which the team is involved. The orienter role may be particularly important in teams involved in work for which the team has autonomy about how to accomplish the work. The devil's advocate role may be particularly important in team contexts in which decisions are "high stakes" in nature. Finally, the energizer role may be most important in team contexts in which the work is important but not intrinsically motivating.

In contrast to task-oriented roles, **team building roles** refer to behaviors that influence the quality of the team's social climate. Examples of team building roles include the harmonizer who steps in to resolve differences among teammates, the encourager who praises the work of teammates, and the compromiser who helps the team see alternative solutions that teammates can accept. As you might have gathered as you read these examples, the presence of members who take on social roles helps teams manage conflicts that could hinder team effectiveness.

Finally, whereas task roles and team building roles focus on activities that benefit the team, **individualistic roles** reflect behaviors that benefit the individual at the expense of the team. For example, the aggressor "puts down" or deflates fellow teammates. The recognition seeker takes credit for team successes. The dominator manipulates teammates to acquire control and power. If you've ever had an experience in a team in which members took on individualistic roles, you probably realize just how damaging they can be. Having to deal with members who take on individualistic roles is dissatisfying and requires time and effort that would otherwise be used to accomplish productive team tasks.

MEMBER ABILITY. Team members possess a wide variety of abilities (see Chapter 10 on Ability for more discussion of such issues). Depending on the nature of the tasks involved in the team's work, some of these may be important to consider in team design. For example, in teams involved in physical work, relevant physical abilities will be important to take into account. Consider the types of abilities that are required of pit crew members in stock car racing, where margins of victory can be one-tenth of a second. When a car pulls into pit row, pit crew members need to leap over the pit wall and lift heavy tires, jacks, and other

TABLE 11-3 — Team and Individualistic Roles

TEAM TASK ROLES	DESCRIPTION
Initiator-contributor	Proposes new ideas
Coordinator	Tries to coordinate activities among team members
Orienter	Determines the direction of the team's discussion
Devil's advocate	Offers challenges to the team's status quo
Energizer	Motivates the team to strive to do better
Procedural-technician	Performs routine tasks needed to keep progress moving

TEAM BUILDING ROLES	DESCRIPTION
Encourager	Praises the contributions of other team members
Harmonizer	Mediates differences between group members
Compromiser	Attempts to find the halfway point to end conflict
Gatekeeper/expediter	Encourages participation from teammates
Standard setter	Expresses goals for the team to achieve
Follower	Accepts the ideas of teammates

INDIVIDUALISTIC ROLES	DESCRIPTION
Aggressor	Deflates teammates, expresses disapproval with hostility
Blocker	Acts stubbornly resistant and disagrees beyond reason
Recognition seeker	Brags and calls attention to him- or herself
Self-confessor	Discloses personal opinions inappropriately
Slacker	Acts cynically, nonchalantly, or goofs off
Dominator	Manipulates team members for personal control

Source: Adapted from K. Benne and P. Sheats, "Functional Roles of Group Members." *Journal of Social Issues* 4 (1948), pp. 41–49.

equipment to get the race car back on the track—ideally in about 14 seconds. In this setting, flexibility, cardiovascular endurance, and explosive strength are required, and in fact, racing teams have hired professional trainers and even built gyms in efforts to improve these abilities.[37]

It's also important to take cognitive abilities into account when designing teams. General cognitive ability is important to many different types of teams. In general, smarter teams perform better because teamwork tends to be quite complex.[38] Team members not only have to be involved in several different aspects of the team's task, but they also have to learn how best to combine their individual efforts to accomplish team goals.[39] In fact, the more that this type of learning is required, the more important member cognitive ability becomes. For example, research has shown that cognitive ability is much more important to teams when team members have to learn from one another to adapt to unexpected changes, compared with contexts in which team members perform their assigned tasks in a routine fashion.[40]

Of course, not every member needs high levels of these physical or cognitive abilities. If you've ever played Trivial Pursuit using teams, you might recall playing against another team in which only one of the team members was smart enough to answer any of the questions correctly. In fact, in tasks with an objectively verifiable best solution, the member who possesses the highest level of the ability relevant to the task will have the most influence on the effectiveness of the team. These types of tasks are called **disjunctive tasks.**[41] You may also recall situations in which it was crucial that everyone on the team possesses the relevant abilities. Returning to the pit crew example, stock cars cannot leave the pit area until all the tires are mounted, and so the length of the pit stop is determined by the physical abilities of the slowest crew member. Tasks like this, for which the team's performance depends on the abilities of the "weakest link," are called **conjunctive tasks.** Finally, there are **additive tasks,** for which the contributions resulting from the abilities of every member "add up" to determine team performance. The amount of money that a Girl Scout troop earns from selling Thin Mints and Samoas is the sum of what each Girl Scout is able to sell on her own.

MEMBER PERSONALITY. Team members also possess a wide variety of personality traits (see Chapter 9 on Personality and Cultural Values for more discussion of such issues). These personality traits affect how teams function and perform as units. For example, team composition in terms of members' conscientiousness is important to teams.[42] After all, almost any team would benefit from having members who tend to be dependable and work hard to achieve team goals. What might be less obvious to you is the strong negative effect on the team of having even one member who is particularly low on conscientiousness.[43] To understand why this is true, consider how you would react to a team member who was not dependable and did not appear to be motivated to work hard toward team goals. If you're like most people, you would find the situation dissatisfying, and you would consider different ways of dealing with it. Some people might try to motivate the person to be more responsible and work harder; others might try to get the person ejected from the team.[44] The problem is that these natural reactions to a low conscientiousness team member not only divert attention away from accomplishing work responsibilities, but they also can result in some very uncomfortable and time-consuming interpersonal conflicts. Moreover, even if you and the other members of the team work harder to compensate for this person,

A task that can go only as quickly as the slowest team member, like a pit stop in a car race, is a conjunctive task.

it would be difficult for your team to perform as effectively as other teams in which all members are more interpersonally responsible and engaged in the team's work.

The agreeableness of team members is also an important consideration. One recent meta-analysis showed that, in team settings, the overall level of members' agreeableness may be even more important than conscientiousness.[45] Why? Because agreeable people tend to be more cooperative and trusting, tendencies that promote positive attitudes about the team and smooth interpersonal interactions. Moreover, because agreeable people may be more concerned about their team's interests than their own, they should work hard on behalf of the team.[46] There is a caveat regarding agreeableness in teams however. Because agreeable people tend to prefer harmony and cooperation over conflict and competition, they may be less apt to speak up and offer constructive criticisms that might help the team improve.[47] Thus, when composed of highly agreeable members, there is a chance that the team will behave in a way that enhances harmony at the expense of task accomplishment.[48]

People who are extraverted tend to perform more effectively in interpersonal contexts and are more positive and optimistic in general.[49] Therefore, it shouldn't surprise you to hear that having extraverted team members is generally beneficial to the social climate of the group, as well as to team effectiveness in the eyes of supervisors.[50] At the same time, however, research has shown that having too many members who are very high on extraversion can hurt the team. The reason for this can be attributed to extraverts' tendency to be assertive and dominant. As you would expect when there are too many members with these types of tendencies, power struggles and unproductive conflict occur with greater frequency.[51]

MEMBER DIVERSITY. Another aspect of team composition refers to the degree to which members are different from one another in terms of any attribute that might be used by someone as a basis of categorizing people. We refer to those differences as **team diversity**.[52] Trying to understand the effects of team diversity is somewhat difficult because there are so many different characteristics that may be used to categorize people. There are also several reasons diversity might influence team functioning and effectiveness, and some of these reasons seem contradictory.

The predominant theory that has been used to explain why diversity has positive effects is called the **value in diversity problem-solving approach.**[53] From this perspective, diversity in teams is beneficial because it provides for a larger pool of knowledge and perspectives from which a team can draw as it carries out its work. Teams that engage in work that is relatively complex and requires creativity benefit most from diversity, and research on teams that are diverse in terms of many different characteristics related to knowledge and perspectives—ethnicity, expertise, personality, attitudes—supports this idea.[54]

A theory that has been used widely to explain why diversity may have detrimental effects on teams is called the **similarity-attraction approach.**[55] According to this perspective, people tend to be more attracted to others who are perceived as more similar. People also tend to avoid interacting with those who are perceived to be dissimilar to reduce the likelihood of having uncomfortable disagreements. Consistent with this perspective, research has shown that diversity on attributes such as cultural background, race, and attitudes are associated with communication problems and ultimately poor team effectiveness.[56]

So it appears that there are two different theories about diversity effects that are relevant to teams, and each has been supported in research. Which perspective is correct? As it turns out, one key to understanding the impact of team diversity requires that you consider both the general type of diversity and the length of time the team has been in existence.[57] **Surface-level diversity** refers to diversity regarding observable attributes such as race, ethnicity, sex, and age.[58] Although this type of diversity may have a negative impact on teams early in their existence because of similarity-attraction issues, those negative effects tend to disappear as members become more knowledgeable about one another. In essence, the stereotypes that members have about one another based on surface differences are replaced with knowledge regarding underlying characteristics that are more relevant to social and task interactions.[59]

Deep-level diversity, in contrast, refers to diversity with respect to attributes that are less easy to observe initially, but that can be inferred after more direct experience. Differences in attitudes, values, and personality are good examples of deep-level diversity.[60] In contrast to the effects of surface-level diversity, time appears to increase the negative effects of deep-level diversity on team functioning and effectiveness.[61] Over time, as team members learn about one another, differences that relate to underlying values and goals become increasingly apparent. Those differences can therefore create problems among team members that ultimately result in reduced effectiveness.

TEAM SIZE. Two adages are relevant to team size: "the more the merrier" or "too many cooks spoil the pot." Which statement do you believe is true in terms of how many members to include on a team? The answer, according to the results of one recent meta-analysis, is that having a greater number of members is beneficial for management and project teams but not for teams engaged in production tasks.[62] Management and project teams engage in work that is complex and knowledge intensive, and these teams therefore benefit from the additional resources and expertise contributed by additional members.[63] In contrast, production teams tend to engage in routine tasks that are less complex. Having additional members beyond what is necessary to accomplish the work tends to result in unnecessary coordination and communication problems. Additional members may therefore be less productive because there is more socializing and they feel less accountable for team outcomes.[64] Although making a claim about the absolute best team size is impossible, research with undergraduate students concluded that team members tend to be most satisfied with their team when the number of members is between 4 and 5.[65] Of course, there are other rules of thumb you can use to keep teams size optimal. Jeff Bezos, the CEO of Amazon.com, uses the two-pizza rule: "If a team can't be fed by two pizzas, it's too large."[66]

SUMMARY: WHAT CHARACTERISTICS CAN BE USED TO DESCRIBE TEAMS?

The preceding sections illustrate that there are a variety of characteristics that can be used to describe teams. As Figure 11-5 illustrates, teams can be described using taxonomies of

Surface-level diversity can sometimes create issues for teams as they begin their tasks, but such problems usually disappear over time.

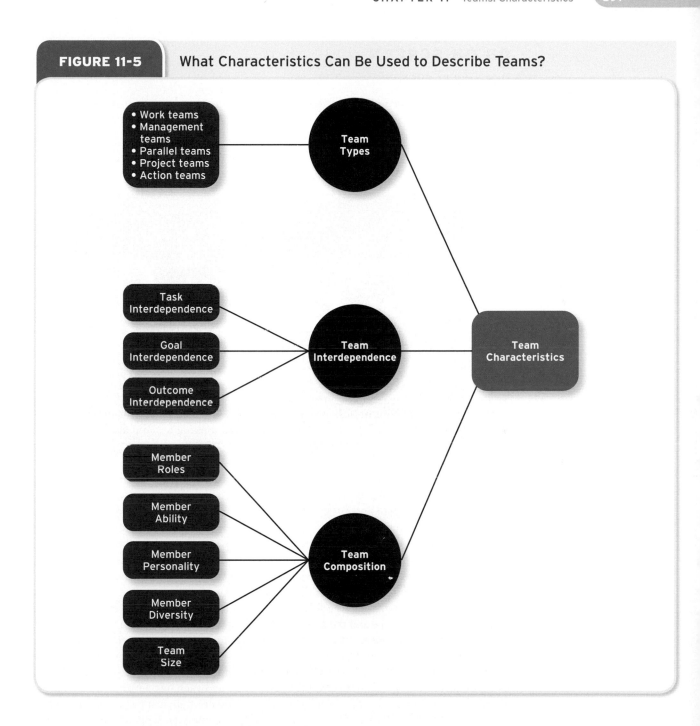

FIGURE 11-5   What Characteristics Can Be Used to Describe Teams?

team types. For example, teams can be described by categorizing them as a work team, a management team, a parallel team, a project team, or an action team. Teams can also be described using the nature of the team's interdependence with regards to the team's task, goals, and outcomes. Finally, teams can be described in terms of their composition. Relevant member characteristics include member roles, member ability, member personality, member diversity, and team size. For an example of all of these characteristics in action, see our **OB on Screen** feature.

OB ON SCREEN

OCEAN'S ELEVEN

Off the top of my head, I'd say you're looking at a Boeski, a Jim Brown, a Miss Daisy, two Jethros, and a Leon Spinks, not to mention the biggest Ella Fitzgerald ever.

With those words, Rusty Ryan (Brad Pitt) tells Danny Ocean (George Clooney) what it's going to take to pull off the biggest heist in the history of Las Vegas in *Ocean's 11* (Dir. Steven Soderbergh, Warner Brothers, 2001).

Ocean's team is composed of 11 members, each of whom possesses a unique skill needed for the heist. For example, the team includes a professional card dealer who takes a job at the casino so he can gain knowledge of the casino's procedures, an electronics expert who sets up surveillance cameras to keep an eye on security personnel, an explosives expert who sets the charges to cause a power outage, and a Chinese acrobat who is able to move around inside the vault without setting off alarms triggered by motion detectors.

Because members interact with a subset of other members during the heist, the team has reciprocal task interdependence. In addition, because each member of the team needs to execute his part of the task perfectly for the team to succeed, the team's task is also conjunctive—one mistake and the heist will fail. Of course, no one on the team wants that. If they fail, they'll be out $150 million and could wind up in jail or tortured, killed, and then tortured again by Terry Benedict (Andy Garcia), the ruthless casino owner. With these strong consequences in mind, Ocean's team has high goal interdependence. Every member understands and is committed to the team's goal, and each has personal goals that are aligned with that objective. Finally, because each member of the team is supposed to share equally in the $150 million take, the team has high outcome interdependence.

How important are those forms of interdependence? Just consider the consequences of poor alignment among the different types of interdependence. What do you think would happen if someone on the team held a different goal during the heist (e.g., if one of them was an undercover police officer)? Similarly, what do you think would happen if Ocean decided that there was not going to be high outcome interdependence—that his and Rusty's split should be $149 million, and everyone else would get a portion of the remainder? In that event, Ocean's 11 would probably become Ocean's 2 fairly quickly.

HOW IMPORTANT ARE TEAM CHARACTERISTICS?

In the previous chapters, we overviewed individual characteristics and mechanisms and discussed how these variables affect individual performance and commitment. In this chapter, we're concerned with team characteristics, and so naturally, we are interested in how they influence team effectiveness. One aspect of team effectiveness is team performance, which may include metrics such as quantity and quality of goods or services produced, customer satisfaction, the effectiveness or accuracy of decisions, victories, completed reports, and successful investigations. Team performance in the context of student project teams most often means the quality with which the team completes assignments and projects, as well as the grades they earn.

A second aspect of team effectiveness is team commitment, which is sometimes called team viability. **Team viability** refers to the likelihood that the team can work together effectively into the future.[67] If the team experience is not satisfying, members may become disillusioned and focus their energy on activities away from the team. Although a team with low viability might be able to work together on short-term projects, over the long run, a team such as this is bound to have significant problems.[68] Rather than planning for future tasks and working through issues that might improve the team, members of a team with low viability are more apt to be looking ahead to the team's ultimate demise.

Of course, it's difficult to summarize the relationship between team characteristics and team performance and commitment when there are so many characteristics that can be used to describe teams. Here we focus our discussion on the impact of task interdependence, because high task interdependence is one of the things that distinguishes true teams from mere groups of individuals. As Figure 11-6 shows, it turns out that the relationship between task interdependence and team performance is moderately positive.[69] That is, task performance tends to be higher in teams in which members depend on one another and have to coordinate their activities rather than when members work more or less independently. It's important to mention that the relationship between task interdependence and team performance is significantly stronger in teams that are responsible for completing complex knowledge work rather than simple tasks. When work is more complex, interdependence is necessary because there is a need for members to interact and share resources and information. When work is simple, sharing information and resources is less necessary because members can do the work by themselves.

In the lower portion of Figure 11-6, you can see that the relationship between task interdependence and team commitment is weaker.[70] Teams with higher task interdependence have only a slightly higher probability of including members who are committed to their team's continued existence. As with the relationship with team performance, task interdependence has a stronger effect on viability for teams doing complex knowledge work. Apparently, sharing resources and information in a context in which it is unnecessary is dissatisfying to members and results in a team with reduced prospects of continued existence.

11.5

How do team characteristics influence team effectiveness?

APPLICATION: TEAM COMPENSATION

Although all team characteristics have implications for managerial practices, outcome interdependence is particularly relevant for two reasons. First, outcome interdependence has obvious connections to compensation practices in organizations,[71] and most of us are

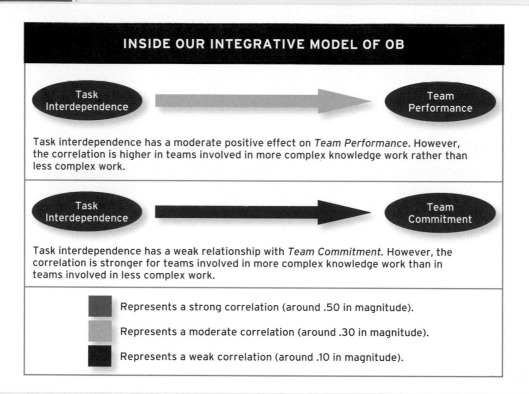

FIGURE 11-6   Effects of Task Interdependence on Performance and Commitment

Sources: M.A. Campion, G.J. Medsker, and A.C. Higgs, "Relations Between Work Group Characteristics and Effectiveness: Implications for Designing Effective Work Groups," *Personnel Psychology* 46 (1993), pp. 823–49; M.A. Campion, E.M. Papper, and G.J. Medsker, "Relations Between Work Team Characteristics and Effectiveness: A Replication and Extension," *Personnel Psychology* 49 (1996), pp. 429–52; G.L. Stewart, "A Meta-Analytic Review of Relationships Between Team Design Features and Team Performance," *Journal of Management* 32 (2006), pp. 29–54.

interested in factors that determine how we get paid. If you work for an organization with compensation that has high outcome interdependence, a higher percentage of your pay will depend on how well your team does. If you work for an organization with compensation that has low outcome interdependence, a lower percentage of your pay will depend on how well your team does.

A second reason outcome interdependence is important to consider is that it presents managers with a tough dilemma. High outcome interdependence promotes higher levels of cooperation because members understand that they share the same fate—if the team wins, everyone wins, and if the team fails, everyone fails.[72] However at the same time, high outcome interdependence may result in reduced motivation, especially among higher performing members. The reason is that high performers may perceive that they are not paid in proportion to what they contributed to the team and that their teammates are taking advantage of this inequity for their own benefit.[73]

One solution to this dilemma has been to design team reward structures with **hybrid outcome interdependence,** which means that members receive rewards that are dependent on both their team's performance and how well they perform as individuals.[74] The majority of

11.6

How can team compensation be used to manage team effectiveness?

organizations that use teams use some sort of hybrid outcome interdependence, and the portion of pay based on team performance is probably lower than you would think. For example, the size of team-based pay in the goods and service sectors is around 10–12 percent of an employee's base pay.[75] It may also surprise you to learn that hybrid outcome interdependence, in and of itself, may not always be that effective. Research conducted at Xerox, for example, showed that service teams with hybrid outcome interdependence were less effective than service teams with very high or very low levels of outcome interdependence.[76]

An alternative approach to solving the dilemma of outcome interdependence has been to implement a level that matches the level of task interdependence. Members tend to be more productive in high task interdependence situations when there is also high outcome interdependence. Similarly, members prefer low task interdependent situations when there is low outcome interdependence.[77] To understand the power of aligning task and outcome interdependence, consider scenarios in which there is not a good match. For example, how would you react to a situation if you worked very closely with your teammates on a team project in one of your classes, and though your professor said the team's project was outstanding, she awarded an A to one of your team members, a B to another, and a C to you? Similarly, consider how you would react to a situation if you scored enough points for an A on your final exam, but your professor averaged everyone's grades together and gave all students a C. Chances are you wouldn't be happy with either scenario.

TAKEAWAYS

11.1 Teams are comprised of two or more people who work interdependently over some time period to accomplish common goals related to some task-oriented purpose. Teams are more interdependent and task focused than groups.

11.2 There are several different types of teams—work teams, management teams, parallel teams, project teams, and parallel teams—but many teams in organizations have characteristics that fit in multiple categories and differ from one another in other ways.

11.3 Teams can be interdependent in terms of the team task, goals, and outcomes. Each type of interdependence has important implications for team functioning and effectiveness.

11.4 Team composition refers to the characteristics of the members who work in the team. These characteristics include roles, ability, personality, and member diversity, as well as the number of team members.

11.5 Depending on the team's task, it may be important to consider the average ability of the members, the ability of the most able, or the ability of the least able.

11.6 The effect of diversity on the team depends on time and whether the diversity is surface-level or deep-level. The effects of surface-level diversity tend to diminish with time, whereas the effects of deep-level diversity tend to increase over time.

11.7 Task interdependence has a moderate positive relationship with team performance and a weak relationship with team commitment.

11.8 Outcome interdependence has important effects on teams, which can be managed with compensation practices that take team performance into account.

KEY TERMS

- Team   p. 372
- Work team   p. 375
- Management team   p. 375
- Parallel team   p. 376
- Project team   p. 376
- Action team   p. 376
- Virtual team   p. 377
- Forming   p. 377
- Storming   p. 377
- Norming   p. 377
- Performing   p. 377
- Punctuated equilibrium   p. 378
- Task interdependence   p. 379
- Pooled interdependence   p. 380
- Sequential interdependence   p. 382
- Reciprocal interdependence   p. 382
- Comprehensive interdependence   p. 382
- Goal interdependence   p. 382
- Outcome interdependence   p. 383
- Team composition   p. 384
- Role   p. 385
- Leader–staff teams   p. 385
- Team task roles   p. 385
- Team building roles   p. 386
- Individualistic roles   p. 386
- Disjunctive tasks   p. 388
- Conjunctive tasks   p. 388
- Additive tasks   p. 388
- Team diversity   p. 389
- Value in diversity problem-solving approach   p. 389
- Similarity-attraction approach   p. 389
- Surface-level diversity   p. 389
- Deep-level diversity   p. 390
- Team viability   p. 393
- Hybrid outcome interdependence   p. 394

DISCUSSION QUESTIONS

11.1 Prior to reading this chapter, would have you made a distinction between groups and teams? After reading this chapter, has your position changed, and if so, how?

11.2 In which types of teams have you worked? Were these teams consistent with the team types discussed in this chapter, or were they a combination of types?

11.3 Are teams used in your profession? Why or why not?

11.4 Think about your student teams. Which aspects of both models of team development apply the most and least to teams in this context?

11.5 Think about a highly successful team with which you are familiar. What types of task, goal, and outcome interdependence does this team have? Describe how changes in task, goal, and outcome interdependence might have a negative impact on this team.

11.6 What type of roles do you normally take on in a team setting? Are there task or social roles that you simply don't perform well? If so, why do you think this is?

11.7 Do you think student teams function best in an additive, disjunctive, or conjunctive manner? What are the advantages and disadvantages of each structure?

11.8 What is the most important team composition factor in your student teams? If a student team has limitations in its composition, what can it do to improve?

11.9 How does diversity relate to the two types of effectiveness in your student teams?

CASE PIXAR

In a little over a decade, Pixar has managed to produce seven blockbuster hits. Its leadership in producing animated motion pictures results from an amalgamation of contributing factors, including the three individuals who lead this innovative organization. Ed Catmull, John Lasseter, and Steve Jobs represent the driving forces behind one of the most cohesive teams in the industry. Pixar consists of three departments: animators, the story department, and the art department. Cross-functional teams comprise members of each of these departments who are integrated together to facilitate communication and thus produce groundbreaking movies.

Companies rise and fall quickly within the moviemaking industry, yet Pixar has managed to pull all of its resources together to create something magical each and every time it produces a movie. How is this success achieved? Pixar has retained the majority of the employees who started with the company at its initiation, which has been a huge advantage. Employees within each team know the strengths and weaknesses of every other team member and therefore can collaborate effectively. Pixar also has established Pixar University to train new employees, which enables them to have an immediate impact after they complete their three-month training program. The success of Pixar thus is rooted in the team atmosphere created by the organization.

11.1 Are cross-functional teams a necessity for the continued success of Pixar? Explain.

11.2 What makes teams at Pixar different from other teams? Explain.

Sources: C. Conley, "Innovation All the Time," *BusinessWeek Online,* September 19, 2006; "Corporate Overview," http://www.pixar.com/companyinfo/about_us/overview.htm (June 26, 2007); S. Dowling, "How Pixar Changed Animation–for Good," October 10, 2003, http://newsvote.bbc.co.uk (June 26, 2007); E. Millard, "What Makes Pixar Run?" May 2004, http://www.technewswolrd.com/story/34107.html (June 26, 2007).

EXERCISE PAPER PLANE CORPORATION

The purpose of this exercise is to analyze the advantages and disadvantages of sequential versus pooled interdependence on a team production project. This exercise uses groups of six participants, so your instructor will either assign you to a group of six or ask you to create your own group of six. The exercise has the following steps.

1. Your professor will supply you with the materials you need to create your final product (as many paper airplanes as you can fold to quality standards in three 5-minute rounds). Instructions for folding the paper airplanes and judging their quality are provided below. Before you start work on your airplanes, do the following:

   a. As a group, select a team manager (who will supervise operations and get additional resources as needed) and a team inspector (who will judge the quality of the work on airplanes).

   b. Familiarize yourself with how to make a paper airplane by folding one according to the instructions shown on the next page.

   c. Be sure you are in a space where all of the team members can work comfortably.

   d. To the extent possible, move away from other groups.

   e. Familiarize yourself with the information about the Paper Plane Corporation.

2. Your group is the complete workforce for the Paper Plane Corporation. Established in 1943, Paper Plane has led the market in paper plane production. Presently under new management, the company is contracting to make aircraft for the U.S. Air Force. You must determine the most efficient method for producing these aircraft. You must make your contract with the Air Force under the following conditions:

   a. The Air Force will pay $200,000 per airplane.
   b. The aircraft must pass a strict inspection by a quality control manager.
   c. A penalty of $250,000 per airplane will be subtracted for failure to meet the production requirements.
   d. Labor and other overhead will be computed at $3,000,000.
   e. Cost of materials will be $30,000 per bid plane. If you bid for 10 but only make 8, you must pay the cost of materials for those you failed to make or those that did not pass inspection.

Plane Folding Instructions

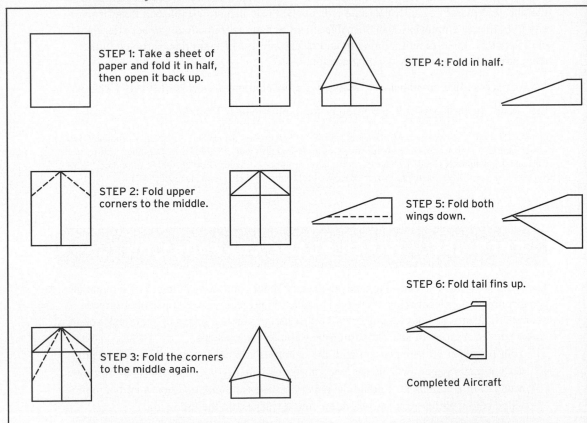

STEP 1: Take a sheet of paper and fold it in half, then open it back up.

STEP 2: Fold upper corners to the middle.

STEP 3: Fold the corners to the middle again.

STEP 4: Fold in half.

STEP 5: Fold both wings down.

STEP 6: Fold tail fins up.

Completed Aircraft

3. In the first round of airplane manufacturing process, the Air Force has asked you to focus on individuality. Each Paper Plane worker should manufacture his or her own planes from start to finish. When each plane is finished, it should be put in a central

location for quality inspection. When time is called, you will record your team profit on the Summary Sheet.

4. In the second round of manufacturing, the Air Force has asked you to give each worker a specific job. In other words, the manufacturing process will take place in an assembly-line fashion. When planes come off the assembly line, they will be given directly to the quality control manager for inspection. When time is called, you will record your team profit on the Summary Sheet.

5. In the final round of manufacturing, the Air Force has asked your team to devise a manufacturing process that will maximize both efficiency and effectiveness. You may do whatever you like in terms of creating paper airplanes. You will have the same amount of time that you did in the two previous rounds. When time is called, you will record your team profit on the Summary Sheet.

Summary Sheet

Round 1

Bid: _____ Aircraft @ $200,000 per aircraft = _____

Results: _____ Aircraft @ $200,000 per aircraft = _____

Subtract: $3,000,000 overhead + _____ × $30,000 cost of raw materials + _____ × $250,000 penalty for not completing a bid plane = _____

Profit: _____

Round 2

Bid: _____ Aircraft @ $200,000 per aircraft = _____

Results: _____ Aircraft @ $200,000 per aircraft = _____

Subtract: $3,000,000 overhead + _____ × $30,000 cost of raw materials + _____ × $250,000 penalty for not completing a bid plane = _____

Profit: _____

Round 3

Bid: _____ Aircraft @ $200,000 per aircraft = _____

Results: _____ Aircraft @ $200,000 per aircraft = _____

Subtract: $3,000,000 overhead + _____ × $30,000 cost of raw materials + _____ × $250,000 penalty for not completing a bid plane = _____

Profit: _____

6. Class discussion (whether in groups or as a class) should center on the following questions:

a. Did pooled interdependence (Round 1) or sequential interdependence (Round 2) work better for your group in terms of the number of planes made correctly? Why do you think you got the result you did?

b. How did you change your work structure in Round 3? Did the changes you implemented help you achieve better productivity? Why or why not?

c. From your perspective, what are the advantages and disadvantages of pooled and/or sequential interdependence?

Sources: Adapted from J.M. Ivancevich, R. Konopaske, and M. Matteson, *Organizational Behavior and Management,* 7th ed. (Chicago: McGraw-Hill/Irwin, 2005). Original exercise by Louis Potheni in F. Luthans, *Organizational Behavior* (New York: McGraw-Hill, 1985), p. 555.

ENDNOTES

11.1 *Box Office Mojo: Finding Nemo,* http://www.boxofficemojo.com/ movies/?id=findingnemo.htm (December 12, 2006).

11.2 Lamonica, P.R. "Disney Buys Pixar," January 25, 2006, http://money. cnn.com/2006/01/24/news/ companies/disney_pixar_deal/index. htm (December 12, 2006).

11.3 Schlender, B. "The Man who Built Pixar's Incredible Innovation Machine." *Fortune* 150, no. 10 November 15, 2004), p. 206. Pro-Quest database (May 28, 2007).

11.4 Ibid.

11.5 Ibid.

11.6 Ilgen, D.R.; D.A. Major; J.R. Hollenbeck; and D.J. Sego. "Team Research in the 1990s." In *Leadership Theory and Research: Perspectives and Directions,* ed. M.M. Chemers and R. Ayman. New York: Academic Press, Inc., 1993, pp. 245–270.

11.7 Devine, D.J.; L.D. Clayton; J.L. Philips; B.B. Dunford; and S.B. Melner. "Teams in Organizations: Prevalence, Characteristics, and Effectiveness." *Small Group Research* 30 (1999), pp. 678–711; Gordan, J. "Work Teams: How Far Have They Come?" *Training* 29 (1992), pp. 59–65; Lawler, E.E., III; S.A. Mohrman, and G.E. Ledford Jr. *Creating High Performance Organizations: Practices and Results of Employee Involvement and Total Quality Management in* Fortune *1000 Companies.* San Francisco: Jossey-Bass, 1995.

11.8 Stewart, G.L.; C.C. Manz, and H.P. Sims Jr. *Team Work and Group Dynamics.* New York: John Wiley & Sons, 1999.

11.9 Ibid.

11.10 Cohen, S.G., and D.E. Bailey. "What Makes Teams Work: Group Effectiveness Research from the Shop Floor to the Executive Suite." *Journal of Management* 23 (1997), pp. 239–90.

11.11 Ibid.

11.12 Ibid.

11.13 Sundstrom, E.; M. McIntyre; T. Halfhill; and H. Richards. "Work Groups: From the Hawthorne Studies to Work Teams of the 1990s and Beyond." *Group Dynamics, Theory, Research, and Practice* 4 (2000), pp. 44–67.

11.14 Treinen, J.J., and S.L. Miller-Frost. "Following the Sun: Case Studies in Global Software Development." *IBM Systems Journal* 45 (2006), pp. 773–83.

11.15 Schiff, D. "Global Teams Rock around the Clock." *Electronic Engineering Times* 1435 (August 7, 2006), pp. 12, 20.

11.16 Godinez, V. "Sunshine 24/7: As EDS' Work Stops in One Time Zone, It Picks Up in Another." *Knight Ridder Tribune Business News,* January 2, 2007. ProQuest database (February 12, 2007); Schiff, "Global Teams Rock"; Treinen and Miller-Frost, "Following the Sun."

11.17 Treinen and Miller-Frost, "Following the Sun."

11.18 Greenhouse, S. "IBM Explores Shift of White-Collar Jobs Overseas." *The New York Times,* July 22, 2003, pp. C1, 2. ProQuest Historical Newspapers database (February 12, 2007).

11.19 Tuckman, B.W. "Developmental Sequence in Small Groups."

Psychological Bulletin 63 (1965), pp. 384–99.

11.20 Gersick, C.J.G. "Time and Transition in Work Teams: Toward a New Model of Group Development." *Academy of Management Journal* 33 (1988), pp. 9–41; Gersick, C.J.G. "Marking Time: Predictable Transitions in Task Groups." *Academy of Management Journal* 32 (1989), pp. 274–309.

11.21 Thompson, J.D. *Organizations in Action.* New York: McGraw-Hill, 1967; Van de Ven, A.H.; A.L. Delbeccq; and R. Koenig. "Determinants of Coordination Modes within Organizations." *American Sociological Review* 41 (1976), pp. 322–38.

11.22 Ibid.

11.23 Thompson, *Organizations in Action.*

11.24 Ibid.

11.25 Ibid.

11.26 Van de Ven et al., "Determinants of Coordination Modes."

11.27 Kelley, T. *The Art of Innovation.* New York: Doubleday, 2001.

11.28 Saavedra, R.; P.C. Earley; and L. Van Dyne. "Complex Interdependence in Task Performing Groups." *Journal of Applied Psychology* 78 (1993), pp. 61–72.

11.29 Deutsch, M. *The Resolution of Conflict.* New Haven, CT: Yale University Press, 1973; Wong, A.; D. Tjosvold; and Zi-you Yu. "Organizational Partnerships in China: Self-Interest, Goal Interdependence, and Opportunism." *Journal of Applied Psychology* 90 (2005), pp. 782–91.

11.30 MacMillan, P.S. *The Performance Factor: Unlocking the Secrets of Teamwork.* Nashville, TN: Broadman & Holman Publishers, 2001.

11.31 Ibid.

11.32 Ibid.

11.33 Shea, G.P., and R.A. Guzzo. "Groups as Human Resources." In *Research in Personnel and Human Resources Management,* Vol. 5, eds. K.M. Rowland and G.R. Ferris. Greenwich CT: JAI Press, 1987, pp. 323–56.

11.34 Erez, A.; J.A. LePine; and H. Elms. "Effects of Rotated Leadership and Peer Evaluation on the Functioning and Effectiveness of Self-Managed Teams: A Quasi-Experiment." *Personnel Psychology* 55 (2002), pp. 929–48.

11.35 Brehmer, B., and R. Hagafors. "Use of Experts in Complex Decision Making: A Paradigm for the Study of Staff Work." *Organizational Behavior and Human Decision Processes* 38 (1986), pp. 181–95.

11.36 Benne, Kenneth, and Paul Sheats. "Functional Roles of Group Members." *Journal of Social Issues* 4 (1948), pp. 41–49.

11.37 Spencer, L. "Conditioning Has Become an Important Tool: Let's Get Physical." *Stock Car Racing.* http://www.stockcarracing.com/howto/stock_car_pit_crew_conditioning/ (February 8, 2007).

11.38 Devine, D.J., and J.L. Philips. "Do Smarter Teams Do Better: A Meta-Analysis of Cognitive Ability and Team Performance." *Small Group Research* 32 (2001), pp. 507–32; Stewart, G.L. "A Meta-Analytic Review of Relationships Between Team Design Features and Team Performance." *Journal of Management* 32 (2006), pp. 29–54.

11.39 LePine, J.A.; J.R. Hollenbeck; D.R. Ilgen; and J. Hedlund. "Effects of Individual Differences on the Performance of Hierarchical Decision-Making Teams: Much More than g." *Journal of Applied Psychology* 82 (1997), pp. 803–11.

11.40 LePine, J.A. "Team Adaptation and Postchange Performance: Effects of Team Composition in Terms of Members' Cognitive Ability and Personality." *Journal of Applied Psychology* 88 (2003), pp. 27–39; LePine, J.A. "Adaptation of Teams in Response to Unforeseen Change: Effects of Goal Difficulty and Team Composition in Terms of Cognitive Ability and Goal Orientation." *Journal of Applied Psychology* 90 (2005), pp. 1153–67.

11.41 Steiner, I.D. *Group Process and Productivity.* New York: Academic Press, 1972.

11.42 Peeters, M.A.G., Tuijl, H.F.J.M. van, Rutte, C.G., Reymen, I.M.M.J. (2006). Personality and Team Performance: A Meta-analysis. *European Journal of Personality,* 20, 377–396.

11.43 Barrick, M.R.; G.L. Stewart; M.J. Neubert; and M.K. Mount. "Relating Member Ability and Personality to Work-Team Processes and Team Effectiveness." *Journal of Applied Psychology* 83 (1998), pp. 377–91; LePine et al., "Effects of Individual Differences"; Neuman, G.A., and J. Wright. "Team Effectiveness: Beyond Skills and Cognitive Ability." *Journal of Applied Psychology,* 84 (1999), pp. 376–89.

11.44 LePine, J.A., and L. Van Dyne. "An Attributional Model of Helping in the Context of Work Groups." *Academy of Management Review* 26 (2001), pp. 67–84.

11.45 Peeters, M. A. G., et al., (2006).

11.46 Comer, D.R. "A Model of Social Loafing in Real Work Groups." *Human Relations* 48 (1995), pp. 647–67; Wagner, J.A., III. "Studies of Individualism–Collectivism: Effects on Cooperation in Groups." *Academy of Management Journal* 38 (1995), pp. 152–72.

11.47 LePine, J.A., and L. Van Dyne. "Voice and Cooperative Behavior as Contrasting Forms of Contextual Performance: Evidence of Differential Relationships with Personality Characteristics and Cognitive Ability." *Journal of Applied Psychology* 86 (2001), pp. 326–36.

11.48 McGrath, J.E. "The Influence of Positive Interpersonal Relations on Adjustment and Interpersonal Relations in Rifle Teams." *Journal of Abnormal and Social Psychology* 65 (1962), pp. 365–75.

11.49 Barrick, M.R., and M.K. Mount. "The Big Five Personality Dimensions and Job Performance: A Meta-Analysis." *Personnel Psychology* 44 (1991), pp. 1–26.

11.50 Barrick et al., "Relating Member Ability and Personality."

11.51 Barry, B., and G.L. Stewart. "Composition, Process, and Performance in Self-Managed Groups: The Role of Personality." *Journal of Applied Psychology* 82 (1997), pp. 62–78.

11.52 Williams, K., and C. O'Reilly. "The Complexity of Diversity: A Review of Forty Years of Research." In *Research in Organizational Behavior,* Vol. 21, eds. B. Staw and R. Sutton. Greenwich, CT: JAI Press, 1998, pp. 77–140.

11.53 Cox, T.; S. Lobel; and P. McLeod. "Effects of Ethnic Group Cultural Differences on Cooperative and Competitive Behavior on a Group Task." *Academy of Management Journal* 34 (1991), pp. 827–47; Mannix, E., and M.A. Neal. "What Differences Make a Difference? The Promise and Reality of Diverse Teams in Organizations." *Psychological Science in the Public Interest* 6 (2005), pp. 31–55.

11.54 Gruenfeld, D.H.; E.A. Mannix; K.Y. Williams; and M.A. Neale. "Group Composition and Decision Making: How Member Familiarity and Information Distribution Affect Processes and Performance." *Organizational Behavior and Human Decision Processes* 67 (1996), pp. 1–15; Hoffman, L. "Homogeneity and Member Personality and Its Effect on Group Problem Solving." *Journal of Abnormal and Social Psychology* 58 (1959), pp. 27–32; Hoffman, L., and N. Maier. "Quality and Acceptance of Problem Solutions by Members of Homogeneous and Heterogeneous Groups." *Journal of Abnormal and Social Psychology* 62 (1961), pp. 401–407; Nemeth, C.J. "Differential Contributions of Majority and Minority Influence." *Psychological Review* 93 (1986), pp. 22–32; Stasster, G.; D. Steward; and G. Wittenbaum. "Expert Roles and Information Exchange During Discussion: The Importance of Knowing Who Knows What." *Journal of Experimental Social Psychology* 57 (1995), pp. 244–65; Triandis, H.; E. Hall; and R. Ewen. "Member Heterogeneity and Dyadic Creativity." *Human Relations* 18 (1965), pp. 33–55; Watson, W.; K. Kuman; and I. Michaelsen. "Cultural Diversity's Impact on Interaction Process and Performance: Comparing Homogeneous and Diverse Task Groups." *Academy of Management Journal* 36 (1993), pp. 590–602.

11.55 Byrne, D. *The Attraction Paradigm.* New York: Academic Press, 1971; Newcomb, T.M. *The Acquaintance Process.* New York: Holt, Rinehart, and Wilson, 1961.

11.56 Byrne, D.; G. Clore; and P. Worchel. "The Effect of Economic Similarity-Dissimilarity as Determinants of Attraction." *Journal of Personality and Social Psychology* 4 (1996), pp. 220–24; Lincoln, J., and J. Miller. "Work and Friendship Ties in Organizations: A Comparative Analysis of Relational Networks." *Administrative Science Quarterly* 24 (1979), pp. 181–99; Triandis, H. "Cognitive Similarity and Interpersonal Communication in Industry." *Journal of Applied Psychology* 43 (1959), pp. 321–26; Triandis, H. "Cognitive Similarity and Communication in a Dyad." *Human Relations* 13 (1960), pp. 279–87.

11.57 Jackson, S.E.; K.E. May; K. Whitney. "Understanding the Dynamics of Diversity in Decision-Making Teams." In *Team Decision-Making Effectiveness in Organizations,* eds. R.A. Guzzo and E. Salas. San Francisco: Jossey-Bass, 1995, pp. 204–61; Milliken, F.J., and L.L. Martins. "Searching for Common Threads: Understanding the Multiple Effects of Diversity in Organizational Groups." *Academy of Management Review* 21 (1996), pp. 402–33.

11.58 Harrison, D.A.; K.H. Price; and M.P. Bell. "Beyond Relational Demography: Time and the Effects of Surface- and Deep-Level Diversity on Work Group Cohesion." *Academy of Management Journal* 41 (1998), pp. 96–107; Harrison, D.A.; K.H. Price; J.H. Gavin; and A.T. Florey. "Time, Teams, and Task Performance: Changing Effects of Surface- and Deep-Level Diversity on Group Functioning." *Academy of Management Journal* 45 (2002), pp. 1029–45.

11.59 Ibid.

11.60 Ibid.

11.61 Ibid.

11.62 Stewart, "A Meta-Analytic Review."

11.63 Kozlowski, S.W.J., and B.S. Bell. "Work Groups and Teams in Organization." In *Comprehensive Handbook of Psychology: Industrial and Organizational Psychology,* Vol. 12, eds. W.C. Borman, D.R. Ilgen, and R.J. Klimoski. New York: John Wiley & Sons, 2003, pp. 333–75.

11.64 Gooding, R.Z., and J.A. Wagner III. "A Meta-Analytic Review of the Relationship Between Size and Performance: The Productivity and Efficiency of Organizations and Their Subunits." *Administrative Science Quarterly* 30 (1985), pp. 462–81; Markham, S.E.; F. Dansereau; and J.A. Alutto. "Group Size and Absenteeism Rates: A Longitudinal Analysis." *Academy of Management Journal* 25 (1982), pp. 921–27.

11.65 Hackman, J.R., and N.J. Vidmar. "Effects of Size and Task Type on Group Performance and Member Reactions." *Sociometry* 33 (1970), pp. 37–54.

11.66 Yank, J.L. "The Power of Number 4.6." *Fortune* 153, no. 11 (June 12, 2006), p. 122. ProQuest database (May 28, 2007).

11.67 Sundstrom, E.; K.P. De Meuse; and D. Futrell. "Work Teams: Applications and Effectiveness." *American Psychologist* 45 (1990), pp. 120–33.

11.68 Stewart, G.L.; C.C. Manz; and H.P. Sims Jr. *Team Work and Group Dynamics.* New York: John Wiley & Sons, 1999.

11.69 Stewart, "A Meta-Analytic Review."

11.70 Campion, M.A.; G.J. Medsker; and A.C. Higgs. "Relations Between Work Group Characteristics and Effectiveness: Implications for Designing Effective Work Groups." *Personnel Psychology* 46 (1993), pp. 823–49; Campion, M.A.; E.M. Papper; and G.J. Medsker. "Relations Between Work Team Characteristics and Effectiveness: A Replication and Extension." *Personnel Psychology* 49 (1996), pp. 429–52.

11.71 DeMatteo, J.S.; L.T. Eby; and E. Sundstrom. "Team-Based Rewards: Current Empirical Evidence and Directions for Future Research." *Research in Organizational Behavior* 20 (1998), pp. 141–83.

11.72 Deutsch, M.A. "A Theory of Cooperation and Competition." *Human Relations* 2 (1949), pp. 199–231.

11.73 Williams, K.; S.G. Harkins; and B. Latane. "Identifiability as a Deterrent to Social Loafing: Two Cheering Experiments." *Journal of Personality and Social Psychology* 40 (1981), pp. 303–11.

11.74 Lawler, E.E. *Strategic Pay: Aligning Organizational Strategies and Pay Systems.* San Francisco: Jossey-Bass, 1990.

11.75 O'Dell, C. *People, Performance, Pay.* American Productivity Institute, 1987, cited in DeMatteo et al., "Team-Based Rewards."

11.76 Wageman, R. "Interdependence and Group Effectiveness." *Administrative Science Quarterly* 40 (1995), pp. 145–80.

11.77 Johnson, D.W.; G. Maruyama; R. Johnson; D. Nelson; and L. Skon. "Effects of Cooperative, Competitive, and Individualistic Goal Structures on Achievement: A Meta-Analysis." *Psychological Bulletin* 89 (1981), pp. 47–62; Miller, L.K., and R.L. Hamblin. "Interdependence, Differential Rewarding and Productivity." *American Sociological Review* 28 (1963), pp. 768–78; Rosenbaum, M.E. "Cooperation and Competition." In *Psychology of Group Influence,* ed. P.B. Paulus. Hillsdale, NJ: Lawrence Erlbaum, 1980.

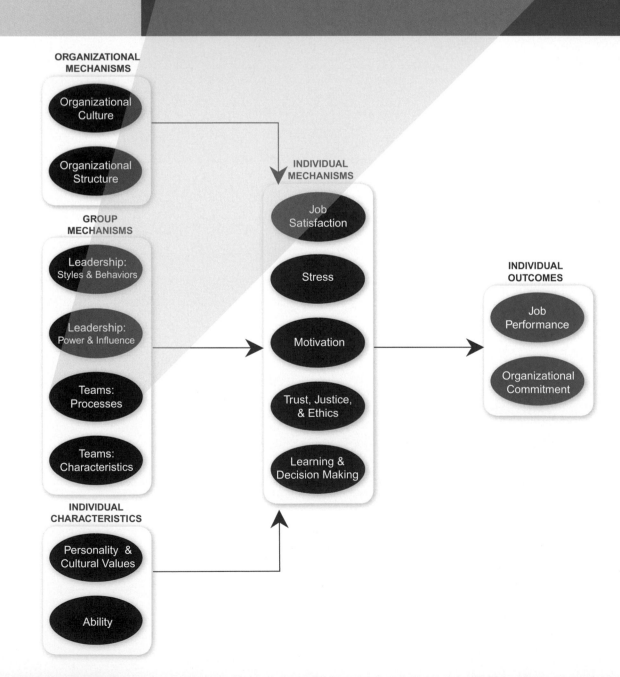

IDEO, a design and innovation firm, relies on the power of team-work to generate new and improved offerings for hundreds of clients including PepsiCo, HBO, Intel, Fisher-Price, Kraft Foods, the Mayo Clinic, Microsoft, NASA, and Whirlpool to name a few. Pictured here is Scott Adams, famed creator of the comic strip DILBERT, standing in "Dilbert's ultimate cubicle" designed by IDEO.

 LEARNING GOALS

After reading this chapter, you should be able to answer the following questions:

12.1 What is team process, and how does it relate to process gain and process loss?

12.2 What are taskwork processes, and what are some examples of team activities that fall into this process category?

12.3 What are teamwork processes, and what are some examples of team activities that fall into this process category?

12.4 What are team states, and what are some examples of the states that fall into this process category?

12.5 How do team processes affect team performance and team commitment?

12.6 What steps can organizations take to improve team processes?

IDEO

If you play golf, cook, travel, play with toys, brush your teeth, wear sunglasses, use a computer, or have been to a hospital recently, you likely have used a product or service designed by IDEO, one of the largest and most successful design firms in the world. IDEO's list of clients numbers in the hundreds and includes many familiar companies: Apple, AT&T, Chevron, Dell, Fisher-Price, Intel, Kraft Foods, the Mayo Clinic, Microsoft, Nestlé, Nike, NASA, Polaroid, Sega, Samsung, Taylormade Golf, and Whirlpool.[1] What

IDEO does best is take an existing product or service and make it better through creativity and innovation.

In 1981, for example, Apple asked the founder of IDEO to design a computer mouse that would be significantly more reliable and 90 percent less costly to produce than the computer mice of the 1970s.[2] Not only did IDEO design new technology to meet those goals, it also added features such as the audible and tactile clicks of the mouse button that have become so familiar. Later, IDEO took those innovations further by helping design the popular Microsoft Mouse. This design moved the rubberized roller ball of the mouse (another IDEO innovation) from under the palm to the fingertips for more precise control. The design also incorporated the now familiar "Dove bar" shape (the original Apple mouse was a squat rectangle). The innovations in these mice were so wildly successful that they served as the foundation for almost all the mechanical mice produced since. Of course, there are many other examples of IDEO innovations—the world's first no-squeeze, stand-up toothpaste tube for Crest, the Oral-B toothbrush, and the Palm V PDA, to name just a few.

How has IDEO become so successful at the business of innovating? Although there are probably several different answers to this question, it's clear that "teams are at the heart of the IDEO method."[3] But it's not just that IDEO uses teams or hires really competent and creative people and assigns them to the right teams. It's that teams at IDEO engage in a fairly specific set of processes in their quest for innovation.[4] IDEO's teams first use a variety of techniques to help them understand the needs and desires of the customer. Teams then meet to generate ideas using short and highly structured brainstorming sessions. During these sessions, wild ideas are encouraged, whereas criticism and negativity are discouraged. Once the team finishes brainstorming, it creates mockups to tease out potential problems and identify solutions.

After this step, teams meet to make refinements to the project, usually with the involvement of the client, with the goal being to choose the best design. Finally, teams implement the final design solution by involving an even wider array of experts from IDEO in fields that are relevant to the solution. Taken together, this series of steps explains why IDEO is so successful in using teams to design new products. In fact, IDEO has become so successful that other companies use IDEO as a consultant. Its consultancy role allows other companies to learn about the team processes IDEO uses to design innovative products and services.[5]

TEAM PROCESSES

12.1

What is team process, and how does it relate to process gain and process loss?

As we described in Chapter 11 on Team Characteristics, a team consists of two or more people who work interdependently over some time period to accomplish common goals related to some task-oriented purpose.[6] The effectiveness of organizations depends to a large extent on the activities and interactions that occur within teams as they move toward their task-related objectives. **Team process** is a term that reflects the different types of activities and interactions that occur within teams that contribute to their ultimate end goals.[7] Team characteristics, like member diversity, task interdependence, team size, and so forth, affect team processes. Team processes, in turn, have a strong impact on team effectiveness.

Some of the team processes we describe in this chapter are observable by the naked eye. At IDEO, an outside observer would be able to see team members gathering information, building on one another's ideas, and collaborating to solve some product problem. Other processes, in contrast, are more invisible. An outside observer wouldn't be able to see the sense of cohesion felt by the IDEO team members or the shared "mental models" that cause them to work together so efficiently. Thus team processes include interactions among members that occur behaviorally, as well as the hard-to-see feelings and thoughts that coalesce as a consequence of member interactions.

WHY ARE SOME TEAMS MORE THAN THE SUM OF THEIR PARTS?

On the one hand, the success of IDEO's teams may not be surprising, because the organization hires very talented, skilled, and hardworking employees. On the other hand, it seems difficult to explain the teams' continued successes just from looking at the rosters of their members, because the teams seem to become "more than the sum of their parts." That is, IDEO's teams seem to benefit from **process gain,** or getting more from the team than you would expect according to the capabilities of its individual members. Process gain is synonymous with "synergy" and is most critical in situations in which the complexity of the work is high or tasks require combinations of members' knowledge, skills, and efforts to solve problems. In essence, process gain is important because it results in useful resources and capabilities that did not exist before the team created them.[8] Our **OB on Screen** feature illustrates vividly how a team that achieves process gain develops capabilities that help it achieve much more than what most people would rationally expect.

Having described process gain, we now consider its polar opposite. Consider this list of names: LeBron James, Dwyane Wade, Carmelo Anthony, Tim Duncan, and Allen Iverson. You don't have to be much more than a casual basketball fan to recognize those names as some of the best in professional basketball. Is that the roster of some all-NBA team? No, it's the roster of the recent USA Men's Basketball team that competed in the 2004 Olympics and 2006 World Championships. With a roster like that, it seems certain that the USA's "Dream Team" would've taken home gold in one or both of those events. Instead, they finished in third place in the 2004 Olympics, behind Argentina and Italy, and in third place again in the 2006 World Championship, behind Spain and Greece. What explains the poor showing? For some reason, the USA Men's Basketball team wound up being "less than the sum of its parts." That is, it seemed to be harmed by **process loss,** or getting less from the team than you would expect based on the capabilities of its individual members.

What factors conspire to create process loss? One factor is that in teams, members have to work to not only accomplish their own tasks but also coordinate their activities with the activities of their teammates.[9] Although this extra effort focused on integrating work is a necessary aspect of the team experience, it is called **coordination loss** because it consumes time and energy that could otherwise be devoted to task activity.[10] Such coordination losses are often driven by **production blocking,** which occurs when members have to wait on one another before they can do their part of the team task.[11] If you've ever worked in a team in which you felt like you couldn't get any of your own work done because of all the time spent in meetings, following up requests for information from other team members, and waiting on team members to do their part of the team task, you already understand how frustrating production blocking (and coordination loss) can be.

The second force that fosters process loss in team contexts is **motivational loss,** or the loss in team productivity that occurs when team members do not work as hard as they could.[12] Why does motivation loss occur in team contexts? One explanation is that it's often quite difficult to gauge exactly how much each team member contributes to the team. Members of teams can work together on projects over an extended period of time, and as a consequence, it's difficult to keep an accurate accounting of who does what. Similarly, members contribute to their team in many different ways, and contributions of some members may

OB ON SCREEN

300

The world will know that free men stood against a tyrant, that few stood against many, and before this battle was over, that even a god-king can bleed.

With those words, King Leonidis (Gerard Butler) announces that his band of 300 Spartan soldiers is capable of pulling off a truly remarkable feat—standing against the Persian army led by Xerxes (Rodrigo Santoro) in *300* (Dir. Zack Snyder, Warner Brothers, 2006). Why would that feat be so remarkable? Because the Persian army includes well over 100,000 soldiers (and a few mutated elephants and rhinos).

The movie centers on the battle of Thermopylae, during which a small band of Spartans employed strategies and tactics that gave them the fighting capabilities of a much larger force. Those tactics represent process gain, because the army was able to achieve more than you'd expect if you simply added up the capabilities of the individual soldiers.

Beyond simply illustrating the concept of process gain, the movie illustrates the role that team processes play in achieving it. The clearest example occurs when the Persian Army "darkens the sky" by launching tens of thousands of arrows simultaneously. When this happens, the Spartans immediately get into a tight formation, lift their shields, and then link them together in a manner that creates a collective shield over the entire formation (think a giant turtle shell, and you get the picture).

Although the movie vividly illustrates the power of process gain, it also alludes to its fragility. For example, as long as each and every soldier executes his part of the process of creating the collective shield, the tactic is effective, and the Spartans can withstand repeated onslaughts of countless arrows. However, if just one Spartan soldier fails to raise his shield on time, it creates a breach in the formation that will only widen as the soldier is struck down (thereby exposing the soldier next to him). Thus, a single soldier's failure in the team process could lead to the destruction of the entire army. This fact was not lost on King Leonidis, who in one scene rejects a volunteer for the Spartan army because the volunteer, though a fierce fighter, could not lift his shield over his head.

be less obvious than others. Finally, members of teams do not always work together at the same time as a unit. Regardless of the reasons for it, uncertainty regarding "who contributes what" results in team members feeling less accountable for team outcomes. Those feelings of reduced accountability, in turn, cause members to exert less effort when working on team tasks than they would if they worked alone on those same tasks. This phenomenon is called **social loafing,**[13] and it can significantly hinder a team's effectiveness.[14] For more information on sources of process loss, see our **OB at the Bookstore** feature.

OB AT THE BOOKSTORE

THE FIVE DYSFUNCTIONS OF A TEAM
by Patrick Lencioni (San Francisco: Jossey-Bass, 2002)

Like so many other aspects of life, teamwork comes down to mastering a set of behaviors that are at once theoretically uncomplicated, but extremely difficult to put into practice day after day. Success comes only for those groups that overcome the all-too-human behavioral tendencies that corrupt teams and breed dysfunctional politics within them.

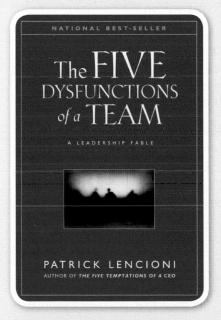

With those words, Lencioni argues that teams face a relatively small number of natural pitfalls, and unless teams are prepared to face them, they often prove lethal.

The book's lessons are centered on a parable of a newly hired 57-year-old CEO named Kathryn Petersen who turns around Decision Tech, a Silicon Valley technology firm that has gone through some tough times. She does so by helping the firm's executive committee overcome five crucial team dysfunctions: absence of trust, fear of conflict, lack of commitment, avoidance of accountability, and inattention to results. So how is Petersen able to accomplish this incredible feat? Beyond having exceptionally high performance standards and being supportive of her employees, Petersen uses several different types of teambuilding assessments, exercises, and guided discussions. In the end, it's easy to come away from the story impressed with the lessons that Petersen taught her team.

How useful are those lessons in the real world? It turns out that the book has caught on in the business world, as well as in some rather unexpected places. For example, current and former National Football League head coaches such as Norv Turner, Marty Schottenheimer, Nick Saban, Romeo Crennel, and Marvin Lewis have read the book and applied its lessons to promote effective teamwork among players and coaching staffs.[15]

How do the five dysfunctions stack up against what we know from OB research? Lencioni based the book on his consulting work with CEOs and executive teams, so the dysfunctions were taken from commonsense knowledge gained from those experiences. Although OB scholars would agree that the dysfunctions are valid concerns for teams, there is no research that supports the idea that these five dysfunctions are the primary drivers of team functioning and effectiveness, that some are more important to overcome than others, or that the techniques Petersen used to approach the dysfunctions are optimal. Nevertheless, the book not only highlights common problems with team processes, it also identifies potential ways of dealing with them.

TASKWORK PROCESSES

✓ 12.2

What are taskwork processes, and what are some examples of team activities that fall into this process category?

Having described process gains and process losses, it's time to describe the particular team processes that can help teams increase their synergy while reducing their inefficiency. One relevant category of team processes is **taskwork processes,** which are the activities of team members that relate directly to the accomplishment of team tasks. In a general sense, taskwork occurs anytime that team members interact with the tools or technologies that are used to complete their work. In this regard, taskwork is similar to the concept of task performance described in Chapter 2 on Job Performance. However, in the context of teams, especially those that engage in knowledge work, three types of taskwork processes are crucially important: creative behavior, decision making, and boundary spanning. These three taskwork processes are shown in Figure 12-1.

CREATIVE BEHAVIOR. When teams engage in creative behavior, their activities are focused on generating novel and useful ideas and solutions.[16] In Chapter 9 on Personality and Cultural Values, we noted that creative behavior is driven in part by the creativity of individual employees, because some employees are simply more original and imaginative than others. However, the team environment is also uniquely suited to fostering creative behavior. As a consequence, organizations like Pixar and IDEO rely on teams to come together and combine their members' unique sets of knowledge and skill in a manner that results in novel and useful ideas. However, achieving such outcomes depends on much more than just putting a diverse mix of people together and letting them go at it. In fact, as we noted in the opening vignette, creative behavior in teams can be fostered when members participate in a specific set of activities.

Perhaps the best known activity that teams use to foster creative behavior is **brainstorming.** Generally speaking, brainstorming involves a face-to-face meeting of team members in which each offers as many ideas as possible about some focal problem or issue.[17] Most brainstorming sessions center around the following rules:

1. Express all ideas that come to mind (no matter how strange).
2. Go for quantity of ideas rather than quality.
3. Don't criticize or evaluate the ideas of others.
4. Build on the ideas of others.

The theory is that if a team follows these rules, it will develop a large pool of ideas that it can use to address the issue at hand.[18] This concept sounds good in theory, and almost all of us have been in some sort of brainstorming meeting at some point. It may surprise you to learn then that such brainstorming sessions rarely work as well as intended. In fact, research

FIGURE 12-1   Taskwork Processes

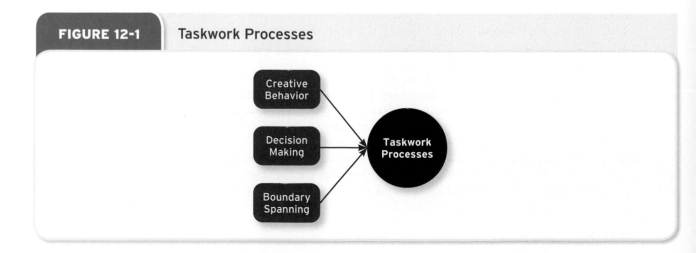

suggests that team members would be better off coming up with ideas on their own, as individuals, before pooling those ideas and evaluating them to arrive at a solution.[19]

Why doesn't brainstorming work as well as individual idea generation? There appear to be at least three reasons.[20] First, there may be a tendency for people to social loaf in group brainstorming contexts. That is, members may not work as hard thinking up ideas as they would if they had to turn in an individually generated list with their name on it. Second, though the brainstorming rules explicitly forbid criticizing others' ideas, members may be hesitant to express ideas that seem silly or not well thought-out. Third, brainstorming results in production blocking because members have to wait their turn to express their ideas. This waiting around consumes time that could otherwise be used by individuals to generate new ideas.

Given the problems associated with brainstorming, why do organizations continue to use it? One reason is that the general idea of brainstorming is well-known, and common sense leads people to believe that it works as advertised. Another reason is that there are benefits of brainstorming beyond just generating ideas. For example, brainstorming builds morale and results in the sharing of knowledge that might otherwise be locked inside the minds of the individual team members.[21] Although this knowledge may not be useful for the particular problem that's being debated, it might be useful for issues that arise in the future. Finally, some companies have had success with brainstorming that follows a somewhat different set of rules. At IDEO, for example, brainstorming meetings often open with a warm-up session, typically a fast-paced word game to clear the minds of the participants.[22] Table 12-1 lists the secrets of better brainstorming, as practiced at IDEO.

TABLE 12-1   IDEO's Secrets for Brainstorming

WHAT TO DO	DESCRIPTION
Have a sharp focus	Begin the brainstorming with a clearly stated problem.
Playful rules	Encourage playfulness, but don't debate or critique ideas.
Number the ideas	Makes it easier to jump back and forth between ideas.
Build and jump	Build on and explore variants of ideas.
The space remembers	Use space to keep track of the flow of ideas in a visible way.
Stretch your brain	Warm up for the session by doing word games.
Get physical	Use drawings and props to make the ideas three-dimensional.

WHAT NOT TO DO	DESCRIPTION
The boss speaks first	Boss's ideas limit what people will say afterwards.
Give everybody a turn	Forcing equal participation reduces spontaneity.
Only include experts	Creative ideas come from unexpected places.
Do it off-site	You want creativity at the office too.
Limit the silly stuff	Silly stuff might trigger useful ideas.
Write down everything	The writing process can reduce spontaneity.

Source: T. Kelley and J. Littman, *The Art of Innovation* (New York: Doubleday, 2001).

One offshoot of brainstorming that addresses some of its limitations is the **nominal group technique.**[23] Similar to a traditional brainstorming session, this process starts off by bringing the team together and outlining the purpose of the meeting. The next step takes place on an individual level however, as members have a set period of time to write down their own ideas on a piece of paper. The subsequent step goes back into the team setting, as members share their ideas with the team in a round-robin fashion. After the ideas are recorded, members have a discussion intended to clarify the ideas and build on the ideas of others. After this, it's back to an individual environment; members rank order ideas on a card that they submit to a facilitator. A facilitator then tabulates the scores to determine the winning idea. From this description, you probably can guess how the nominal group technique addresses the problems with brainstorming. By making people write down ideas on their own, it decreases social loafing and production blocking. Although team members might still be hesitant about expressing wild ideas to the group, doing so might be less threatening than having nothing to contribute to the group. In addition, ranking items as individuals makes people less apprehensive about going "against the grain" of the group by voicing support for an unpopular idea.

DECISION MAKING. In Chapter 8 on Learning and Decision Making, we described how people use information and intuition to make specific decisions. In team contexts, however, decision making involves multiple members gathering and considering information that is relevant to their area of specialization, and then making recommendations to a team leader who is ultimately responsible for the final decision.[24] If you ever watched the TV show *The Apprentice,* you should be able to understand this process quite clearly. The show typically begins with Donald Trump assigning two teams a fairly complex task. A member from each team then volunteers to be project leader, and this person assigns roles like marketing, logistics, and sales to the other team members. Throughout the project, members make suggestions and recommendations to the leader, who ultimately is responsible for making the decisions that determine the success of the project. Of course, project success is important because someone from the losing team—most often the project leader—gets to hear Trump say those famous words: "You're fired."

What factors account for a team's ability to make effective decisions? At least three factors appear to be involved.[25] The first factor is **decision informity,** which reflects whether members possess adequate information about their own task responsibilities. Project teams

Like many teams in the real world, the teams on the popular television show *The Apprentice* often struggle to make good decisions.

on *The Apprentice* often fail, for example, because the team member in charge of marketing does not gather information necessary to help the team understand the desires and needs of the client. The second factor is **staff validity,** which refers to the degree to which members make good recommendations to the leader. Team members can possess all the information needed to make a good recommendation but then fail to do so because of a lack of ability, insight, or good judgment. The third factor is **hierarchical sensitivity,** which reflects the degree to which the leader effectively weighs the recommendations of the members. Whom does the leader listen to, and whom does the leader ignore? Teams that make good decisions tend to have leaders that do a good job giving recommendations the weight they deserve. Although these three variables play a large role in how effective teams are in terms of their decision making,[26] our **OB Internationally** feature describes additional considerations that need to be taken into account in culturally diverse teams.[27]

The decision informity, staff validity, and hierarchical sensitivity concepts can be used to make specific recommendations for improving team decision making. For example, research shows that more experienced teams tend to make better decisions because they

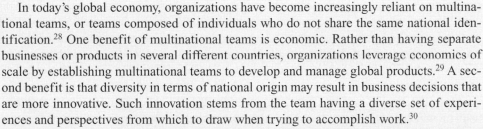

OB INTERNATIONALLY

In today's global economy, organizations have become increasingly reliant on multinational teams, or teams composed of individuals who do not share the same national identification.[28] One benefit of multinational teams is economic. Rather than having separate businesses or products in several different countries, organizations leverage economics of scale by establishing multinational teams to develop and manage global products.[29] A second benefit is that diversity in terms of national origin may result in business decisions that are more innovative. Such innovation stems from the team having a diverse set of experiences and perspectives from which to draw when trying to accomplish work.[30]

Of course, few things in life are free. Along with these benefits of multinational teams come costs in terms of potential problems with team processes. The most obvious problem is language barriers that prevent team members from communicating effectively with one another. Beyond simple misunderstandings, communication barriers can result in difficulties in coordinating tasks and may hinder members from receiving or understanding the information they need to make good recommendations and decisions.[31] So what can multinational teams do to address some of these problems?

One solution is *group decision support systems,* which involve the use of computer technology to help the team structure its decision-making process.[32] As an example, members of a multinational team might meet in rooms, where each member sits at a networked laptop. At different points during the meeting, members are directed to provide their ideas and recommendations into the computer. These inputs are then summarized and shared visually with the entire team on their computer screens. Advantages of this approach are that the system keeps the meeting focused squarely on the task, and information can be presented in a logical sequence at a pace that makes it easier to digest. Moreover, no single member can dominate the meeting. As a consequence of these advantages, team members may participate more uniformly in the meeting and develop a more consistent understanding of the information that was exchanged. Another advantage is that the technique can be modified and used when members are geographically dispersed. The downside of group decision support systems, especially if the meetings are held virtually, is that the process is depersonalized, and members may leave the meetings feeling less connected to the team and its decisions.[33]

develop an understanding of the information that's needed and how to use it, and leaders develop an understanding of which members provide the best recommendations.[33] As another example, team decision making may be improved by giving members feedback about the three variables involved in the decision-making process.[34] For example, a team can improve its decision making if the members are told that they have to share and consider additional pieces of information before making recommendations to the leader. Although this recommendation may seem obvious, all too often teams only receive feedback about their final decision. In addition, there may be a benefit to separating the process of sharing information from the process of making recommendations and final decisions, at least in terms of how information is communicated among members.[35] Whereas teams tend to share more information when they meet face to face, leaders do a better job considering recommendations and making final decisions when they're away from the members. Once they're separated, they don't have to deal with pressure from members who may be more assertive or better at articulating and defending their positions.

BOUNDARY SPANNING. The third type of taskwork process is **boundary spanning,** which involves activities with individuals and groups other than those who are considered part of the team. **Ambassador activities** refer to communications that are intended to protect the team, persuade others to support the team, or obtain important resources for the team. As you might have guessed from this description, members who engage in ambassador activities typically communicate with people who are higher up in the organization. For example, a member of a marketing team might meet with senior management to request an increase in the budget for an expanded television ad campaign. **Task coordinator activities** involve communications that are intended to coordinate task-related issues with people or groups in other functional areas. Continuing with the marketing team example, a member of the team might meet with someone from manufacturing to work out how a coupon might be integrated into the product packaging materials. Finally, **scout activities** refer to things team members do to obtain information about technology, competitors, or the broader marketplace. The marketing team member who meets with an engineer to seek information about new materials is engaging in scout activities. Taken together, research suggests that these boundary-spanning activities may be as important to determining team success as the processes that occur entirely within the team.[36]

boundary spanning activities

TEAMWORK PROCESSES

12.3
What are teamwork processes, and what are some examples of team activities that fall into this process category?

Another category of team processes that helps teams increase their process gain while minimizing their process loss is teamwork processes. **Teamwork processes** refer to the interpersonal activities that facilitate the accomplishment of the team's work but do not directly involve task accomplishment itself.[37] You can think of teamwork processes as the behaviors that create the setting or context in which taskwork can be carried out. So what types of behaviors do teamwork processes involve? Figure 12-2 summarizes the set of teamwork processes discussed in this chapter.[38]

TRANSITION PROCESSES. Teamwork processes become important right when teams first begin their work. **Transition processes** are teamwork activities that focus on preparation for future work. For example, mission analysis involves an analysis of the team's task, the challenges that face the team, and the resources available for completing the team's work. Strategy formulation refers to the development of courses of action and contingency plans, and then adapting those plans in light of changes that occur in the team's environment. Finally, goal specification involves the development and prioritization of goals related to the team's mission and strategy. Each of these transition processes is relevant before the team actually begins to conduct the core aspects of its work. However, these transition processes also may be important between periods of work activity. For example,

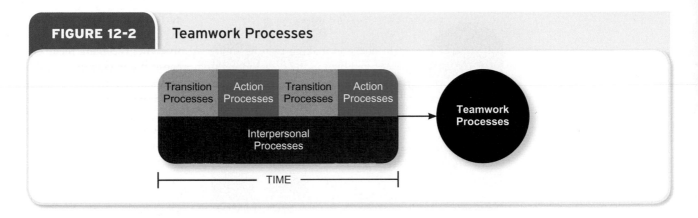

FIGURE 12-2   Teamwork Processes

think about the halftime adjustments made by a basketball team that is losing a game badly. The team could consider the strengths of its opponent and develop a new strategy intended to neutralize them. In this way, teams may switch from transition processes to taskwork, then back to transition processes.

ACTION PROCESSES. Whereas transition processes are important before and between periods of taskwork, **action processes** are important as the taskwork is being accomplished. One type of action process involves monitoring progress toward goals. Teams that pay attention to goal-related information—perhaps by charting the team's performance relative to team goals—are typically in a good position to realize when they are "off-track" and need to make changes. Systems monitoring involves keeping track of things that the team needs to accomplish its work. A team that does not engage in systems monitoring may fail because it runs out of inventory, time, or other necessary resources. Helping behavior involves members going out of their way to help or back up other team members. Team members can provide indirect help to their teammates in the form of feedback or coaching, as well as direct help in the form of assistance with members' tasks and responsibilities. Coordination refers to synchronizing team members' activities in a way that makes them mesh effectively and seamlessly. Poor coordination results in team members constantly having to wait on others for information or other resources necessary to do their part of the team's work.[39]

INTERPERSONAL PROCESSES. The third category of teamwork processes is called **interpersonal processes.** The processes in this category are important before, during, or in between periods of taskwork, and each relates to the manner in which team members manage their relationships. The first type of interpersonal process is motivating and confidence building, which refers to things team members do or say that affect the degree to which members are motivated to work hard on the team's task. Expressions that create a sense of urgency and optimism are examples of communications that would fit in this category. Similarly, affect management involves activities that foster a sense of emotional balance and unity. If you've ever worked in a team in which members got short tempered when facing pressure or blamed one another when there were problems, you have firsthand experience with poor affect management.

Another important interpersonal process is conflict management, which involves the activities that the team uses to manage conflicts that arise in the course of its work. Conflict tends to have a negative impact on a team, but the nature of this effect depends on the focus of the conflict as well as the manner in which the conflict is managed.[40] **Relationship conflict** refers to disagreements among team members in terms of interpersonal relationships or incompatibilities with respect to personal values or preferences. This type of conflict centers on issues that are not directly connected to the team's task. Relationship conflict is not only dissatisfying to most people, it also tends to result in reduced team

For task conflict to be productive, team members must feel free to express their opinions and know how to manage conflict effectively.

performance. **Task conflict,** in contrast, refers to disagreements among members about the team's task. In the abstract, this type of conflict can be beneficial to teams if it stimulates conversations that result in the development and expression of new ideas.[41] Research findings, however, indicate that task conflict tends to result in reduced team effectiveness unless two conditions are present.[42] First, members need to trust one another and be confident that they can express their opinions openly without fear of reprisals. Second, team members need to engage in effective conflict management processes. (For more discussion of conflict management issues, see Chapter 13 on Leadership: Power and Influence.)

What does effective conflict management involve? First, when trying to manage conflict, it's important for members to stay focused on the team's mission. If members do this, they can rationally evaluate the relative merits of each position.[43] Second, any benefits of task conflict disappear if the level of the conflict gets too heated, if parties appear to be acting in self-interest rather than in the best interest of the team, or if there is high relationship conflict.[44] Third, to effectively manage task conflict, members need to discuss their positions openly and be willing to exchange information in a way that fosters collaborative problem solving.[45] If you've ever had an experience in an ongoing relationship in which you tried to avoid uncomfortable conflict by ignoring it, you probably already understand that this strategy only tends to make things worse in the end. Our **OB for Students** feature provides an example of how conflict management can have a significant impact on the effectiveness of student teams.

TEAM STATES

12.4

What are team states, and what are some examples of the states that fall into this process category?

A third category of team processes that helps teams increase their process gain while minimizing their process loss is less visible to the naked eye. **Team states** refer to specific types of feelings and thoughts that coalesce in the minds of team members as a consequence of their experience working together. Although there are many types of team states that we could review in this chapter, Figure 12-3 summarizes the set of team states we discuss.

COHESION. For a number of different reasons, members of teams can develop strong emotional bonds to other members of their team and to the team itself. This emotional attachment, which is called **cohesion,**[47] tends to foster high levels of motivation and commitment to the team, and as a consequence, cohesiveness tends to promote higher levels of team performance.[48] But is a cohesive team necessarily a good team? According to researchers, the answer to this question is no. In highly cohesive teams, members may try to maintain harmony by striving toward consensus on issues without ever offering, seeking, or seriously considering alternative viewpoints and perspectives. This drive toward conformity at the expense of other team priorities is called **groupthink** and is thought to be associated with feelings of overconfidence about the team's capabilities.[49] In the end, groupthink has been blamed for decision-making fiascos in politics as well as in business. Some famous examples include John F. Kennedy's decision to go forward with the Bay of Pigs invasion of Cuba,[50] NASA's decision to launch the space shuttle Challenger in unusually cold weather,[51] and Enron's Board of Directors' decisions to ignore illegal accounting practices.[52]

OB FOR STUDENTS

Conflict among team members about the team's task can result in improved team performance, for several reasons. Primarily, task conflict can foster the sharing of information that results in superior solutions to the problems that arise in the team's work. However, if you have experience working in student teams in your courses, you know that this type of conflict can have some really negative consequences—not the least of which is the discomfort it provokes and the huge waste of time that can ensue. To avoid this dissatisfying experience, many students try to avoid conflict in their team. One strategy that that may be familiar to you involves splitting up parts of the assignment, performing the work independently, and finally slapping the parts together to produce the team outcome. Although a team might be able to complete assignments using this strategy, the end product tends not to be as good as it could be.

Might there be a better way for student teams to manage task conflict? One study of teams of undergraduate business students investigated the role that task conflict had on two important team outcomes—the grade on a semester-long team project and members' satisfaction with the team experience.[46] The results of the study indicated that the effects of task conflict on these two outcomes depended a lot on the way the team managed its conflict.

First, higher levels of task conflict tended to result in higher scores on team projects, but only for teams that approached the conflict proactively. Members of these teams openly discussed points of disagreement and tried to resolve their disagreements collaboratively. In contrast, teams tended to perform less well on team projects when the members managed high levels of task conflict in a more passive way. These teams tended to avoid openly expressing disagreements or ended potential disagreement prematurely by being overly accommodating of other members' positions.

Second, higher levels of task conflict resulted in higher levels of satisfaction with the team experience, but only for teams that managed conflict in an agreeable manner. Individuals in these teams expressed opposing positions in a relaxed and nonconfrontational way. When members expressed their positions harshly or in a more emotional way, higher levels of task conflict tended to reduce member satisfaction.

FIGURE 12-3 **Team States**

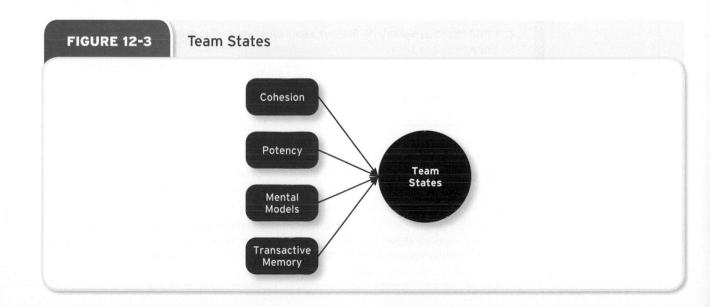

So how do you leverage the benefits of cohesion without taking on the potential costs? One way is to acknowledge that cohesion can potentially have detrimental consequences. A good first step in this regard would be to assess the team's cohesion using a scale such as the one in our **OB Assessments** feature. A high score on this sort of assessment indicates the team may be vulnerable to groupthink. A second step in preventing problems associated with cohesion would be to formally institute the role of devil's advocate. The person filling this role would be responsible for evaluating and challenging prevailing points of view in a constructive manner and also bringing in fresh perspectives and ideas to the

OB ASSESSMENTS

COHESION

How cohesive is your team? This assessment is designed to measure cohesion—the strength of the emotional bonds that develop among members of a team. Think of your current student project team or an important team that you belong to in your job. Answer each question using the response scale provided. Then subtract your answers to the bold-faced questions from 8, with the difference being your new answers for those questions. For example, if your original answer for question 6 was "5", your new answer is "3" (8 − 5). Then sum up your answers for the eight questions.

1	2	3	4	5	6	7
STRONGLY DISAGREE	DISAGREE	SLIGHTLY DISAGREE	NEUTRAL	SLIGHTLY AGREE	AGREE	STRONGLY AGREE

1. **If given a chance, I would choose to leave my team to join another.** _____

2. The members of my team get along well together. _____

3. The members of my team will readily defend each other from criticism. _____

4. I feel that I am really a part of my team. _____

5. I look forward to being with the members of my team every day. _____

6. **I find that I generally do not get along with other members of my team.** _____

7. I enjoy belonging to this team because I am friends with many members. _____

8. The team to which I belong is a close one. _____

SCORING

If your scores sum up to 48 or above, you feel a strong bond to your team, suggesting that your team is cohesive. If your scores sum up to less than 48, you feel a weaker bond to your team, suggesting that your team is not as cohesive.

Source: G.H. Dobbins and S.J. Zacarro, "The Effects of Group Cohesion and Leader Behavior on Subordinate Satisfaction," *Group and Organization Management* 11 (1986), pp. 203–19. Copyright © 1986 Sage Publications Inc. Reproduced via permission from Copyright Clearance Center.

team. Although the devil's advocate role could be filled by an existing team member, it's also possible that the team could bring in an outsider to fill that role.

POTENCY. The second team state, **potency,** refers to the degree to which members believe that the team can be effective across a variety of situations and tasks.[53] When a team has high potency, members are confident that their team can perform well, and as a consequence, they focus more of their energy on achieving team goals. When a team has low potency, members are not as confident about their team, and so they begin to question the team's goals and one another. Ultimately, this reaction can result in members focusing their energies on activities that don't benefit the team. As a result, research studies have shown that potency has a strong positive impact on team performance.[54] So how does high potency develop in teams? Team members' confidence in their own capabilities, their trust in other members' capabilities, and feedback about past performance are all likely to play a role. Specifically, team potency is promoted in teams in which members are confident in themselves and their teammates and when the team has found success in the past.

MENTAL MODELS. Mental models refer to the level of common understanding among team members with regard to important aspects of the team and its task.[55] A team may have shared mental models with respect to the capabilities that members bring to the team as well as the processes the team needs to use to be effective.[56] How can these two types of mental models foster team effectiveness? When team members share in their understanding of one another's capabilities, they're more likely to know where to go for the help they might need to complete their work. In addition, they should be able to anticipate when another member needs help to do his or her work. When members have a shared understanding of which processes are necessary to help the team be effective, they can carry out these processes efficiently and smoothly. To help you understand why this is true, consider what would happen in a team of students who had different understandings about how the team should manage conflict. Few disagreements would get resolved if some of the members believed that direct confrontation was best, whereas others believed that avoidance was best.

TRANSACTIVE MEMORY. Whereas mental models refer to the degree to which the knowledge is shared among members, **transactive memory** refers to how specialized knowledge is distributed among members in a manner that results in an effective system of memory for the team.[57] This concept takes into account the idea that not everyone on a team has to possess the same knowledge. Instead, team effectiveness requires that members understand when their own specialized knowledge is relevant to the team and how their knowledge should be combined with the knowledge of other members to accomplish team goals. If you've ever worked on a team that had effective transactive memory, you may have noticed that work got done very efficiently.[58] Everyone focused on his or her specialty and what he or she did best, members knew exactly where to go to get information when there were gaps in their knowledge, and the team produced synergistic results. Of course, transactive memory can also be fragile because the memory system depends on each and every member.[59] If someone is slow to respond to another member's request for information or forgets something important, the team's system of memory fails. Alternatively, if a member of the team leaves, you lose an important node in the memory system.

SUMMARY: WHY ARE SOME TEAMS MORE THAN THE SUM OF THEIR PARTS?

So what explains why some teams become more than the sum of their parts (whereas other teams become less)? As shown in Figure 12-4, teams become more than the sum of their parts if their team process achieves process gain rather than process loss. Teams can accomplish that goal by engaging in activities that are involved in taskwork processes, team-work processes, and team states. Important taskwork processes include creative behavior, decision making, and boundary spanning. Important teamwork processes include transition processes, action processes, and interpersonal processes. Finally, team states refer to variables such as cohesion, potency, mental models, and transactive memory. In contrast to the taskwork and teamwork processes, team states offer less visible and observable reasons why some teams possess an effective synergy whereas others seem quite inefficient.

FIGURE 12-4	Why Are Some Teams More than the Sum of Their Parts?

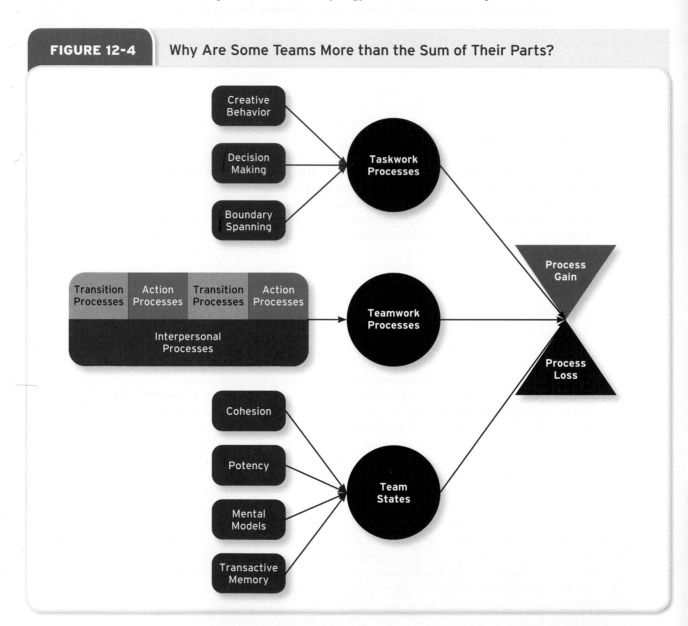

HOW IMPORTANT ARE TEAM PROCESSES?

Do team processes affect performance and commitment? Answering this question is somewhat complicated for two reasons. First, as in Chapter 11 on Team Characteristics, when we say "performance and commitment," we are not referring to the performance of individuals or their attachment to the organization. Instead, we are referring to the performance of teams and the degree to which teams are capable of remaining together as ongoing entities. In the jargon of research on teams, this form of commitment is termed "team viability." Second, as have we described throughout this chapter, there are several different types of team processes that we could consider in our summary. In Figure 12-5, we characterize the relationship between team processes and performance and commitment by focusing specifically on research involving teamwork processes. The figure therefore represents a summary of existing research on transition processes, action processes, and interpersonal processes.

Research conducted in a wide variety of team settings has shown that teamwork processes have a moderate positive relationship with team performance.[60] This same moderate positive relationship appears to hold true, regardless of whether the research examines transition processes, action processes, or interpersonal processes. Why might the relationships between these different types of processes and team performance be so similarly positive? Apparently, effectiveness with respect to a wide variety of interactions is needed to help teams achieve process gain and, in turn, perform effectively. The interpersonal activities that prepare teams for future work appear to be just as important as those that help members integrate their taskwork and those that build team confidence and a positive team climate.

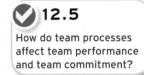

12.5

How do team processes affect team performance and team commitment?

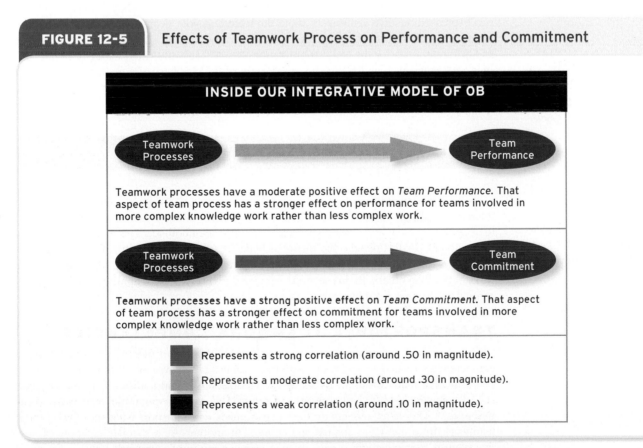

| FIGURE 12-5 | Effects of Teamwork Process on Performance and Commitment |

Source: J.A. LePine, R.F. Piccolo, C.L. Jackson, J.E. Mathieu, and J.R. Saul, "A Meta-Analysis of Team Process: Towards a Better Understanding of the Dimensional Structure and Relationships with Team Effectiveness Criteria," *Personnel Psychology* (in press).

A rare orchestra that performs without a conductor, the Orpheus Chamber Orchestra exhibits such teamwork and commitment that it has had a successful history of over 35 years of performance. While all members of the orchestra help refine the interpretation and execution of each work in its repertoire, they also select a concertmaster and principal players to lead each piece.

Research also indicates that teamwork processes have a strong positive relationship with team commitment.[61] In other words, teams that engage in effective teamwork processes tend to continue to exist together into the future. Why should teamwork and team commitment be so strongly related? One reason is that people tend to be satisfied in teams in which there are effective interpersonal interactions, and as a consequence, they go out of their way to do things that they believe will help the team stick together. Think about a team situation that you've been in when everyone shared the same goals for the team, work was coordinated smoothly, and everyone was positive, pleasant to be around, and willing to do their fair share of the work. If you've ever actually been in a situation like this—and we hope that you have—chances are that you did your best to make sure the team could continue on together. It's likely that you worked extra hard to make sure that the team achieved its goals. It's also likely that you expressed positive sentiments about the team and your desire for the team to remain together. Of course, just the opposite would be true in a team context in which members had different goals for the team, coordination was difficult and filled with emotional conflict, and everyone was pessimistic and disagreeable. Members of a team like this would not only find the situation dissatisfying but, also make it known that they would be very open to a change of scenery.

APPLICATION: TRAINING TEAMS

12.6

What steps can organizations take to improve team processes?

Team-based organizations invest a significant amount of resources into training that is intended to improve team processes. These types of investments seem to be a smart thing to do, given that team processes have a positive impact on both team performance and team commitment. Unfortunately, the intended benefits of investments in team training have not always been realized. It therefore becomes important to understand which approaches work better than others. In this section, we review several different approaches that organizations use to train team processes.

TRANSPORTABLE TEAMWORK COMPETENCIES

One approach to training teams is to help individual team members develop general competencies related to teamwork activities. Table 12-2 shows that this type of training could involve many different forms of knowledge, skills, and abilities.[62] Taken together, such knowledge, skills, and abilities are referred to as **transportable teamwork competences.**[63] This label reflects the fact that trainees can transport what they learn about teamwork from one team context and apply it in another. As a specific example of how this type of training might work, consider a recent study of teamwork training for naval aviators in an advanced pilot training program.[64] In this study, one group of pilots went through two days of training, during which they received instruction on preferred communication practices, communicating suggestions and asking questions, and communicating

| TABLE 12-2 | Examples of Knowledge, Skills, and Abilities for Teamwork |

	COMPETENCY	DESCRIPTION
1.	Conflict resolution	Can distinguish between desirable and undesirable conflict. Encourages desirable conflict and discourages undesirable conflict. Uses win-win strategies to manage conflict.
2.	Collaborative problem solving	Can identify situations requiring participative problem solving. Uses the appropriate degree of participation. Recognizes and manages obstacles to collaborative problem solving.
3.	Communications	Understands communication networks. Communicates openly and supportively. Listens without making premature evaluations. Uses active listening techniques. Can interpret nonverbal messages of others. Engages in ritual greetings and small talk.
4.	Goal setting and performance management	Helps establish specific and difficult goals for the team. Monitors, evaluates, and provides performance-related feedback.
5.	Planning and task coordination	Coordinates and synchronizes activities among team members. Establishes expectations to ensure proper balance of workload within the team.

Source: Adapted from M.J. Stevens and M.A. Campion, "The Knowledge, Skill, and Ability Requirements for Teamwork: Implications for Human Resource Management," *Journal of Management* 20 (1994), pp. 503–30.

about potential problems. The pilots who went through the training believed that in addition to building teamwork knowledge and skills, the training would increase their mission effectiveness and flight safety. Most important, teams that were composed of pilots who went through the training were significantly more effective than teams composed of pilots who did not go through the training. Effectiveness was judged by performance in dangerous scenarios, such as ice buildup on the aircraft wings and instructions from the air traffic control tower that were conflicting or ambiguous.

CROSS-TRAINING

A second type of team training involves training members in the duties and responsibilities of their teammates. The idea behind this type of training, which is called **cross-training,**[65] is that team members can develop shared mental models of what is involved in each of the roles in the team and how the roles fit together to form a system.[66] What exactly does cross-training involve? Researchers have found that cross-training may involve instruction at three different levels of depth.[67] At the shallowest level, there is **personal clarification.** With this type of training, members simply receive information regarding the roles of the other team members. As an example, the highly specialized members of surgical teams—surgeons, anesthesiologists, operating room nurses—might meet so that they can learn about others' roles and how each contributes to the team's goal of achieving overall patient well-being.

At the next level of cross-training, there is **positional modeling,** which involves team members observing how other members perform their roles. In the case of the surgical teams, the surgeons might spend a day shadowing operating room nurses as they perform their duties. The shadowing not only helps the surgeons gain a better understanding of what the job of a nurse entails, but also may provide insight into how the activities involved in their respective jobs could be integrated more effectively.

Finally, the deepest level of cross-training involves **positional rotation.** This type of training gives members actual experience carrying out the responsibilities of their teammates. Although this type of hands-on experience could expand skills of members so that they might actually perform the duties of their teammates if they had to, the level of training required to achieve proficiency or certification in many situations may be prohibitive. For example, because it takes years of specialized training to become a surgeon, it would be impractical to train an operating room nurse to perform this job for the purposes of positional rotation.

TEAM PROCESS TRAINING

Cross-training and training in transportable teamwork competencies focus on individual experiences that promote individual learning. **Team process training,** in contrast, occurs in the context of a team experience that facilitates the team being able to function and perform more effectively as an intact unit. One type of team process training is called **action learning.** With this type of training, which has been used successfully at companies such as Motorola and General Electric, a team is given a real problem that is relevant to the organization and then held accountable for analyzing the problem, developing an action plan, and finally carrying out the action plan.[68] How does this type of experience develop effective team processes? First, the team receives coaching to help facilitate more effective processes during different phases of the project. Second, there are meetings during which team members are encouraged to reflect on the team processes they have used as they worked on the project. In these meetings, the members not only discuss what they observed and learned from their experiences, but also what they would do differently in the future.

A second type of team process training involves experience in a team context when there are task demands that highlight the importance of effective teamwork processes. As an example, in an effort to decrease the amount of time airliners spend on the ground between flights, United Airlines used pit crew training for their ramp crews.[69] Although teams of ramp workers at an airline like United must work with luggage, belt loaders, and baggage carts, there are parallels with the work of NASCAR pit crews that work with tires, jacks, and air guns. Primarily, effective performance in both contexts means performing work safely within tight time constraints. Moreover, in both of these contexts, achieving goals requires teamwork, communication, and strict adherence to standardized team procedures. The real value of the pit crew training to the ramp crews is that it conveys the lessons of teamwork in a very vivid way. If a team fails to follow procedures and work together when trying to change tires, tools will be misplaced, parts will be dropped, and members will get in one another's way. As a consequence, a pit stop may last for minutes rather than seconds.

TEAM BUILDING

The fourth general type of team process training is called **team building.** This type of training is normally conducted by a consultant and intended to facilitate the development of team processes related to goal setting, interpersonal relations, problem solving, and role clarification.[70] The ropes course is a very popular task used in team building. It requires team members to work together to traverse wooden beams, ropes, and zip lines while dangling in a harness 20–50 feet in the air. Other examples include laser tag and paintball,[71]

WhirlyBall (think lacrosse played in bumper cars with a whiffle ball and plastic scoops),[72] whitewater rafting, scavenger hunts, and beating drums in a drum circle.[73] Team-building activities such as these are hugely popular with organizations of all sizes, and they do seem like an awful lot of fun.

But can you really build effective teams by having them participate in enjoyable activities that seem so unrelated to their jobs? In fact, this was the basis for Senators Byron Dorgan's and Ron Wyden's request that the Inspector General of the U.S. Postal Service be fired.[74] In their letter to the Chairman of the Post Office Board of Governors, they wrote that the inspector general "has spent millions of agency dollars on expensive and silly 'team building' exercises, diverting massive resources from the task of finding waste and improving efficiency . . . . On tapes, you see images of public servants dressed up as the Village People, wearing cat costumes, doing a striptease, and participating in mock trials—all on official time, all at the public's expense."[75] Although it is somewhat difficult to gauge the effectiveness of team-building interventions because so many different types of exercises have been used, research has been conducted that provides mixed support for the senators' claim. The findings of one meta-analysis found that team building did not have a significant effect on team performance when performance was defined in terms of productivity.[76] However, the research found that team building is most likely to have positive effects for smaller teams and when the exercise emphasizes the importance of clarifying role responsibilities.

TAKEAWAYS

12.1 Team process reflects the different types of activities and interactions that occur within teams that contribute to their ultimate end goals. When teams have process gain, they become more than the sum of their parts through interactions that create synergy among members. When teams have process loss, they become less than the sum of their parts through interactions that create inefficiencies between members.

12.2 Taskwork processes are the activities of team members that relate directly to the accomplishment of team tasks. Taskwork processes include creative behavior, decision making, and boundary spanning.

12.3 Teamwork processes refer to the interpersonal activities that facilitate the accomplishment of the team's work but do not directly involve task accomplishment itself. Teamwork processes include transition processes, action processes, and interpersonal processes.

12.4 Team states refer to specific types of feelings and thoughts that coalesce in the minds of team members as a consequence of their experience working together. Team states include cohesion, potency, mental models, and transactive memory.

12.5 Teamwork processes have a moderate positive relationship with team performance and a strong positive relationship with team commitment.

12.6 Organizations can use training interventions to improve team processes. Such interventions may include training in transportable teamwork competencies, cross-training, team process training, and team building.

KEY TERMS

- Team process   *p. 408*
- Process gain   *p. 409*
- Process loss   *p. 409*
- Coordination loss   *p. 409*
- Production blocking   *p. 409*
- Motivational loss   *p. 409*
- Social loafing   *p. 411*
- Taskwork processes   *p. 412*
- Brainstorming   *p. 412*
- Nominal group technique   *p. 414*
- Decision informity   *p. 414*
- Staff validity   *p. 415*
- Hierarchical sensitivity   *p. 415*
- Boundary spanning   *p. 416*
- Ambassador activities   *p. 416*
- Task coordinator activities   *p. 416*
- Scout activities   *p. 416*
- Teamwork processes   *p. 416*
- Transition processes   *p. 416*
- Action processes   *p. 417*
- Interpersonal processes   *p. 417*
- Relationship conflict   *p. 417*
- Task conflict   *p. 418*
- Team states   *p. 418*
- Cohesion   *p. 418*
- Groupthink   *p. 418*
- Potency   *p. 421*
- Mental models   *p. 421*
- Transactive memory   *p. 421*
- Transportable teamwork competencies   *p. 424*
- Cross-training   *p. 425*
- Personal clarification   *p. 425*
- Positional modeling   *p. 425*
- Positional rotation   *p. 426*
- Team process training   *p. 426*
- Action learning   *p. 426*
- Team building   *p. 426*

DISCUSSION QUESTIONS

12.1 Before reading this chapter, how did you define teamwork? How did this definition correspond to the definition outlined in this book?

12.2 Think of a team you worked in that performed poorly. Were any of the causes of the poor performance related to the forces that tend create process loss? If so, which force was most particularly problematic? What steps, if any, did your team take to deal with the problem?

12.3 Think of a team you worked in that performed exceptionally well. What type of taskwork process did the team engage in? Which teamwork processes did the team seem to depend on most to produce the exceptional results?

12.4 Think about the team states described in this chapter. If you joined a new team, how long do you think it would take you to get a feel for those team states? Which states would you be able to gauge first? Which would take longer?

12.5 Describe boundary-spanning activities in the context of a student team. Have student teams you worked in done any of these effectively? Are there boundary-spanning activities that you could engage in that would promote your learning, grades, or overall satisfaction?

12.6 Which types of teamwork training would your student team benefit most from? What exactly would this training cover? What specific benefits would you expect? What would prevent a team from training itself on this material?

CASE IDEO

Innovation is what separates one business from another, which may be why IDEO's services are so highly sought after. David Kelly, founder of IDEO, uses mind maps, a method that freely associates seemingly unrelated ideas together, to foster creativity, as well as innovative products and services. This approach to creativity has proven widely successful in Silicon Valley and at IDEO.

IDEO has set the benchmark for brainstorming with its innovative business tactics and knack for success. Brainstorming generates ideas, but not all brainstorming sessions are created equal. IDEO uses cross-functional project teams to gather input from employees with diverse skill sets. Within these teams, everybody is actively involved in generating ideas. The brainstorming process at IDEO is successful because of the teams' ability to work as a cohesive unit to discover new possibilities.

Empathy also provides a significant source of IDEO's ability to continually push the envelope of innovation in various industries. IDEO believes it is vital for its teams to understand the consumer psyche prior to designing a product or service. This understanding is normally the first step IDEO teams take when given a project. In contrast, most companies start a project by creating an elaborate design drawing; however, this approach limits the creative possibilities of a project. IDEO is a leader in innovation not just because of its talented individual employees but also because of the employees' ability to work as a team toward a common goal.

12.1 Is creative behavior based on individual or team performance within IDEO? Explain.

12.2 What makes IDEO's brainstorming sessions more productive than those of other companies? Explain.

Sources: "Eight Rules to Brilliant Brainstorming," *BusinessWeek Online*, September 25, 2006, www.business-week.com (June 21, 2007); "Online Extra: IDEO's Innovation Ideas," *BusinessWeek Online*, October 24, 2005, www.businessweek.com (June 21, 2007); "In Mind," *BusinessWeek*, September 25, 2006; D.H. Pink, "Out of the Box," *Fast Company*, October 2003.

EXERCISE WILDERNESS SURVIVAL

The purpose of this exercise is to experience team processes during a decision-making task. This exercise uses groups of six participants, so your instructor will either assign you to a group of six or ask you to create your own group of six. The exercise has the following steps:

1. Working individually, read the following scenario:

You have gone on a Boundary Waters canoe trip with five friends to upper Minnesota and southern Ontario in the Quetico Provincial Park. Your group has been traveling Saganagons Lake to Kawnipi Lake, following through Canyon Falls and Kennebas Falls and Kenny Lake. Fifteen to eighteen miles away is the closest road, which is arrived at by paddling through lakes and rivers and usually portaging (taking the land path) around numerous falls. Saganagons Lake is impossible to cross in bad weather, generally because of heavy rain. The nearest town is Grand Marais, Minnesota, 60 miles away. That town has plenty of camping outfitters but limited medical help, so residents rely on hospitals farther to the south.

The terrain is about 70 percent land and 30 percent water, with small patches of land here and there in between the lakes and rivers. Bears are not uncommon in this region. It is now mid-May, when the (daytime) temperature ranges from about 25° to 70°, often in the same day. Nighttime temperatures can be in the 20s. Rain is frequent during the day (nights, too) and can be life threatening if the temperature is cold. It is unusual for the weather to stay the same for more than a day or two. Generally, it will rain one day and be warm and clear the next, with a third day windy—and it is not easy to predict what type of weather will come next. In fact, it may be clear and warm, rainy and windy, all in the same day.

Your group of six was in two canoes going down the river and came to some rapids. Rather than taking the portage route on land, the group foolishly decided to shoot the rapids by canoe. Unfortunately, everyone fell out of the canoes, and some were banged against the rocks. Luckily no one was killed, but one person suffered a broken leg, and several others had cuts and bruises. Both canoes were damaged severely. Both were bent in half, one with an open tear of 18 inches, while the other suffered two tears of 12 and 15 inches long. Both have broken gunwales (the upper edges on both sides). You lost the packs that held the tent, most clothing, nearly all the food, cooking equipment, and fuel, the first aid kit, and the flashlight. Your combined possessions include the items shown in the table on the opposite page.

You had permits to take this trip, but no one knows for sure where you are, and the closest phone is in Grand Marais. You were scheduled back four days from now, so it is likely a search party would be sent out in about five days (because you could have been delayed a day or so in getting back). Just now it has started to drizzle, and it looks like rain will follow. Your task is to figure out how to survive in these unpredictable and possibly harsh conditions until you can get help.

2. Working individually, consider how important each of the items in the table would be to you in this situation. Begin with the most important item, giving it a rank of "1," and wind up with the least important item, giving it a rank of "14." Put your rankings in Column B.

3. In your groups, come to a consensus about the ranking of the items. Put those consensus rankings in Column C. Group members should not merely vote or average rankings together. Instead, try to get everyone to more or less agree on the rankings. When someone disagrees, try to listen carefully. When someone feels strongly, that person should attempt to use persuasive techniques to create a consensus.

4. The instructor will post the correct answers and provide the reasons for those rankings, according to two experts (Jeff Stemmerman and Ken Gieske of REI Outfitters, both of whom act as guides for many canoe trips in the Boundary Waters region). Put those expert rankings in Column D. At this point, the Individual Error scores in Column A can be computed by taking the absolute difference between Column B and Column D. The Group Error scores in Column E can also be computed by taking the absolute difference between Column C and Column D. Finally, the Persuasion scores can be computed by taking the absolute difference between Column B and Column C. Remember that all of the differences are absolute differences—there should not be any negative numbers in the table. After completing all these computations, fill in the three scores below the table: the Individual Score (total of Column A), the Group Score (total of Column E), and the Persuasion Score (total of Column F). The Persuasion

	A	B	C	D	E	F
	INDIVIDUAL ERROR (B − D)	YOUR RANKING	GROUP RANKING	EXPERT RANKING	GROUP ERROR (C − D)	PERSUASION SCORE (B − C)
Fanny pack of food (cheese, salami, etc.)						
Plastic-covered map of the region						
Six personal flotation devices						
Two fishing poles (broken)						
Set of clothes for three (wet)						
One yellow Frisbee						
Water purification tablets						
Duct tape (one 30' roll)						
Whiskey (one pint, 180 proof)						
Insect repellant (one bottle)						
Matches (30, dry)						
Parachute cord (35')						
Compass						
Six sleeping bags (synthetic)						

Individual Score: (Total all numbers in Column A): _____

Group Score: (Total all numbers in Column E): _____

Persuasion Score: (Total all numbers in Column F): _____

score measures how much you are able to influence other group members to match your thinking.

5. The instructor will create a table similar to the one that follows in an Excel file in the classroom or on the chalkboard. All groups should provide the instructor with their Average Member Score (the average of all of the Individual Scores for the group), the Group Score, their Best Member Score (the lowest of all the Individual Scores for the group), and that member's Persuasion Score (the Persuasion Score for the member who had the lowest Individual Score).

GROUPS	1	2	3	4	5	6	7	8
Average Member Score								
Group Score								
Best Member Score								
Best Member's Persuasion								
Process Gain? (Yes or No)								

6. Fill in a "Yes" for the Process Gain row if the Group Score was lower than the Average Member Score. This score would reflect a circumstance in which the group discussion actually resulted in more accurate decisions—when "the whole" seemed to be more effective than "the sum of its parts." Fill in a "No" for the Process Gain row if the Group Score was higher than the Average Member Score. In this circumstance, the group discussion actually resulted in less accurate decisions—and the group would have been better off if no talking had occurred.

7. Class discussion (whether in groups or as a class) should center on the following questions: Did most groups tend to achieve process gain in terms of group scores that were better than the average individual scores? Were the group scores usually better than the best member's score? Why not; where did the groups that lacked synergy tend to go wrong? In other words, what behaviors led to process loss rather than process gain? What role does the best member's persuasion score play in all of this? Did groups that tended to listen more to the best member (as reflected in lower persuasion numbers) have more frequent instances of process gain?

ENDNOTES

12.1 IDEO, Corporate Web Site, http://www.ideo.com/portfolio/ (February 27, 2007).

12.2 IDEO, Corporate Web Site, http://www.ideo.com/portfolio/re.asp?x = 50184 (February 27, 2007).

12.3 Kelley, T., and J. Littman. *The Art of Innovation* New York: Doubleday, 2001, p. 69.

12.4 Nessbaum, B. "The Power of Design." *BusinessWeek,* May 17, 2004.

12.5 Ibid.

12.6 Ilgen, D.R.; D.A. Major; J.R. Hollenbeck; and D.J. Sego. "Team Research in the 1990s." In *Leadership Theory and Research: Perspectives and Directions,* eds. M.M. Chemers and R. Ayman. New York: Academic Press, Inc., 1993.

12.7 "Process." Merriam-Webster online dictionary, http://www.merriam-webster.com/dictionary/process (May 27, 2007).

12.8 Hackman, J.R. "The Design of Work Teams." In *Handbook of Organizational Behavior,* ed. J.W. Lorsch.

Englewood Cliffs, NJ: Prentice Hall, 1987, pp. 315–42.

12.9 Steiner, I.D. *Group Processes and Productivity.* New York: Academic Press, 1972.

12.10 Hackman, "The Design of Work Teams."

12.11 Lamm, H., and G. Trommsdorff. "Group Versus Individual Performance on Tasks Requiring Ideational Proficiency (Brainstorming)." *European Journal of Social Psychology* 3 (1973), pp. 361–87.

12.12 Hackman, "The Design of Work Teams."

12.13 Latane, B.; K. Williams; and S. Harkins. "Many Hands Make Light the Work: The Causes and Consequences of Social Loafing." *Journal of Personality and Social Psychology* 37 (1979), pp. 822–32.

12.14 Latane et al., "Many Hands"; Jackson, C.L., and J.A. LePine. "Peer Responses to a Team's Weakest Link: A Test and Extension of LePine and Van Dyne's Model." *Journal of Applied Psychology* 88 (2003), pp. 459–75; Sheppard, A. "Productivity Loss in Performance Groups: A Motivation Analysis." *Psychological Bulletin* 113 (1993), pp. 67–81.

12.15 Jones, D. "Business Leadership Book Wins Fans in NFL." *USA Today,* November 29, 2005, http://www.usatoday.com/money/books/2005-11-27-nfl-book-usat_x.htm (May 29, 2007).

12.16 Shalley, C.E.; J. Zhou; and G.R. Oldham. "The Effects of Personal and Contextual Characteristics on Creativity: Where Should We Go from Here?" *Journal of Management* 30 (2004), pp. 933–58.

12.17 Osborn, A.F. *Applied Imagination* (Revised ed.). New York: Scribner, 1957.

12.18 Ibid.

12.19 Diehl, M., and W. Stroebe. "Productivity Loss in Brainstorming Groups: Toward a Solution of a Riddle." *Journal of Personality and Social Psychology* 53 (1987), pp. 497–509; Mullen, B.; C. Johnson; and E. Salas. "Productivity Loss in Brainstorming Groups: A Meta-Analytic Investigation." *Basic and Applied Social Psychology* 12 (1991), pp. 3–23.

12.20 Diehl and Stroebe, "Productivity Loss."

12.21 Sutton, R.I., and A. Hargadon. "Brainstorming Groups in Context: Effectiveness in a Product Design Firm." *Administrative Science Quarterly* 41 (1996), pp. 685–718.

12.22 Kelley and Littman, *The Art of Innovation.*

12.23 Delbecq, A.L., and A.H. Van de Ven. "A Group Process Model for Identification and Program Planning." *Journal of Applied Behavioral Sciences* 7 (1971), pp. 466–92; Geschka, H.; G.R. Schaude; and H. Schlicksupp. "Modern Techniques for Solving Problems." *Chemical Engineering,* August 1973, pp. 91–97.

12.24 Brehmer, B., and R. Hagafors. "Use of Experts in Complex Decision Making: A Paradigm for the Study of Staff Work." *Organizational Behavior and Human Decision Processes* 38 (1986), pp. 181–95; Ilgen, D.R.; D. Major; J.R. Hollenbeck; and D. Sego. "Raising an Individual Decision Making Model to the Team Level: A New Research Model and Paradigm." In *Team Effectiveness and Decision Making in Organizations,* eds. R. Guzzo and E. Salas. San Francisco: Jossey-Bass, 1995, pp. 113–48.

12.25 Hollenbeck, J.R.; J.A. Colquitt; D.R. Ilgen; J.A. LePine; and J. Hedlund. "Accuracy Decomposition and Team Decision Making: Testing Theoretical Boundary Conditions." *Journal of Applied Psychology* 83 (1998), pp. 494–500; Hollenbeck, J.R.; D.R. Ilgen; D.J. Sego; J. Hedlund; D.A. Major; and J. Phillips. "Multilevel Theory of Team Decision Making; Decision Performance in Teams Incorporating Distributed Expertise." *Journal of Applied Psychology* 80 (1995), pp. 292–316.

12.26 Humphrey, S.E.; J.R. Hollenbeck; C.J. Meyer; and D.R. Ilgen. "Hierarchical Team Decision Making." *Research in Personnel and Human Resources Management* 21 (2002), pp. 175–213.

12.27 Ilgen, D.R.; J.A. LePine; and J.R. Hollenbeck. "Effective Decision Making in Multinational Teams." In *New Perspectives in International Industrial–Organizational Psychology,* eds. P.C. Earley and M. Erez. San Francisco: Jossey-Bass, 1997, pp. 377–409.

12.28 Dwyer, P.; P. Engardio; S. Schiller; and S. Reed. "The New Model: Tearing up Today's Organization Chart." *BusinessWeek,* November 18, 1994, pp. 80–90.

12.29 Cox, T.; S. Lobel; and P. McLeod. "Effects of Ethnic Group Cultural Differences on Cooperative and Competitive Behavior on a Group Task." *Academy of Management Journal* 34 (1991), pp. 827–47; Mannix, E., and M.A. Neal. "What Differences Make a Difference? The Promise and Reality of Diverse Teams in Organizations." *Psychological Science in the Public Interest* 6 (2005), pp. 31–55.

12.30 Ilgen et al., "Effective Decision Making."

12.31 Prieto Zamora, J.M., and R. Martinez Arias. "Those Things Yonder Are not Giants, but Decision Makers in International Teams." In *New Perspectives on International Industrial and Organizational Psychology,* eds. P.C. Earley and M. Erez. San Francisco: New Lexington Press, 1997, pp. 410–45.

12.32 Ibid; Hollenbeck et al., "Accuracy Decomposition."

12.33 Hollenbeck et al., "Multilevel Theory of Team Decision Making"; Hollenbeck, J.R.; D.R. Ilgen; J.A. LePine; J.A. Colquitt; and J. Hedlund. "Extending the Multilevel Theory of Team Decision Making. Effects of Feedback and Experience in Hierarchical Teams." *Academy of Management Journal* 41 (1998), pp. 269–82.

12.34 Hollenbeck et al., "Extending the Multilevel Theory."

12.35 Hedlund, J.; D.R. Ilgen; and J.R. Hollenbeck. "Decision Accuracy in Computer-Mediated vs. Face-to-Face Decision Making Teams." *Organizational Behavior and Human Decision Processes* 76 (1998), pp. 30–47.

12.36 Ancona, D.G. "Outward Bound: Strategies for Team Survival in an Organization." *Academy of Management Journal* 33 (1990), pp. 334–65.

12.37 LePine, J.A.; R.F. Piccolo; C.L. Jackson; J.E. Mathieu; and J.R. Saul. "A Meta-Analysis of Team Process: Towards a Better Understanding of the Dimensional Structure and Relationships with Team Effectiveness Criteria." *Personnel Psychology* (in press); Marks, M.A.; J.E. Mathieu; and S.J. Zaccaro. "A Temporally Based Framework and Taxonomy of Team Processes." *Academy of Management Review* 26 (2001), pp. 356–76.

12.38 Marks et al. 2001. Please note that this entire section on teamwork processes is largely based on this body of work.

12.39 Kozlowski, S.W.J., and B.S. Bell. "Work Groups and Teams in Organizations." In *Handbook of Psychology,* Vol. 12: Industrial and Organizational Psychology, eds. W.C. Borman, D.R. Ilgen, and R.J. Klimoski. Hoboken, NJ: John Wiley & Sons, Inc., 2003, pp. 333–75.

12.40 De Dreu, C.K.W., and L.R. Weingart. "Task Versus Relationship Conflict, Team Performance, and Team Member Satisfaction: A Meta-Analysis." *Journal of Applied Psychology* 88 (2003), pp. 741–49.

12.41 Jehn, K. "A Multimethod Examination of the Benefits and Detriments of Intergroup Conflict." *Administrative Science Quarterly* 40 (1995), pp. 256–82.

12.42 De Dreu and Weingart, "Task Versus Relationship Conflict."

12.43 Thompson, L.L. *Making the Team: A Guide for Managers,* 2nd ed. Upper Saddle River, NJ: Pearson Prentice Hall, 2004.

12.44 De Church, L.A., and M.A. Marks. "Maximizing the Benefits of Task Conflict: The Role of Conflict Management." *The International Journal of Conflict Management* 12 (2001), pp. 4–22; De Dreu and Weingart, "Task Versus Relationship Conflict"; Van de Vliert, E., and M.C. Euwema. "Agreeableness and Activeness as Components of Conflict Behaviors." *Journal of Personality and Social Psychology* 66 (1994), pp. 674–87.

12.45 De Church and Marks, "Maximizing the Benefits"; Van de Vliert and Euwema, "Agreeableness and Activeness."

12.46 De Church and Marks, "Maximizing the Benefits."

12.47 Festinger, L. "Informal Social Communication." *Psychological Review* 57 (1950), pp. 271–82.

12.48 Beal, D.J.; R.R. Cohen; M.J. Burke; and C.L. McLendon. "Cohesion and Performance in Groups: A Meta-Analytic Clarification of Construct Relations." *Journal of Applied Psychology* 88 (2003), pp. 989–1004; Mullen, B., and C. Copper. "The Relation Between Group Cohesiveness and Performance: An Integration." *Psychological Bulletin* 115 (1994), pp. 210–27.

12.49 Janis, I.L. *Victims of Groupthink: A Psychological Study of Foreign Policy Decisions and Fiascoes.* Boston, MA: Houghton Mifflin, 1972.

12.50 Janis (1972).

12.51 Hirokawa, R.; Gouran, D.; and Martz, A. "Understanding the Sources of Faulty Group Decision Making: A Lesson from the *Challenger* Disaster." *Small Group Behavior* 19 (1988), pp. 411–433; Esser, J., and Linoerfer, J. "Groupthink and the Space Shuttle *Challenger* Accident: Toward a Quantitative Case Analysis." *Journal of Behavioral Decision Making* 2 (1989), pp. 167–177; Moorhead, G.; Ference, R.; and Neck, C. "Group Decision Fiascoes Continue: Space Shuttle *Challenger* and a Revised Groupthink Framework." *Human Relations* 44 (1991), pp. 539–550.

12.52 Stephens, J., and Behr, P. "Enron Culture Fed Its Demise." *Washington Post,* June 27, 2002, pp. A1–2.

12.53 Shea, G.P., and R.A. Guzzo. "Groups as Human Resources." In *Research in Personnel and Human Resource Management,* Vol. 5, eds. K.M. Rowland and G.R. Ferris. Greenwich, CT: JAI Press, 1987, pp. 323–56.

12.54   Gully, S.M.; K.A. Incalcaterra; A. Joshi; and J.M. Beubien. "A Meta-Analysis of Team-Efficacy, Potency, and Performance: Interdependence and Level of Analysis as Moderators of Observed Relationships." *Journal of Applied Psychology* 87 (2002), pp. 819–32.

12.55   Klimoski, R.J., and S. Mohammed. "Team Mental Model: Construct or Metaphor?" *Journal of Management* 20 (1994), pp. 403–37.

12.56   Cannon-Bowers, J.A.; E. Salas; and S.A. Converse. "Shared Mental Models in Expert Team Decision Making." *Individual and Group Decision Making,* ed. N.J. Castellan. Hillsdale, NJ: Erlbaum, 1993, pp. 221–46.

12.57   Wegner, D.M. "Transactive Memory: A Contemporary Analysis of the Group Mind." In *Theories of Group Behavior,* ed. B. Mullen and G.R. Goethals. New York: Springer-Verlag, 1986, pp. 185–208.

12.58   Hollingshead, A.B. "Communication, Learning, and Retrieval in Transactive Memory Systems." *Journal of Experimental Social Psychology* 34 (1998), pp. 423–42.

12.59   Wegner, "Transactive Memory."

12.60   LePine et al., "A Meta-Analysis of Team Process."

12.61   Ibid.

12.62   Stevens, M.J., and M.A. Campion. "The Knowledge, Skill, and Ability Requirements for Teamwork: Implications for Human Resource Management." *Journal of Management* 20 (1994), pp. 503–30.

12.63   Ibid.; Ellis, A.P.J.; B. Bell; R.E. Ployhart; J.R. Hollenbeck; and D.R. Ilgen. "An Evaluation of Generic Teamwork Skills Training with Action Teams: Effects on Cognitive and Skill-Based Outcomes."

Personnel Psychology 58 (2005), pp. 641–72.

12.64   Stout, R.J.; E. Salas; and J.E. Fowlkes. "Enhancing Teamwork in Complex Environments through Team Training." *Group Dynamics: Theory, Research, and Practice* 1 (1997), pp. 169–82.

12.65   Volpe, C.E.; J.A. Cannon-Bowers; E. Salas; and P.E. Spector. "The Impact of Cross-Training on Team Functioning: An Empirical Investigation." *Human Factors* 38 (1996), pp. 87–100.

12.66   Marks, M.A.; M.J. Sabella; C.S. Burke; and S.J. Zaccaro. "The Impact of Cross-Training on Team Effectiveness." *Journal of Applied Psychology* 87 (2002), pp. 3–13.

12.67   Blickensderfer, E., Cannon-Bowers, J. A., and Salas, E. Cross-Training and Team Performance. In J. A. Cannon-Bowers and E. Salas eds. Making Decision Under Stress: Implications for Individual and Team Training. Washington, DC: APA Press, 1998, pp. 299–311.

12.68   Dotlich, D., and J. Noel. *Active Learning: How the World's Top Companies Are Recreating their Leaders and Themselves.* San Francisco: Jossey-Bass, 1998; Marquardt, M. "Harnessing the Power of Action Learning." *T&D* 58 (June 2004), pp. 26–32.

12.69   Carey, S. "Racing to Improve; United Airlines Employees Go to School for Pit Crews to Boost Teamwork, Speed." *The Wall Street Journal,* Eastern Edition, March 24, 2006, p. B.1.

12.70   Salas, E.; D. Bozell; B. Mullen; and J.E. Driskell. "The Effect of Team Building on Performance: An Integration." *Small Group Research* 30 (1999), pp. 309–29.

12.71 Berman, D. "Zap! Pow! Splat!; Laser Tag and Paintball Can Enhance Teamwork, Communications, and Planning." *BusinessWeek* 3564 (February 9, 1998), p. ENT22. Proquest Database. Retrieved April 19, 2007.

12.72 Rasor, M. "Got Game? Bring It On: WhirlyBall Helps Workers Develop Drive, Teamwork." *Knight Ridder Tribune Business News,* April 3, 2006, p. 1. Proquest Database (May 7, 2006).

12.73 Regan, M.P. "Team Players: From Drums to Daring Getaways, Workers Embark on Team-Building Exercises." *Gainesville Sun,* February 15, 2004, pp. 5G, 6G.

12.74 Ballard, T.N. "Postal IG Under Fire for Unusual 'Team-Building' Activities." GovernmantExecutive.com, 2003, http://www.govexec.com/dailyfed/0503/050203t1.htm (October 15, 2003).

12.75 Dorgan, B.L., and R. Widen. "Letter to Chairman Fincman," May 1, 2003, http://www.govexec.com/pdfs/corcoran.pdf.

12.76 Salas et al., "The Effect of Team Building."

Leadership: Power and Influence

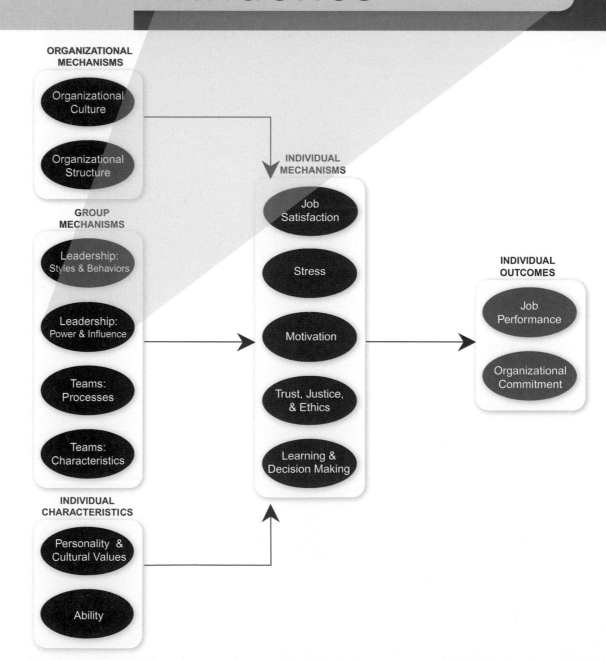

ORGANIZATIONAL MECHANISMS

Organizational Culture

Organizational Structure

GROUP MECHANISMS

Leadership: Styles & Behaviors

Leadership: Power & Influence

Teams: Processes

Teams: Characteristics

INDIVIDUAL CHARACTERISTICS

Personality & Cultural Values

Ability

INDIVIDUAL MECHANISMS

Job Satisfaction

Stress

Motivation

Trust, Justice, & Ethics

Learning & Decision Making

INDIVIDUAL OUTCOMES

Job Performance

Organizational Commitment

Mark Hurd, CEO of Hewlett-Packard, uses power very differently from his predecessor, Carly Fiorina. Hurd's low-key approach to leadership and his interpersonal strategies for building commitment among employees demonstrate just one way in which managers can lead. Fiorina's more assertive style was another; both have their advantages.

After reading this chapter, you should be able to answer the following questions:

13.1 What is leadership? What is power? What role does power play in leadership?

13.2 What are the different types of power that leaders possess, and when can they use those types most effectively?

13.3 What behaviors do leaders exhibit when trying to influence others? Which of these behaviors is most effective?

13.4 What is organizational politics? When is political behavior most likely to occur?

13.5 How do leaders use their power and influence to resolve conflicts in the workplace?

13.6 How do power and influence affect job performance and organizational commitment?

13.7 What are the ways in which leaders negotiate in the workplace?

HEWLETT-PACKARD

When Mark Hurd took over the responsibilities as CEO of Hewlett-Packard (HP), the California-based maker of printers and computers in 2005, the company was in the midst of the largest crisis in its history. HP was faced with seemingly insurmountable financial and strategic obstacles, employed a completely demoralized workforce, and was saddled with a board of directors rife with political battles (the result of which was a highly publicized corporate spying scandal in 2006).[1] Doesn't that sound like a job everyone would want? Fortunately for HP, Mark Hurd was just the kind of leader it needed at the time. In the span of two years, Hurd, through the smart use of power and influence, turned HP around to take its place as the largest technology company in the world with $92 billion in sales.

Part of Hurd's mystique as a leader is that he is the complete opposite of the CEO who preceded him: Carleton ("Carly") Fiorina. Dismissed three months prior to Hurd's arrival by the board of directors, Fiorina was known as a very smooth, polished, out-in-front CEO who enjoyed the limelight. However, she was also more of a top-down, power-conscious leader who attempted to change a deeply instilled culture within HP by setting a vision that employees came to resent and resist.[2] In fact, Hurd became known as the "Un-Carly," as he took on the role of coach in opposition to Fiorina's quarterbacking.[3] He took a decidedly different approach to leadership and used his power and influence in ways that better fit the culture of the company he took over. Company insiders state that Hurd is "low-key, self-effacing, and a bread-and-butter business guy."[4] Using more personal forms of power and "softer" methods of influence to lead, Hurd was able to build commitment among employees and investors. He didn't walk in the door with set ideas and a grandiose vision for the organization. In fact, Hurd changed nothing when he first arrived—the CEO's office remained exactly the way it was when Fiorina left. Moreover, to this day, Hurd refuses to pose for pictures that will place him on the cover of magazines by himself.[5]

Hurd came to HP from NCR, the California-based manufacturer of retail and financial technology, a position that afforded him "outsider" status at HP. Hurd therefore made it a point to consult with his employees to formulate a plan for HP's future. He encouraged employees to contact him directly with ideas, receiving over 5,000 e-mails. Using his own areas of expertise and supplying rational arguments to help drive decisions, he generated a level of commitment among his workforce that hadn't been seen in years.[6] Hurd also made a point of visiting and collecting information from all areas of the company while maintaining an open mind. Explained Hurd, "I never like people to think I'm interviewing them. I either want to bring them towards the view I've formed, or better, yet, have them argue me down."[7]

Hurd also did his best to tear down some of the uncertainty that had created a highly charged political atmosphere within HP. He brought in outsiders to play key roles in the company, simplified reward systems, and refused to use outside consultants in an effort to minimize the coalitions that had formed within the organization.[8] He also refused to be unduly influenced by political behaviors, noting, "When someone gets a job, it better be clear what they did to get it. If the organization thinks it's because they gave good PowerPoint presentations or because they were nice to Hurd when he showed up, you've got a problem. But if it's because she built a strong team and delivered strong operating results, the next person may think, 'Well, that's what I ought to do'."[9] Part of his ability to influence as a leader is the creation of common goals, as Hurd explained: "In the end, we've got to do what's best for the company, not what's best for its CEO or the management, or what's best for any single one person."[10]

LEADERSHIP: POWER AND INFLUENCE

As evidenced by the turnaround at Hewlett-Packard, leaders within organizations can make a huge difference to the success of an organization or group. It would be easy after reading the opening example to anoint Mark Hurd as a great leader and dismiss Carly Fiorina as a bad one. However, things aren't quite that simple. In fact, Fiorina exhibited many of the most touted leadership characteristics and behaviors that have been proven successful at other organizations. As we will discover in the next two chapters, there are many different types of leaders, many of whom can excel given the right circumstances. Indeed, many believe that Mark Hurd's leadership approach would not have been successful without many of the changes that Fiorina put in place during her tenure as CEO (a belief that Mark Hurd himself does not dispute).

There is perhaps no subject that's written about more in business circles than the topic of leadership. A quick search on Amazon.com of the topic "leadership" will generate a list of more than 200,000 books! That number doesn't even count the myriad of videos, calendars, cassette tapes, and other items, all designed to help people become better leaders. Given all the interest in this topic, a natural question becomes, "What exactly is a leader?" We define **leadership** as the use of power and influence to direct the activities of followers toward goal achievement.[11] That direction can affect followers' interpretation of events, the organization of their work activities, their commitment to key goals, their relationships with other followers, and their access to cooperation and support from other work units.[12] This chapter focuses on how leaders *get* the power and influence they use to direct others; Chapter 14 will focus on how leaders actually *use* their power and influence to help followers achieve their goals.

13.1
What is leadership? What is power? What role does power play in leadership?

WHY ARE SOME LEADERS MORE POWERFUL THAN OTHERS?

What exactly comes to mind when you think of the term "power"? Does it raise a positive or negative image for you? Certainly it's easy to think of leaders who have used power for what we would consider good purposes, but it's just as easy to think of leaders who have used power for unethical or immoral purposes. For now, try not to focus on how leaders use power but instead on how they acquire that power. **Power** can be defined as the ability to influence the behavior of others and resist unwanted influence in return.[13] Note that this definition gives us a couple of key points to think about. First, just because a person has the ability to influence others does not mean he or she will actually choose to do so. In fact, many times in organizations, the most powerful employees don't even realize how influential they could be! Second, in addition to influencing others, power can be seen as the ability to resist the influence attempts of others.[14] This resistance could come in the form of the simple voicing of a dissenting opinion, the refusal to perform a specific behavior, or the organization of an opposing group of coworkers.[15] Sometimes leaders need to resist the influence of other leaders or higher-ups to do what's best for their own unit. Other times leaders need to resist the influence of their own employees to avoid being a "pushover" when employees try to go their own way.

ACQUIRING POWER

13.2

What are the different types of power that leaders possess, and when can they use those types most effectively?

Think about the people you currently work with or have worked with in the past, or think of students that are involved in many of the same activities you are. Do any of those people seem to have especially high levels of power, meaning that they had the ability to influence your behavior? What is it that gives them that power? In some cases, their power may come from some formal position (e.g., supervisor, team leader, teaching assistant, resident advisor). However, sometimes the most powerful people we know lack any sort of formal authority. It turns out that power in organizations can come from a number of different sources. Specifically, there are five major types of power that can be grouped along two dimensions: organizational power and personal power.[16] These types of power are illustrated in Figure 13-1.

ORGANIZATIONAL POWER. The three types of organizational power derive primarily from a person's position within the organization. These types of power are considered to be more formal in nature.[17] **Legitimate power** is derived from a position of authority inside the organization and is sometimes referred to as "formal authority." People with legitimate power have some title—some term on an organizational chart or on their door that says, "Look, I'm supposed to have influence over you." Those with legitimate power have the understood right to ask others to do things that are considered within the scope of their authority. When a manager asks an employee to stay late to work on a project, work on one task instead of another, or work faster, they are exercising legitimate power. The higher up in an organization a person is, the more legitimate power he or she generally possesses. *Fortune* magazine provides rankings of the most powerful women in business. As shown in Table 13-1, all of those women possess legitimate power, in that they hold a title that affords them the ability to influence others.

Legitimate power does have its limits, however. It doesn't generally give a person the right to ask employees to do something outside the scope of their jobs or roles within the

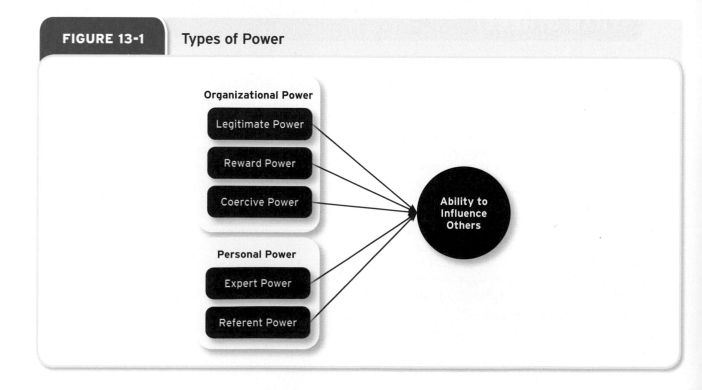

FIGURE 13-1   Types of Power

	NAME	COMPANY	POSITION	AGE
1	Indra Nooyi	PepsiCo	CEO	50
2	Anne Mulcahy	Xerox	Chairperson and CEO	53
3	Meg Whitman	eBay	CEO and President	50
4	Pat Woertz	Archer Daniels Midland	CEO and President	53
5	Irene Rosenfeld	Kraft Foods	CEO	53
6	Brenda Barnes	Sara Lee	Chairperson and CEO	52
7	Andrea Jung	Avon	Chairperson and CEO	48
8	Oprah Winfrey	Harpo, Inc.	Chairperson	52
9	Sally Krawcheck	Citigroup	CFO, Head of Strategy	41
10	Susan Arnold	Procter & Gamble	Vice Chair, Beauty and Health	52
11	Christine Poon	Johnson & Johnson	Vice Chair, Medicines & Nutritionals	53
12	Judy McGrath	MTV Networks Viacom	Chairperson and CEO	54
13	Anne Sweeney	Disney-ABC	President	48
14	Ann Livermore	Hewlett-Packard	Executive Vice President	48
15	Ann Moore	Time Inc.	Chairperson and CEO	56

TABLE 13-1   Fortune's 15 Most Powerful Women in Business in 2006

Source: E. Levenson, C. Tkaczyk, and J.L. Yang, "Indra Rising," 50 Most Powerful Women in Business *Fortune* (October 16, 2006), p. 145. Copyright © 2006 Time Inc. All rights reserved.

organization. For example, if a manager asked an employee to wash her car or mow his lawn, it would likely be seen as an inappropriate request. As we'll see later in this chapter, there is a big difference between having legitimate power and using it effectively. When used ineffectively, legitimate power can be a very weak form of power. In our opening example, Mark Hurd and Carly Fiorina each had the same level of legitimate power inside Hewlett-Packard, but the ways in which they used that power were quite different. As a result, the perceptions of them as leaders and the reactions they received were also quite different.

The next two forms of organizational power are somewhat intertwined with legitimate power. **Reward power** exists when someone has control over the resources or rewards another person wants. For example, managers generally have control over raises, performance evaluations, awards, more desirable job assignments, and the resources an employee might require to perform a job effectively. Those with reward power have the ability to influence others if those being influenced believe they will get the rewards by behaving in a certain way. **Coercive power** exists when a person has control over punishments in an organization. Coercive power operates primarily on the principle of fear. It exists when one person believes that another has the ability to punish him or her and is willing to use that power. For example, a manager might have the right to fire, demote, suspend, or lower the pay of an employee. Sometimes the limitations of a manager to impose punishments are formally spelled out in an organization. However, in many instances, managers

"Hank, when you're finished firing this gentleman I have some rather unfortunate news for you as well."

have a considerable amount of leeway in this regard. Coercive power is generally regarded as a poor form of power to use regularly, because it tends to result in negative feelings toward those that wield it.

PERSONAL POWER. Of course, the women in Table 13-1 do not appear on that list just because they have some formal title that affords them the ability to reward and punish others. There's something else about them as people that provides them additional capabilities to influence others. Personal forms of power capture that "something else." **Expert power** is derived from a person's expertise, skill, or knowledge on which others depend. When people have a track record of high performance, the ability to solve problems, or specific knowledge that is necessary to accomplish tasks, they are more likely to be able to influence other people who need that expertise. Consider a lone programmer who knows how to operate a piece of antiquated software, a machinist who was recently trained to operate a new piece of equipment, or the only engineer who has experience working on a specific type of project. All of these individuals will have a degree of expert power because of what they individually bring to the organization. Pat Woertz, the CEO of Archer Daniels Midland (ADM), the Illinois-based agricultural firm, appears on Table 13-1 largely because of her expert power. ADM hired Woertz as CEO because it felt that her time at Chevron would provide energy expertise that could help the firm in its push for renewable fuels.[18] There is perhaps no place where expert power comes into play more than in Silicon Valley where it is largely perceived that the best leaders are those with significant technological experience and expertise. Yahoo! employees recently celebrated the return of Jerry Yang, one of the cofounders of the company, as he took over as CEO in the summer of 2007. Yang's expert power gives him immediate levels of authority that the prior CEO never had.[19] At Intel, CEO Andy Grove "fostered a culture in which 'knowledge power' would trump 'position power.' Anyone could challenge anyone else's idea, so long as it was about the idea and not the person—and so long as you were ready for the demand 'Prove it.' That required data."[20]

Referent power exists when others have a desire to identify and be associated with a person. This desire is generally derived from an affection, admiration, or loyalty toward a specific individual.[21] Although our focus is on individuals within organizations, there are many examples of political leaders, celebrities, and sports figures who seem to possess high levels of referent power. Bill Clinton, Angelina Jolie, and Peyton Manning all possess referent power to some degree because others want to emulate them. The same could be said of leaders in organizations who possess a good reputation, attractive personal qualities, or a certain level of charisma. Oprah Winfrey, the Chairperson of Harpo, Inc., clearly wields an incredible amount of referent power. The people who watch Oprah on TV or listen to her on satellite radio admire her views and often seek to emulate her actions. Just consider what happens when Oprah mentions a book on her show—it rockets up the bestseller list almost immediately. If only she was looking for a good organizational behavior text . . . . For more discussion of referent power (and legitimate power), see our **OB on Screen** feature.

OB ON SCREEN

THE QUEEN

> Queen Elizabeth: *I rather envy you being able to vote. Not the actual ticking of the box, although, I suppose, it would be nice to experience that ONCE. But the sheer joy of being partial.*
>
> Artist: *Yes. One forgets that as Sovereign, you are not entitled to vote.*
>
> Queen Elizabeth: *No.*
>
> Artist: *Still, you won't catch me feeling sorry for you. You might not be allowed to vote, Ma'am. But it IS your Government.*
>
> Queen Elizabeth: *Yes… I suppose that is some consolation.*

These words at the very beginning of the movie help explicate the seemingly contradictory and confusing forms of power that permeate The Queen (Dir. Stephen Frears, Miramax Films, 2006). The movie itself is primarily a story about the week during which Diana,

Princess of Wales, was killed in a Paris car crash. Queen Elizabeth II (Helen Mirren) is initially adamant that the princess's funeral will be a private affair and not a public one. What the Queen incorrectly estimates is the affection the public had toward Diana and the outpouring of public support she would receive.

The movie is a stark portrayal of the reactions some people have toward various forms of power. The Queen clearly perceives herself as having a great deal of legitimate power due to her royal position. However, in a real sense, her duties and responsibilities are largely ceremonial, as she has no real formal authority to do anything. What she slowly must come to grips with is that people's responses to legitimate power aren't quite the same as those to more personal forms of power.

Tony Blair (Michael Sheen) correctly estimates that the public has much larger affections toward Diana than the Queen perceives and attempts to counsel her to that effect. He goes so far as to dub Diana the "people's princess." The Queen is baffled throughout the movie at the outpouring of support for the princess, because she never realized the extreme level of referent power that Diana possessed. Diana's entry into the royal family through marriage, her high-profile support of charitable causes, and her charisma caused the larger public to identify with and develop an emotional attachment to her to a degree they never could with the Queen.

Of course, it's possible for a person to possess all of the forms of power at the same time. In fact, the most powerful leaders—like those in Table 13-1—have bases of power that include all five dimensions. From an employee's perspective, it's sometimes difficult to gauge what form of power is most important. Why exactly do you do what your boss asks you to do? Is it because the boss has the formal right to provide direction, because the boss controls your evaluations, or because you admire and like the boss? Many times, we don't know exactly what type of power leaders possess until they attempt to use it. Generally speaking, the personal forms of power are more strongly related to organizational commitment and job performance than are the organizational forms. If you think about the authorities for whom you worked the hardest, they probably possessed some form of expertise and charisma, rather than just an ability to reward and punish. Some useful guidelines for wielding each of the forms of power can be found in Table 13-2.

TABLE 13-2	Guidelines for Using Power
TYPE OF POWER	**GUIDELINES FOR USE**
Legitimate	Make polite, clear requests. Explain the reason for the request. Don't exceed your scope or authority. Follow up to verify compliance. Insist on compliance if appropriate.
Reward	Offer the types of rewards people desire. Offer rewards that are fair and ethical. Don't promise more than you can deliver. Explain the criteria for giving rewards and keep it simple. Provide rewards as promised if requirements are met. Don't use rewards in a manipulative fashion.
Coercive	Explain rules and requirements and ensure people understand the serious consequences of violations. Respond to infractions promptly and without favoritism. Investigate to get facts before following through. Provide ample warnings. Use punishments that are legitimate, fair, and commensurate with the seriousness of noncompliance.
Expert	Explain the reasons for a request and why it's important. Provide evidence that a proposal will be successful. Don't make rash, careless, or inconsistent statements. Don't exaggerate or misrepresent the facts. Listen seriously to the person's concerns and suggestions. Act confidently and decisively in a crisis.
Referent	Show acceptance and positive regard. Act supportive and helpful. Use sincere forms of ingratiation. Defend and back up people when appropriate. Do unsolicited favors. Make self-sacrifices to show concern. Keep promises.

Source: Adapted and partially reprinted G. Yukl, *Leadership in Organization,* 5th ed. (Upper Saddle River, NJ: Prentice Hall, 2002).

CONTINGENCY FACTORS. There are certain situations in organizations that are likely to increase or decrease the degree to which leaders can use their power to influence others. Most of these situations revolve around the idea that the more other employees depend on a person, the more powerful that person becomes. A person can have high levels of expert and referent power, but if he or she works alone and performs tasks that nobody sees, the ability to influence others is greatly reduced. That being said, there are four factors that have an effect on the strength of a person's ability to use power to influence others.[22] These factors are summarized in Table 13-3. **Substitutability** is the degree to which people have alternatives in accessing resources. Leaders that control resources to which no one else has access can use their power to gain greater influence. **Discretion** is the degree to which managers have the right to make decisions on their own. If managers are forced to follow organizational policies and rules, their ability to influence others is reduced. **Centrality** represents how important a person's job is and how many people depend on that person to accomplish their tasks. Leaders who perform critical tasks and interact with others regularly have a greater ability to use their power to influence others. **Visibility** is how aware others are of a leader's power and position. If everyone knows that a leader has a certain level of power, the ability to use that power to influence others is likely to be high.

Ken Loughridge, an information technology manager working for MWH Global—an environmental and engineering consulting firm based in England—took these ideas to heart when he changed jobs within the organization. He used a survey the company had done to map out the "social network" within his organization. He used that network map to tell where his employees went for information, who possessed certain types of expertise, and who offered the most help to his employees. He then went to each of the most well-connected individuals so that he could meet them face-to-face. In a sense, he was seeking out and networking with the individuals in his organization that were likely to have the most power.[23] Companies are increasingly using such networking maps to understand the power structures in their organizations.

USING INFLUENCE

Up until now, we have discussed the types of power leaders possess and when their opportunities to use that power will grow or diminish. Now we turn to the specific strategies that leaders use to translate that power into actual influence.

Recall that having power increases our *ability* to influence behavior. It does not mean that we will use or exert that power. **Influence** is the use of an actual behavior that causes behavioral or attitudinal changes in others.[24] There are two important aspects of influence to

TABLE 13-3	The Contingencies of Power
CONTINGENCY	**LEADER'S ABILITY TO INFLUENCE OTHERS INCREASES WHEN . . .**
Substitutability	There are no substitutes for the rewards or resources the leader controls.
Centrality	The leader's role is important and interdependent with others in the organization.
Discretion	The leader has the freedom to make his or her own decisions without being restrained by organizational rules.
Visibility	Others know about the leader and the resources he or she can provide.

keep in mind. First, influence can be seen as directional. It most frequently occurs downward (managers influencing employees) but can also be lateral (peers influencing peers) or upward (employees influencing managers). Second, influence is all relative. The absolute power of the "influencer" and "influencee" isn't as important as the disparity between them.[25]

INFLUENCE TACTICS. Leaders depend on a number of tactics to cause behavioral or attitudinal changes in others. In fact, there are 10 types of tactics that leaders can use to try to influence others.[26] These tactics and their general levels of effectiveness are illustrated in Figure 13-2. The four most effective tactics have been shown to be rational persuasion, inspirational appeals, consultation, and collaboration. **Rational persuasion** is the use of logical arguments and hard facts to show the target that the request is a worthwhile one. Research shows that rational persuasion is most effective when it helps show that the proposal is important and feasible.[27] Rational persuasion is particularly important because it's the only tactic that is consistently successful in the case of upward influence.[28] Returning to our Hewlett-Packard example, Mark Hurd suggests that he uses this tactic most often to influence others and that it is the tactic that most often influences him when used by employees.[29] An **inspirational appeal** is a tactic designed to appeal to the target's values and ideals, thereby creating an emotional or attitudinal reaction. To use this tactic effectively, leaders must have insight into what kinds of things are important to the target. **Consultation** occurs when the target is allowed to participate in deciding how to carry out or implement a request. This tactic increases commitment from the target, who now has a stake in seeing that his or her opinions were right. A leader uses **collaboration** by attempting to make it easier for the target to complete the request. Collaboration could involve the leader helping complete the task, providing required resources, or removing obstacles that make task completion difficult.[30]

Four other influence tactics are sometimes effective and sometimes not. **Ingratiation** is the use of favors, compliments, or friendly behavior to make the target feel better about the influencer. You might more commonly hear this referred to this as "sucking up," especially when used in an upward influence sense. Ingratiation has been shown to be more effective when used as a long-term strategy and not nearly as effective when used immediately prior to making an influence attempt.[31] **Personal appeals** are when the requestor asks for something based on personal friendship or loyalty. The stronger the friendship, the more

13.3

What behaviors do leaders exhibit when trying to influence others? Which of these behaviors is most effective?

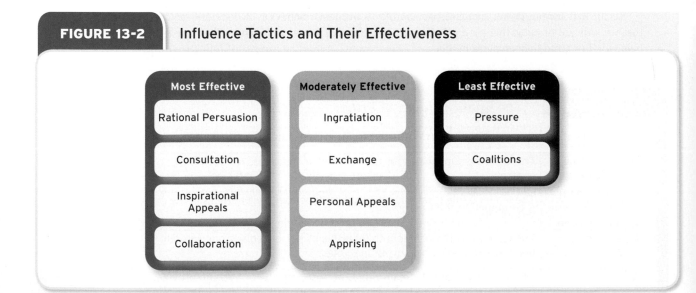

FIGURE 13-2 Influence Tactics and Their Effectiveness

Most Effective	Moderately Effective	Least Effective
Rational Persuasion	Ingratiation	Pressure
Consultation	Exchange	Coalitions
Inspirational Appeals	Personal Appeals	
Collaboration	Apprising	

successful the attempt is likely to be. As described in our **OB Internationally** feature, there are cultural differences when it comes to this kind of an appeal, as there are with other influence attempts. An **exchange tactic** is used when the requestor offers a reward or resource to the target in return for performing a request. This type of request requires that the requestor have something of value to offer.[32] Finally, **apprising** occurs when the requestor clearly explains why performing the request will benefit the target personally. It differs from rational persuasion in that it focuses solely on the benefit to the target as opposed to simple logic or benefits to the group or organization. It differs from exchange in that the benefit is not necessarily something that the requestor gives to the target but rather something that results from the action.[33]

OB INTERNATIONALLY

When Google hired Kai-Fu Lee to be vice president of engineering and president of Google Greater China, with a more than $10 million compensation package, the company was counting on his continued ability to use the same skills that allowed him to be a huge success at Microsoft. What was it that Lee possessed that made him so worthwhile? Lee argues that it was his understanding of *guanxi* (pronounced gwan-she).[34] In the Chinese culture, guanxi (literally translated "relationships") is the ability to influence decisions by creating obligations between parties based on personal relationships.

Guanxi represents a relationship between two people that involves both sentiment and obligation.[35] Individuals with high levels of guanxi tend to be tied together on the basis of shared institutions, such as kinship, places of birth, schools attended, and past working relationships.[36] Although such shared institutions might "get someone in the door" in the United States, in China, they become a higher form of obligation. Influence through guanxi just happens—it's an unspoken obligation that must be followed through on.[37] It is, in a sense, a blending of both formal and personal relationships that exists at a different level than in the United States. There is no such thing as a "business-only" relationship, and the expectation is simply that if you take, you must also give back.[38]

American managers who go to work overseas must be conscious of these different but influential relationships. In addition to understanding the power of guanxi, evidence suggests that Chinese managers from different areas of the country (e.g., Hong Kong, Taiwan, Mainland China) have different beliefs when it comes to which influence tactics are the most effective.[39] If anything, it goes to show that managers need to be acutely aware of both general and more specific cultural differences when trying to influence others in China.

The two tactics that have been shown to be least effective and could result in resistance from the target are pressure and coalitions. Of course this does not mean that they aren't used or can't be effective at times. **Pressure** is the use of coercive power through threats and demands. As we have discussed previously, coercion is a poor way to influence others and may only bring benefits over the short term. The last tactic is the formation of coalitions. **Coalitions** occur when the influencer enlists other people to help influence the target. These people could be peers, subordinates, or one of the target's superiors. Coalitions are generally used in combination with one of the other tactics. For instance, if rational persuasion is not strong enough, the influencer might bring in another person to show that that person agrees with the logic of the argument.

Two points should be noted about leaders' use of influence tactics. First, influence tactics tend to be most successful when used in combination.[40] Many tactics have some limitations or weaknesses that can be overcome using other tactics. Second, the influence tactics that tend to be most successful are those that are "softer" in nature. Rational persuasion, consultation, inspirational appeals, and collaboration take advantage of personal rather than organizational forms of power. Leaders that are the most effective at influencing others will generally rely on the softer tactics, make appropriate requests, and ensure the tactics they use match the types of power they have.

RESPONSES TO INFLUENCE TACTICS. As illustrated in Figure 13-3, there are three possible responses people have to influence tactics.[41] **Engagement** occurs when the target of influence agrees with and becomes committed to the influence request.[42] For a leader, this is the best outcome, because it results in employees putting forth the greatest level of effort in accomplishing what they are asked to do. Engagement reflects a shift in both the behaviors and the attitudes of employees. **Compliance** occurs when targets of influence are willing to do to what the leader asks, but they do it with a degree of ambivalence. Compliance reflects a shift in the behaviors of employees but not their attitudes. This behavior is the most common response to influence attempts in organizations, because anyone with some degree of power who makes a reasonable request is likely to achieve compliance. That response allows leaders to accomplish their purpose but it doesn't bring about the highest levels of employee effort and dedication. Still, it's clearly preferable to **resistance,** which occurs when the target refuses to perform the influence request and puts forth an effort to avoid having to do it. Employee resistance could come in the form of making excuses, trying to influence the requestor in return, or simply refusing to carry out the request. Resistance is most likely when the influencer's power is low relative to the target or when the request itself is inappropriate or unreasonable.[43]

POWER AND INFLUENCE IN ACTION

In this section, we look at two major areas in which leaders have the ability to use power to influence others. The first is through navigating the environment of organizational politics within the organization. The second is through using power and influence to help solve conflicts within the organization. As it turns out, it's easy for these two areas to coincide with each other.

FIGURE 13-3   Responses to Influence Attempts

Engagement
Target agrees with and becomes committed to request
(Behavioral and attitudinal changes)

Compliance
Target is willing to perform request, but does so with indifference
(Behavioral change only)

Resistance
Target is opposed to request and attempts to avoid doing it
(No change in behavior or attitude)

Most Effective

Least Effective

"You have no idea how political this place is."

ORGANIZATIONAL POLITICS. If there was perhaps one term that had a more negative connotation than power, it might be politics. You've probably had people give you career advice such as, "Stay away from office politics" or "Avoid being seen as political." The truth is that you cannot escape it; politics are a fact of life in organizations![44] Although you might hear company executives, such as former Vodaphone CEO Sir Christopher Gent, make statements such as, "[When I was CEO], we were mercifully free of company politics and blame culture,"[45] you can be pretty sure that wasn't actually the case—especially given that Vodaphone is one of the world's largest mobile phone operators. Most leaders, such as Allison Young, vice president of Blue Cross and Blue Shield of Louisiana, will tell you that "You have to assess the political situation early on and make decisions on forward-looking strategy not only on the facts, but also the political landscape."[46] Whether we like it or not, organizations are filled with independent, goal-driven individuals who must take into account the possible actions and desires of others to get what they want.[47]

Organizational politics can be seen as actions by individuals that are directed toward the goal of furthering their own self-interests.[48] Although there's generally a negative perception of politics, it's important to note that this definition doesn't imply that furthering one's self-interests is necessarily in opposition to the company's interests. A leader needs to be able to push his or her own ideas and influence others through the use of organizational politics. Research has recently supported the notion that, to be effective, leaders must have a certain degree of political skill.[49] In fact, universities and some organizations such as Becton, Dickinson, and Company—a leading global medical technology company based in the United States—are training their future leaders to be attuned to their political environment and develop their political skill.[50]

Political skill is the ability to effectively understand others at work and use that knowledge to influence others in ways that enhance personal and/or organizational objectives.[51] Two aspects of political skill are networking ability, or an adeptness at identifying and developing diverse contacts, and social astuteness, or the tendency to observe others and accurately interpret their behavior.[52] To see where you stand on these two dimensions, see our **OB Assessments** feature. Political skill also involves two other capabilities. Interpersonal influence involves having an unassuming and convincing personal style that is flexible enough to adapt to different situations.[53] Apparent sincerity involves appearing to others as having high levels of honesty and genuineness.[54] Taken together, these four skills provide a distinct advantage when navigating the political environments in organizations.

Although organizational politics can lead to positive outcomes, people's perceptions of politics are generally negative. This perception is certainly understandable, as anytime someone acts in a self-serving manner, it is potentially to the detriment of others.[55] In a highly charged political environment in which people are trying to capture resources and influence one another toward potentially opposing goals, it's only natural that some employees will feel stress about the uncertainty they face at work. Environments that are perceived as extremely political have been shown to cause lower job satisfaction, increased

13.4

What is organizational politics? When is political behavior most likely to occur?

OB ASSESSMENTS

POLITICAL SKILL

How much political skill do you have? This assessment is designed to measure two dimensions of political skill. Please write a number next to each statement that indicates the extent to which it accurately describes your attitude toward work while you were on the job. Alternatively, consider the statements in reference to school rather than work. Answer each question using the response scale provided. Then sum up your answers for each of the dimensions.

1	2	3	4	5
STRONGLY DISAGREE	DISAGREE	NEUTRAL	AGREE	STRONGLY AGREE

1. I spend a lot of time and effort networking with others. _____

2. I know a lot of important people and am well connected. _____

3. I am good at using my connections and networks to make things happen. _____

4. I have developed a large network of colleagues and associates whom I can call on for support when I really need to get things done. _____

5. I spend a lot of time making connections. _____

6. I always seem to instinctively know the right thing to say or do to influence others. _____

7. I have a good intuition or savvy about how to present myself to others. _____

8. I am particularly good at sensing the motivations and hidden agendas of others. _____

9. I pay close attention to people's facial expressions. _____

10. I understand people very well. _____

SCORING AND INTERPRETATION

Networking Ability: Sum up items 1–5. _____
Social Astuteness: Sum up items 6–9. _____

For networking ability, scores of 18 or more are above average and scores of 17 or less are below average. For social astuteness, scores of 19 or more are above average and scores of 18 or less are below average.

Source: Adapted from G.R. Ferris, D.C. Treadway, R.W. Kolodinsky, W.A. Hochwarter, C.J. Kacmar, C. Douglas, and D.D. Frink, "Development and Validation of the Political Skill Inventory," *Journal of Management* 31 (2005), pp. 126–52.

strain, lower job performance, and lower organizational commitment among employees.[56] In fact, high levels of organizational politics have even been shown to be detrimental to company performance as a whole.[57]

As a result, organizations (and leaders) do their best to minimize the perceptions of self-serving behaviors that are associated with organizational politics. This goal requires identifying the particular organizational circumstances that cause politics to thrive. As illustrated in Figure 13-4, organizational politics are driven by both personal characteristics and organizational characteristics. Some employees have a strong need for power that provides them with an incentive to engage in political behaviors. Others are high in self-monitoring, meaning that they have a tendency to be closely guarded in their actions and behaviors.[58] Still others have "Machiavellian" tendencies, meaning that they are willing to manipulate and deceive others to acquire power.[59] If you have these sorts of characteristics, or if you're especially interested in organizational politics, chances are good you've already read the book in this chapter's **OB at the Bookstore** feature.

Organizational factors that are the most likely to increase politics are those that raise the level of uncertainty in the environment. When people are uncertain about an outcome or event, they will generally act in ways that help reduce that uncertainty. A number of events can trigger uncertainty, including limited or changing resources, ambiguity in role requirements, high performance pressures, or unclear performance evaluation measures.[61] These sorts of organizational factors generally have a much stronger effect on political behavior than do personal factors. That's actually a good thing for organizations, because it may be

FIGURE 13-4   The Organizational Politics Process

OB AT THE BOOKSTORE

THE 48 LAWS OF POWER
by Robert Greene (New York: Penguin Books, 2000).

Law 1: Never outshine the master.

Law 3: Conceal your intentions.

Law 7: Get others to do the work for you, but always take the credit.

Law 15: Crush your enemy totally.

Law 17: Keep others in suspended terror: cultivate an air of unpredictability.

Law 33: Discover each man's thumbscrew.

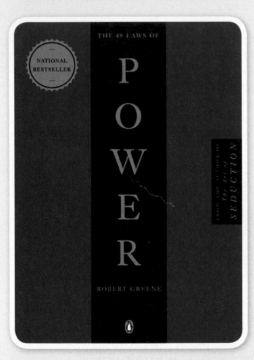

As is evident by this selection of laws from *The 48 Laws of Power,* it isn't your typical business book. It is essentially, as the author would put it, a "handbook on the arts of indirection." To Greene, every action people perform either increases or decreases their power. The laws he sets forth are amoral in nature; that is, there are no morals. Indeed, he instructs readers that they should disavow themselves of notions of good and evil, except to the degree that one needs to act "good" to get ahead. Greene argues that power is gained by always having your own best interests at heart. If you don't, you can be assured that others are simply taking advantage of you. Understanding the weaknesses of others and influencing them without their knowledge are some of the keys to gaining power. Upward influence tactics such as ingratiation abound in the book, as evidenced by this quote: "Always make those above you feel comfortably superior. In your desire to please and impress them, do not go too far in displaying your talents or you might accomplish the opposite: inspire fear and insecurity. Make your masters appear more brilliant than they are and you will attain the heights of power."

Greene cites historical figures such as Machiavelli (whom he considers the master), Sun-Tzu, Talleyrand, Catherine the Great, and others who notoriously used power to their own advantage. In some sense, the book is really about what we would see as the ultimate in political behavior. Of course, you might be thinking, who would ever buy such a book? The underlying premise of it is essentially to behave unethically to self-servingly gain power. However, the book has now sold over 2,000,000 copies. In fact, it has developed a cult following among the hip-hop community, including devotees Busta Rhymes, 50 Cent, and Kanye West.[60] Needless to say, the information we've presented in this chapter so far would argue that, if most workers behaved in the manner prescribed by Greene, we would have a very dissatisfied, uncommitted, and stressed out workforce. But perhaps that makes us the suckers . . . ?

easier to clarify performance measures and roles than it is to change the personal characteristics of a workforce.

CONFLICT RESOLUTION. In addition to using their power to shape office politics, leaders can use their influence in the context of conflict resolution. Conflict arises when two or more individuals perceive that their goals are in opposition (see Chapter 12 on Team Processes for more discussion of such issues). Conflict and politics are clearly intertwined, because the pursuit of one's own self-interests often breeds conflict in others. When conflict arises in organizations, leaders have the ability to use their power and influence to resolve it. As illustrated in Figure 13-5, there are five different styles a leader can use when handling conflict, each of which is appropriate in different circumstances.[62] The five styles can be viewed as combinations of two separate factors: how *assertive* leaders want to be in pursuing their own goals and how *cooperative* they are with regard to the concerns of others.

Competing (high assertiveness, low cooperation) occurs when one party attempts to get his or her own goals met without concern for the other party's results. It could be considered a win–lose approach to conflict management. Competing occurs most often when one party has high levels of organizational power and can use legitimate or coercive power to settle the conflict. It also generally involves the hard forms of influence, such as pressure or coalitions. Although this strategy for resolving conflict might get the result initially, it won't win a leader many friends, given the negative reactions that tend to accompany such tactics. It's best used in situations in which the leader knows he or she is right and a quick decision needs to be made.

Avoiding (low assertiveness, low cooperation) occurs when one party wants to remain neutral, stay away from conflict, or postpone the conflict to gather information or let things cool down. Avoiding usually results in an unfavorable result for everyone, including the organization, and may result in negative feelings toward the leader. Most important, avoiding never really resolves the conflict. **Accommodating** (low assertiveness, high cooperation) occurs when one party gives in to the other and acts in a completely unselfish way. Leaders will typically use an accommodating strategy when the issue is really not that important to them but is very important to the other party. It's also an important strategy to think about when the leader has less power than the other party. If leaders

13.5

How do leaders use their power and influence to resolve conflicts in the workplace?

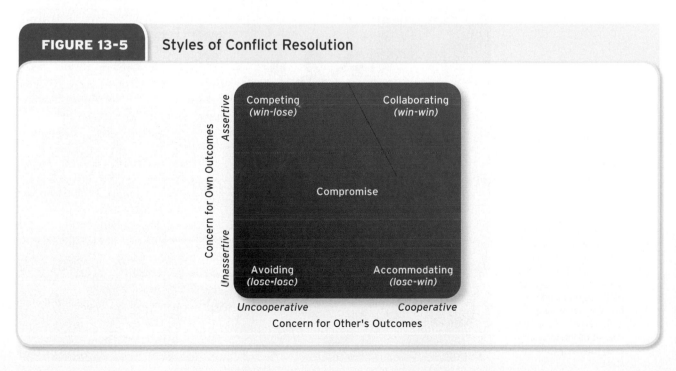

| FIGURE 13-5 | Styles of Conflict Resolution |

Concern for Own Outcomes (Assertive / Unassertive)

Competing (win–lose)

Collaborating (win–win)

Compromise

Avoiding (lose–lose)

Accommodating (lose–win)

Uncooperative — Cooperative
Concern for Other's Outcomes

know they are going to lose the conflict due to their lack of power anyway, it might be a better long-term strategy to give in to the demands from the other party.

Collaboration (high assertiveness, high cooperation) occurs when both parties work together to maximize outcomes. Collaboration is seen as a win–win form of conflict resolution. Collaboration is generally regarded as the most effective form of conflict resolution, especially in reference to task-oriented rather than personal conflicts.[63] However, it's also the most difficult to come by because it requires full sharing of information by both parties, a full discussion of concerns, relatively equal power between parties, and a lot of time investment to arrive at a resolution. However, this style also results in the best outcomes and reactions from both parties. **Compromise** (moderate assertiveness, moderate cooperation) occurs when conflict is resolved through give-and-take concessions. Compromise is perhaps the most common form of conflict resolution whereby each party's losses are offset by gains and vice versa. It is seen as an easy form of resolution, maintains relations between parties, and generally results in favorable evaluations for the leader.[64] For more discussion of when to use the various conflict resolution strategies, see Table 13-4.

One recent and unique example of conflict resolution is occurring through the One Laptop Per Child project. Nicolas Negroponte is the founder and chairperson of this nonprofit organization whose mission is to make millions of $100 laptops for undereducated children in the world's poorest nations. Needless to say, manufacturing a $100 laptop (named the XO) is no small feat. Negroponte is leading a network of vastly different individuals, all working on their own time or on loan from other organizations, through a painstaking collaboration process of design and manufacturing. The process hasn't always been easy. There have been times when Negroponte has had to adopt a competing style of conflict resolution to make a custom wireless system for the laptop function. This competitive response upset a faction of volunteers who subsequently quit the project. However, other times Negroponte has facilitated collaboration among very disparate groups. As a leader with varying degrees of power, Negroponte constantly has to balance the needs of the project with the needs of individuals and attempt to resolve conflict effectively.[65]

The One Laptop Per Child project intends to provide millions of $100 laptops for the world's poorest children. Founder and director Nicholas Negroponte has put together a large team of volunteers and "borrowed" workers from many different organizations and has worked to establish an effective collaboration among them by adopting a wide variety of conflict-resolution strategies, even the competing style.

TABLE 13-4	When to Use Conflict Resolution Styles
RESOLUTION STYLE	**USE DURING THE FOLLOWING SITUATIONS:**
Competing	• When quick decisive action is vital (i.e. emergencies). • On important issues for which unpopular actions need implementation. • On issues vital to company welfare when you know you're right. • Against people who take advantage of noncompetitive people.
Avoiding	• When an issue is trivial or more important issues are pressing. • When you perceive no chance of satisfying your concerns. • When potential disruption outweighs the benefits of resolution. • To let people cool down and regain perspective. • When gathering information supercedes an immediate decision. • When others can resolve the conflict more effectively. • When issues seem tangential or symptomatic of other issues.
Collaborating	• To find an integrative solution when both sets of concerns are too important to be compromised. • When your objective is to learn. • To merge insights from people with different perspectives. • To gain commitment by incorporating concerns into a consensus. • To work through feelings that have interfered with a relationship.
Accommodating	• When you find you are wrong, to allow a better position to be heard, to learn, and to show your reasonableness. • When issues are more important to others than yourself, to satisfy others and maintain cooperation. • To build social credits for later issues. • To minimize loss when you are outmatched and losing. • When harmony and stability are especially important. • To allow subordinates to develop by learning from mistakes.
Compromising	• When goals are important but not worth the effort of potential disruption of more assertive modes. • When opponents with equal power are committed to mutually exclusive goals. • To achieve temporary settlements to complex issues. • To arrive at expedient solutions under time pressure. • As a backup when collaboration or competition is unsuccessful.

Source: Reprinted from K.W. Thomas, "Toward Multi-Dimensional Values in Teaching: The Example of Conflict Behaviors," *Academy of Management Review* 2 (1977), pp. 484–90. Copyright © 1977 Academy of Management. Reproduced via permission from Copyright Clearance Center.

SUMMARY: WHY ARE SOME LEADERS MORE POWERFUL THAN OTHERS?

So what explains why some leaders are more powerful and influential than others? As shown in Figure 13-6, answering that question requires an understanding of the types of power leaders acquire, what kinds of influence tactics they have available to them, and how they can use that influence to alter the attitudes and behaviors of their employees. Leaders acquire both organizational (legitimate, reward, coercive) and personal (expert, referent) forms of power, which gives them the ability to influence others. They can then use that power to influence others through influence tactics. Those tactics can help achieve

FIGURE 13-6   Why Are Some Leaders More Powerful Than Others?

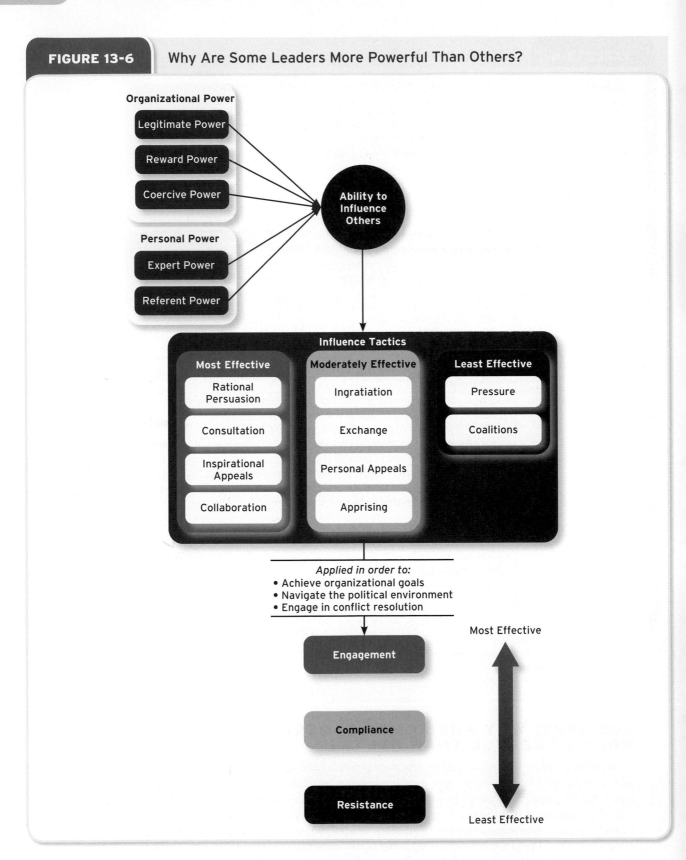

organizational goals or may be applied more specifically to dealing with organizational politics or conflict resolution situations. In the end, there are three possible responses to influence attempts: engagement, compliance, and resistance. The effectiveness of those attempts will depend on leaders' skill at performing them and how well they match the forms of power they have with the appropriate types of influence.

HOW IMPORTANT ARE POWER AND INFLUENCE?

How important is a leader's ability to use power and influence? In other words, does a leader's power and influence correlate with job performance and organizational commitment? Figure 13-7 summarizes the research evidence linking power and influence to job performance and organizational commitment. The figure reveals that power and influence are moderately correlated with job performance. When used correctly and focused

13.6

How do power and influence affect job performance and organizational commitment?

FIGURE 13-7   Effects of Power and Influence on Performance & Commitment

INSIDE OUR INTEGRATIVE MODEL OF OB

Power and Influence → **Job Performance**

Power and influence have a moderate positive effect on Performance. When used effectively, they can increase engagement and compliance, which facilitates *Task Performance*. The engagement and compliance facilitated by power and influence can also increase *Citizenship Behavior* and decrease *Counterproductive Behavior*.

Power and Influence → **Organizational Commitment**

Power and influence can have a moderate positive effect on Commitment. The use of personal forms of power, such as expert and referent, is associated with increased *Affective Commitment*. It should be noted, however, that more organizational forms of power, or hard influence tactics, can decrease that form of commitment. Not much is known about the impact of power and influence on *Continuance Commitment* or *Normative Commitment*.

- Represents a strong correlation (around .50 in magnitude).
- Represents a moderate correlation (around .30 in magnitude).
- Represents a weak correlation (around .10 in magnitude).

Sources: R.T. Sparrowe, B.W. Soetjipto, and M.L. Kraimer, "Do Leaders' Influence Tactics Relate to Members' Helping Behavior? It Depends on the Quality of the Relationship," *Academy of Management Journal* 49 (2006), pp. 1194–1208; G. Yukl, H. Kim, and C.M. Falbe, "Antecedents of Influence Outcomes," *Journal of Applied Psychology* 81 (1996), pp. 309–17; P.P. Carson, K.D. Carson, and C.W. Rowe, "Social Power Bases: A Meta-Analytic Examination of Interrelationships and Outcomes," *Journal of Applied Social Psychology* 23 (1993), pp. 1150–69.

on task-related outcomes, power and influence can create engagement in workers such that they are both behaviorally and attitudinally focused on high levels of task performance. That engagement also helps increase citizenship behavior, whereas the compliance associated with power and influence can decrease counterproductive behavior. These job performance benefits make sense given that the effective use of power and influence can increase the *motivation* levels of employees, whereas the ineffective use of power and influence can increase *stress* levels of employees.

Figure 13-7 also reveals that power and influence are moderately related to organizational commitment. When a leader draws on personal sources of power, such as expert power and referent power, a stronger emotional bond can be created with the employee, boosting affective commitment. The effective use of such power should increase *job satisfaction* and a sense of *trust* in the leader, all of which are associated with increased commitment levels. As with job performance, however, it is important to note that an ineffective use of power can also decrease commitment levels. In particular, repeated uses of coercive power or repeated reliance on hard influence tactics such as pressure or coalitions could actually decrease organizational commitment levels.

APPLICATION: NEGOTIATIONS

13.7

What are the ways in which leaders negotiate in the workplace?

There is perhaps no better place for leaders to use their power, influence, political, and conflict resolution skills than when conducting negotiations. **Negotiation** is a process in which two or more interdependent individuals discuss and attempt to come to an agreement about their different preferences.[66] Negotiations can take place inside the organization or when dealing with organizational outsiders. Negotiations can involve settling a contract dispute between labor and management, determining a purchasing price for products, haggling over a performance review rating, or determining the starting salary for a new employee. Clearly, negotiations are a critical part of organizational life, for both leaders and employees.

There are two general strategies leaders must choose between when it comes to negotiations: distributive bargaining and integrative bargaining.[67] **Distributive bargaining** involves win–lose negotiating over a "fixed-pie" of resources.[68] That is, when one person gains, the other person loses (also known as a "zero-sum" condition). The classic example of a negotiation in which distributive bargaining is used is the purchasing of a car. When you walk into a car dealership, there's a stated price on the side of the car that's known to be negotiable. In these circumstances though, every dollar you save is a dollar the dealership loses. Similarly, every dollar the salesperson negotiates for, you lose. Distributive bargaining is similar in nature to a competing approach to conflict resolution. Some of the most visible negotiations that have traditionally been approached with a distributive bargaining tactic are union–management labor negotiations. Whether it be automobile manufacturers, airlines, or nurses at hospitals, the negotiations for these sessions are typically viewed through a win–lose lens. For an example of a negotiation that might interest you, see this chapter's **OB for Students** feature.

Many negotiations within organizations, including labor–management sessions, are beginning to occur with a more integrative bargaining strategy. **Integrative bargaining** is aimed at accomplishing a win–win scenario.[73] It involves the use of problem solving and mutual respect to achieve an outcome that is satisfying for both parties. Leaders who thoroughly understand the conflict resolution style of collaboration are likely to thrive in these types of negotiations. In general, integrative bargaining is a preferable strategy whenever possible, because it allows a long-term relationship to form between the parties (because neither side feels like the loser). In addition, integrative bargaining has a tendency to produce a higher level of outcome favorability when both parties' views are considered than

OB FOR STUDENTS

Nine out of ten recruiters say that their initial compensation offer to a job candidate is lower than they are prepared to pay.[69] Many of you are in the midst of or starting to consider a job search as you graduate. Research has plenty to say about your ability to negotiate and secure an acceptable salary. One major issue is that the majority of us never attempt to negotiate the offered salary.[70] A second major issue is that those who do negotiate do a pretty poor job of it. Although the conventional wisdom that men negotiate more often than women is false, a study of MBA students showed that men do perhaps negotiate more effectively than their female counterparts and that these differences could account for a lot of money over time.[71] Regardless, here are some suggestions for negotiating your salary:[72]

1. Know your worth going in. You should know the approximate salaries for others within your major or functional area. You can ask your career center for this information in many cases.
2. You need to know your "BATNA," or your best alternative to a negotiated agreement. What is the lowest possible offer that you would be willing to accept? At what point would you be willing to walk away? Negotiators with a clear BATNA generally walk away with higher results.
3. What is your goal for a salary? Do not be afraid to put this number on the table. Avoid vague responses such as, "I want more money," which does nothing to help further the negotiation process.
4. You need to be prepared to sell yourself. What value do you bring to the table that they might not know about? If you want to convince the company that raising your offer is a win–win result, you need to be able to convince the company that your value is more significant than it thought it was.
5. Last but not least: Don't threaten to leave the table unless you really are prepared to do it. Do you indeed have a worthwhile backup plan?

distributive bargaining.[74] However, not all situations are appropriate for integrative bargaining. Integrative bargaining is most appropriate in situations in which multiple outcomes are possible, there is an adequate level of trust, and parties are willing to be flexible.[75] Please don't approach your next used car purchase with an integrative bargaining strategy!

TAKEAWAYS

13.1 Leadership is the use of power and influence to direct the activities of followers toward goal achievement. Power is the ability to influence the behavior of others and resist unwanted influence in return. Power is necessary, in that it gives leaders the ability to influence others.

13.2 Leaders have five major types of power. There are three organizational forms of power: Legitimate power is based on authority or position, reward power is based on the distribution of resources or benefits, and coercive power is based on the handing out of punishments. There are two personal forms of power: Expert power is derived from expertise and knowledge, whereas referent power is based on the attractiveness and charisma of the leader. These types of power can be used most effectively when leaders are central to the work process, highly visible, have discretion, and are the sole controllers of resources and information.

13.3   Leaders can use 10 different influence tactics to achieve their objectives. The most effective are rational persuasion, consultation, inspirational appeals, and collaboration. The least effective are pressure and the forming of coalitions. Tactics with moderate levels of effectiveness are ingratiation, exchange, personal appeals, and apprising.

13.4   Organizational politics are individual actions that are directed toward the goal of furthering a person's own self-interests. Political behavior is most likely to occur in organizational situations in which individual outcomes are uncertain.

13.5   Leaders use power and influence to resolve conflicts through five conflict resolution styles: avoidance, competing, accommodating, collaborating, and compromising. The most effective and also most difficult tactic is collaboration.

13.6   Power and influence have moderate positive relationships with job performance and organizational commitment. However, for these beneficial effects to be realized, leaders must wield their power effectively and rely on effective influence tactics.

13.7   Leaders use both distributive and integrative bargaining to negotiate outcomes.

KEY TERMS

- Leadership — p. 441
- Power — p. 441
- Legitimate power — p. 442
- Reward power — p. 443
- Coercive power — p. 443
- Expert power — p. 444
- Referent power — p. 444
- Substitutability — p. 447
- Discretion — p. 447
- Centrality — p. 447
- Visibility — p. 447
- Influence — p. 447
- Rational persuasion — p. 448
- Inspirational appeal — p. 448
- Consultation — p. 448
- Collaboration — p. 448
- Ingratiation — p. 448
- Personal appeals — p. 448
- Exchange tactic — p. 449
- Apprising — p. 449
- Pressure — p. 449
- Coalitions — p. 449
- Engagement — p. 450
- Compliance — p. 450
- Resistance — p. 450
- Organizational politics — p. 451
- Political skill — p. 451
- Competing — p. 455
- Avoiding — p. 455
- Accommodating — p. 455
- Collaboration — p. 456
- Compromise — p. 456
- Negotiation — p. 460
- Distributive bargaining — p. 460
- Integrative bargaining — p. 460

DISCUSSION QUESTIONS

13.1   Can a leader influence others without power? How exactly would that influence take place?

13.2   Which forms of power do you consider to be the strongest? Which types of power do you currently have? How could you go about obtaining higher levels of the forms that you're lacking?

13.3   Who is the most influential leader you have come in contact with personally? What forms of power did he or she have and which types of influence did he or she use to accomplish objectives?

13.4   Think of a time when you resisted an influence attempt at work. What made you resist? Could the person attempting to influence you have done anything differently to get you to behave the way he or she wanted?

13.5   What would it take to have a "politically free" environment? Is that possible?

13.6   Think about the last serious conflict you had with a coworker or group member. How was that conflict resolved? Which approach did you take to resolve it?

13.7   Think of a situation in which you negotiated an agreement. Which approach did you take? Was it the appropriate one? How might have the negotiation process gone more smoothly?

CASE   HEWLETT-PACKARD

Hewlett-Packard had to make a tough decision to replace Carly Fiorina to guide the company out of a crisis. The board appointed Mark Hurd, a low-profile CEO with a proven record of success. Hurd's personality was the complete opposite of Fiorina's and exactly what the company needed. Fiorina was a celebrity CEO with a flare for marketing, whereas Hurd is a straight-edged CEO who frequently seeks the inputs of his employees from every level of the organization. Hurd's leadership style has been embraced by his internal and external constituencies.

Only several months into his tenure, Hurd has made several significant moves that have positively affected the company. First, Hurd is changing the culture that focused on innovating the next big thing every day. Instead, he is attempting to recreate HP's culture to focus on execution and accountability and thus rebuild the company's reputation as a consistent performer. Second, he has simplified the bonus system to reflect the performance of employees' business units and the overall company. Third, Hurd made a strategic decision to undergo a restructuring process that would cut HP's costs and make the company leaner. Therefore, HP decided to lay off 14,500 employees from its 150,000-employee workforce. This cost-cutting decision will allow the company to be more competitive in the long term. It seems evident so far that Hurd's personality and business sense will lead HP back to its once prestigious stature.

13.1 What type of powers did Hurd exert after becoming the CEO of Hewlett-Packard?

13.2 Was Hurd's visibility the difference in turning the company around from its position under the previous CEO?

Sources: P. Burrow, "HP Says Goodbye to Drama," *BusinessWeek,* 2005, www.businessweek.com; P. Burrows and B. Elgin, "HP's New Low-Profile Boss," *BusinessWeek,* 2005, www.businessweek.com; A. Hesseldahl, "The Cuts Aren't Over at HP," *BusinessWeek,* 2006, www.businessweek.com; P. Thibodeau, "Dunn Out at HP; Hurd Put on Hot Seat," *Computerworld* 40 (2006), pp. 1–14.

EXERCISE   LOBBYING FOR INFLUENCE

The purpose of this exercise is to give you experience in using influence tactics to modify the behavior of others. This exercise uses groups of six participants, so your instructor will either assign you to a group of six or ask you to create your own group of six. The exercise has the following steps:

1. During this exercise, your objective is to get other people in the class to give you their points. If you get more than 50 percent of the total number of points distributed to the whole class, you will win. Each person in the class has a different number of points, as shown in the class list. You can keep or give away your points in whatever manner you choose, as long as you follow the rules for each round of the process. There are five rounds, described next.

   Round 1. In this round, you will write memos to your classmates. You can say whatever you want in your memos, and write them to whomever you choose, but for the 10-minute writing period, there will be no talking, only writing. You will deliver all your messages at one time, at the end of the 10-minute writing period.

   Round 2. In this round, you will respond in writing to the messages you received in the first round. You can also write new memos as you see fit. Again, there is to be no talking! At the end of 15 minutes, you can distribute your memos.

   Round 3. In Round 3, you can talk as much as you like. You will have 15 minutes to talk with anyone about anything.

   Round 4. In this round, you will create ballots to distribute your points any way you see fit. To distribute your points, put a person's name on an index card, along with the number of points you want that person to have. If you choose to keep any of your points, put your own name on the card, along with the number of points you want to keep. Do not hand in your cards until asked to do so by the professor.

   Round 5. If there is no clear winner, Round 5 will be used to repeat steps 3 and 4.

2. Either individually or in your groups, answer the following discussion questions:

   • What kinds of social influence attempts did you make during this exercise?
   • How successful were you at influencing others to go along with you?
   • What kinds of influence did others use on you?
   • What was the most successful way you saw someone else use influence during the memo-writing and discussion sections?
   • What other factors determined how you voted?

Source: Adapted from "Voting for Dollars," in the Instructor's Manual for D.A. Whetten and K.S. Cameron, *Developing Management Skills,* 7th ed. (Englewood Cliffs, NJ: Prentice Hall, 2007).

ENDNOTES

13.1 Stewart, J. "The Kona Files: How an Obsession with Leaks Brought Scandal to Hewlett-Packard." *The New Yorker* 83, no. 1 (2007), pp. 152–67; Hardy, Q. "The UnCarly." *Forbes* 179, no. 5 (2007), pp. 82–90.

13.2 Murray, A. "H-P Lost Faith in Fiorina, but Not in Merger." *The Wall Street Journal,* May 24, 2006, p. A2.

13.3 Hardy, "The UnCarly."

13.4 Malone, M.S. "Hurd Instinct." *The Wall Street Journal,* September 14, 2006, p. A20.

13.5 Lashinsky, A. "The Hurd Way." *Fortune* 153 (2006), pp. 92–99; Hardy, "The UnCarly."

13.6 Lashinsky, A. "Mark Hurd Takes His First Swing at HP." *Fortune* 152 (2005), p. 24.

13.7 Tam, P. "Rewiring Hewlett-Packard." *The Wall Street Journal,* July 20, 2005, p. B1.

13.8 Burrows, P., and B. Elgin. "The UnCarly Reveals his Game Plan." *BusinessWeek,* June 27, 2005, p. 36.

13.9 Burrows, P. "HP Says Goodbye to Drama." *BusinessWeek,* September 12, 2005, p. 83.

13.10 Lashinsky, "Mark Hurd."

13.11 Yukl, G. *Leadership in Organizations.* 4th ed. Englewood Cliffs, NJ: Prentice-Hall, 1998.

13.12 Ibid.

13.13 McMurray, V.V. "Some Unanswered Questions on Organizational Conflict." *Organization and Administrative Sciences* 6 (1975), pp. 35–53; Pfeffer, J. *Managing with Power.* Boston: Harvard Business School Press, 1992.

13.14 Cotton, J.L. "Measurement of Power-Balancing Styles and Some of their Correlates." *Administrative Science Quarterly* 21 (1976), pp. 307–19; Emerson, R.M. "Power-Dependence Relationships." *American Sociological Review* 27 (1962), pp. 29–41.

13.15 Ashforth, B.E., and F.A. Mael. "The Power of Resistance." In *Power and Influence in Organizations,* eds. R.M. Kramer and M.E. Neal. Thousand Oaks, CA: Sage, 1998, pp. 89–120.

13.16 French, Jr., J.R.P., and B. Raven. "The Bases of Social Power." In *Studies in Social Power,* ed. D. Cartwright. Ann Arbor: University of Michigan, Institute for Social Research, 1959, pp. 150–67; Yukl, G., and C.M. Falbe. "The Importance of Different Power Sources in Downward and Lateral Relations." *Journal of Applied Psychology* 76 (1991), pp. 416–23.

13.17 Yukl, G. "Use Power Effectively." In *Handbook of Principles of Organizational Behavior,* ed. E.A. Locke. Madden, MA: Blackwell, 2004, pp. 242–47.

13.18 Levenson, E.; C. Tkaczyk; and J.L. Yang, "Indra Rising," *Fortune* 154, no. 8 (2006), p. 145.

13.19 Hof, R.D. "Back to the Future at Yahoo!." *BusinessWeek,* July 2, 2007, pp. 35-36.

13.20 Tedlow, R.S. "The Education of Andy Grove." *Fortune,* December 12, 2005, pp. 117–38:

13.21 French and Raven, "The Bases of Social Power."

13.22 Hickson, D.J.; C.R. Hinings; C.A. Lee; R.E. Schneck; and J.M.

Pennings. "A Strategic Contingencies Theory of Intraorganizational Power." *Administrative Science Quarterly* 16 (1971), pp. 216–27; Hinings, C.R.; D.J. Hickson; J.M. Pennings; and R.E. Schneck. "Structural Conditions of Intraorganizational Power." *Administrative Science Quarterly* 19 (1974), pp. 22–44; Salancik, G.R., and J. Pfeffer. "Who Gets Power and How They Hold on to It: A Strategic Contingency Model of Power." *Organizational Dynamics* 5 (1977), pp. 3–21.

13.23 McGregor, J. "The Office Chart That Really Counts." *BusinessWeek,* February 27, 2006, pp. 48–49.

13.24 Somech, A., and A. Drach-Zahavy. "Relative Power and Influence Strategy: The Effects of Agent/Target Organizational Power on Superiors' Choices of Influence Strategies." *Journal of Organizational Behavior* 23 (2002), pp. 167–79; Stahelski, A.J., and C.F. Paynton. "The Effects of Status Cues on Choices of Social Power and Influence Strategies." *Journal of Social Psychology* 135 (1995), pp. 553–60.

13.25 Yukl, *Leadership in Organizations.*

13.26 Yukl, G.; C. Chavez; and C.F. Seifert. "Assessing the Construct Validity and Utility of Two New Influence Tactics." *Journal of Organizational Behavior* 26 (2005), pp. 705–25; Yukl, G. *Leadership in Organizations,* 5th ed. (Upper Saddle River, NJ: Prentice Hall, 2002).

13.27 Yukl, G.; H. Kim; and C. Chavez. "Task Importance, Feasibility, and Agent Influence Behavior as Determinants of Target Commitment." *Journal of Applied Psychology* 84 (1999), pp. 137–43.

13.28 Yukl, *Leadership in Organizations.*

13.29 Hardy, "The UnCarly"; Malone, "Hurd Instinct."

13.30 Yukl et al., "Task Importance."

13.31 Wayne, S.J., and G.R. Ferris. "Influence Tactics, Affect, and Exchange Quality in Supervisor–Subordinate Interactions: A Laboratory Experiment and Field Study." *Journal of Applied Psychology* 75 (1990), pp. 487–99.

13.32 Kelman, H.C. "Compliance, Identification, and Internalization: Three Processes of Attitude Change." *Journal of Conflict Resolution* 2 (1958), pp. 51–56.

13.33 Yukl et al., "Assessing the Construct Validity."

13.34 Buderi, R. "The Talent Magnet." *Fast Company* 106 (2006), pp. 80–84.

13.35 Chen, C.C.; Y.R. Chen: and K. Xin. "Guanxi Practices and Trust in Management: A Procedural Justice Perspective." *Organization Science* 15 (2004), pp. 200–209.

13.36 Yang, M.M. *Gifts, Favors, and Banquets: The Art of Social Relationships in China.* Ithaca, NY: Cornell University Press, 1994.

13.37 Fu, P.P.; T.K. Peng; J.C. Kennedy; and G. Yukl. "A Comparison of Chinese Managers in Hong Kong, Taiwan, and Mainland China." *Organizational Dynamics* 33 (2003), pp. 32–46.

13.38 Buderi, "The Talent Magnet."

13.39 Fu et al., "A Comparison."

13.40 Falbe, C.M., and G. Yukl. "Consequences for Managers of Using Single Influence Tactics and Combinations of Tactics." *Academy of Management Journal,* August 1992, pp. 638–52.

13.41 Yukl, G. *Leadership in Organizations.* 5th ed. Upper Saddle River, NJ: Prentice Hall, 2002.

13.42 Note: Engagement is more commonly referred to as "commitment" in this context. We have changed the original term to avoid any confusion with organizational commitment.

13.43 Somech and Drach-Zahavy, "Relative Power and Influence Strategy"; Yukl, *Leadership in Organizations,* 5th ed.; Yukl, "Use Power Effectively."

13.44 Mintzberg, H. "The Organization as Political Arena." *Journal of Management Studies* 22 (1985), pp. 133–54.

13.45 Bryan-Low, C., and J. Singer. "Vodafone Group Life President Resigns over Management Flap." *The Wall Street Journal,* March 13, 2006, p. B3.

13.46 Ramel, D. "Protégé Profiles." *Computerworld* 39 (2005), p. 50.

13.47 Bacharach, S.B., and E.J. Lawler. "Political Alignments in Organizations." In *Power and Influence in Organizations,* eds. R.M. Kramer and M.E. Neal. Thousand Oaks, CA: Sage, 1998, pp. 67–88.

13.48 Kacmar, K.M., and R.A. Baron. "Organizational Politics: The State of the Field, Links to Related Processes, and an Agenda for Future Research." In *Research in Personnel and Human Resources Management,* Vol. 17, ed. G.R. Ferris. Greenwich, CT: JAI Press, 1999, pp. 1–39.

13.49 Ferris, G.R.; D.C. Treadway; P.L. Perrewe; R.L. Brouer; C. Douglas; and S. Lux. "Political Skill in Organizations." *Journal of Management* 33 (2007), pp. 290–320; Treadway, D.C.; G.R. Ferris; A.B. Duke; G.L. Adams; and J.B. Thatcher. "The Moderating Role of Subordinate Political Skill on Supervisors' Impressions of Subordinate Ingratiation and Ratings of Subordinate Interpersonal Facilitation." *Journal of Applied Psychology* 92 (2007), pp. 848–55.

13.50 Seldman, M., and E. Betof. "An Illuminated Path." *T + D* 58 (2004), pp. 34–39.

13.51 Ferris, G.R.; D.C. Treadway; R.W. Kolokinsky; W.A. Hochwarter; C.J. Kacmar; and D.D. Frink. "Development and Validation of the Political Skill Inventory." *Journal of Management* 31 (2005), pp. 126–52.

13.52 Ferris et al., "Political Skill in Organizations"; Ferris et al., "Development and Validation."

13.53 Ibid.

13.54 Ibid.

13.55 Ferris, G.R.; D.D. Frink; D.P.S. Bhawuk; J. Zhou; and D.C. Gilmore. "Reactions of Diverse Groups to Politics in the Workplace." *Journal of Management,* no. 1 (1996), pp. 23–44.

13.56 Kacmar and Baron, "Organizational Politics"; Hochwarter, W.A. "The Interactive Effects of Pro-Political Behavior and Politics Perceptions on Job Satisfaction and Commitment." *Journal of Applied Social Psychology* 33 (2003), pp. 1360–78; Randall, M.L.; R. Cropanzano; C.A. Bormann; and A. Birjulin. "Organizational Politics and Organizational Support as Predictors of Work Attitudes, Job Performance, and Organizational Citizenship Behavior." *Journal of Organizational Behavior* 20 (1999), pp. 159–74; Witt, L.A. "Enhancing Organizational Goal Congruence: A Solution to Organizational Politics." *Journal of Applied Psychology* 83 (1998), pp. 666–74.

13.57 Eisenhardt, K.M., and L.J. Bourgeois. "Politics of Strategic Decision Making in High-Velocity Environments: Toward a Midrange Theory." *Academy of Management Journal* 31 (1988), pp. 737–70.

13.58 Biberman, G. "Personality and Characteristic Work Attitudes of Persons with High, Moderate, and Low Political Tendencies." *Psychological Reports* 60 (1985), pp. 1303–10; Ferris et al., "Reactions of Diverse Groups"; O'Connor, W.E., and T.G. Morrison. "A Comparison of Situational and Dispositional Predictors of Perceptions of Organizational Politics." *Journal of Psychology* 135 (2001), pp. 301–12.

13.59 Valle, M., and P.L. Perrewe. "Do Politics Perceptions Relate to Political Behaviors? Tests of an Implicit Assumption and Expanded Model." *Human Relations* 53 (2000), pp. 359–86.

13.60 Paumgarten, N. "Fresh Prince." *The New Yorker* 82, no. 36 (2006), pp. 55–66.

13.61 Fandt, P.M., and G.R. Ferris. "The Management of Information and Impressions: When Employees Behave Opportunistically." *Organizational Behavior and Human Decision Processes* 45 (1990), pp. 140–58; O'Connor and Morrison, "A Comparison of Situational and Dispositional Predictors"; Poon, J.M.L. "Situational Antecedents and Outcomes of Organizational Politics Perceptions." *Journal of Managerial Psychology* 18 (2003), pp. 138–55.

13.62 Lewicki, R.J., and J.A. Litterer. *Negotiations.* Homewood, IL: Irwin, 1985; Thomas, K.W. "Conflict and Negotiation Processes in Organizations." In *Handbook of Industrial and Organizational Psychology,* 2nd ed., Vol. 3, eds. M.D. Dunnette and L.M. Hough. Palo Alto, CA: Consulting Psychologists Press, pp. 651–717.

13.63 Weingart, L., and K.A. Jehn. "Manage Intra-Team Conflict Through Collaboration." *Handbook of Principles of Organizational Behavior,* ed.

E.A. Locke. Madden, MA: Blackwell, 2004, pp. 226–38.

13.64 Thomas, K.W. "Toward Multi-Dimensional Values in Teaching: The Example of Conflict Behaviors." *Academy of Management Review* 2 (1977), pp. 484–90; de Dreu, C.K.W.; A. Evers; B. Beersma; E.S. Kluwer; and A. Nauta. "A Theory-Based Measure of Conflict Management Strategies in the Workplace." *Journal of Organizational Behavior* 22 (2001), pp. 645–68.

13.65 Fahey, J. "The Soul of a Laptop." *Forbes,* May 7, 2007, pp. 100–104.

13.66 Adapted from Neale, M.A., and M.H. Bazerman. "Negotiating Rationally: The Power and Impact of the Negotiator's Frame." *Academy of Management Executive* 2 (1992), pp. 42–51.

13.67 Bazerman, M.H., and M.A. Neale. *Negotiating Rationally.* New York: The Free Press, 1992; Pinkley, R.L.; T.L. Griffeth; and G.B. Northcraft. "Fixed Pie a la Mode: Information Availability, Information Processing, and the Negotiation of Suboptimal Agreements." *Organizational Behavior and Human Decision Processes* 50 (1995), pp. 101–12.

13.68 Pinkley et al., "Fixed Pie a la Mode."

13.69 Donkin, R. "So What Do You Think You're Worth? The Evidence Seems to Support a New Book's Contention That If You Want a Good Salary, You Had Better Negotiate for It. But Recognize That It Takes Practice." *Financial Times,* November 18, 2004, p. 11.

13.70 Pinkley, R.L., and G.B. Northcraft. *Get Paid What You're Worth: The Expert Negotiators' Guide to Salary and Compensation.* New York: St. Martin's Griffin, 2003.

13.71 Gerhart, B., and S. Rynes. "Determinants and Consequences of Salary Negotiations by Male and Female MBA Graduates." *Journal of Applied Psychology* 76 (1991), pp. 256–62.

13.72 Adapted from Thompson, L.L. *The Mind and Heart of the Negotiator.* 3rd ed. Upper Saddle River, NJ: Prentice Hall, 2005; Pinkley and Northcraft, *Get Paid.*

13.73 Kolb, D.M., and J. Williams. "Breakthrough Bargaining." *Harvard Business Review,* February 2001, pp. 88–97.

13.74 Pinkley et al., "Fixed Pie a la Mode."

13.75 Thomas, "Conflict and Negotiation Processes."

Leadership: Styles and Behaviors

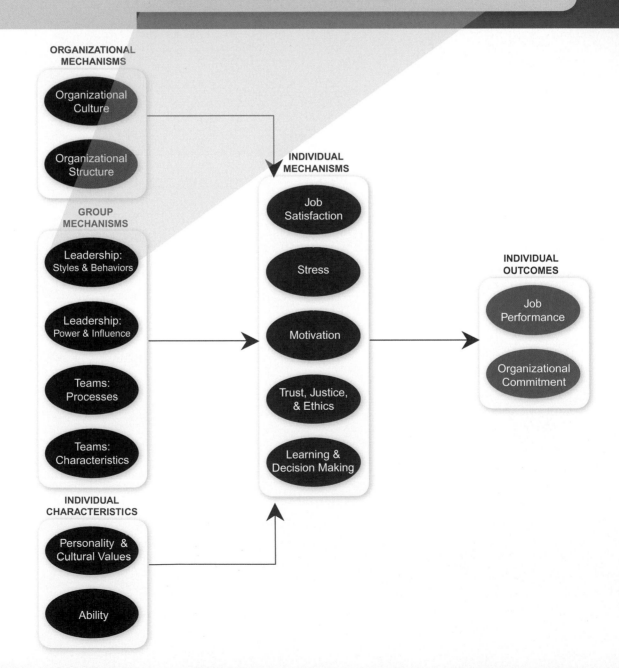

ORGANIZATIONAL MECHANISMS

- Organizational Culture
- Organizational Structure

GROUP MECHANISMS

- Leadership: Styles & Behaviors
- Leadership: Power & Influence
- Teams: Processes
- Teams: Characteristics

INDIVIDUAL CHARACTERISTICS

- Personality & Cultural Values
- Ability

INDIVIDUAL MECHANISMS

- Job Satisfaction
- Stress
- Motivation
- Trust, Justice, & Ethics
- Learning & Decision Making

INDIVIDUAL OUTCOMES

- Job Performance
- Organizational Commitment

The strikingly original commercial introducing the Macintosh computer during the 1984 Super Bowl is still the most famous spot ever made. The development of the Mac showcased what was best (and worst) about the hard-driving leadership style of CEO Steve Jobs.

 LEARNING GOALS

After reading this chapter, you should be able to answer the following questions:

14.1 What is leadership? What does it mean for a leader to be "effective"?

14.2 What traits and characteristics are related to leader emergence? What traits and characteristics are related to leader effectiveness?

14.3 What four styles can leaders use to make decisions? According to the time-driven model of leadership, what factors combine to make some styles more effective in a given situation?

14.4 What two dimensions capture most of the day-to-day leadership behaviors that leaders engage in?

14.5 How does transformational leadership differ from transactional leadership? What kinds of behaviors underlie transformational leadership?

14.6 How does leadership affect job performance and organizational commitment?

14.7 Can leaders be trained to be more effective?

APPLE

It was the third quarter of Super Bowl XVIII in Tampa, Florida, on January 22, 1984. As CBS faded to a commercial from the Raiders' 38-9 victory over the Redskins, the image of a blonde heroine running down a dark hallway carrying a sledgehammer soon came into view. After entering an auditorium in which rows and rows of workers are being brainwashed by a huge image of Big Brother,[1] she hurls the sledgehammer at the video screen. As the screen smashes, a voice-over reads: "On January 24th, Apple Computer will introduce Macintosh. And you'll understand why 1984 won't be like *1984*." The Macintosh was going to liberate the world from the "green text on a black screen" that characterized the computers of the time, including the IBM PC. The commercial—directed by Ridley Scott, whose screen credits include *Alien, Blade Runner,* and *Gladiator*—became arguably the most famous commercial ever, ushering in a new age of Super Bowl advertising, though it aired only once on a national basis.[2]

The Macintosh represented the marriage of two different visions.[3] The first vision belonged to Steve Jobs, who cofounded Apple with Steve Wozniak and who wanted to introduce the graphical user interface and mouse developed at Xerox's Palo Alto Research Center to mainstream computing. The second vision belonged to Jef Raskin, the computer scientist who chose the Macintosh name and wanted to create an "all-in-one" computer that customers could just plug in to get started. The Macintosh began as a fringe product for Apple, which was still focused on updating the Apple II—the computer that had essentially started the personal computer industry in 1977 and remained the market leader before being eclipsed by the IBM PC. To stave off IBM's threat, Jobs knew that Apple needed a product that would be "so important that it will make a dent in the universe."[4]

The development of the Macintosh was dominated by Jobs's leadership, for better and for worse.[5] Two phrases captured the spirit he created within the Macintosh team. "Let's Be Pirates" reflected the renegade nature of the group as it fought against the rest of the industry and even Apple's existing products. "Working 90 Hours a Week and Loving It!" reflected the impossible odds the team faced in bringing the Macintosh to market in only two years. One team member described Jobs's leadership style as "hands-on management," saying that Jobs "would march right into your cubicle, invade your space, sit right down, and start playing with whatever you were working on." Jobs's impatience and legendary temper were balanced only by his considerable charisma. As one Apple employee noted, "He doesn't know that anything is impossible because, well, he's always been able to do anything he wanted. So even as he's being a jerk, he's got this incredibly seductive aura around him that keeps you bound to him, keeps you near his flame, keeps you on the team."

The introduction of the Macintosh should have been a crowning achievement for Jobs. Apple sold 70,000 units in the 100 days following the Super Bowl, meeting even the most optimistic expectations.[6] However, sales declined sharply over the summer as customers realized that the Macintosh didn't have enough memory, wasn't expandable, and didn't have enough software, particularly for business customers. Market research could have warned of such problems, but Jobs chose not to do any research because of his ambitious timetable and his own belief that he knew what consumers wanted. As Jobs explained, "Did Alexander Graham Bell do any market research when he invented the telephone? Of course not." Such sentiments were reinforced by Apple's marketing director who noted, "Steve did his market research by looking into the mirror every morning." Added to those missteps was the fateful decision to ask Microsoft, the company founded by Bill Gates and Paul Allen, to develop a word processing program for the Macintosh. Although Microsoft delivered the program on time, its experience with the Macintosh enabled it eventually to incorporate the graphical user interface into its Windows operating system, seriously damaging the Macintosh's market niche. Less than two years later, Jobs lost an internal power struggle and left the company he cofounded.

Of course, that's not the end of the story. Fast-forward a decade later and Apple found itself in dire straits—a company with a meager 2 percent market share in computers,[7] no new products,[8] and a CEO in Gil Amelio who didn't fit the company's culture.[9] Desperate for a new operating system to satisfy Apple's customers and certain that his in-house talent couldn't provide it, Amelio began looking outside the company for help. Enter Steve Jobs. During the preceding decade, Jobs had founded NeXT, a computer company that had initially specialized in upscale hardware for educational environments but was now more notable for its NeXTSTEP software. Jobs also bought a computer graphics company from George Lucas, the creator of the *Star Wars* franchise. Although Jobs was initially attracted to the company's hardware and software, it was Pixar's animation division that wound up making Jobs's investment so profitable. Fresh off Pixar's debut of *Toy Story,* Apple acquired NeXT, and Steve Jobs was back where he belonged, eventually assuming the role of Apple's CEO in 1997. Jobs quickly fast-tracked some innovative new hardware offerings, including the iMac, which returned to the all-in-one roots of the original Macintosh while also demonstrating a new appreciation for software with the development of programs like iPhoto, iMovie, and iTunes.[10] Of course, the masterstroke of Jobs's second go-around was the realization that online music would be the "next big thing" and that existing music players were about as user friendly as the IBM PC had once been. Demonstrating a new willingness to go outside Apple for designs, Jobs hired a company called PortalPlayer to develop a revolutionary product that would complement iTunes—a product that eventually became the iPod. As the iPod set the stage for the iPhone, the return of Steve Jobs set Apple up as a significant player in three different industries.

Apple's Steve Jobs, then and now—on the left with the original Macintosh, on the right with the iPod.

LEADERSHIP: STYLES AND BEHAVIORS

14.1

What is leadership? What does it mean for a leader to be "effective"?

This is the second of two chapters on **leadership,** defined as the use of power and influence to direct the activities of followers toward goal achievement.[11] That direction can affect followers' interpretation of events, the organization of their work activities, their commitment to key goals, their relationships with other followers, or their access to cooperation and support from other work units.[12] The last chapter described how leaders *get* the power and influence needed to direct others. In the case of Steve Jobs, his power is derived from his formal role as Apple's CEO; his symbolic role as its cofounder; his expertise in hardware, software, and the user experience; and his remarkable charisma. This chapter describes how leaders actually *use* their power and influence in an effective way. Since his return, Jobs has clearly used his power and influence effectively, as Apple's stock price has climbed 1,025 percent since the launch of the iPod, reaching a total market value of $72 billion as of 2007.[13]

Of course, most leaders can't judge their performance by pointing to changes in stock price. In fact, it turns out that leader effectiveness can be gauged in a number of ways. Leaders can be judged by objective evaluations of unit performance, such as profit margins, market share, sales, returns on investment, productivity, quality, costs in relation to budgeted expenditures, and so forth.[14] If those sorts of indices are unavailable, the leader's superiors may judge the performance of the unit on a more subjective basis. Other approaches to judging leader effectiveness center more on followers, including indices such as absenteeism, retention of talented employees, grievances filed, requests for transfer, and so forth.[15] Those sorts of indices can be complemented by employee surveys that assess the perceived performance of the leader, the perceived respect and legitimacy of the leader, and employee commitment, satisfaction, and psychological well-being. The top panel of Table 14-1 provides one example of these sorts of measures.

One source of complexity when judging leader effectiveness, particularly with more subjective employee-centered approaches, is "Whom do you ask?" The members of a given unit often disagree about how effective their leader is. **Leader–member exchange theory,** which describes how leader–member relationships develop over time on a dyadic basis, can explain why those differences exist.[16] The theory argues that new leader–member relationships are typically marked by a **role taking** phase, during which a manager describes role expectations to an employee and the employee attempts to fulfill those expectations with his or her job behaviors.[17] In this period of sampling and experimentation, the leader tries to get a feel for the talent and motivation levels of the employee. For some employees, that initial role taking phase may eventually be supplemented by **role making,** during which the employee's own expectations for the dyad get mixed in with those of the leader.[18] The role making process is marked by a free-flowing exchange in which the leader offers more opportunities and resources and the employee contributes more activities and effort.

Over time, the role taking and role making processes result in two general types of leader–member dyads, as shown in Figure 14-1. One type is the "high-quality exchange" dyad, marked by the frequent exchange of information, influence, latitude, support, and attention. Those dyads form the leader's "ingroup" and are characterized by higher levels of mutual trust, respect, and obligation.[19] The other type is the "low-quality exchange" dyad, marked by a more limited exchange of information, influence, latitude, support, and attention. Those dyads form the leader's "outgroup" and are characterized by lower levels of trust, respect, and obligation.[20] Tests of the theory suggest that employees who are competent, likable, and similar to the leader in personality will be more likely to end up

TABLE 14-1	Employee-Centered Measures of Leader Effectiveness

Unit-Focused Approach

Ask all members of the unit to fill out the following survey items, then average the responses across the group to get a measure of leader effectiveness.

1. My supervisor is effective in meeting our job-related needs.

2. My supervisor uses methods of leadership that are satisfying.

3. My supervisor gets us to do more than we expected to do.

4. My supervisor is effective in representing us to higher authority.

5. My supervisor works with us in a satisfactory way.

6. My supervisor heightens our desire to succeed.

7. My supervisor is effective in meeting organizational requirements.

8. My supervisor increases our willingness to try harder.

9. My supervisor leads a group that is effective.

Dyad-Focused Approach

Ask members of the unit to fill out the following survey items in reference to their particular relationship with the leader. The responses are not averaged across the group; rather, differences across people indicate differentiation into "ingroups" and "outgroups" within the unit.

1. I always know how satisfied my supervisor is with what I do.

2. My supervisor understands my problems and needs well enough.

3. My supervisor recognizes my potential.

4. My supervisor would use his/her power to help me solve work problems.

5. I can count on my supervisor to 'bail me out' at his/her expense if I need it.

6. My working relationship with my supervisor is extremely effective.

7. I have enough confidence in my supervisor to defend and justify his/her decisions when he/she is not present to do so.

Sources: Adapted from B. Bass and B. Avolio, *MLQ Manual* (Menlo Park, CA: Mind Garden, Inc., 2004); G.B. Graen and M. Uhl-Bien, "Relationship-Based Approach to Leadership: Development of Leader–Member Exchange (LMX) Theory of Leadership over 25 Years: Applying a Multi-Level Multi-Domain Perspective," *Leadership Quarterly* 6 (1995), pp. 219–47.

in the leader's ingroup, with those factors proving more impactful than age, gender, or racial similarity.[21] Leader–member exchange theory would suggest that leader effectiveness should be judged by gauging how effective the most critical leader–member dyads appear to be. The bottom panel of Table 14-1 provides one example of this sort of measure, with more agreement indicating a higher-quality exchange relationship and thus, higher levels of leader effectiveness on a dyadic basis.[22]

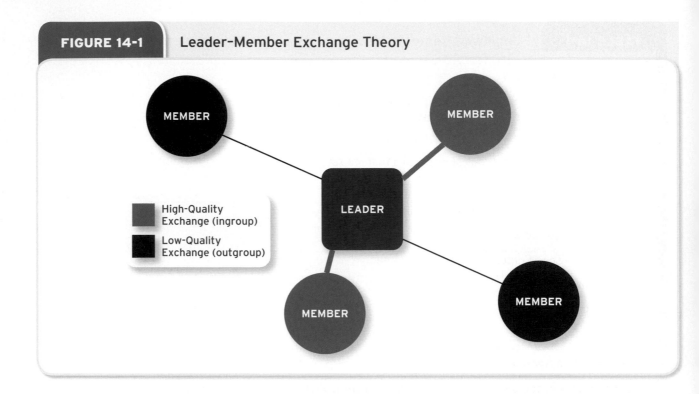

FIGURE 14-1   Leader–Member Exchange Theory

WHY ARE SOME LEADERS MORE EFFECTIVE THAN OTHERS?

For our purposes, **leader effectiveness** will be defined as the degree to which the leader's actions result in the achievement of the unit's goals, the continued commitment of the unit's employees, and the development of mutual trust, respect, and obligation in leader–member dyads. Now that we've described what it means for a leader to be effective, we turn to the critical question in this chapter: "Why are some leaders more effective than others?" That is, why exactly are some leaders viewed as more effective on a unitwide basis, and why exactly are some leaders better at fostering high-quality exchange relationships? Beginning as far back as 1904, research on leadership has attempted to answer such questions by looking for particular traits or characteristics of effective leaders.[23] The search for traits and characteristics is consistent with "great person" theories of leadership that suggest that "leaders are born, not made."[24] Early research in this area frequently focused on physical features (e.g., gender, height, physical attractiveness, energy level), whereas subsequent research focused more squarely on personality and ability (see Chapter 9 on Personality and Cultural Values and Chapter 10 on Ability for more discussion of those topics).

After a century of research, leadership scholars now acknowledge that there is no generalizable profile of effective leaders from a trait perspective.[25] In fact, most studies have concluded that traits are more predictive of **leader emergence** (i.e., who becomes a leader in the first place) than they are of leader effectiveness (i.e., how well people actually do in a leadership role). Table 14-2 reviews some of the traits and characteristics frequently examined in organizational behavior research in general and leadership research in particular. The table draws a distinction between traits and characteristics that predict leader emergence and those that predict leader effectiveness. Although a number of traits and characteristics are relevant to leadership, two limitations of this work have caused leadership

14.2

What traits and characteristics are related to leader emergence? What traits and characteristics are related to leader effectiveness?

TABLE 14-2	Traits/Characteristics Related to Leader Emergence and Effectiveness	
DESCRIPTION OF TRAIT/ CHARACTERISTIC	**LINKED TO EMERGENCE?**	**LINKED TO EFFECTIVENESS?**
High conscientiousness	√	
Low agreeableness	√	
Low neuroticism		
High openness to experience	√	√
High extraversion	√	√
High general cognitive ability	√	√
High energy level	√	√
High stress tolerance	√	√
High self-confidence	√	√

Sources: Adapted from T.A. Judge, J.E. Bono, R. Ilies, and M.W. Gerhardt, "Personality and Leadership: A Qualitative and Quantitative Review," *Journal of Applied Psychology* 87 (2002), pp. 765–80; T.A. Judge, A.E. Colbert, and R. Ilies, "Intelligence and Leadership: A Quantitative Review and Test of Theoretical Propositions," *Journal of Applied Psychology* 89 (2004), pp. 542–52; G. Yukl, *Leadership in Organizations,* 4th ed. (Englewood Cliffs, NJ: Prentice-Hall, 1998).

research to move in a different direction. First, many of the trait–leadership correlations are weak in magnitude, particularly when leader effectiveness serves as the outcome. Second, the focus on leader traits holds less practical relevance than a focus on leader actions. What exactly can leaders *do* that can make them more effective? This chapter will review three types of leader actions: decision-making styles, day-to-day behaviors, and behaviors that fall outside of a leader's typical duties.

LEADER DECISION-MAKING STYLES

Of course, one of the most important things leaders do is make decisions. Think about the job you currently hold or the last job you had. Now picture your boss. How many decisions did he or she have to make in a given week? How did he or she go about making those decisions? A leader's decision-making style reflects the process the leader uses to generate and choose from a set of alternatives to solve a problem (see Chapter 8 on Learning and Decision Making for more on such issues). Decision-making styles capture *how* a leader decides as opposed to *what* a leader decides.

The most important element of a leader's decision-making style is this: Does the leader decide most things for him- or herself, or does the leader involve others in the process? We've probably all had bosses (or professors, or even parents) who made virtually all decisions by themselves, stopping by to announce what had happened once the call had been made. We've probably also had other bosses (or professors, or parents) who tended to do the opposite—involving us, asking our opinions, or seeking our vote even when we didn't even care about what was being discussed. It turns out that this issue of leader versus follower control can be used to define some specific decision-making styles. Figure 14-2 shows those styles, arranged on a continuum from high follower control to high leader control.

 14.3

What four styles can leaders use to make decisions? According to the time-driven model of leadership, what factors combine to make some styles more effective in a given situation?

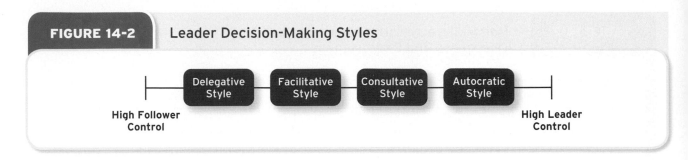

| **FIGURE 14-2** | Leader Decision-Making Styles |

Delegative Style — Facilitative Style — Consultative Style — Autocratic Style

High Follower Control   **High Leader Control**

DEFINING THE STYLES. With an **autocratic style,** the leader makes the decision alone without asking for the opinions or suggestions of the employees in the work unit.[26] The employees may provide information that the leader needs but are not asked to generate or evaluate potential solutions. In fact, they may not even be told about the decision that needs to be made, knowing only that the leader wants information for some reason. This decision-making style seems to be a favorite of Mike Jeffries, the quirky CEO of Abercrombie & Fitch, the Ohio-based clothing retailer best known for its racy catalog and preppy but edgy styles.[27] Jeffries is incredibly superstitious, leaving his black Porsche with the doors unlocked and the keys between the seats at the same angle in the parking lot each day and putting on a pair of lucky Italian loafers stored in his secretary's desk whenever he looks at the business numbers. That superstitious nature may explain why he developed a controlling style even in his first job, working for a now defunct New York department store chain. A colleague during that period spoke critically of Jeffries's desire to do it all himself, noting, "A gifted guy who does it himself is different from a gifted guy who helps people help him do it."[28] Even as CEO, Jeffries interviews every model used in the company's catalog, approves all merchandise in the stores, and describes how clothes should be folded on store tables.

The next two styles in Figure 14-2 offer more employee involvement. With a **consultative style,** the leader presents the problem to individual employees or a group of employees, asking for their opinions and suggestions before ultimately making the decision him- or herself.[29] With this style, employees do "have a say" in the process, but the ultimate authority still rests with the leader. That ultimate authority changes with a **facilitative style,** in which the leader presents the problem to a group of employees and seeks consensus on a solution, making sure that his or her own opinion receives no more weight than anyone else's.[30] With this style, the leader is more facilitator than decision maker. Disney CEO Bob Iger seems to embrace a combination of consultative and facilitative styles.[31] Since taking over for Michael Eisner, Iger has made meetings with his division heads less autocratic. Whereas Eisner held court, Iger encourages a conversation. Iger describes his style this way: "You put good people in jobs and give them room to run. . . . You involve yourself in a responsible way, but not to the point where you are usurping their authority. I don't have the time or concentration—and you could argue maybe even the talent—to do that."[32]

Mike Jeffries (on the left), CEO of Abercrombie & Fitch, appears to have an autocratic leadership style.

"I'd like your honest, unbiased and possibly career-ending opinion on something."

Source: © The New Yorker Collection 2003 Alex Gregory from cartoonbank.com.
All rights reserved.

With a **delegative style,** the leader gives an individual employee or a group of employees the responsibility for making the decision within some set of specified boundary conditions.[33] The leader plays no role in the deliberations unless asked, though he or she may offer encouragement and provide necessary resources behind the scenes. Phil Knight, the chairman of Nike, the Oregon-based athletic apparel company, often embraces a delegative style.[34] A quiet and enigmatic figure, Knight has been described as the ultimate delegator, with executives interpreting his silences and nods as the freedom to make their own decisions, even when those decisions take the company in different directions. It's a mystery to employees what Knight actually does in his managing role at Nike, other than to serve as a father figure and visionary. When the copresident of the Nike brand was asked how frequently he met with Knight, he estimated, "Once a week . . . and we probably did that twice a month."[35] The management style that has defined Knight's approach over the past 40 years is straightforward: Find people who care about the product and let them handle the details. Given his delegative style, it's ironic that Knight has had trouble ceding the CEO position to others during his tenure at Nike.[36]

WHEN ARE THE STYLES MOST EFFECTIVE? Which decision-making style is best? As you may have guessed, there is no one decision-making style that's effective across all situations, and all styles have their pluses and minuses. There are many factors to consider when leaders choose a decision-making style.[37] The most obvious consideration is the quality of the resulting decision, because making the correct decision is the ultimate means of judging the leader. However, leaders also have to consider whether employees will accept and commit to their decision. Research studies have repeatedly shown that allowing employees to participate in decision making increases their job satisfaction.[38] Such participation also helps develop employees' own decision-making skills.[39]

Of course, such participation has a downside for employees because it takes up time. Many employees view meetings as an interruption of their work. One recent study found that employees spend, on average, six hours a week in scheduled meetings, and that time spent in meetings was negatively related to job satisfaction when employees didn't depend on others in their jobs, were focused on their own task accomplishment, and felt that meetings were run ineffectively.[40] Consider the case of Paul Pressler, whose five-year term as

CEO of Gap Inc., the California-based apparel company, ended in 2007.[41] Pressler had been hired from Disney to use his expertise to bring discipline to the struggling company. His tenure was criticized for its increase in meetings, with employees asked to explain incredibly specific details to Gap Inc.'s new chief financial officer. One former employee describes the demands as "the antithesis of being creative and nimble. It was talking about the work vs. doing the work." Criticisms about decision-making style were also leveled at Cynthia Harriss, whom Pressler had hired to lead the Gap brand. "She made no decisions," says one employee. "She defaulted to Paul, who made no decisions."

How can leaders effectively manage their choice of decision-making styles? The **time-driven model of leadership** offers one potential guide.[42] The model suggests that the focus should shift away from autocratic, consultative, facilitative, and delegative *leaders* to autocratic, consultative, facilitative, and delegative *situations.* More specifically, the model suggests that seven factors combine to make some decision-making styles more effective in a given situation and other styles less effective. Those seven factors include:

- *Decision significance:* Is the decision significant to the success of the project or the organization?
- *Importance of commitment:* Is it important that employees "buy in" to the decision?
- *Leader expertise:* Does the leader have significant knowledge or expertise regarding the problem?
- *Likelihood of commitment:* How likely is it that employees will trust the leader's decision and commit to it?
- *Shared objectives:* Do employees share and support the same objectives, or do they have an agenda of their own?
- *Employee expertise:* Do the employees have significant knowledge or expertise regarding the problem?
- *Teamwork skills:* Do the employees have the ability to work together to solve the problem, or will they struggle with conflicts or inefficiencies?

Figure 14-3 illustrates how these seven factors can be used to illustrate the most effective decision-making style in a given situation. The figure asks whether levels of each of the seven factors are "high" (H) or "low" (L). The figure functions like a funnel moving from left to right, with each answer bringing you closer to the eventual recommended style (dashes mean that a given factor can be skipped with that combination). Although the model seems complex on first look, the principles within it are straightforward. Autocratic styles are reserved for decisions that are insignificant or decisions for which employee commitment is unimportant. The only exception is when the leader's expertise is high and the leader is trusted. Going with the autocratic style in these situations should result in an accurate decision that makes the most efficient use of employees' time. Delegative styles are reserved for circumstances in which employees have strong teamwork skills and aren't likely to just commit to whatever decision the leader provides. Deciding between the remaining two styles—consultative and facilitative—is more nuanced and requires a more complete consideration of all seven factors.

Research has tended to support many of the time-driven model's propositions, particularly when the research uses practicing managers as participants.[43] For example, one study asked managers to recall past decisions, the context surrounding those decisions, and the eventual successes (or failures) of their decisions.[44] When managers used the decision-making styles recommended by the model, those decisions were rated as successful 68 percent of the time. When managers went against the model's prescriptions, their decisions were only rated as successful 22 percent of the time. It's also interesting to note that studies suggest that managers tend to choose the style recommended by the model only around 40 percent of the time and exhibit less variation in styles than the

FIGURE 14-3 — The Time-Driven Model of Leadership

START HERE → ... → END HERE

Decision Significance	Importance of Commitment	Leader Expertise	Likelihood of Commitment	Shared Objectives	Employee Expertise	Teamwork Skills	
H	H	H	H	-	-	-	Autocratic
			L	H	H	H	Delegative
						L	Consultative
					L	-	
				L	-	-	
		L	H	H	H	H	Facilitative
						L	Consultative
					L	-	
				L	-	-	
			L	H	H	H	Facilitative
						L	Consultative
					L	-	
				L	-	-	
	L	H	-	-	-	-	Autocratic
		L	-	H	H	H	Facilitative
						L	Consultative
					L	-	
				L	-	-	
L	H	-	H	-	-	-	Autocratic
			L	-	-	H	Delegative
						L	Facilitative
	L	-	-	-	-	-	Autocratic

Source: Adapted from V.H. Vroom, "Leadership and the Decision-Making Process," *Organizational Dynamics* 28 (2000), pp. 82–94.

model suggests they should.[45] In particular, managers seem to overuse the consultative style and underutilize autocratic and facilitative styles. For a more informal test (and "test drive") of the model, see our **OB on Screen** feature.

DAY-TO-DAY LEADERSHIP BEHAVIORS

Leaving aside how they go about making decisions, what do leaders *do* on a day-to-day basis? When you think about bosses that you've had, what behaviors do they tend to perform as part of their daily leadership responsibilities? A series of studies at Ohio State in the 1950s attempted to answer that question. Working under grants from the Office of Naval Research and the International Harvester Company, the studies began by generating a list of all the behaviors leaders engage in—around 1,800 in all.[46] Those behaviors were trimmed down to 150 specific examples, then grouped into several categories, as shown in Table 14-3.[47] The table reveals that many leaders spend their time engaging in a mix of initiating, organizing, producing, socializing, integrating, communicating, recognizing, and representing behaviors. Although eight categories are easier to remember than 1,800 behaviors, further analyses suggested that the categories in Table 14-3 really boil down to just two dimensions: initiating structure and consideration.[48]

OB ON SCREEN

THIRTEEN DAYS

There's something immoral about abandoning your own judgment.

With those words, President John F. Kennedy (Bruce Greenwood) foreshadows the decision-making style he's going to use during the Cuban missile crisis, as depicted in *Thirteen Days* (Dir. Roger Donaldson, New Line, 2001). During a conversation with his brother, Robert Kennedy (Steven Culp), and his chief-of-staff, Kenny O'Donnell (Kevin Costner), Kennedy voices regret over his past decision to support the Bay of Pigs invasion, when U.S.-backed Cuban refugees attempted to overthrow the government of Fidel Castro. He doesn't want to repeat the same mistakes when dealing with a new crisis: the installation of Soviet missiles in Cuba. Kennedy assembles the best team of advisors he can to deal with the crisis, but the question remains: What decision-making style should he use?

If we work our way through Figure 14-3, it seems clear that the decision is significant (the missiles can reach every major city in the United States, except for Seattle). O'Donnell himself notes how important it is for U.S. generals to commit to the decision, and it's clear that Kennedy doesn't have the expertise needed to drive the discussions.

Unfortunately for Kennedy, the movie's depiction of the events shows that his generals don't trust him (they view him as an "appeaser," like his father was), resulting in a low likelihood of commitment. To make matters worse, the generals appear to have their own objectives, seeming to want to use the missile crisis as an excuse to invade Cuba and take out Castro once and for all. If you're scoring at home, our journey through Figure 14-3 results in H-H-L-L-L, suggesting that the most effective decision-making style for Kennedy is consultative.

Did Kennedy use that style? In the end, Kennedy's advisors present him with two feasible options. One is an invasion of Cuba to take out the missiles, and the other is a blockade, an action that prevents additional missiles from being delivered while giving the Russians a chance to pull back from the brink of war. Once those options are delivered, Kennedy doesn't call for a show of hands and makes no attempt to bring the room to consensus. He asks his speechwriters to get time on the network news the next day and write up speeches for invasion and for blockade. Then he tells the room he'll give them *his decision* in the morning. Thus, Kennedy did exactly what the time-driven model of leadership suggests he should have done: Gather the opinions and suggestions of others but maintain the ultimate authority for himself.

Initiating structure reflects the extent to which the leader defines and structures the roles of employees in pursuit of goal attainment.[49] Leaders who are high on initiating structure play a more active role in directing group activities and prioritize planning, scheduling, and trying out new ideas. They might emphasize the importance of meeting deadlines, describe explicit standards of performance, ask employees to follow formalized procedures,

TABLE 14-3	Day-to-Day Behaviors Performed by Leaders
BEHAVIOR	**DESCRIPTION**
Initiating Structure	
Initiation	Originating, facilitating, and sometimes resisting new ideas and practices
Organization	Defining and structuring work, clarifying leader versus member roles, coordinating employee tasks
Production	Setting goals and providing incentives for the effort and productivity of employees
Consideration	
Membership	Mixing with employees, stressing informal interactions, and exchanging personal services
Integration	Encouraging a pleasant atmosphere, reducing conflict, promoting individual adjustment to the group
Communication	Providing information to employees, seeking information from them, showing an awareness of matters that affect them
Recognition	Expressing approval or disapproval of the behaviors of employees
Representation	Acting on behalf of the group, defending the group, and advancing the interests of the group

Source: J.K. Hemphill and A.E. Coons, "Development of the Leader Behavior Description Questionnaire," in *Leader Behavior: Its Description and Measurement,* eds. R.M. Stogdill and A.E. Coons. (Columbus, OH: Bureau of Business Research, Ohio State University, 1957), pp. 6–38.

and criticize poor work when necessary.[50] **Consideration** reflects the extent to which leaders create job relationships characterized by mutual trust, respect for employee ideas, and consideration of employee feelings.[51] Leaders who are high on consideration create a climate of good rapport and strong, two-way communication and exhibit a deep concern for the welfare of employees. They might do personal favors for employees, take time to listen to their problems, "go to bat" for them when needed, and treat them as equals.[52]

The Ohio State studies argued that initiating structure and consideration were (more or less) independent concepts, meaning that leaders could be high on both, low on both, or high on one and low on the other. That view differed from a series of studies conducted at the University of Michigan during the same time period. Those studies identified concepts similar to initiating structure and consideration, calling them production-centered (or task-oriented) and employee-centered (or relations-oriented) behaviors.[53] However, the Michigan studies framed their task-oriented and relations-oriented concepts as two ends of one continuum, implying that leaders couldn't be high on both dimensions.[54] In fact, a recent meta-analysis of 78 studies showed that initiating structure and consideration are only weakly related—knowing whether a leader engages in one brand of behavior says little about whether he or she engages in the other brand.[55] To see how much initiating structure and consideration you engage in during leadership roles, see our **OB Assessments** feature.

14.4

What two dimensions capture most of the day-to-day leadership behaviors that leaders engage in?

OB ASSESSMENTS

INITIATING STRUCTURE AND CONSIDERATION

How do you act when you're in a leadership role? This assessment is designed to measure the two dimensions of leaders' day-to-day behaviors: initiating structure and consideration. Please write a number next to each statement that reflects how frequently you engage in the behavior described. Answer each question using the response scale provided. Then subtract your answers to the bold-faced question from 6, with the difference being your new answer for that question. For example, if your original answer for question 16 was "4," your new answer is "2" (6 − 4). Then sum up your answers for each of the dimensions.

1	2	3	4	5
NEVER	SELDOM	OCCASIONALLY	OFTEN	ALWAYS

1. I let group members know what is expected of them. _____

2. I encourage the use of uniform procedures. _____

3. I try out my ideas in the group. _____

4. I make my attitudes clear to the group. _____

5. I decide what shall be done and how it shall be done. _____

6. I assign group members to particular tasks. _____

7. I make sure that my part in the group is understood by the group members. _____

8. I schedule the work to be done. _____

9. I maintain definite standards of performance. _____

10. I ask group members to follow standard rules and regulations. _____

11. I am friendly and approachable. _____

12. I do little things to make it pleasant to be a member of the group. _____

13. I put suggestions made by the group into operation. _____

14. I treat all group members as equals. _____

15. I give advance notice of changes. _____

16. **I keep to myself.** _____

17. I look out for the personal welfare of group members. _____

18. I am willing to make changes. _____

19. **I refuse to explain my actions.** _____

20. **I act without consulting the group.** _____

SCORING AND INTERPRETATION:

Initiating Structure: Sum up items 1–10.
Consideration: Sum up items 11–20.

(continued)

For initiating structure, scores of 38 or more are above average, and scores of 37 or less are below average. For consideration, scores of 40 or more are above average, and scores of 39 or less are below average.

Source: R.M. Stogdill, *Manual for the Leader Behavior Description Questionnaire–Form XII* (Columbus, OH: Bureau of Business Research, The Ohio State University, 1963).

After an initial wave of research on initiating structure and consideration, leadership experts began to doubt the usefulness of the two dimensions for predicting leadership effectiveness.[56] More recent research has painted a more encouraging picture, however. A meta-analysis of 103 studies showed that initiating structure and consideration both had beneficial relationships with a number of outcomes.[57] For example, consideration had a strong positive relationship with perceived leader effectiveness, employee motivation, and employee job satisfaction. It also had a moderate positive relationship with overall unit performance. For its part, initiating structure had a strong positive relationship with employee motivation and moderate positive relationships with perceived leader effectiveness, employee job satisfaction, and overall unit performance.

Although initiating structure and consideration tend to be beneficial across situations, there may be circumstances in which they become more or less important. The **life cycle theory of leadership** (sometimes also called the situational model of leadership) argues that the optimal combination of initiating structure and consideration depends on the readiness of the employees in the work unit.[58] **Readiness** is broadly defined as the degree to which employees have the ability and the willingness to accomplish their specific tasks.[59] As shown in Figure 14-4, the theory suggests that readiness varies from R1 (unable and unwilling) to R2 (unable but willing) to R3 (able but unwilling) to R4 (able and willing). It is important to note that employees may be unwilling to perform their tasks because they lack commitment or motivation or merely because they are insecure due to a lack of experience.[60]

FIGURE 14-4   The Life Cycle Theory of Leadership

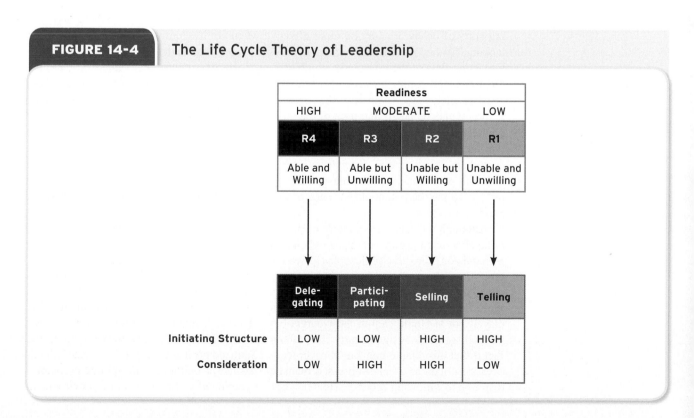

Readiness			
HIGH	MODERATE		LOW
R4	**R3**	**R2**	**R1**
Able and Willing	Able but Unwilling	Unable but Willing	Unable and Unwilling

	Dele-gating	Partici-pating	Selling	Telling
Initiating Structure	LOW	LOW	HIGH	HIGH
Consideration	LOW	HIGH	HIGH	LOW

To find the optimal behavioral combination for those levels of readiness, put your finger on the relevant R level then move it straight down to the recommended combination. For example, the optimal combination for the R1 readiness level is **telling**—high initiating structure and low consideration—in which case the leader provides specific instructions and closely supervises performance.[61] Here the leader tells employees what to do, where to do it, and how to do it, because such guidance and direction is needed in the absence of employee ability, motivation, or confidence. The optimal combination for the R2 readiness level is **selling**—high initiating structure and high consideration—so the leader explains key issues and provides opportunities for clarification.[62] Some guidance and direction is still needed due to a lack of employee ability, but the increased explanation and persuasion can help foster the emerging motivation and confidence.

As employees gain more ability, the nature of their job becomes more complex, potentially renewing concerns about their confidence. The optimal combination for the R3 readiness level is **participating**—low initiating structure and high consideration—as the leader shares ideas and tries to help the group conduct its affairs.[63] Here guidance is no longer needed because employee ability is high. What is needed is some combination of collaborating and facilitating to support employees during this shift in their role requirements. Finally, the optimal combination for the R4 readiness level is **delegating**—low initiating structure and low consideration—such that the leader turns responsibility for key behaviors over to the employees.[64] Here the leader "gives them the ball and lets them run with it." All that is needed from the leader is some degree of observation and monitoring to make sure that the group's efforts stay on track.

Estimates suggest that the life cycle theory has been incorporated into leadership training programs at around 400 of the firms in the *Fortune* 500, with more than one million managers exposed to it annually.[65] Unfortunately, the application of the theory has outpaced scientific testing of its propositions. The research that has been conducted supports the theory's predictions only for low readiness situations, suggesting that telling and selling sorts of behaviors may be more effective when ability, motivation, or confidence are lacking.[66] When readiness is higher, these tests suggest that leader behaviors simply matter less, regardless of their particular combinations. Tests also suggest that leaders only use the recommended combinations of behaviors between 14 and 37 percent of the time,[67] likely because many leaders adhere to the same leadership philosophy regardless of the situation. It should also be noted that tests of the theory have been somewhat more supportive when conducted on an across-job, rather than within-job, basis. For example, research suggests that the performance of lower ranking university employees (e.g., maintenance workers, custodians, landscapers) depends more on initiating structure and less on consideration than the performance of higher ranking university employees (e.g., professors, instructors).[68] To see the potential relevance of the life cycle theory for students, see our **OB for Students** feature.

Although the scientific validity of the life cycle theory remains in question, its predictions often seem to play out in professional sports. General managers often hire coaches with a "hands-on" directive philosophy for youthful teams with several rookies or new starters. Over time, those teams mature and become more experienced, at which point the coach's style begins to wear on the veterans. The general managers then bring in coaches with a more "hands-off" style (often referred to as a "player's coach"). This same dynamic recently played out at Home Depot, the Georgia-based hardware retailer. Controversial CEO Bob Nardelli agreed to resign in early 2007 after a six-year tenure, with one observer noting, "the fact is that this retail organization never really embraced his leadership style."[72] Nardelli has been described as a detail-obsessed manager devoted to building a disciplined corps predisposed to following orders.[73] He believes in a command-and-control sort of environment

OB FOR STUDENTS

Even if you aren't currently working and haven't worked in the past, the life cycle theory of leadership has some relevance to you. After all, you've experienced at least two kinds of leaders already: parents and teachers.

The originators of the life cycle theory suggest that it offers predictions for how parenting behaviors should vary over the course of a child's time at home.[69] Telling should be effective early in life, because initiating structure is needed as children learn to navigate their daily lives. As the child enters school and begins to demonstrate his or her own responsibility and work ethic, telling should give way to selling to build trust and mutual respect. As the child moves into high school and college, the responsibility for key decisions becomes his or her own, with the parent offering mostly support in accordance with a participating style. Finally, as the now young adult makes his or her own living and starts a family, a delegating style seems most appropriate.

Although those predictions have never been formally tested, research has supported the importance of parenting behaviors to academic success in college. One study of 236 undergraduates asked the students to rate their parents on three types of behaviors: consideration, demandingness (one aspect of initiating structure), and autonomy granting (reflecting the use of a more participating and delegating style).[70] The students were asked to rate those behaviors in reference to two time periods: now and during their childhood (around 8 years old). As would be expected based on the life cycle theory, current levels of autonomy granting were significantly related to student GPA, but childhood levels were not. However, autonomy granting at both time periods was related to students' confidence, persistence, involvement, and rapport with instructors. Its importance did not vary, as would be expected by the theory. Similarly, the study showed that consideration was related to students' confidence and persistence in the classroom and their rapport with their instructors, again regardless of whether the behaviors occurred currently or in childhood. For its part, demandingness had little impact on student outcomes, regardless of the relevant time period.

It's also possible to use the life cycle theory to examine the different teaching styles that students encounter during their college careers.[71] Instructors may use a telling style in freshman courses, because students are still adjusting to college life. As prerequisites give way to electives, more student participation is offered, as a selling and participating style is used more frequently. Finally, in graduate study—particularly Ph.D. programs—more of a delegating style is practiced as students engage in more self-directed studies of topics of their choosing.

and is fond of saying, "Facts are friendly."[74] You can probably already guess the adjectives associated with Nardelli's replacement. The cofounder of Home Depot describes new CEO Frank Blake as more "people oriented," lacking Nardelli's sharp edges while playing the role of consensus builder.[75]

TRANSFORMATIONAL LEADERSHIP BEHAVIORS

By describing decision-making styles and day-to-day leader behaviors, we've covered a broad spectrum of what it is that leaders do. Still, something is missing. Take a small piece of scrap paper and jot down five people who are famous for their effective leadership. They can come from inside or outside the business world and can be either living people

Mother Teresa's inspiring humanitarian work with India's sick and poor, and her founding of the influential Missionaries of Charity, became known around the world and suggest that she was a transformational leader. She was awarded the Nobel Peace Prize in 1979.

or historical figures. All that's important is that their name be practically synonymous with great leadership. Once you've compiled your list, take a look at the names. Do they appear on your list because they tend to use the right decision-making styles in the right situations and engage in effective levels of consideration and initiating structure? What about the case of Steve Jobs? Do decision-making styles and day-to-day leadership behaviors explain his importance to the fortunes of Apple?

The missing piece of this leadership puzzle is what leaders do to motivate their employees to perform beyond expectations. **Transformational leadership** involves inspiring followers to commit to a shared vision that provides meaning to their work while also serving as a role model who helps followers develop their own potential and view problems from new perspectives.[76] Transformational leaders heighten followers' awareness of the importance of certain outcomes while increasing their confidence that those outcomes can be achieved.[77] What gets "transformed" is the way followers view their work, causing them to focus on the collective good more than just their own short-term self-interests and to perform beyond expectations as a result.[78] Former President Dwight D. Eisenhower once noted, "Leadership is the ability to decide what is to be done, and then to get others to want to do it."[79] Former President Harry S. Truman similarly observed, "A leader is a man who has the ability to get other people to do what they don't want to do, and like it."[80] Both quotes capture a transformation in the way followers view their work and what motivates them on the job.

Transformational leadership is viewed as a more motivational approach to leadership than other managerial approaches. Figure 14-5 contrasts various approaches to leadership according to how active or passive they are and, ultimately, how effective they prove to be. The colored cubes in the figure represent five distinct approaches to motivating employees, and the depth of the cubes represent how much a leader prioritizes each of the approaches. The figure therefore represents an optimal leadership approach that prioritizes more effective and more active behaviors. That optimal approach includes low levels of **laissez-faire** (i.e., hands-off) leadership, represented by the red cube, which is the avoidance of leadership altogether.[81] Important actions are delayed, responsibility is ignored, and power and influence go unutilized. One common measure of leadership reflects laissez-faire styles with this statement: "The leader avoids getting involved when important issues arise."[82]

FIGURE 14-5	Laissez-Faire, Transactional, and Transformational Leadership

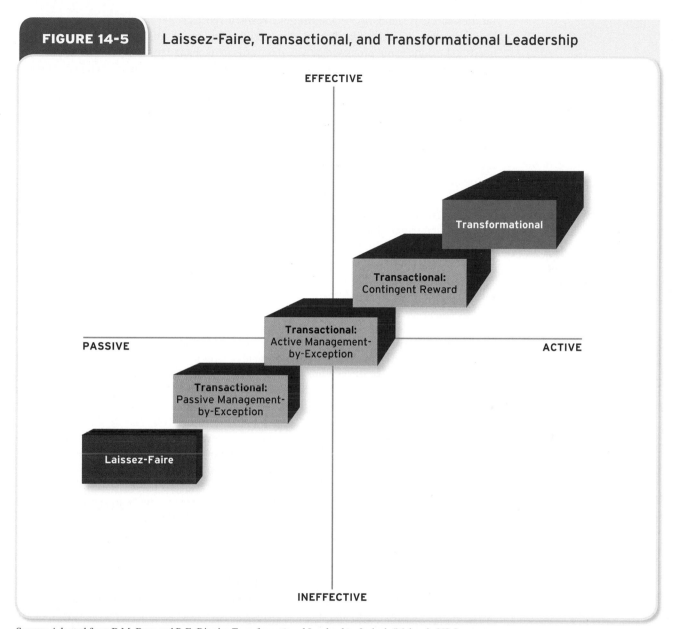

Source: Adapted from B.M. Bass and R.E. Riggio, *Transformational Leadership,* 2nd ed. (Mahwah, NJ: Lawrence Erlbaum Associates, 2006).

The three yellow cubes represent **transactional leadership,** which occurs when the leader rewards or disciplines the follower depending on the adequacy of the follower's performance.[83] With **passive management-by-exception,** the leader waits around for mistakes and errors, then takes corrective action as necessary.[84] After all, "if it ain't broke, don't fix it!"[85] This approach is represented by statements like: "The leader takes no action until complaints are received."[86] With **active management-by-exception,** the leader arranges to monitor mistakes and errors actively and again takes corrective action when required.[87] This approach is represented by statements like: "The leader directs attention toward failures to meet standards."[88] **Contingent reward** represents a more active and effective brand of transactional leadership, in which the leader attains follower agreement on what needs to be done using promised or actual rewards in exchange for adequate performance.[89] Statements like "The leader makes clear what one can expect to receive when performance goals are achieved" exemplify contingent reward leadership.[90]

Transactional leadership represents the "carrot-and-stick" approach to leadership, with management-by-exception providing the "sticks" and contingent reward supplying the "carrots." Of course, transactional leadership represents the dominant approach to motivating employees in most organizations, and research suggests that it can be effective. A meta-analysis of 87 studies showed that contingent reward was strongly related to follower motivation and perceived leader effectiveness[91] (see Chapter 6 on Motivation for more discussion of contingent reward issues). Active management-by-exception was only weakly related to follower motivation and perceived leader effectiveness, however, and passive management-by-exception seems to actually harm those outcomes.[92] Such results support the progression shown in Figure 14-5, with contingent reward standing as the most effective approach under the transactional leadership umbrella.

Finally, the green cube represents transformational leadership—the most active and effective approach in Figure 14-5. How effective is transformational leadership? Well, we'll save that discussion for the "How Important Is Leadership" section that concludes this chapter, but suffice it to say that transformational leadership has the strongest and most beneficial effects of any of the leadership variables described in this chapter. It's also the leadership approach that is most universally endorsed across cultures, as described in our **OB Internationally** feature. In addition, it probably captures the key qualities of the famous leaders we asked you to list a few paragraphs back. To understand why it's so powerful, we need to dig deeper into the specific kinds of actions and behaviors that leaders can utilize to become more transformational. It turns out that the full spectrum of transformational leadership can be summarized using four dimensions: idealized influence, inspirational motivation, intellectual stimulation, and individualized consideration. Collectively, these four dimensions of transformational leadership are often called "the Four I's."[93]

Idealized influence involves behaving in ways that earn the admiration, trust, and respect of followers, causing followers to want to identify with and emulate the leader.[98] Idealized influence is represented by statements like: "The leader instills pride in me for being associated with him/her."[99] Idealized influence is synonymous with *charisma*—a Greek word that means "divinely inspired gift"—which reflects a sense among followers that the leader possesses extraordinary qualities.[100] Charisma is a word often associated with Steve Jobs. One observer noted that, even though Jobs could be very difficult to work with, his remarkable charisma created a mysterious attraction that drew people to him, keeping them loyal to his collective sense of mission.[101]

To some extent, discussions of charisma serve as echoes of the "great person" view of leadership that spawned the trait research described in Table 14-2. In fact, research suggests that there is a genetic component to charisma specifically and to transformational leadership more broadly. Studies on identical twins reared apart show that such twins have very similar charismatic profiles, despite their differing environments.[102] Indeed, such research suggests that almost 60 percent of the variation in charismatic behavior can be explained by genes. One explanation for such findings is that genes influence the personality traits that give rise to charisma. For example, research suggests that extraversion, openness to experience, and agreeableness have significant effects on perceptions of leader charisma,[103] and all three of those personality dimensions have a significant genetic component (see Chapter 9 on Personality and Cultural Values for more discussion of such issues).

14.5

How does transformational leadership differ from transactional leadership? What kinds of behaviors underlie transformational leadership?

OB INTERNATIONALLY

Does the effectiveness of leader styles and behaviors vary across cultures? Answering that question is one of the objectives of *Project GLOBE* (Global Leadership and Organizational Behavior Effectiveness), a collection of 170 researchers from 62 cultures who have studied leadership with 17,300 managers in 951 organizations since 1991.[94] In part, Project GLOBE represents a test of *culturally endorsed implicit leadership theory,* which argues that effective leadership is "in the eye of the beholder" and that cultural variables can alter how people define such leadership.[95] To test that theory, the GLOBE researchers asked participants to rate a number of leader styles and behaviors using a 1–7 scale, where 1 represents the perception that the style or behavior inhibits a person from being an outstanding leader and 7 represents the perception that the style or behavior contributes greatly to a person being an outstanding leader. The figure below shows how three of the styles and behaviors described in this chapter were rated across 10 different regions (note that the term "Anglo" represents people of English ethnicity, including the United States, Great Britain, and Australia).

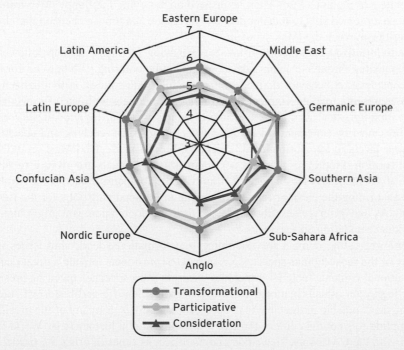

It turns out that transformational leadership is the most universally accepted approach to leadership of any of the concepts studied by Project GLOBE,[96] receiving an average rating near 6 among the citizens of every region except the Middle East. That universal appeal is likely explained by that fact that transformational leaders appeal to values like idealism and virtue that are accepted and endorsed in almost all countries.[97] The figure also shows that participative decision-making styles are favorably viewed in most countries, though more variation is evident, with the Middle East and Asia endorsing that style less than European and Anglo regions. Even more variation is seen with consideration behaviors, which are endorsed a bit less across the board but especially in Europe. These results suggest that participative styles and consideration behaviors appeal to cultural values that differ across regions. Understanding these kinds of results can help organizations select, counsel, and train managers who will better fit the profile of an effective leader in a given region.

Inspirational motivation involves behaving in ways that foster an enthusiasm for and commitment to a shared vision of the future.[104] That vision is transmitted through a sort of "meaning-making" process in which the negative features of the status quo are emphasized while highlighting the positive features of the potential future.[105] Inspirational motivation is represented by statements like: "The leader articulates a compelling vision of the future."[106] At Apple, Steve Jobs is renowned for spinning a "reality distortion field" that reshapes employees' views of the current work environment.[107] One Apple employee explained, "Steve has this power of vision that is almost frightening. When Steve believes in something, the power of that vision can literally sweep aside any objections, problems, or whatever. They just cease to exist."[108]

Intellectual stimulation involves behaving in ways that challenge followers to be innovative and creative by questioning assumptions and reframing old situations in new ways.[109] Intellectual stimulation is represented by statements like: "The leader gets others to look at problems from many different angles."[110] Intellectual stimulation has been a staple of Jobs's tenure at Apple. He pushed for a different power supply on the Apple II so that the fan could be removed, preventing it from humming and churning like other computers of the time. Years later, he insisted on removing the floppy drive from the iMac because it seemed silly to transfer data one megabyte at a time, a decision that drew merciless criticism when the iMac debuted.

Individualized consideration involves behaving in ways that help followers achieve their potential through coaching, development, and mentoring.[111] Not to be confused with the consideration behavior derived from the Ohio State studies, individualized consideration represents treating employees as unique individuals with specific needs, abilities, and aspirations that need to be tied into the unit's mission. Individualized consideration is represented by statements like: "The leader spends time teaching and coaching."[112] Of the four facets of transformational leadership, Steve Jobs seems lowest on individualized consideration. Employees who are not regarded as his equals are given a relatively short leash and sometimes face an uncertain future in the company. In fact, some Apple employees resist riding the elevator for fear of ending up trapped with Jobs for the ride between floors. As one observer describes it, by the time the doors open, you might have had your confidence undermined for weeks.[113]

One interesting domain for examining transformational leadership issues is politics. Many of the most famous speeches given by U.S. presidents include a great deal of transformational content. Table 14-4 includes excerpts from speeches given by presidents that rank highly on transformational content based on scientific and historical study.[114] One theme that's notable in the table is the presence of a crisis, as many of the presidents were attempting to steer the country through a difficult time in history (e.g., World War II, the Cold War, the Civil War). That's not a coincidence, as times of crisis are particularly conducive to the emergence of transformational leadership.[115] Times of stress and turbulence cause people to long for charismatic leaders, and encouraging, confident, and idealistic visions resonate more deeply during such times. Some recent support for this suggestion comes from President George W. Bush's speeches before and after the tragedies on 9/11. Coding of his major speeches, public addresses, and radio addresses shows a significant increase in the transformational content of his rhetoric after the 9/11 attacks, including more focus on a collective mission and more articulation of a value-based vision.[116]

SUMMARY: WHY ARE SOME LEADERS MORE EFFECTIVE THAN OTHERS?

So what explains why some leaders are more effective than others? As shown in Figure 14-6, answering that question requires an understanding of the particular styles that

TABLE 14-4	Transformational Rhetoric among U.S. Presidents

PRESIDENT	TERM	REMARK	WHICH "I"?
Abraham Lincoln	1861–1865	"Fourscore and seven years ago our forefathers brought forth on this continent, a new nation, conceived in Liberty, and dedicated to the proposition that all men are created equal."	Idealized influence
Franklin Roosevelt	1933–1945	"First of all, let me assert my firm belief that the only thing we have to fear is fear itself—nameless, unreasoning, unjustified terror which paralyzes needed efforts to convert retreat into advance."	Inspirational motivation
John F. Kennedy	1961–1963	"And so, my fellow Americans . . . ask not what your country can do you for you—ask what you can do for your country. My fellow citizens of the world: Ask not what America will do for you, but what together we can do for the freedom of man."	Intellectual stimulation
Lyndon Johnson	1963–1969	"If future generations are to remember us more with gratitude than sorrow, we must achieve more than just the miracles of technology. We must also leave them a glimpse of the world as it was created, not just as it looked when we got through with it."	Idealized influence
Ronald Reagan	1981–1989	"General Secretary Gorbachev, if you seek peace, if you seek prosperity for the Soviet Union and Eastern Europe, if you seek liberalization: Come here to this gate! Mr. Gorbachev, open this gate! Mr. Gorbachev, tear down this wall!"	Idealized influence
Bill Clinton	1993–2001	"To realize the full possibilities of this economy, we must reach beyond our own borders, to shape the revolution that is tearing down barriers and building new networks among nations and individuals, and economies and cultures: globalization. It's the central reality of our time."	Intellectual stimulation

Sources: Names of presidents high in transformational content taken from J.S. Mio, R.E. Riggio, S. Levin, and R. Reese, "Presidential Leadership and Charisma: The Effects of Metaphor," *Leadership Quarterly* 16 (2005), pp. 287–94. Quotes retrieved from http://www.usa-patriotism.com/quotes/_list.htm.

leaders use to make decisions and the behaviors they perform in their leadership role. In terms of decision-making styles, do they choose the most effective combination of leader and follower control in terms of the autocratic, consultative, facilitative, and delegative styles, particularly considering the importance of the decision and the expertise in the unit? In terms of day-to-day behaviors, do they engage in adequate levels of initiating structure and consideration? Finally, do they utilize an effective combination of transactional leadership behaviors, such as contingent reward, and transformational leadership behaviors, such as idealized influence, inspirational motivation, intellectual stimulation, and individualized consideration?

| FIGURE 14-6 | Why Are Some Leaders More Effective Than Others? |

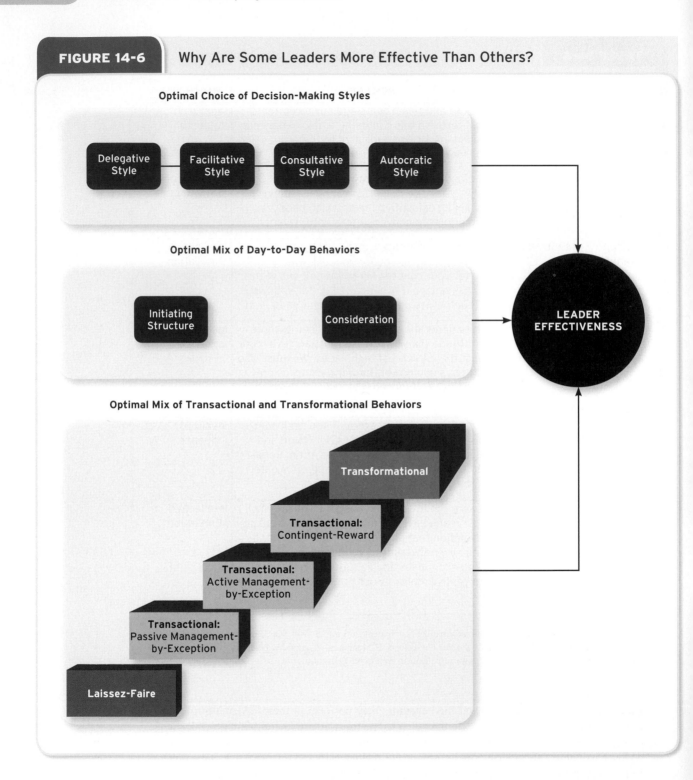

HOW IMPORTANT IS LEADERSHIP?

How important is leadership? As with some other topics in organizational behavior, that's a complicated question because "leadership" isn't just one thing. Instead, all of the styles and behaviors summarized in Figure 14-6 have their own unique importance. However, transformational leadership stands apart from the rest to some extent, with particularly strong effects in organizations. For example, transformational leadership is more strongly related to unit-focused measures of leadership effectiveness, like the kind shown in the top panel of Table 14-1.[117] Units led by a transformational leader tend to be more financially successful and bring higher quality products and services to market at a faster rate.[118] Transformational leadership is also more strongly related to dyad-focused measures of leader effectiveness, like the kind shown in the bottom panel of Table 14-1. Transformational leaders tend to foster leader–member exchange relationships that are of higher quality, marked by especially strong levels of mutual respect and obligation.[119]

What if we focus specifically on the two outcomes in our integrative model of OB: performance and commitment? Figure 14-7 summarizes the research evidence linking transformational leadership to those two outcomes. The figure reveals that transformational leadership indeed affects the job performance of the employees who report to the leader. Employees with transformational leaders tend to have higher levels of task performance and engage in higher levels of citizenship behaviors.[120] Why? One reason is that employees with transformational leaders have higher levels of *motivation* than other employees.[121] They feel a stronger sense of psychological empowerment, feel more self-confident, and set more demanding work goals for themselves.[122] They also *trust* the leader more, making them willing to exert extra effort even when that effort might not be immediately rewarded.[123]

Figure 14-7 also reveals that employees with transformational leaders tend to be more committed to their organization.[124] They feel a stronger emotional bond with their organization and a stronger sense of obligation to remain present and engaged in their work. Why? One reason is that employees with transformational leaders have higher levels of *job satisfaction* than other employees.[125] One study showed that transformational leaders can make employees feel that their jobs have more variety and significance, enhancing intrinsic satisfaction with the work itself.[126] Other studies have shown that charismatic leaders express positive emotions more frequently and that those emotions are "caught" by employees through a sort of "emotional contagion" process.[127] For example, followers of transformational leaders tend to feel more optimism and less frustration during their workday, which makes it a bit easier to stay committed to work.

Although leadership is very important to unit effectiveness and the performance and commitment of employees, there are contexts in which the importance of the leader can be reduced. The **substitutes for leadership model** suggests that certain characteristics of the situation can constrain the influence of the leader, making it more difficult for the leader to influence employee performance.[128] Those situational characteristics come in two varieties, as shown in Table 14-5. **Substitutes** reduce the importance of the leader while simultaneously providing a direct benefit to employee performance. For example, a cohesive work group can provide its own sort of governing behaviors, making the leader less relevant, while providing its own source of motivation and job satisfaction. **Neutralizers,** in contrast, only reduce the importance of the leader—they themselves have no beneficial impact on performance.[129] For example, spatial distance lessens the impact of a leader's behaviors and styles, but distance itself has no direct benefit for employee job performance.

14.6

How does leadership affect job performance and organizational commitment?

FIGURE 14-7 Effects of Transformational Leadership on Performance and Commitment

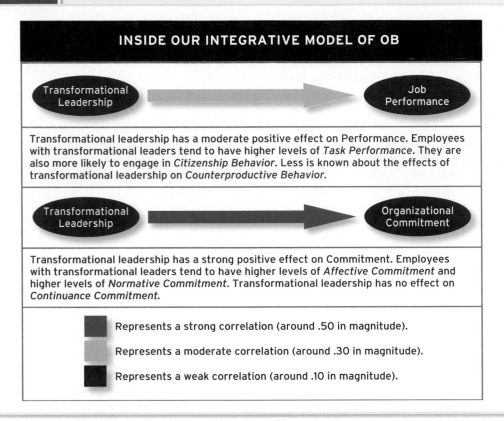

Sources: T.A. Judge and R.F. Piccolo, "Transformational and Transactional Leadership: A Meta-Analytic Test of Their Relative Validity," *Journal of Applied Psychology* 89 (2004), pp. 755–68; J.P. Meyer, D.J. Stanley, L. Herscovitch, and L. Topolnytsky, "Affective, Continuance, and Normative Commitment to the Organization: A Meta-Analysis of Antecedents, Correlates, and Consequences," *Journal of Vocational Behavior* 61 (2002), pp. 20–52; P.M. Podsakoff, S.B. MacKenzie, J.B. Paine, and D.G. Bachrach, "Organizational Citizenship Behaviors: A Critical Review of the Theoretical and Empirical Literature and Suggestions for Future Research," *Journal of Management* 26 (2000), pp. 513–63.

The substitutes for leadership model offers a number of prescriptions for a better understanding of leadership in organizations. First, it can be used to explain why a leader who seemingly "does the right things" doesn't seem to be making any difference.[130] It may be that the leader's work context possesses high levels of neutralizers and substitutes. Second, it can be used to explain what to do if an ineffective person is in a leadership role with no immediate replacement waiting in the wings.[131] If the leader can't be removed, perhaps the organization can do things to make that leader more irrelevant. Studies on the substitutes for leadership model have been inconsistent in showing that substitutes and neutralizers actually make leaders less influential in the predicted manner.[132] What is more clear is that the substitutes in Table 14-5 have beneficial effects on the job performance and organizational commitment of employees. In fact, the beneficial effects of the substitutes is sometimes even greater than the beneficial effects of the leader's own behaviors and styles. Some leadership experts even recommend that leaders set out to create high levels of the substitutes in their work units wherever possible, even if the units might ultimately wind up "running themselves."[133]

TABLE 14-5	Leader Substitutes and Neutralizers

SUBSTITUTES	DESCRIPTION
• Task feedback	Receiving feedback on performance from the task itself
• Training & experience	Gaining the knowledge to act independently of the leader
• Professionalism	Having a professional specialty that offers guidance
• Staff support	Receiving information and assistance from outside staff
• Group cohesion	Working in a close-knit and interdependent work group
• Intrinsic satisfaction	Deriving personal satisfaction from one's work
NEUTRALIZERS	
• Task stability	Having tasks with a clear, unchanging sequence of steps
• Formalization	Having written policies and procedures that govern one's job
• Inflexibility	Working in an organization that prioritizes rule adherence
• Spatial distance	Being separated from one's leader by physical space

Source: Adapted from S. Kerr and J.M. Jermier, "Substitutes for Leadership: Their Meaning and Measurement," *Organizational Behavior and Human Performance* 22 (1978), pp. 375–403.

APPLICATION: LEADERSHIP TRAINING

Given the importance of leadership, what can organizations do to maximize the effectiveness of their leaders? One method is to spend more time training them. Estimates suggest that U.S. companies spent $56 billion on training programs in 2006, with 29 percent of that devoted to management and supervisory training.[134] One training analyst explains the increasing emphasis on leadership training this way: "The biggest problem that companies face today is an acute shortage of midlevel managers. They look around and just don't have enough qualified people." The same analyst notes that hiring leaders away from competitors isn't an option "because they probably don't have enough managers either."[135]

Leadership training programs often focus on very specific issues, like conducting more accurate performance evaluations, being a more effective mentor, structuring creative problem solving, or gaining more cultural awareness and sensitivity.[136] However, training programs can also focus on much of the content covered in this chapter. For example, content could focus on contextual considerations that alter the effectiveness of decision-making styles or particular leader behaviors, such as initiating structure and consideration. What about transformational leadership? Given how dependent charisma is on personality and genetic factors, is it possible that transformational leaders can only be born, not made? See our **OB at the Bookstore** feature for one answer to that question.

It turns out that many training programs focus on transformational leadership content, and research suggests that those programs can be effective.[137] One study of transformational leadership training occurred in one of the largest bank chains in Canada.[138] Managers at all of the branches in one region were randomly assigned to either a transformational training group or a control group. The managers in the training group took part in a one-day training session that began by asking the managers to describe the best and worst

14.7

Can leaders be trained to be more effective?

OB AT THE BOOKSTORE

THE LEADERSHIP CHALLENGE

4th ed., by James M. Kouzes and Barry Z. Posner (San Francisco, CA: Jossey Bass, 2007).

> *Good leadership is an understandable and universal process. Though each leader is a unique individual, there are patterns to the practice that are shared. And that can be learned.*

With those words, Kouzes and Posner lay out their "field guide for leaders"—a book that describes five practices of exemplary leadership, provides case studies of real people who use those practices, and offers specific recommendations for learning how to use them. So what exactly are the five practices? They include:

1. *Model the Way:* Be a model of the behavior you expect of others in order to gain commitment.
2. *Inspire a Shared Vision:* Forge a unity of purpose by describing a dream that is for the common good.
3. *Challenge the Process:* Be willing to step out into the unknown to innovate, grow, and improve.
4. *Enable Others to Act:* Foster a sense of collaboration and trust to build teamwork.
5. *Encourage the Heart:* Create a culture of celebration to show appreciation for contributions.

A quick glance at the five practices reveals that Kouzes and Posner's exemplary leadership has much in common with the Four Is of transformational leadership. In particular, the first three practices are quite similar to idealized influence, inspirational motivation, and intellectual stimulation.

The book devotes two chapters to each of the five practices, with each chapter describing eight specific steps to take to get better at a given practice. For example, some of the steps involved in inspiring a shared vision include reading a biography of a visionary leader, determining the "something" you want to do, writing a vision statement, expanding your communication skills, and learning to be a better listener. In all, the book includes 80 specific steps that can be taken to become a more transformational leader. The book also includes information on the Leadership Practices Inventory (LPI), which can offer a "before and after" look at your proficiency with the five practices. The popularity of Kouzes and Posner's book is testament to the view that transformational leaders can indeed be made, not just born.

leaders they had ever encountered. Where applicable, the behaviors mentioned as belonging to the best leaders were framed around transformational leadership. The transformational dimensions were then described in a lecture-style format. Participants set goals for how they could behave more transformationally and engaged in role-playing exercises to practice those behaviors. The managers then created specific action plans, with progress on those plans monitored during four "booster sessions" over the next month. The results of the study showed that managers who participated in the training were rated as more transformational afterward. More important, their employees reported higher levels of organizational commitment, and their branches enjoyed better performance in terms of personal loan sales and credit card sales.

TAKEAWAYS

14.1 Leadership is defined as the use of power and influence to direct the activities of followers toward goal achievement. An "effective leader" improves the performance and well-being of his or her overall unit, as judged by profit margins, productivity, costs, absenteeism, retention, employee surveys, and so forth. An "effective leader" also cultivates high-quality leader–member exchange relationships on a dyadic basis through role taking and role making processes.

14.2 Leader emergence has been linked to a number of traits, including conscientious-ness, disagreeableness, openness, extraversion, general cognitive ability, energy level, stress tolerance, and self-confidence. Of that set, the last six traits also predict leader effectiveness.

14.3 Leaders can use a number of styles to make decisions. Beginning with high leader control and moving to high follower control, they include autocratic, consultative, facilitative, and delegative styles. According to the time-driven model of leadership, the appropriateness of these styles depends on decision significance, the importance of commitment, leader expertise, the likelihood of commitment, shared objectives, employee expertise, and teamwork skills.

14.4 Most of the day-to-day leadership behaviors that leaders engage in are examples of either initiating structure or consideration. Initiating structure behaviors include initiation, organization, and production sorts of duties. Consideration behaviors include membership, integration, communication, recognition, and representation sorts of duties.

14.5 Transactional leadership emphasizes "carrot-and-stick" approaches to motivating employees, whereas transformational leadership fundamentally changes the way employees view their work. More specifically, transformational leadership inspires them to commit to a shared vision or goal that provides meaning and challenge to their work. The specific behaviors that underlie transformational leadership include the "Four Is": idealized influence, inspirational motivation, intellectual stimulation, and individualized consideration.

14.6 Transformational leadership has a moderate positive relationship with job perfor-mance and a strong positive relationship with organizational commitment. It has stronger effects on these outcomes than other leadership behaviors.

14.7 Leaders can be trained to be effective. In fact, such training can be used to increase transformational leadership behaviors, despite the fact that charisma is somewhat dependent on personality and genetic factors.

KEY TERMS

- Leadership   *p. 474*
- Leader–member exchange
  theory   *p. 474*
- Role taking   *p. 474*
- Role making   *p. 474*
- Leader effectiveness   *p. 476*
- Leader emergence   *p. 476*
- Autocratic style   *p. 478*
- Consultative style   *p. 478*
- Facilitative style   *p. 478*

- Delegative style   *p. 479*
- Time-driven model of
  leadership   *p. 480*
- Initiating structure   *p. 482*
- Consideration   *p. 483*
- Life cycle theory of leadership   *p. 485*
- Readiness   *p. 485*
- Telling   *p. 486*
- Selling   *p. 486*
- Participating   *p. 486*
- Delegating   *p. 486*
- Transformational leadership   *p. 488*
- Laissez-faire leadership   *p. 488*
- Transactional leadership   *p. 489*
- Passive management-by-
  exception   *p. 489*
- Active management-by-
  exception   *p. 489*
- Contingent reward   *p. 490*
- Idealized influence   *p. 490*
- Inspirational motivation   *p. 492*
- Intellectual stimulation   *p. 492*
- Individualized consideration   *p. 492*
- Substitutes for leadership model *p. 495*
- Substitutes   *p. 495*
- Neutralizers   *p. 495*

DISCUSSION QUESTIONS

14.1 Before reading this chapter, which statement did you feel was more accurate: "Leaders are born" or "Leaders are made"? How do you feel now, and why do you feel that way?

14.2 The time-sensitive model of leadership argues that leaders aren't just concerned about the accuracy of their decisions when deciding among autocratic, consultative, facilitative, and delegative styles; they're also concerned about the efficient use of time. What other considerations could influence a leader's use of the four decision-making styles?

14.3 The time-sensitive and life cycle models of leadership both potentially suggest that leaders should use different styles and behaviors for different followers. Can you think of any negative consequences of that advice? How could those negative consequences be managed?

14.4 Consider the four dimensions of transformational leadership: idealized influence, inspirational motivation, intellectual stimulation, and individualized consideration. Which of those dimensions would you respond to most favorably? Why?

14.5 Can you think of any potential "dark sides" to transformational leadership? What would they be?

CASE   APPLE

Steve Jobs has managed single-handedly to change the entire world with his innovative products. His vision to place digital media in the hands of the common public became a reality in the past decade while he served as CEO of Apple. Lee Clow, chairman of TBWA/Chiat/Day, stated that "from the time he was a kid, Steve thought his products could change the world." The leadership persona of Steve Jobs is well-known throughout the company, as well as to the public. Jobs is a perfectionist who likes to have a hand in every major project, from start to finish. The influence exerted by Jobs has turned Apple into the most innovative company in the world for the past three years.

Obviously Steve Jobs has the desire to innovate great products to revolutionize the world. But what separates him from everyone else? He has an uncanny ability to execute his strategies. This ability appears to be becoming a lost art in the world of business. Jobs also has the focus to take an idea and transform it into a product. This focus is what drives his employees to achieve high standards. A recent poll by *BusinessWeek* revealed that fans of Apple believe Steve Jobs is the "king." Nearly 90 percent of respondents consider him either very good or excellent. Apple has a bright future ahead of it in the hands of a man who has made a career out of innovation and success.

14.1 How effective is Steve Jobs as the leader of Apple? Explain.

14.2 Would you consider Steve Jobs to be a transformational leader? Explain.

Sources: "Grading Steve Jobs," *BusinessWeek,* April 24, 2002, www.businessweek.com; "Steve Jobs' Magic Kingdom," *BusinessWeek,* February 6, 2006, www.businessweek.com; "Steve Jobs: He Thinks Different," *BusinessWeek,* November 1, 2004, www.businessweek.com; "The World's 25 Most Innovative Companies," *BusinessWeek,* May 14, 2007.

EXERCISE   EMPLOYEE INVOLVEMENT

The purpose of this exercise is to use the Time-Driven Model of Leadership (shown in Figure 14-3) to determine whether or not to involve employees in various decisions. This exercise uses groups of six participants, so your instructor will either assign you to a group of six or ask you to create your own group of six. The exercise has the following steps:

1. Review the two cases below, then answer the discussion questions that appear in Step 2 by yourself.

Case 1: The Sugar Substitute Research Decision

You are the head of research and development (R&D) for a major beer company. While working on a new beer product, one of the scientists in your unit seems to have tentatively identified a new chemical compound that has few calories but tastes more like sugar than current sugar substitutes. The company has no foreseeable need for this product, but it could be patented and licensed to manufacturers in the food industry.

The sugar substitute discovery is in its preliminary stages, and considerable time and resources would be required before it would be commercially viable. Therefore, some resources would be taken away from other projects in the lab. The sugar substitute project is beyond your technical expertise, but some of the R&D lab researchers are familiar with that field of chemistry. As with most forms of research, the amount of research required to identify and perfect the sugar substitute is difficult to determine. You do not know how much demand is expected for this product. Your department has a decision process for funding projects that are behind schedule, but there are no rules or precedents about funding projects that would be licensed but not used by the organization.

The company's R&D budget is limited, and other scientists in your work group have recently complained that they require more resources and financial support to get their projects completed. Some of these other R&D projects hold promise for future beer sales. You believe that most researchers in the R&D unit are committed to ensuring that the company's interests are achieved.

Case 2: Coast Guard Cutter Decision Problem

You are the captain of a 200-foot Coast Guard cutter, with a crew of 16, including officers. Your mission is general search and rescue at sea. At 2:00 this morning, while en route to your home port after a routine 28-day patrol, you received word from the nearest Coast Guard station that a small plane had crashed 60 miles offshore. You obtained all the available information about the location of the crash, informed your crew of the mission, and set a new course at maximum speed for the scene to commence a search for survivors and wreckage.

You have now been searching for 20 hours. Your search operation has been increasingly impaired by rough seas, and there is evidence of a severe storm building. The atmospherics associated with the deteriorating weather have made communications with the Coast Guard station impossible. A decision must be made shortly about whether to abandon the search and place your vessel on a course that would ride out the storm (thereby protecting the vessel and your crew but relegating any possible survivors to almost certain death from exposure) or continue a potentially futile search and the risks it would entail.

Before losing communications, you received an updated weather advisory about the severity and duration of the storm. Although your crew members are extremely conscientious about their responsibilities, you believe they would be divided on the decision of leaving or staying.

2. Come to a group consensus on the following questions:

a. To what extent should your subordinates be involved in making this decision? Select one of the following levels of involvement:

- *No involvement:* You make the decision alone without any participation from subordinates.
- *Low involvement:* You ask one or more subordinates for information relating to the problem, but you don't ask for their recommendations and might not mention the problem to them.
- *Medium involvement:* You describe the problem to one or more subordinates (alone or in a meeting) and ask for any relevant information as well as their recommendations on the issue. However, you make the final decision, which might or might not reflect their advice.
- *High involvement:* You describe the problem to subordinates. They discuss the matter, identify a solution without your involvement (unless they invite your ideas), and implement that solution. You have agreed to support their decision.

b. What factors led you to choose this level of employee involvement rather than the others?

3. Class discussion (whether in groups or as a class) should focus on this question: What problems might occur if less or more involvement was granted in these cases?

Sources: S.L. McShane and M.A. Von Glinow, Organizational Behavior, 3rd ed. (New York: McGraw-Hill, 2005). Used with permission. Case 1 prepared by Steven L. McShane © 2002; Case 2 adapted from *The New Leadership: Managing Participation in Organizations*, by V.H. Vroom and A.G. Jago, 1987.

ENDNOTES

14.1 Orwell, G. *Nineteen Eighty-Four.* Orlando, FL: Harcourt, Inc., 1949.

14.2 Young, J.S., and W.L. Simon. *iCon: Steve Jobs—The Greatest Second Act in the History of Business.* Hoboken, NJ: Wiley, 2005.

14.3 Ibid.

14.4 Ibid.

14.5 Ibid.

14.6 Ibid.

14.7 Schlender, B. "How Big Can Apple Get?" *Fortune,* February 21, 2005, pp. 66–76.

14.8 Burrows, P., and R. Grover. "Steve Jobs' Magic Kingdom." *Business-Week,* February 6, 2006, pp. 63–69.

14.9 Young and Simon, *iCon.*

14.10 Schlender, "How Big Can Apple Get?"

14.11 Yukl, G. *Leadership in Organizations,* 4th ed. Englewood Cliffs, NJ: Prentice-Hall, 1998.

14.12 Ibid.

14.13 Burrows, P. "The Teflon Factor: Is Steve Jobs Untouchable?" *Business-Week,* January 15, 2007, pp. 28–31.

14.14 Yukl, *Leadership in Organizations*.

14.15 Ibid.

14.16 Dansereau, F. Jr.; G. Graen; and W.J. Haga. "A Vertical Dyad Linkage Approach to Leadership Within Formal Organizations: A Longitudinal Investigation of the Role Making Process." *Organizational Behavior and Human Performance* 13 (1975), pp. 46–78; Graen, G.; M. Novak; and P. Sommerkamp. "The Effects of Leader-Member Exchange and Job Design on Productivity and Satisfaction: Testing a Dual Attachment Model." *Organizational Behavior and Human Performance* 30 (1982), pp. 109–31; Graen, G.B., and M. Uhl-Bien. "Relationship-Based Approach to Leadership: Development of Leader-Member Exchange (LMX) Theory of Leadership over 25 Years: Applying a Multi-Level Multi-Domain Perspective."*Leadership Quarterly* 6 (1995), pp. 219–47; Liden, R.C.; R.T. Sparrowe; and S.J. Wayne. "Leader-Member Exchange Theory: The Past and Potential for the Future." In *Research in Personnel and Human Resources Management,* Vol. 15, ed. G.R. Ferris. Greenwich, CT: JAI Press, 1997, pp. 47–119.

14.17 Graen, G.B., and T. Scandura. "Toward a Psychology of Dyadic Organizing." In *Research in Organizational Behavior,* Vol. 9, eds. L.L. Cummings and B.M. Staw. Greenwich, CT: JAI Press, 1987, pp. 175–208.

14.18 Ibid.

14.19 Graen and Uhl-Bien, "Relationship-Based Approach to Leadership."

14.20 Ibid.

14.21 Bauer, T.N., and S.G. Green. "Development of Leader-Member Exchange: A Longitudinal Test." *Academy of Management Journal* 39 (1996), pp. 1538–67; Gerstner, C.R., and D.V. Day. "Meta-Analytic Review of Leader-Member Exchange Theory: Correlates and Construct Issues." *Journal of Applied Psychology* 82 (1997), pp. 827–44; Liden, R.C.; S.J. Wayne; and D. Stillwell. "A Longitudinal Study on the Early Development of Leader-Member Exchanges." *Journal of Applied Psychology* 78 (1993), pp. 662–74.

14.22 Graen and Uhl-Bien, "Relationship-Based Approach to Leadership."

14.23 Stogdill, R.M. "Personal Factors Associated with Leadership: A Survey of the Literature." *Journal of Applied Psychology* 54 (1948), pp. 259–69.

14.24 Den Hartog, D.N., and P.L. Koopman. "Leadership in Organizations." In *Handbook of Industrial, Work, and Organizational Psychology,* Vol. 2, eds. N. Anderson, D.S. Ones, H.K. Sinangil, and C. Viswesvaran. Thousand Oaks, CA: Sage, 2002, pp. 166–87.

14.25 Yukl, *Leadership in Organizations;* Zaccaro, S.J. "Trait-Based Perspectives of Leadership." *American Psychologist* 62 (1998), pp. 6–16.

14.26 Vroom, V.H. "Leadership and the Decision-Making Process." *Organizational Dynamics* 28 (2000), pp. 82–94; Yukl, *Leadership in Organizations.*

14.27 Berner, R. "Flip-Flops, Torn Jeans—and Control." *BusinessWeek,* May 30, 2005, pp. 68–70.

14.28 Ibid.

14.29 Vroom, "Leadership and the Decision-Making Process"; Yukl, *Leadership in Organizations.*

14.30 Ibid.

14.31 Grover, R. "How Bob Iger Unchained Disney." *BusinessWeek,* February 5, 2007, pp. 74–79.

14.32 Ibid.

14.33 Vroom, "Leadership and the Decision-Making Process"; Yukl, *Leadership in Organizations.*

14.34 Roth, D. "Can Nike Still Do It Without Phil Knight?" *Fortune,* April 4, 2005, pp. 59–68.

14.35 Ibid.

14.36 Holmes, S. "Inside the Coup at Nike." *BusinessWeek,* February 6, 2006, pp. 34–37.

14.37 Vroom, "Leadership and the Decision-Making Process."

14.38 Miller, K.I., and P.R. Monge. "Participation, Satisfaction, and Productivity: A Meta-Analytic Review." *Academy of Management Journal* 29 (1986), pp. 727–53; Wagner, J.A. III. "Participation's Effects on Performance and Satisfaction: A Reconsideration of Research Evidence." *Academy of Management Review* 19 (1994), pp. 312–30.

14.39 Vroom, "Leadership and the Decision-Making Process."

14.40 Rogelberg, S.G.; D.J. Leach; P.B. Warr; and J.L. Burnfield. "'Not Another Meeting!' Are Meeting Time Demands Related to Employee Well-Being?" *Journal of Applied Psychology* 91 (2006), pp. 86–96.

14.41 Lee, L. "Paul Pressler's Fall from The Gap." *BusinessWeek,* February 26, 2007, pp. 80–84.

14.42 Vroom, "Leadership and the Decision-Making Process"; Vroom, V.H., and A.G. Jago. *The New Leadership: Managing Participation in Organizations.* Englewood Cliffs, NJ: Prentice Hall, 1988; Vroom, V.H., and A.G. Jago. "Decision Making as a Social Process: Normative and Descriptive Models of Leader Behavior." *Decision Sciences* 5 (1974), pp. 743–69; Vroom, V.H., and P.W. Yetton. *Leadership and Decision-Making.* Pittsburgh, PA: University of Pittsburgh Press, 1973.

14.43 Aditya, R.N.; R.J. House; and S. Kerr. "Theory and Practice of Leadership: Into the New Millennium." In *Industrial and Organizational Psychology: Linking Theory with Practice,* eds. C.L. Cooper and E.A. Locke. Malden, MA: Blackwell, 2000, pp. 130–65; House, R.J., and R.N. Aditya. "The Social Scientific Study of Leadership: Quo Vadis?" *Journal of Management* 23 (1997), pp. 409–73; Yukl, *Leadership in Organizations.*

14.44 Vroom, V.H., and A.G. Jago. "On the Validity of the Vroom-Yetton Model." *Journal of Applied Psychology* 63 (1978), pp. 151–62. See also Vroom and Yetton, *Leadership and Decision Making;* Vroom and Jago, *The New Leadership;* Field, R.H.G.

"A Test of the Vroom-Yetton Normative Model of Leadership." *Journal of Applied Psychology* 67 (1982), pp. 523–32.

14.45 Vroom and Yetton, *Leadership and Decision Making.*

14.46 Hemphill, J.K. *Leader Behavior Description.* Columbus, OH: Ohio State University, 1950. Cited in Fleishman, E.A.; E.F. Harris; and H.E. Burtt. *Leadership and Supervision in Industry: An Evaluation of a Supervisory Training Program.* Columbus, OH: Bureau of Educational Research, Ohio State University, 1955.

14.47 Hemphill, J.K., and A.E. Coons. "Development of the Leader Behavior Description Questionnaire." In *Leader Behavior: Its Description and Measurement,* eds. R.M. Stogdill and A.E. Coons. Columbus, OH: Bureau of Business Research, Ohio State University, 1957, pp. 6–38.

14.48 Fleishman, E.A. "The Description of Supervisory Behavior." *Journal of Applied Psychology* 37 (1953), pp. 1–6; Fleishman et al., *Leadership and Supervision in Industry;* Hemphill and Coons, "Development of the Leader Behavior Description Questionnaire"; Halpin, A.W., and B.J. Winer. *Studies in Aircrew Composition: The Leadership Behavior of the Airplane Commander* (Technical Report No. 3). Columbus, OH: Personnel Research Board, Ohio State University, 1952. Cited in Fleishman et al.

14.49 Fleishman, "The Description of Supervisory Behavior"; Fleishman et al., *Leadership and Supervision in Industry;* Fleishman, E.A., and D.R. Peters. "Interpersonal Values, Leadership Attitudes, and Managerial 'Success." *Personnel Psychology* 15 (1962), pp. 127–43.

14.50 Yukl, *Leadership in Organizations.*

14.51 Fleishman, "The Description of Supervisory Behavior"; Fleishman et al., *Leadership and Supervision in Industry;* Fleishman and Peters, "Interpersonal Values."

14.52 Yukl, *Leadership in Organizations.*

14.53 Katz, D.; N. Maccoby; and N. Morse. *Productivity, Supervision, and Morale in an Office Situation.* Ann Arbor, MI: Institute for Social Research, University of Michigan, 1950; Katz, D.; N. Maccoby; G. Gurin; and L. Floor. *Productivity, Supervision, and Morale among Railroad Workers.* Ann Arbor, MI: Survey Research Center, University of Michigan, 1951; Katz, D., and R.L. Kahn. "Some Recent Findings in Human-Relations Research in Industry." In *Readings in Social Psychology,* eds. E. Swanson, T. Newcomb, and E. Hartley. New York: Holt, pp. 650–65; Likert, R. *New Patterns of Management.* New York: McGraw-Hill, 1961; Likert, R. *The Human Organization.* New York: McGraw-Hill, 1967.

14.54 Fleishman, E.A. "Twenty Years of Consideration and Structure." In *Current Developments in the Study of Leadership,* eds. E.A. Fleishman and J.G. Hunt. Carbondale, IL: Southern Illinois Press, 1973, pp. 1–37.

14.55 Judge, T.A.; R.F. Piccolo; and R. Ilies. "The Forgotten Ones? The Validity of Consideration and Initiating Structure in Leadership Research." *Journal of Applied Psychology* 89 (2004), pp. 36–51.

14.56 Aditya et al., "Theory and Practice of Leadership"; Den Hartog and Koopman, "Leadership in Organizations"; House and Aditya, "The

Social Scientific Study of Leadership"; Korman, A.K. "'Consideration,' 'Initiating Structure,' and Organizational Criteria—A Review." *Personnel Psychology* 19 (1966), pp. 349–61; Yukl, *Leadership in Organizations;* Yukl, G., and D.D. Van Fleet. "Theory and Research on Leadership in Organizations." In *Handbook of Industrial and Organizational Psychology,* Vol. 3, eds. M.D. Dunnette and L.M. Hough. Palo Alto, CA: Consulting Psychologists Press, 1992, pp. 147–97.

14.57 Judge et al., "The Forgotten Ones?"

14.58 Hersey, P., and K.H. Blanchard. "Life Cycle Theory of Leadership." *Training and Development Journal,* May 1969, pp. 26–34; Hersey, P., and K.H. Blanchard. "So You Want to Know Your Leadership Style?"*Training and Development Journal,* February 1974, pp. 22–37; Hersey, P., and K.H. Blanchard. *Management of Organizational Behavior,* 6th ed. Englewood Cliffs, NJ: Prentice Hall, 1993.

14.59 Hersey and Blanchard, *Management of Organizational Behavior.*

14.60 Ibid.

14.61 Ibid.

14.62 Ibid.

14.63 Ibid.

14.64 Ibid.

14.65 Fernandez, C.F., and R.P. Vecchio. "Situational Leadership Revisited: A Test of an Across-Jobs Perspective." *Leadership Quarterly* 8 (1997), pp. 67–84.

14.66 Vecchio, R.P. "Situational Leadership Theory: An Examination of a Prescriptive Theory." *Journal of Applied Psychology* 72 (1987),

pp. 444–51; Norris, W.R., and R.P. Vecchio. "Situational Leadership Theory: A Replication." *Group and Organization Management* 17 (1992), pp. 331–42.

14.67 Vecchio, "Situational Leadership Theory"; Norris and Vecchio, "Situational Leadership Theory: A Replication"; Blank, W.; J.R. Weitzel; and S.G. Green. "A Test of Situational Leadership Theory." *Personnel Psychology* 43 (1990), pp. 579–97.

14.68 Fernandez and Vecchio, "Situational Leadership Theory Revisited."

14.69 Hersey and Blanchard, "Life Cycle Theory of Leadership"; Hersey and Blanchard, *Management of Organizational Behavior.*

14.70 Strage, A., and T.S. Brandt. "Authoritative Parenting and College Students' Academic Adjustment and Success." *Journal of Educational Psychology* 91 (1999), pp. 146–56.

14.71 Hersey and Blanchard, "Life Cycle Theory of Leadership"; Hersey and Blanchard, *Management of Organizational Behavior.*

14.72 Grow, B. "Out at Home Depot." *BusinessWeek,* January 15, 2007, pp. 56–62.

14.73 Grow, B. "Renovating Home Depot." *BusinessWeek,* March 6, 2006, pp. 50–58.

14.74 Ibid.; Grow, "Out at Home Depot."

14.75 Sellers, P. "Six Sigma Man: Another GE Vet Atop Home Depot." *Fortune,* January 22, 2007, p. 30; Grow, "Renovating Home Depot."

14.76 Bass, B.M., and R.E. Riggio. *Transformational Leadership,* 2nd ed. Mahwah, NJ: Lawrence Erlbaum Associates, 2006; Bass, B.M. *Leadership and Performance Beyond*

Expectations. New York: The Free Press, 1985; Burns, L.M. *Leadership.* New York: Harper & Row, 1978.

14.77 Bass, *Leadership and Performance Beyond Expectations.*

14.78 Ibid.

14.79 Larson, A. *The President Nobody Knew.* New York: Popular Library, 1968, p. 68. Cited in Ibid.

14.80 Truman, H.S. *Memoirs.* New York: Doubleday, 1958. Cited in Bass, *Leadership and Performance Beyond Expectations.*

14.81 Bass and Riggio, *Transformational Leadership.*

14.82 Ibid.; Bass, B.M., and B.J. Avolio. *MLQ: Multifactor Leadership Questionnaire.* Redwood City, CA: Mind Garden, 2000.

14.83 Bass and Riggio, *Transformational Leadership;* Bass, *Leadership and Performance Beyond Expectations;* M. (1985). Burns, *Leadership.*

14.84 Bass and Riggio, *Transformational Leadership.*

14.85 Bass, *Leadership and Performance Beyond Expectations.*

14.86 Bass and Riggio, *Transformational Leadership;* Bass and Avolio, *MLQ.*

14.87 Bass and Riggio, *Transformational Leadership.*

14.88 Ibid; Bass and Avolio, *MLQ.*

14.89 Bass and Riggio, *Transformational Leadership.*

14.90 Ibid.; Bass and Avolio, *MLQ.*

14.91 Judge, T.A., and R.F. Piccolo. "Transformational and Transactional Leadership: A Meta-Analytic Test of their Relative Validity." *Journal of Applied Psychology* 89 (2004), pp. 755–68.

14.92 Ibid.

14.93 Bass and Riggio, *Transformational Leadership.*

14.94 House, R.J.; P.J. Hanges; M. Javidan; P.W. Dorfman; and V. Gupta. *Culture, Leadership, and Organizations.* Thousand Oaks, CA: Sage, 2004.

14.95 Dorfman, P.W.; P.J. Hanges; and F.C. Brodbeck. "Leadership and Cultural Variation: The Identification of Culturally Endorsed Leadership

Profiles." In *Culture, Leadership, and Organizations,* eds. R.J. House, P.J. Hanges, M. Javidan, P.W. Dorfman, and V. Gupta. Thousand Oaks, CA: Sage, 2004, pp. 669–720.

14.96 Javidan, M.; R.J. House; and P.W. Dorfman. "A Nontechnical Summary of GLOBE Findings." In *Culture, Leadership, and Organizations,* eds. R.J. House, P.J. Hanges, M. Javidan, P.W. Dorfman, and V. Gupta. Thousand Oaks, CA: Sage, 2004, pp. 29–48.

14.97 Dorfman et al., "Leadership and Cultural Variation."

14.98 Bass and Riggio, *Transformational Leadership.*

14.99 Ibid.; Bass and Avolio, *MLQ.*

14.100 Conger, J.A. "Charismatic and Transformational Leadership in Organizations: An Insider's Perspective on these Developing Research Streams." *Leadership Quarterly* 10 (1999), pp. 145–79.

14.101 Young and Simon, *iCon.*

14.102 Johnson, A.M.; P.A. Vernon; J.M. McCarthy; M. Molso; J.A. Harris; and K.J. Jang. "Nature vs. Nurture: Are Leaders Born or Made? A Behavior Genetic Investigation of

Leadership Style." *Twin Research* 1 (1998), pp. 216–23.

14.103   Judge, T.A., and J.E. Bono. "Five-Factor Model of Personality and Transformational Leadership." *Journal of Applied Psychology* 85 (2000), pp. 751–65.

14.104   Bass and Riggio, *Transformational Leadership.*

14.105   Conger, "Charismatic and Transformational Leadership in Organizations."

14.106   Bass and Riggio, *Transformational Leadership;* Bass and Avolio, *MLQ.*

14.107   Young and Simon, *iCon.*

14.108   Ibid.

14.109   Bass and Riggio, *Transformational Leadership.*

14.110   Ibid.; Bass and Avolio, *MLQ.*

14.111   Bass and Riggio, *Transformational Leadership.*

14.112   Ibid.; Bass and Avolio, *MLQ.*

14.113   Young and Simon, *iCon.*

14.114   Mio, J.S.; R.E. Riggio; S. Levin; and R. Reese. "Presidential Leadership and Charisma: The Effects of Metaphor." *Leadership Quarterly* 16 (2005), pp. 287–94.

14.115   Conger, "Charismatic and Transformational Leadership in Organizations."

14.116   Bligh, M.C.; J.C. Kohles; and J.R. Meindl. "Charisma under Crisis: Presidential Leadership, Rhetoric, and Media Responses Before and After the September 11th Terrorist Attacks." *Leadership Quarterly* 15 (2004), pp. 211–39.

14.117   Lowe, K.B.; K.G. Kroeck; and N. Sivasubramaniam. "Effectiveness Correlates of Transformational and Transactional Leadership: A Meta-Analytic Review of the MLQ Literature." *Leadership Quarterly* 7 (1996), pp. 385–425.

14.118   Howell, J.M., and B.J. Avolio. "Transformational Leadership, Transactional Leadership, Locus of Control, and Support for Innovation: Key Predictors of Consolidated-Business-Unit Performance." *Journal of Applied Psychology* 78 (1993), pp. 891–902; Howell, J.M.; D.J. Neufeld; and B.J. Avolio. "Examining the Relationship of Leadership and Physical Distance with Business Unit Performance." *Leadership Quarterly* 16 (2005), pp. 273–85; Keller, R.T. "Transformational Leadership, Initiating Structure, and Substitutes for Leadership: A Longitudinal Study of Research and Development Project Team Performance." *Journal of Applied Psychology* 91 (2006), pp. 202–10; Waldman, D.A.; G.G. Ramirez; R.J. House; and P. Puranam. "Does Leadership Matter? CEO Leadership Attributes and Profitability under Conditions of Perceived Environmental Uncertainty." *Academy of Management Journal* 44 (2001), pp. 134–43.

14.119   Howell, J.M., and K.E. Hall-Merenda. "The Ties That Bind: The Impact of Leader-Member Exchange, Transformational and Transactional Leadership, and Distance on Predicting Follower Performance." *Journal of Applied Psychology* 84 (1999), pp. 680–94; Piccolo, R.F., and J.A. Colquitt. "Transformational Leadership and Job Behaviors: The Mediating Role of Core Job Characteristics." *Academy of Management Journal* 49 (2006), pp. 327–40; Wang, H.; K.S. Law; R.D. Hackett; D. Wang; and Z.X. Chen. "Leader-Member Exchange as a Mediator of the Relationship Between Transformational Leadership and Followers'

Performance and Organizational Citizenship Behavior." *Academy of Management Journal* 48 (2005), pp. 420–32.

14.120   Judge and Piccolo, "Transformational and Transactional Leadership"; Podsakoff, P.M.; S.B. MacKenzie; J.B. Paine; and D.G. Bachrach. "Organizational Citizenship Behaviors: A Critical Review of the Theoretical and Empirical Literature and Suggestions for Future Research." *Journal of Management* 26 (2000), pp. 513–63.

14.121   Judge and Piccolo, "Transformational and Transactional Leadership."

14.122   Avolio, B.J.; W. Zhu; W. Koh; and P. Bhatia. "Transformational Leadership and Organizational Commitment: Mediating Role of Psychological Empowerment and Moderating Role of Structural Distance." *Journal of Organizational Behavior* 25 (2004), pp. 951–68; Kirkpatrick, S.A., and E.A. Locke. "Direct and Indirect Effects of Three Core Charismatic Leadership Components on Performance and Attitudes." *Journal of Applied Psychology* 81 (1996), pp. 36–51; Shamir, B.; E. Zakay; E. Breinin; and M. Popper. "Correlates of Charismatic Leader Behaviors in Military Units: Subordinates' Attitudes, Unit Characteristics, and Superiors' Appraisals of Leader Performance." *Academy of Management Journal* 41 (1998), pp. 387–409.

14.123   Podsakoff, P.M.; S.B. MacKenzie; and W.H. Bommer. "Transformational Leader Behaviors and Substitutes for Leadership as Determinants of Employee Satisfaction, Commitment, Trust, and Organizational Citizenship Behaviors."

Journal of Management 22 (1996), pp. 259–98; Podsakoff, P.M.; S.B. MacKenzie; R.H. Moorman; and R. Fetter. "Transformational Leader Behaviors and their Effects on Followers' Trust in Leader, Satisfaction, and Organizational Citizenship Behaviors." *Leadership Quarterly* 1 (1990), pp. 107–42; Shamir et al., "Correlates of Charismatic Leader Behaviors."

14.124   Meyer, J.P.; D.J. Stanley; L. Herscovitch; and L. Topolnytsky. "Affective, Continuance, and Normative Commitment to the Organization: A Meta-Analysis of Antecedents, Correlates, and Consequences." *Journal of Vocational Behavior* 61 (2002), pp. 20–52.

14.125   Judge and Piccolo, "Transformational and Transactional Leadership."

14.126   Piccolo and Colquitt, "Transformational Leadership and Job Behaviors." See also Bono, J.E., and T.A. Judge. "Self-Concordance at Work: Toward Understanding the Motivational Effects of Transformational Leaders." *Academy of Management Journal* 46 (2003), pp. 554–71; Shin, S.J., and J. Zhou. "Transformational Leadership, Conservation, and Creativity: Evidence from Korea." *Academy of Management Journal* 46 (2003), pp. 703–14.

14.127   Bono, J.E., and R. Ilies. "Charisma, Positive Emotions, and Mood Contagion." *Leadership Quarterly* 17 (2006), pp. 317–34; McColl-Kennedy, J.R., and R.D. Anderson. "Impact of Leadership Style and Emotions on Subordinate Performance." *Leadership Quarterly, 13* (2002), pp. 545-559.

14.128   Kerr, S., and J.M. Jermier. "Substitutes for Leadership: Their Meaning and Measurement." *Organizational Behavior and Human*

Performance 22 (1978), pp. 375–403.

14.129   Howell, J.P.; P.W. Dorfman; and S. Kerr. "Moderator Variables in Leadership Research." *Academy of Management Review* 11 (1986), pp. 88–102.

14.130   Kerr and Jermier, "Substitutes for Leadership"; Jermier, J.M.; and S. Kerr. "'Substitutes for Leadership: Their Meaning and Measurement': Contextual Recollections and Current Observations." *Leadership Quarterly* 8 (1997), pp. 95–101.

14.131   Howell, J.P.; D.E. Bowen; P.W. Dorfman; S. Kerr; and P.M. Podsakoff. "Substitutes for Leadership: Effective Alternatives to Ineffective Leadership." *Organizational Dynamics* Summer 1990, pp. 21–38.

14.132   Podsakoff, P.M., and S.B. MacKenzie. "Kerr and Jermier's Substitutes for Leadership Model: Background, Empirical Assessment, and Suggestions for Future Research." *Leadership Quarterly* 8 (1997), pp. 117–25; Podsakoff, P.M.; B.P. Niehoff; S.B. MacKenzie; and M.L. Williams. "Do Substitutes for Leadership Really Substitute for Leadership? An Empirical Examination of Kerr and Jermier's Situational Leadership Model." *Organizational Behavior and Human Decision Processes* 54 (1993), pp. 1–44; Podsakoff et al., "Transformational Leadership Behaviors and Substitutes for Leadership"; Podsakoff, P.M.; S.B. MacKenzie; M. Ahearne; and W.H. Bommer. "Searching for a Needle in a Haystack: Trying to Identify the Illusive Moderators of Leadership Behavior." *Journal of Management* 21 (1995), pp. 422–70.

14.133   Howell et al., "Substitutes for Leadership: Effective Alternatives."

14.134   Kranz, G. "A Higher Standard for Managers." *Workforce,* June 11, 2007, pp. 21–26.

14.135   Ibid.

14.136   Gist, M.E., and D. McDonald-Mann. "Advances in Leadership Training and Development." In *Industrial and Organizational Psychology: Linking Theory with Practice,* ed. C.L. Cooper and E.A. Locke. Malden, MA: Blackwell, 2000, pp. 52–71.

14.137   Ibid.; Dvir, T.; D. Eden; B.J. Avolio; and B. Shamir. "Impact of Transformational Leadership on Follower Development and Performance: A Field Experiment." *Academy of Management Journal* 45 (2000), pp. 735–44; Barling, J.; T. Weber; and E.K. Kelloway. "Effects of Transformational Leadership Training on Attitudinal and Financial Outcomes: A Field Experiment." *Journal of Applied Psychology* 81 (1996), pp. 827–32.

14.138   Barling, J.; T. Weber; and E.K. Kelloway.

ORGANIZATIONAL MECHANISMS

CHAPTER 15:
Organizational Structure

CHAPTER 16:
Organizational Culture

Organizational Structure

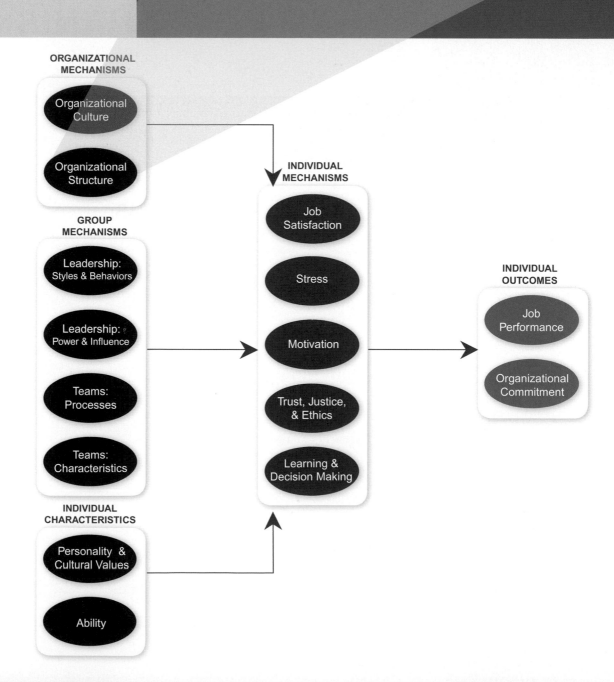

Howard Stringer, Sony's CEO, faces the challenge of helping the company recover its leadership position while addressing organizational structure problems that have hurt it in the past. Sony has 160,000 employees in its various departments.

LEARNING GOALS

After reading this chapter, you should be able to answer the following questions:

15.1 What is an organization's structure, and what does it consist of?

15.2 What are the major elements of an organizational structure?

15.3 What is organizational design? What factors does the organizational design process depend on?

15.4 What are some of the more common organizational forms that an organization might adopt for its structure?

15.5 When an organization makes changes to its structure, how does that restructuring affect job performance and organizational commitment?

15.6 What steps can organizations take to reduce the negative effects of restructuring efforts?

SONY CORPORATION

Sir Howard Stringer. Perhaps not the name you would expect for the CEO of Sony Corporation. Stringer, 63, was previously the head of Sony's U.S. music and film operations. He is now the first non-Japanese head of Sony, handpicked by outgoing CEO Nobuyuki Idei.[1] Stringer took over what some have argued is one of the most bureaucratic organizations in the world. At the time, Sony consisted of multiple, diverse business units that, for the most part, operated independently and without regard for one another. As a result, Sony's performance had slipped dramatically in both profits and market share. Indeed, the once proud and respected technology giant was now considered a laggard, and its 160,000-employee workforce lacked the ability to work together toward common goals.[2]

One of the major reasons for Sony's problems was the development of "silos" or "fiefdoms" that divided up the company's business. Many of these silos were created by separating workers according to the type of work that they performed. In Sony's case, one of the biggest problems originated from separating hardware engineers from software developers. Sony grouped its hardware engineers together to encourage them to be creative and focus on major technological advances. This strategy worked very well for a long time as Sony developed hardware, like the Sony Walkman, that was smaller and lighter than that offered by its competitors.[3] However, significant environmental changes required better integration between the hardware engineers and software developers. Specifically, consumers began to want their various electronic devices to "talk to one another" and be easier to use than ever before. Both of those new demands required hardware engineers and software developers to collaborate—something that Sony had inadvertently discouraged.

One of the greatest capitalizers on this networking trend was Apple, whose iPod became the epitome of everything people wanted in a portable, personal music player. Much of this appeal emerged because the iPod's software allowed even the most computer illiterate user to download and network digital music. Apple had beaten Sony at its own game. One of the biggest disappointments for Sony was its development of the digital-based "Network Walkman"—two years prior to the creation of the iPod! However, because Sony's engineers and software developers didn't communicate or work together, the Network Walkman was unbelievably complicated to use. The way Sony organized its workers—its organizational structure—had essentially kept the company from taking advantage of the biggest shift in music media in the past 20 years.

Even today, Sony has an incredibly complex organizational structure. Entertainment units are split by geographic regions and operate completely independently of one another. Consumer electronics divisions each have their own marketing departments that often compete for the same customer![4] However, using the same structure that cost it in its competition with Apple also allowed Sony to finish producing the most advanced gaming system in the world: the new Playstation 3. Howard Stringer's challenge is to find a way to organize Sony to take advantage of what many believe is the greatest accumulation of assets in the entertainment industry. He has to find a way to structure the organization so that it builds synergy between the company's movie, games, music, and consumer electronics divisions—all while preparing Sony to react to the "next big change" in entertainment.

ORGANIZATIONAL STRUCTURE

As the preceding example illustrates, an organization's structure can have a significant impact on its financial performance and ability to manage its employees. The decisions that Howard Stringer makes regarding Sony's organizational structure will have an impact on how employees communicate and cooperate with one another, how power is distributed, and how individuals view their work environment. In fact, an organization's structure dictates more than you might think. We've spent a great deal of time in this book talking about how employee attitudes and behaviors are shaped by individual characteristics, such as personality and ability, and group mechanisms, such as teams and leaders. In this and the following chapter, we discuss how the organization as a whole affects employee attitudes and behavior.

Think about some of the jobs you've held in the past (or perhaps the job you hope to have after graduation). What types of employees did you interact with on a daily basis? Were they employees who performed the same tasks that you performed? Or maybe they didn't do exactly what you did, but did they serve the same customer? How many employees did your manager supervise? Was every decision you made scrutinized by your supervisor, or were you given a "long leash"? The answers to all of these questions are influenced by organizational structure. An **organizational structure** formally dictates how jobs and tasks are divided and coordinated between individuals and groups within the company. Organizational structures can be relatively simple when a company only has 5–20 employees but grow incredibly complex in the case of Sony's 160,000 employees who produce thousands of different kinds of products.

15.1

What is an organization's structure, and what does it consist of?

"No, now all of our pillaging is done electronically from a centralized office."

WHY DO SOME ORGANIZATIONS HAVE DIFFERENT STRUCTURES THAN OTHERS?

One way of getting a feel for an organization's structure is by looking at an organizational chart. An **organizational chart** is a drawing that represents every job in the organization and the formal reporting relationships between those jobs. It helps organizational members and outsiders understand and comprehend how work is structured within the company. Figure 15-1 illustrates two sample organizational charts. In a real chart, the boxes would generally be filled with actual names and job titles. As you can imagine, as companies grow

FIGURE 15-1   Two Sample Organizational Structures

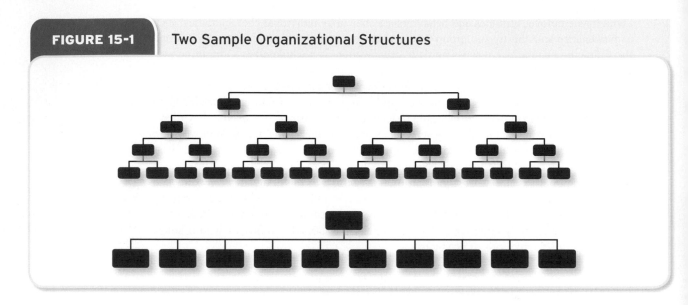

larger, their organizational charts get more complex. Can you imagine drawing an organizational chart that included every one of Sony's 160,000 employees? Not only would that require a lot of boxes and a lot of paper, it would probably take a couple of years to put together (plus, as soon as someone left the organization, it would be time to update the chart!).

ELEMENTS OF ORGANIZATIONAL STRUCTURE

The organizational charts described in this chapter are relatively simple and designed to illustrate specific points (if you want to see how complex some of these charts can get, do a search on the Internet for "organizational chart," and you'll begin to see how varied organizations can be in the way they design their company). Specifically, charts like those in Figure 15-1 can illustrate the five key elements of an organization's structure. Those five key elements, summarized in Table 15-1, describe how work tasks, authority relationships,

TABLE 15-1   Elements of Organizational Structure

ORGANIZATIONAL STRUCTURE DIMENSION	DEFINITION
Work Specialization	The degree to which tasks in an organization are divided into separate jobs.
Chain of Command	Answers the question of "who reports to whom?" and signifies formal authority relationships.
Span of Control	Represents how many employees each manager in the organization has responsibility for.
Centralization	Refers to where decisions are formally made in organizations.
Formalization	The degree to which rules and procedures are used to standardize behaviors and decisions in an organization.

and decision-making responsibilities are organized within the company. These elements will be discussed in the next several sections.

WORK SPECIALIZATION. **Work specialization** is the way in which tasks in an organization are divided into separate jobs. In some organizations, this categorization is referred to as a company's division of labor. How many tasks does any one employee perform? To some degree, work specialization is a never-ending trade-off among productivity, flexibility, and worker motivation. Take an assembly line worker at Ford as an example. Henry Ford was perhaps the earliest (and clearly most well-known) believer in high degrees of work specialization. He divided tasks among his manufacturing employees to such a degree that each employee might only perform one single task, over and over again, all day long. Having only one task to perform allowed those employees to be extremely productive at doing that one thing. It also meant that training new workers was much easier when replacements were needed.

However, there are trade-offs when organizations make jobs highly specialized. Highly specialized jobs can cause organizations to lose the ability for their employees to be flexible in what they do. By spending all their time performing specialized tasks well, employees fail to update or practice other skills. Accounting majors, for example, might specialize in taxes or auditing. Some larger companies might hire these graduates for their ability to do either auditing or tax—but not both. Other companies might be looking for an accountant who can perform either aspect well, depending on how they divide up accounting duties within their organization. Still other companies might want to hire "general managers" who understand accounting, finance, management, marketing, and operations as a part of their job. Thus, high levels of specialization may be acceptable in larger firms with more employees but can be problematic in smaller firms in which employees must be more flexible in their job duties.

Organizations may also struggle with employee job satisfaction when they make jobs highly specialized. If you recall Chapter 4 on Job Satisfaction, we discussed five core characteristics of jobs that significantly affect satisfaction. One of those characteristics was variety, or the degree to which the job requires a number of different activities involving a number of different skills and talents.[5] Employees tend to be more satisfied with jobs that require them to perform a number of different kinds of activities. Even though you might be very efficient and productive performing a job

Charlie Chaplin in *Modern Times* (1932) has a job with an extremely high degree of work specialization.

with only one task, how happy would you be to perform that job on a daily basis? One of the most famous films in early motion picture history was *Modern Times,* a film in which Charlie Chaplin was relegated to performing the same task over and over, very quickly. The movie ridiculed work specialization and the trend of treating employees as machines.

CHAIN OF COMMAND. The **chain of command** within an organization essentially answers the question "Who reports to whom?" Every employee in a traditional organizational structure has one person to whom they report. That person then reports to someone else, and on and on, until the buck stops with the CEO (though in a public company, even the CEO is responsible to the Board of Directors). The chain of command can be seen as the specific flow of authority down through the levels of an organization's structure.

15.2

What are the major elements of an organizational structure?

Organizations depend on this flow of authority to attain order, control, and predictable performance.[6] Some newer organizational structures make this chain of command a bit more complex. It has become common to have positions that report to two or more different managers. For example, Intel recently placed two people apiece in charge of the two largest divisions of their organization. Questions have arisen as to how their duties will be split up and whether employees will know who it is to whom they should report.[7]

SPAN OF CONTROL. A manager's **span of control** represents how many employees he or she is responsible for in the organization. The organizational charts in Figure 15-1 provide an illustration of the differences in span of control. In the top chart, each manager is responsible for leading two subordinates. In most instances, this level would be considered a narrow span of control. In the bottom chart, the manager is responsible for 10 employees. Typically, this number would be considered a wide span of control. Of course, the key question in many organizations is how many employees one manager can supervise effectively. Answering that question requires a better understanding of the benefits of narrow and wide spans of control.

Narrow spans of control allow managers to be much more hands-on with employees, giving them the opportunity to use directive leadership styles while developing close mentoring relationships with employees. A narrow span of control is especially important if the manager has substantially more skill or expertise than the subordinates. Early writings on management assumed that the narrower the span of control, the more productive employees would become.[8] However, a narrow span of control requires organizations to hire many managers, which can significantly increase labor costs. Moreover, if the span of control becomes too narrow, employees can become resentful of their close supervision and long for more latitude in their day-to-day decision making. In fact, current research suggests that a moderate span of control is best for an organization's productivity.[9] This relationship is illustrated in Figure 15-2. Note that organizational performance increases as span of control increases, but only up to the point that managers no longer have the ability to coordinate and supervise the large numbers of employees underneath them. Most organizations work hard to try to find the right balance, and this balance differs for every organization, depending on its unique circumstances. However, there is no question that spans of control in organizations have increased significantly in recent years.[10] Organizations such as Coca-Cola have vice presidents with up to 90 employees reporting to them![11]

An organization's span of control affects how "tall" or "flat" its organizational chart becomes. For example, the top panel of Figure 15-1 depicts a tall structure with many hierarchical levels and a narrow span of control, whereas the bottom panel depicts a flat organization with few levels and a wide span of control. Think about what happens when an organization becomes "taller." First, more layers of management means having to pay more management salaries. Second, communication in the organization becomes more complex as each new layer becomes one more point through which information must pass when traveling upward or downward. Third, the ability for an organization to make decisions becomes slower because approval for decisions has to be authorized at every step of the hierarchy.

Throughout the 1990s and into the current decade, organizations have worked to become flatter to reduce the costs associated with multiple layers of management and increase their ability to adapt to their environment. Intel, for example, recently announced a reduction in its managerial ranks of 1,000 positions (or 1 percent of its 100,000 employees). A spokesperson from Intel announced that "This [layoff] is designed to improve costs and improve decision making and communications across the company."[12] Putnam Investment Company also went through a flattening of its organization recently, reducing the workforce by 11 percent—including 25 of its 50 highest-paid executives. Putnam CEO

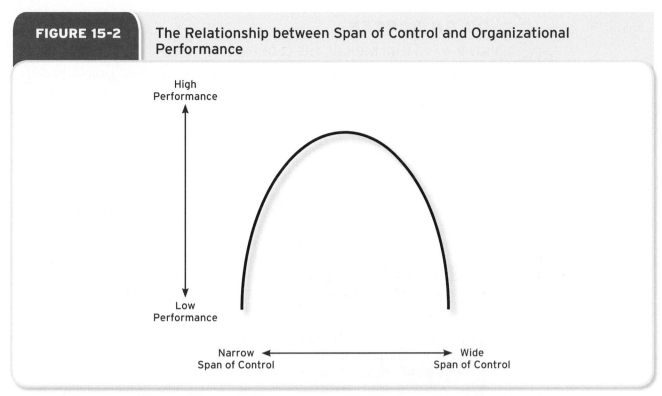

FIGURE 15-2 | The Relationship between Span of Control and Organizational Performance

Source: Adapted from N.A. Theobald and S. Nicholson-Crotty, "The Many Faces of Span of Control: Organizational Structure Across Multiple Goals," *Administration and Society* 36 (2005), pp. 648–60.

Ed Haldeman noted, "To attract and retain the best people, it's necessary to provide them with the autonomy and independence to make decisions."[13]

CENTRALIZATION. Centralization reflects where decisions are formally made in organizations. If only the top managers within a company have the authority to make final decisions, we would say that the organization has a highly "centralized" structure. In contrast, if decision-making authority is pushed down to lower-level employees and these employees feel empowered to make decisions on their own, an organization has a "decentralized" structure. Decentralization becomes necessary as a company grows larger. Sooner or later, the top management of an organization cannot make every single decision within the organization. Centralized organizational structures tend to concentrate power and authority within a relatively tight group of individuals in the firm, because they are the ones who have formal authority over important decisions. This point is illustrated at a cosmic level in our **OB on Screen** feature.

Many organizations are moving toward a more decentralized structure. A manager can't have 20 employees reporting to him or her if those employees aren't allowed to make some decisions on their own. However, it's also important to realize that some organizations might choose to centralize a few functions while leaving other decisions in the hands of lower-level managers. Aon Insurance is a perfect example of this approach. Through a series of mergers and acquisitions over the past 20 years, Aon had grown to a size of 47,000 employees in 500 locations around the world. Each of those offices had the authority to make its own decisions regarding human resource practices, such as who to hire and how to pay people. This decentralization led to employees being treated differently depending

OB ON SCREEN

STAR WARS II: ATTACK OF THE CLONES

"It is with great reluctance that I have agreed to this calling. I love democracy . . . . I love the Republic. But I am mild by nature, and I do not desire to see the destruction of democracy. The power you give me I will lay down when this crisis has abated, I promise you. And as my first act with this new authority, I will create a grand army of the Republic to counter the increasing threats of the separatists."

With those words, Supreme Chancellor Palpatine (Ian McDiarmid) takes control of the Republic in *Star Wars II: Attack of the Clones* (Dir. George Lucas, 20th Century Fox, 2002). Even in distant worlds, organizations are a way of life. Although the six Star Wars movies during the past 30 years have included a lot of space battles, they have also witnessed the formation, transformation, and ruling of a galaxy through the use of organizational structure.

One of the main plot lines in Episodes I through III of the Star Wars saga revolves around Chancellor Palpatine. He is the elected leader of the Galactic Senate, which serves as the governing body for the Galactic Republic (a group of hundreds of planets whose members agreed to form an organization for mutual protection and economic alliance). The Jedi Order is a group of mystical warriors that exist to protect the Republic. Unfortunately for Palpatine, his powers as Chancellor are extremely limited because all his decisions require a vote from all participating senators. Moreover, the Jedi are loyal to the Senate, not to him.

Unbeknownst to those around him, Chancellor Palpatine is really a Sith Lord named Darth Sidious. The Sith are an evil group of Jedi who use their mystical powers—known as "The Force"— for evil purposes. Palpatine secretly controls a group known as the Trade Federation, which he uses to attack and threaten members of the Republic. Episodes II and III of the Star Wars saga show Palpatine using this threat to have the Republic grant him centralized decision-making authority. That centralized authority gives him the power and authority needed to create a grand Army of the Republic. Once that army is created, they get transformed into Storm Troopers who help him change the Republic into his own personal Empire. That centralized authority (together with his ability to shoot "force lightning"), helps Palpatine rule the galaxy—until one Luke Skywalker comes along . . . .

on the location where they worked, creating feelings of animosity and unfairness. These inconsistent decisions could have been made more efficiently by the organization as a whole. Aon recently elected to centralize certain employee-related decisions within the organization.[14] Have the organizations where you have worked been largely centralized or decentralized? See our **OB Assessments** feature to find out.

OB ASSESSMENTS

CENTRALIZATION

Have you experienced life inside an organization with a highly centralized structure? This assessment is designed to measure two facets of what would be considered a centralized organizational structure. Those two facets are hierarchy of authority, which reflects the degree to which managers are needed to approve decisions, and participation in decision making, which reflects how involved rank-and-file employees are in day-to-day deliberations. Think about the last job you held (even if it was a part-time or summer job). Alternatively, think about a student group of yours that seems to have a definite "leader." Then answer each question using the response scale provided.

1 STRONGLY DISAGREE	2 DISAGREE	3 UNCERTAIN	4 AGREE	5 STRONGLY AGREE

1. There can be little action here until a supervisor approves a decision. _____

2. A person who wants to make his own decisions would be quickly discouraged. _____

3. Even small matters have to be referred to someone higher up for a final answer. _____

4. I have to ask my boss before I do almost anything. _____

5. Any decision I make has to have my boss' approval. _____

6. I participate frequently in the decision to adopt new programs. _____

7. I participate frequently in the decision to adopt new policies and rules. _____

8. I usually participate in the decision to hire or adopt new group members. _____

9. I often participate in decisions that affect my working environment. _____

SCORING

Hierarchy of Authority: Sum up items 1-5. _____
Participation in Decision Making: Sum up items 6-9. _____

INTEPRETATION

A centralized structure would be one in which Hierarchy of Authority is high and Participation in Decision Making is low. If your score is above 20 for Hierarchy of Authority and below 8 for Participation in Decision Making, your organization (or student group) has a highly centralized structure. Think about the implications that this structure has on your view toward work and your interactions with your coworkers or boss.

Source: Adapted from M. Schminke, R. Cropanzano, and D.E. Rupp, "Organization Structure and Fairness Perceptions: The Moderating Effects of Organizational Level," *Organizational Behavior and Human Decision Processes* 89 (2002), pp. 881–905.

FORMALIZATION. A company is high in **formalization** when there are many specific rules and procedures used to standardize behaviors and decisions. Although not something you can necessarily see on an organizational chart, the impact of formalization is felt throughout the organization. Rules and procedures are a necessary mechanism for control in every organization. Although the word "formalization" has a somewhat negative connotation, think about your reaction if every McDonald's made its French fries in different ways at each location. Or think about this: Would it bother you if every time you called Dell for technical support, you got an operator who treated you differently and gave you conflicting answers? Formalization is a necessary coordination mechanism that organizations rely on to get a standardized product or deliver a standardized service.

Alcoa's Michigan Casting Center, a leading automotive part supplier, was plagued by the fact that it could have two machine operators running the same machine on two different shifts and get up to a 50 percent performance difference in output and quality between the workers. The company conducted a study to identify the best practices for each machine in its plant. These best practices became standard operating procedures for each worker, and that formalization allowed the company to get a more predictable level of output.[15] Companies such as W.L. Gore, the manufacturer of Gore-Tex and hundreds of other products, fall at the other extreme when it comes to formalization. Whereas most companies have titles for their jobs and job descriptions that specify the tasks each job is responsible for, Bill Gore (company founder) felt that such formalization stifles communication and creativity. After one of his employees mentioned that she needed to put some kind of job title on a business card to hand out at an outside conference, Gore replied that she could put "supreme commander" on the card for all he cared. She liked the title so much that she followed through on his suggestion, and it became a running joke throughout the company.[16]

ELEMENTS IN COMBINATION. You might have noticed that some elements of an organization's structure seem to go hand-in-hand with other elements. For example, wide spans of control tend to be associated with decentralization in decision making. A high level of work specialization tends to bring about a high level of formalization. Moreover, if you take a closer look at the elements, you might notice that many of the elements capture the struggle between efficiency and flexibility. **Mechanistic organizations** are efficient, rigid, predictable, and standardized organizations that thrive in stable environments. Mechanistic organizations are typified by a structure that relies on high levels of formalization, a rigid and hierarchical chain of command, high degrees of work specialization, centralization of decision making, and narrow spans of control. In contrast, **organic organizations** are flexible, adaptive, outward-focused organizations that thrive in dynamic environments. Organic organizations are typified by a structure that relies on low levels of formalization, weak or multiple chains of command, low levels of work specialization, and wide spans of control. Table 15-2 sums up the differences between the two types of organizations.

If you think about the differences between the two types, it probably wouldn't be too difficult to come up with a few companies that fall more toward one end of the continuum or the other. However, it is important to remember that few organizations are perfect examples of either of these extremes. Most fall somewhere near the middle, with certain areas within the organization having mechanistic qualities and others being more organic in nature. Although it is tempting to label mechanistic as "bad" and organic as "good," this perception is not necessarily true. Being mechanistic is the only way for many organizations to survive, and it can be a highly appropriate and fruitful way to structure work functions. To find out why that's the case, we need to explore why organizations develop the kinds of structures they do.

TABLE 15-2	Characteristics of Mechanistic vs. Organic Structures

MECHANISTIC ORGANIZATIONS	ORGANIC ORGANIZATIONS
High degree of work specialization; employees are given a very narrow view of the tasks they are to perform.	Low degree of work specialization; employees are encouraged to take a broad view of the tasks they are to perform.
Very clear lines of authority; employees know exactly whom they report to.	Although there might be a specified chain of command, employees think more broadly in terms of where their responsibilities lie.
High levels of hierarchical control; employees are not encouraged to make decisions without their manager's consent.	Knowledge and expertise are decentralized; employees are encouraged to make their own decisions when appropriate.
Information is passed through vertical communication between an employee and his or her supervisor.	Lateral communication is encouraged, focusing on information and advice as opposed to orders.
Employees are encouraged to develop firm-specific knowledge and expertise within their area of specialization.	Employees are encouraged to develop knowledge and expertise outside of their specialization.

Source: Adapted from T. Burns and G.M. Stalker, G.M. *The Management of Innovation* (London: Tavistock, 1961).

ORGANIZATIONAL DESIGN

Organizational design is the process of creating, selecting, or changing the structure of an organization. Ideally, organizations don't just "let" a structure develop on its own; they proactively design it to match their specific circumstances and needs. However, some organizations aren't that proactive and find themselves with a structure that has unintentionally developed on its own, without any careful planning. Those organizations may then be forced to change their structure to become more effective. A number of factors influence the process of organizational design. Those factors include the environment in which the organization does business, its strategy and technology, and the size of the firm.

BUSINESS ENVIRONMENT. An organization's **business environment** consists of its customers, competitors, suppliers, distributors, and other factors external to the firm, all of which have an impact on organizational design. One of the biggest factors in an environment's effect on structure is whether the outside environment is stable or dynamic. Stable environments do not change frequently, and any changes that do occur happen very slowly. Stable environments allow organizations to focus on efficiency and require little change over time. In contrast, dynamic environments change on a frequent basis and require organizations to have structures that are more adaptive.[16] In the opening example for this chapter, Sony failed to meet the needs of its changing business environment to match Apple's iPod. Because it took it so long to recognize and adapt to that environmental shift, Sony has struggled to be profitable. Some would argue that the world is changing so fast that the majority of companies can no longer keep up. For some good examples of the changes occurring in today's business environment, see our **OB at the Bookstore** feature.

COMPANY STRATEGY. A **company strategy** describes an organization's objectives and goals and how it tries to capitalize on its assets to make money. Although the myriad

 15.3

What is organizational design? What factors does the organizational design process depend on?

OB AT THE BOOKSTORE

THE WORLD IS FLAT: A BRIEF HISTORY OF THE TWENTY-FIRST CENTURY
by Thomas L. Friedman (New York: Farrar, Straus and Giroux, 2002)

"Here's the truth that no one wanted to tell you. The world has been flattened. As a result [commerce has] been made cheaper, more friction-free, and more productive for more people from more corners of the earth than at any time in the history of the world."

With these words, Thomas Friedman sums up what just might be the biggest driving force for structure change in organizations over the next decade: major environmental shifts. Although there are many environmental factors at play to which companies need to adapt their structure over time, *The World Is Flat* details what is perhaps the most significant of these changes: rapid advances in technology. Friedman's book gives many examples of the changes companies have made to take advantage of these changes. For example, did you know that when you order a hamburger at the McDonald's drive-through in Cape Girardeau, Missouri, the person taking your order is actually sitting in Colorado (900 miles away)? You place your order to someone in Colorado who then beams it back to the actual McDonald's in whose drive-through lane you are sitting. Talk about work specialization! When your Toshiba laptop computer needs fixing and the UPS driver comes by to pick it up, guess who's actually doing the repairs? In many instances, an employee in "funny brown shorts" at UPS is the one actually taking it apart and putting it back together. It's a way in which Toshiba and UPS have "virtually" structured themselves to take advantage of changes in supplier/distributor skill sets.

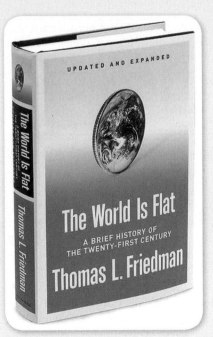

The World Is Flat also provides a glimpse into the future to which companies will have to adjust to survive. One of the big environmental shifts is what Friedman terms "offshoring," or the ability of firms to send work overseas that used to be done in their home countries. Indian accounting firms completed 400,000 American tax returns in 2005, with that number expected to grow rapidly. Do you think U.S. firms such as H&R Block will need to find ways to adjust their structure to take advantage of this reality? In addition, U.S. hospitals are having CAT scans interpreted by Indian or Australian radiologists during their waking hours while your primary doctor is snoozing. Radiology practices in the United States will have to adjust work patterns and flows to deal with this shift.

All of these environmental factor changes can mean radical shifts in the way companies structure themselves to provide services or manufacture products more efficiently. Friedman details the 10 forces he believes have "flattened" the world. He also believes that U.S. companies will have to flatten with it or be prepared to be left behind. Most haven't. Adapting to these rapid changes requires that companies become more organic in their structures and adopt a willingness to change to meet the quickly changing environmental factors that surround them.

of organizational strategies is too cumbersome to discuss here, two common strategies revolve around being either a low-cost producer or a differentiator.[18] Companies that focus on a low-cost producer strategy rely on selling products at the lowest possible cost. To do this well, they have to focus on being as efficient as they can be. Such companies are more likely to take a mechanistic approach to organizational design. Other companies might follow a differentiation strategy. Rather than focusing on supplying a product or service at the lowest cost, these companies believe that people will pay more for a product that is unique in some way. It could be that their product has a higher level of quality or offers features that a low-cost product doesn't. A differentiation strategy often hinges on adjusting to changing environments quickly, which often makes an organic structure more appropriate.

TECHNOLOGY. An organization's **technology** is the method by which it transforms inputs into outputs. Very early on in the study of organizations, it was assumed that technology was the major determinant of an organization's structure.[19] Since then, the picture has become less clear regarding the appropriate relationship between technology and structure.[20] Although not completely conclusive, research suggests that the more routine a technology is, the more mechanistic a structure should be. In many ways, this suggestion makes perfect sense: If a company makes the exact same thing over and over, it should focus on creating that one thing as efficiently as possible by having high levels of specialization, formalization, and centralization. However, if technologies need to be changed or altered to suit the needs of various consumers, it follows that decisions would be more decentralized and the rules and procedures the organization relies on would need to be more flexible.

COMPANY SIZE. There is no question that there is a significant relationship between **company size,** or total number of employees, and structure.[21] As organizations become larger, they need to rely on some combination of specialization, formalization, and centralization to control their activities and thus become more mechanistic in nature. When it comes to organizational performance, however, there is no definite answer as to when an organization's structure should be revised, or "how big is too big."[22] As many organizations get bigger, they attempt to create smaller units within the firm to create a "feeling of smallness." W.L. Gore did just that by attempting to prevent any one location in the company from having more than 150 employees. Top management was convinced that a size of 150 would still allow all the employees to talk to one another in the hallways. However, even W.L. Gore hasn't been able to keep that goal as it has grown to encompass 7,300 employees in 45 locations.[23]

COMMON ORGANIZATIONAL FORMS

Our discussion of organizational design describes how an organization's business environment, strategy, technology, and size conspire to make some organizational structures more effective than others. Now we turn our attention to a logical next question: What structures do most organizations utilize? The sections that follow describe some of the most common organizational forms. As you read their descriptions, think about whether these forms would fall on the mechanistic or organic side of the structure continuum. You might also consider what kinds of design factors would lead an organization to choose that particular form.

SIMPLE STRUCTURES. Simple structures are perhaps the most common form of organizational design, primarily because there are more small organizations than large ones. In fact, more than 80 percent of employing organizations have fewer than 19 employees.[24] Small accounting and law firms, family-owned grocery stores, individual-owned retail outlets, independent churches, and landscaping services are all organizations that are

15.4

What are some of the more common organizational forms that an organization might adopt for its structure?

likely to use a simple structure. Figure 15-3 shows a simple structure for a manager-owned restaurant. The figure reveals that simple structures are just that: simple. Simple structures are generally used by extremely small organizations in which the manager, president, and owner are all the same person. A simple structure is a flat organization with one person as the central decision-making figure; it is not large enough to have a high degree of formalization and will only have very basic differences in work specialization.

A simple structure makes perfect sense for a small organization, because employees can come and go with no major ripple effects on the organization. However, as the business grows, the coordinating efforts on the part of the owner/manager become increasingly more complex. In the case of our restaurant, let's assume that the growth of the restaurant requires the owner to spend time doing lots of little things to manage the employees. Now the manager has lost the ability to spend time focusing on the actual business at hand. The manager then decides to add a supervisor to handle all of the day-to-day organizing of the restaurant. This arrangement works well until the owner decides to open a second restaurant that needs to have its own supervisor. Now let's assume that this second restaurant is much larger, leading the owner to decide to have separate supervisors directly in charge of the waitstaff and the kitchen. All of the sudden, our little restaurant has three layers of management!

BUREAUCRATIC STRUCTURES. When you think of the word "bureaucracy," what thoughts come to mind? Stuffy, boring, restrictive, formal, hard to change, and needlessly complex are some of the terms that have a tendency to be associated with bureaucracies. Those unflattering adjectives aside, chances are very good that you either currently work in a bureaucracy or will after you graduate. A **bureaucratic structure** is an organizational form that exhibits many of the facets of the mechanistic organization. Bureaucracies are designed for efficiency and rely on high levels of work specialization, formalization, centralization of authority, rigid and well-defined chains of command, and relatively narrow spans of control. As mentioned previously, as an organization's size increases, it is incredibly difficult not to develop some form of bureaucracy. How attractive might bureaucratic structures be to you? See our **OB for Students** feature to find out.

There are numerous types of bureaucratic structures on which we might focus. The most basic of these is the **functional structure.** As shown in Figure 15-4, a functional structure groups employees by the functions they perform for the organization. For example, employees with marketing expertise are grouped together, those with finance duties are grouped together, and so on. The success of the functional structure is based on the efficiency advantages that come with having a high degree of work specialization that

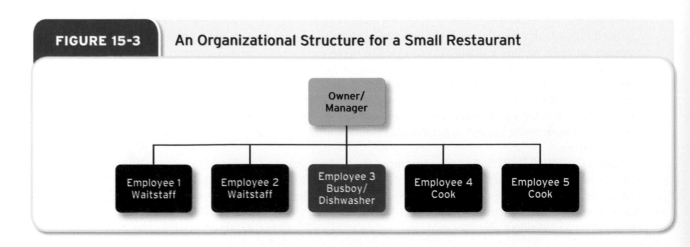

FIGURE 15-3   **An Organizational Structure for a Small Restaurant**

Owner/ Manager

Employee 1 Waitstaff

Employee 2 Waitstaff

Employee 3 Busboy/ Dishwasher

Employee 4 Cook

Employee 5 Cook

OB FOR STUDENTS

Whether it's obvious to you or not, structure has a significant effect on you as a student. What organizations are you a part of? Fraternities, sororities, professional associations, student government, and other campus organizations all have structures that influence how decisions are made, where the power lies, and how involved members are in the day-to-day goings on. Indeed, even your university as a whole affects you by the way it is structured.

As you begin to search for jobs, there is some evidence that you will be attracted to certain organizations on the basis of their organizational structure. On the whole, college-level job seekers tend to find centralization in organizations an unattractive company characteristic. It's not hard to picture why. Most job seekers like the idea of being able to work in an organization in which they will be able to make decisions on their own without someone else's approval.

Does anyone find centralization attractive? Not usually, but there is evidence that some job seekers are less affected by centralization than others. For example, research has shown that job seekers with high self-esteem are less bothered by centralization.[25] That is, the negative effect of centralization on organizational attractiveness is weaker for them. Perhaps they feel confident that they can "fight the bureaucracy" if they need to!

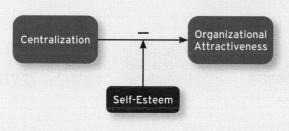

Regardless, when you begin your search for a job, some good questions to ask in an interview might revolve around the organizational structure of the company. How many people will be working for your immediate supervisor? How does the group you are looking to work for fit in with the rest of the organization? Will you be working for one direct supervisor or have reporting responsibilities to a number of managers? You are likely to find that questions like these will impress your interviewer. Understanding these aspects of organizational structure might also help you make a decision between multiple job offers.

is centrally coordinated.[26] Managers have expertise in an area and interact with others with the same type of expertise to create the most efficient solutions for the company. As illustrated in our previous example of the fast-growing restaurant, many small companies naturally evolve into functionally based structures as they grow larger.

However, small companies experiencing rapid growth are not the only organizations to benefit from a functional structure. Smurfit-Stone Container Corporation, a leading paper and packaging manufacturer with 25,000 employees at 140 locations, is moving toward a more traditional functional structure. Smurfit-Stone was organized like other companies in the paper industry, with a structure relying on a large number of plants operating under different general managers. CEO Patrick Moore made the decision to move toward a more functional structure, noting that the move "allows us to drive a standardization of operating practices within the organization, which is critical. In addition, it allows us to drive scale and efficiency, which has suffered with the series of acquisitions that provided too many smaller, inefficient plants."[27] Smurfit-Stone hopes that the efficiencies generated by the change in structure will afford it enough cost savings to get a jump on its competitors.

FIGURE 15-4   Functional and Multi-Divisional Structures

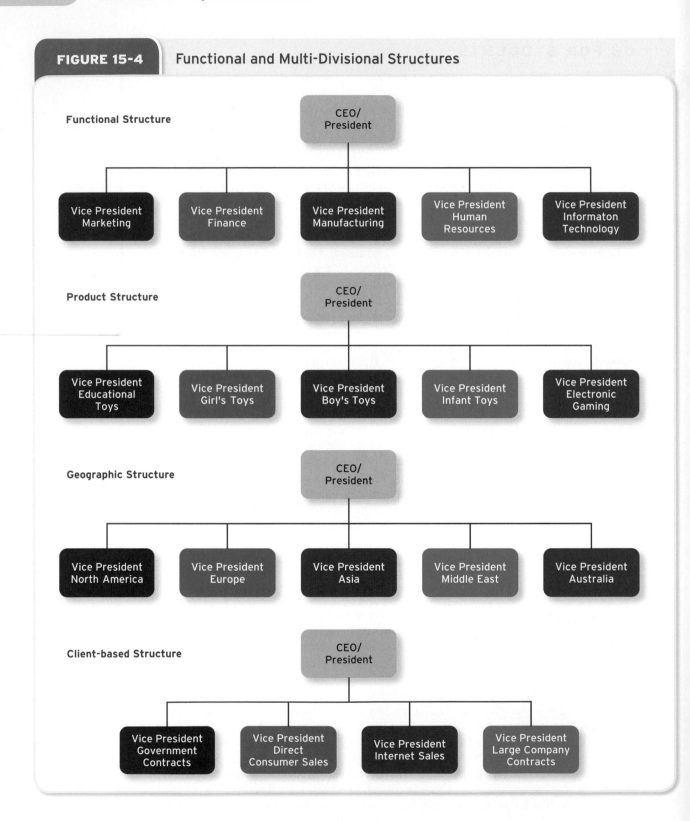

Functional structures are extremely efficient when the organization as a whole has a relatively narrow focus, fewer product lines or services, and a stable environment. The biggest weaknesses of a functional structure tend to revolve around the fact that individuals within each function get so wrapped up in their own goals and viewpoints that they lose sight of the bigger organizational picture. In other words, employees don't communicate as well across functions as they do within functions. The Sony example describes this danger, as the hardware engineers failed to communicate with the software developers. That lack of communication prevented the hardware and software people from seeing all the pieces of the puzzle.

In contrast to functional structures, **multi-divisional structures** are bureaucratic organizational forms in which employees are grouped into divisions around products, geographic regions, or clients (see Figure 15-4). Each of these divisions operates relatively autonomously from the others and has its own functional groups. Multi-divisional structures generally develop from companies with functional structures whose interests and goals become too diverse for that structure to handle. For example, if a company with a functional structure begins to add customers that require localized versions of its product, the company might adopt a geographic structure to handle the product variations. Which form a company chooses will likely depend on where the diversity in its business lies.

Product structures group business units around different products that the company produces. Each of those divisions becomes responsible for manufacturing, marketing, and doing research and development for the products in its own division. Boeing, Procter & Gamble, Hewlett-Packard, and Sony are companies that have developed product structures. Product structures make sense when firms diversify to the point that the products they sell are so different that managing them becomes overwhelming. CEO Mark Hurd changed Hewlett-Packard's organizational structure to become more product-based. He was inspired to do so because his sales force (in a centralized functional structure) simply had way too many products to sell (from the largest servers to the smallest printers). Shifting the sales force into three different product-based divisions allowed the salespeople to concentrate on a core set of products, reinvigorating the Hewlett-Packard sales force.[28]

However, there are downsides to a product structure. One of those downsides arises when the products are not really that different. Mattel ran into this problem with its product-based structure. Mattel was organized into girl's brands (Barbie), boy's brands (HotWheels), the American Girl line, and Fisher-Price (educational toys, Dora the Explorer). When Mattel CEO Robert Eckert took over the company, he found that each of the divisions not only had its own unique culture and ways of doing business, but they were actually competing against one another! Mattel has since combined three of the four divisions to push a "One Mattel" philosophy, hoping the more centralized and functional structure will help the company become more profitable.[29]

Mattel recently centralized its operations by combining three of its four divisions. CEO Robert Eckert hopes the new organization will reduce competition between divisions and make the company more profitable.

Geographic structures are generally based around the different locations where the company does business. The functions required to serve a business are placed under a manager who is in charge of a specific location. Reasons for developing a geographic structure revolve around the different tastes of customers in different regions, the size of the locations that need to be covered by different salespeople, or the fact that the manufacturing and distribution of a product are better served by a geographic breakdown. When the Regus Group (a U.K.-based company) and HQ Global Workplaces (a U.S.-based company) merged, they came together to form the world's largest supplier of meeting spaces and office suites. The new Regus group now has 750 office-suite facilities in 350 cities in 60 countries. When they merged, HQ and Regus had different structures. Given its necessarily geographic-based type of business (i.e., the distances between facilities and the range of their customers), the new Regus group is structured by geographic region.[30] Many global companies are also organized by geographic location. IBM was one of the first, but that might be changing, as described in our **OB Internationally** feature.

One last form of multi-divisional structure is the **client structure.** When organizations have a number of very large customers or groups of customers that all act in a similar way, they might organize their businesses around serving those customers. For example, small banks traditionally organize themselves into divisions such as personal banking, small business banking, personal lending, and commercial lending. Similarly, consulting firms often organize themselves into divisions that are responsible for small business clients, large business clients, and federal clients.

OB INTERNATIONALLY

Traditionally, IBM has structured its 200,000 employee organization along geographic lines. In fact some might argue that IBM was the company that pioneered the first multinational geographic structure by setting up mini-IBMs in countries around the globe. Each country in which IBM operated had its own workforce and management team that reacted to the clients for whom it provided services in each country. It was a structure that made perfect sense in a world where consultants needed to be on location with their clients when those customers were having software or computer issues. However, IBM's environmental factors are changing rapidly. Competitors, such as those out of India, are providing many of the same services for significantly less money.

To change with its competitors and the "flattening world" (see this chapter's OB at the Bookstore), IBM is reorganizing its workforce by creating and utilizing what it calls "competency centers." These centers will group employees from around the world on the basis of the specific skill sets that they have to offer clients. Some workers will be grouped into one location that can service clients all over the world through the use of technology. In Boulder, Colorado, IBM employs 6,200 professionals as part of a "call center" that monitors clients' computing functions worldwide. If something goes wrong in one of IBM's 426 data centers, employees in Boulder will more than likely be the ones to handle it or send it to someone who can. Other IBM workers will be grouped by broader geographic locations so that they can still be in relatively close proximity to their customers. When these employees are needed by a client, IBM has a computer database that allows it to put together teams of highly specialized consultants by examining the skill sets listed on 70,000 IBM resumes.

Does this change in structure sound familiar to you? It should—though IBM is maintaining some of it geographical structure, its organizational structure is becoming more functional. As the world becomes flatter through technology, clients expect the best talent from around the world, not just the best talent that happens to be sitting in their city. These structural changes will allow IBM to give clients just that. For IBM, these are the necessary changes that come with being a global company. It's not just about structure though, according to IBM Senior Vice President Robert W. Moffat Jr.: "Globalization is more than that. Our customers need us to put the right skills in the right place at the right time."[31]

Matrix structures are more complex forms of organizational design that try to take advantage of two types of structures at the same time. Companies such as Xerox, General Electric, and Dow Corning were among the first to adopt this type of structure.[32] Figure 15-5 provides an example of a matrix structure. In this example, employees are distributed into teams or projects within the organization on the basis of both their functional expertise and the product that they happen to be working on. Thus, the matrix represents a combination of a functional structure and a product structure. There are two important points to understand about the matrix structure. First, the matrix allows an organization to put together very flexible teams based on the experiences and skills of their employees.[33] This flexibility enables the organization to adjust much more quickly to the environment than a traditional burcaucratic structure would.

Second, the matrix gives each employee two chains of command, two groups with which to interact, and two sources of information to consider. This doubling of traditional structural elements can create high stress levels for employees if the demands of their functional grouping are at odds with the demands of their product- or client-based grouping.[34] The situation can become particularly stressful if one of the two groupings has more power than the other. For example, it may be that the functional manager assigns employees to

FIGURE 15-5 Matrix Structure

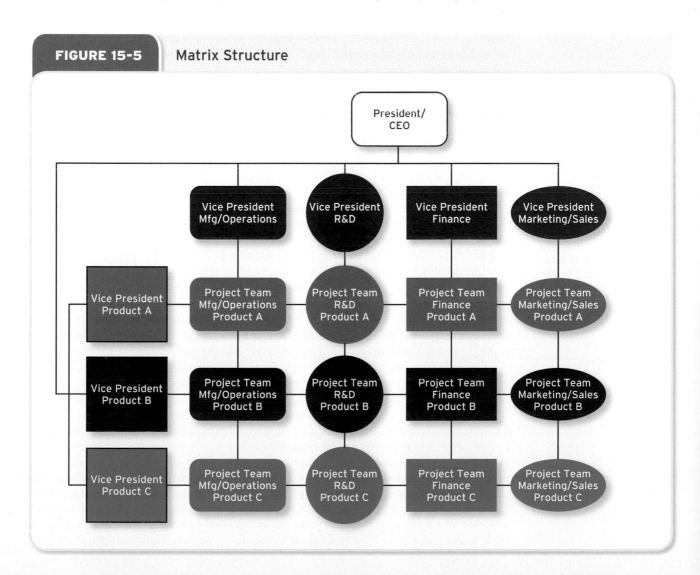

teams, conducts performance evaluations, and decides raises—making that manager more powerful than the product- or client-based manager.[35] Although matrix structures have been around for an extremely long time, the number of organizations using them is growing as teams become a more common form of organizing work. They have also become more common in global companies, with the functional grouping balanced by a geographic grouping. For example, Areva NP, a French company that designs and builds nuclear power plants, has a matrix structure based on products (plants, fuel, services, and equipment) and geographical locations (France, Germany, and North America).[36]

SUMMARY: WHY DO SOME ORGANIZATIONS HAVE DIFFERENT STRUCTURES THAN OTHERS?

So why do some organizations have different structures? As shown in Figure 15-6, differences in the business environment, company strategy, technology, and firm size cause some organizations to be designed differently than others. These differences create variations in the five elements of organizational structure: work specialization, chain of command, span of control, centralization, and formalization. These elements then combine to form one of a number of common organizational forms, including: (1) a simple structure; (2) a bureaucratic structure, which may come in functional, product, geographic, or client forms; or (3) a matrix structure. Some of these forms are more mechanistic, whereas others are more organic. Taken together, these structures explain how work is organized within a given company.

HOW IMPORTANT IS STRUCTURE?

15.5

When an organization makes changes to its structure, how does that restructuring affect job performance and organizational commitment?

To some degree, an organization's structure provides the foundation for almost everything in organizational behavior. Think about some of the things that organizational structure affects: communication patterns between employees, the tasks an employee performs, the types of groups an organization uses, the freedom employees have to innovate and try new things, how power and influence are divided up in the company . . . we could go on and on. Picture the walls of a house. The occupants within those walls can decorate or personalize the structure as best they can. They can make it more attractive according to their individual preferences by adding and taking away furniture, but at the end of the day, they are still stuck with that structure. They have to work within the confines that the builder envisioned (unless they are willing to tear down walls or build new ones at considerable time, effort, and expense!). Organizational structures operate in much the same way for employees and their managers. A given manager can do many things to try to motivate, inspire, and set up an effective work environment so that employees have high levels of performance and commitment. At the end of the day, however, that manager must work within the structure created by the organization.

Given how many organizational forms there are, it is almost impossible to give an accurate representation of the impact of organizational structure on job performance. In fact, we might even say that an organization's structure determines what job performance is supposed to look like! In addition, the elements of structure are not necessarily good or bad for performance. For example, a narrow span of control is not necessarily better than a broad one; rather, the organization must find the optimal "middle ground." One thing we can say, as illustrated in Figure 15-7, is that changes to an organization's structure can have negative effects on the employees who work for the company, at least in the short term. The process of changing an organization's structure is called

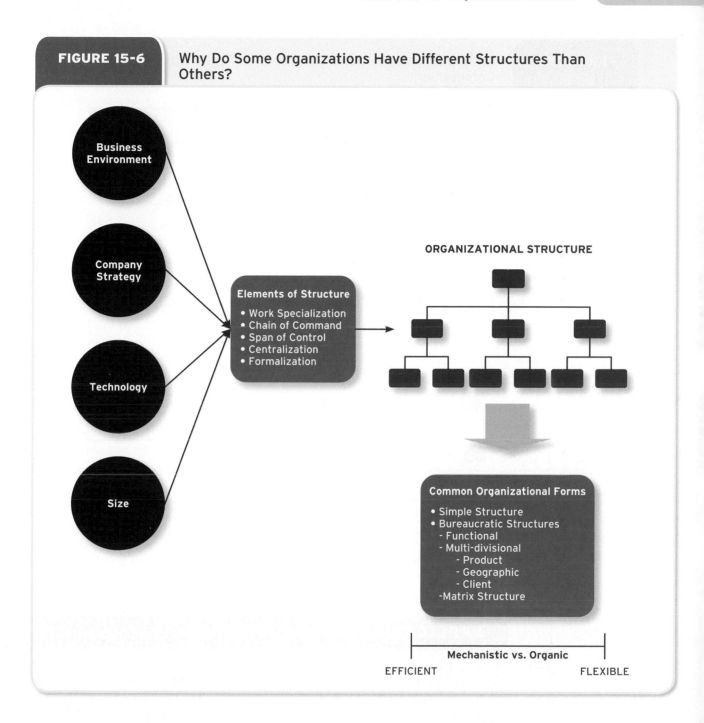

FIGURE 15-6   Why Do Some Organizations Have Different Structures Than Others?

restructuring. Research suggests that restructuring has a small negative effect on task performance, likely because changes in specialization, centralization, or formalization may lead to confusion about how exactly employees are supposed to do their jobs, which hinders *learning* and *decision making.* Restructuring has a more significant negative effect on organizational commitment however. Restructuring efforts can increase *stress* and jeopardize employees' *trust* in the organization. There is some evidence that the end result is a lower level of affective commitment on the part of employees, because they feel less emotionally attached to the firm.

| FIGURE 15-7 | Effects of Organizational Structure on Performance and Commitment |

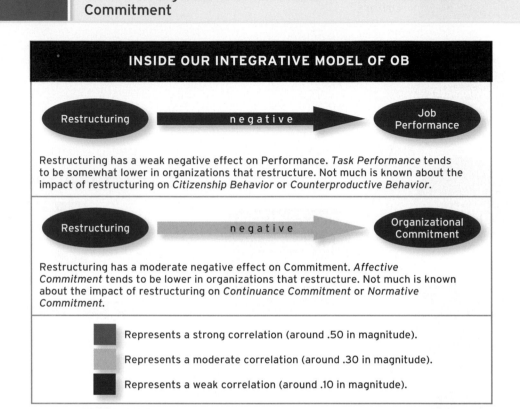

Sources: C. Gopinath and T.E. Becker, "Communication, Procedural Justice, and Employee Attitudes: Relationships under Conditions of Divestiture," *Journal of Management* 26 (2000), pp. 63–83; J. Brockner, G. Spreitzer, A. Mishra, W. Hockwarter, L. Pepper, and J. Weinberg, "Perceived Control as an Antidote to the Negative Effects of Layoffs on Survivors' Organizational Commitment and Job Performance," *Administrative Science Quarterly* 49 (2004), pp. 76–100.

APPLICATION: RESTRUCTURING

As you have read through our discussion of organizational structure, you may have noticed how important it is for organizations to adapt to their environment. The first step in adapting is recognizing the need to change. The second (and sometimes much more problematic) step is actually doing it by restructuring. Organizations attempt to restructure all the time—in fact, it's difficult to pick up a copy of *BusinessWeek* or *Fortune* without reading about some organization's restructuring initiatives. General Motors has undertaken a massive restructuring effort no less than 6 times over the past 20 years![37] Indeed, most of the examples we put into this chapter center on organizations that were restructuring.

Restructuring efforts come in a variety of shapes and sizes. Organizations may change from a product-based structure to a functional structure, from a functional structure to a geographic-based structure, and on and on. However, the most common kind of restructuring in recent years has been a "flattening" of the organization. Why do so many organizations do this? Primarily to show investors that they are reducing costs to become more profitable. Think back to our discussion of tall and flat organizational hierarchies, in which we noted that taller organizations have more layers of management. Many restructuring efforts are designed to remove one or more of those layers to reduce costs. Of course, removing such layers doesn't just mean deleting boxes on an organizational chart; there are actual people within those boxes! Thus, efforts to flatten require organizations to lay off several of the managers within the company.

When employees get a sense that their company might be getting ready to restructure, it causes a great deal of stress because they become worried that they will be one of those to lose their jobs. As a perfect example we return to our Chapter 13 example of Hewlett-Packard. When ex-CEO Carly Fiorina decided to restructure Hewlett-Packard, it caused widespread fear and panic among employees. For the 60 days prior to the actual restructuring announcement, work came to a standstill at the company—tales of high stress, low motivation, political battles, and power struggles abounded.[38] It is estimated that Hewlett-Packard as a company lost an entire quarter's worth of productivity.[39] Not a great way to run a business, especially when, not two years later, the new CEO Mark Hurd essentially undid everything that had previously been restructured! He unmerged units that had been merged, decentralized the company where it had been centralized, and flattened the layers of management from 11 to 8 levels.[40]

One of the ways in which managers can do their best to help a restructuring succeed is to help manage layoff survivors (employees that remain with the company following a layoff). Many layoff survivors are known to experience a great deal of guilt and remorse following an organization's decision to remove some employees from the company.[41] Researchers and practitioners recently have been trying to understand layoff survivors better, as well as how to help them adjust more quickly. One of the major problems for layoff survivors is the increased job demands placed on them. After all, that coworker or boss the employee had was doing *something*. Layoff survivors are generally burdened with having to pick up the leftover tasks that used to be done by somebody else.[42] This burden creates a sense of uncertainty and stress. Recent research suggests that one of the best ways to help layoff survivors adjust is to do things that give them a stronger sense of control.[43] Allowing survivors to have a voice in how to move forward or help set the plans about how to accomplish future goals are two ways managers can help employees feel more in control. In addition, honest and frequent communication with layoff survivors greatly helps reduce their feelings of uncertainty and stress.[44]

15.6

What steps can organizations take to reduce the negative effects of restructuring efforts?

TAKEAWAYS

15.1 An organization's structure formally dictates how jobs and tasks are divided and coordinated between individuals and groups within the organization. This structure, partially illustrated through the use of organizational charts, provides the foundation for organizing jobs, controlling employee behavior, shaping communication channels, and providing a lens through which employees view their work environment.

15.2 There are five major elements to an organization's structure: work specialization, chain of command, span of control, centralization of decision making, and formalization. These elements can be organized in such a way as to make an organization more mechanistic in nature, which allows it to be highly efficient in stable environments, or more organic in nature, which allows it to be flexible and adaptive in changing environments.

15.3 Organizational design is the process of creating, selecting, or changing the structure of an organization. Factors to be considered in organizational design include a company's business environment, its strategy, its technology, and its size.

15.4 There are literally thousands of organizational forms. The most common is the simple structure, which is used by most small companies. Larger companies adopt a more bureaucratic structure. This structure may be functional in nature, such that employees are grouped by job tasks, or multi-divisional, such that employees are grouped by product, geography, or client. Organizations may also adopt a matrix structure that combines functional and multi-divisional grouping.

15.5 Organizational restructuring efforts have a weak negative effect on job performance. They have a more significant negative effect on organizational commitment, because employees tend to feel less emotional attachment to organizations that are restructuring.

15.6 To reduce the negative effects of restructuring, organizations should focus on managing the stress levels of the employees who remain after the restructuring. Providing employees with a sense of control can help them learn to navigate their new work environment.

KEY TERMS

- Organizational structure   *p. 517*
- Organizational chart   *p. 517*
- Work specialization   *p. 519*
- Chain of command   *p. 519*
- Span of control   *p. 520*
- Centralization   *p. 521*
- Formalization   *p. 524*
- Mechanistic organizations   *p. 524*
- Organic organizations   *p. 524*
- Organizational design   *p. 525*
- Business environment   *p. 525*
- Company strategy   *p. 525*
- Technology   *p. 527*
- Company size   *p. 527*
- Simple structure   *p. 527*
- Bureaucratic structure   *p. 528*
- Functional structure   *p. 528*
- Multi-divisional structure   *p. 531*
- Product structure   *p. 531*
- Geographic structure   *p. 531*
- Client structure   *p. 532*
- Matrix structure   *p. 533*
- Restructuring   *p. 535*

DISCUSSION QUESTIONS

15.1 Is it possible to be a great leader of employees in a highly mechanistic organization? What special talents or abilities might be required?

15.2 Why do the elements of structure, such as work specialization, formalization, span of control, chain of command, and centralization, have a tendency to change together? Which of the five do you feel is the most important?

15.3 Which is more important for an organization: the ability to be efficient or the ability to adapt to its environment? What does this say about how an organization's structure should be set up?

15.4 Which of the organizational forms described in this chapter do you think leads to the highest levels of motivation among workers? Why?

15.5 If you worked in a matrix organization, what would be some of the career development challenges that you might face? Does the idea of working in a matrix structure appeal to you? Why or why not?

15.6 Should an organization consult with rank-and-file employees before it restructures? Should it be open about its intentions to restructure or more secretive about key details? Why?

CASE SONY CORPORATION

Sir Howard Stringer, the new CEO of Sony, could not have arrived at a more critical time for the company. Sony's organizational structure has become bloated with multiple "silos" that divide the company into seemingly separate entities. The different silos are not committed to a common Sony vision, which has caused the organization to fail to capitalize on market shifts. Sony also includes a number of noncore businesses that have taken capital away from key areas that historically were successful. Thus, Sony's organizational structure is not integrated with its organizational strategy.

Currently, Sony is attempting to create a leaner company to combat the competitive problems facing its core businesses. The television division represents a significant portion of its revenue and is in need of restructuring. Stringer will attempt to revitalize this division by focusing plant production on HDTV products rather than cathode ray tube TV products. Sony also will begin integrating the various divisions of the company to create, build, and market HDTV products. Another division within Sony needing restructuring is the computer entertainment arm. Sony's PlayStation3 is struggling to break even in fiscal 2007, largely due to the lack of communication among various departments of the company. Because the various divisions of Sony are separate, the company cannot effectively compete with its competitors. Stringer will have an uphill battle to restructure Sony to integrate the various divisions of the company to regain its stature in the industry.

15.1 Evaluate Sony's organizational structure in terms of its inability to compete effectively with its competitors.

15.2 Why has Sony been missing the mark with its recent product releases?

Sources: B. Bremner, "Is a Slimmer Sony Coming?" *BusinessWeek,* September 16, 2005; E. Rusli, "Game Over for Father of PlayStation," *Forbes,* April 27, 2007, www.forbes.com (June 26, 2007); "Time for Sony to Call the TV Repairman," *BusinessWeek,* August 15, 2005; J. Yang, "What Should Sony Spin Off?" *BusinessWeek,* April 13, 2005.

EXERCISE   CREATIVE CARDS, INC.

The purpose of this exercise is to demonstrate the effects of structure on organizational efficiency. Creative Cards, Inc., is a small but growing company, started 10 years ago by Angela Naom, a graphic designer. The company has added many employees over the years but without a master plan. Now Angela wants to reorganize the company. The current structure of Creative Cards, Inc. looks like this:

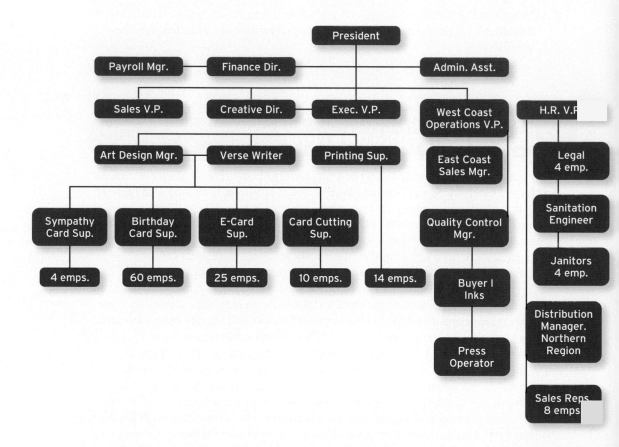

This exercise uses groups of six participants, so your instructor will either assign you to a group of six or ask you to create your own group of six. The exercise has the following steps:

1. Review the organizational chart and identify at least 10 problems with the design of Creative Cards, Inc. Be sure to consider work specialization, chain of command, span of control, centralization, and formalization in developing your answer.

2. Create a new organizational design that you think would help the company operate more efficiently and effectively.

ENDNOTES

15.1 Brenner, B. "Sony's Sudden Samurai." *BusinessWeek,* March 21, 2005, pp. 28–32.

15.2 Singer, M. "Stringer's Way." *The New Yorker,* June 5, 2006, pp. 46–57.

15.3 Kane, Y.I., and P. Dvorak. "Howard Stringer, Japanese CEO." *The Wall Street Journal,* March 3, 2007, pp. A1, A6.

15.4 Singer, "Stringer's Way."

15.5 Hackman, J. R., and G. R. Oldham. *Work Redesign.* Reading, MA: Addison-Wesley, 1980.

15.6 Simon, H. *Administrative Behavior.* New York: Macmillan, 1947.

15.7 Edwards, C. "Shaking Up Intel's Insides." *BusinessWeek*, January 31, 2005, p. 35.

15.8 Meier, K.J., and J. Bohte. "Ode to Luther Gulick: Span of Control and Organizational Performance." *Administration and Society* 32 (2000), pp. 115–37.

15.9 Theobald, N.A., and S. Nicholson-Crotty. "The Many Faces of Span of Control: Organizational Structure Across Multiple Goals." *Administration and Society* 36 (2005), pp. 648–60.

15.10 Child, J., and M. McGrath. "Organizations Unfettered: Organizational Forms in an Information-Intensive Economy." *Academy of Management Journal* 44 (2001), pp. 1135–48.

15.11 Hymowitz, C. "Today's Bosses Find Mentoring Isn't Worth the Time and Risks." *The Wall Street Journal,* March 13, 2006, p. B1.

15.12 Nuttal, C. "Intel Cuts 1,000 Management Jobs." *Financial Times,* July 14, 2006, p. 23.

15.13 Marquez, J. "Taking a Longer View." *Workforce Management,* May 22, 2006, pp. 18–22.

15.14 Marquez, J. "Many Businesses, but One Mission." *Workforce Management,* June 12, 2006, pp. 32–36.

15.15 Groszkiewicz, D., and B. Warren. "Alcoa's Michigan Casting Center Runs the Business from the Bottom Up." *Journal of Organizational Excellence,* Spring 2006, pp. 13–23.

15.16 Kiger, P. "Power of the Individual." *Workforce Management,* February 27, 2006, p. 1, 22–27.

15.17 Scott, W.R., and G. F. Davis. *Organizations and Organizing: Rational, Natural, and Open System Perspectives.* New Jersey: Pearson Prentice Hall, 2007.

15.18 Porter, M. *Competitive Strategy.* New York: The Free Press, 1980.

15.19 Woodward, J. *Industrial Organization: Theory and Practice.* London: Oxford University Press, 1965.

15.20 Miller, C.C.; W.H. Glick; Y. Wang; and G.P. Huber. "Understanding Technology–Structure Relationships: Theory Development and Meta-Analytic Theory Testing." *Academy of Management Journal* 34 (1991), pp. 370–99.

15.21 Gooding, J.Z., and J.A. Wagner III. "A Meta-Analytic Review of the Relationship Between Size and Performance: The Productivity and Efficiency of Organizations and their Subunits." *Administrative Science Quarterly* 30 (1985), pp. 462–81. See also Bluedorn, A.C. "Pilgrim's Progress: Trends and Convergence in Research on Organizational Size and Environments." *Journal of Management* 21 (1993), pp. 163–92.

15.22 Lawler, E.E., III. "Rethinking Organizational Size." *Organizational Dynamics,* 26 (1997), pp. 24–35.

15.23 Kiger, "Power of the Individual."

15.24 Scott and Davis, *Organizations and Organizing.*

15.25 Turban, D.B., and T.L. Keon. "Organizational Attractiveness: An Interactionist Perspective." *Journal of Applied Psychology* 78 (1993), pp. 184–93.

15.26 Miles, R.E., and C.C. Snow. *Organizational Strategy, Structure, and Process.* New York: McGraw-Hill, 1978.

15.27 Shaw, M. "Boxing It Up the Right Way." *Pulp & Paper,* September 2006, pp. 31–34.

15.28 Lashinsky, A. "The Hurd Way: How a Sales-Obsessed CEO Rebooted HP." *Fortune,* April 17, 2006, pp. 92–102.

15.29 Ruiz, G. "Shaking up the Toyshop." *Workforce Management,* June 26, 2006, pp. 27–34.

15.30 Hosford, C. "Behind the Regus-HQ Merger: A Clash of Cultures that Wasn't." *Sales and Marketing Management,* March 2006, pp. 47–48.

15.31 Hamm, S. "Big Blue Shift." *BusinessWeek,* June 5, 2006, pp. 108–10.

15.32 Burns, L.R., and D.R. Wholey. "Adoption and Abandonment of Matrix Management Programs: Effects of Organizational Characteristics and Interorganizational Programs." *Academy of Management Journal* 36 (1993), pp. 106–38.

15.33 Hackman, J.R. "The Design of Work Teams." In *Handbook of Organizational Behavior,* ed. J.W. Lorsch. New Jersey: Prentice Hall, 1987, pp. 315-342.

15.34 Larson, E.W., and D.H. Gobeli. "Matrix Management: Contradictions and Insight." *California Management Review* 29 (1987), pp. 126–38.

15.35 Rees, D.W., and C. Porter. "Matrix Structures and the Training Implications." *Industrial and Commercial Training* 36 (2004), pp. 189–93.

15.36 http://www.areva-np.com. Accessed April 26, 2007.

15.37 Taylor, A., III. "GM Gets Its Act Together. Finally." *Fortune,* April 5, 2004, pp. 136–46.

15.38 Gopinath, C. "Businesses in a Merger Need to Make Sense Together." *Businessline,* June 26, 2006, p. 1.

15.39 Hamm, J. "The Five Messages Leaders Must Manage." *Harvard Business Review,* May 2006, pp. 114–23.

15.40 Lashinsky, "The Hurd Way."

15.41 Noer, D.M. *Healing the Wounds.* San Francisco: Jossey-Bass, 1993; Mishra, K.; G.M. Spreitzer; and A. Mishra. "Preserving Employee Morale During Downsizing." *Sloan Management Review* 39 (1998), pp. 83–95.

15.42 Conlin, M. "The Big Squeeze on Workers; Is There a Risk to Wringing More from a Smaller Staff?" *BusinessWeek,* May 13, 2002, p. 96.

15.43 Brockner, J.; G. Spreitzer; A. Mishra; W. Hockwarter; L. Pepper; and J. Weinberg. "Perceived Control as an Antidote to the Negative Effects of Layoffs on Survivors' Organizational Commitment and Job Performance." *Administrative Science Quarterly* 49 (2004), pp. 76–100.

15.44 Brockner, J. "The Effects of Work Layoffs on Survivors: Research, Theory and Practice." In *Research in Organizational Behavior,* Vol. 10, eds. B.M. Staw and L.L. Cummings. Berkeley: University of California Press, 1988, pp. 213–55.

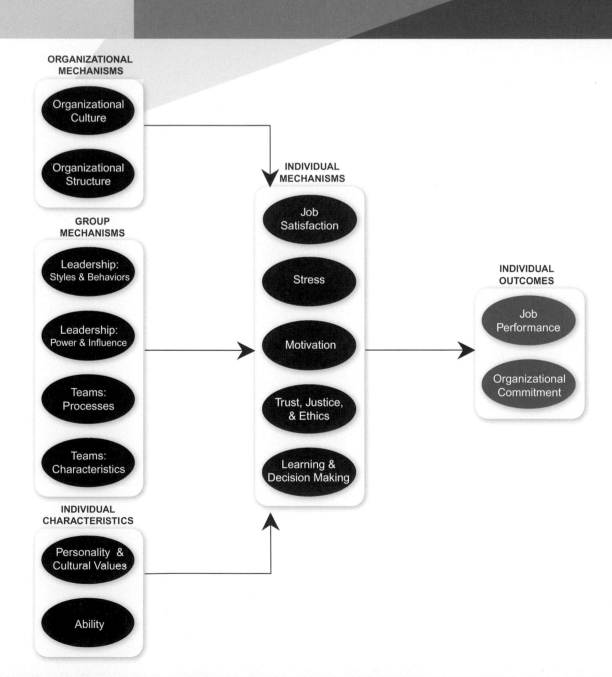

The company practices of General Electric (led by Jack Welch) and of Enron (led by Jeff Skilling) had many similarities, despite the dramatically different fates of the two firms.

 LEARNING GOALS

After reading this chapter, you should be able to answer the following questions:

16.1 What is organizational culture, and what are its components?

16.2 What general and specific types can be used to describe an organization's culture?

16.3 What is a strong culture, and what makes a culture strong? Is a strong culture necessarily good?

16.4 How do organizations maintain their culture? How do they change it?

16.5 What is person-organization fit? How does fitting with an organization's culture affect job performance and organizational commitment?

16.6 What steps can organizations take to make sure that newcomers will fit with their culture?

GENERAL ELECTRIC AND ENRON

General Electric. Enron. Not two companies that you would expect to be mentioned in the same breath at the beginning of a textbook chapter. After all, General Electric was recently named "The World's Most Admired Company" by *Fortune* magazine,[1] and Enron will go down in history as one of the greatest organizational failures and financial scandals in U.S. corporate history.[2] So why would we mention both of these firms together?

Because the fact is that throughout the 1990s and into the early 2000s, these companies actually approached their businesses and treated their employees in very similar ways. Both were extremely successful enterprises whose stock performance rewarded investors handsomely and caused them to be recognized as companies of excellence by numerous publications of all types.[3,4] On the surface, both companies used terms like "creativity," "competitiveness," "people," "integrity," and "excellence" to describe their core values. On an annual basis, GE and Enron both fired managers who were at the bottom of their performance scales, with Enron removing the bottom 20 percent of performers and GE removing the bottom 10 percent. Employees were paid well above average market levels, and managers received large bonuses that were tied directly to performance goals. Both had strong-minded and well-respected leaders—GE was led by Jack Welch, who has been described as a legend, a hero, and the world's greatest business leader,[5] and Enron was led by Jeff Skilling, known as a brilliant visionary and perhaps one of the smartest CEOs on the planet.[6]

Underneath the surface though, these two organizations could not have been more different. What was it that made these two companies move in such opposite directions? One potential answer lies with organizational culture. Whereas GE's culture led to continued success, high levels of employee commitment and performance, low employee turnover, and generally a perception as one of the top companies in world, Enron's culture failed miserably over the long term on almost every level. Many blame Enron's failure on a culture of greed that favored maximizing real or perceived profits to boost stock prices.[7] In the late 1990s, an Enron taskforce put together to help communicate Enron's "Visions and Values" considered replacing words such as "integrity," "excellence," "trust," and "respect" with words like "smart," "bold," and "aggressive."[8] The changes were never made, but the fact that they were considered says quite a bit about the underlying culture within Enron. There was also no doubt that the culture at Enron had a powerful effect on employees. Jeff Skilling told others, "People didn't just go to work for Enron; it became a part of your life, just as important as your family. *More* important than your family."[9]

ORGANIZATIONAL CULTURE

In almost every chapter up to this point, we have simply given you definitions of important topics. However, in this case, it is important for you to understand that there are just about as many definitions of organizational culture as there are people who study it. In fact, research on organizational culture has produced well over 50 different definitions![10] It seems that the term "culture" means a great many things to a great many people. Definitions of culture have ranged from as broad as, "The way we do things around here"[11] to as specific as . . . well, let's just suffice it to say that they can get complicated. Not surprisingly, the various definitions of organizational culture stem from how people have studied it. Sociologists study culture using a broad lens and anthropological research methods, like those applied to study tribes and civilizations. Psychologists tend to study culture and its effects on people using survey methods. In fact, many psychologists actually prefer the term "climate," but for our purposes, we'll use the two terms interchangeably. In this chapter, we define **organizational culture** as the shared social knowledge within an organization regarding the rules, norms, and values that shape the attitudes and behaviors of its employees.[12]

"I don't know how it started, either. All I know is that it's part of our corporate culture."

Source: © The New Yorker Collection 1994 Mick Stevens from cartoonbank.com.

This definition helps highlight a number of facets of organizational culture. First, culture is social knowledge among members of the organization. Employees learn about most important aspects of culture through other employees. This transfer of knowledge might be through explicit communication, simple observation, or other, less obvious methods. In addition, culture is shared knowledge, which means that members of the organization understand and have a degree of consensus regarding what the culture is. Second, culture tells employees what the rules, norms, and values are within the organization. What are the most important work outcomes to focus on? What behaviors are appropriate or inappropriate at work? How should a person act or dress while at work? Indeed, some cultures even go so far as to say how employees should act when they aren't at work. Third, organizational culture shapes and reinforces certain employee attitudes and behaviors by creating a system of control over employees.[13] There is evidence that your individual goals and values will grow over time to match those of the organization for which you work.[14] This development really isn't that hard to imagine, given how much time employees spend working inside an organization.

 16.1

What is organizational culture, and what are its components?

WHY DO SOME ORGANIZATIONS HAVE DIFFERENT CULTURES THAN OTHERS?

One of the most common questions people ask when you tell them where you are employed is, "So, tell me . . . what's it like there?" The description you use in your response is likely to have a lot to do with what the organization's culture is all about. In calculating your response to the question, you might consider describing the kinds of people who work at your company. More than likely, you will do your best to describe the work atmosphere on a regular day. Perhaps you will painstakingly describe the facilities you work in or how you feel the employees are treated. You might even go as far as to describe what it is that defines "success" at your company. All of those answers give clues that help organizational outsiders understand what a company is actually like. To give you a feel for the full range of potential answers to the "what's it like there?" question, it's necessary to review the facets of culture in more detail.

CULTURE COMPONENTS

There are three major components to any organization's culture: observable artifacts, espoused values, and basic underlying assumptions. You can understand the differences among these three components if you view culture like an onion, as in Figure 16-1. Some components of an organization's culture are readily apparent and observable, like the skin of an onion. However, other components are less observable to organizational outsiders or newcomers. Such outsiders can observe, interpret, and make conclusions based on what they see on the surface, but the inside remains a mystery until they can peel back the outside layers to gauge the values and assumptions that lie beneath. The sections that follow review the culture components in more detail.

OBSERVABLE ARTIFACTS. Observable artifacts are the manifestations of an organization's culture that employees can easily see or talk about. They supply the signals that employees interpret to gauge how they should act during the workday. Artifacts supply the primary means of transmitting an organization's culture to its workforce. It is difficult to overestimate the importance of artifacts, because they help show not only current employees but also potential employees, customers, shareholders, and investors what the organization is all about. There are six major types of artifacts: symbols, physical structures, language, stories, rituals, and ceremonies.[15]

Symbols can be found throughout an organization, from its corporate logo to the images it places on its Web site to the uniforms its employees wear. Think about what Nike's "swoosh" represents: speed, movement, velocity. What might that symbol convey about Nike's culture? Or consider Apple Computer's "apple" logo. That symbol brings to mind Newton's discovery of gravity under the apple tree, conveying the importance of innovation within Apple's culture. When you think of the words "dark suit, white shirt, tie," what company do you think of? For many, the symbol represents IBM because that represents the company's long-standing dress code. Even though that dress code hasn't been in place at IBM for 10 years, it still symbolizes a formal, bureaucratic, and professional culture. For more on IBM's culture, see our **OB at the Bookstore** feature.

FIGURE 16-1	The Three Components of Organizational Culture

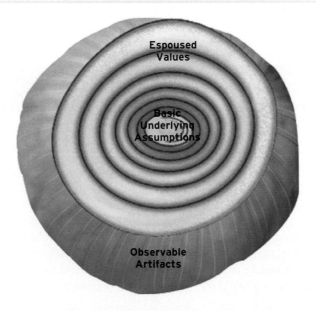

OB AT THE BOOKSTORE

WHO SAYS ELEPHANTS CAN'T DANCE?
by Louis V. Gerstner, Jr. (New York: Harper Business, 2002)

Until I came to IBM, I probably would have told you that culture was just one among several important elements in any organization's makeup and success—along with vision, strategy, marketing, financials, and the like . . . . I came to see, in my time at IBM, that culture isn't just one aspect of the game; it is the game. In the end, an organization is nothing more than the collective capacity of its people to create value.

With those words, Louis Gerstner, seen by many as one of the greatest CEOs of all time, sums up his view of what is important for success in organizations: Culture!

When Gerstner arrived on the scene as chairman and CEO of IBM in 1993, he felt like he had been transported back into the 1950s. At this moment in time, IBM was in a severe financial crisis and at the doorstep of bankruptcy. Gerstner was a force for change in the company over the following 10 years as he accomplished what no one thought he could, namely, transforming what was seen by many as the most rigid organization in the world. Needless to say, leading culture change is not easy. As one IBM executive said, "Reengineering is like starting a fire on your head and putting it out with a hammer."

Gerstner clearly demonstrates in the book that he understands how culture is created in the first place, how it is valuable, how it can become an impediment to change, and how to go about changing it. Gerstner speaks about how the observable artifacts of culture are important symbols and send messages to employees and customers alike. Gerstner made changes like removing the old "dark suit and tie" dress code and stopping the "special language" that IBMers understood but their customers did not. Most important though, he understood that espoused values and underlying assumptions are not the same. Gerstner puts it best: "You've probably found, as I have, that most companies say their cultures are about the same things—outstanding customer service, excellence, teamwork, shareholder value, responsible corporate behavior, and integrity. But, of course, these kinds of values don't necessarily translate into the same kind of behavior in all companies—how people actually go about their work, how they interact with one another, what motivates them. That's because . . . most of the really important rules aren't written down anywhere."

Physical structures also say a lot about a culture. Is the workplace open? Does top management work in a separate section of the building? Is the setting devoid of anything unique, or can employees express their personalities? Bloomberg, an information services, news, and media company based in New York, built its new headquarters in Manhattan primarily out of steel and glass, resembling what workers call a "beehive." It has no private offices, no cubicles, and even the conference rooms have glass walls. CEO Lex Fenwick sits on the third floor, surrounded by his sales and customer service staff. He believes this setup leads to

The ability to set up your own work space, as at the think tank IDEO, is a hallmark of an open corporate culture. Would this environment suit your working style?

instantaneous communication among employees.[16] IDEO, a creative think tank, also has an open office environment, though IDEO lets employees set up their offices however they like. When you walk around their work areas, you'll be walking underneath bicycles hanging over your head and crazy objects and toys in every direction.[17]

Language reflects the jargon, slang, and slogans used within the walls of an organization. Do you know what a CTR, CPC, or Crawler is? Chances are you don't. If you worked for Yahoo, however, those terms would be second nature to you. CTR stands for click-through rate, CPC stands for cost-per-click, and a Crawler is a computer program that gathers information from other Web sites. Home Depot maintains a "stack it high and watch it fly" slogan, which reflects its approach to sales. Yum Brands Inc., which owns Pizza Hut, Taco Bell, KFC, and other fast-food restaurants, expects employees to be "customer maniacs"[18]—language that conveys its culture for customer interaction.

Stories consist of anecdotes, accounts, legends, and myths that are passed down from cohort to cohort within an organization. When the London-based, global conglomerate Unilever purchased Ben & Jerry's Homemade Inc. in 2001, the Unilever chairman first walked into the Vermont-based company to a sight he didn't often see: All the employees were wearing togas![19] This story captures the cultural differences between Unilever and Ben & Jerry's and serves to illustrate the unique identity shared by the ice cream company's employees.

Rituals are the daily or weekly planned routines that occur in an organization. Employees at New Belgium Brewing in Colorado, home of Fat Tire Ale, receive a case of beer a week after a year on the job, conveying the importance of both employees and the company's product.[20] At UPS, every driver and package handler attends a mandatory "three-minute meeting" with their managers to help with communication. The 180-second time limit helps enforce the importance of punctuality in the UPS culture. The Men's Wearhouse pays managers quarterly bonuses when theft (referred to as "shrink") is kept low. That ritual sends a message that "when workers steal from you, they are stealing from themselves and their colleagues."[21]

Ceremonies are formal events, generally performed in front of an audience of organizational members. In the process of turning around the company, Continental Airlines held a ceremony to burn an employee-despised 800-page policy manual. Gordon Bethune, then-CEO of Continental, put together a task force that came up with a new 80-page manual.[22] Other types of ceremonies revolve around celebrations for meeting quality goals, reaching a certain level of profitability, or launching a new product.

ESPOUSED VALUES. Espoused values are the beliefs, philosophies, and norms that a company explicitly states. Espoused values can range from published documents, such as a company's vision or mission statement, to verbal statements made to employees by executives and managers. Examples of some of UPS's outward representations of espoused values can be found in Table 16-1. What do each of these statements tell you about UPS and what it cares about?

It is certainly important to draw a distinction between espoused values and enacted values. It is one thing for a company to outwardly say something is important; it is another thing for employees to consistently act in ways that support those espoused values. When a company holds to its espoused values over time and regardless of the situations it operates in, the values become more believable both to employees and outsiders. However, in times of economic downturns, staying true to espoused values is not always easy. Our opening example of Enron helps to illustrate the differences between espoused and enacted values.

TABLE 16-1   The Espoused Values of UPS

Below is a sample of some of the 37 values that spell out UPS's vision for managing its workforce. These values are spelled out in a "policy book" that is handed out to the company's management team.

1. We build our organization around people.
2. We place great value on diversity.
3. We treat our people fairly and without favoritism.
4. We insist upon integrity in our people.
5. We promote from within.
6. We promote the good health of our people.
7. We look for people who have potential for development.
8. We have meaningful discussions with our people .
9. We promote an open-door approach to managing people.
10. We respect each employee's point of view.
11. We encourage participation and suggestions.
12. We stress safety throughout our company.
13. We keep our buildings and equipment clean.
14. We expect our people to be neat in appearance.
15. We prohibit the use of company time, facilities, or materials for personal benefit.

Source: "UPS's 37 Principles for Managing People," *Workforce Management Online,* May 2005, www.workforce.com (Accessed February 24, 2007). Reprinted with permission. Copyright © 2005 Crain Communications Inc.

BASIC UNDERLYING ASSUMPTIONS. Basic underlying assumptions are taken-for-granted beliefs and philosophies that are so ingrained that employees simply act on them rather than questioning the validity of their behavior in a given situation.[23] These assumptions represent the deepest and least observable part of a culture and may not be consciously apparent, even to organizational veterans. Edgar Schein, one of the preeminent scholars on the topic of organizational culture, uses the example of safety in an engineering firm. He states, "In an occupation such as engineering, it would be inconceivable to deliberately design something that is unsafe; it is a taken-for-granted assumption that things should be safe."[24] Whatever a company's underlying assumptions are, its hidden beliefs are those that are the most likely to dictate employee behavior and affect employee attitudes. They are also the aspects of an organizational culture that are the most long-lasting and difficult to change.[25]

GENERAL CULTURE TYPES

What general and specific types can be used to describe an organization's culture?

If we can consider the combination of an organization's observable artifacts, espoused values, and underlying assumptions, we can begin to classify its culture along various dimensions. Of course, there are many different types of organizational cultures, just like there are many different types of personalities. Many researchers have tried to create general typologies that can be used to describe the culture of any organization. For instance, one popular general typology divides organizational culture along two dimensions: solidarity and sociability. Solidarity is the degree to which group members think and act alike, and sociability represents how friendly employees are to one another.[26] Figure 16-2 shows how we might describe organizations that are either high or low on these dimensions. Organizations that are low on both dimensions have a **fragmented culture** in which employees are distant and disconnected from one another. Organizations that have cultures in which employees think alike but aren't friendly to one another can be considered **mercenary cultures.** These types of organizations are likely to be very political, "what's in it for me"

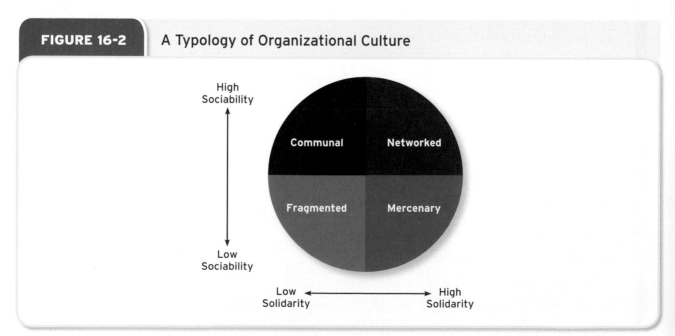

FIGURE 16-2   **A Typology of Organizational Culture**

Source: Adapted from R. Goffee and G. Jones, *The Character of a Corporation* (New York: Harper Business, 1998).

environments. Cultures in which all employees are friendly to one another, but everyone thinks differently and does his or her own thing, are **communal cultures.** Many highly creative organizations have a communal culture. Organizations with friendly employees who all think alike are **networked cultures.**

SPECIFIC CULTURE TYPES

The typology shown in Figure 16-2 is general enough to be applied to almost any organization. However, there are obviously other ways to classify an organization's culture. In fact, many organizations attempt to manipulate observable artifacts and espoused values to create specific cultures that help them achieve their organizational goals. Some of these specific cultures are more relevant in some industries than in others. Although the number of specific cultures an organization might strive for are virtually endless, we focus on four examples: customer service cultures, safety cultures, diversity cultures, and creativity cultures.

Many organizations try to create a **customer service culture** focused on service quality. After all, 65 percent of the gross domestic product in the United States is generated by service-based organizations.[27] Organizations that have successfully created a service culture have been shown to change employee attitudes and behaviors toward customers.[28] These changes in attitudes and behaviors then manifest themselves in higher levels of customer satisfaction and sales.[29] Figure 16-3 illustrates the process of creating a service culture and the effects it has on company results. Numerous companies claim that the sole reason for their continued existence is their ability to create a service culture in their organization when it wasn't originally present.[30] Other companies, such as Circuit City, have tried to reinvigorate customer service by recreating a service culture within their stores. After falling way behind rival Best Buy, the retailer has been inching its way back to respectability by making changes such as shifting its mostly commission-based workforce to an hourly pay rate. This shift was a big change for a company that for many years had maintained that commission-based salespeople provided better customer service. Circuit City also closed underperforming retailers and made a service culture its top priority at the stores that remained.[31]

It is not uncommon for manufacturing or medical companies to go through a string of accidents or injuries that potentially harm their employees. For these organizations, creating a **safety culture** is of paramount importance. There is a clear difference between organizations in terms of the degree to which safe behaviors at work are viewed as expected and valued.[32] A positive safety culture has been shown to reduce accidents and increase safety-based citizenship behaviors.[33] A safety culture also reduces treatment errors in medical settings.[34] GE recently instigated an investigation into some of

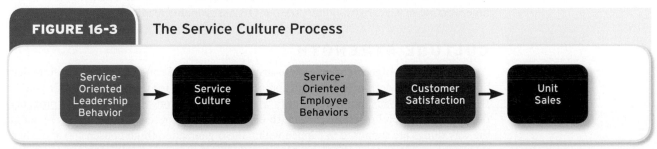

FIGURE 16-3 | The Service Culture Process

Service-Oriented Leadership Behavior → Service Culture → Service-Oriented Employee Behaviors → Customer Satisfaction → Unit Sales

Source: Adapted from B. Schneider, M.G. Ehrhart, D.M. Mayer, J.L. Saltz, and K. Niles-Jolly, "Understanding Organization–Customer Links in Service Settings," *Academy of Management Journal* 48 (2005), pp. 1017–32.

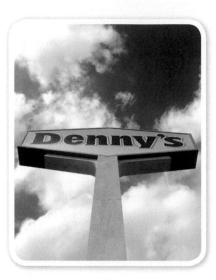

Denny's has worked hard to recover from lawsuits charging it discriminated against minorities. In the process it developed techniques to encourage diversity that other firms have now adopted.

its service centers that were suffering unacceptable levels of accidents and injuries. Plants that were having problems went through a process of energizing their safety cultures through a series of two-day meetings during which safety problems and potential solutions were identified. Although GE doesn't expect that all of its problems will be fixed overnight, it is so satisfied with the new culture created at these plants that it is working on rolling out similar programs in all of its 67 service centers across the United States.[35] As with many changes, it is very important that what management says about safety is also how it acts. One study found that employees were highly cynical of a safety program when they perceived a mismatch between espoused and enacted safety values by management.[36]

There are a number of reasons why an organization might want to foster a **diversity culture.** What images come to mind when you think of Denny's? Do you think of the nation's largest family-style, full-service restaurant chain in the country and the Grand Slam breakfast, or do you think of race discrimination? Although the lawsuits that charged company discrimination against African Americans were settled back in 1994, the stigma of Denny's discrimination complaints still lingers. Since 1994, Denny's has maintained a position within the company of Chief Diversity Officer whose sole responsibility is to help create a culture of diversity. Denny's has since become a prime example of how to aggressively lead a charge toward a diversity culture. What used to be an all-white, all-male organization has tried to transform itself by hiring a large number of new minority managers and franchise owners, replacing half of the all-male board of directors with women, conducting diversity sensitivity training sessions, and performing a whole host of other symbolic actions. Many of the techniques used by Denny's are now recognized as key elements in successful corporate diversity initiatives.[37]

Given the importance of new ideas and innovation in many industries, it is understandable that some organizations focus on fostering a **creativity culture.** Creativity cultures have been shown to affect both the quantity and quality of creative ideas within an organization.[38] Google recently put policies in place that will allow its engineers to spend 20 percent of their working time pursuing projects that they feel passionate about to foster innovation at the organization.[39] In part to foster a culture of creativity, Pfizer Canada has banned all e-mails and voice mails on weekends and after 6:00 p.m. on weekdays to keep their employees fresh while they are on the job. The company feels this 12-hour break has led to a higher-quality flow of ideas and provided a morale boost to go along with it.[40] To see whether you've spent time working in a creativity culture, see our **OB Assessments** feature.

CULTURE STRENGTH

Although most organizations seem to strive for one, not all companies have a culture that creates a sense of definite norms and appropriate behaviors for their employees. If you've worked for a company and can't identify whether it has a strong culture or not, it probably doesn't. A high level of **culture strength** exists when employees definitively agree about the way things are supposed to happen within the organization (high consensus) and when their subsequent behaviors are consistent with those expectations (high intensity).[41] As

OB ASSESSMENTS

CREATIVITY CULTURE

Have you experienced a creativity culture? This assessment is designed to measure two facets of that type of culture. Think of your current job, or the last job that you held (even if it was a part-time or summer job). If you haven't worked, think of a current or former student group that developed strong norms for how tasks should be done. Answer each question using the response scale provided. Then subtract your answers to the bold-faced questions from 6, with the difference being your new answer for that question. For example, if your original answer for question 7 was "4," your new answer is "2" (6 − 4). Then sum up for your scores for the two facets.

1 STRONGLY DISAGREE	2 DISAGREE	3 UNCERTAIN	4 AGREE	5 STRONGLY AGREE

1. New ideas are readily accepted here. _____

2. This company is quick to respond when changes need to be made. _____

3. Management here is quick to spot the need to do things differently. _____

4. This organization is very flexible; it can quickly change procedures to meet new conditions and solve problems as they arise. _____

5. People in this organization are always searching for new ways of looking at problems. _____

6. It is considered extremely important here to follow the rules. _____

7. **People can ignore formal procedures and rules if it helps to get the job done.** _____

8. Everything has to be done by the book. _____

9. **It is not necessary to follow procedures to the letter around here.** _____

10. **Nobody gets too upset if people break the rules around here.** _____

SCORING

Innovation: Sum up items 1-5. _____
Formalization: Sum up items 6-10. _____

INTERPRETATION

If your score is 22 or above for either facet, your organization or workgroup is high on that particular dimension. Creative cultures tend to be high on innovation and low on formalization. So if your score was 22 or above for innovation and 21 or below for formalization, then chances are you've experienced a strong creativity culture.

Source: M.G. Patterson, M.A. West, V.J. Shackleton, J.F. Dawson, R. Lawthom, S. Maitlis, D.L. Robinson, and A.M. Wallace, "Validating the Organizational Climate Measure: Links to Managerial Practices, Productivity and Innovation," *Journal of Organizational Behavior* 26 (2005), pp. 379–408. Copyright © 2005 John Wiley & Sons Limited. Reproduced with permission.

shown in Figure 16-4, a strong culture serves to unite and direct employees. Weak cultures exist when employees disagree about the way things are supposed to be or what is expected of them, meaning that there is nothing to unite or direct their attitudes and actions.

Strong cultures take a long time to develop and are very difficult to change. Individuals working within strong cultures are typically very aware of it. However, this discussion brings us to an important point: "Strong" cultures are not always "good" cultures. Strong cultures guide employee attitudes and behaviors, but that doesn't always mean that they guide them toward the most successful organizational outcomes. As such, it is useful to recognize some of the positive and negative aspects of having a strong organizational culture. Table 16-2 lists some of the advantages and disadvantages.[42] You might have noticed that all of the advantages in the left-hand column of Table 16-2 allow the organization to become more efficient at whatever aspect of culture is strong within the organization. The right-hand column's disadvantages all lead toward an organization's inability to adapt.

In some cases, the culture of an organization is not really strong or weak. Instead, there might be **subcultures** that unite a smaller subset of the organization's employees. These subgroups may be created because there is a strong leader in one area of the company that engenders different norms and values or because different divisions in a company act independently and create their own cultures. As shown in Figure 16-4, subcultures exist when the overall organizational culture is supplemented by another culture governing a more specific set of employees. Subcultures are more likely to exist in large organizations than they are in small companies.[43] Most organizations don't mind having subcultures, to

16.3

What is a strong culture, and what makes a culture strong? Is a strong culture necessarily good?

FIGURE 16-4   **Culture Strength and Subcultures**

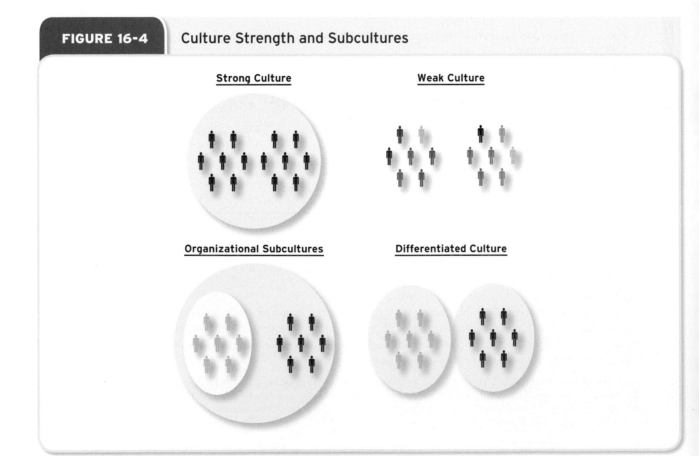

TABLE 16-2	Pros and Cons of a Strong Culture	
ADVANTAGES OF A STRONG CULTURE	**DISADVANTAGES OF A STRONG CULTURE**	
Differentiates the organization from others	Makes merging with another organization more difficult	
Allows employees to identify themselves with the organization	Attracts and retains similar kinds of employees, thereby limiting diversity of thought	
Facilitates desired behaviors among employees	Can be "too much of a good thing" if it creates extreme behaviors among employees	
Creates stability within the organization	Makes adapting to the environment more difficult	

the degree that they do not interfere with the values of the overall culture. In fact, subcultures can be very useful for organizations if there are certain areas of the organization that have different demands and needs for their employees.[44] However, when their values don't match those of the larger organization, we call subcultures **countercultures.** Countercultures can sometimes serve a useful purpose by challenging the values of the overall organization or signifying the need for change.[45] In extreme cases however, countercultures can split the organization's culture right down the middle, resulting in the differentiated culture in Figure 16-4.

MAINTAINING AN ORGANIZATIONAL CULTURE

Clearly an organization's culture can be described in many ways, from espoused values and underlying assumptions, to general dimensions such as solidarity or sociability, to more specific types such as service cultures or safety cultures. No matter how we describe an organization's culture, however, that culture will be put to the test when an organization's founders and original employees begin to recruit and hire new members. If those new members do not fit the culture, then the culture may become weakened or differentiated. However, two processes can conspire to help keep cultures strong: attraction–selection–attrition and socialization.

16.4

How do organizations maintain their culture? How do they change it?

ATTRACTION–SELECTION–ATTRITION (ASA). The **ASA framework** holds that potential employees will be attracted to organizations whose cultures match their own personality, meaning that some potential job applicants won't apply due to a perceived lack of fit.[46] In addition, organizations will select candidates based on whether their personalities fit the culture, further weeding out potential "misfits." Finally, those people who still don't fit will either be unhappy or ineffective when working in the organization, which leads to attrition (i.e., voluntary or involuntary turnover).

Several companies can provide an example of ASA in action. FedEx has worked hard to create a culture of ethics. The executives at FedEx believe that a strong ethical culture will attract ethical employees who will strengthen moral behavior at FedEx.[47] The Cheesecake Factory believes that selection is where maintaining a culture begins. Management suggests that its heavily service-oriented culture calls for certain types of employees. They believe that teaching people how to perform regular restaurant duties is possible, but teaching people to have the right personality and attitudes is not. As a company, it consistently tries to identify the traits that allow employees to thrive in a Cheesecake Factory environment.[48] Of course, attraction and selection processes do not always align employees' personalities with organizational culture—one reason voluntary and involuntary turnover occurs in every organization.

SOCIALIZATION. In addition to taking advantage of attraction–selection–attrition, organizations also maintain an organizational culture by shaping and molding new employees. Starting a new job with a company is a stressful, complex, and challenging undertaking for both employees and organizations.[49] In reality, no outsider can fully grasp or understand the culture of an organization simply by looking at artifacts visible from outside the company. A complete understanding of organizational culture is a process that happens over time. **Socialization** is the primary process by which employees learn the social knowledge that enables them to understand and adapt to the organization's culture. It is a process that begins before an employee starts work and doesn't end until an employee leaves the organization.[50] What is it that an employee needs to learn and adapt to in order to be socialized into his or her new role within an organization? Most of the important information can be grouped into six dimensions, highlighted in Figure 16-5.[51] Research shows that each of these six dimensions is an important area in the process of socialization. Each has unique contributions to job performance, organizational commitment, and person–organization fit.[52]

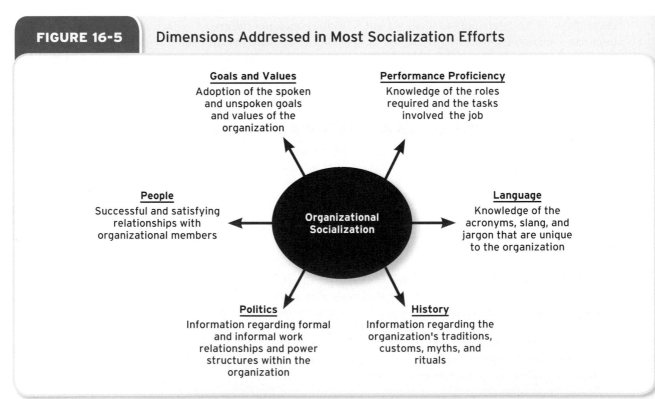

FIGURE 16-5   Dimensions Addressed in Most Socialization Efforts

Goals and Values
Adoption of the spoken and unspoken goals and values of the organization

Performance Proficiency
Knowledge of the roles required and the tasks involved the job

People
Successful and satisfying relationships with organizational members

Organizational Socialization

Language
Knowledge of the acronyms, slang, and jargon that are unique to the organization

Politics
Information regarding formal and informal work relationships and power structures within the organization

History
Information regarding the organization's traditions, customs, myths, and rituals

Source: G.T. Chao, A.M. O'Leary-Kelly, S. Wolf, H.J. Klein, and P.D. Gardner, "Organizational Socialization: Its Content and Consequences," *Journal of Applied Psychology* 79 (1994), pp. 730–43. Copyright © 1994 by the American Psychological Association. Adapted with permission. No further reproduction or distribution is permitted without written permission from the American Psychological Association.

Socialization happens in three relatively distinct stages. The **anticipatory stage** happens prior to an employee spending even one second on the job. It starts the moment a potential employee hears the name of the organization. When you see the company name "Microsoft," what does it make you think about? What are the images that come to your mind? Anticipatory socialization begins as soon as a potential employee develops an image of what it must be like to work for a given company. The bulk of the information acquired during this stage occurs during the recruitment and selection processes employees go through prior to joining an organization. Relevant information includes the way employees are treated during the recruitment process, the things that organizational insiders tell them about the organization, and any other information employees acquire about what the organization is like and what working there entails.

The **encounter stage** begins the day an employee starts work. There are some things about an organization and its culture that can only be learned once a person becomes an organizational insider. During this stage, new employees compare the information they acquired as outsiders during the anticipatory stage with what the organization is really like now that they are insiders. To the degree that the information in the two stages is similar, employees will have a smoother time adjusting to the organization. Problems occur when the two sets of information don't quite match. This mismatch of information is called **reality shock.** Reality shock is best exemplified by hearing an employee say something to the effect of, "Working at this company is not nearly what I expected it to be." Surveys suggest that as many as one-third of new employees leave an organization within the first 90 days as a result of unmet expectations.[53] The goal of the organization's socialization efforts should be to minimize reality shock as much as possible. We'll describe some ways that organizations can do this effectively in our Application section that concludes this chapter.

The final stage of socialization is one of **understanding and adaptation.** During this stage, newcomers come to learn the content areas of socialization and internalize the norms and expected behaviors of the organization. The important part of this stage is change on the part of the employee. By looking back at the content areas of socialization in Figure 16-5, you can begin to picture what a perfectly socialized employee looks like. The employee has adopted the goals and values of the organization, understands what the organization has been through, and can converse with others in the organization using technical language and specific terms that only insiders would understand. In addition, the employee enjoys and gets along with other employees in the organization, knows who to go to in order to make things happen, and understands and can perform the key functions of his or her job. Talk about the perfect employee! Needless to say, that is quite a bit of information to gain—it is not a process that happens overnight. Some would say that this last stage of socialization never truly ends, as an organization's culture continues to change and evolve over time.[54] However, organizations also know that the more quickly and effectively an employee is socialized, the sooner that employee becomes a productive worker within the organization.

It is important to note that the length of the socialization process varies depending on the characteristics of the employee, not just the company. For example, some employees might progress more rapidly through the stages because of the knowledge they possess, their ability to recognize cultural cues, or their adaptability to their environment. In fact, there is growing evidence that proactivity on the part of employee being socialized has a significant effect on socialization outcomes.[55] Some organizations might help their employees socialize more quickly because they have stronger cultures or cultures that are more easily understandable. The biggest difference though is that some organizations simply work harder at socializing their employees than others.

CHANGING AN ORGANIZATIONAL CULTURE

Given all the effort it takes to create and maintain a culture, changing a culture once one has been established is perhaps even more difficult. In fact, estimates put the rate of successful major culture change at less than 20 percent.[56] Mark Fields, head of Ford Motor Company's North and South American auto operations, knows how difficult it can be to change the culture at an organization. Prior CEOs at Ford have tried, unsuccessfully, to change a culture that current employees call "toxic," "cautious," "hierarchical," and "cliquish." To instigate a change, Fields took drastic measures, including purposefully creating a sense of stress and crisis among employees. Ford is calling its new attempt at major culture change the "Way Forward." In the "Way Forward" war room (where Fields and colleagues map out the drastic changes the company needs to make), big sheets of white paper hang on the wall reading, "Culture eats strategy for breakfast," and "Culture is unspoken, but powerful. It develops over time—difficult to change." Fields has gone to many extremes to create a climate for change among those responsible for helping him with the plans to overhaul Ford's culture. He has banned PowerPoint presentations, uses phrases such as "change or die" in meetings, and makes employees wear blue wristbands with "Red, White and Bold" inscripted on them, signifying a new Ford.[57] In practice, there are two primary ways to change a culture: changes in leadership and mergers or acquisitions.

CHANGES IN LEADERSHIP. There is perhaps no bigger driver of culture than the leaders and top executives of organizations. Just as the founders and originators of organizations set the tone and develop the culture of a new company, subsequent CEOs and presidents leave their mark on the culture. Many times, leaders are expected simply to sustain the culture that has already been created.[58] At other times, leaders have to be the driving force for change as the environment around the organization shifts. This expectation is one of the biggest reasons organizations change their top leadership. For example, Nortel Networks recently hired two former Cisco executives into the roles of chief operating officer and chief technology officer. It is Nortel's hope that these executives will help bring some of Cisco's culture of aggressiveness to Nortel and thus allow it to compete more effectively in the high-technology industry environment.[59]

MERGERS AND ACQUISITIONS. Merging two companies with two distinct cultures is a surefire way to change the culture in an organization. The problem is that there is just no way to know what the culture will look like after the merger takes place. What the new culture will resemble is a function of both the strength of the two cultures involved in the merger and how similar they are to each other.[60] Ideally, a new culture would be created out of a compromise in which the best of both companies is represented by the new culture. There are many stories that have arisen from the mergers of companies with very different cultures: AOL/Time Warner, Exxon/Mobil, HP/Compaq, and RJR/Nabisco, to name a few. Unfortunately, very few of these stories are good ones. Mergers rarely result in the strong culture that managers hope will appear when they make the decision to merge. In fact, most merged companies operate under a differentiated culture for an extended period of time. Some of them never really adopt a new identity, and when they do, many of them are seen as failures by the outside world. This perception is especially true in global mergers, in which each of the companies not only has a different organizational culture but is from a different country as well. See our **OB Internationally** box for more details.

Merging two different cultures has major effects on the attitudes and behaviors of organizational employees. Companies merge for many different strategic reasons, and though many managers and executives may realize its importance, whether the cultures will match is rarely the deciding criterion.[65] Slightly less troublesome but still a major hurdle to overcome are acquisitions. In most instances, the company doing the acquiring has a dominant culture to which the other is expected to adapt. A recent example is the acquisition of Mail

OB INTERNATIONALLY

As mentioned in the chapter, there is perhaps no more perilous journey for a company to take than merging with or acquiring another large firm. These problems are exacerbated when the two companies are from different countries. As few as 30 percent of international mergers and acquisitions create shareholder value.[61] Nevertheless, 2006 set a record pace for global mergers and acquisitions.[62] Why is this the case? Hopefully, we've illustrated the inherent difficulties of simply trying to merge two different cultures when the organizations are in the same country. These cultural differences can be magnified when international culture plays a role as well. Chances are good that your experiences in college have shown you that different countries have different cultures, just like organizations. People that come from different countries tend to view the world differently and have different sets of values as well. For instance, DaimlerChrysler bought a controlling stake in Mitsubishi Motors, thinking that a strong alliance between the two would result in high levels of value for both companies. Unfortunately, this merger was recently broken up for reasons that have been attributed to international culture differences between the two firms (Japan vs. U.S. and Germany).[63] Japanese managers had a tendency to avoid "unpleasant truths" and stay away from major change efforts—a tendency that DaimlerChrysler never confronted.

There are many stories of failed international mergers, and one of the greatest reasons for them is that corporations do not recognize the impact that national culture differences (in addition to organizational culture differences) have on their ability to be successful. One such merger that doesn't intend to fall victim to this issue is the creation of a joint venture between telecommunication giants Nokia (Finland) and Siemens (Germany). This merger between two very different firms is projected to earn annual sales of $20 billion. The CEOs of the two companies (Siemens's Klaus Kleinfeld and Nokia's Olli-Pekka Kallasvuo) are determined not to let differences in national or organizational cultures cause the merger fatal problems. Toward this end, cultural integration has been in the forefront of their minds. Although much of the main business will be located in Germany, headquarters for the new company will be in Helsinki. Both CEOs are determined for each company to learn from the other.[64]

Boxes Etc. by UPS. Strategically, the acquisition had many advantages and was supposed to allow UPS to compete better with FedEx and the U.S. Postal Service. However, the culture clash between the efficiency and rigidness of UPS and the entrepreneurial spirit of Mail Boxes Etc. franchisees has caused UPS some major headaches.[66] We've noted how difficult it is just to get one person to adapt to an established culture through the socialization process. Can you imagine how difficult it is to change an entire organization at the same time? See our **OB on Screen** feature for one potential answer.

SUMMARY: WHY DO SOME ORGANIZATIONS HAVE DIFFERENT CULTURES THAN OTHERS?

So why do some organizations have different cultures than others? As shown in Figure 16-6, attraction–selection–attrition processes, socialization, changes in leadership, and mergers and acquisitions shape the three components of organizational culture: basic underlying assumptions, espoused values, and observable artifacts. Specific combinations of those culture components then give rise to both general and specific culture types. For example, cultures can be categorized on the basis of solidarity and sociability into

OB ON SCREEN

IN GOOD COMPANY

I'm not sure I understand what you are talking about. . . . What I mean is, what do computers have to do with sports? Are you literally saying that there should be a section in the magazine about computers? Who's going to want to read that?

By interjecting those words, Dan Forman (Dennis Quaid) interrupts Globecom CEO Teddy K (Malcom McDowell) in the middle of a divisionwide speech during *In Good Company* (Dir. Paul Wietz, Universal, 2005). Globecom purchased *Sports America* magazine in a hostile takeover, hoping that the company would be a cash cow. However, problems arise when the two cultures of the companies don't mesh. Dan's words at the meeting speak volumes about what every *Sports America* employee is thinking but don't say out of fear for their jobs: "We simply don't fit the Globecom culture!"

Teddy K's Globecom is a no-holds barred, dog-eat-dog, profit-means-everything type of firm whose employees use language like "synergy" to describe what leads to success. In fact, it very much resembles a mercenary culture. One telling example of the culture emerges when Globecom appoints an inexperienced, 26-year old Carter Duryea (Topher Grace) to take 51-year-old Dan Forman's place because the CEO remembered that Carter had done "something with cell phones." Carter soon finds that *Sports America* is a more traditional, family-oriented company that values employees and relationships with customers. His fast-talking, smooth-moving ways don't exactly go over well with his new subordinates. And it really doesn't help when he starts dating Dan's daughter (Scarlett Johansson).

The lack of fit between Globecom and *Sports America* isn't unlike many acquisitions that take place in corporate America. Two very different cultures that value different things are thrown together for the sake of "potential." Carter is essentially expected to change the *Sports America* culture to fit with Globecom. However, he actually finds that he likes the *Sports America* culture much better, as it seems to have a better "fit" with his own personality. In the end, the culture clash between the two firms is too much, and Globecom sells *Sports America*. You'll have to rent the movie to find out what happens to Dan and Carter.

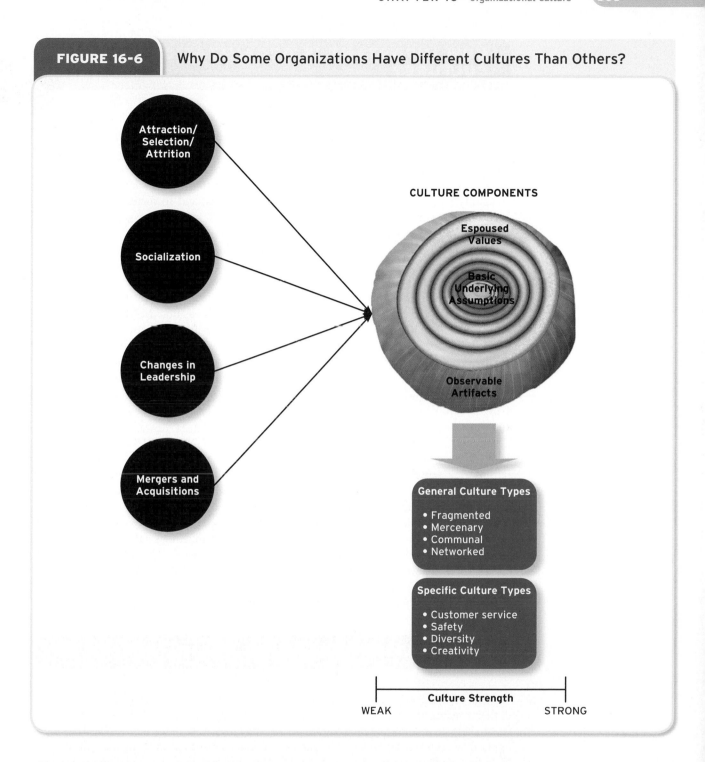

FIGURE 16-6   Why Do Some Organizations Have Different Cultures Than Others?

fragmented, mercenary, communal, and networked types. Cultures can also be categorized into more specific types such as customer service, safety, diversity, and creativity. Finally, those general and specific types can be further classified according to the strength of the culture. Taken together, these processes explain "what it's like" within the hallways of a given organization.

HOW IMPORTANT IS ORGANIZATIONAL CULTURE?

Normally, this section is where we summarize the importance of organizational culture by describing how it affects job performance and organizational commitment—the two outcomes in our integrative model of OB. However (similar to organizational structure in Chapter 15), it's difficult to summarize the importance of culture in this way because there are so many different types and dimensions of the concept. High solidarity cultures, high sociability cultures, diversity cultures, creativity cultures, and so forth all have different effects on performance and commitment—effects that likely vary across different types of organizations and industries.

 16.5

What is person-organization fit? How does fitting with an organization's culture affect job performance and organizational commitment?

Regardless of the type of culture we're talking about however, one concept remains important for any employee in any business: fit. Think for a moment about working for an organization whose culture doesn't match your own values. Maybe you work for an organization that produces a product that you don't believe in or that might be harmful to others, such as Phillip Morris, Budweiser, or Harrah's casinos. Maybe your employer is an organization that expects you to perform questionable behaviors from an ethical standpoint or produces a product that is of poor quality. **Person–organization fit** is the degree to which a person's personality and values match the culture of an organization. Employees judge fit by thinking about the values they prioritize the most, then judging whether the organization shares those values. Table 16-3 provides a set of values that many people have used to judge fit. Which of these values would you say are the most important to you?

A recent meta-analysis illustrated the importance of person–organization fit to employees.[67] When employees feel that their values and personality match those of the organization, they experience higher levels of *job satisfaction* and feel less *stress* about their day-to-day tasks. They also feel higher levels of *trust* toward their managers. Taken together, those results illustrate why person–organization fit is so highly correlated with organizational commitment, one of the two outcomes in our integrative model of OB (see Figure 16-7). When employees feel they fit with their organization's culture, they are much more likely to develop an emotional attachment to the company. The effects of fit on job performance are weaker however. In general, person–organization fit is more related to citizenship behaviors than task performance. Employees who sense a good fit are therefore more likely to help their colleagues and "go the extra mile" to benefit the company.

APPLICATION: MANAGING SOCIALIZATION

Most organizations recognize the importance of having employees adapt to the culture of their organization quickly. Luckily, there are a number of actions that organizations can take to help their employees adapt from the first day they walk in the door. Table 16-4 highlights some of the different tactics organizations can use when socializing their employees. Note that companies can take two very different approaches to the socialization process. The left-hand column represents a view of socialization in which the goal of the process is to have newcomers adapt to the organization's culture. This view assumes that the organization has a strong culture and definite norms and values that it wants employees to adopt, which is not always the case. Some organizations don't have a strong culture that they

TABLE 16-3	Values Used to Judge Fit with an Organizational Culture

PERSONAL AND CULTURAL VALUES

Flexibility	Adaptability
Stability	Predictability
Being innovative	Take advantage of opportunities
A willingness to experiment	Risk taking
Being careful	Autonomy
Being rule oriented	Being analytical
Paying attention to detail	Being precise
Being team oriented	Sharing information freely
Emphasizing a single culture	Being people oriented
Fairness	Respect for the individual's rights
Tolerance	Informality
Being easy going	Being calm
Being supportive	Being aggressive
Decisiveness	Action orientation
Taking initiative	Being reflective
Achievement orientation	Being demanding
Taking individual responsibility	High expectations for performance
Opportunities for growth	High pay for good performance
Security of employment	Offers praise for good performance
Low level of conflict	Confronting conflict directly
Developing friends at work	Fitting in
Working in collaboration with others	Enthusiasm for the job
Working long hours	Not being constrained by rules
Having an emphasis on quality	Being distinctive from others
Having a good reputation	Being socially responsible
Being results oriented	Having a clear guiding philosophy
Being competitive	Being highly organized

Source: C.A. O'Reilly, J.A. Chatman, and D.F. Caldwell, "People and Organizational Culture: A Profile Comparison Approach to Assessing Person–Organization Fit," *Academy of Management Journal* 34 (1991), pp. 487–516. Copyright © 1991 Academy of Management. Reproduced via permission from Copyright Clearance Center.

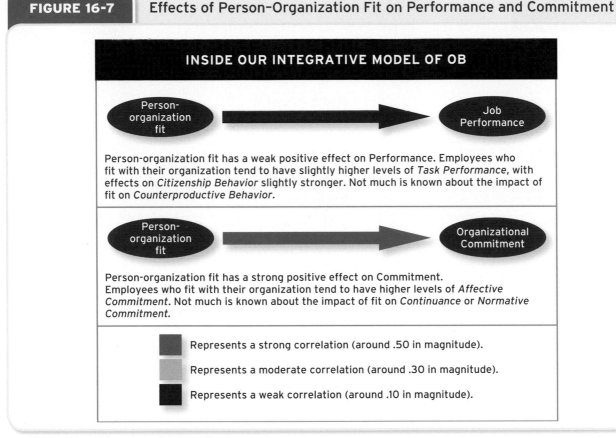

FIGURE 16-7   Effects of Person–Organization Fit on Performance and Commitment

Sources: A.L. Kristof-Brown, R.D. Zimmerman, and E.C. Johnson, "Consequences of Individuals' Fit at Work: A Meta-Analysis of Person–Job, Person–Organization, Person–Group, and Person–Supervisor Fit," *Personnel Psychology* 58 (2005), pp. 281–342. Reprinted with permission of Blackwell Publishing.

want employees to adapt to or they might be trying to change their culture and want new employees to come in and "shake things up." The socialization tactics listed in the right-hand column of Table 16-4 might be more appropriate in such circumstances. In addition to the socialization tactics listed in the table, there are three other major ways in which organizations routinely and effectively help speed up the socialization process of new-comers: realistic job previews, orientation programs, and mentoring.

REALISTIC JOB PREVIEWS. One of the most inexpensive and effective ways of reducing early turnover among new employees is the use of **realistic job previews.**[68] Realistic job previews (RJPs) occur during the anticipatory stage of socialization during the recruitment process. These RJPs involve making sure a potential employee has an accurate picture of what working for an organization is going to be like by providing both the positive *and* the negative aspects of the job.[69] Kal Tire, a leading Canadian automotive retail outlet, allows job candidates to spend an entire day inside the company becoming familiar with the organization and the job they are applying for. By allowing applicants to see what the organization's idea of customer service is and the job demands of road tire repairs, Kal Tire is effectively reducing the likelihood of significant reality shock and shortening the encounter stage that generally accompanies initial employment.[70]

 16.6

What steps can organizations take to make sure that newcomers will fit with their culture?

TABLE 16-4	Tactics Organizations Use to Socialize New Employees

TACTICS DESIGNED TO <u>ENCOURAGE</u> ADAPTATION TO THE ORGANIZATION'S CULTURE	TACTICS DESIGNED TO <u>DISCOURAGE</u> ADAPTATION TO THE ORGANIZATION'S CULTURE
Orient new employees along with a group of other new employees.	Orient new employees by themselves.
Put newcomers through orientation apart from current organizational members.	Allow newcomers to interact with current employees while they are being oriented.
Provide hurdles that are required to be met prior to organizational membership.	Allow organizational membership regardless of whether any specific requirements have been met.
Provide role models for newcomers.	Use no examples of what an employee is supposed to be like.
Constantly remind newcomers that they are now part of a group and that this new group helps define who they are.	Constantly affirm to newcomers that they are to be themselves and that they were chosen for the organization based on who they are.

Source: Adapted from G.R. Jones, "Socialization Tactics, Self-Efficacy, and Newcomers' Adjustments to Organizations," *Academy of Management Journal* 29 (1986), pp. 262–79; J. Van Maanen and E.H. Schein, "Toward a Theory of Organizational Socialization," *Research in Organizational Behavior* 1 (1979), pp. 209–64.

ORIENTATION PROGRAMS. One effective way to start the socialization process is by having new employees attend some form of **newcomer orientation** session. Apparently most organizations agree, given that 64–93 percent of all organizations use some form of orientation training process.[71] Not all orientation programs are alike however, and different types of orientation training can be more effective than others.[72] Orientation programs have been shown to be effective transmitters of socialization content, such that those employees who complete orientation have higher levels of satisfaction, commitment, and performance than those who don't.[73] General Motors has a unique orientation program set up for its new hires in the Michigan area, called JumpStart. The program is designed to indoctrinate new employees into the GM culture, which GM believes will allow these employees to become productive much more quickly. Each new employee is able to join up to five different committees that represent a different aspect of GM's culture, in which they learn about key values, network with employees from different areas of the country, and interact with business leaders.[74]

MENTORING. One of the most popular pieces of advice given to college students as they begin their careers is that they need to find a mentor or coach within their organization.[75] **Mentoring** is a process by which a junior-level employee (protégé) develops a deep and long-lasting relationship with a more senior-level employee (mentor) within the organization. The mentor can provide social knowledge, resources, and psychological support to the protégé both at the beginning of employment and as the protégé continues his or her career with the company. Mentoring has always existed in companies on an informal basis. However, as organizations continue to learn about the strong benefits of these relationships, they are more frequently instituting mentoring programs that formally match newcomers with mentors.[76] Formal programs allow the company to provide consistent information, train mentors, and ensure that all newcomers have the opportunity to develop one of these fruitful relationships. The Chubb Group of insurance companies based in New Jersey plans to start a group mentoring program among female employees in which multiple protégés meet regularly with multiple mentors.[77] This process has worked well for Budco, a marketing services and distribution firm that works with GM and Disney, which pairs four protégés with two mentors and has them meet twice a month. Group mentoring at the 850-employee company has significantly reduced turnover among new hires.[78] Mentoring does not just occur in business organizations, however. See our **OB for Students** feature for a discussion of mentoring for university students.

OB FOR STUDENTS

What does culture mean for you as a student? Think back on all the things you had to learn and all the ambiguity you faced during your first semester in college. Just as organizational newcomers experience reality shock when they enter an organization, so do freshmen when they initially enter the university culture. Just as organizations have a culture that affects employees, universities have a culture that affects students. One recent study at a university investigated whether it was worthwhile to help socialize students in much the same way that organizations socialize new employees. The university set up a mentoring program to help facilitate the transition toward being a successful student.

As shown in the diagram below, whether a freshman was provided a mentor and the quality of the relationship he or she had with that mentor positively affected both satisfaction with and commitment to the university. In turn, levels of satisfaction with and commitment to the university had positive effects on the student's intention to graduate.

Of course, many of you are now wondering why your university didn't do this for you! Many of you probably had some type of informal mentor to rely on to some degree. Some of you, however, might have lacked such a resource. That disadvantage explains why formal mentoring programs can be important: Formal programs help ensure equal access for everyone. If your university doesn't have a formal mentoring program or orientation session, you might consider being an informal mentor to an incoming freshman.

Source: Adapted from R.J. Sanchez, T.N. Bauer, and M.E. Paronto, "Peer-Mentoring Freshmen: Implications for Satisfaction, Commitment, and Retention to Graduation," *Academy of Management Learning and Education* 5 (2006), pp. 25–37.

TAKEAWAYS

16.1 Organizational culture is the shared social knowledge within an organization regarding the rules, norms, and values that shape the attitudes and behaviors of its employees. There are three components of organizational culture: observable artifacts, espoused values, and basic underlying assumptions. Observable artifacts include symbols, physical structures, language, stories, rituals, and ceremonies.

16.2 An organization's culture can be described on dimensions such as solidarity and sociability to create four general culture types: networked, communal, fragmented, and mercenary. Organizations often strive to create a more specific cultural emphasis, as in customer service cultures, safety cultures, diversity cultures, and creativity cultures.

16.3 Strong cultures have the ability to influence employee behaviors and attitudes. Strong cultures exist when employees agree on the way things are supposed to happen and their behaviors are consistent with those expectations. Strong cultures are not necessarily good or bad. Generally, a culture's effectiveness depends on how well it matches the company's outside environment. To this degree, adaptive cultures can be very useful.

16.4 Organizations maintain their cultures through attraction, selection, and attrition processes and socialization practices. Organizations change their cultures by changing their leadership or through mergers and acquisitions.

16.5 Person–organization fit is the degree to which a person's values and personality match the culture of the organization. Person–organization fit has a weak positive effect on job performance and a strong positive effect on organizational commitment.

16.6 There are a number of practices organizations can utilize to improve the socialization of new employees, including realistic job previews, orientation programs, and mentoring.

KEY TERMS

- Organizational culture — p. 546
- Observable artifacts — p. 548
- Symbols — p. 548
- Physical structures — p. 549
- Language — p. 550
- Stories — p. 550
- Rituals — p. 550
- Ceremonies — p. 550
- Espoused values — p. 551
- Basic underlying assumptions — p. 552
- Fragmented cultures — p. 552
- Mercenary cultures — p. 552
- Communal cultures — p. 553
- Networked cultures — p. 553
- Customer service culture — p. 553
- Safety culture — p. 553
- Diversity culture — p. 554
- Creativity culture — p. 554
- Culture strength — p. 554
- Subcultures — p. 556
- Countercultures — p. 557
- ASA framework — p. 557
- Socialization — p. 558
- Anticipatory stage — p. 559
- Encounter stage — p. 559
- Reality shock — p. 559
- Understanding and adaptation — p. 559
- Person–organization fit — p. 564
- Realistic job previews — p. 566
- Newcomer orientations — p. 567
- Mentoring — p. 567

DISCUSSION QUESTIONS

16.1 Have you or a family member worked for an organization that you would consider to have a strong culture? If so, what made the culture strong? Did you or they enjoy working there? What do you think led to that conclusion?

16.2 Is it possible for an employee to have personal values that are inconsistent with the values of the organization? If so, how is this inconsistency likely to affect the employee's behavior and attitudes while at work?

16.3 If you had to describe the culture of your university, what would it be like? What observable artifacts are present to be perceived by students? Are there any underlying assumptions that guide your behavior at your university?

16.4 How can two companies with very different cultures that operate in the same industry both be successful? Shouldn't one company's culture automatically be a better fit for the environment?

16.5 If an organization wanted to foster a diversity culture, what steps might management take to ensure that employees will support the new culture? What observable artifacts might a company change to instill this culture?

16.6 When you think of the U.S. Postal Service's culture, what kinds of words come to mind? Where do these impressions come from? Do you think your impressions are accurate? What has the potential to make them inaccurate?

16.7 Think about the last job you started. What are some unique things that companies might do to reduce the amount of reality shock that new employees encounter? Are these methods likely to be expensive?

CASE   GENERAL ELECTRIC AND ENRON

General Electric and Enron can be compared on the basis of their seemingly similar company practices throughout the 1990s and into the early 2000s. From the outside looking in, both companies attracted the best and the brightest by offering premium wages and other financial bonuses. Each company had a similar policy to retain only their best performing employees; Enron annually retained its top 80 percent of employees, whereas General Electric retained its top 90 percent. Both companies also developed cultures driven by success. But Enron's culture actually caused its downward spiral that led to its ultimate demise.

Was it Enron's accounting practices, initiated at the top of the company, that caused its organizational failure? Although accounting was a major piece of the equation, another factor really enabled one of the largest financial scandals in U.S. corporate history. The so-called "entrepreneurial culture" emphasized the importance of financial performance and aggressive employee initiatives. The ends justified the means at Enron, which may explain why a distinct lack of controls monitored the performance of employees.

General Electric's fixation on bottom line performance and risk taking is complemented by its core values, which include a high sense of ethical behavior. The culture that Jack Welch helped establish at GE remains relatively the same, even since the new CEO,

Jeffrey R. Immelt, took control of the company. Immelt has realized that GE's culture, focused on teamwork, innovation, ethics, and financial performance, is a culture that can continue to give the company a competitive advantage in the future.

16.1 Is corporate culture the underlying cause of corporate scandals? Explain.

16.2 Is General Electric's absolute employee evaluation process (firing the bottom 10 percent) a good strategic decision? Explain.

Sources: "At Enron, 'the Environment Was Ripe for Abuse'," *BusinessWeek,* February 25, 2002; "The Immelt Revolution," *BusinessWeek,* March 28, 2005; "What Really Went Wrong with Enron? A Culture of Evil?" 2002, http://www.scu.edu/ethics/publications/ethicalperspectives/enronpanel.html (June 26, 2007).

EXERCISE   UNIVERSITY CULTURE

The purpose of this exercise is to explore how organizational culture is transmitted through observable artifacts. This exercise uses groups of six participants, so your instructor will either assign you to a group of six or ask you to create your own group of six. The exercise has the following steps:

1. Consider the observable artifacts that transmit the organizational culture of your university.

Symbols	Think about the logo and images associated with your university. What message do they convey about the university's culture?
Physical Structures	Think about the most visible physical structures on campus. What do those structures say about your university's culture?
Language	Think about the jargon, slang, slogans, and sayings associated with your university. What insights do they offer into the university's culture?
Stories	What anecdotes, accounts, legends, and myths are associated with your university? What messages do they convey about your university's culture?
Rituals	What are the daily or weekly routines that occur at your university, and what do they say about the culture?
Ceremonies	What are the formal events and celebrations that occur at your university, and what cultural signals do they convey?

2. Consider the sorts of values listed in Table 16-3. If you consider the symbols, physical structures, language, stories, rituals, and ceremonies identified in Step 1, what core values seem to summarize your university's culture? Using a transparency, laptop, or chalkboard, list the one value that seems to be most central to your university's culture. Then list the three cultural artifacts that are most responsible for transmitting that core value. Present your results to the class.

3. Discuss (in groups or as a class) two main questions. First, do you like how your university's culture is viewed, as represented in the group presentations? Why or why not? Second, if you wanted to change the university's culture to represent other sorts of values, what process would you use to change the culture?

ENDNOTES

16.1 Useem, J. "America's Most Admired Companies. *Fortune,* March 7, 2005, p. 67.

16.2 McLean, B., and P. Elkind. *Smartest Guys in the Room: The Amazing Rise and Scandalous Fall of Enron.* New York: Portfolio Publishing, 2003.

16.3 Useem, J. "Another Boss, Another Revolution." *Fortune,* April 5, 2004, pp. 112–17.

16.4 Haasen, A., and G.F. Shea. *New Corporate Cultures that Motivate.* Westport, CT: Praeger, 2003.

16.5 Lear, R.W. "Jack Welch Speaks: Wisdom from the World's Greatest Business Leader." *Chief Executive,* July/August 1998, p. 64.

16.6 McLean and Elkind, *Smartest Guys.*

16.7 Haasen and Shea, *New Corporate Cultures.*

16.8 Fowler, T. "The Pride and Fall of Enron." *Houston Chronicle,* Oct. 20, 2002. Accessed on www.chron.com on January 29, 2007.

16.9 McLean and Elkind, *Smartest Guys.*

16.10 Verbeke, W.; M. Volgering; and M. Hessels. "Exploring the Conceptual Expansion within the Field of Organizational Behavior: Organizational Climate and Organizational Culture." *Journal of Management Studies* 35 (1998), pp. 303–29.

16.11 Deal, T.E., and A.A. Kennedy. *Corporate Cultures: The Rites and Rituals of Corporate Life.* Reading, MA: Addison-Wesley, 1982.

16.12 Adapted from O'Reilly, C.A., III; J. Chatman; and D.L. Caldwell. "People and Organizational Culture: A Profile Comparison Approach to Assessing Person–Organization Fit."*Academy of Management Journal* 34 (1991), pp. 487–516; Tsui, A.S.; Z. Zhang; W. Hui; K.R. Xin, and J.B. Wu. "Unpacking the Relationship between CEO Leadership Behavior and Organizational Culture." *The Leadership Quarterly* 17 (2006), pp. 113–37.

16.13 O'Reilly, C.A., and Jennifer A. Chatman. " Culture as Social Control: Corporations, Cults, and Commitment." In *Research in Organizational Behavior,* Vol. 18, eds. Barry M. Staw and L.L. Cummings. Stamford, CT: JAI Press, 1996, pp. 157–200.

16.14 Chatman, J.A. "Matching People and Organizations: Selection and Socialization in Public Accounting Firms." *Administrative Science Quarterly* 36 (1991), pp. 459–84.

16.15 Trice, H.M., and J.M. Beyer. *The Cultures of Work Organizations.* Englewood Cliffs, NJ: Prentice Hall, 1993.

16.16 Kaihla, P. "Best-Kept Secrets of the World's Best Companies." *Business 2.0* 7 (2006), pp. 82–87.

16.17 Stibbe, M. "Mothers of Invention." *Director* 55 (2002), pp. 64–68.

16.18 Shuit, D. P. "Yum Does a 360." *Workforce Management,* April 2005, pp. 59–60.

16.19 Kiger, P.J. "Corporate Crunch." *Workforce Management,* April 2005, pp. 32–38.

16.20 Jacobson, D. "Extreme Extras." *Money Magazine,* April 7, 2006, p. 99.

16.21 Kaihla, "Best Kept Secret."

16.22 Higgins, J.M., and C. McAllaster. "If You Want Strategic Change, Don't Forget to Change Your Cultural

Artifacts." *Journal of Change Management* 4 (2004), pp. 63–74.

16.23 Schein, E.H. "Organizational Culture." *American Psychologist* 45 (1990), pp. 109–19.

16.24 Schein, E. H. *Organization Culture and Leadership.* San Francisco, CA: Jossey-Bass, 2004.

16.25 Schein, E.H. "What Is Culture?" In *Reframing Organizational Culture,* ed. P.J. Frost, L.F. Moore, M.R. Louis, C.C. Lundberg, and J. Martin. Beverly Hills, CA: Sage, 1991, pp. 243–53.

16.26 Goffee, R., and G. Jones. *The Character of a Corporation.* New York: Harper Business, 1998.

16.27 Lum, S., and B.C. Moyer. "Gross Product by Industry, 1995–1997." *Survey of Current Business,* November 1998, pp. 20–40.

16.28 Schneider, B.; D.E. Bowen; M.G. Ehrhart; and K.M. Holcombe. "The Climate for Service: Evolution of a Construct." In *Handbook of Organizational Culture and Climate,* eds. N.M. Ashkanasy, C. Wilderom, and M.F. Peterson. Thousand Oaks, CA, Sage, 2000.

16.29 Schneider, B.; M.G. Ehrhart; D.M. Mayer; J.L. Saltz; and K. Niles-Jolly. "Understanding Organization–Customer Links in Service Settings." *Academy of Management Journal* 48 (2005), pp. 1017–32.

16.30 du Gay, P., and G. Salaman. "The Cult(ure) of the Customer." In *Strategic Human Resource Management,* eds. C. Mabey, G. Salaman, and J. Storey. London: Sage, 1998, pp. 58–67.

16.31 Heller, L. "Will Circuit City Find its Way to Turnaround City?" *DSN Retailing Today* January 9, 2006, pp. 17–19.

16.32 Zohar, D., and G. Luria. "Climate as a Social-Cognitive =Construction of Supervisory Safety Practices: Scripts as a Proxy of Behavior Patterns." *Journal of Applied Psychology* 89 (2004), pp. 322–33.

16.33 Hofmann, D.A.; F.P. Morgeson; and S.J. Gerras. "Climate as a Moderator of the Relationship Between Leader-Member Exchange and Content Specific Citizenship: Safety Climate as an Exemplar." *Journal of Applied Psychology* 88 (2003), pp. 170–78.

16.34 Katz-Navon, T.; E. Naveh; and Z. Stern. "Safety Climate in Healthcare Organizations: A Multi-Dimensional Approach." *Academy of Management Journal* 48 (2005), pp. 1075–89.

16.35 Liss, H.J., and R.J. Wagner. "GE's Crash Course in Culture Change." *Occupational Hazards,* September , 2004, pp. 83–88.

16.36 Clarke, S. "Perceptions of Organizational Safety: Implications for the Development of Safety Culture." *Journal of Organizational Behavior* 20 (1999), pp. 185–98.

16.37 Speizer, I. "Diversity on the Menu." *Workforce Management,* November 2004, pp. 41–45.

16.38 McLean, L.D. "Organizational Culture's Influence on Creativity and Innovation: A Review of the Literature and Implications for Human Resource Development." *Advances in Developing Human Resources* 7 (2005), pp. 226–46.

16.39 Frauenheim, E. "On the Clock but Off on Their Own: Pet-Project Programs Set to Gain Wider Acceptance." *Workforce Management* April 24, 2006, pp. 40–41.

16.40 Poulton, T. "Got a Creative Creative Process? Fostering Creativity in an ROI-Focused Cubicle-Ridden

Environment Ain't Easy. Here's How to Get your Team's Juices Flowing." *Strategy,* April 2006, p. 11.

16.41 O'Reilly, C.A. "Corporations, Culture, and Commitment: Motivation and Social Control in Organizations." *California Management Review* 31 (1989), pp. 9–25.

16.42 O'Reilly et al., "People and Organizational Culture."

16.43 Schein, E.H. "Three Cultures of Management: The Key to Organizational Learning." *Sloan Management Review* 38 (1996), pp. 9–20.

16.44 Boisner A., and J. Chatman. "The Role of Subcultures in Agile Organizations." In *Leading and Managing People in Dynamic Organizations,* eds. R. Petersen and E. Mannix. Mahwah, NJ: Lawrence Erlbaum Associates, 2003.

16.45 See Howard-Grenville, J.A. "Inside the 'BLACK BOX': How Organizational Culture and Subcultures Inform Interpretations and Actions on Environmental Issues." *Organization & Environment* 19 (2006) , pp. 46–73; Jermier, J.; J. Slocum; L. Fry; and J. Gaines. "Organizational Subcultures in a Soft Bureaucracy: Resistance Behind the Myth and Façade of an Official Culture." *Organizational Science* 2 (1991), pp. 170–94.

16.46 Schneider, B.; H.W. Goldstein; and D.B. Smith. "The ASA Framework: An Update." *Personnel Psychology* 48 (1995), pp. 747–73.

16.47 Graf, A.B. "Building Corporate Cultures." *Chief Executive,* March 2005, p. 18.

16.48 Ruiz, G "Tall Order." *Workforce Management,* April 2006, pp. 22–29.

16.49 For good summaries of socialization, see Fisher, C.D. "Organizational Socialization: An Integrative View." *Research in Personnel and Human Resource Management* 4 (1986), pp. 101–45; Bauer, T. N.; E.W. Morrison; and R.R. Callister. "Organizational Socialization: A Review and Directions for Future Research." In *Research in Personnel and Human Resource Management,* Vol. 16, ed. G.R. Ferris. Greenwich, CT: JAI Press, 1998, pp. 149–214.

16.50 Cable, D.M.; L. Aiman-Smith; P.W. Mulvey; and J.R. Edwards. "The Sources and Accuracy of Job Applicants' Beliefs about Organizational Culture."*Academy of Management Journal* 43 (2000), pp. 1076–85; Louis, M.R. "Surprise and Sense-Making: What Newcomers Experience in Entering Unfamiliar Organizational Settings." *Administrative Science Quarterly* 25 (1980), pp. 226–51.

16.51 Chao, G.T.; A. O'Leary-Kelly; S. Wolf; H.J. Klein; and P.D. Gardner. "Organizational Socialization: Its Content and Consequences." *Journal of Applied Psychology* 79 (1994), pp. 450–63.

16.52 Ibid. ; Klein, H., and N. Weaver. "The Effectiveness of an Organizational-Level Orientation Training Program in the Socialization of New Hires." *Personnel Psychology,* Spring 2000, pp 47–66; Wesson, M. J., and C.I. Gogus. "Shaking Hands with a Computer: An Examination of Two Methods of Organizational Newcomer Orientation." *Journal of Applied Psychology* 90 (2005), pp. 1018–26.

16.53 Gravelle, M. "The Five Most Common Hiring Mistakes and How to Avoid Them." *The Canadian Manager* 29 (2004), pp. 11–13.

16.54 Van Maanen, J., and E.H. Schein. "Toward a Theory of Organizational Socialization." *Research in*

Organizational Behavior 1 (1979), pp. 209–64.

16.55 Ashford, S.J., and J.S. Black. "Proactivity During Organizational Entry: The Role of Desire for Control." Journal of Applied Psychology, 81 (1996), pp. 199–214; Kim, T.; D.M. Cable, and S. Kim. "Socialization Tactics, Employee Proactivity, and Person–Organization Fit." *Journal of Applied Psychology* 90 (2005), pp. 232–41.

16.56 Mourier, P., and M. Smith. *Conquering Organizational Change: How to Succeed Where Most Companies Fail.* Atlanta: CEP Press, 2001.

16.57 McCracken, J. "'Way Forward' Requires Culture Shift at Ford." *The Wall Street Journal,* January 23, 2006, p. B1.

16.58 Schein, *Organization Culture and Leadership.*

16.59 Gubbins, E. "Nortel's New Execs Bring Cisco Experience." *Telephony,* April 11, 2005. pp. 14–15.

16.60 Weber, Y. "Measuring Cultural Fit in Mergers and Acquisitions." In *Handbook of Organizational Culture and Climate,* eds. N.M. Ashkanasy, C. Wilderom, and M.F. Peterson. Thousand Oaks, CA; Sage, pp. 309–20.

16.61 Brahy, S. "Six Solution Pillars for Successful Cultural Integration of International M&As." *Journal of Organizational Excellence,* Autumn 2006, pp. 53–63.

16.62 Platt, G. "Global Merger Activity Sets Record Pace." *Global Finance* 20 (2006), p. 60.

16.63 Edmondson, G. "Auf Wiedersehen, Mitsubishi." *BusinessWeek,* November 11, 2005, Accessed through www.businessweek.com on February 9, 2007; Bremmer, B. "A Tale of Two Auto Mergers." *Busi-*

nessWeek, April 29, 2004, Accessed through www.businessweek.com on February 9, 2007.

16.64 Ewing, J. "Nokia and Siemens: Exciting the Market." *BusinessWeek,* June 19, 2006.

16.65 Stahl, G.K., and M.E. Mendenhall. *Mergers and Acquisitions: Managing Culture and Human Resources.* Stanford, CA: Stanford University Press, 2005.

16.66 Gibson, R. "Package Deal: UPS's Purchase of Mail Boxes Etc. Looked Great on Paper. Then Came the Culture Clash." *The Wall Street Journal,* May 8, 2006, p. R13.

16.67 Kristof-Brown, A.L.; R.D. Zimmerman; and E.C. Johnson, "Consequences of Individuals' Fit at Work: A Meta-Analysis of Person–Job, Person–Organization, Person–Group, and Person–Supervisor Fit," *Personnel Psychology* 58 (2005), pp. 281–342.

16.68 Barber, A.E. *Recruiting Employees: Individual and Organizational Perspectives.* Thousand Oaks, CA: Sage, 1998.

16.69 Wanous, J.P. *Organizational Entry: Recruitment, Selection, Orientation and Socialization of Newcomers.* Reading, MA: Addison-Wesley, 1992.

16.70 Gravelle, "The Five Most Common Hiring Mistakes."

16.71 Anderson, N.R.; N.A. Cunningham-Snell; and J. Haigh. "Induction Training as Socialization: Current Practice and Attitudes to Evaluation in British Organizations," International Journal of Selection and Assessment, 4 (1996), pp. 169–83.

16.72 Wesson and Gogus, "Shaking Hands with a Computer."

16.73 Ibid.; Klein and Weaver, "The Effectiveness."

16.74 Marquez, J. "Despite Job Cuts, GM May Expand New-Hire Networking Program." *Workforce Management,* March 27, 2006, p. 16.

16.75 Wanberg, C.R.; E.T. Welsh; and S.A. Hezlett. "Mentoring Research: A Review and Dynamic Process Model." *Research in Personnel and Human Resources Management* 22 (2003), pp. 39–124.

16.76 Allen, T.D.; L.T. Eby; M.L. Poteet; E. Lentz; and L. Lima. "Outcomes Associated with Mentoring Protégés: A Meta-Analysis." *Journal of Applied Psychology* 89 (2004), pp. 127–36.

16.77 Tahmincioglu, E. "Group Mentoring: A Cost Effective Option." *Workforce Management Online,* December 2004, Accessed March 2, 2007.

16.78 Ibid.

A

ability Relatively stable capabilities of people for performing a particular range of related activities.

ability to focus The degree to which employees can devote their attention to work.

absenteeism A form of physical withdrawal in which employees do not show up for an entire day of work.

abuse Employee assault or endangerment from which physical and psychological injuries may occur.

accommodating A conflict resolution style by which one party gives in to the other and acts in a completely unselfish way.

accomplishment striving A strong desire to accomplish task-related goals as a means of expressing one's personality.

action learning Team process training in which a team has the opportunity to work on an actual problem within the organization.

action processes Teamwork processes, such as helping and coordination, that aid in the accomplishment of teamwork as the work is actually taking place.

action team A team of limited duration that performs complex tasks in contexts that tend to be highly visible and challenging.

active management-by-exception When the leader arranges to monitor mistakes and errors actively and takes corrective action when required.

adaptive task performance Thoughtful responses by an employee to unique or unusual task demands.

additive tasks Tasks for which the contributions from every member add up to determine team performance.

affect-based trust Trust that depends on feelings toward the authority that go beyond any rational assessment of trustworthiness.

affective commitment An employee's desire to remain a member of an organization due to a feeling of emotional attachment.

agreeableness One of the "Big Five" dimensions of personality reflecting traits like being kind, cooperative, sympathetic, helpful, courteous, and warm.

ambassador activities Boundary-spanning activities that are intended to protect the team, persuade others to support the team, or obtain important resources for the team.

anticipatory stage A stage of socialization that begins as soon as a potential employee develops an image of what it would be like to work for a company.

apathetics Employees with low commitment levels and low task performance levels who exert the minimum amount of effort needed to keep their jobs.

apprising An influence tactic in which the requestor clearly explains why performing the request will benefit the target personally.

ASA framework A theory (Attraction-Selection-Attrition) that states that employees will be drawn to organizations with cultures that match their personality, organizations will select employees that match, and employees will leave or be forced out when they are not a good fit.

auditory attention The ability to focus on a single sound in the presence of many other sounds.

autocratic style A leadership style where the leader makes the decision alone without asking for opinions or suggestions of the employees in the work unit.

autonomy The degree to which a job allows individual freedom and discretion regarding how the work is to be done.

availability bias The tendency for people to base their judgments on information that is easier to recall.

avoiding A conflict resolution style by which one party wants to remain neutral, stay away from conflict, or postpone the conflict to gather information or let things cool down.

B

basic underlying assumptions The ingrained beliefs and philosophies of employees.

behavior modeling training A formalized method of training in which employees observe and learn from employees with significant amounts of tacit knowledge.

behavioral coping Physical activities used to deal with a stressful situation.

behavioral modeling When employees observe the actions of others, learn from what they observe, and then repeat the observed behavior.

behavioral strains Patterns of negative behaviors that are associated with other strains.

behaviorally anchored rating scales (BARS) Use of examples of critical incidents to evaluate an employee's job performance behaviors directly.

benevolence The belief that an authority wants to do good for an employee, apart from any selfish or profit-centered motives.

benign job demands Job demands that are not appraised as being stressful.

Big Five The five major dimensions of personality including conscientiousness, agreeableness, neuroticism, openness to experience, and extraversion.

boosterism Positively representing the organization when in public.

boundary spanning Interactions among team members and individuals and groups who are not part of the team.

bounded rationality The notion that people do not have the ability or resources to process all available information and alternatives when making a decision.

brainstorming A team process used to generate creative ideas.

bureaucratic structure An organizational form that exhibits many of the facets of a mechanistic organization.

burnout The emotional, mental, and physical exhaustion from coping with stressful demands on a continuing basis.

business environment The outside environment, including customers, competitors, suppliers, and distributors, which all have an impact on organizational design.

C

centrality How important a person's job is and how many people depend on that person to accomplish their tasks.

centralization Refers to where decisions are formally made in organizations.

ceremonies Formal events, generally performed in front of an audience of organizational members.

chain of command Answer to the question of "who reports to whom?" and signifies formal authority relationships.

challenge stressors Stressors that tend to be appraised as opportunities for growth and achievement.

character The perception that an authority adheres to a set of values and principles that the trustor finds acceptable.

citizens Employees with high commitment levels and low task

performance levels who volunteer to do additional activities around the office.

citizenship behavior Voluntary employee behaviors that contribute to organizational goals by improving the context in which work takes place.

civic virtue Participation in company operations at a deeper-than-normal level through voluntary meetings, readings, and keeping up with news that affects the company.

clear purpose tests Integrity tests that ask about attitudes toward dishonesty, beliefs about the frequency of dishonesty, desire to punish dishonesty, and confession of past dishonesty.

client structure An organizational form in which employees are organized around serving customers.

climate for transfer An organizational environment that supports the use of new skills.

coalitions An influence tactic in which the influencer enlists other people to help influence the target.

coercive power A form of organizational power based on the ability to hand out punishment.

cognition-based trust Trust that is rooted in a rational assessment of the authority's trustworthiness.

cognitive abilities Capabilities related to the use of knowledge to make decisions and solve problems.

cognitive coping Thoughts used to deal with a stressful situation.

cognitive distortion A reevaluation of the inputs an employee brings to a job, often occurring in response to equity distress.

cognitive moral development As people age and mature, they move through several states of moral development, each more mature and sophisticated than the prior one.

cognitive-behavioral techniques Various practices that help workers cope with life's stressors in a rational manner.

cohesion A team state that occurs when members of the team develop strong emotional bonds to other members of the team and to the team itself.

collaboration Seen as both a conflict resolution style and an influence tactic whereby both parties work together to maximize outcomes.

communal cultures An organizational culture type in which employees are friendly to one another, but everyone thinks differently and does his or her own thing.

communion striving A strong desire to obtain acceptance in personal relationships as a means of expressing one's personality.

communities of practice Groups of employees who learn from one another through collaboration over an extended period of time.

company size The number of employees in a company.

company strategy An organization's objectives and goals and how it tries to capitalize on its assets to make money.

comparison other Another person who provides a frame of reference for judging equity.

compensatory forms model A model indicating that the various withdrawal behaviors are negatively correlated—that engaging in one type of withdrawal makes one less likely to engage in other types.

competence The capability to perform work tasks successfully.

competing A conflict resolution style by which one party attempts to get his or her own goals met without concern for the other party's results.

compliance When targets of influence are willing to do what the leader asks but do it with a degree of ambivalence.

comprehensive interdependence A form of task interdependence in which team members have a great deal of discretion in terms of what they do and with whom they interact in the course of the collaboration involved in accomplishing the team's work.

compromise A conflict resolution style by which conflict is resolved through give-and-take concessions.

conjunctive tasks Tasks for which the team's performance depends on the abilities of the team's weakest link.

conscientiousness One of the "Big Five" dimensions of personality reflecting traits like being dependable, organized, reliable, ambitious, hardworking, and persevering.

consensus Used by decision makers to attribute cause; whether other individuals behave the same way under similar circumstances.

consideration A pattern of behavior where the leader creates job relationships characterized by mutual trust, respect for employee ideas, and consideration of employee feelings.

consistency Used by decision makers to attribute cause; whether this individual has behaved this way before under similar circumstances.

consultation An influence tactic whereby the target is allowed to participate in deciding how to carry out or implement a request.

consultative style A leadership style where the leader presents the problem to employees asking for their opinions and suggestions before ultimately making the decision him- or herself.

contingencies of reinforcement Four specific consequences used by organizations to modify employee behavior.

contingent reward When the leader attains follower agreement on what needs to be done using rewards in exchange for adequate performance.

continuance commitment An employee's desire to remain a member of an organization due to an awareness of the costs of leaving.

continuous reinforcement A specific consequence follows each and every occurrence of a certain behavior.

control movement abilities The ability to make precise adjustments using machinery to complete work effectively.

coordination loss Process loss due to the time and energy it takes to coordinate work activities with other team members.

coping Behaviors and thoughts used to manage stressful demands and the emotions associated with the stressful demands.

corporate social responsibility A perspective that acknowledges that the responsibility of a business encompasses the economic, legal, ethical, and citizenship expectations of society.

correlation The statistical relationship between two variables. Abbreviated r, it can be positive or negative and range from 0 (no statistical relationship) to ± 1 (a perfect statistical relationship).

countercultures When a subcultures' values do not match those of the organization.

counterproductive behavior Employee behaviors that intentionally hinder organizational goal accomplishment.

courtesy Sharing important information with coworkers.

coworker satisfaction Employees' feelings about their coworkers, including their abilities and personalities.

creativity Capacity to generate novel and useful ideas and solutions.

creativity culture A specific culture type focused on fostering a creative atmosphere.

cross-training Training team members in the duties and responsibilities of their teammates.

cultural values Shared beliefs about desirable end states or modes of conduct in a given culture that influence the expression of traits.

culture strength The degree to which employees agree about how things should happen within the organization and behave accordingly.

customer service culture A specific culture type focused on service quality.

cyberloafing A form of psychological withdrawal in which employees surf the Internet, e-mail, and instant message to avoid doing work-related activities.

D

daily hassles Minor day-to-day demands that interfere with work accomplishment.

daydreaming A form of psychological withdrawal in which one's work is interrupted by random thoughts or concerns.

decision informity The degree to which team members possess adequate information about their own task responsibilities.

decision making The process of generating and choosing from a set of alternatives to solve a problem.

deductive reasoning The ability to solve problems by applying general rules.

deep-level diversity Diversity of attributes that are inferred through observation or experience, such as one's values or personality.

delegating When the leader turns responsibility for key behaviors over to employees.

delegative style A leadership style where the leader gives the employee the responsibility for making decisions within some set of specified boundary conditions.

depth perception The ability to judge relative distances between things accurately.

differential exposure Being more likely to appraise day-to-day situations as stressful, thereby feeling that stressors are encountered more frequently.

differential reactivity Being less likely to believe that one can cope with the stressors experienced on a daily basis.

discretion The degree to which managers have the right to make decisions on their own.

disjunctive tasks Tasks with an objectively verifiable best solution for which the member with the highest level of ability has the most influence on team effectiveness.

disposition-based trust Trust that is rooted in one's own personality, as opposed to a careful assessment of the trustee's trustworthiness.

distinctiveness Used by decision makers to attribute cause; whether the person being judged acts in a similar fashion under different circumstances.

distributive bargaining A negotiation strategy in which one person gains and the other person loses.

distributive justice The perceived fairness of decision-making outcomes.

diversity culture A specific culture type focused on fostering or taking advantage of a diverse group of employees.

dynamic flexibility The ability to quickly and repeatedly execute bends, twists, stretches, or reaches to complete a job.

dynamic strength The ability to exert force for a prolonged period of time without becoming overly fatigued and giving out.

E

economic exchange Work relationships that resemble a contractual agreement by which employees fulfill job duties in exchange for financial compensation.

embeddedness An employee's connection to and sense of fit in the organization and community.

emotion regulation The ability to recover quickly from emotional experiences.

emotional contagion The idea that emotions can be transferred from one person to another.

emotional cues Positive or negative feelings that can help or hinder task accomplishment.

emotional intelligence A set of abilities related to the understanding and use of emotions that affect social functioning.

emotional labor When employees manage their emotions to complete their job duties successfully.

emotional support The empathy and understanding that people receive from others that can be used to alleviate emotional distress from stressful demands.

emotion-focused coping Behaviors and cognitions of an individual intended to help manage emotional reactions to the stressful demands.

emotions Intense feelings, often lasting for a short duration, that are clearly directed at someone or some circumstance.

encounter stage A stage of socialization beginning the day an employee starts work, during which the employee compares the information as an outsider to the information learned as an insider.

engagement In the context of mood, it represents how active or sluggish a mood is. In the context of influence tactics, it occurs when one agrees and becomes committed to an influencer's request.

equity distress An internal tension that results from being overrewarded or underrewarded relative to some comparison other.

equity theory A theory that suggests that employees create a mental ledger of the outcomes they receive for their job inputs, relative to some comparison other.

erosion model A model that suggests that employees with fewer bonds with coworkers are more likely to quit the organization.

escalation of commitment A common decision-making error in which the decision maker continues to follow a failing course of action.

espoused values The beliefs, philosophies, and norms that a company explicitly states.

ethical ideology Principles used by individuals during ethical decision making.

ethical sensitivity The ability to recognize that a decision has ethical content.

ethics The degree to which the behaviors of an authority are in accordance with generally accepted moral norms.

ethnocentrism One who views his or her cultural values as "right" and values of other cultures as "wrong."

exchange tactic An influence tactic in which the requestor offers a reward in return for performing a request.

exit A response to a negative work event by which one becomes often absent from work or voluntarily leaves the organization.

expectancy The belief that exerting a high level of effort will result in successful performance on some task.

expectancy theory A theory that describes the cognitive process employees go through to make choices among different voluntary responses.

expert power A form of organizational power based on expertise or knowledge.

expertise The knowledge and skills that distinguish experts from novices.

explicit knowledge Knowledge that is easily communicated and available to everyone.

explosive strength The ability to move or move things in short bursts of energy.

extent flexibility The ability to execute extreme ranges of bends, twists, stretches, or reaches to complete a job.

external comparison Comparing oneself to someone in a different company.

extinction The removal of a positive outcome following an unwanted behavior.

extraversion One of the "Big Five" dimensions of personality reflecting traits like being talkative, sociable, passionate, assertive, bold, and dominant.

extrinsic motivation Desire to put forth work effort due to some contingency that depends on task performance.

F

facilitative style A leadership style where the leader presents the problem to a group of employees and seeks consensus on a solution, making sure that his or her own opinion receives no more weight than anyone else's.

faking Exaggerating responses to a personality test in a socially desirable fashion.

family time demands The amount of time committed to fulfilling family responsibilities.

feedback In job characteristics theory, it refers to the degree to which the job itself provides information about how well the job holder is doing. In goal setting theory, it refers to progress updates on work goals.

fine manipulative abilities The ability to keep the arms and hands steady while using the hands to do precise work.

fixed interval schedule Reinforcement occurs at fixed time periods.

fixed ratio schedule Reinforcement occurs following a fixed number of desired behaviors.

focus of commitment The people, places, and things that inspire a desire to remain a member of an organization.

formalism The view that ethical actions are defined using a set of guiding principles.

formalization The degree to which rules and procedures are used to standardize behaviors and decisions in an organization.

forming The first stage of team development, during which members try to get a feel for what is expected of them, what types of behaviors are out of bounds, and who's in charge.

fragmented cultures An organizational culture type in which employees are distant and disconnected from one another.

functional structure An organizational form in which employees are grouped by the functions they perform for the organization.

fundamental attribution error The tendency for people to judge others' behaviors as being due to internal factors such as ability, motivation, or attitudes.

G

general adaptation syndrome (GAS) The process that the body uses to adapt to stressful demands so that it can continue to function effectively.

general mental ability The general level of cognitive ability that plays an important role in determining the more narrow cognitive abilities.

geographic structure An organizational form in which employees are grouped around the different locations where the company does business.

goal commitment The degree to which a person accepts a goal and is determined to reach it.

goal interdependence The degree to which team members have a shared goal and align their individual goals with that vision.

goal setting theory A theory that views goals as the primary drivers of the intensity and persistence of effort.

gossiping Casual conversations about other people in which the facts are not confirmed as true.

gross body coordination The ability to synchronize the movements of the body, arms, and legs to do something while the whole body is in motion.

gross body equilibrium The ability to maintain the balance of the body in unstable contexts or when changing directions.

groupthink Behaviors that support conformity and team harmony at the expense of other team priorities.

growth need strength The degree to which employees desire to develop themselves further.

H

harassment Unwanted physical contact or verbal remarks from a colleague.

health and wellness programs Employee assistance programs that help workers with personal problems such as alcoholism and other addictions.

hearing sensitivity The ability to discriminate sounds that vary in terms of loudness and pitch.

helping Assisting coworkers who have heavy workloads, aiding them with personal matters, and showing new employees the ropes when they are first on the job.

heuristics Simple and efficient rules of thumb that allow one to make decisions more easily.

hierarchical sensitivity The degree to which the team leader effectively weighs the recommendations of the members.

hindrance stressors Stressors that tend to be appraised as thwarting progress toward growth and achievement.

history A collective pool of experience, wisdom, and knowledge created by people that benefits the organization.

human resource management Field of study that focuses on the applications of OB theories and principles in organizations.

hybrid outcome interdependent When team members receive rewards based on both their individual performance and that of the team to which they belong.

hypotheses Written predictions that specify relationships between variables.

I

idealism Embracing the notion of universal moral rules.

idealized influence When the leader behaves in ways that earn the admiration, trust, and respect of followers, causing followers to want to identify with and emulate the leader.

identity The degree to which a job offers completion of a whole, identifiable piece of work.

impact The sense that a person's actions "make a difference"—that progress is being made toward fulfilling some important purpose.

incivility Communication that is rude, impolite, discourteous, and lacking in good manners.

independent forms model A model that predicts that the various withdrawal behaviors are uncorrelated—that engaging in one type of withdrawal has little bearing on engaging in other types.

individualism-collectivism The degree to which a culture has a loosely knit social framework (individualism) or a tight social framework (collectivism).

individualistic roles Behaviors that benefit the individual at the expense of the team.

individualized consideration When the leader behaves in ways that help followers achieve their potential through coaching, development, and mentoring.

inductive reasoning The ability to consider several pieces of information and then reach a more general conclusion regarding how those pieces are related.

influence The use of behaviors to cause behavioral or attitudinal changes in others.

informational justice The perceived fairness of the communications provided to employees from authorities.

ingratiation The use of favors, compliments, or friendly behavior to make the target feel better about the influencer.

inimitable Incapable of being imitated or copied.

initiating structure A pattern of behavior where the leader defines and structures the roles of employees in pursuit of goal attainment.

inspirational appeal An influence tactic designed to appeal to one's values and ideals, thereby creating an emotional or attitudinal reaction.

inspirational motivation When the leader behaves in ways that foster an enthusiasm for and commitment to a shared vision of the future.

instrumental support The help people receive from others that can be used to address a stressful demand directly.

instrumentality The belief that successful performance will result in the attainment of some outcome(s).

integrative bargaining A negotiation strategy that achieves an outcome that is satisfying for both parties.

integrity tests Personality tests that focus specifically on a predisposition to engage in theft and other counterproductive behaviors (sometimes also called "honesty tests").

intellectual stimulation When the leader behaves in ways that challenge followers to be innovative and creative by questioning assumptions and reframing old situations in new ways.

interests Expressions of personality that influence behavior through preferences for certain environments and activities.

internal comparisons Comparing oneself to someone in your same company.

interpersonal citizenship behavior Going beyond normal job expectations to assist, support, and develop coworkers and colleagues.

interpersonal justice The perceived fairness of the interpersonal treatment received by employees from authorities.

interpersonal processes Teamwork processes, such as motivating and confidence building, that focus on the management of relationships among team members.

intrinsic motivation Desire to put forth work effort due to the sense that task performance serves as its own reward.

intuition An emotional judgment based on quick, unconscious, gut feelings.

J

job analysis A process by which an organization determines requirements of specific jobs.

job characteristics theory A theory that argues that five core characteristics (variety, identity, significance, autonomy, and feedback) combine to result in high levels of satisfaction with the work itself.

job enrichment When job duties and responsibilities are expanded to provide increased levels of core job characteristics.

job performance Employee behaviors that contribute either positively or negatively to the accomplishment of organizational goals.

job satisfaction A pleasurable emotional state resulting from the appraisal of one's job or job experiences. It represents how a person feels and thinks about his or her job.

job sharing When two people share the responsibilities of a single job.

justice The perceived fairness of an authority's decision making.

K

knowledge and skill The degree to which employees have the aptitude and competence needed to succeed on their job.

knowledge of results A psychological state indicating the extent to which employees are aware of how well or how poorly they are doing.

knowledge transfer The exchange of knowledge between employees.

knowledge work Jobs that primarily involve cognitive activity versus physical activity.

L

laissez-faire leadership When the leader avoids leadership duties altogether.

language The jargon, slang, and slogans used within an organization.

leader effectiveness The degree to which the leader's actions result in the achievement of the unit's goals, the continued commitment of the unit's employees, and the development of mutual trust, respect, and obligation in leader-member dyads.

leader emergence The process of becoming a leader in the first place.

leader-member exchange theory A theory describing how leader-member relationships develop over time on a dyadic basis.

leadership The use of power and influence to direct the activities of followers toward goal achievement.

leader-staff teams A type of team that consists of members who make recommendations to the leader who is ultimately responsible for team decisions.

learning A relatively permanent change in an employee's knowledge or skill that results from experience.

learning orientation A predisposition or attitude according to which building competence is deemed more important by an employee than demonstrating competence.

legitimate power A form of organizational power based on authority or position.

life cycle theory of leadership A theory stating that the optimal combination of initiating structure and consideration depends on the readiness of the employees in the work unit.

life satisfaction The degree to which employees feel a sense of happiness with their lives in general.

locus of control Whether one believes the events that occur around him or her are driven by him- or herself or the external environment.

lone wolves Employees with low commitment levels and high task performance levels who focus on their own career rather than what benefits the organization.

long breaks A form of physical withdrawal in which employees take longer-than-normal lunches or breaks to spend less time at work.

looking busy A form of psychological withdrawal in which one attempts to appear consumed with work when not performing actual work tasks.

loyalty A passive response to a negative work event in which one publicly supports the situation but privately hopes for improvement.

M

management by objectives (MBO) A management philosophy that bases employee evaluations on whether specific performance goals have been met.

management team A relatively permanent team that participates in managerial-level tasks that affect the entire organization.

masculinity-femininity The degree to which a culture values stereotypically male traits (masculinity) or stereotypically female traits (femininity).

mathematical reasoning The ability to choose and apply formulas to solve problems that involve numbers.

matrix structure A complex form of organizational structure that combines a functional and multidivisional grouping.

maximum performance Performance in brief, special circumstances that demand a person's best effort.

meaning of money The idea that money can have symbolic value (e.g., achievement, respect, freedom) in addition to economic value.

meaningfulness A psychological state reflecting one's feelings about work tasks, goals, and purposes, and the degree to which they contribute to society and fulfill one's ideals and passions.

mechanistic organizations Efficient, rigid, predictable, and standardized organizations that thrive in stable environments.

mental models The degree to which team members have a shared understanding of important aspects of the team and its task.

mentoring The process by which a junior-level employee develops a deep and long-lasting relationship with a more senior-level employee within the organization.

mercenary cultures An organizational culture type in which employees think alike but are not friendly to one another.

meta-analysis A method that combines the results of multiple scientific studies by essentially calculating a weighted average correlation across studies (with larger studies receiving more weight).

method of authority Knowing something because a respected official, agency, or source has said it is so.

method of experience Knowing something because it is consistent with one's own experience and observations.

method of intuition Knowing something because it seems obvious or self-evident.

method of science Knowing something because scientific studies have replicated the result using a series of samples, settings, and methods.

missing meetings A form of physical withdrawal in which employees neglect important work functions while away from the office.

moods States of feeling that are mild in intensity, last for an extended period of time, and are not directed at anything.

moonlighting A form of psychological withdrawal in which employees use work time and resources to do nonwork-related activities.

moral awareness When an authority recognizes that a moral issue exists in a situation.

moral identity The degree to which a person views him- or herself as a moral person.

moral intensity The degree to which an issue has ethical urgency.

moral intent An authority's degree of commitment to the moral course of action.

moral judgment When an authority can accurately identify the "right" course of action.

motivation A set of energetic forces that determine the direction, intensity, and persistence of an employee's work effort.

motivational loss Process loss due to team members' tendency to put forth less effort on team tasks than they could.

multi-divisional structure An organizational form in which employees are grouped by product, geography, or client.

Myers-Briggs type indicator (MBTI) A personality framework that evaluates people on the basis of four types or preferences: extraversion versus introversion, sensing versus intuition, thinking versus feeling, and judging versus perceiving.

N

near and far vision The ability to see things up close and at a distance.

needs Groupings or clusters of outcomes viewed as having

critical psychological or physiological consequences.

negative affectivity A dispositional tendency to experience unpleasant moods such as hostility, nervousness, and annoyance.

negative emotions Employees' feelings of fear, guilt, shame, sadness, envy, and disgust.

negative life events Events such as a divorce or death of a family member that tend to be appraised as a hindrance.

negative reinforcement An unwanted outcome is removed following a desired behavior.

neglect A passive, destructive response to a negative work event in which one's interest and effort in work decline.

negotiation A process in which two or more interdependent individuals discuss and attempt to reach agreement about their differences.

networked cultures An organizational culture type in which employees are friendly to one another and all think alike.

neuroticism One of the "Big Five" dimensions of personality reflecting traits like being nervous, moody, emotional, insecure, jealous, and unstable.

neutralizers Situational characteristics that reduce the importance of the leader and do not improve employee performance in any way.

newcomer orientations A common form of training during which new hires learn more about the organization.

night vision The ability to see things in low light.

nominal group technique A team process used to generate creative ideas, whereby team members individually write down their ideas and then take turns sharing them with the group.

nonprogrammed decision Decisions made by employees when a problem is new, complex, or not recognized.

normative commitment An employee's desire to remain a member of an organization due to a feeling of obligation.

norming The third stage of team development, during which members realize that they need to work together to accomplish team goals and consequently begin to cooperate.

number facility The capability to do simple math operations such as adding and subtracting.

numerous small decisions People making many small decisions every day that are invisible to competitors.

O

observable artifacts Aspects of an organization's culture that employees and outsiders can easily see or talk about.

occupational information network An online database containing job tasks, behaviors, required knowledge, skills, and abilities.

openness to experience One of the "Big Five" dimensions of personality reflecting traits like being curious, imaginative, creative, complex, refined, and sophisticated.

oral comprehension The ability to understand spoken words and sentences.

oral expression The ability to communicate ideas by speaking.

organic organizations Flexible, adaptive, outward-focused organizations that thrive in dynamic environments.

organizational behavior (OB) Field of study devoted to understanding, explaining, and ultimately improving the attitudes and behaviors of individuals and groups in organizations.

organizational chart A drawing that represents every job in the organization and the formal reporting relationships between those jobs.

organizational citizenship behavior Going beyond normal expectations to improve operations of the organization, as well as defending the organization and being loyal to it.

organizational commitment An employee's desire to remain a member of an organization.

organizational culture The shared social knowledge within an organization regarding the rules, norms, and values that shape the attitudes and behaviors of its employees.

organizational design The process of creating, selecting, or changing the structure of an organization.

organizational politics Individual actions directed toward the goal of furthering a person's own self-interests.

organizational structure Formally dictates how jobs and tasks are divided and coordinated between individuals and groups within the company.

originality The ability to develop clever and novel ways to solve problems.

other awareness The ability to recognize and understand the emotions that other people are feeling.

outcome interdependence The degree to which team members share equally in the feedback and rewards that result from the team achieving its goals.

P

parallel team A team composed of members from various jobs within the organization that meets to provide recommendations about important issues.

participating When the leader shares ideas and tries to help the group conduct its affairs.

passive management-by-exception When the leader waits around for mistakes and errors, then takes corrective action as necessary.

past accomplishments The level of success or failure with similar job tasks in the past.

pay satisfaction Employees' feelings about the compensation for their jobs.

perceptual speed The ability to examine and compare numbers, letters, and objects quickly.

performance-avoid orientation A predisposition or attitude by which employees focus on demonstrating their competence so that others will not think poorly of them.

performance-prove orientation A predisposition or attitude by which employees focus on demonstrating their competence so that others think favorably of them.

performing The final stage of team development, during which members are comfortable working within their roles, and the team makes progress toward goals.

personal aggression Hostile verbal and physical actions directed toward other employees.

personal appeals An influence tactic in which the requestor asks for something based on personal friendship or loyalty.

personal clarification Training in which members simply receive information regarding the roles of the other team members.

personal development Participation in activities outside of work that foster growth and learning.

personality The structures and propensities inside a person that explain his or her characteristic patterns of thought, emotion, and behavior. Personality reflects what people are like and creates their social reputation.

person-organization fit The degree to which a person's values and personality match the culture of the organization.

physical structures The organization's buildings and internal office designs.

physical withdrawal A physical escape from the work environment.

physiological strains Reactions from stressors that harm the human body.

pleasantness The degree to which an employee is in a good versus bad mood.

political deviance Behaviors that intentionally disadvantage other individuals.

political skill The ability to understand others and the use of that knowledge to influence them to further personal or organizational objectives.

pooled interdependence A form of task independence in which group members complete their work assignments independently, and then their work is simply added together to represent the group's output.

positional modeling Training that involves observations of how other team members perform their roles.

positional rotation Training that gives members actual experience carrying out the responsibilities of their teammates.

positive affectivity A dispositional tendency to experience pleasant, engaging moods such as enthusiasm, excitement, and elation.

positive emotions Employees' feelings of joy, pride, relief, hope, love and compassion.

positive life events Events such as marriage or the birth of a child that tend to be appraised as a challenge.

positive reinforcement When a positive outcome follows a desired behavior.

potency A team state reflecting the degree of confidence among team members that the team can be effective across situations and tasks.

power The ability to influence the behavior of others and resist unwanted influence in return.

power distance The degree to which a culture prefers equal power distribution (low power distance) or an unequal power distribution (high power distance).

pressure An influence tactic in which the requestor attempts to use coercive power through threats and demands.

primary appraisal Evaluation of whether a demand is stressful and, if it is, the implications of the stressor in terms of personal goals and well-being.

problem sensitivity The ability to sense that there is or will be a problem.

problem-focused coping Behaviors and cognitions of an individual intended to manage the stressful situation itself.

procedural justice The perceived fairness of decision-making processes.

process gain When team outcomes are greater than expected based on the capabilities of the individual members.

process loss When team outcomes are less than expected based on the capabilities of the individual members.

product structure An organizational form in which employees are grouped around different products that the company produces.

production blocking A type of coordination loss resulting from team members having to wait on each other before completing their own part of the team task.

production deviance Intentionally reducing organizational efficiency of work output.

programmed decision Decisions that are somewhat automatic because the decision maker's knowledge allows him or her to recognize the situation and the course of action to be taken.

progression model A model indicating that the various withdrawal behaviors are positively correlated—that engaging in one type of withdrawal makes one more likely to engage in other types.

project team A team formed to take on one-time tasks, most of which tend to be complex and require input from members from different functional areas.

projection bias The faulty perception by decision makers that others think, feel, and act the same way as they do.

promotion satisfaction Employees' feelings about how the company handles promotions.

property deviance Behaviors that harm the organization's assets and possessions.

psychological empowerment An energy rooted in the belief that tasks are contributing to some larger purpose.

psychological strains Negative psychological reactions from stressors such as depression, anxiety, and anger.

psychological withdrawal Mentally escaping the work environment.

punctuated equilibrium A sequence of team development during which not much gets done until the halfway point of a project, after which teams make necessary changes to complete the project on time.

punishment When an unwanted outcome follows an unwanted behavior.

Q

quitting A form of physical withdrawal in which employees voluntarily leave the organization.

R

rare A resource that is difficult to come by.

rational decision-making model A step-by-step approach to making decisions that is designed to maximize outcomes by examining all available alternatives.

rational persuasion The use of logical arguments and hard facts to show someone that a request is worthwhile.

readiness The degree to which employees have the ability and the willingness to accomplish their specific tasks.

realistic job previews The process of ensuring that a potential employee understands both the positive and negative aspects of the potential job.

reality shock A mismatch of information that occurs when an employee finds that aspects of working at a company are not what the employee expected it to be.

reciprocal interdependence A form of task interdependence in which group members interact with only a limited subset of other members to complete the team's work.

referent power A form of organizational power based on the attractiveness and charisma of the leader.

relationship conflict Disagreements among team members with regard to interpersonal relationships or incompatibilities in personal values or preferences.

relativism The view that there are no universal moral rules.

relaxation techniques Calming activities to reduce stress.

resistance When a target refuses to perform a request and puts forth an effort to avoid having to do it.

resource-based view A model that argues that rare and inimitable resources help firms maintain competitive advantage.

response orientation The ability to choose the right action quickly in response to several different signals.

response time The ability to respond to signaling information after it occurs.

responsibility for outcomes A psychological state indicating the degree to which employees feel they are key drivers of the quality of work output.

restructuring The process of changing an organization's structure.

reward power A form of organizational power based on the control of resources or benefits.

RIASEC model An interest framework summarized by six different personality types including realistic, investigative, artistic, social, enterprising, and conventional.

rituals The daily or weekly planned routines that occur in an organization.

role The behavior a person is generally expected to display in a given context.

role ambiguity When an individual has a lack of direction and information about what needs to be done.

role conflict When others have conflicting expectations of what an individual needs to do.

role making The phase in a leader-follower relationship when a follower voices his or her own expectations for the relationship, resulting in a free-flowing exchange of opportunities and resources for activities and effort.

role overload When an employee has too many demands to work effectively.

role taking The phase in a leader-follower relationship when a leader provides an employee with job expectations and the follower tries to meet those expectations.

routine task performance Well-known or habitual responses by employees to predictable task demands.

rule of one-eighth The belief that at best one-eighth or 12 percent of organizations will actually do what is required to build profits by putting people first.

S

S.M.A.R.T. goals Acronym that stands for Specific, Measurable, Achievable, Results-Based, Time-Sensitive goals.

sabotage Purposeful destruction of equipment, organizational processes, or company products.

safety culture A specific culture type focused on the safety of employees.

satisfaction with the work itself Employees' feelings about their actual work tasks.

satisficing When a decision maker chooses the first acceptable alternative considered.

schedules of reinforcement The timing of when contingencies are applied or removed.

scout activities Boundary-spanning activities that are intended to obtain information about technology, competitors, or the broader marketplace.

secondary appraisal When people determine how to cope with the various stressors they face.

selective perception The tendency for people to see their environment only as it affects them and as it is consistent with their expectations.

self-awareness The ability to recognize and understand the emotions in oneself.

self-determination A sense of choice in the initiation and continuation of work tasks.

self-efficacy The belief that a person has the capabilities needed to perform the behaviors required on some task.

self-serving bias When one attributes one's own failures to external factors and success to internal factors.

self-set goals The internalized goals that people use to monitor their own progress.

selling When the leader explains key issues and provides opportunities for clarification.

sequential interdependence A form of task interdependence in which group members perform different tasks in a prescribed sequence, and members only depend on the member who comes before them in the sequence.

service work Providing a service that involves direct verbal or physical interactions with customers.

short-term vs. long-term orientation The degree to which a culture stresses values that are past- and present-oriented (short-term orientation) or future-oriented (long-term orientation).

significance The degree to which a job really matters and impacts society as a whole.

similarity-attraction approach A theory explaining that team diversity can be counterproductive because people tend to avoid interacting with others who are unlike them.

simple structure An organizational form that features one person as the central decision-making figure.

situational strength The degree to which situations have clear behavioral expectations, incentives, or instructions that make differences between individuals less important.

social exchange Work relationships that are characterized by mutual investment, with employees willing to engage in "extra mile" sorts of behaviors because they trust that their efforts will eventually be rewarded.

social identity theory A theory that people identify themselves based on the various groups to which they belong and judge others based on the groups they associate with.

social influence model A model that suggests that employees with direct linkages to coworkers who leave the organization will themselves become more likely to leave.

social learning theory Theory that argues that people in organizations learn by observing others.

social loafing A type of motivational loss resulting from members feeling less accountable for team outcomes relative to independent work that results in individually identifiable outcomes.

social support The help people receive from others when they are confronted with stressful demands.

socialization The primary process by which employees learn the social knowledge that enables them to understand and adapt to the organization's culture.

socializing A form of psychological withdrawal in which one verbally chats with coworkers about nonwork topics.

socially complex resources Resources created by people, such as culture, teamwork, trust, and reputation. The source of competitive advantage is known, but the method of replicating the advantage is unclear.

span of control Represents how many employees each manager in the organization has responsibility for.

spatial organization A good understanding of where one is relative to other things in the environment.

specific and difficult goals Goals that stretch an employee to perform at his or her maximum level while still staying within the boundaries of his or her ability.

speech recognition The ability to identify and understand the speech of another person.

speed and flexibility of closure The ability to pick out a pattern of information quickly in the presence of distractions, even without all the information present.

sportsmanship Maintaining a positive attitude with coworkers through good and bad times.

staff validity The degree to which team members make good recommendations to the team leader.

stamina The ability to work effectively while engaging in physical activity.

stars Employees with high commitment levels and high task performance levels who serve as role models within the organization.

static strength The ability to lift, push, or pull very heavy objects such as boxes or heavy equipment.

status striving A strong desire to obtain power and influence within a social structure as a means of expressing one's personality.

stereotype Assumptions made about others based on their social group membership.

stories Anecdotes, accounts, legends, and myths passed down from cohort to cohort within an organization.

storming The second stage of team development, during which conflict occurs due to members' ongoing commitment to ideas they bring with them to the team.

strains Negative consequences of the stress response.

strategic management Field of study devoted to exploring the product choices and industry characteristics that affect an organization's profitability.

stress The psychological response to demands when there is something at stake for the individual, and where coping with these demands would tax or exceed the individual's capacity or resources.

stress audit An assessment of the sources of stress in the workplace.

stressors Demands that cause the stress response.

subculture A culture created within a small subset of the organization's employees.

substance abuse The abuse of drugs or alcohol before coming to work or while on the job.

substitutability The degree to which people have alternatives in accessing the resources a leader controls.

substitutes Situational characteristics that reduce the importance of the leader while simultaneously providing a direct benefit to employee performance.

substitutes for leadership model A model that suggests that characteristics of the situations can constrain the influence of the leader which makes it more difficult for the leader to influence employee performance.

supervision satisfaction Employees' feelings about their boss, including his or her competency, communication, and personality.

supportive practices Ways in which organizations help employees manage and balance their demands.

surface-level diversity Diversity of observable attributes such as race, gender, ethnicity, and age.

symbols The images an organization uses, which generally convey messages.

T

tacit knowledge Knowledge that employees can only learn through experience.

tardiness A form of physical withdrawal in which employees arrive late to work or leave work early.

task complexity The degree to which the information and actions needed to complete a task are complicated.

task conflict Disagreements among members about the team's task.

task coordinator activities Boundary-spanning activities that are intended to coordinate task-related issues with people or groups in other functional areas.

task interdependence The degree to which team members interact with and rely on other team members for information, materials, and resources needed to accomplish work for the team.

task performance Employee behaviors that are directly involved in the transformation of organizational resources into the goods or services that the organization produces.

task strategies Learning plans and problem-solving approaches used to achieve successful performance.

taskwork processes The activities of team members that relate directly to the accomplishment of team tasks.

team Two or more people who work interdependently over some time period to accomplish common goals related to some task-oriented purpose.

team building Fun activities that facilitate team problem solving, trust, relationship building, and the clarification of role responsibilities.

team building roles Behaviors that influence the quality of the team's social climate.

team composition The mix of the various characteristics that describe the individuals who work in the team.

team diversity The degree to which team members are different from one another.

team process The different types of activities and interactions that occur within a team as the team works toward its goals.

team process training The use of team experiences that facilitates the team's ability to function and perform more effectively as an intact unit.

team states Specific types of feelings and thoughts that coalesce in the minds of team members as a consequence of their experience working together.

team task roles Behaviors that directly facilitate the accomplishment of team tasks.

team viability Team commitment; the likelihood a team can work together effectively into the future.

teamwork processes The interpersonal activities that promote the accomplishment of team tasks but do not involve task accomplishment itself.

technology The method by which an organization transforms inputs to outputs.

telling When the leader provides specific instructions and closely supervises performance.

theft Stealing company products or equipment from the organization.

theory A collection of verbal and symbolic assertions that specify how and why variables are related, as well as the conditions in which they should (and should not) be related.

360-degree feedback A performance evaluation system that uses ratings provided by supervisors, coworkers, subordinates, customers, and the employees themselves.

time pressure The sense that the amount of time allotted to do a job is not quite enough

time-driven model of leadership A model that suggests that seven factors, including the importance of the decision, the expertise of the leader, and the competence of the followers, combine to make some decision-making styles more effective than others in a given situation.

training A systematic effort by organizations to facilitate the learning of job-related knowledge and behavior.

training interventions Practices that increase employees' competencies and skills.

trait activation The degree to which situations provide cues that trigger the expression of a given personality trait.

traits Recurring trends in people's responses to their environment.

transactional leadership A pattern of behavior where the leader rewards or disciplines the follower based on performance.

transactive memory The degree to which team members' specialized knowledge is integrated into an effective system of memory for the team.

transfer of training Occurs when employees retain and demonstrate the knowledge, skills, and behaviors required for their job after training ends.

transformational leadership A pattern of behavior where the leader inspires followers to commit to a shared vision that provides meaning to their work while also serving as a role model who helps followers develop their own potential and view problems from new perspectives.

transition processes Teamwork processes, such as mission analysis and planning, that focus on preparation for future work in the team.

transportable teamwork competencies Team training that involves helping people develop general teamwork competencies that they can transport from one team context to another.

trust The willingness to be vulnerable to an authority based on positive expectations about the authority's actions and intentions.

trust propensity A general expectation that the words, promises, and statements of individuals can be relied upon.

trustworthiness Characteristics or attributes of a person that inspire trust, including competence, character, and benevolence.

type A behavior pattern People who tend to experience more stressors, appraise more demands as stressful, and be prone to experiencing more strains.

typical performance Performance in the routine conditions that surround daily job tasks.

U

uncertainty avoidance The degree to which a culture tolerates ambiguous situations (low uncertainty avoidance) or feels threatened by them (high uncertainty avoidance).

understanding and adaptation The final stage of socialization, during which newcomers come to learn the content areas of socialization and internalize the norms and expected behaviors of the organization.

use of emotions The degree to which people can harness emotions and employ them to improve their chances of being successful in whatever they are seeking to do.

utilitarianism The view that ethical actions are defined as those that achieve the most valuable ends.

V

valence The anticipated value of the outcome(s) associated with successful performance.

value in diversity problem-solving approach A theory that supports team diversity because it provides a larger pool of knowledge and perspectives.

value-percept theory A theory that argues that job satisfaction depends on whether the employee perceives that his or her job supplies those things that he or she values.

values Things that people consciously or unconsciously want to seek or attain.

variable interval schedule Reinforcement occurs at random periods of time.

variable ratio schedule Behaviors are reinforced after a varying number of them have been exhibited.

variety The degree to which a job requires different activities and skills.

veiled purpose tests Integrity tests that do not directly ask about dishonesty, instead assessing more general personality traits associated with dishonest acts.

verbal persuasion Pep talks that lead employees to believe that they can "get the job done".

vicarious experiences Observations of and discussions with others who have performed some work task.

virtual team A team in which the members are geographically dispersed, and interdependent activity occurs through e-mail, Web conferencing, and instant messaging.

visibility How aware others are of a leader and the resources that leader can provide.

visual color discrimination The ability to perceive colors accurately.

visualization The ability to imagine how separate things will look if they were put together in a particular way.

voice When an employee speaks up to offer constructive suggestions for change, often in reaction to a negative work event.

W

wasting resources Using too many materials or too much time to do too little work.

whistle-blowing When employees expose illegal actions by their employer.

withdrawal behavior Employee actions that are intended to avoid work situations.

Wonderlic Personnel Test A 12-minute test of general cognitive ability used to hire job applicants.

work complexity The degree to which job requirements tax or just exceed employee capabilities.

work responsibility The number and importance of the obligations that an employee has to others.

work specialization The degree to which tasks in an organization are divided into separate jobs.

work team A relatively permanent team in which members work together to produce goods and/or provide services.

work-family conflict A form of role conflict in which the demands of a work role hinder the fulfillment of the demands in a family role (or vice versa).

written comprehension The ability to understand written words and sentences.

written expression The ability to communicate ideas in writing.

Z

zero acquaintance Situations in which two people have just met.

Chapter 1

Page 5: © Reuters / Corbis; page 9: © Knight Rider / Tribune / Newscom; page 12: Photo courtesy of Hyundai Motor America; page 19: Harvard Business School Press; Jacket design by Mike Fender; page 20: © Corbis SYGMA; page 24: Chris Rank / Bloomberg News / Landov

Chapter 2

Page 35: © David Young-Wolff / PhotoEdit; page 39: © Disney Enterprises, Inc. / Pixar Animation Studios / Photofest NYC; page 42: United States Department of Labor; page 49: © BananaStock / PunchStock; page 53: © AP / Wide World Photos; page 54: © Warner Business Books. All Rights Reserved

Chapter 3

Page 65: Dennis Van Tine / Landov; page 70: Liquidlibrary / JupiterImages; page 73: © AP / Wide World Photos; page 75: © François Duhamel / Sygma / Corbis; page 86: © Harvard Business School Press; page 89: © Lou Dematteis / Reuters / Corbis

Chapter 4

Page 103: Courtesy of Wegmans; page 109: Photo courtesy of Quik Trip Convenience Stores; page 116: © TongRo Image Stock / Alamy; page 122: © Perseus Books; page 124: © Warner Bros. / Photofest

Chapter 5

Page 141: © AP / Wide World Photos; page 145: © Image Source Pink / Alamy; page 147: © 1997 Richard Carlson, Ph.D. Reprinted by permission of Hyperion. All Rights Reserved; page 149: © PhotoFest Inc.; page 153:

© RF / Corbis; page 158: Ryan McVay / Getty Images

Chapter 6

Page 177: © AP / Wide World Photos; page 179 (top left): Steve Mason / Getty Images; page 179 (middle left): Ryan McVay / Getty Images; page 179 (bottom left): Nick Koudis / Getty Images; page 179 (top middle): © Daniel Goodchild / Alamy; page 179 (top right): Ryan McVay / Getty Images; page 185: © Sony Pictures Entertainment / Photofest; page 189: Kimimasa Mayama / Bloomberg News / Landov; page 199: The McGraw-Hill Companies, Inc. / Rick Brady, photographer; page 200: From FISH! By Stephen C. Lundin, Ph.D. Harry Paul and John Christensen. Copyright © 2000 by Stephen Lundin, PhD., Harry Paul and John Christensen. Reprinted by permission of Hyperion. All Rights Reserved.

Chapter 7

Page 217: © The McGraw-Hill Companies, Inc. / John Flournoy, photographer; page 221: © Brand X Pictures / PunchStock; page 225: © Photofest Inc.; page 231: Steven Brahms / Bloomberg News / Landov; page 235: © AP / Wide World Photos; page 242: © Simon & Schuster, Inc.

Chapter 8

Page 255: © Mark Peterson / Redux; page 257: Dynamic Graphics / JupiterImages; page 259: © Digital Vision; page 263: © AP / Wide World Photos; page 267: Courtesy of Little Brown Publishing. All Rights Reserved.; page 269: PARAMOUNT / THE KOBAL COLLECTION / MARKS, ELLIOTT; page 275:

© Kevin Moloney / The New York Times / Redux

Chapter 9

Page 291: Jean Christian Bourcart / Photo features Joey Stalzer, a 2004 Greater New Orleans Corp member; page 294: © RF / Corbis; page 299: © Universal Studios / Photofest; page 304: © RF / Corbis; page 306: © AP / Wide World Photos; page 315: Courtesy of Simon & Schuster. All Rights Reserved.

Chapter 10

Page 335: ©Norbert von der Groeben / The Image Works; page 337: Fox Searchlight Pictures / Photofest; page 338: © Columbia Pictures / Photofest; page 341: © NBC Photographer: Paul Drinkwater / Photofest; page 344: Courtesy of Harper Collins. All Rights Reserved.; page 346: © Digital Vision; page 349: © AP / Wide World Photos; page 353: © 2006 Cabrillo Festival of Contemporary Music. All Rights Reserved.

Chapter 11

Page 371: © Walt Disney Pictures / Photofest; page 374: Courtesy of Random House. All Rights Reserved.; page 376: Stockbyte / Getty Images; page 383: © AP / Wide World Photos; page 388: © George Tiedemann / Corbis; page 390: © Ryan McVay / Getty Images; page 392: © Warner Bros. / Photofest

Chapter 12

Page 407: © AP / Wide World Photos; page 410: © Warner Bros. / Photofest; page 411: Copyright William James Warren 2007. All other rights are reserved.; page 414: TRUMP PROD. /

MARK BURNETT PROD. / THE KOBAL COLLECTION; page 418: © SuperStock; page 424: © The New York Times

Chapter 13

Page 439: © AP / Wide World Photos; page 445: © Miramax / Photofest; page 454: Courtesy of The Penguin Group. All Rights Reserved.; page 456: Courtesy of One Laptop Per Child

Chapter 14

Page 471: © Apple Computer, Inc. Used with permission. All rights reserved. Apple ® and the Apple logo are registered trademarks of Apple Computer, Inc.; page 473 (left): © AP / Wide World Photos; page 473 (right): © Krista Kennell / ZUMA / Corbis; page 478: © Mark Peterson / Redux; page 482: © New Line / Photofest; page 488: Tim Graham / Getty Images. Page 498: The Leadership Challenge 3/e by Jim Kouzes and Barry Posner. Copyright © 2006. Reprinted with permission of John Wiley & Sons, Inc.

Chapter 15

Page 515: © AP / Wide World Photos; page 519: © Sunset Boulevard / Corbis; page 522: LUCASFILM/20TH CENTURY FOX / THE KOBAL COLLECTION; page 526: Courtesy of Farrar, Straus, Giroux, LLC. All Rights Reserved.; page 531: YOSHIKAZU TSUNO / AFP / Getty Images

Chapter 16

Page 545 (left): THOMAS LOHNES / AFP / Getty Images; page 545 (right): © Richard Carson / Reuters / Corbis; page 549: © Harper Collins. All Rights Reserved.; page 550: © IDEO / Nicholas Zurcher; page 554: © james cheadle / Alamy; page 562: © Universal Studios / Photofest

Page numbers with n indicate notes.

A

Abraham, L. M., 326
Abush, R., 172
Adams, G. L., 467
Adams, J. S., 194n, 212, 227n, 249
Aditya, R. N., 504, 505
Adler, S., 330
Aguinis, H., 31, 212
Ahearne, M., 61, 510
Ahlrichs, N. S., 93
Aiman-Smith, L., 214, 574
Albright, L., 326
Aldana, S. G., 170
Alderfer, C. P., 183n, 210
Alge, B. J., 191n, 211
Allan, B., 287
Allen, N. J., 30, 71n, 93, 94
Allen, Paul, 472
Allen, T. D., 62, 576
Alliger, G. M., 277n, 286
Allport, G. W., 324
Alsop, Marin, 353
Alterman, T., 170, 174
Alutto, J. A., 404
Ambrose, M. L., 252
Ancona, D. G., 434
Anderson, D. K., 60
Anderson, N., 63, 94, 138, 503
Anderson, N. R., 575
Anderson, R. D., 509
Andersson, L. M., 63
Andrews, A. O., 32
Ang, S., 365
Anthony, W. P., 284
Arad, S., 40n, 60
Arbaugh, J. B., 287
Armenakis, A., 173
Armour, S., 63
Armstrong, L., 31
Armstrong, T., 330
Arthaud-Day, M. L., 136
Arvey, R. D., 325, 326
Asendorpf, J. B., 326, 327
Ashford, S. J., 575
Ashforth, B. E., 285, 465
Ashkanasy, N. M., 138, 573, 575
Aston, A., 253
Atalla, A. M., 60
Atanasoff, L., 328
Athos, G., 249
Atkin, R. S., 96
Audia, P. G., 212
Auletta, K., 63
Austin, A., 365
Austin, N. K., 174
Austin, W. G., 248
Avalos, J., 365
Averbrook, J., 286

Avila, R. A., 62
Avolio, B., 475n, 507, 508, 509, 510
Ayman, R., 400, 432

B

Bacharach, S. B., 467
Bachiochi, P. D., 132n, 139
Bachrach, D. G., 61, 496n, 509
Bacon, F., 32
Bailey, D. E., 375n, 400
Baine, J. B., 61
Baldwin, T. T., 136, 139
Ballard, T. N., 437
Ballmer, Steve, 196
Balzer, W. K., 132n, 139
Bandura, A., 182n, 209, 284
Barbee, A. P., 331
Barber, A. E., 575
Barksdale, K., 252
Barling, J., 510
Barney, J. B., 31
Barnum, D. T., 214
Baron, J., 272n
Bar-On, R., 364, 365
Baron, R. A., 138, 467
Barra, A., 366
Barrett, A., 95, 211
Barrick, M. R., 138, 314n, 325, 326, 327, 328, 329, 330, 402
Barros, E., 138
Barry, B., 402
Barsky, A. P., 326
Bartol, K. M., 214
Bass, B., 475n
Bass, B. M., 489, 506–507, 508
Bates, S., 249
Bauer, T. N., 503, 568n, 574
Baynes, H. G., 328
Bazerman, M. H., 227n, 250, 468
Beal, D. J., 138, 435
Beaubien, J. M., 284–285
Bebeau, M. J., 251
Becker, H. S., 94
Becker, L. C., 249
Becker, T. E., 536n
Becker, W. S., 210
Beda, Joe, 66
Bedeian, A. G., 173
Beehr, T. A., 97
Beersma, B., 468
Behr, P., 435
Bell, B. S., 404, 435, 436
Bell, M. P., 403
Benne, K., 387n
Benne, Kenneth, 401
Bennett, R. J., 48n, 62
Bennett, W., Jr., 277n, 286
Benson, Herbert, 165
Benson, L., 250
Bergey, P. K., 214

Berkowitz, L., 194n, 212, 227n, 249, 285
Berliner, D. C., 324
Berman, D., 437
Bernardin, H. J., 331
Berner, R., 247, 504
Bernieri, F., 363
Berns, G., 137
Bernstein, A., 247
Berry, C. M., 314n
Bethune, Gordon, 551
Betof, E., 467
Beubien, J. M., 436
Beyer, J. M., 572
Bezos, Jeff, 390
Bhaskar-Shrinivas, P., 172
Bhatia, P., 509
Bhawuk, D.P.S., 467
Bianco, A., 247
Biberman, G., 468
Bies, R. J., 227n, 250, 251
Bilodeau, E. A., 365
Birger, J., 247
Birjulin, A., 467
Birkeland, S. A., 331
Black, J. S., 97, 171, 328, 575
Blake, Frank, 487
Blanchard, K. H., 506
Blank, W., 506
Blau, G., 95
Blau, P., 252
Blickensderfer, E., 436
Bliese, P. D., 327
Bligh, M. C., 508
Bluedorn, A. C., 542
Bobocel, D. R., 183n, 210
Bohte, J., 541
Boisner, A., 574
Bolger, N., 327
Bommer, W. H., 136, 509, 510
Bond, M. H., 309n
Bono, J. E., 127n, 138, 326, 327, 477n, 508, 509
Boodoo, G., 363
Borgen, F. H., 328
Borman, W. C., 60, 61, 174, 314n, 329, 340n, 352n, 363, 404, 435
Borman, W. S., 366
Bormann, C. A., 467
Borrows, P., 465
Boswell, W. R., 173, 355n, 366
Bouchard, T. J., Jr., 325, 326, 363
Boudreau, J. W., 173, 355n, 366
Bourgeois, L. J., 467
Bowen, D. E., 510, 573
Boykin, A. W., 363
Boyle, M., 245n
Bozell, D., 436
Bradley, J. C., 327
Brady, F. N., 252
Brahy, S., 575
Brandt, T. S., 506

Brannick, M. T., 110n, 136, 139, 331
Breaugh, J. A., 137
Breen, B., 332
Brehmer, B., 401, 433
Breinin, E., 509
Bremner, B., 539n
Brenner, B., 541
Brett, J. F., 264n
Bretz, R. D., 355n, 366
Brief, A. P., 138
Briggs, S. R., 248
Brin, Sergey, 336
Brinkmann, J., 284, 329
Brockmann, E. N., 284
Brockner, J., 209, 250, 286, 536n, 543
Brodbeck, F. C., 507
Brody, N., 363
Brouer, R. L., 467
Brown, K. G., 210
Bryan-Low, C., 467
Bryant, F. B., 172
Buckingham, M., 330
Buderi, R., 466
Buffett, Warren, 196, 268
Buford, B., 283
Bunker, B. B., 226n, 248, 249
Burd, Gary, 66
Burke, C. S., 436
Burke, M. E., 156n, 164n, 173, 174
Burke, M. J., 435
Burkhead, E. J., 172
Burnett, D. D., 330
Burnfield, J. L., 504
Burns, L. M., 507
Burns, L. R., 542
Burns, T., 525n
Burris, L. R., 331
Burrows, P., 464n, 503
Burt, R. S., 247
Burtt, H. E., 505
Bush, George W., 492
Buss, A. H., 26n
Butcher, J. N., 324
Butterfield, K. D., 251
Byham, W. C., 284
Byosiere, P., 172, 173
Byrne, D., 403
Byrne, Z. S., 183n, 210
Byrnes, N., 98, 209, 213, 253

C

Cable, D. M., 574
Cacioppo, J. T., 138
Caldwell, D. L., 565n, 572
Callahan, C., 331
Callister, R. R., 574
Camara, W. J., 365
Camerer, C., 247
Cameron, K. S., 464n
Campbell, D. P., 328
Campbell, D. T., 32

Campbell, J. P., 32, 60
Campion, M. A., 96, 137, 380n, 394n, 404, 425n, 436
Cannon, W. B., 172
Cannon-Bowers, J. A., 436
Cappelli, P., 98
Capps, M. H., 331
Carey, S., 436
Carlson, Richard, 147
Carnevale, A. P., 286
Carroll, A. B., 252–253
Carroll, J. B., 364
Carroll, S. J., 329
Carson, K. D., 459n
Carson, K. P., 139
Carson, P. P., 459n
Cartwright, D., 465
Caruso, D., 349n
Cascio, W. F., 97
Castellan, N. J., 436
Catania, A., 96
Catmull, Ed, 372, 397
Cattell, R. B., 364
Cavanaugh, M. A., 173
Cayne, James, 196
Ceci, S. J., 363
Cellar, D. F., 327
Cellitti, D. R., 63
Chao, G. T., 558n, 574
Chaplin, Charlie, 519
Charness, N., 284
Chatman, J. A., 572, 574
Chavez, C., 466
Chemers, M. M., 400, 432
Chen, C. C., 466
Chen, Y. R., 466
Chen, Z. X., 508
Cherniss, C., 364, 365
Chernyshenko, O. S., 326
Cherrington, D., 95
Chess, W. A., 173
Child, J., 541
Chiu, C., 285
Christal, R. E., 324
Christensen, John, 200
Christiansen, N. D., 97, 331
Church, A. H., 136
Clark, M. S., 137–138
Clark, R. C., 287
Clarke, S., 573
Clayton, L. D., 400
Clinton, Bill, 444, 493
Clore, G., 403
Clow, Lee, 500
Coblin, James, 178
Coffman, C., 330
Cohen, Ben, 89
Cohen, J., 325
Cohen, R. R., 435
Cohen, S., 173
Cohen, S. G., 375n, 400

Cohen-Charash, Y., 203n, 213, 250
Colarelli, S. M., 355n, 366
Colbert, A. E., 210, 477n
Colella, A., 213
Coleman, V. I., 61
Colligan, M., 170, 173
Collins-Nakai, R., 97
Colquitt, J. A., 60, 203n, 213, 240n, 249, 250, 251, 277n, 286, 312n, 327, 329, 366, 434, 508
Comer, D. R., 402
Conger, J. A., 507, 508
Conley, C., 297n
Conlin, M., 203n, 252, 542
Conlon, D. E., 213, 249, 286
Conte, J. M., 365
Converse, S. A., 436
Cook, T. D., 32
Cooke, D. K., 331
Coon, H. M., 329
Coons, A. E., 483n, 505
Cooper, C. L., 136, 173, 174, 214, 504, 510
Cooper, E. A., 212
Cooper, H., 327
Cooper-Hakim, A., 127n, 139, 330
Copper, C., 435
Corio, P., 213
Cortina, J. M., 332
Costa, P. T., Jr., 293n, 325
Costanza, D. P., 340n, 352n, 363
Cote, S., 364, 365
Cotton, J. L., 173, 465
Couch, L. L., 248
Covey, S.M.R., 251
Cox, T. H., 329, 402, 434
Coy, P., 97
Criqui, M. H., 325
Cropanzano, R., 183n, 210, 248, 250, 251, 467, 523n
Crossley, C. D., 132n, 139
Crouter, A., 171
Crump, C. E., 170
Csikszentmihalyi, Mihaly, 122
Cullen, M. J., 223n, 330
Cummings, L. L., 184n, 210, 286, 325, 330, 503, 543, 572
Cunningham, D. A., 173, 174
Cunningham, M. R., 331
Cunningham-Snell, N. A., 575
Curry, J., 61

D

Dalal, R. S., 127n, 138
Dalessio, A., 139
Dane, E., 285
Daniels, C., 172, 174, 229n, 247
Dansereau, F., 404, 503
Dante, Dolores, 117
Daus, C. S., 138
Davenport, T., 283

Davies, M., 364
Davis, G. F., 541, 542
Davis, J. H., 220n, 222n, 226n, 247
Davison, H. K., 332
Dawis, R. V., 106n, 136
Dawson, C., 31
Dawson, J. F., 555n
Day, D. V., 503
Deal, T. E., 572
Dean, M. A., 365
Dean, R. A., 355n, 366
Dearborn, M. J., 173
de Chermont, K., 326
De Church, L. A., 435
Deci, E. L., 183n, 210, 213
Decker, Frank, 114
Decker, P. T., 324
De Dreu, C.K.W., 435, 468
Defrank, R. S., 172, 174
Delbecq, A. L., 401, 433
Delery, J. E., 97
De Long, D. W., 283
Delongis, A., 171
DeMatteo, J. S., 404
De Meuse, K. P., 375n, 404
DeNeve, K. M., 327
Den Hartog, D. N., 503, 505
Dessler, G., 97
Detterman, D. K., 365
Deutsch, M., 401, 404
Devadoss, S., 96
Devine, D. J., 400, 401
Devine, K., 97
DeVore, C. J., 63, 138
Dewe, P. J., 173
Dickter, D. N., 355n, 366
Diehl, M., 433
Diener, E., 121n, 137, 138, 139, 326
Digman, J. M., 324
DiMicco, Daniel, 208
Dineen, B. R., 249
Dirks, K. T., 240n, 252
Dixon, P., 330, 331
Dobbins, G. H., 329, 420n
Docter, P., 60
Doke, D., 168n
Donkin, R., 468
Donnellan, M. B., 296n
Donovan, J. J., 211
Donovan, M. A., 40n, 60
Dorfman, P. W., 507, 510
Dorgan, B. L., 437
Dorgan, Byron, 427
Dosier, L. N., 61
Dotlich, D., 436
Dougherty, P., 366
Douglas, C., 452n, 467
Douma, B., 252
Doverspike, D. D., 327
Dowling, S., 397n
Drach-Zahavy, A., 466, 467

Drasgow, F., 32, 120n
Driskell, J. E., 436
Drucker, P. F., 63
du Gay, P., 573
Duke, A. B., 467
Duncan, T. E., 184n
Dunford, B. B., 400
Dunkel-Schetter, C., 171
Dunnette, M. D., 32, 60, 93, 106n, 136, 172, 262n, 283, 324, 468, 506
Durham, C. C., 214
Dvir, T., 510
Dvorak, P., 541
Dwyer, P., 434
Dychtwald, Ken, 86

E

Earley, P. C., 212, 250, 365, 401, 434
Ebert, Larry, 142
Eby, L. T., 327, 329, 404, 576
Echternacht, G., 365
Eckert, Robert, 531
Eden, D., 510
Edmondson, G., 327, 575
Edwards, C., 541
Edwards, J. R., 574
Ehrhart, M. G., 553n, 573
Eisenhardt, K. M., 467
Eisenhower, Dwight D., 488
Eisner, Michael, 478
Eldam, M., 31
Eldridge, L. D., 170
Elgin, B., 93, 363, 465
Elkind, P., 572
Ellis, A.P.J., 436
Elms, H., 401
Emerson, R. M., 465
Emo, A. K., 364
Endler, N. S., 330
Engardio, P., 434
Erez, A., 60, 127n, 138, 191n, 327, 366, 401
Erez, M., 94, 212, 434
Erickson, E. H., 248
Erickson, Tamara J., 86
Ericsson, K. A., 284
Esser, J., 435
Eucker, T. R., 284
Eustace, A., 363
Euwema, M. C., 435
Evans, M., 332
Evanson, Paul, 195
Evers, A., 468
Ewen, R., 403
Ewing, J., 575
Exner, J. E., Jr., 248

F

Fahey, J., 468
Falbe, C. M., 459n, 465, 466
Fandt, P. M., 468

Farrell, D., 94, 95
Feist, G. J., 327
Feltovich, P. J., 284
Fenigstein, A., 26n
Fenwick, Lex, 549–550
Ference, R., 435
Ferguson, C. H., 363
Fern, E. F., 62
Fernandez, C. F., 506
Ferrin, D. L., 240n, 252
Ferris, G. R., 137, 214, 330, 401, 435, 452n, 466, 467, 468, 503, 574
Festinger, L., 435
Fetter, R., 62, 509
Fichman, M., 96
Field, R.H.G., 504–505
Fields, Mark, 560
Finn, R. H., 212
Fiorina, Carly, 440, 443, 463, 537
Fisher, A., 95, 97, 98, 219n, 247, 283, 364
Fisher, C. D., 574
Fishman, C., 247
Fitzgerald, M. P., 117n, 137
Fleishman, E. A., 340n, 352n, 363, 365, 505
Fletcher, S., 322n
Floor, L., 505
Florey, A. T., 403
Fogli, L., 329
Folger, R., 249, 251
Folkers, D., 286
Folkman, S., 170, 171, 172
Foltz, J., 96
Ford, Henry, 519
Forger, G., 30
Forsyth, D. R., 252
Fowler, T., 572
Fowlkes, J. E., 436
Frankfort, Lew, 195
Frauenheim, E., 330, 331, 573
Freeman, Bud, 115–116
Frei, R. L., 326
Freidberg, J., 60
Freidberg, K., 60
French, J.R.P., Jr., 465
Frese, M., 174
Frey, M. C., 365
Fried, Y., 137
Friedman, H. S., 325
Friedman, M., 172, 327
Friedman, Thomas L., 13, 31, 526
Frink, D. D., 452n, 467
Frone, M. R., 171
Frost, P. J., 573
Fry, L., 574
Fu, P. P., 466
Fujita, F., 326
Fulmer, I. S., 32
Funder, D. C., 324
Furnham, A., 314n, 329
Fusilier, M. R., 173
Futrell, D., 375n, 404

G

Gabarro, J. J., 249
Gaertner, S., 95, 96
Gaines, J., 574
Galbraith, J., 184n
Gale, S. F., 30, 31
Galton, F., 364
Gannon, M. J., 172, 212, 223n, 251, 324
Ganster, D. C., 171, 172, 173
Gardner, H., 364
Gardner, P. D., 558n, 574
Gardner, W. L., 328
Garland, H., 286
Gates, Bill, 76, 472
Gavin, J. H., 403
Gavin, M. B., 252
Gebhardt, D. L., 170
Gellar, A., 331
Gent, Christopher, 451
George, G., 281n
George, J. M., 138, 327
Gergen, K., 249
Gerhardt, M. W., 326, 477n
Gerhart, B., 32, 210, 214, 469
Gerras, S. J., 573
Gersick, C.J.G., 401
Gerstner, C. R., 503
Gerstner, Louis V., Jr., 549
Geschka, H., 433
Gibson, C. B., 212, 309n, 328
Gibson, R., 575
Gibson, W. M., 110n, 136, 139
Gigernzer, P. M., 272n
Gilbreth, F. B., 136
Gillers, G., 324
Gilliland, S., 248, 250, 332
Gilmore, D. C., 467
Gist, M. E., 182n, 210, 510
Gladwell, Malcolm, 267
Glazerman, S., 324
Glick, W. H., 541
Gloeckler, G., 213
Glomb, T. M., 250
Gobeli, D. H., 542
Godinez, V., 400
Goethals, G. R., 436
Goff, S., 366
Goffee, R., 552n, 573
Goffin, R. D., 331
Gogoi, P., 245n
Gogus, C. I., 574, 575
Gold, E., 30
Goldbacher, E., 184n
Goldberg, L. R., 293n, 324, 325, 326
Golden, D., 286
Goldenhar, L., 170, 174
Goldsmith, M., 92n
Goldstein, D. L., 172
Goldstein, H. W., 574
Goldstein, N. B., 332

Goleman, D., 364
Gooding, J. Z., 541
Gooding, R. Z., 404
Goodman, P. S., 96
Gopinath, C., 536n, 542
Gordan, J., 400
Gore, Bill, 524
Goslin, D. A., 251
Gosling, S. D., 326
Gouran, D., 435
Graen, G. B., 475n, 503
Graf, A. B., 574
Grant, S., 330
Gravelle, M., 574, 575
Graziano, W. G., 326
Green, H., 184n
Green, S. G., 503, 506
Greenberg, J., 31, 212, 213, 232n, 247, 248, 250, 251
Greenberg, M., 249
Greene, J., 93
Greene, Robert, 454
Greenfield, Jerry, 89
Greenhouse, S., 400
Griffeth, R. W., 78n, 95, 96
Griffeth, T. L., 468
Groszkiewicz, D., 541
Grove, Andy, 444
Grover, R., 503, 504
Grow, B., 94, 506
Grubb, P., 170, 174
Gruen, R. J., 171
Gruenfeld, D. H., 403
Gubbins, E., 575
Gully, S. M., 436
Gunther, M., 247, 253
Gupta, N., 97
Gupta, V., 507
Gurin, G., 505
Guzzo, R. A., 401, 403, 433, 435

H

Haasen, A., 572
Hachiya, D., 95
Hackett, R. D., 508
Hackman, J. R., 120n, 136, 137, 213, 404, 432, 433, 541, 542
Hafner, K., 362n
Haga, W. J., 503
Hagafors, R., 401, 433
Haigh, J., 575
Hair, E. C., 326
Haldeman, Ed, 521
Halfhill, T., 400
Hall, D., 281n
Hall, E., 403
Hall-Merenda, K. E., 508
Halpern, D. F., 363
Halpin, A. W., 505
Hamblin, R. L., 404

Hamilton, A., 170, 174
Hamm, J., 542
Hamm, S., 542
Hamper, B., 80, 96
Hanges, P. J., 507
Hanisch, K. A., 139
Hansen, F., 214, 250
Haran, 174
Hardy, Q., 465, 466
Hargadon, A., 433
Harkins, S. G., 404, 433
Harper, D., 63
Harris, E. F., 505
Harris, J. A., 507–508
Harris, M. J., 363
Harris, M. M., 331
Harris, V. A., 285
Harrison, D. A., 97, 127n, 139, 172, 355n, 366, 403
Harriss, Cynthia, 480
Hart, R., 31
Hartel, C.E.J., 138
Hartley, E., 505
Harvey, S., 92n
Hastings, J. E., 173
Hatfield, E., 138
Haugland, S. N., 330
Havlovic, S. J., 151n, 171
Hayashi, A. M., 285
Hayward, Louis, 115
Hazelwood, Joseph, 273
Hechanova, R., 97
Hecker, D., 63
Hedlund, J., 401, 434
Heller, D., 326
Heller, L., 573
Helm, B., 253
Hemphill, J. K., 483n, 505
Henderson, Naomi, 154, 165
Henle, C. A., 31, 212
Herscovitch, L., 93, 94, 127n, 139, 203n, 277n, 286, 496n, 509
Hersey, P., 506
Herzberg, F., 32
Hesseldahl, A., 464n
Hessels, M., 572
Hezlett, S. A., 576
Hickson, D. J., 465–466
Higgins, C. A., 325
Higgins, J. M., 572
Higgs, A. C., 394n, 404
Hill, J. M., 96
Hinings, C. R., 465–466
Hirokawa, R., 435
Hirschman, A. O., 95
Hochschild, A. R., 138
Hochwarter, W., 452n, 467, 543
Hockwarter, L., 536n
Hof, R. D., 465
Hoffman, L., 403

Hoffman, R. R., 284
Hofmann, D. A., 573
Hofstede, G., 62, 308, 309n, 328
Hoft, S., 331
Hogan, J., 326
Hogan, R., 24n, 248
Hogan, R. T., 324
Hogg, M. A., 285
Holcombe, K. M., 573
Holland, B., 326
Holland, J. L., 308n, 328
Hollenbeck, J. R., 191n, 211, 400, 401, 432, 433, 434, 436
Hollinger, R. C., 63
Hollingshead, A. B., 436
Hollweg, Lewis, 63
Holmes, S., 253, 504
Holmes, T. H., 150n, 171
Holtom, B. C., 94
Hom, P. W., 96
Homans, G. C., 212
Hong, Y., 285
Hosford, C., 542
Hough, J.M.R., 172
Hough, L. M., 32, 60, 93, 106n, 136, 262n, 283, 314n, 324, 329, 468, 506
House, R. J., 504, 505, 507, 508
Howard, J. A., 285
Howard, J. H., 173
Howard-Grenville, J. A., 574
Howell, J. M., 508, 510
Howell, J. P., 510
Huber, G. P., 541
Huber, V. L., 284
Hui, W., 572
Hulin, C. L., 93, 95, 136, 250
Hull, C. L., 209
Hull, R. R., 328
Humphrey, S. E., 434
Hunnicutt, D., 170
Hunt, J. G., 505
Hunt, S. D., 251
Hunter, J. E., 332, 366
Hurd, Mark, 439, 440, 441, 443, 463, 531, 537
Hurrell, J., Jr., 170, 173
Huselid, M. A., 16n, 32
Hymowitz, C., 541

I

Idaszak, J. R., 120n
Iger, Bob, 478
Ihlwan, M., 31
Ilgen, D. R., 60, 174, 210, 314n, 329, 400, 401, 404, 432, 433, 434, 435, 436
Ilies, R., 326, 329, 477n, 505, 509
Immelt, Jeffrey R., 571
Incalcaterra, K. A., 436
Irani, Ray, 195
Ironson, G. H., 110n, 136, 139

Irwin, J. L., 132n, 139
Isen, A. M., 138
Ivancevich, J. M., 172, 174, 399n

J

Jackson, C. L., 61, 170, 312n, 329, 423n, 433, 434
Jackson, S. E., 31, 403
Jacobson, B. H., 170
Jacobson, D., 572
Jago, A. G., 504
Jang, K. J., 507–508
Janis, I. L., 435
Jardine, L., 32
Javidan, M., 507
Jayaratne, S., 173
Jeanneret, P. R., 340n, 352n, 363
Jeffries, Mike, 478
Jehn, K., 435, 468
Jenkins, C. D., 157n
Jenkins, Charles, Jr., 196
Jenkins, G. D., Jr., 97
Jennings, K. R., 173
Jensen-Campbell, L. A., 326
Jermier, J. M., 497n, 509, 510, 574
Jimeno, D. I., 96
Jobs, Steve, 372, 397, 471–473, 474, 490, 492, 500–501
Johns, G., 94, 96, 552n
Johnson, A. M., 507–508
Johnson, C., 433
Johnson, D. E., 127n, 138
Johnson, D. W., 404
Johnson, E. C., 566n, 575
Johnson, G., 63
Johnson, J. J., 223n
Johnson, J. S., 248
Johnson, K., 286
Johnson, L., 168n
Johnson, Lyndon, 493
Johnson, R., 404
Johnson, S. M., 139
Johnson, S. R., 170
Johnston, J., 170, 174
Jolie, Angelina, 444
Jones, A. P., 173
Jones, D., 433
Jones, E. E., 285, 286
Jones, G., 573
Jones, G. R., 567n
Jones, T. M., 236n, 251
Jones, W. H., 248
Joshi, A., 436
Judd, C. M., 285
Judge, T. A., 127n, 136, 138, 139, 302n, 314n, 325, 326, 327, 329, 330, 355n, 366, 477n, 496n, 505, 506, 507, 508, 509
Jung, Carl, 306, 328
Jung, K. G., 139

K

Kacmar, C. J., 452n, 467
Kacmar, K. M., 467
Kafry, D., 172
Kahn, R., 171, 172
Kahn, R. L., 172, 173, 505
Kahneman, D., 129n, 139, 270n, 272n, 285
Kaihla, P., 572
Kallasvuo, Olli-Pekka, 561
Kane, Y. I., 541
Kanfer, R., 250
Kanter, R. M., 94
Kaplan, M.D.G., 60
Kaplan, S. A., 326
Karatz, Bruce, 196
Katz, D., 505
Katz-Navon, T., 573
Kavanaugh, M. J., 287
Kaye, Beverly, 91
Kazmi, S., 365
Keller, R. T., 508
Kelley, H. H., 286
Kelley, T., 401, 413n, 432
Kelloway, E. K., 510
Kelly, David, 429
Kelman, H. C., 466
Kemmelmeier, M., 329
Kendall, L. M., 136
Kendell, J., 364
Kennedy, A. A., 572
Kennedy, J. C., 466
Kennedy, John F., 418, 482, 493
Kenny, D. A., 326
Keon, T. L., 542
Kerlinger, F. N., 32
Kerr, S., 497n, 504, 509–510
Keys, J. B., 61
Kiger, P., 95, 541, 542, 572
Kiker, D. S., 62
Kim, H., 459n, 466
Kinicki, A. J., 139
Kirkland, R., 213
Kirkman, B. L., 309n, 328
Kirkpatrick, S. A., 509
Kisamore, J. L., 331
Klawsky, J. D., 327
Klein, H. J., 191n, 211, 558n, 574, 575
Kleinfeld, Klaus, 561
Klimoski, R. J., 174, 314n, 329, 404, 435, 436
Kluwer, E. S., 468
Knight, Phil, 479
Kobasa, S., 173
Koenig, R., 401
Koh, W., 509
Kohlberg, L., 251
Kohles, J. C., 508
Kohn, M. L., 363

Kolb, D. M., 469
Kolokinsky, R. W., 452n, 467
Konopaske, R., 399n
Konstans, C., 355n, 366
Koopman, P. L., 503, 505
Kopp, Wendy, 292, 322n
Kopytoff, V., 363
Korbin, J. L., 365
Koretz, G., 136
Korman, A. K., 506
Korsgaard, M. A., 250
Koslowsky, M., 95, 97
Kouzes, James M., 498
Kowalski, R. M., 210
Kozlowski, D., 170
Kozlowski, S.W.J., 404, 435
Kraiger, K., 286
Kraimer, M. L., 459n
Kramer, R. M., 226n, 248, 465, 467
Krantz, L., 143n
Kranz, G., 510
Krausz, M., 95, 97
Kreitner, R., 284
Krilowicz, T. J., 62
Kristof-Brown, A. L., 566n, 575
Kroeck, K. G., 508
Krueger, A. B., 129n, 139
Kulmann, T. M., 172
Kuman, K., 403
Kurek, K. E., 138

L

Laczko-Kerr, I., 324
Lamm, H., 433
Lamonica, P. R., 400
Landy, F. J., 210
Langan-Fox, J., 330
Langton, L., 63
LaRocco, J. M., 173
Larsen, R. J., 121n, 137
Larson, A., 507
Larson, E. W., 542
Lashinsky, A., 465, 542
Lasseter, John, 372, 397
Latack, J. C., 151n, 171
Latane, B., 404, 433
Latham, G. P., 32, 188n, 189n, 190n, 191n, 209, 211, 212, 214, 284
Latham, S., 214
Lavelle, L., 213
Law, K. S., 350n, 364, 365, 508
Lawler, E. E., III, 136, 184n, 211, 214, 400, 404, 542
Lawler, E. J., 467
Lawrence, P. R., 137
Lawson, C., 284
Lawthom, R., 555n
Layard, R., 139
Layton, W. L., 328
Lazarus, R. S., 138, 170, 171, 172

Leach, D. J., 504
Lear, R. W., 572
Ledford, G. E., Jr., 400
Lee, C. A., 465–466
Lee, H. B., 32
Lee, Kai-Fu, 66, 449
Lee, L., 504
Lee, S. M., 212
Lee, T. W., 94, 96
Lefevre, Mike, 114
Lehmann, A. C., 284
Lei, B.Y.C., 287
Leitner, K., 172
Leno, Jay, 12
Lentz, E., 576
Leonard, B., 281n
LePine, J. A., 45n, 60, 61, 127n, 138, 161n, 170, 173, 174, 240n, 277n, 286, 327, 366, 401, 402, 423n, 433, 434, 436
LePine, M. A., 161n, 170, 173, 174
Levenson, E., 443n, 465
Leventhal, G. S., 227n, 249
Levering, R., 17n, 30, 31, 32, 93, 94, 95, 97, 98, 135, 136, 138, 249
Levesque, M. J., 326
Levin, S., 493n, 508
Lewicki, R. J., 226n, 227n, 248, 249, 250, 468
Lewis, D., 287
Lewis, J. D., 249
Liden, R. C., 503
Likert, R., 505
Lim, V.K.G., 95
Lima, L., 576
Lin, L. F., 110n, 136, 139
Lincoln, Abraham, 493
Lincoln, J., 403
Lind, E. A., 248, 249, 250
Linoerfer, J., 435
Liss, H. J., 573
Litterer, J. A., 468
Littman, J., 413n, 432
Lobel, S. A., 329, 402, 434
Locke, E. A., 32, 136, 138, 188n, 189n, 190n, 191n, 203n, 211, 213, 214, 327, 332, 366, 465, 468, 504, 509, 510
Locke, K., 32
Lockwood, N. R., 283
Loehlin, J. C., 325, 363
Loher, B. T., 117n, 137
Lombardo, M. M., 171
Looper, G., 61
Lorenzi, E., 284
Lorsch, J. W., 432, 542
Loughridge, Ken, 447
Louis, M. R., 573, 574
Lowe, K. B., 309n, 328, 508
Lowery, C. M., 62
Lubinski, D., 365
Lucas, R. E., 138
Lucovsky, Mark, 66

Luk, D. M., 172
Lum, S., 573
Lundberg, C. C., 573
Lundin, Stephem, 200
Luria, G., 573
Luthans, F., 32, 203n, 213, 284, 399n
Lux, S., 467
Lynch, P., 252

M

Mabey, C., 573
Maccoby, N., 505
MacDermid, S. M., 138
Mackay, David, 263
MacKenzie, S. B., 61, 62, 496n, 509, 510
MacMillan, P., 61
MacMillan, P. S., 384n, 401
MacMullan, J., 61
Mael, F., 285
Mael, F. A., 465
Magnus, K., 326
Magnusson, D., 330
Maier, N., 403
Maier, N.R.F., 209
Mainous, A. G., III, 95
Maitlis, S., 555n
Major, D. A., 400, 432, 433, 434
Malloy, T. E., 326
Malone, M. S., 465
Mandel, M., 171
Mann, O. K., 62
Manning, Peyton, 444
Mannix, E. A., 402, 403, 434, 574
Manson, T. M., 331
Manz, C. C., 400, 404
March, J. G., 285
Marcus, B., 331
Markham, S. E., 404
Marks, M. A., 434, 435, 436
Marquardt, M., 436
Marquez, J., 247, 541, 576
Marshall-Mies, J., 340n, 352n, 363
Martin, J., 573
Martin, L. R., 325
Martinez Arias, R., 434
Martinko, M. J., 328
Martins, L. L., 403
Martocchio, J. J., 96
Martz, A., 435
Maruyama, G., 404
Maslow, A. H., 183n, 210
Mason, B., 258n, 284
Mathieu, J. E., 94, 330, 423n, 434
Matteson, M., 399n
Matthews, G., 364
Matthieu, J. E., 314n
Mausner, B., 32
May, K. E., 403
Mayer, D. M., 553n
Mayer, D. P ., 324

Mayer, J., 349n
Mayer, J. D., 364
Mayer, J. L., 573
Mayer, R. C., 220n, 222n, 226n, 247, 248, 249, 252
Mayes, B. T., 173
Mazzetti, M., 31
McAdam, R., 258n, 284
McAdams, D. P., 324, 328
McAllaster, C., 572
McAllister, D. J., 248, 249
McAuley, E., 184n
McCabe, D. L., 252
McCall, M. W., 171
McCarthy, J. M., 507–508
McCartney, K., 363
McCaulley, M. H., 328
McClelland, C. L., 137
McColl-Kennedy, J. R., 509
McCracken, J., 575
McCrae, R. R., 293n, 325, 328
McCrory, J., 258n, 284
McDaniel, M. A., 326
McDonald-Mann, D., 510
McFarlin, D. B., 171
McGee-Cooper, A., 61
McGrath, J. E., 402
McGrath, M., 541
McGregor, J., 214, 466
McIntyre, M., 400
McKee-Ryan, F. M., 139
McKenna, J. F., 195n, 212
McLean, B., 251, 572
McLean, L. D., 573
McLendon, C. L., 435
McLeod, P. L., 329, 402, 434
McMurray, V. V., 465
Medsker, G. J., 380n, 394n, 404
Mehl, M. R., 326
Meier, K. J., 541
Meindl, J. R., 508
Melner, S. B., 400
Mendenhall, M., 97, 171, 172, 575
Menkes, Justin, 344
Menon, T., 285
Mento, A. J., 203n, 211, 213
Meyer, C. J., 434
Meyer, J. P., 30, 71n, 93, 94, 127n, 139, 203n, 277n, 286, 496n, 509
Meyers, D. G., 272n
Michaelsen, I., 403
Mickel, A. E., 210
Miles, R. E., 542
Milewski, G. B., 365
Millard, E., 397n
Miller, C., 184n
Miller, C. C., 541
Miller, H. E., 96
Miller, J., 170, 171, 172, 174, 403
Miller, K. I., 504

Miller, L. K., 404
Miller, M., 170, 171, 172, 174
Miller, M. L., 327
Miller-Frost, S. L., 400
Milliken, F. J., 403
Miner, A. G., 250
Miner, J. B., 331, 332
Miners, C.T.H., 364, 365
Minette, K. A., 210
Minkoff, H. B., 214
Mintzberg, H., 467
Mio, J. S., 493n, 508
Mischel, W., 330
Mishra, A., 536n, 542, 543
Mishra, K., 542
Mitchell, T. R., 94, 96, 182n, 210
Moag, J. G., 227n, 250, 251
Mobley, W., 96
Moeller, M., 92n
Moeller, N. L., 117n, 137
Moffat, Robert W., Jr., 532
Mohammed, S., 436
Mohrman, S. A., 400
Mokoto, R., 31
Mol, S., 329
Molso, M., 507–508
Monge, P. R., 504
Moon, H., 286
Mooney, C. H., 136
Moore, L. F., 573
Moore, Patrick, 529
Moorhead, G., 435
Moorman, R. H., 509
Morgan, William, 43
Morgeson, F. P., 573
Morison, Robert, 86
Morris, B., 63, 250
Morris, J. R., 97
Morris, M. W., 285
Morris, W. N., 137
Morrison, A. M., 171
Morrison, E. W., 62, 574
Morrison, T. G., 468
Morse, N., 505
Mosakowski, E., 365
Moskowitz, M., 17n, 30, 31, 32, 93, 94, 95, 97, 98, 135, 136, 138, 249
Motowidlo, S. J., 60, 61, 62, 366
Mount, M. K., 314n, 325, 326, 327, 328, 329, 330, 402
Mourier, P., 575
Mowday, R. T., 93, 94, 209
Moyer, B. C., 573
Muchinsky, P. M., 96, 328
Mullen, B., 433, 435, 436
Mulvey, P. W., 574
Mumford, M. D., 340n, 352n, 363
Murphy, K. R., 138, 364, 365
Murphy, L., 170, 173
Murphy, L. R., 174

Murphy, V., 92n
Murray, A., 465
Murray, S. S., 174
Myers, J. B., 328

N

Nardelli, Robert, 195, 486
Narvaez, D., 251
Nash, John, 36
Nauta, A., 468
Naveh, E., 573
Naylor, J. C., 210
Neal, M. A., 402, 434
Neal, M. E., 465, 467
Neale, M. A., 403, 468
Near, J. P., 136
Neck, C., 435
Negroponte, Nicholas, 456
Neihoff, B. P., 61
Neisser, U., 363
Nelson, B., 30, 31
Nelson, D., 404
Nemeth, C. J., 403
Nessbaum, B., 432
Neubert, M. J., 402
Neufeld, D. J., 508
Neufeld, S., 171, 174
Neuman, G. A., 402
Newcomb, T., 505
Newman, D., 139
Newman, D. A., 127n
Newman, K. L., 172, 212, 223n, 251, 324
Ng, K. Y., 203n, 213, 249
Ng, T.W.H., 327
Nicholson, N., 96
Nicholson-Crotty, S., 521n, 541
Niehoff, B. P., 510
Niles-Jolly, K., 553n, 573
Nisbett, R. E., 272n
Noe, N. L., 117n, 277n
Noe, R. A., 137, 286, 287
Noel, J., 436
Noel, T. W., 252
Noeldner, S., 142, 170
Noer, D. M., 542
Nonaka, I., 284
Norman, W. T., 324, 325
Norris, W. R., 506
Northcraft, G. B., 468, 469
Novak, M., 503
Noyce, J., 174
Nuttal, C., 541

O

O'Connor, A., 171
O'Connor, W. E., 468
Odbert, H. S., 324
Oddou, G., 97, 171
O'Dell, C., 404
O'Driscoll, M. P., 173

Oh, H., 252
Oldham, G. R., 120n, 136, 137, 213, 327, 433, 541
O'Leary-Kelly, A., 558n, 574
Olsen, R. N., 214
Olson-Buchanan, J. B., 173
Ones, D. S., 63, 94, 138, 314n, 318n, 331, 332, 503
Ordonez, L., 252
O'Reilly, C. A., III, 41n, 60, 402, 565n, 572, 574
Orey, M., 251
Organ, D. W., 61
Orwell, G., 502
Osborn, A. F., 433
Osland, J. S., 172
Oswald, B. M., 296n
Overholt, A., 330, 331
Oyserman, D., 329

P

Padgett, M. Y., 139
Paetzold, R. L., 213
Page, Larry, 336
Paine, J., 62, 509
Paine, J. B., 496n
Palmeri, C., 61
Palmeri, D., 326
Pals, J. L., 324, 328
Papper, E. M., 380n, 394n, 404
Park, B., 285
Park, O. S., 62
Parker-Pope, T., 170
Paronto, M. E., 568n
Parra, L. F., 132n, 139
Patrick, Tom, 115
Patterson, M. G., 555n
Patton, G. K., 127n, 138, 330
Paul, Harry, 200
Paul, K. B., 110n, 136, 139
Paulus, P. B., 404
Paumgarten, N., 468
Paunonen, S. V., 326
Pavot, W., 326
Payne, S. C., 284–285, 332
Paynton, C. F., 466
Pearce, J., 171
Pearson, C. M., 63
Peeters, M.A.G., 402
Peng, T. K., 466
Pennebaker, J. W., 326
Pennings, J. M., 465–466
Pepper, L., 536n, 543
Perkins, A., 173
Perloff, R., 363
Perrewé, P. L., 171, 467, 468
Persaud, J., 92n
Pescuric, A., 284
Peters, D. R., 505
Petersen, Kathryn, 411
Petersen, R., 574

Peterson, M. F., 573, 575
Peterson, N. G., 340n, 352n, 363
Peterson, S. J., 32
Pfeffer, J., 19, 32, 41n, 60, 465, 466
Philip, S., 184n
Philips, J. L., 400, 401, 434
Piccolo, R. F., 61, 423n, 434, 496n, 505, 507, 508, 509
Pike, Rob, 361
Pinder, C. C., 209, 210
Pines, A., 172
Pinkley, R. L., 468, 469
Piotrowski, C., 330
Piotrowski, M., 325, 326
Plamondon, K. E., 40n, 60
Platt, G., 575
Ployhart, R. E., 436
Podsakoff, N. P., 161n, 170, 173, 174
Podsakoff, P. M., 61, 62, 496n, 509, 510
Poon, M.J.L., 468
Pope, J., 322n
Popper, M., 509
Porter, C., 542
Porter, C.O.L.H., 203n, 213, 249
Porter, L. W., 93, 94, 96
Porter, M., 541
Posner, Barry Z., 498
Postman, L., 209
Poteet, M. L., 576
Potheni, Louis, 399n
Poulton, T., 573
Pratt, M. G., 285
Pressler, Paul, 479–480
Price, K. H., 403
Prieto Zamora, J. M., 434
Pritchard, D. R., 210
Pulakos, E. D., 40n, 60
Puranam, P., 508

Q

Quinn, R., 171

R

Radosevich, D. J., 211
Rafaeli, A., 138
Rahe, R. H., 150n, 171
Ramamoorthy, N., 329
Ramel, D., 467
Ramirez, G. G., 508
Randall, M. L., 467
Rapson, R. L., 138
Rasinski, K.A., 250
Rasor, M., 437
Raven, B., 465
Rayman, J., 328
Raymond, M., 322n
Reade, C., 97
Reagan, Ronald, 493
Reay, T., 97
Rechnitzer, P. A., 173

Reed, S., 434
Rees, D. W., 542
Reese, R., 493n, 508
Regan, M. P., 437
Reilly, M. E., 365
Resch, M. G., 172
Rest, J. R., 233n, 251
Reymen, I.M.M.J., 402
Reynolds, Lilith, 116
Reynolds, S. J., 248
Rice, R. W., 171
Richards, H., 400
Riediger, M., 331
Riggio, R. E., 489n, 493n, 506, 507, 508
Roberson, L., 250
Roberts, B. W., 297n, 325, 326
Roberts, R. D., 364
Robertson, D. C., 251
Robie, C., 132n, 139
Robinson, D. C., 555n
Robinson, S. L., 48n, 62
Rode, J. C., 136
Roehling, M. V., 173
Rogelberg, S. G., 504
Roger, C., 222n
Rogers, C., 95
Rokeach, M., 324
Roosevelt, Franklin, 493
Rosen, S. D., 214
Rosenbaum, M. E., 404
Rosenbaum, W. B., 212
Rosenberg, M., 248
Rosenman, R. H., 157n, 172, 327
Rosenthal, R. A., 171
Ross, J., 286
Ross, L., 272n, 285
Rosse, J. G., 96, 97
Roth, D., 94, 504
Roth, P. L., 127n, 139
Rotter, J. B., 248, 303n, 327
Rotundo, M., 62
Rounds, J., 328
Rousseau, D. M., 247
Rowe, C. W., 459n
Rowland, K. M., 401, 435
Roznowski, M., 95, 355n, 366
Rubin, R. S., 136
Ruffolo, Robert, 189
Ruiz, G., 542, 574
Rupp, D. E., 523n
Rupp, D. R., 183n, 210
Rusbult, C. E., 94, 95
Rush, M. C., 62
Rusli, E., 539n
Russell, Eugene, 113, 121n
Russell, J. A., 137
Russell, S. S., 110n, 136, 139
Ryan, A. M., 138, 330
Ryan, R. M., 183n, 210, 213
Rynes, S. L., 210, 469

S

Saari, L. M., 139, 211
Saavedra, R., 401
Sabella, M. J., 436
Sablynski, C. J., 94
Sackett, P. R., 62, 63, 138, 314n, 318n, 329, 330, 331
Sager, J. K., 95
Sagie, A., 95, 97
St. Jude Children's Hospital, 60
Salaman, G., 573
Salancik, G. R., 466
Salas, E., 403, 433, 436, 437
Salgado, J. G., 314n, 330
Salovey, P., 349n, 364
Saltz, J. L., 553n, 573
Sanchez, R. J., 568n
Sanchez-Runde, C. J., 324
Saucier, G., 293n, 325
Saul, J. R., 170, 423n, 434
Sauter, S., 170, 173
Sauve, E., 287
Scandura, T., 503
Scharf, F., Jr., 170, 173
Schaubroeck, J., 173
Schaude, G. R., 433
Scheier, M. F., 26n
Schein, E. H., 552, 567n, 573, 574, 575
Schepers, D. H., 250
Schiff, D., 400
Schiller, S., 434
Schilling, Curt, 43
Schkade, D. A., 129n, 139
Schlender, B., 247, 332, 400, 503
Schlicksupp, H., 433
Schmidt, F. L., 331, 332, 366
Schminke, M., 252, 523n
Schmit, M. J., 60, 366
Schmitt, N., 32
Schneck, R. E., 465–466
Schneider, B., 553n, 573, 574
Schoeff, J., Jr., 253
Scholl, R. W., 195n, 212
Schooler, C., 363
Schoorman, F. D., 220n, 222n, 226n, 247
Schriesheim, C. A., 139
Schuler, R. S., 31
Schwartz, J. E., 325
Schwartz, S. J., 184n
Schwartz, T., 365
Schwarz, N., 129n, 139
Schweitzer, M. E., 252
Scott, B. A., 240n
Scott, K. S., 32
Scott, Lee, 243
Scott, Ridley, 472
Scott, S., 248
Scott, W. R., 541, 542
Scullen, S. E., 214

Scullen, S. M., 328
Segal, N. L., 326
Sego, D. J., 432, 433, 434
Seifert, C. F., 466
Seldman, M., 467
Seligman, D., 365
Sellaro, C. L., 96
Sellers, P., 324, 506
Selye, H., 172
Semel, Terry, 195
Serwer, A., 31, 247
Seyle, H., 154n
Shackleton, V. J., 555n
Shadish, W. R., 32
Shaffer, M. A., 97, 172
Shalley, C. E., 327, 433
Shamir, B., 509, 510
Shapira, Z., 286
Shapiro, D., 209
Shaw, J. C., 251
Shaw, J. D., 97
Shaw, K. N., 211, 212
Shaw, M., 542
Shea, G. F., 572
Shea, G. P., 401, 435
Sheats, P., 387n, 401
Sheppard, A., 433
Sheppard, B. H., 227n, 250
Shimoff, E., 96
Shin, S. J., 509
Shore, L. M., 252
Shotland, A., 277n, 286
Shuit, D. P., 572
Silverman, D., 60
Silverthorne, M., 32
Simon, H., 541
Simon, H. A., 270n, 285
Simon, W. L., 502, 507, 508
Simons, T., 249
Simpson, Beryl, 115
Sims, H. P., Jr., 62, 400, 404
Sims, R. R., 284
Sinangil, H. K., 63, 94, 138, 503
Sinar, E. F., 132n, 139
Sinclair, R., 170, 174
Singer, A. D., 95, 97
Singer, J., 467
Singer, M., 541
Sitkin, S. B., 247
Sitzman, T., 286
Sivasubramaniam, N., 508
Skarlicki, D., 248
Skarlicki, D. P., 251
Skilling, Jeff, 545, 546
Skinner, B. F., 258
Skon, L., 404
Slocum, J., 574
Slovic, P., 272n, 285
Smith, C. A., 94
Smith, D. B., 574

Smith, J. L., 132n
Smith, M. A., 331, 575
Smith, P. C., 110n, 136, 139
Snoek, J., 171
Snow, C. C., 542
Snyder, L., 210
Snyderman, B. B., 32
Soetjipto, B. W., 459n
Somech, A., 466, 467
Sommerkamp, P., 503
Song, L. J., 350n, 364
Sonnentag, S., 174
Sorensen, K. L., 327
Sparks, J. R., 251
Sparrowe, R. T., 459n, 503
Spearman, C., 364
Spector, P. E., 203n, 213, 250, 436
Speizer, I., 210, 573
Spencer, L., 401
Spielberger, C. D., 324
Spitzmuller, C., 110n, 136, 139
Spodick, N., 250
Spreitzer, G., 536n
Spreitzer, G. M., 213, 542, 543
Stack, L. C., 248
Stahelski, A. J., 466
Stahl, G. K., 575
Stainton, L., 97
Stajkovic, A. D., 32, 203n, 213
Stalker, G. M., 525n
Stallings, Phil, 112
Stamps, D., 287
Stankov, L., 364
Stanley, D. J., 93, 94, 127n, 139, 203n, 277n, 286, 496n, 509
Stanton, J. M., 110n, 132n, 136, 139
Stark, S., 326
Stasster, G., 403
Staw, B. M., 210, 286, 325, 330, 402, 503, 543, 572
Stead, D., 210
Stebbins, R. A., 94
Steers, R. M., 93, 94, 96, 209, 324
Steiner, D., 248
Steiner, I. D., 402, 433
Stephens, J., 435
Stern, Z., 573
Sternberg, R. J., 284, 363, 364
Stevens, M. J., 425n, 436
Steward, D., 403
Stewart, D., 286
Stewart, G. L., 325, 326, 394n, 400, 401, 402, 404
Stewart, J., 465
Stibbe, M., 572
Stillings, J., 210
Stillwell, D., 503
Stinson, Dave, 255
Stogdill, R. M., 483n, 485n, 503, 505
Stone, A. A., 129n, 139

Stöppler, M. C., 172
Storey, J., 573
Stout, R. J., 436
Strage, A., 506
Strauss, J. P., 325
Stringer, Howard, 515
Stroebe, W., 433
Strong, E. K., 328
Suh, E., 139
Suh, E. M., 329
Sulkowicz, K., 213
Sundstrom, E., 375n, 400, 404
Suttle, J. L., 184n, 211
Sutton, R. I., 138, 250, 402, 433
Swanson, E., 505
Swanson, N., 170, 173

T

Tahmincioglu, E., 576
Tai, B., 283
Tait, M., 139
Takemoto-Chock, N. K., 324
Tam, P., 465
Tams, S., 212
Tan, H. S., 287
Tang, T. L., 210, 211
Tannenbaum, S. I., 277n, 286, 287
Taylor, A., III, 542
Taylor, F. W., 32, 136
Tedlow, R. S., 465
Tellegen, A., 121n, 137
Tepper, B. J., 250
Terkel, S., 112, 137
Terracciano, A., 328
Terry, D. J., 285
Tetrick, L. E., 252
Tett, R. P., 330
Thatcher, J. B., 467
Theobald, N. A., 521n, 541
Thibaut, J., 227n, 249
Thibodeau, P., 464n
Thierry, H., 203n, 213
Thoma, S. J., 251
Thomas, K. W., 210, 213, 457n, 468
Thompson, J. D., 401
Thompson, L. L., 435, 469
Thoreson, C. J., 127n, 138, 325, 326, 327
Thoreson, J. D., 327
Thorndike, E. L., 209
Thorndike, R. K., 364
Thurstone, L. L., 364
Tisdale, J., 170, 174
Tjosvold, D., 401
Tkaczyk, C., 443n, 465
Toll, Robert, 195
Tomlinson, E. C., 249
Tomlinson-Keasey, C., 325
Topolnytsky, L., 93, 94, 127n, 139, 203n,
    277n, 286, 496n, 509

Tracey, J. B., 287
Traver, H., 277n, 286
Treadway, D. C., 452n, 467
Treinen, J. J., 400
Trevino, L. K., 248, 251, 252
Triandis, H. C., 172, 329, 403
Trice, H. M., 572
Tripodi, T., 173
Trist, E. L., 96
Truman, H. S., 507
Tsui, A. S., 572
Tsui, L., 365
Tucker, J. S., 325
Tuckman, B. W., 400
Tuijl, H.F.J.M., 402
Tupes, E. C., 324
Turban, D. B., 542
Turner, A. N., 137
Tversky, A., 272n, 285
Tyler, K., 287
Tyler, T. R., 226n, 248, 250

U

Uhl-Bien, M., 475n, 503
Unkrich, L., 60
Urbina, S., 363
Useem, J., 247, 572

V

Valle, M., 468
Van Blerkom, M. L., 96
Van Den Bos, K., 248, 249
Van der Zee, K. I., 329
Van de Ven, A. H., 401, 433
Van de Vliert, E., 435
VandeWalle, D., 264n, 284
Van Dyne, L., 45n, 61, 401, 402
Van Eerde, W., 203n, 213
Van Fleet, D. D., 506
Van Maanen, J., 567n, 574
Van Oudenhoven, J. P., 329
van Rutte, C. G., 402
Van Scotter, J. R., 62
Vecchio, R. P., 506
Veiga, F., 32
Velthouse, B. A., 210, 213
Verbeke, W., 572
Vernon, P. A., 507–508
Vernon, P. E., 364
Vidmar, N. J., 404
Viechtbauer, W., 297n, 325
Viswesvaran, C., 63, 94, 127n, 139, 330, 331,
    332, 503
Vogelstein, F., 364
Volgering, M., 572
Volpe, C. E., 436
Vroom, V. H., 181n, 209, 210, 211, 213,
    481n, 504, 505

W

Wageman, R., 404
Wagner, J. A., III, 402, 404, 504, 541
Wagner, R. J., 573
Wagner, R. K., 284
Wah, L., 284
Waldman, D. A., 508
Walker, L., 227n, 249
Wallace, A. M., 555n
Walster, W., 227n, 249
Walton, K. E., 297n, 325
Walz, S. M., 61
Wanberg, C. R., 576
Wanek, J. E., 318n, 331
Wang, D., 508
Wang, H., 508
Wang, Y., 541
Wanous, J. P., 575
Warr, P. B., 504
Warren, B., 541
Warren, C. R., 326
Watanabe, S., 139
Waterman, A. S., 184n
Watson, D., 121n, 137, 403
Wayne, S. J., 466, 503
Weaver, G. R., 248, 251
Weaver, N., 574, 575
Webb, W. M., 248
Weber, G., 30
Weber, J., 61, 253, 284
Weber, T., 510
Weber, Y., 575
Wegman, Danny, 134
Wegman, Robert, 104
Wegner, D. M., 436
Weigert, A., 249
Weinberg, J., 536n, 543
Weingart, L. R., 435, 468
Weiss, H. M., 138, 262n, 283,
    284, 330
Weitz, J., 302n
Weitzel, J. R., 506
Welbourne, T. M., 32
Welch, Jack, 54, 55, 545, 546, 570
Welsh, E. T., 576
Wesson, M. J., 191n, 203n, 211, 213, 249,
    312n, 329, 574, 575
West, M. A., 555n
Wheeler, G. E., 252
Wheeler, L., 325
Whetten, D. A., 32, 464n
Whitney, K., 403
Wholey, D. R., 542
Widen, R., 437
Wiener, Y., 94
Wild, R. E., 251
Wilder, John, 195
Wilderom, C., 573, 575

Wilke, H.A.M., 248
Williams, J., 469
Williams, K., 402, 404, 433
Williams, K. D., 183n, 210
Williams, K. Y., 403
Williams, M. L., 510
Williams, S. W., 270n
Willis, R., 249
Wilpers, S., 326, 327
Winer, B. J., 505
Winfrey, Oprah, 444
Wingard, D. L., 325
Wisher, R., 286
Witt, L. A., 467
Wittenbaum, G., 403
Woertz, Pat, 444
Wolf, S., 558n, 574
Wolfe, D., 171
Wong, A., 401
Wong, C. S., 350n, 364
Wong, D. T., 331
Wood, R. E., 211, 213
Woodley, Butch, 255
Woodward, J., 541
Worchel, P., 248, 403
Wraith, S., 184n
Wright, J., 402

Wrightsman, L. S., Jr., 248
Wu, J. B., 572
Wyatt, J., 366
Wyden, Ron, 427

X

Xie, J. L., 62
Xin, K., 466
Xin, K. R., 572

Y

Yang, J., 332, 539n
Yang, J. L., 443n, 465
Yang, Jerry, 444
Yang, M. M., 466
Yank, J. L., 404
Yarnold, P. R., 172
Yetton, P. W., 504, 505
Young, Allison, 451
Young, C. E., 97
Young, J. S., 502, 507, 508
Young, M. I., 285
Young, Vince, 359
Youngcourt, S., 284–285
Yukl, G., 446n, 459n, 465, 466, 467, 477n, 503, 504, 505, 506

Z

Zacarro, S. J., 420n
Zaccaro, S. J., 434, 436, 504
Zajac, D. M., 94, 314n, 330
Zakay, E., 509
Zander, Edward, 196
Zapata-Phelan, C. P., 312n, 329
Zardkoohi, A., 213
Zedeck, S., 329
Zeidner, M., 364
Zemba, Y., 285
Zhang, Z., 572
Zhao, Y., 286–287
Zhou, J., 327, 433, 467, 509
Zhu, W., 509
Zimmerman, R. D., 566n, 575
Zi-you Yu, 401
Zohar, D., 573
Zuckerman, A., 327
Zyzanski, S. J., 157n

Company Index

A

Abercrombie & Fitch, 478
A.G. Edwards, 89
Alcoa, 524
Alcon Labs, 74
Allegheny Energy, 195
Amazon.com, 390
American Express, 347
American League Championship Series
    (ALCS), 43
Apple Computer, 471–474, 492, 500–501,
    516, 525, 548
Archer Daniels Midland (ADM), 444

B

Babbo, 257
Bank of America, 163
Bayer, 243
Bear Sterns, 196
Becton, Dickinson, and Company, 451
Ben & Jerry's, 88, 89, 550
Berkshire Hathaway, 196
Best Buy, 553
Bloomberg, 549
BMW, 305–306
Boeing, 531
Bowl Championship Series (BCS), 228–230
Bright Horizons, 107
Budco, 568

C

Capital One, 141–142, 163, 168
Cheesecake Factory, 557–558
Chevron, 444
Chubb Group, 568
Circuit City, 553
Cisco Systems, 72, 560
Coach, 195
Computer Associates International, 241
The Container Store, 9–11
Continental Airlines, 550–551
Corning, 165

D

DaimlerChrysler, 561
Delta Airlines, 14
Denny's, 554
Disco-Vision, 47
Disney, 478, 568
Dow Corning, 533
DuPont, 243

E

Electronic Data Systems, 378
Enron, 545–546, 570–571
Exxon, 273

F

FedEx, 557, 561
Fleet Bank, 163
Ford Motor Company, 560

G

Gap, Inc., 480
General Electric (GE), 54, 426, 533, 545–
    546, 553–554, 570–571
General Motors (GM), 80, 536, 567, 568
Google, 66, 335–336, 361–362, 449
Griffin Hospital, 123

H

Hewlett-Packard, 439–440, 443, 463–464,
    531, 537
Hilton New Orleans Riverside, 43
Home Depot, 195, 486, 487, 550
Honda, 12
HQ Global Workplaces, 532
Hyundai, 12

I

IBM, 48, 89, 308, 378, 532, 548
IDEO, 407–409, 413, 429, 550
IDS Life Insurance, 347
Intel, 444, 520
International Harvester Company, 481

J

Japan Airlines, 273
JetBlue Airlines, 14
J.M. Smuckers, 243

K

Kal Tire, 566
KB Home, 196
Kellogg's, 263
KFC, 550

L

Logitech, 378

M

Mail Boxes Etc., 560–561
Mattel, 531
MCA, 47, 48
Men's Wearhouse, 41
Microsoft, 65–66, 76, 91–92, 196, 449,
    472
Mind/Body Medical Institute (Boston),
    165
Mitsubishi Motor Manufacturing, 50, 561
Monsanto, 88
Motorola, 196, 426
MWH Globe, 447

N

NASA, 418
NASCAR, 426
Netimpact.org, 76
New York Yankees, 43
NeXT, 473
Nike, 243, 479, 548
Nissan, 12
Nokia, 561
Nortel Networks, 560
Nucor Steel, 177–178, 199, 207–208

O

Occidental Petroleum, 195
Orpheus Chamber Orchestra, 424

P

PepsiCo, 88
Pfizer Canada, 554
Pixar, 371–372, 397, 473
Pizza Hut, 550
PricewaterhouseCoopers, 226
Principal Financial Group, 89
Procter & Gamble, 88, 531
Publix Supermarkets, 196
Putnam Investment Company, 520–521

Q

Qualcomm, 76
QuickTrip, 107–108

R

RadioShack, 231
Red Cross, 76
Red Sox, 43
Regus Group, 532
RIVA, 154

S

Salary.com, 195
SAS Institute, 122, 124
Siemens, 561
Smurfit-Stone Container Corporation, 529
Society for Human Resource Management,
    66, 285
Song, 14, 15
Sony Corporation, 515–517, 525, 531, 539
Southwest Airlines, 14, 42–43, 46
St. Jude Children's Research Hospital, 35–36,
    58
Starbucks, 5, 29

T

Taco Bell, 550
Target, 243
Teach for America (TFA), 291–292, 322–323

Tennessee Valley Authority, 255–256, 263, 281
Toll Brothers, 195
Toyota, 12
TXU, 195

U

Unicru, 316
Unilever, 550
United Airlines, 275, 426
United Parcel Services, 165
U.S. Air Force, 46, 347
U.S. Army, 46
U.S. Navy, 241–242

U.S. Postal Service, 426, 561
UPS, 551, 561
USA Men's Basketball Team, 409

V

Valassis, 109
Vodaphone, 451

W

Wal-Mart, 217–219, 241, 243, 245
Wegmans, 103–104, 134–135
W.L. Gore, 524, 527
Wyeth, 189–190

X

Xerox, 165, 395, 533

Y

Yahoo, 195, 205
Yum Brands, Inc., 550

Subject Index

A

Abilities
  cognitive, 339–343
  emotional, 344–348
  explanation of, 336–337, 339
  importance of, 354–357
  physical, 348, 351–354
  team-member, 386–388
Ability tests, 357–359
Ability to focus, 240
Absenteeism, 80
Abuse, 50
Accommodating, 455–457
Accomplishment striving, 297
Acquisitions, 560–561
Action learning, 426
Action processes, 417
Action teams, 375, 376
Active management-by-exception, 489–490
Adaptability, 40
Adaptive task performance, 38, 40–41
Additive tasks, 388
Affect-based trust, 221, 224
Affective commitment
  assessment of, 71
  explanation of, 68
  factors promoting, 77–78
  function of, 70–72
  initiatives to foster, 88
African Americans, 228, 554
Agreeableness
  as personality dimension, 298
  of team members, 389
Ambassador activity, 416
Anticipatory stage of socialization, 559
Apathetics, 78
Appraising, 449
Artifacts, 548–551
Assessment
  of affective commitment, 71
  of core job characteristics, 119–120
  of creativity culture, 555
  of emotional intelligence, 347–350
  of goal orientation, 264
  of helpfulness, 45
  of interdependence, 380
  of leadership behavior, 484–485
  of meaning of money, 187
  of organizational structure, 523
  of personality, 295–296
  of political skill, 452
  reliability and validity of, 26
  of stress, 163
  of team cohesion, 420
  of trust propensity, 222
  of Type A behavior, 157

Attraction–selection–attrition (ASA) framework, 557–558
Auditory attention, 353
Autocratic style, 478
Autonomy, 115–116
Availability bias, 271
Avoiding, 455, 457

B

Baby Boomers, 85
Basic underlying assumptions, 552
Behavioral coping, 151–152
Behaviorally anchored rating scales (BARS), 55–56
Behavioral modeling, 262–263
Behavioral strains, 155–156
Behavior modeling training, 279
Benevolence, 224
Benign job demands, 144
Bias
  availability, 271
  decision-making, 271–273
  projection, 271
  self-serving, 273
Big Five Taxonomy
  agreeableness and, 298
  conscientiousness and, 296–298
  explanation of, 293–294, 296
  extroversion and, 298, 300–301
  neuroticism and, 301, 303–304
  openness to experience and, 304–306
Blink: The Power of Thinking Without Thinking (Gladwell), 267
Boosterism, 46
Boundary spanning, 416
Bounded rationality, 268, 270
Brainstorming
  explanation of, 412
  limitations of, 413–414
The Break-Up, 299
Bureaucratic structure, 528
Burnout, 155
Business environment, 525

C

Centrality, 447
Centralization
  explanation of, 521–522
  personal preferences regarding, 529
Ceremonies, 550–551
Chain of command, 519–520
Challenge stressors
  explanation of, 145
  function of, 163–164
  on students, 162
Character, as dimension of trustworthiness, 223–224

Charisma, 490
Chief executive officers (CEOs)
  function of, 519
  salaries of, 195–197
Citizens, 77
Citizenship behavior
  effect of trust on, 241
  explanation of, 43–44
  importance of, 46
  interpersonal, 44–45
  job satisfaction and, 128
  national culture and, 47
  organizational, 45–46
Civic virtue, 45–46
Clear purpose tests, 317
Client structure, 532
Climate for transfer, 279
Coalitions, 449
Coercive power, 443–444
Cognition-based trust
  explanation of, 221–224
  function of, 239
Cognitive abilities
  explanation of, 339–340
  factors related to, 337
  of team members, 387
  types and facets of, 340–343
Cognitive-behavioral techniques, 165
Cognitive coping, 151
Cognitive cultural intelligence, 348
Cognitive distortion, 193
Cognitive moral development, 236, 237
Cohesion
  consequences of, 420–421
  explanation of, 418
Collaboration, 456, 457
Collective group members, 312
Commitment. *See also* Organizational commitment
  effect of cognitive abilities on, 355–357
  effect of learning on, 277
  effect of personality on, 313, 314
  effect of person–organization fit on, 566
  effect of power and influence on, 459–460
  effect of strains on, 160–161
  effect of task interdependence on, 394
  effect of team process on, 423
  effect of transformational leadership on, 495, 496
  effect of trust on, 240
Communal cultures, 553
Communion striving, 298
Communities of practice, 279
Company size, 527, 528
Company strategy, 525, 527

Comparison others, 192–195
Compensation. *See also* Salaries
    gender and race and, 228
    negotiation of, 461
    outcome interdependence and, 393–394
Compensation plans, 204–205
Compensatory forms model, 82
Competence, 199, 223
Competing, 455, 457
Compliance, 450
Comprehensive interdependence, 382
Compromise, 456, 457
Conflict
    relationship, 417–418
    role, 145
    task, 418
    work–family, 148
Conflict resolution
    explanation of, 455
    styles used in, 455–457
Conjunctive tasks, 388
Conscientiousness
    as dimension of personality, 296–298
    effect on job performance, 313, 314
    of team members, 389
Consensus, 274
Consideration, 483
Consistency, 274
Consultation, 448
Consultative style, 478, 481
Contingencies of reinforcement, 259, 260
Contingent reward, 490
Continuance commitment
    explanation of, 69
    function of, 72–74
    initiatives to foster, 88
Continuous reinforcement, 260, 262
Control movement abilities, 353
Coordination loss, 409
Coping
    behavioral, 151–152
    choosing strategy for, 153–154
    cognitive, 151
    emotion-focused, 152
    explanation of, 151
    problem-focused, 151
Corporate social responsibility, 241–243
Correlation, 23, 24
Countercultures, 557
Counterproductive behavior
    behavior patterns associated with, 52
    effect of trust on, 241
    explanation of, 46–47
    types of, 47–51
Courtesy, 44
Coworkers, 6
Coworker satisfaction, 109
Creativity, 304–305
Creativity culture, 554, 555

Cross-cultural organizational behavior, 13
Cross-training, 425–426
Cultural diversity. *See also* Diversity;
        Globalization; Organizational culture
    assignment of blame and, 273
    business ethics and, 234
    citizenship behavior and, 47
    cultural intelligence and, 348
    life satisfaction and, 130
    motivation and, 192
    organizational commitment and, 87
    values and, 308
Cultural intelligence, 348
Cultural values
    dimensions of, 308, 309
    explanation of, 292, 293
    function of, 307
    importance of, 313–314
Culture. *See* Organizational culture
Culture strength, 554, 556–557
Customer service culture, 553
Cyberloafing, 79

D

Daily hassles, 146
Daydreaming, 79
Decentralization, 521–522
Decision informity, 414–415
Decision making
    bias in, 272
    decentralization in, 524
    ethical, 233–238
    explanation of, 256
    by leaders, 477–481
    learning and, 256, 257
    methods of, 265, 268
    problems related to, 268, 270–271,
        273–275
    team, 414–416
    variations in, 275, 276
Decisions
    nonprogrammed, 266–268
    programmed, 265, 266
Deductive reasoning, 342
Deep-level diversity, 390
Delegating, 486
Delegative style, 479
Depth perception, 353
Deviance
    political, 49
    production, 49
    property, 47–48
Differential exposure, 303
Differential reactivity, 303
Discretion, 447
Disjunctive tasks, 388
Disposition-based trust, 220–221
Distinctiveness, 274
Distributive bargaining, 460

Distributive justice
    explanation of, 226
    importance of, 228–229
Diversity. *See also* Cultural diversity
    deep-level, 390
    management of, 13
    surface-level, 389–390
    of team members, 389–390
    workforce, 83, 85
Diversity culture, 554
Don't Sweat the Small Stuff at Work
        (Carlson), 147
Dopamine, 114
Downsizing
    effects of, 85, 87–88
    explanation of, 85
Dynamic flexibility, 351
Dynamic strength, 351

E

Economic exchange, 241
Effort, 178–180
Embeddedness, 73
Emotional ability
    components of, 345–348
    explanation of, 344–345
Emotional contagion, 125
Emotional cues, 180
Emotional cultural intelligence, 348
Emotional intelligence
    application of, 346 347
    assessment of, 347–350
    explanation of, 345–346
Emotional labor, 125
Emotional Quotient Inventory (EQ-i), 347
Emotional regulation, 346
Emotional support, 158
Emotion-focused coping, 152
Emotions
    explanation of, 123
    types of, 123, 125
    use of, 346
Employees
    changing relationship between employers
        and, 85, 87–88
    effects of restructuring on, 535–537
Empowerment, psychological, 197–200
Encounter stage of socialization, 559
Engagement
    explanation of, 118, 120
    influence and, 450
Equilibrium
    gross body, 351
    punctuated, 378–379
Equity distress, 193
Equity theory, 191–197
Erosion model, 72
Escalation of commitment, 274–275
Espoused values, 551

Ethical decision making
    explanation of, 233, 235
    moral awareness and, 235–236
    moral intent and, 238
    moral judgment and, 236–237
Ethical ideologies, 237
Ethical sensitivity, 235
Ethics
    explanation of, 219
    research on, 233
    for students, 238
Ethnocentrism, 308, 310
Exchange tactic, 449
Executive intelligence, 344
*Executive Intelligence: What All Great
    Leaders Have* (Menkes), 344
Exit, 77
Expatriates. *See also* Cultural diversity;
    Globalization; Multinational
    corporations
    adjustment of, 87
    effectiveness of, 152
    factors affecting, 13
Expectancy, 180–182
Expectancy theory
    expectancy and, 180–182
    explanation of, 180
    motivational force and, 186
    valence and, 182–184, 186
Expertise, 257
Expert power, 444
Explicit knowledge, 257, 258
Explosive strength, 351
Extent flexibility, 351
External comparisons, 194
Extinction, 260
Extrinsic motivation, 183
Extroversion, 298, 300–301

F

Facilitative style, 478
Faking, 318–320
Family time demands, 150
Far vision, 353
Feedback
    cultural differences in responses to, 192
    explanation of, 116–117
    on goal attainment, 188
*Finding Flow: The Psychology of
    Engagement with Everyday Life*
    (Csikszentmihalyi), 122
Fine manipulative abilities, 353
The Firm, 75
*Fish! A Remarkable Way to Boost Morale
    and Improve Results* (Lundin et al.),
    200
The Five Dysfunctions of a Team (Lencioni),
    411
Fixed interval schedule, 260

Fixed ratio schedule, 260
Flattening, organizational, 537
Focus, ability to, 240
Focus of commitment, 70
Formalism, 237
Formalization, 524
Forming, 377
The 48 Laws of Power (Greene), 454
Fragmented culture, 552
Functional structure, 528–529
Fundamental attribution error, 273–274

G

Gainsharing, 205
Gattaca, 338–339
Gender, 228. *See also* Women
General adaptation syndrome (GAS),
    154–156
General mental ability, 343
Geographic structure, 531–532
g-factor, 343
Globalization. *See also* Cultural diversity;
    Multinational corporations
    expatriate assignments and, 13, 87, 152
    impact of, 13
    influence tactics and, 449
    leadership styles and, 491
    mergers and acquisitions and, 561
    organizational structure and, 532
    technology and, 532
    virtual teams and, 378
Goal commitment, 190
Goal interdependence, 382–383
Goal orientation, 264, 265
Goals
    cultural differences in, 192
    self-set, 188
    S.M.A.R.T., 190
    specific and difficult, 186
Goal setting theory
    explanation of, 186, 188
    goal commitment and, 190
    task performance and, 188–190
Gossiping, 49
Grand Theft Auto: San Andreas, 235, 236
Gross body coordination, 351
Gross body equilibrium, 351
Group members, collective, 312
Groupthink, 418
Growth need strength, 117

H

Harassment, 50
Health and wellness programs, 166
Hearing sensitivity, 353
Helpfulness, assessment of, 45
Helping, 44
Heuristics, 271
Hierarchical sensitivity, 415

Hindrance stressors
    explanation of, 145–146
    function of, 163–164
    on students, 162
History, 13–14
*The Human Equation: Building Profits by
    Putting People First* (Pfeffer), 19
Human resource management, 7
Hurricane Katrina, 43, 226
Hybrid outcome interdependence, 394–395
Hypotheses, 22

I

Idealism, 237
Idealized influence, 490
Identity, 114
Impact, 199
Incivility, 49
Independent forms model, 82
Individualism–collectivism, 308, 309
Individualistic roles, 386, 387
Individualized consideration, 492
Inductive reasoning, 342
Influence
    conflict resolution and, 455–457
    explanation of, 447–448
    importance of, 459–460
    of leaders, 457, 459
    organizational politics and, 355, 451, 453
    use of, 450
Influence tactics, 448–450
Informational justice, 231–232
In Good Company, 562
Ingratiation, 448
Inimitable, 13
Initial public offerings (IPOs), 15
Initiating structure, 482
Inspirational appeal, 448
Inspirational motivation, 492
Instrumentality, 181–182
Instrumental support, 158
Integrative bargaining, 460–461
Integrative model of organizational behavior,
    7–11, 536
Integrity tests, 317–320
Intellectual stimulation, 492
Intelligence quotient (IQ), 343
Interdependence
    assessment of, 380
    comprehensive, 382
    goal, 382–383
    outcome, 383–384, 393–395
    pooled, 380–381
    reciprocal, 382
    sequential, 382
    task, 379–380
Interests, 307
Internal comparisons, 194
Interpersonal citizenship behavior, 44–45

Interpersonal justice
    effect of, 232
    explanation of, 230–231
Interpersonal processes, 417–418
Intrinsic motivation, 183
Intuition, 265
The Island, 124

J

Jack: Straight from the Gut (Welch), 54–55
Job analysis, 41
Job characteristics
    assessment of, 119–120
    autonomy as, 115–116
    feedback as, 116–117
    identity as, 114
    job satisfaction and, 117–118
    significance as, 114–115
    variety as, 112–114
Job characteristics theory, 112, 113
Job Descriptive Index (JDI), 131–132
Job enrichment, 118
Job in General (JIG) Scale, 131, 132
Job performance
    citizenship behavior and, 43–46
    counterproductive behavior and, 46–51
    effect of cognitive abilities on,
        355–357
    effect of job satisfaction on, 127–128
    effect of learning on, 276–277
    effect of personality on, 313, 314
    effect of person–organization fit and,
        566
    effect of power and influence on,
        459–460
    effect of strains on, 160–161
    effect of task interdependence on, 394
    effect of transformational leadership on,
        495, 496
    effect of trust on, 240
    elements of, 9, 38, 51
    explanation of, 36–37
    interest in, 7
    management of, 54–56
    social recognition and, 22–25
    of students, 52
    task performance and, 38–43
    workplace trends affecting, 51–53
Job satisfaction. *See also* Satisfaction
    assessment of, 131–132
    effect of mood and emotions on, 118,
        120–121, 123, 125
    explanation of, 104–105
    hourly fluctuation in, 120
    importance of, 125–128
    life satisfaction and, 128–129
    neuroticism and, 301, 302
    organizational culture and, 564
    for students, 111

Job satisfaction—*Cont.*
    value fulfillment and, 107–110
    variations in, 105–106, 126
    with work tasks, 111–118
Job sharing, 163
Justice
    explanation of, 219, 226, 233
    informational, 231–232
    interpersonal, 230–231
    procedural, 226–230

K

Knowledge
    explicit, 257, 258
    need for, 117
    of results, 112
    tacit, 258
Knowledge transfer, 279
Knowledge work, 52–53

L

Laissez-faire leadership, 488, 489
Language, 550
Layoffs, 537
Leader–member exchange theory, 474–476
Leaders
    decision-making styles of, 477–481
    effectiveness of, 474–477, 492–494
    emergence of, 476, 477
    importance of power and influence in,
        459–460
    influence of, 447–450, 457, 459
    negotiations by, 460–461
    power of, 441–447, 458
    use of power and influence by, 450–451,
        453, 455–456
Leadership
    explanation of, 441
    importance of, 495–496
    laissez-faire, 488, 489
    life cycle theory of, 485–487
    organizational culture and, 560
    time-driven model of, 480, 481
    transactional, 489, 490
    transformational, 488–490, 492, 493,
        495–498
Leadership behaviors
    cultural diversity and, 491
    day-to-day, 481–483, 485–487
    explanation of, 474
The Leadership Challenge (Kouzes &
        Posner), 498
Leadership training, 497–498
Leader–staff teams, 385
Learning
    action, 426
    decision making and, 256, 257
    explanation of, 256
    goal orientation and, 265

Learning—*Cont.*
    importance of, 276–278
    through observation, 262–263
    through reinforcement, 258–262
Learning orientation, 265
Legitimate power, 442–443
Life cycle theory of leadership, 485–487
Life events, 148, 150
Life satisfaction
    explanation of, 128–129
    international data on, 130
Locus of control, 303
Lone wolves, 78
Long breaks, 80
Looking busy, 79
Loyalty, 77

M

Management by objectives (MBO), 55
Management teams, 375
Masculinity–femininity, 308, 309
Mathematical reasoning, 341
Matrix structure, 533–534
Maximum performance, 313
Mayer-Salovey-Caruso Emotional
        Intelligence Test, 349
Meaningfulness
    explanation of, 198
    of work, 112
Meaning of money
    assessment of, 187
    explanation of, 184, 186
Mechanistic organizations, 524, 525
Mental models, 421
Mentoring, 567–568
Mercenary culture, 552
Mergers, 560, 561
Merit pay, 205
Meta-analysis, 25
Method of authority, 21
Method of experience, 21
Method of intuition, 21
Method of science, 21
Minorities, 228, 229, 554
Missing meetings, 80
Mission statements, 383, 384
Money, meaning of, 184, 186, 187
Monsters, Inc., 39
Moods
    attempts to foster positive, 121, 123
    explanation of, 118
    job satisfaction and, 118, 120–121
    types of, 121
Moonlighting, 79
Moral awareness, 235–236
Moral identity, 238
Moral intensity, 236
Moral intent, 238
Moral judgment, 236–237

Motivation
  compensation systems and, 204–205
  effort and, 178–180
  equity theory and, 191–197
  expectancy theory and, 180–184,
    186
  explanation of, 178, 180
  extrinsic, 183
  goal setting theory and, 186–191
  importance of, 202, 203
  inspirational, 492
  intrinsic, 183
  origins of, 9
  psychological empowerment and,
    197–200
  in students, 197
  universals in, 192
  variations in, 200, 201
Motivational force, 186
Motivational loss, 409
Multicultural personality questionnaire, 310
Multidivisional structure, 531
Multinational corporations. *See also* Cultural
    diversity; Globalization
  ethnocentrism and, 310
  expatriates and, 13, 87, 152
  geographic structure in, 532
  organizational behavior in, 13
  organizational commitment in, 87
Myers-Briggs Type Indicator, 306–307, 313

N

Near vision, 353
Needs, 182
Negative affectivity, 301
Negative emotions, 123
Negative life events, 148
Negative reinforcement, 259
Neglect, 77
Negotiation, 460–461
Networked cultures, 553
Neuroticism, 301, 303–304
Neutralizers, 495, 497
Newcomer orientation, 567
Night vision, 353
Nominal group technique, 414
Nonprogrammed decisions, 265, 267, 268
Nonwork challenge stressors, 150
Nonwork hindrance stressors, 148
Normative commitment
  explanation of, 69
  factors promoting, 77–78
  function of, 74, 76
  initiatives to foster, 89
Norming, 377
Now, Discover Your Strengths (Buckingham
    & Clifton), 315
Number facility, 341
Numerous small decisions, 14

O

Observable artifacts, 548
Occupational Information Network
    (O*Net), 42
Occupations, rated by stress levels, 143
Ocean's Eleven, 390
The Office, 344–345
One Laptop Per Child project, 456
Openness to experience, 304–306
Operant conditioning, 258, 259
Oral comprehension, 340–341
Oral expression, 341
Organic organizations, 524, 525
Organizational Behavior at the Bookstore
  *Blink: The Power of Thinking Without
    Thinking* (Gladwell), 267
  Don't Sweat the Small Stuff at Work
    (Carlson), 147
  *Executive Intelligence: What All Great
    Leaders Have* (Menkes), 344
  *Finding Flow: The Psychology of
    Engagement with Everyday Life*
    (Csikszentmihalyi), 122
  *Fish! A Remarkable Way to Boost Morale
    and Improve Results* (Lundin
    et al.), 200
  The Five Dysfunctions of a Team
    (Lencioni), 411
  The 48 Laws of Power (Greene), 454
  *The Human Equation: Building Profits
    by Putting People First* (Pfeffer),
    19
  Jack: Straight from the Gut (Welch),
    54–55
  The Leadership Challenge (Kouzes &
    Posner), 498
  Now, Discover Your Strengths
    (Buckingham & Clifton), 315
  *The Speed of Trust: The One Thing That
    Changes Everything* (Covey),
    242
  Who Says Elephants Can't Dance?
    (Gerstner), 549
  The Wisdom of Crowds (Surowiecki),
    374
  *Workforce Crisis: How to Beat the
    Coming Shortage of Skills and
    Talent* (Dychtwald et al.), 86
  *The World Is Flat: A Brief History of the
    Twenty-First Century* (Friedman),
    526
Organizational behavior (OB)
  explanation of, 7
  impact of globalization on, 13
  integrative model of, 7–11, 536
  methods for learning about, 21–25
  research in, 7, 15–19
  value in studying, 12–15, 18

Organizational Behavior on Screen
  The Break-Up, 299
  The Firm, 75
  Gattaca, 338–339
  In Good Company, 562
  The Island, 124
  Monsters, Inc., 39
  Ocean's Eleven, 390
  Office Space, 20
  Pirates of the Caribbean, 225
  Pushing Tin, 149–150
  The Screen, 445
  Star Trek: First Contact, 269
  Star Wars II: Attack of the Clones, 522
  Talladega Nights, 185
  Thirteen, 482
  300, 410
Organizational charts, 517–518
Organizational citizenship behavior, 45–46
Organizational commitment. *See also*
    Commitment
  background of, 67–68
  changing employee–employer
    relationship and, 85, 87–88
  effect of restructuring on, 535, 536
  elements of, 9, 84
  explanation of, 66–67
  interest in, 7
  job satisfaction and, 128
  in multinational corporations, 87
  organizational culture and, 564
  strategies to maximize, 88–89
  types of, 68–74, 76
  withdrawal behavior and, 76–83
  workforce diversity and, 83, 85
Organizational culture
  basic underlying assumptions and, 552
  creativity, 554, 555
  customer service, 553
  diversity, 554
  effect of leadership change on, 560
  effect of mergers and acquisitions on,
    560–561
  effect on students, 568
  espoused values and, 551
  explanation of, 546–547
  fragmented, 552
  importance of, 564
  mercenary, 552–553
  methods to maintain, 557–560
  observable artifacts and, 548–551
  safety, 553–554
  socialization and, 564, 566–568
  strength of, 554, 556–557
  subcultures within, 556–557
  values to judge fit with, 565
  variations in, 547, 553, 561
Organizational design, 525, 527
Organizational politics, 355, 451, 453

Organizational power, 442–444
Organizational structure
    assessment of, 523
    bureaucratic, 528–531
    chain of command and, 519–520
    changes in, 536–537
    elements of, 518–519, 524
    formalization and, 524
    function of, 516–517, 534
    geographic, 531–532
    importance of, 534–536
    matrix, 533–534
    multinational, 532
    product, 531
    simple, 527–528
    span of control and, 520–522
    technology and, 527
    work specialization and, 519
Organizations
    changing relationship between employees
        and, 85, 87–88
    flattening of, 537
    mechanistic, 524, 525
    organic, 524, 525
    role of technology in, 527
    size of, 527, 528
Orientation programs, 567
Originality, 342
Other awareness, 345–346
Outcome, 112
Outcome interdependence
    compensation and, 393–394
    hybrid, 394–395

P

Parallel teams, 375, 376
Participating, 486
Passive management-by-exception, 489
Past accomplishments, 180
Pay satisfaction, 107
Perceptual ability, 342
Perceptual speed, 342
Performance-avoid orientation, 265
Performance management, 53, 55
Performance-prove orientation, 265
Performing, 377
Personal aggression
    costs of, 50
    explanation of, 50
Personal appeals, 448–449
Personal clarification, 425
Personal development, 150
Personality
    agreeableness and, 298
    assessment of, 295–296
    conscientiousness and, 296–298
    dimensions of, 293–294
    of employees, 311, 313
    explanation of, 292

Personality—*Cont.*
    extroversion and, 298, 300–301
    genetic basis of, 294
    importance of, 313–314
    Myers-Briggs Type Indicator of, 306–307
    neuroticism and, 301, 303–304
    openness to experience and, 304–306
Personality tests
    effectiveness of, 318, 320
    explanation of, 316–317
    types of, 317–318
Personal power, 444, 446
Person organization fit
    effect on performance and commitment,
        566
    explanation of, 564
    values and, 565
Physical abilities
    explanation of, 348, 351
    of team members, 386, 387
    types of, 351–354
Physical cultural intelligence, 348
Physical structures, 549–550
Physical withdrawal, 80–82
Physiological strains, 155–156
Pirates of the Caribbean, 225
Pleasantness, 118
Political deviance, 49
Political skills, 451
Pooled interdependence, 380–381
Positional modeling, 425–426
Positional rotation, 426
Positive affectivity, 300–301
Positive emotions, 123
Positive life events, 150
Positive reinforcement, 259
Potency, 421
Power
    conflict resolution and, 455–457
    contingencies of, 447
    explanation of, 441
    guidelines for using, 446
    importance of, 459–460
    organizational, 442–444
    organizational politics and, 355, 451, 453
    personal, 444, 446
    use of, 450
Power distance, 308, 309
Pressure, 449
Primary appraisal, 144
Problem-focused coping, 151
Problem sensitivity, 342
Procedural justice
    compensation data and, 228
    explanation of, 226–228
    importance of, 228–230
Process gain, 409
Process loss, 409
Production blocking, 409

Production deviance, 49
Product structure, 531
Profit sharing, 205
Programmed decisions, 265, 266
Progression model, 82
Project GLOBE, 491
Projection bias, 271
Project teams, 375, 376
Promotion satisfaction, 107–108
Property deviance, 47–48
Psychological empowerment
    elements of, 198–200
    explanation of, 197–198
Psychological strains, 155–156
Psychological withdrawal, 78–80
Psychomotor abilities, 353
Punctuated equilibrium, 378–379
Punishment, 259–260
Pushing Tin, 149–150

Q

Quantitative ability, 341
Quitting, 80–81

R

Rational decision-making model, 268, 270
Rational persuasion, 448
Readiness, 485
Realistic job previews (RJPs), 566
Reality shock, 559
Reasoning ability, 341–342
Reciprocal interdependence, 382
Referent power, 444, 446
Reinforcement
    contingencies of, 259, 260
    continuous, 260, 262
    explanation of, 258
    negative, 259
    positive, 259
    schedules of, 260–262
Relationship conflict, 417–418
Relativism, 237
Relaxation techniques, 165
Resistance, 450
Resource-based view, 13
Response orientation, 353
Response time, 353
Responsibility for outcomes, 112
Restructuring
    explanation of, 534–535
    types of, 536–537
Results, knowledge of, 112
Reward power, 443
Rewards, 192
RIASEC model, 307, 308, 313
Rituals, 550
Riverhead: Tales of the Assembly Line
    (Hamper), 80
Role ambiguity, 146

Role conflict, 145
Role making, 474
Role overload, 146–147
Roles, 385–386
Role taking, 474
Routine task performance, 38
Rule of one-eighth, 18

S

Sabotage, 47
Safety culture, 553–554
Salaries, 195–197. *See also* Compensation;
    Compensation plans
Satisfaction. *See also* Job satisfaction
    coworker, 109
    life, 128–129
    pay, 107
    promotion, 107–108
    supervision, 107–108
    with work itself, 109–110
Satisficing, 270
Schedules of reinforcement, 260–262
Scholastic Assessment Test (SAT), 340, 341,
    356
Scientific management, 112
Scout activities, 416
Secondary appraisal, 151
Selective perception, 270–271
Self-awareness, 345
Self-determination, 198–199
Self-efficacy, 180, 199
Self-serving bias, 273
Self-set goals, 188
Selling, 486
Sensory abilities, 353–354
Service work, 53
Short-term vs. long-term orientation, 308,
    309
Significance, 114–115
Similarity-attraction approach, 389
Simple structure, 527–528
Situational strength, 313
Skills, need for, 117
S.M.A.R.T. goals, 190
Social exchange, 241
Social identity theory, 271
Social influence model, 72
Socialization
    explanation of, 558–559
    management of, 564, 566–568
Socializing, 79
Social learning theory, 262
Social loafing, 411
Socially complex resources, 14–15
Social recognition, 22–25
Social support, 158, 159
Span of control, 520
Spatial ability, 342
Spatial organization, 342

Specific and difficult goals, 186
Speech recognition, 353
Speed and flexibility of closure, 342
*The Speed of Trust: The One Thing
    That Changes Everything*
    (Covey), 242
Sportsmanship, 44–45
Staff validity, 415
Stamina, 351
Stars, 77
Star Trek: First Contact, 269
Star Wars II: Attack of the Clones, 522
Static strength, 351
Status striving, 300
Stereotypes, 271
Stories, 550
Storming, 377
Strains
    behavioral, 155–156
    effects of, 161
    explanation of, 143
    physiological, 155–156
    psychological, 155–156
    reduction of, 165–166
    relationship between stress and,
        154–155
Strategic management, 7
Strength, physical, 351
Stress
    assessment of, 163
    explanation of, 142–143
    importance of, 160–161
    neuroticism and, 303
    organizational culture and, 564
    strain resulting from, 154–156
    strategies for coping with, 151–154
    on students, 162
    variations in levels of, 156–160
Stress audits, 163
Stress management
    resources for, 163–165
    strain reduction for, 165–166
    stressor reduction for, 163
Stressors
    coping with, 151–154
    evaluation of, 144–145
    explanation of, 143
    nonwork challenge, 150
    nonwork hindrance, 148
    reduction of, 163
    types of, 145
    work challenge, 146
    work hindrance, 145–147
Subcultures, 556–557
Substance abuse, 49
Substitutability, 447
Substitutes, leader, 495, 497
Substitutes for leadership model, 495
Supervision satisfaction, 108

Supportive practices, to reduce stress,
    164–165
Surface-level diversity, 389–390
Survivor syndrome, 88
Symbols, 548

T

Tacit knowledge, 258
Talladega Nights, 185
Tardiness, 80
Task complexity, 189–190
Task conflict, 418
Task coordinator activities, 416
Task interdependence
    effect on job performance and
        commitment, 394
    explanation of, 379–380
    types of, 380–382
Task performance
    adaptive, 38, 40–41
    effect of restructuring on, 535, 536
    explanation of, 38
    identifying behaviors associated with,
        41–43
    routine, 38
Task strategies, 188
Taskwork processes
    creative behavior and, 412–414
    decision making and, 414–416
    explanation of, 412
Team building, 426–427
Team building roles, 386, 387
Team diversity, 389–390
Team members
    abilities of, 386–388
    diversity of, 389–390
    personality traits of, 388–389
    roles of, 385–386
Team process
    explanation of, 408–409
    function of, 409–411
    gain in, 409
    importance of, 422–424
    loss in, 409
    taskwork processes and, 412–416
    team states and, 418–421
    teamwork processes and, 416–418
Team process training, 426
Teams
    composition of, 384–390
    decision making on, 414–416
    development of, 377–379
    explanation of, 372–373
    function of characteristics of, 390, 391,
        393
    interdependence in, 379–384
    outcome interdependence of, 393–395
    size of, 390
    students working in, 385, 419

Teams—*Cont.*
    training, 424–427
    types of, 373, 375–377, 385
    variations in, 377–379
    virtual, 377, 378
Team states, 418–421
Team task roles, 385–386
Team viability, 393
Teamwork processes
    explanation of, 416
    types of, 416–418, 421–422
Technology
    globalization and, 532
    organizational structure and, 527
    virtual teams and, 377, 378
Telling, 486
Theft, 49
Theory, 21–22
Thirteen, 482
300, 410
360-degree feedback, 56
Time-driven model of leadership, 480, 481
Time pressure, 146
Training
    cultural intelligence, 348
    explanation of, 278–279
    leadership, 497–498
    team, 425–427
Training interventions, 164
Training teams
    cross-training, 425–426
    team building, 426–427
    team process, 426
    transportable teamwork competencies
        and, 424–425
Trait activation, 313–314
Traits, 292
Transactional leadership, 489, 490
Transactive memory, 421
Transfer of training, 279
Transformational leadership
    effects of, 495, 496
    explanation of, 488–490, 492
    of presidents, 493
    training in, 497–498
Transition processes, 416–417

Transportable teamwork competencies,
        424–425
Trivial Pursuit, 345
Trust
    affect-based, 224
    in authority, 238–239
    cognition-based, 221–224, 239
    disposition-based, 220–221
    explanation of, 219
    importance of, 240–241
    organizational culture and, 564
    over time, 226
Trust propensity, 221, 222
Trustworthiness
    dimensions of, 223–224
    evidence of, 239
    explanation of, 221–222
Type A behavior pattern, 156–160
Typical performance, 313

U

Uncertainty avoidance, 308, 309
Understanding and adaptation stage of
        socialization, 559
Use of emotions, 346
Utilitarianism, 237

V

Valence, 182–184, 186
Value in diversity problem-solving approach,
        389
Value-percept theory, 107–110
Values
    collective, 312
    cultural, 292, 293, 307–309, 313–314
    espoused, 551
    explanation of, 105–106
    job satisfaction and, 107
    organization fit and, 564, 565
Variable interval schedule, 260
Variable ratio schedule, 260
Variety
    explanation of, 112
    in jobs, 112–114
Veiled purpose tests, 317
Verbal ability, 340–341

Verbal persuasion, 180
Vicarious experiences, 180
Virtual teams, 377, 378
Visibility, 447
Visual color discrimination, 353
Visualization, 342
Voice, 45, 77

W

Wasting resources, 49
Whistle-blowing, 233
Who Says Elephants Can't Dance?
        (Gerstner), 549
The Wisdom of Crowds (Surowiecki), 374
Withdrawal behavior
    explanation of, 67, 76–77
    models of, 82–83
    physical, 80–82
    psychological, 78–80
    in students, 81
Women
    compensation for, 228
    list of powerful, 443
Wonderlic Personnel Test, 357–359
Work, 112
Work challenge stressors, 146
Work complexity, 148
Work family conflict, 148
Workforce diversity, 83, 85. *See also* Cultural
        diversity; Diversity
Work hindrance stressors, 145 147
*Working: People Talk About What They Do All
        Day and How They Feel About What
        They Do* (Terkel), 112
Work responsibility, 148
Work specialization, 519
Work tasks
    job characteristics model and,
        112–118
    satisfaction with, 109–110
Work teams, 375
Written comprehension, 341
Written expression, 341

Z

Zero acquaintance, 298